THE OXFORD HANDBOOK OF

CIVIL SOCIETY

THE OXFORD HANDBOOK OF

CIVIL SOCIETY

Edited by

MICHAEL EDWARDS

OXFORD
UNIVERSITY PRESS

OXFORD

UNIVERSITY PRESS

Oxford University Press is a department of the University of Oxford.
It furthers the University's objective of excellence in research, scholarship,
and education by publishing worldwide.

Oxford   New York
Auckland   Cape Town   Dar es Salaam   Hong Kong   Karachi
Kuala Lumpur   Madrid   Melbourne   Mexico City   Nairobi
New Delhi   Shanghai   Taipei   Toronto

With offices in
Argentina   Austria   Brazil   Chile   Czech Republic   France   Greece
Guatemala   Hungary   Italy   Japan   Poland   Portugal   Singapore
South Korea   Switzerland   Thailand   Turkey   Ukraine   Vietnam

Oxford is a registered trade mark of Oxford University Press
in the UK and certain other countries.

Published in the United States of America by
Oxford University Press
198 Madison Avenue, New York, NY 10016

© Oxford University Press 2011

First issued as an Oxford University Press paperback, 2013.

Library of Congress Cataloging-in-Publication Data
The Oxford handbook of civil society / edited by Michael Edwards.
p.   cm.
ISBN 978-0-19-539857-1 (hardcover); 978-0-19-933014-0 (paperback)
1. Civil society.   I. Edwards, Michael, 1957-
JC337.O94 2011

300—dc22   2010046063

Printed in the United States of America
on acid-free paper

Contents

Part III Geographical Perspectives

Part IV The Norms Of Civil Society

Contributors

Clifford Bob is Associate Professor of Political Science at Duquesne University. He is the author of *The Marketing of Rebellion: Insurgents, Media, and International Activism* (Cambridge University Press, 2005) and is writing a new book on transnational clashes between ideologically opposed civil society groups.

Catherine Bolzendahl is an Assistant Professor of Sociology at the University of California, Irvine. Her research largely focuses on gender, political power, citizenship, and social policy in Western democracies.

Harry C. Boyte is founder and codirector of the Center for Democracy and Citizenship at Augsburg College, and a Senior Fellow at the University of Minnesota's Humphrey Institute. He is the author of many books including *Everyday Politics: Reconnecting Citizens and Public Life* (Pennsylvania University Press, 2005).

Craig Calhoun is President of the U.S. Social Science Research Council and University Professor at New York University. His books include *Cosmopolitanism and Belonging* (Routledge, 2011) and *Possible Futures* (New York University Press, 2011).

Neera Chandhoke is Professor of Political Science at Delhi University and the author of *The Conceits of Civil Society* (Oxford University Press, 2003), *Beyond Secularism* (Oxford University Press India, 1999) and *State and Civil Society* (Sage, 1995).

Hilde Coffé is an Assistant Professor of Sociology at Utrecht University. Her main research interests include civic and political attitudes and participation, and partisan politics.

Evelina Dagnino holds a Ph.D. in Political Science from Stanford University and is Professor of Political Science at the University of Campinas in Sao Paulo, Brazil.

Mario Diani is ICREA Research Professor in the Department of Political and Social Sciences at the Universitat Pompeu Fabra in Barcelona.

Michael Edwards is a Distinguished Senior Fellow at Demos in New York, and directed the Ford Foundation's Governance and Civil Society Program between

1999 and 2008. His books include *Civil Society* (second edition, Polity Press, 2009) and *Small Change: Why Business Won't Save the World* (Berrett-Koehler, 2010).

John Ehrenberg is Senior Professor of Political Science at the Brooklyn Campus of Long Island University. He is the author of several books including *Civil Society: The Critical History of an Idea* (New York University Press, 1999).

Nina Eliasoph is an Associate Professor of Sociology at the University of Southern California. She is the author of *Avoiding Politics: How Americans Produce Apathy in Everyday Life* (Cambridge University Press, 1998) and *Making Volunteers: Civic Life After Welfare's End* (Princeton University Press, 2011).

Omar G. Encarnación is Professor and Chair of Political Studies at Bard College, where he teaches comparative politics and Iberian and Latin American politics. He is the author of *The Myth of Civil Society* (Palgrave Macmillan, 2003) and *Spanish Politics: Democracy after Dictatorship* (Polity, 2008).

Alan Fowler holds professorial appointments at the Erasmus University in the Netherlands and the University of KwaZulu Natal in South Africa. He is an author and co-editor of many books on civic-driven change and NGO management.

John Gaventa is Professor at the Institute of Development Studies, University of Sussex and a member of the Participation, Power, and Social Change team there. He is the author of *Power and Powerlessness: Quiescence and Rebellion in an Appalachian Valley* (University of Illinois Press, 1980) and more recent books on citizen action.

Claudia Horwitz is the founding director of stone circles at The Stone House in Mebane, North Carolina. She is the author of *The Spiritual Activist* (Penguin, 2002).

Marc Morjé Howard is Professor of Government at Georgetown University. He is the author of two award-winning books, *The Weakness of Civil Society in Post-Communist Europe* (Cambridge University Press, 2003) and *The Politics of Citizenship in Europe* (Cambridge University Press, 2009), and he has published articles in numerous academic journals.

Jude Howell is Professor and Director of the Centre for Civil Society at the London School of Economics. She is the coauthor (with Jeremy Lind) of *Counter-Terrorism, Aid and Civil Society: Before and After the War on Terror* (Palgrave Macmillan, 2010) and editor of *Governance in China* (Rowan and Littlefield, 2003).

David Hulme is Professor of Development Studies at the Institute for Development Policy and Management, and Director of the Brooks World Poverty

Institute and the Chronic Poverty Research Centre, all at the University of Manchester.

Solava Ibrahim is a Research Fellow in Global Poverty Reduction at the Brooks World Poverty Institute and Chronic Poverty Research Centre at the University of Manchester.

Lisa Jordan is Executive Director of the Bernard van Leer Foundation and previously oversaw the Ford Foundation's Global Civil Society Program. She is the coeditor of *NGO Accountability; Politics, Principles and Innovations* (Earthscan, 2006) and has published numerous articles on civil society and global governance.

Eberhard Kienle is a research professor at the Centre National de la Recherche Scientifique (CNRS) in Paris and teaches at the Institut d'Etudes Politiques in Grenoble. From 2007 to 2010 he was the Program Officer for Governance and Civil Society in the Ford Foundation's Cairo office.

Sally Kohn is a community organizer, writer, and political satirist. She is the Chief Agitation Officer of the Movement Vision Lab, a grassroots think tank based in Brooklyn, New York.

Frances Kunreuther is the Director of the Building Movement Project and a Fellow at New York University's Research Center for Leadership and Action. She has coauthored two books, *From the Ground Up* (ILR Press, 2007) and *Working Across Generations* (Jossey-Bass, 2009).

Roberta G. Lentz is an Assistant Professor in the Department of Art History and Communication Studies at McGill University, and a former Program Officer in Electronic Media Policy at the Ford Foundation from 2001 to2007.

Charles H. T. Lesch is a graduate student in the Department of Government at Harvard University.

Peter Levine is Director of the Center for Information and Research on Civic Learning and Engagement at the Jonathan M. Tisch College of Citizenship and Public Service, Tufts University. His books include *The Future of Democracy*, *Engaging Young People in Civic Life* (Tufts University Press, 2007) and *Reforming the Humanities* (Palgrave Macmillan, 2009).

Charles Lewis is a professor and the founding executive editor of the Investigative Reporting Workshop at American University in Washington, D.C. He earlier founded the Center for Public Integrity, where he began the International Consortium of Investigative Journalists (1997), Global Integrity (1999), and the Fund for Independence in Journalism (2003).

Donald E. Miller is Professor of Religion and Director of the Center for Religion and Civic Culture at the University of Southern California, Los Angeles.

Alex Nicholls is University Lecturer in Social Entrepreneurship at the Said Business School and Fellow in Management at Harris Manchester College at the University of Oxford.

Ebenezer Obadare is an Associate Professor of Sociology at the University of Kansas, Lawrence, and holds a Ph.D. in Social Policy from the London School of Economics and Political Science. He is the coeditor of *Encountering the Nigerian State* (Palgrave Macmillan, 2010).

Jenny Pearce is Professor of Latin American Politics and Director of the International Centre for Participation Studies at the University of Bradford. She is the coauthor of *Civil Society and Development: A Critical Exploration* (Lynne Rienner, 2001) and *Participation and Democracy in the Twenty-First Century City* (Palgrave Macmillan, 2010).

Donatella della Porta is Professor of Sociology in the Department of Political and Social Sciences at the European University Institute in Firenze.

Nancy L. Rosenblum is Senator Joseph Clark Professor of Ethics in Politics and Government in the Department of Government at Harvard University. She is the author of *Membership and Morals: The Personal Uses of Pluralism in America* (2000) and *On the Side of the Angels: An Appreciation of Parties and Partisanship* (2008), both from Princeton University Press.

Albert Ruesga is President and CEO of the Greater New Orleans Foundation. His articles have appeared in *Social Theory and Practice*, the *Journal of Popular Culture*, the *Boston Book Review*, and other publications. He is the founding editor of the White Courtesy Telephone, a popular blog about nonprofits and philanthropy.

William A. Schambra is the Director of the Hudson Institute's Bradley Center for Philanthropy and Civic Renewal. He has written extensively on the theory and practice of civil society, and is the editor of several volumes including *As Far as Republican Principles Will Admit: Collected Essays of Martin Diamond* (AEI Press, 1992).

Krista Shaffer is a research fellow with Hudson Institute's Bradley Center for Philanthropy and Civic Renewal.

Mark Sidel is Professor of Law, Faculty Scholar, and Lauridsen Family Fellow at the University of Iowa, and President of the International Society for Third Sector Research (ISTR). He is the author of *Regulation of the Voluntary Sector: Freedom and Security in an Era of Uncertainty* (Routledge, 2009).

Theda Skocpol is the Victor S. Thomas Professor of Government and Sociology at Harvard University. She has written about public policies and civic engagement in the United States, and her newest book is *Health Care Reform and American Politics: What Everyone Needs to Know* (Oxford University Press, 2010).

Steven Rathgeb Smith is Professor of Public Policy and Waldemar A. Nielsen Chair in Philanthropy at the Georgetown Public Policy Institute, Georgetown University.

Mark E. Warren is the Harold and Dorrie Merilees Professor for the Study of Democracy at the University of British Columbia.

Michael Woolcock is Senior Social Scientist in the World Bank's Development Research Group, where he has worked since 1998. From 2007 to 2009 he was Professor of Social Science and Development Policy, and founding Research Director of the Brooks World Poverty Institute at the University of Manchester.

Simon Zadek is a Visiting Senior Fellow at the Centre for Government and Business of the J. F. Kennedy School of Government, Harvard University, Associate Senior Fellow at the International Institute of Sustainable Development, and Honorary Professor at the Centre for Corporate Citizenship of the University of South Africa.

THE OXFORD HANDBOOK OF

CIVIL SOCIETY

PART I

INTRODUCTION

CHAPTER 1

INTRODUCTION: CIVIL SOCIETY AND THE GEOMETRY OF HUMAN RELATIONS

MICHAEL EDWARDS

CIVIL society is one of the most enduring and confusing concepts in social science, and for that reason it is an excellent candidate for the analytic explorations that an Oxford handbook can provide. The concept is enduring because it offers a malleable framework through which to examine the "geometry of human relations," as John Ehrenberg puts it in chapter 2—the patterns of collective action and interaction that provide societies with at least partial answers to questions of structure and authority, meaning and belonging, citizenship and self-direction. From the time of classical Greece, thinkers have returned to civil society as one way of generating new energy and ideas around old and familiar questions as the world has changed around them. But civil society is also a confusing and contested concept because so many different definitions and understandings exist (often poorly connected to and articulated with the others), and because the claims that are sometimes made for its explanatory power never quite match up to the complexities and contingencies of real cultures and societies, especially when interpretations fashioned at one time or in one part of the world are transported to another.

Hence, if civil society does shed light on the changing geometry of human relations, it does so not by substantiating any universal patterns, formulae, or equations, but by providing frames and spaces in which the agency and imagination of individuals can be combined to address the key issues of the day. In this respect, and borrowing from Michael Walzer's (1998, 123–24) oft-quoted definition, civil society is the sphere of uncoerced human association between the individual and the state, in which people undertake collective action for normative and substantive purposes, relatively independent of government and the market. What levels of "coercion" actually exist in practice, how "independent" civil society can be from these other spheres of action, which "norms" are reproduced and represented, and what "purposes" are pursued to what effect, are, of course, the stuff of continued and necessary debates, but the beauty of this definition is that it can encompass many different answers and interpretations while calling attention to a set of core mechanisms and concerns. For this reason it provides the best starting point for the discussion that follows.

1. The Rise and Fall of Civil Society

Although the theory and history of civil society are very broad, the ways in which these ideas have been applied in policy, politics, and practice have been much narrower and more restrictive, causing further confusion and creating rising dissatisfaction in some quarters with the concept as a whole. Indeed, most of the problems of the contemporary civil society debate stem from a powerful but unreflectively reductive approach that posits a mechanical relationship between certain forms of voluntary citizen action, the norms and commitments they are presumed to generate, and the achievement of macro-level goals such as democratization and poverty reduction. In this sense, although ideas about civil society have grown in popularity among politicians and policy makers since the late 1980s, scholarly support has fallen away, or at least has given way to rising suspicion and critical questioning. As is common with other concepts in social science such as "participation" and "development," the more that ideas are appropriated in this way the muddier they become, and the greater the need to subject them to critical interrogation in the ways that the contributors to this handbook all seek to do. Indeed, this is the crucial task if the promise of civil society is to be rescued from the confusion and manipulation that have grown up around it.

After the fall of the Berlin Wall in 1989 and the worldwide democratic openings that followed, the idea of civil society returned to the center of intellectual and political debate, and it continued to gain in prominence throughout the 1990s. Everyone, it seemed, saw a "strong civil society" as one of the cornerstones of democracy, "good governance," pluralism, and the achievement of important social and economic goals. Perhaps it was even the "big idea" for the twenty-first century, enjoying support across the political spectrum, in many different parts of the world, and among theorists, activists, and policy makers alike (Edwards 2009). In this sense civil society was the undoubted beneficiary of broader political and intellectual trends that sought alternatives to the deadening effects of state centralization—the dominant motif of the 1960s and 1970s—and the human consequences of an over-reliance on the market: the defining theme of the twenty years that followed. Civil society became the missing link in attempts to address the problems that these paradigms created—the magic ingredient that might correct generations of state and market "failure" and resolve the tensions between social cohesion and capitalism that have preoccupied social scientists at least since the publication of Karl Polanyi's book *The Great Transformation* in 1944 (Polanyi [1944] 2001).

This sense of optimism was carried through the first decade of the twenty-first century under the rubric of "third-way" politics, "compassionate conservatism," communitarian thinking, and other calls for greater citizen participation, devolution, and local empowerment across the United States, most of Europe, and a good part of the "developing" world, at least in rhetorical terms. Perhaps it was no surprise then that these ideas became formally embedded in state policy in the United Kingdom in 2010 under the slogan of the "big society," as defined by the Conservative and Liberal Democratic parties. Even that most bureaucratic of institutions, the European Union, began to encourage more participation in its political structures in 2010 in the form of legislation to encourage petitions and other forms of citizen involvement.[1] And "building civil society" across the Middle East has been an explicit goal of U.S. foreign policy since the terrorist attacks on New York and Washington, D.C. of September 11th, 2001, aiming to cement democracy and siphon discontent into more positive avenues for action in Iraq, Afghanistan, and elsewhere.

These are ambitious—and some would say foolish—aspirations, which civil society, or indeed any set of concepts and ideas, could never hope to meet, except by reducing the richness and diversity of the concept to a set of predefined, actionable instruments of limited value and coherence in those areas that are amenable to external funding and support. The result has been the proliferation of government-sponsored volunteering programs, "capacity-building" for nongovernmental organizations (NGOs), and the replacement of civil society by a set of narrower concepts that are easier to operationalize such as the "third sector," the "nonprofit sector," and the "social economy." Debates about the cultural and political significance of civil society have been displaced by arguments about its economic role, particularly the supposed benefits that accrue from providing health, education, and other goods and services on a not-for-profit basis to lower income groups as states continue to retreat from their social obligations. What began as an *additional* category to the state and the market—a distinct source of both value and values—has been relegated to the status of a *residual*—something that exists only because these other institutions have blind spots and weaknesses, greatly reducing its potential to act as a force for structural or systemic change. Despite the continued rhetoric of public participation, intrusive regulation by governments—and at times outright repression—remains commonplace. And what was once a conversation about democracy and self-expression has become increasingly technocratic, dominated by elites who seek to shape civil society for their own ends and increasingly mimicking the language and practices of businesses and market-based investment (Edwards 2010). Of course, there has been tension for many years between radical and neo-liberal interpretations of civil society, the former seeing it is the ground from which to challenge the status quo and build new alternatives, and the latter as the service-providing not-for-profit sector necessitated by "market failure," but the increasing influence of the latter is leading to growing skepticism in some quarters about the power of collective action, social movements, democratic decision making, community organizing and the noncommercial values of solidarity, service and cooperation.

Will these trends undermine civil society's transformative potential by reducing the ability or willingness of citizens' groups to hold public and private power accountable for its actions, generate alternative ideas and policy positions, push for fundamental changes in the structures of power, and organize collective action on a scale large enough to force through long-term shifts in politics, economics, and social relations? Perhaps, but on a more positive note the 2000s have also seen increasing interest in new avenues for citizen organizing (often based around the Internet and stimulated by other forms of information technology), and in the potential of participatory, direct, and deliberative forms of democracy, in which civil society has a central role to play. These trends have their roots in two developments. The first is the inability of conventional, representative forms of democracy to activate, channel, and aggregate the diverse voices of citizens in modern societies, making additional avenues essential to the successful functioning of the polity. The second is the continued popularity of citizen protest and other forms of direct organizing and engagement despite attempts to weaken, repress, or suppress them in both authoritarian and democratic regimes. Perhaps there is something written into the genetic code of human beings that resists attempts to bureaucratize the self-organizing principles of civil society or reduce citizen action to a subset of the market. Either way, these innovations, if they continue to grow and deepen, might provide a counterweight to continued privatization and top-down government control, returning some of the richness and radical intent of much civil society thinking and practice to the mainstream.

Given these developments, it is all the more important that scholars bring their traditional virtues of rigor, critical independence, long engagement, and historical depth to the continuing debate about civil society and its many meanings, in order to encourage a more analytical approach to its potential as a vehicle for understanding and changing key elements of our world, but without dismissing or desiccating the ability of ideas that are straightforward in their essence to inspire successive generations in their struggles for a better life. This is the approach of all the contributors to the *Oxford Handbook of Civil Society*, who, while recognizing the contestation and cooptation that surround this concept, are not imprisoned or immobilized by the conceptual and empirical difficulties this presents. Instead, they search for insights that both "live" in particular settings and have something to say about civil society in broader terms across a range of contexts and approaches, though it is fair to say that North American authors and experiences are somewhat overrepresented. These insights help to create a more expansive vision of civil society's many possibilities, while guarding against the misuse or monopolization of the term by any one set of interests or school of thought. And the starting point of this process is to break apart the confusion and conflation that surrounds civil society in contemporary usage in order to create a strong foundation for reintegrating diverse perspectives into a coherent set of theories, policies and practices.

2. THE FORMS OF CIVIL SOCIETY

One of the reasons for the continued confusion of the civil society debate is that this is such an elastic concept, seen by many as a part of society (the world of voluntary associations), by some as a kind of society (marked out by certain social norms), and by others as a space for citizen action and engagement (described as the public square or sphere). Rather than seeing these definitions as mutually exclusive or linked together in rigid, universal ways, it is more useful to explore how they relate to each other in different contexts and theoretical approaches.

To that end, sections II and III of this handbook explore the debate from the perspective of the first of these definitions—the *forms* of civil society—across a widely contrasting set of organizational and geographical conditions. This is important because much current civil society research, funding, and policy making is highly ethnocentric, informed by a partial reading of work dating back to the writings of Alexis de Tocqueville in mid-nineteenth-century America which placed voluntary associations of various kinds at the center of civil society thinking and action, but later translated to settings with completely different cultures of collective action, histories, and contemporary conditions. It is this sense of mimicry that has stimulated the export of models developed in North America and Western Europe to other parts of the world with unsurprisingly disappointing results. I have deliberately chosen contexts such as China, India, sub-Saharan Africa, and the Middle East as key locations in which ideas about civil society are being contested and reimagined, alongside more "predictable" contexts such as Eastern Europe, Latin America, and the United States. Lisa Jordan's chapter on global civil society explores the increasingly important terrain of transnational or cross-border citizen organizing that is adding yet more diversity to these patterns.

In the popular imagination, as well as in the minds of most funders and policy makers, it is the forms of civil society that immediately spring to mind, often conflated with particular norms and achievements that they are assumed to produce or generate. Certainly, citizen action, participation, and deliberation all require a physical infrastructure through which they can be expressed, and in that sense a focus on voluntary and quasi-voluntary organizations is not only appropriate but extremely important. Two caveats apply. The first is that civil society organizations cover a huge range of entities of different types, sizes, purposes, and levels of formality, including community or grassroots associations, social movements, labor unions, professional groups, advocacy and development NGOs, formally registered nonprofits, social enterprises, and many others. What is important about these organizations is less their individual existence, identity, or functioning than the ways in which they interact with each other and with the institutions of the state and the market in complex civil society assemblages, ecologies, or "ecosystems," which vary widely in their details from one context to another. As in a real, biological ecosystem, each element is related to the others and gains strength from the system's diversity and organic growth, so that all members of society can activate their interests and intents through associational life. Conversely, any move towards greater homogeneity weakens the civil society ecosystem and leads to its erosion, and eventually its collapse. This is why an over-reliance on any particular form—such as NGOs with weak roots in society, for example—is so dangerous.

The second caveat is that associational ecosystems rarely lead to predictable effects, because they are organic, constantly evolving human creations, most successful when they are most embedded in the "soil and water" of local conditions and mechanisms of support. Studying the gaps and disconnections of real associational ecosystems is therefore likely to pay significant dividends, even if it also complicates the lessons that can be learned for policy and practice. Most important of all, it is clear from an examination of any empirical setting that associations exhibit support for a broad range of different norms, policies, and beliefs, especially at the level of implementation—the means by which even widely agreed norms are assumed to be achieved in practice across the institutions of the state, market, and civil society. Therefore, the links between "forms and norms" that are often taken for granted in analyses of civil society may be much weaker, or perhaps may not exist at all, outside of particular historical and contemporary settings.

3. THE NORMS OF CIVIL SOCIETY

Civil society is often used as shorthand for the *kind* of society in which people want to live, marked out by norms, values, and achievements that they consider to be positive and important. Indeed, these normative aspirations are the most powerful source of energy that drives collective action, though they may take a very pragmatic or prosaic form in meeting the day-to-day needs of individuals and their communities. But it is clear that the forms of civil society do not automatically produce these norms and achievements, first because opinions of what is "positive" vary so widely within and between societies, and second because both societal progress and normative consensus result from the interaction of all the institutions in which our dispositions are formed and action is taken, including those of the state and the market. The idea that a "natural" transmission belt exists between a "strong civil society," measured in terms of the strength and density of voluntary associations, a "society that is strong and civil," measured in terms of positive social norms such as trust, tolerance, and cooperation, and a "good society," measured by its macro-level achievements in addressing poverty, inequality, discrimination, and other large-scale ills, has been heavily criticized by civil society scholars, particularly in the aftermath of Robert Putnam's (1993; 2000) well-known claims about "social capital" and its effects. Historical and empirical evidence also confirms that voluntary associations can play roles which are widely considered to be retrogressive, as in Weimar Germany, the Lebanese "civil wars," and ethnic cleansing in Rwanda, to name but three examples.

However, to say that norms vary among citizens and their associations is a statement of the obvious, and does little to advance the civil society debate, though it is sometimes seized on by critics as a key weakness that invalidates the utility of these ideas. Of more interest is to pose a series of questions about normative diversity and conflict that create space to consider whether and why these differences might be significant, how they might be reconciled, and whether any objective boundaries can or should be drawn between the "civil" and the "uncivil"—something of a "fool's errand" if Clifford Bob is to be believed in chapter 17. Without accepting that all associations have to be "schools of democratic citizenship," what impact do different kinds of civic participation have on social norms? Without accepting that all "good citizens" must sign up to a standard normative agenda, what values do they hold in common, and what tradeoffs do they make between different values such as equality and freedom? And without accepting that all differences have to be negotiated to some sort of consensus in order to preserve democracy, what do the theory and practice of civil society have to say about the mediating effects of the associational ecosystems described in brief above?

Section IV explores these questions through contributions that deal with what one might call the "contested core" values of civil society such as civility, diversity, and equality, and through the ambiguous terrain of social capital, religion, and spirituality, where normative questions are especially significant. These values are core to the notion of civil society because without some level of agreement on and attachment to them, collective action, associational life, and processes of participation and deliberation are unlikely to produce the results that theory predicts. For example, large-scale inequality or discrimination will privilege some interests and agendas over others and distort the public sphere. However, these core values will also be contested, both in their own meaning and in the weight that different groups attach to them. In some normative critiques of civil society, examples such as the mafia and Al-Qaeda are used to prove this point, but they offer little of use to the debate because they are so extreme—close to the forms of civil society in some senses but closer to straightforward criminal, military, or paramilitary activities that work against even the broadest interpretation of these core norms.

Of more interest are the normative differences that exist between "ordinary" associations of various kinds, which are the inevitable result of the diversity that civil society is supposed to encourage and protect. These variations are rooted not only in culture, faith, and ideology, but in much deeper social differences such as gender and ethnicity, which color ideas about civil society itself in more fundamental ways. Hilde Coffé and Catherine Bolzendahl explore the impact of such differences through the prism of gender in chapter 20. However, even these deep-rooted differences pose no threat to the utility or integrity of civil society thinking, so long as it embraces the theory of the public sphere.

4. The Spaces of Civil Society

A strong tradition of civil society thinking emphasizes the *spaces* in which citizens engage with one another and with the institutions of the state and the market, rather than the forms or the norms of civil society in and of themselves. This tradition is less visible in the discourse of most politicians and funders, perhaps because it leads to fewer immediate avenues for action beyond support for the independent media and conflict resolution projects, but it is critical to the utility of civil society as a conceptual frame, particularly because it offers a mechanism by which differences between associations and their agendas can be held and, in some cases, sorted through, to create a new sense of the public interest—a new public—that is strong enough to break through the logjam of embedded power relations and politics. Anchored in Antonio Gramsci's thinking about civil society as a site for the development of hegemony and contestation, in John Dewey's philosophy of pragmatic public engagement and deliberation, and in Jürgen Habermas's theory of the "public sphere," this approach puts the spotlight on the processes of citizen participation which do so much to determine outcomes, and on the structural conditions which frame, expand, or contract them for different groups at different times. Indeed, without the insights and practical possibilities offered by the public sphere, civil society would signify little more than a disaggregated collection of activities and beliefs.

This last point is especially important, because it refocuses our attention away from micro-level studies of, and support for, individual associations, towards the macro-level issues that funders, policy makers and even some academics often ignore when they think about civil society and its effects. These macro-level issues—such as insecurity, inequality, factionalism, the structure of communications, and the extent of civil and political liberties—shape the ability of any population to activate their citizenship through public processes; to undertake projects of "public work" together, as Harry Boyte puts it in chapter 26; and to engage with each other across the lines of difference in order to fashion alliances, networks, and social movements strong enough to exert sufficient pressure for reforms in public policy and the market. Section V explores the forces that strengthen and erode these public spaces and the processes they contain, through which citizens engage with each other, argue and deliberate about the issues of the day, build consensus around the future direction of their societies, and participate in democracy, governance, and "dialogic politics."

In modern, market-based societies, threats to the public sphere come from many different sources, though all are related in some way to the continued privatization and commercialization of human activity from which civil society is far from immune—this being part of the general "decline of the public" in every sphere of life that characterizes the course of contemporary capitalism (Marquand 2004). Once seen as a counterweight to these threats, the distinctive forms and norms of voluntary associations and of philanthropy are being increasingly submerged within the market itself, as business principles are used to promote "more effective" performance, usually in terms of service provision by not-for-profit groups. The "hyper-individualism" that characterizes the marketplace offers no support for collective action or processes of public work, and provides nothing to hold communities together in the face of increasing economic and social stress. Rising levels of insecurity, risk, and inequality make civic participation much more difficult and demanding, further skewing the public sphere towards the interests of elites. Secondary and higher education policies favor a narrow band of technical skills rather than broader capacities for "civic knowledge," as Peter Levine puts it in chapter 29, thereby eroding the ability of ordinary people to make their voices heard. And despite the rhetoric of official support for civil society and "public-private partnership," government attitudes in most countries continue to veer from social engineering to straightforward repression, especially with regard to large-scale citizen mobilization, advocacy, and protest.

Of course, there are also opportunities for greater engagement in the public sphere as a result of new information technologies, community media, "public journalism," and the new forms of civil society organizing that are being developed around these innovations. Attitudes towards these innovations vary from wild optimism to undue pessimism, with the truth lying somewhere in between, but even the most successful find it difficult to reverse the structural inequalities of the public sphere, especially because so much new communication is virtual rather than face-to-face, and may therefore be less effective as a tool for confronting the raw realities of politics and power and for reshaping—as opposed to reinforcing—existing norms and values among communities of interest. The "cyber-optimists" that Roberta Lentz describes in chapter 27 may disagree, but the balance sheet of the public sphere in most countries leans more heavily towards the losses than the gains, imperiling the ability of public spaces to promote democratic engagement and consensus-building and placing a question mark over civil society's ultimate achievements.

5. THE ACHIEVEMENTS OF CIVIL SOCIETY

Each of these theoretical approaches to the forms, norms, and spaces of civil society has much to offer, but it is the *achievements* of civil society that are most important, and understanding those achievements rests on combining insights from all these different schools of thought in each particular setting. How do the structures of associational life and the dynamics of the public sphere help or hinder the achievement of "good society" goals? This is the most important question in the civil society debate, and also the least explored—perhaps because it is so complex, refusing to yield any easy answers or straightforward policy prescriptions. All the contributors to this handbook struggle with this question, and unsurprisingly they end up in very different places. But posing the question in this way already helps to move the conversation away from two responses that have bedeviled the debate thus far. The first is a rigid adherence to one of these approaches to the exclusion of the others, and the second is a tendency to tie each approach together in universal terms, prompting scholars and policy makers to overgeneralize in their conclusions—most commonly, the conclusion that "building" more civil society organizations will automatically cement "positive" social norms and practices, thereby contributing in a similarly linear fashion to the deepening of democracy, the eradication of poverty, and the achievement of other macro-social goals.

This conclusion is not, of course, completely incorrect, but when one examines how democracy has actually been deepened, poverty reduced, peace restored or maintained, and power relations and market economies transformed—as the contributors to section VI all attempt to do—it is clear that civil society is only one of many forces at work, and that it has often been a progenitor of these problems as well as a contributor to their resolution. In unpicking these complicated patterns of cause and effect, all the richness and diversity of civil society thinking must be brought to bear on the analysis. Understanding the *forms* of civil society helps to illumine which kinds of collective action are most important around specific issues and their contexts, and where gaps or disconnects in the associational ecosystem may require attention. For example, evidence from Bangladesh suggests that the growth of service-providing NGOs has extended access to health, education, and economic services among the poor but has failed to achieve any significant impact on social mobilization or political empowerment—areas which are fundamental to large-scale, long-term progress (Kabeer, Mahmud, and Castro 2010). Understanding the *norms* of civil society takes us on a journey into just these areas, penetrating more deeply into the forces that drive social change such as the values, beliefs, and ideologies that exert their influence beneath the surface of citizen action and underpin the success or failure of social movements and other attempts to shift the rules of the game. And understanding the *spaces* of civil society is vital if we are to get to grips with the tasks of debate and consensus-building around these norms, and of contesting and reshaping the power relations that ultimately determine the success of social action. When the analysis of forms, norms, and spaces is incorporated into a single, integrated framework, new light can be shed on civil society's achievements even in the most complicated and difficult of circumstances. Seen in this way, civil society is simultaneously a goal to aim for, a means of achieving it, and a framework for engaging with each other about ends and means.

If this is true, than the practical task of nurturing or encouraging civil society becomes much more complex, way beyond the usual agenda of organizational development and support for greater citizen participation. Therefore it is fitting that this handbook closes with three contributions in section VII that look at the record of efforts to promote civil society through various forms of philanthropy and foreign aid, a task which has occupied the attention of many donor agencies especially since the fall of the Berlin Wall. The verdict of these authors is somewhat pessimistic, largely because foundations and other funders have mis-specified the tasks involved and exaggerated their potential influence. Paradoxically, civil society may be nurtured most effectively when donors do less, not more, stepping back to allow citizens themselves to dictate the agenda and evolve a variety of civil societies to suit their contexts and concerns.

6. CONCLUSION

The goal of this introduction has been to lay out the basic parameters of the civil society debate in order to help the reader situate the many different contributions that follow in a wider context. Necessarily, this has involved abandoning any one particular understanding, interpretation, or point of view, beyond the idea that civil society is a composite of forms, norms, and spaces in the sense of Michael Walzer's definition of "uncoerced human association" between the individual and the state. This may seem overly complex or unduly vague, but it represents a much better starting point than framing the debate only in terms of Habermas, deTocqueville, or any of the other icons of the civil society pantheon. Once liberated from the idea that civil society must mean one thing in every context, it is easier to engender a wide-ranging conversation about the core elements of this idea as well as its contested peripheries, while still relating theory to practice in actionable ways.

There is unlikely to be a specific endpoint or winner in the civil society debate, because the concept of civil society is continually being reshaped and reinterpreted by new actors in new contexts—yet the idea that voluntary collective action can influence the world for the better is unlikely to dissipate or be defeated. Many different varieties of civil society will be created in this way in the future, containing hybrid organizational forms, norms which may depart from traditional notions of cooperation and solidarity, and spaces which are occupied by a wider range of cross-sector partnerships and alliances. Scholars must bring to bear the widest possible array of tools and approaches to interpret the costs and benefits of these changes—free, as far as is humanly possible, from ethnocentric and other assumptions. This task is likely to be framed by increasing pressures from governments, businesses, and others to redefine the conventional roles, rights, and responsibilities of civil society associations, the public sphere, and their associated values. And these pressures will test and reshape the practice of citizen action in service to the good society in both positive and negative ways that are sure to have important implications for civil society theory. I hope that the *Oxford Handbook of Civil Society* will help readers of all persuasions to chart a course through these uncertain waters with greater understanding, insight, and success.

NOTE

1. "Europe Turns Ear Toward Voice of the People," by S. Daley and S. Castle, New York Times July 22, 2010.

REFERENCES

Edwards, M. 2009. *Civil Society*. 2nd ed. Cambridge: Polity Press.

———. 2010. *Small Change: Why Business Won't Save the World*. San Francisco: Berrett-Koehler.

Kabeer, N., S. Mahmud, and J. Castro. 2010. *NGO Strategies and the Challenge of Development and Democracy in Bangladesh*. Institute for Development Studies Working Paper 343. Brighton Institute for Development Studies.

Marquand, D. *The Decline of the Public*. 2004. Cambridge: Polity Press.

Polanyi, M. [1944] 2001. *The Great Transformation*. Boston: Beacon Press.

Putnam, R. 1993. *Making Democracy Work: Civic Traditions in Modern Italy*. Princeton, N.J.: Princeton University Press.

———. 2000. *Bowling Alone: The Collapse and Revival of American Community*. New York: Simon & Schuster.

Walzer, M. 1998. "The Idea of Civil Society: A Path to Social Reconstruction," in E. J. Dionne (ed.) *Community Works: The Revival of Civil Society in America*. Washington, D.C.: Brookings Institution Press.

CHAPTER 2

THE HISTORY OF CIVIL SOCIETY IDEAS

JOHN EHRENBERG

GREEK and Roman thinkers began talking about civil society as part of a more general attempt to establish a geometry of human relations. Their tendency to privilege political matters drove them to think of "civility" as an orientation toward the common good and the requirements of effective citizenship rather than as a matter of domestic relations or good manners, a trend that culminated in the classical identification of civil society with the political commonwealth. At the same time, a recognition that life is lived in different spheres that have their own internal logic drove toward a more nuanced approach that made possible a recognition of social complexity and the limits of political life.

1. CIVIL SOCIETY AS THE ORGANIZED COMMONWEALTH

Plato's desire to organize an invariant ethical center for public life tended to subsume private affairs to the requirements of civic health and moral renewal. His affinity for a unitary community made him suspicious of particular interests and domestic affairs, and his understanding of civil society was defined by his search for the first principles that would frame the community's moral life. He established the general categories which could assist in an analysis of the particular, but it was left to his greatest student, Aristotle, to craft an understanding of civil society that respected the multiple spheres in which life is lived even as it retained the dedication to a comprehensive political association that defined the moral life of its members.

Aristotle understood that humans live in different spheres, all of which contribute to moral development and political stability. Plato's notion of "the Good" identified that which is worthy of pursuit for its own sake, but Aristotle knew that habits and preferences limited the sweep of grand plans for moral regeneration. Having moved away from his teacher's orientation toward unitary explanations, he developed a notion of civil society based on a respect for variation that also expressed a desire for comprehensiveness. If less developed processes have their own logic, it is also true that they derive their meaning from their relation to the more developed wholes to which they contribute and which frame their possibilities. Civil society receives its most general meaning in the political community but Aristotle knew that individuals act for particular reasons and that subsidiary levels of organization contribute to the welfare of the whole. If the polis is the broadest of all human associations because it alone exists for the sake of the "good life," it is no less true that the spheres of intimacy, production, and nature are spheres of moral action. Their range is restricted and their effects conditioned by inequality, dependence, and necessity, but they help set the conditions for the full realization of human potential and share in the ethical content of the polis.

But it is the political sphere's deliberation, self-rule, and mutual recognition that defined Aristotle's civil society—an emphasis that reflected the embedded nature of subordinate spheres and the material limits that made impossible the appearance of a distinct arena of self-interested economic life. Aristotle's famous suspicion of untrammeled economic affairs, a moral aversion that characterized all Christian thought during the Middle Ages, fortified his sense that civil society was rooted in the aristocratic, face-to-face interactions of friends whose leisurely benevolence drove their discovery and articulation of the public good. Animated by informed debate and populated by a broad middle class, Aristotle's civil society was constituted by the life of noble action.

For all its limits, Aristotle's recognition that a polis is a union of unlike elements implied that there is no single vision of excellence that is common to all. If Plato sought an undifferentiated unity that would always generate a given course of action, Aristotle's suggestion that different virtues are appropriate to different situations would prove to be his lasting contribution to theories of civil society. But Aristotle's dictum that only politics could provide the full measure of possibilities for moral action and the Good Life should not be forgotten. The common interest can be grasped with relative precision, and Aristotle's celebrated classification of states aimed at a moderate constitutional order that could protect public action even as it recognized that civil societies are composed of different families, classes, occupations, circumstances of birth, and orders of merit. Aristotle's preference for a mixed constitution expressed his recognition that plurality was the foundation of unity. He was sure that a state whose structure took account of subordinate spheres would enhance the deliberative life of citizenship conditioned life in subordinate spheres.

The slow decline and eventual disappearance of the independent city-states that had nurtured Plato and Aristotle encouraged the Roman claim that a universal empire could transcend Greek parochialism. An integrated notion of a world community gave rise to the late Stoic ideal of a universal civil society organized by reason. As permanent crisis and instability marked the transition to empire, Cicero sought to rescue civic virtue by rooting justice in a conception of law-governed nature. Equally hostile to self-serving aristocratic corruption and grasping popular movements, he tried to develop a defense of civil society that was rooted in natural law and conditioned the *res publica*, the "people's possession." Civil society was now an organization of public power that made civilization possible, and justice was its organizing principle. It rested on the universal human capacity to share in the right reason that is consonant with nature, exists independently of human contingency, and orders the universe. The requirements of a politically constituted commonwealth would continue to drive private pursuits toward the public by limiting the private sphere's disintegrative tendencies. Reason and right thinking were indispensable to civic health but effective institutions animated by republican ideals were indispensable to the never-ending struggle against the impulse to seek private advantage.

Cicero's conviction that Aristotle's mixed constitution could protect particular differences while organizing the common good marked his chief contribution to medieval constitutionalism and to Enlightenment notions of civil society. In the shorter run, his notion of the common good envisaged a civil society that rested on the peasant-soldiers who defended the republic against domestic exploitation and foreign threat. Even as the empire's universal aspirations claimed to represent a finality and universality to which alternative systems of private and public life could not pretend, the Roman notion of a *res publica* soon implied a *res privata* as a correlative sphere. Constituted by family and property and protected by a network of rights, it marked the area of intimate associations and particular interests. Private law regulated the relations between individuals, provided legal definition to the family and to property, and established a legally recognized zone of domestic life. The later distinction between private persons and public citizens provided the background for the truism that Roman law stopped at the household's doorstep. The republican notion of civil society as a sphere of property, reason, justice, and privacy continued to seek a universal and public understanding of citizenship even as it recognized a powerful private center of gravity. Even if the empire finally proved unable to protect Rome, classical notions of civil society continued the effort to rescue mankind from barbarism and secure for it the benefits of a politically organized civilization.

The Roman Empire was gradually succeeded by a centralized state backed by the Byzantine Church in Constantinople and a multiplicity of tribally based territorial kingdoms in the West. If the universal empire now existed in memory, it was Christianity that supplied the West with whatever social and ideological unity it had for a millennium following the fall of Rome. It did so by providing a basis for a common spiritual fellowship and by articulating a consistent theory of the state and civil society as two mutually defined elements of an integrated Christian Commonwealth.

Religion had been subordinated to the requirements of the political order in Greece and Rome, but it assumed a stronger independent standing in the more decentralized environment of the Middle Ages. Augustine's powerful attack on the classical ideal of self-sufficiency located dependence at the center of politics, theology, and history. Theories of universal knowledge and universal commonwealths claimed to organize the whole of public and private life in a single comprehensive totality, and an increasingly centralized Church provided the legitimacy for state structures and political authority. But the development of broader markets, stronger kings, and more assertive local bodies made it increasingly difficult to maintain an overarching framework within which civil society could be understood. In the end, the Church's ecclesiastical theory could not withstand the disintegrative forces of individual interest, the sanctity of the conscience, or the calculations of opportunistic princes. As the Christian Commonwealth's traditional notion of two spheres and two powers collapsed before the logic of undivided sovereignty flowing from a single point of power, it became impossible for an avowedly religious authority to organize the whole of public life. Religion's long retreat to the sphere of private belief meant that the spiritual truths proclaimed, guarded, and advanced by the Church ceased to have any compelling public force apart from the state's organizing and coercive power. By the end of the Middle Ages, a more secular conception of politics was beginning to develop, accompanied by a notion of civil society that was now understood in economic terms.

2. The Transition to Modernity

Niccolo Machiavelli was unable to theorize civil society outside the traditional categories of Roman republicanism, but his secular economy of power anticipated the appearance of the interest-bearing individual that would form the core for the bourgeois understanding of civil society articulated by John Locke and Adam Smith. In the meantime, it was important to learn from Rome. If political power held human affairs together, then the mixed constitution would protect the vibrant civic life that could protect the republic, ensure stability, and organize a long-lasting politics. Civic institutions, a vigorous public life, creative leadership, and "good laws" can mitigate the inevitable disputes that arise from class conflict and the strivings for individual advantage. Only a mixed constitution that reflected the organization of society could preserve the autonomy of the part and safeguard the integrity of the whole.

Thomas Hobbes wasn't so sure. Obsessed by the constant threat of civil war and barbarism, he was convinced that only a single point of undivided sovereign power could constitute civil society and make it possible for his calculating individual to live his life free of mortal danger. In a world that was being defined by the religious claims of the individual conscience and the pursuit of private interest, only state power can make civilization possible. Domestic peace required the presence of the "artificial man" who made it possible for real men to construct a human life free of the constant threat of annihilation. Equally alarmed by the English Revolution and the Protestant Reformation, Hobbes sought refuge in a state that was coterminous with a civil society now conceived as the arena in which interest-bearing individuals pursued their private goals. If the "natural condition" of mankind feeds the "desire of power after power" in an environment of equal vulnerability and pervasive insecurity, then nothing is possible until the threat of endless war is brought under control. This requires a "common power" that will enforce standards of behavior and make it possible for people to go about their business in peace. If people can safely anticipate that others will control themselves, then all can surrender their propensity to act as if they are the only people in the world. If they can live with a measure of assurance that they will be safe, they can make the calculation that a mutual and universal transfer of rights is in everyone's interest.

The sword stands behind the original agreement to leave the chaos of nature, and it is this common commitment to public power that makes civilization possible. It brings industry, agriculture, justice, navigation, science, morality, and culture into human history. Hobbes's civil society is made possible by sovereign power, is constituted by politics, and cannot be distinguished from the state. Inhabited by individuals who share a desire for the material, cultural, and moral benefits of civil society, it requires a coercive mechanism that can compel isolated, fearful, and competitive individuals to act as if they trusted one another.

For all his emphasis on the need for a single source of sovereign power, Hobbes knew that economic activity, science, and arts and letters require respect for the private realm of individual desire and autonomy. But even as he made it clear that civil society existed at the pleasure of the sovereign, he was equally sure that it was a recognizable sphere of self-interested activity with which the state need not interfere unless civic order was threatened. Even if he was unwilling to invest the private sphere with the moral content or economic creativity that would characterize Locke, the distinction that he drew between public political power and the private arena of desire marked an important contribution to modern theories of the state and of civil society.

Hobbes marked an end—and a beginning. European society would continue to fracture, and the spread of markets accompanied the development of modern forms of centralized and bureaucratic political organization. As the arguments for an autonomous and protected economic sphere began to gain traction, notions of princely power and classical republicanism yielded to the cold logic of self-interest. It would not be long before civil society would be defined in distinctly bourgeois terms.

3. THE CIVIL SOCIETY OF "ECONOMIC MAN"

Locke announced the appearance of a modern theory of civil society. Hobbes didn't have to rely on a powerful state to protect civil society, Locke suggested, since all the preconditions for prosperity and peace were present in the state of nature. Our natural condition is one of freedom, sociability, and reason, and the collective decision to establish a disinterested authority to adjudicate disputes does nothing more than address the "inconvenience" occasioned by the temptation to use the collective power of the community to advance oneself. Locke's resident of civil society is an economic person first and foremost; the state exists to protect the rights of acquisition and accumulation that were already present and lacked only an effective enforcement mechanism. The celebrated "rule of law" is designed to protect and structure the economic activity of the self-interested members of civil society. Drawing on Locke's work and Adam Ferguson's moral economy, Smith expressed the bourgeois confidence that the laws of economics made it possible to organize civil society around individual advantage while bringing the blessings of civilization to everyone. The material processes of social life were replacing the political community and sovereign power as the constitutive forces of civil society.

Hobbes had privileged politics in the transition from barbarism to civilization, but Locke was sure that economic forces could organize civil society if allowed to function in conditions of freedom, if structured by the rule of law, and if protected by a state with limited coercive power. Citizenship could now be based on property, and Locke's announcement that the state existed to protect a set of prepolitical natural rights took theories of civil society into new territory. Locke agreed that political power organized civilization in the broad sense, but he wanted to rest civil society on a stronger foundation than an understanding of the common good. The priority that he accorded to private interests illustrated liberalism's suggestion that it is the creation, accumulation, and use of wealth that is really important. A limited state and the rule of law would now make it possible for rights-bearing individuals to pursue their interests without being forced to kill each other. The state and the economy were separating out from the wider social organism, and the gradual disappearance of the embedded economy meant that political power could now be theoretically distinguished from the production, accumulation, and distribution of wealth. If Locke was correct and property was both a natural right and a condition for moral independence and personal autonomy, then it should be possible to develop an understanding of civil society that would reserve pride of place to economic laws and processes.

It was Smith who first articulated a fully developed bourgeois theory of civil society. Economic processes now constitute the anatomy of civilized life, and Smith's celebrated attack on the political regulation of economic affairs anticipated modern conceptions of civil society as a sphere of private striving that stands apart from the state. Smith didn't ignore public matters, suggesting that political authority is necessary to provide for defense, organize the rule of law, and provide public goods that cannot produce a profit for private investors. But *The Wealth of Nations* is organized around the proposition that civil society is organized by economic processes. Resting as they do on the division of labor, markets allow individuals to multiply and develop their particular skills and apply their inclinations in a way that fosters mutual dependence—particularly in conditions where they do not mean to do so.

The formal expression of the "law of unanticipated consequences," civil society transforms the self-interested exchanges of free men into a mutually beneficial civilized life for all through the operations of an "invisible hand" that acts behind our backs to produce results that we do not intend. Contract theory was unnecessary, replaced by Smith's assurance that a natural "propensity to truck, barter, and exchange one thing for another" was the real foundation of civil society.

Smith shared Locke's sentiment that the activity of people in markets, rather than in politics, is the real glue of civil society. The state's formal separation from the economy was more apparent than real, but Smith's break with mercantilism signaled that close public supervision was no longer necessary to organize and protect civil society. He did have some some reservations about the social price that market-induced inequality would demand, but it fell to Georg Wilhelm Friedrich Hegel and Karl Marx to generate a new theory of civil society that would more fully take account of modernity's economics and politics.

4. BEYOND CIVIL SOCIETY

Hegel, along with Immanuel Kant, shared Adam Smith's view that civil society was organized and constituted by economic processes, but they weren't as confident that the market would be able to translate the chaos of private desire into the common good. Drawing considerable moral force from Jean-Jacques Rousseau, Kant sought to base civil society on an intrinsic sense of moral duty that unites all humans, but he also wanted to move past the Scots' naïve assumption of innate moral sentiments. His claim that civilization requires universal categories of right that are accessible to all sought to derive a minimal universal ethic appropriate to people who are fully self-governing in moral affairs. If rules are requirements that people impose on themselves, then the path from dependence to autonomy is the path toward freedom. But political institutions and the rule of law can make possible a civil society that can generate universal moral principles, and that is why Kant's civil society rests on a law-governed foundation of coercion and obedience. A republic committed to publicity and protective of rights could make it possible for reason to serve the public good, free mankind from authority and dogma, and organize a civil society of mutual recognition in a "kingdom of ends."

But Kant's formalism prevented him from probing deeply into the network of material relations that constituted civil society, and Hegel took pains to demonstrate that equality before the law, republican institutions, and civil liberties were not enough to protect moral autonomy and freedom. Conscious control of individual and collective lives requires action in accordance with the requirements of reason. Freedom is now a determinate structure of interactions in the world and the three spheres of social life—the family, civil society, and the state—are different structures of ethical development, separate and related "moments of freedom."

Civil society transcends the family's moral content by moving beyond the ties of sentiment and loyalty that constitute domestic institutions but suppress difference and individuality. The first stirrings of independent consciousness precipitate the ethical moment of civil society. Its foundation in subjectivity, property, competition, and particularity means that its inhabitants act with their own interests in mind and are concerned with the satisfaction of their own needs. Hegel had read his political economy. The paradox of his civil society is that self-serving individuals behave selfishly and instrumentally toward each other but cannot help satisfying one another's needs and advancing their mutual interests in the process. Civil society is a moment in moral freedom, but is a limited and dangerous moment because it drives toward making itself the only determination for social life. Hegel shared philosophy's long suspicion of untrammeled economic activity. This is what led him to look to the universal state to transcend the limits of the "system of needs."

Like Smith, Hegel knew that bourgeois civil society constantly generated inequality, illustrating the paradoxical motion from choice, self-interest, and autonomy to isolation, dependence, and subservience. In the end civil society is an alienated, unfree and unjust sphere where autonomy and freedom can no longer suffice to constitute a moral life worthy of human habitation and ethical self-determination. Poverty and inequality signal that Kant was wrong, Hegel announced. Civil society cannot overcome nature because freedom requires more than liberation from the constraints of feudalism.

Marx transformed Hegel's theory of the state into a critique of civil society and of the bourgeois economic order that sustained it. Drawing on the British political economists, Hegel had discovered that civil society was constituted by bourgeois class relations and increasingly characterized by instability, pauperism, and moral degradation. He looked to the "universal" state to transcend civil society's particularism in a more comprehensive moment of liberation, but Marx's early work led him to conclude that Hegel's state was a false universal that could not be the final moment in human freedom. Hegel's idealism had blinded him. He was right that the great bourgeois revolutions had freed the state from the formal constraints of civil society, but he had failed to appreciate the implications of their freeing civil society from the state. If public life now functioned in formal separation from feudal determinations of property, religion, class, and the like, it was no less true that property, religion, and class were now free to develop in formal isolation from political determinations and constraints. Their hold on people had not been weakened by all the genuine advances of the great anti-feudal revolutions; as the United States revealed, they had been strengthened. The American constitution had insisted upon the formal separation of church from state as a condition for strengthening religion and protecting it from political interference. The paradoxical result was that the United States was simultaneously the country that was most formally free from the political influence of religion, but was also the most deeply religious in matters of belief.

Marx's discovery that civil society itself had to be democratized is what carried him beyond Hegel—indeed, beyond all previous conceptions. His extension of emancipation from politics to economics, from the state to civil society, from the formal to the substantial, constitutes his most important contribution to theories of civil society. Hegel had theorized the state as freedom from the antagonisms and limits of civil society, but Marx criticized the state as part of a more general critique of the civil society on which it rested. The new understanding required transcending civil society as such by uprooting its material base in private property. This was a crucial step in the development of modern democratic and socialist thought, for it led directly to the discovery of the proletariat as the alternative to Hegel's state. Hegel had thought that civil society could be transcended from the outside. Marx looked at the constitutive processes of civil society itself and found the universal class there, in the person of the property-less proletariat. Even so, he was as much an enemy of the bourgeois state as of bourgeois civil society and never harbored any illusions that human freedom would be served by merely strengthening the former at the expense of the latter. When he hailed the Paris Commune as the germ of a communist society, he celebrated its assault on bourgeois civil society as enthusiastically as its break with bourgeois political understandings and institutions. Democratizing civil society requires abolishing it and moving toward an "association" that transcends the chaos, antagonism, inequality, and arbitrariness of market society. Liberalism developed a theory of civil society because it wanted to democratize the state. Marxism developed a theory of the state because it wanted to democratize civil society. The twists and turns of contemporary history would bring them face-to-face in Eastern Europe.

5. CIVIL SOCIETY AND ASSOCIATIONS

The roots of the contemporary interest in civil society lie in the contention of some dissident East European intellectuals during the 1980s that communism's crisis could only be understood as a "revolt of civil society against the state." Driven by the central socialist desire to transform the conditions of material life, they said, a bureaucratized and grasping state apparatus relentlessly interfered with society and repeatedly proved itself immune to democratic initiative or control. A sustained criticism of Marxism's supposed lack of limits, its tendency to politicize everything, its suspicion of popular democracy, and its drive to direct, suppress, or absorb all spontaneous activity originating in civil society evolved into a deep theoretical hostility to the state. This position found a powerful echo in the West, where a right-wing attack on the welfare state was beginning to develop. As is often the case in conservative periods, Alexis de Tocqueville was suddenly in favor.

A critic of the centralizing French monarchy, the baron de Montesquieu had drawn on Aristotle and Cicero as he located intermediate bodies at the heart of his aristocratic theory of civil society. Edmund Burke shared his fear of centralized leveling political power, and his famous attack on the French Revolution was organized around a defense of local privilege and inequality. But it was Tocqueville's famous claim that voluntary activity connected individualistic, self-serving Americans to the common good that proved particularly powerful. Worried about the reach of a democratic state in an egalitarian society, Tocqueville sought to preserve local privilege and nurture traditions of self-government. He was confident that the Americans had learned to defend liberty without surrendering to democratic excess precisely because their interests tended to be narrow and parochial. A vibrant culture of local activity contrasted favorably with Europeans' love of routine, uniformity, and moderation. Echoing James Madison, he hoped that civil society would serve liberty by diluting the influence of any single interest, weakening the majority, and guarding against excess. Equality, localism, and materialism could coexist in Tocqueville's expanded notion of civil society as localism, voluntarism, and association. In an age when democracy and egalitarianism could threaten liberty, Tocqueville looked to civil society to protect freedom with inequality.

Tocqueville's assurance that American society was characterized by widespread equality let him avoid the problem that had proven so important to Hegel, Marx, and others: how inequality of condition might inhibit voluntary activity for those with neither the time nor the resources to spend on it. Under such conditions, civil society becomes a sphere of self-reinforcing inequality and privilege. It is not clear that Tocqueville was right about American equality when he visited, but there is no doubt that contemporary conditions call some of his fundamental assumptions into question. The United States is the most unequal advanced nation on earth, and easy assertions that localism and voluntarism provide formally equal citizens with the opportunity to better their condition and influence public life have yielded to more sober reflections about how civil society may reinforce privilege, serve inequality, and damage democracy. Tocqueville's admiration for the New England town meeting notwithstanding, there is abundant evidence that small and intimate organizations stifle divisive conflict, reinforce existing inequalities, and defer to the leadership of the already powerful. There is no convincing evidence that the local and the intimate are necessarily more democratic just because they are small. Indeed, it is entirely possible that the real threat to equality and democracy comes from private power and that the only way to mitigate this threat is through broad, comprehensive regulation and redistribution—exactly the sort of politically driven interference against which much of the contemporary fascination with civil society ranges itself.

Thirty years of conservative hegemony have been built on a rhetorical hostility to the state and a celebration of the local. Now civil society is supposed to revive communities, train citizens, build habits of cooperation, provide an alternative to bureaucratic meddling, and reinvigorate public life—all this in an era of small government and parochial politics. This simplistic view has hidden the state-led redistribution of wealth through regressive fiscal and monetary policies, deregulation, and privatization. It also obscures the presence of a different and no less authentically American tradition of broad state action to address the inequalities of civil society—a view that fed important periods of democratic reform from the Progressive Era through the New Deal, the Civil Rights Movement and the Great Society. Barack Obama's election might signal a changed orientation, but a narrowed sense of public purpose and a restricted sense of political possibilities continue to bedevil efforts to democratize economic life. It is important to understand what is at stake. Understanding civil society as a nonstate, nonmarket sphere of voluntary activity cannot help us make distinctions between bowling leagues and neighborhood associations on the one hand, and Greenpeace, the National Organization of Women, and the White Citizens Council on the other. It is not enough to say that democracy requires a strengthened civil society and leave it at that. As important as they are, local activity, voluntary organizations, and good manners cannot protect equality or advance democracy in conditions of historic inequality and gigantic centers of private power. They cannot take on the historic concentrations of wealth and privilege that dominate contemporary life and distort democracy. Now as before, there is no substitute for broad, sustained, and democratic political action.

REFERENCES

Cohen, J. and Arato, A. 1994. *Civil Society and Political Theory.* Cambridge, Mass.: MIT Press.

Eberle, D. 2000. *The Essential Civil Society Reader: The Classic Essays.* Lanham, Md.: Rowman and Littlefield.

Edwards, M. *Civil Society.* 2009 2nd ed. Cambridge: Polity Press.

Ehrenberg, J. 1999. *Civil Society: The Critical History of an Idea.* New York: NYU Press.

Habermas, J. 1989. *The Structural Transformation of the Public Sphere: An Inquiry into a Category of Bourgeois Society.* Cambridge, Mass.: MIT Press.

Kaldor, M. 2003. *Global Civil Society: An Answer to War.* Cambridge: Polity Press.

Keane, J. (ed.) 1988. *Democracy and the State: New European Perspectives.* London: Verso.

Mansbridge, J. 1983. *Beyond Adversary Democracy.* Chicago: University of Chicago Press.

McConnell, G. 1966. *Private Power and American Democracy.* New York: Knopf.

Putnam, R. 2001. *Bowling Alone: The Collapse and Revival of American Community.* New York: Simon & Schuster.

Sandel, M. 1998. *Democracy's Discontent: America in Search of a Public Philosophy.* Cambridge, Mass.: Harvard University Press.

Verba, S., Schlozman, K.L. and Brady, H. 1995. *Voice and Equality: Civic Voluntarism in American Politics.* Cambridge, Mass.: Harvard University Press.

PART II

THE FORMS OF CIVIL SOCIETY

CHAPTER 3

THE NONPROFIT SECTOR

STEVEN RATHGEB SMITH

THE role of the nonprofit sector in society is on the rise throughout the world (Salamon, Sokolowski and Lis 2004; Salamon 2010; Phillips and Smith 2011). In the United States, nonprofit organizations play a central role in providing key public services, often with government funding. Widespread attention has been devoted to the importance of faith-based and neighborhood organizations in addressing important social problems. The administration of President Barack Obama has established a federal Office of Social Innovation to support emergent nonprofit organizations with proven records of effectiveness, and in the United Kingdom, public-private partnerships with community and nonprofit involvement form a key component of the "Big Society" envisaged by the political coalition between Conservative and Liberal Democratic parties that came to power in 2010, just as they were a decade earlier under the "Third Way" policy agenda of "New Labor," though the specifics of policy implementation obviously vary. The European Union has placed engagement with civil society at the heart of its pursuit of democratic legitimacy, integration, and enlargement (European Commission 2001; Dunn 2011). So too have many countries in transition, where legal, policy, and regulatory reforms are linked to processes of modernization and democratization, and where civil society organizations are establishing a stronger role as more stable democracies develop. Even countries that have long ignored or openly repressed civil society groups are taking steps to develop new nonprofit and charity legislation. Political rhetoric abounds, but it has also been accompanied by substantial reform in many countries. The result has been both an expansion of and a wide variety of reforms in the nonprofit sector, especially in relation to the roles that nonprofits play in service delivery. This chapter explores the place of the nonprofit sector in the broader field of civil society, analyzes a number of different theories which aim to account for the rise of nonprofits, and highlights an emerging set of issues and dilemmas that arise from the ways in which nonprofit organizations are being positioned.

1. WHAT IS THE NONPROFIT SECTOR?

A connecting thread that runs through many different definitions is that civil society is the space of voluntary association and activity that exists in relative separation from the state and the market (Cohen and Arato 1992; Barber 1998; Salamon, Sokolowski, and List 2004). As noted by Putnam (1993), a vibrant civil society is characterized by a rich mixture of voluntary groups that provide ongoing opportunities for citizen engagement and participation in associational affairs, as well as more broadly in the public policy process. Nonprofit organizations (or "nonprofits") form a specific category of associational life in civil society, and are usually defined by their high level of formality in terms of legal registration, by the preponderance of external funding in their budgets (as opposed to membership support), and by their roles as intermediaries that sit between grassroots constituencies and communities, and government and other agencies. Nonprofits constitute an important element in the ecosystems of civil society, but the two should not be conflated.

Robert Putnam's (1993; 2000) widely publicized work argued that voluntary associations can produce cooperative social networks, or social capital, which in turn can promote more effective government, higher levels of economic development, and a more satisfied citizenry. Putnam's work also calls attention to the role of nonprofit organizations in supporting civil society more broadly. The attraction of nonprofits also reflects the growing worldwide interest in civic and community service, including volunteering. In the United States, the Serve America Act of 2009 could potentially fund over 250,000 paid "volunteers" through the federal Corporation for National and Community Service. In the United Kingdom, the Home Office issued a white paper on police reform in 2010 that called for the greater use of volunteers in public safety (Home Office 2010). More broadly, David Cameron, who was elected as Prime Minister in the same year, made plans for sharply increased levels of volunteering among the population to anchor his vision of the "Big Society." Overall, volunteering appears to be growing worldwide, especially among young people (McBride, et al. 2004; 2006). Most, but not all, volunteering occurs in the nonprofit sector.

In the United States, high-profile nonprofits such as Teach for America, the Harlem Children's Zone, and YouthBuild have received widespread attention for their focus on outcomes and improved program performance, which, it is claimed, distinguishes them from more traditional civil society groups. Many innovative nonprofits in the United States and elsewhere have also generated interest as a result of their mix of nonprofit and for-profit elements. These so-called social enterprises tend to rely in part on fees or on earned income, and they actively participate in the market economy as a way of helping the users of their programs to advance (Alter 2010; Light 2008; Bornstein 2007; Crutchfield and Grant 2008; Cordes and Steuerle 2009; Nicholls, chapter 7 in this volume). Outside of the United States, similar organizations are also on the rise, including microcredit groups such as the Grameen Bank.

Global social and demographic trends are also shaping the role of the nonprofit sector, with the aging of the population in many countries creating sharply higher levels of demand for community care programs including home care, home health, and transitional living. Support for work opportunities for the disabled, the unemployed, and the disadvantaged has led naturally to rising interest in community living and workforce development programs, in which nonprofits usually play a central part. Indeed, except in a small number of highly repressive regimes such as Myanmar and Cuba, the absolute size of the nonprofit sector has increased significantly over the past twenty years in all parts of the world, though substantial differences exist in the relative importance and character of the sector in different countries. For example, over 14 percent of the labor force works in the nonprofit sector in the Netherlands compared to 7.1 percent in Sweden and less than one percent in Poland (Salamon, Sokolowski, and List 2004: 19). In the developing world these variations are much wider, ranging, for example, from 1.2 million nonprofit organizations in India to between 15,000 and 20,000 in Egypt (Kienle and Chandhoke, chapters 12 and 14 in this volume). What explains these cross-country differences?

2. Theories of the Nonprofit Sector

a. From Welfare States to Social Origins

One key reference point for understanding cross-national differences in the nonprofit sector is the literature on the development of the welfare state. In particular, Esping-Andersen (1990) argued in his influential book that welfare state regimes could be classified into three different categories: *liberal, corporatist,* and *social-democratic. Liberal* regimes include countries such as the United States, the United Kingdom, New Zealand, and Australia, and are characterized by minimal social support from the state and extensive means-testing. *Corporatist* regimes include Germany and the Netherlands and typically offer extensive social benefits through a mix of market and state mechanisms for support, with the state often working in conjunction with market organizations such as employers. *Social democratic* regimes are committed to universal benefits largely provided by the state, with a deliberate disconnect between eligibility for social benefits and the market (sometimes known as "de-commodification"). Countries in this category include Denmark, Sweden, and Norway.

Esping-Andersen's profoundly influential welfare state regime typology was based on his research into income maintenance programs such as pensions and unemployment insurance. Relatively little attention was devoted to nonprofit organizations. Salamon and Anheier (1998) addressed this gap in their "social origins" theory, which draws on Esping-Andersen as well as the work of Barrington Moore (1966). Social origins theory details four different nonprofit regime types: *liberal* regimes such as the United States, with low government social welfare spending and a large nonprofit sector; *social democratic* regimes such as the Scandinavian countries, with extensive state services and smaller numbers of service-providing nonprofit organizations; *corporatist* regimes such as Germany, with broad-based social benefits and a long tradition of state-supported organizations in an extensive nonprofit sector; and *statist* regimes such as Japan, in which the government exercises substantial power and autonomy but rarely on behalf of lower-income groups so that both social benefits and the nonprofit sector tend to be limited (Anheier and Salamon 2006).

Hence, the key components of the social origins theory are the following: first, an inverse relationship between the extent of social spending and the size of the nonprofit sector; second, the critical importance of key historical moments in a country's history that establish specific institutional configurations that influence the development of the nonprofit sector, including the relationship between church and state and the role of the working class in state formation; and third, a focus on service agencies, as opposed to sports clubs, choral societies, and other types of largely volunteer organizations which receive little revenue from public or private sources. Furthermore, nonprofit revenue is divided into three basic categories: private philanthropy, fees, and government funding.

Also relevant to any understanding of the historical development of the nonprofit sector's service role is the research of Jens Alber (1995), who proposed a model and a set of propositions to explain differences in social service provision across Europe, based on research into elder care services. Alber's model identifies four key institutional variables that influence the structure of social services: the type of regulation; the structure of financing; the public/private mix of providers; and the religious structure of the country. Further, he links the type of providers to consumer power. For example, German social services are dominated by large nonprofit providers linked to religious institutions and receiving large-scale funding from the state. This arrangement reflects the heterogeneous religious culture of Germany and, as a result, the reliance on large religious providers to supply social services to different religious communities. By contrast, Denmark, Alber notes, is a religiously homogeneous country, and therefore religiously based providers have never established the strong presence that evolved in Germany or the Netherlands. As a consequence, the expansion of health and social services in twentieth-century Denmark was channeled into the public sector.

Understanding the relative importance of nonprofit organizations within the welfare state is of increasing significance given the shift that is taking place—to varying degrees in different countries—from cash assistance to services provided by nonprofit and for-profit organizations in areas such as poverty assistance and unemployment. In the United States, for example, the landmark welfare reform legislation of 1996 led to a marked decline in cash assistance and a substantial increase in funding for nonprofit social service agencies providing an array of programs such as workforce development (Allard 2009; Smith 2011). Similar shifts have occurred in many other countries including the United Kingdom, Australia, and New Zealand.

Nonprofit organizations are now firmly established on the front lines of social policy implementation, and are critical to the life-chances of much of the citizenry, especially in times of acute economic crisis and high levels of unemployment.

b. The "New Public Management"

Perhaps one of the most important influences in the changing size and role of the nonprofit sector has been the adoption by many countries of the New Public Management agenda (NPM)—a term that refers to the restructuring of public management using market-oriented strategies to provide for social needs and increase the effectiveness, efficiency, and responsiveness of public services (Rhodes 1996; Hood 1991; Lynn 1998; Osborne 2006; Osborne, Mclaughlin, and Ferlie 2002). These strategies include competitive contracting for services, public-private partnerships, the use of vouchers among purchasers, and the introduction of more consumer choice. The shift to NPM has had profound effects on the size and role of the nonprofit sector. Nonprofits have increasingly been funded through contracts to provide vital public services, from community care to substance abuse treatment to home health care for the elderly (Smith 2010). The restructuring of the state has in turn drawn nonprofits into greater engagement with the public policy process, especially through intermediary associations that represent large numbers of local organizations such as the National Council of Voluntary Organizations (NCVO) in the United Kingdom and the Maryland Association of Nonprofits in the United States. In some countries, such as the United Kingdom and Australia, this evolving relationship between government and the nonprofit sector has led to the adoption of formal "compacts" that provide a structured forum for the discussion and resolution of mutual areas of concern (Plowden 2003; Casey, et al. 2010).

The emphasis on citizen engagement and responsiveness within the tenets of NPM has also spurred governments to promote the representation of neighborhoods, ethnic groups, or approaches to service delivery in the policy process. As a result, neighborhood-based and other specialized nonprofits have increased substantially in many countries, and in some, such as the United States, they provide an opportunity for citizens to participate in the governance of the services they receive. In addition, many newer nonprofit service agencies are linked to immigrant groups or disadvantaged populations, and they often partner with government agencies as part of a broader approach to addressing problems such as HIV/AIDS, affordable housing, economic development, and community care. NPM is also closely linked to the devolution of public programs to lower levels of government and society, a shift that has led to a more prominent role for nonprofits which are often seen to be closer to their communities. Finally, NPM is also part of a broader movement to improve the performance and effectiveness of government. The increased utilization of nonprofits is an integral component of this effort since they are assumed to be more innovative and effective than traditional public programs in many countries.

c. The Limitations of NPM and Theories of the Welfare State

To be sure, marked differences still exist across countries in the position of the non-profit sector. First, it is apparent that the institutional logic of a welfare state regime—an important underlying assumption of the Esping-Anderson typology—has important and enduring effects on welfare state development and therefore on the sector's size and positioning (see also Alber 2010). The public-private mix affects the trajectory of the welfare state, and fundamental reforms are required to change its funding and organizational dynamics. Despite the pressures of NPM and other new ideas on social policy, for example, the service-providing nonprofit sector in Scandinavian countries such as Denmark and Sweden remains relatively small (Henriksen and Bundesen 2004; Svedberg, and Olsson 2010). By contrast, the number of nonprofit public charities in the United States that are tax-exempt and can accept tax deductible contributions has more than doubled in the last fifteen years (NCCS 2010).

Second, the enormous influence of the welfare-state regime typology has tended to minimize the importance of nonprofit organizations in other fields such as the arts, sports and recreation, and social clubs. For example, Sweden has a small non-profit social welfare presence but a very sizable segment of the population is engaged in nonprofit sports clubs and their activities (Norberg 2010; Lundstrom and Wijkstrom 1997; Kuhnle and Selle 1992). And in the United Kingdom, philanthropy has emerged in the last twenty-five years as a key force in the world of arts and culture (Pharaoh 2010). Trade unions also tend to be excluded from consideration as nonprofit organizations because of the dominance of theories of the welfare state. But as noted by Norberg (2010), labor unions in Sweden are one of the key forms of voluntary participation by the citizenry. In the U.S. context, social clubs are considered to be part of civil society more broadly defined, especially as a result of Putnam's work on the importance of voluntary organizations such as choral societies in building social capital. However, labor unions have remained largely absent from discussions of the nonprofit sector despite their tax-exempt status.

Third, the welfare state regime typology has difficulty in capturing the evolving situation of the nonprofit sector in Eastern and Central Europe, Russia, and many developing countries, whose authoritarian and semiauthoritarian regimes had banned nonprofit organizations from providing significant services or representing citizen interests. The advent of democracy in many of these countries has wrought profound shifts in the position of nonprofits, fueled in part by the influence of NPM as well as outside funding institutions including European and American philanthropic foundations. However, many countries have wrestled with finding an appropriate legal and regulatory framework for nonprofits and a satisfactory model for their role in society. Poland, for example, continues to debate the merits of a German-style corporatist framework consisting of close cooperation between government and large umbrella nonprofit organizations, as opposed to a British model that is more reliant on private philanthropy (Krzyszkowski 2010). In Hungary, the government has struggled to balance the goal of more efficiency and accountability with the goal of engaging nonprofit organizations and civil society in the policy process (Kuti 2011).

Overall, despite the pressure for policy convergence that stems from NPM and other forces, each country's institutional legacy has had a major influence on the role of nonprofits and the relationship between government and the nonprofit sector in particular. More specifically, the structure of government and the system for funding the provision of social services influences the opportunities for nonprofit formation and affects their ongoing relationships with the state. This conclusion builds on theories which suggest that the institutions of government influence the goals and priorities of private actors and organizations. In this model, nonprofit organizations are formed based on the mix of incentives they face from government as well as other societal institutions (Pierson 2004; Smith and Lipsky 1993). As the nonprofit sector grows, it creates a supply of organizations that then affect the implementation choices of government officials. Importantly, however, regime characteristics also blur and mix with the so-called pillars of the welfare state—markets, the state, the family, and the community—so that countries such as Poland, the United Kingdom, Australia, and the United States come to rely on the interaction of these pillars in surprising and increasingly complicated ways (Goodin and Rein 2001).

3. Common Issues and Dilemmas

The growing prominence of nonprofits throughout the world has raised similar policy and management issues for government and the nonprofit sector itself. First, the economic crisis of 2008–10 has had profound effects on government and private funders, although the severity of this impact varies substantially across countries. In the United States and the United Kingdom, the crisis has produced a wave of funding cutbacks, forcing many nonprofit agencies to reduce services, sometimes drastically. The severity of these cutbacks has been exacerbated by reductions in funding from foundations and private donors. The withdrawal of foundation support from the new democracies of Eastern and Central Europe has added to these effects.

Second, nonprofits are facing increasing demands for accountability and improved performance. Public funding programs in many countries including the United States, the United Kingdom, Australia, New Zealand, and Germany now require performance contracts which tie reimbursement for nonprofits to the meeting of specified indicators and results such as placement in permanent employment (Smith and Smyth 2010; Zimmer and Smith 2010; Lyons and Dalton 2011). Importantly for agencies receiving public funds, performance contracting can significantly change the incentives for nonprofit agencies to serve certain types of clients, and can force agencies to alter their program models in order to meet performance targets and their accompanying payment arrangements. Overall, government and private funders are placing much greater emphasis on evaluation and performance measurement. Consequently, nonprofits face markedly higher expectations in terms of their transparency and levels of reporting for their programmatic and financial operations. The push for more accountability, combined with ongoing financial pressures on nonprofits, means that they are engaged in complex and sometimes contradictory relationships with other agencies in their field. Funding cutbacks often prompt nonprofits to join together to influence public policy, sometimes through formal coalitions and associations that represent their interests. In some service fields, agencies have tried to promote voluntary means of accountability and quality improvement, and cost-sharing strategies such as the sharing of program locations and staff are attracting widespread interest, although the actual number of nonprofits engaged in these strategies is relatively small.

Nonetheless, performance contracting and the sheer numbers of nonprofit agencies in many communities encourage more competition for funding and for "clients." This trend is reinforced by the shift to a greater emphasis on client choice and responsiveness, another ripple effect of the New Public Management (Alber 2010; Phillips and Smith 2011; Lyons and Dalton 2011). Vouchers for services such as child care and housing are one manifestation of these changes, but the increased use of health insurance reimbursement such as Medicaid in the United States, where funding is tied to the client, is another reflection of this trend. These policy tools tend to be procompetitive since nonprofit agencies are no longer assured of their funding levels, unlike under previous contracting arrangements. More competition is also abetted by the growing inroads made by for-profit service providers in many fields that were previously dominated by nonprofits, such as community care for the disabled and aged, hospitals, mental health care, and substance abuse treatment (Bode 2011; Smith 2011). For example, home care was provided almost exclusively by nonprofit organizations in the United States in the 1970s; today, this field is dominated by for-profit providers. In Germany, commercial hospitals have essentially taken over the public facilities of the former East Germany (Zimmer and Smith 2010). In Australia, recent governments have actually favored for-profit organizations, resulting in a long-term decline in the relative service role of nonprofits (Lyons and Dalton 2011). The rise of for-profits in many service fields is due to several factors: growing demand for services such as community care; the undercapitalization of many nonprofits which erodes their ability or unwillingness to scale up to meet increased demand; and the efficiencies that can accrue to larger for-profit agencies compared to smaller community-based organizations, especially in more routine services such as home care. Greater competition also places pressure on nonprofits to be more commercial and market-oriented (Eikenberry and Kluver 2004; Bode 2011).

The surge in smaller, community-based nonprofits in recent years in an environment of increased competition and accountability has generated widespread concern, and greater attention to issues of nonprofit capacity, infrastructure, and sustainability, especially among funders (Smith 2011; Ryan 2001). Many of these newer and smaller agencies have relatively small boards and staff, lack substantial capital, and may be highly dependent on a relatively restricted revenue base. Many are also at a stage in their organizational development at which they need to develop a more sustainable financial plan. Capacity building is also vital for both government and the nonprofit sector because the changing political and funding environment demands new skills from managers that were not previously emphasized, including negotiation and conflict resolution, collaboration, outreach, openness, and organizational development. Increasingly, nonprofit agencies are part of complex networks of public, nonprofit, and sometimes for-profit organizations, so a detailed knowledge of how these networks operate and can be managed is essential if services are to be sustained and effective.

Governments can provide help with capacity building directly and indirectly by supporting nonprofits on important issues such as strategic planning, the development of business plans, and assistance with improving board governance. Towards this end, some countries have established formal offices to work with nonprofit organizations. Examples include the Office of the Third Sector (now Civil Society) in the United Kingdom, and the Office for the Community and Voluntary Sector in New Zealand. In the United Kingdom, the formal "compact" between government and the nonprofit sector is properly staffed and provides a wide variety of support services to local government and to nonprofit staff and volunteers. While compacts like these have arguably provided a structured vehicle for the discussion of important issues, they will remain insufficient unless nonprofits are skilled advocates of citizen interests. Nonprofits are valued for their potential to represent their communities and provide valued feedback to policymakers on important public policy matters. Yet many encounter serious internal and external constraints to engaging in sustained advocacy. Many agencies worry that advocacy will create legal and political problems, given the restrictions on advocacy that are enshrined in legislation in many countries. Service providers may worry that advocacy will have a deleterious effect on their relationships with government, including future funding and regulatory decisions. Newer and smaller community organizations often lack the resources and expertise to be effective advocates, and some nonprofit agencies such as emergency shelters or food banks may not necessarily view political activity, or even broad civic engagement, as priorities given their missions and program goals (see Smith and Lipsky 1993; Lewis 1999; Bass, Arons, Guinane, and Carter 2007; Lyons and Dalton 2011).

In essence, the challenge of nonprofit advocacy reflects the restructuring of the state and the consequent increase in the service role of the nonprofit sector. Inevitably, this role has created a complex relationship with government whereby nonprofits are dependent on the state for funding and worry that their advocacy will have a deleterious effect on future support. Fiscal crises and increasingly competitive environments for public and private funding tend to heighten these levels of anxiety and lead to greater caution by nonprofits in their advocacy work. In order to tackle this problem, nonprofits could usefully rethink their governance and funding models to help promote sustainability and reduce dependence so that they can hold governments accountable for their obligation to fund key public services. But in order to cope with—and hopefully influence—these emerging funding and regulatory environments, nonprofits will need to be more creative and innovative in their programming, organizational structures, and their relations with other organizations.

4. CONCLUSION

Social and demographic trends, state restructuring, the push for more individual choice in public service delivery, and the advance of the New Public Management would appear to ensure that the nonprofit sector will become even more important in the future. But these developments also create new risks and challenges for nonprofits and for society as a whole. As service providers, nonprofits have complicated relationships with the state, affecting their ability to be responsive to community needs and act as conduits for citizen pressure. Issues of scale, capacity, and sustainability pose questions about the macro-level impact of nonprofit service provision, and major differences within and across countries are likely to persist, despite pressures to conform to universal roles and standards. If it is to advance civil society and not simply substitute for the state, the nonprofit sector will need to maintain a careful balance between dependence and independence, and find ways of blending service delivery with other roles such as advocacy and community organizing.

REFERENCES

Alber, Jens. 1995. "A Framework for the Comparative Study of Social Services." *Journal of European Social Policy* 5(2): 131–49.

——. 2010. "What the European and American Welfare States have in Common and Where they Differ: Facts and Fiction in Comparisons of the European Social Model and the United States." *Journal of European Social Policy* vol. 20(2): 102–25.

Allard, S. W. 2009. *Out of Reach: Place, Poverty, and the New American Welfare State.* New Haven, Conn.: Yale University Press.

Alter, K. S. 2010. "Social Enterprise Typology." Portland, Oregon: Virtue Ventures. Available at http://www.4lenses.org/setypology.

Anheier, H. K., and L. M. Salamon. 2006. "The Nonprofit Sector in Comparative Perspective," in Walter W. Powell and Richard Steinberg (eds.) *The Nonprofit Sector. A Research Handbook.* New Haven, Conn.: Yale University Press.

Barber, B. 1998. *A Place for Us: How to Make Society Civil and Democracy Strong.* New York: Hill and Wang.

Bass, G., D. Arons, K. Guinane, and M. Carter. 2007. *Seen But Not Heard: Strengthening Nonprofit Advocacy.* Washington, D.C.: Aspen Institute.

Bode, I. 2011. "Creeping Marketization and Post-Corporatist Governance: The Transformation of State–Nonprofit Relations in Continental Europe," in S. D. Phillips and S. R. Smith (eds.) *Governance and Regulation in the Third Sector*. London: Routledge.

Bornstein, D. 2007. *How to Change the World: Social Entrepreneurs and the Power of New Ideas*. New York: Oxford University Press.

Casey, J., B. Dalton, R. Melville, and J. Onyx. 2010. "Strengthening Government–Nonprofit Relations with Compacts: International Experiences." *Voluntary Sector Review* vol. 1(1) (March): 59–76.

Cohen, J. and A. Arato. 1992. *Civil Society and Political Theory*. Cambridge, Mass.: MIT Press.

Cordes, J. J., and C. Eugene Steuerle (eds.) 2009. *Nonprofits and Business*. Washington, D.C.: Urban Institute.

Crutchfield, L. R., and H. McLeod Grant. 2008. *Forces for Good: The Six Practices of High-Impact Nonprofits*. San Francisco: Jossey-Bass.

Dunn, A. 2011. "Gatekeeper Governance: The European Union and Civil Society Organizations," in S. Phillips and S.R. Smith (eds.) op. cit.

Eikenbery, A. M., and J. D. Kluver. 2004. "The Marketization of the Nonprofit Sector: Civil Society at Risk?" *Public Administration Review* vol. 64, 2 (April): 132–40.

Esping-Andersen, G. 1990. *The Three Worlds of Welfare Capitalism*. Princeton, N.J.: Princeton University Press.

European Commission. 2001. *European Governance—A White Paper*. Brussels: European Commission.

Goodin, R., and M. Rein. 2001. "Regimes on Pillars: Alternative Welfare State Logics and Dynamics." *Public Administration* vol. 79(4): 769–801.

Henriksen, L. S., and P. Bundesen. 2004. "The Moving Frontier in Denmark: Voluntary-State Relationships since 1850." *Journal of Social Policy* vol. 33(4): 605–25.

Home Office. 2010. "Policing in the 21st Century: Reconnecting Police and the People." Available at http://www.homeoffice.gov.uk/publications/consultations/policing-21st-century/policing-21st-full-pdf?view=Binary.

Hood, C. 1991. "A Public Management for All Seasons." *Public Administration* vol. 69: 3–19.

Krzyszkowski, J. 2010. "Third Sector Organizations in Social Services in Poland: Old Problems and New Challenges," in A. Evers and A. Zimmer (eds.) *Third Sector Organizations Facing Turbulent Environments: Sports, Culture and Social Services in Five European Countries*. Baden-Baden, Germany: Nomos.

Kuhnle, S., and P. Selle (eds.) 1992. *Government and Voluntary Organizations: A Relational Perspective*. Aldershot: Avebury.

Kuti, E. 2011. "Government-Nonprofit Sector Relations in Hungary: Aspirations, Efforts, and Impacts," in S. Phillips and S.R. Smith (eds.), op. cit.

Lewis, J. 1999. "Reviewing the Relationship Between the Voluntary Sector and the State in Britain in the 1990s." *Voluntas* vol. 10(3): 255–70.

Light, P. C. 2008. *The Search for Social Entrepreneurship*. Washington, D.C.: Brookings Institute.

Lundstrom, T., and F. Wijkstrom. 1997. *The Nonprofit Sector in Sweden*. Manchester: Manchester University Press.

Lynn, L. E. Jr. 1998. "The New Public Management: How to Transform a Theme into a Legacy." *Public Administration Review* vol. 58 (May-June): 231–37.

Lyons, M., and B. Dalton. 2011. "Australia: A Continuing Love Affair with the New Public Management," in S. Phillips and S.R. Smith (eds.), op. cit.

McBride, A. M., M. Sherraden, C. Benítez, and E. Johnson. 2004. "Civic Service Worldwide: Defining a Field, Building a Knowledge Base." *Nonprofit and Voluntary Sector Quarterly* vol. 33: 8S–21S.

McBride, A. M., and M. Sherraden (eds.) 2006. *Civic Service Worldwide: Impacts and Inquiry.* Armonk, N.Y.: M. E. Sharpe.

Moore, B.. 1966. *Social Origins of Dictatorship and Democracy: Lord and Peasant in the Making of the Modern World.* Boston: Beacon Press.

National Center for Charitable Statistics (NCCS). 2010. "Number of Nonprofit Organizations in the United States, Selected Years." Washington, D.C.: Urban Institute. Available at http://nccs.urban.org/index.cfm.

Norberg, J. R. 2010. "The Development of the Swedish Sports Movement between State, Market and Civil Society—Some Remarks," in A. Evers and A. Zimmer (eds.), op. cit.

Osborne, S. P. 2006. "The New Public Governance?" *Public Management Review* vol. 8(3): 277–87.

Osborne, S. P., K. Mclaughlin, and E. Ferlie (eds.) 2002. *New Public Management: Current Trends and Future Prospects.* London: Routledge.

Pharaoh, C. 2010. "Arts and Culture in the U.K.: Funding Structures, Shifting Boundaries, and the Creation of a Sector," in A. Evers and A. Zimmer (eds.), op. cit.

Phillips, S. D. and S. R. Smith (eds.). 2011. *Governance and Regulation in the Third Sector.* London: Routledge.

Phillips, S. D., and S. R. Smith. 2011. "Between Governance and Regulation: Evolving Government-Third Sector Relationships," in S. Phillips and S.R. Smith (eds.), op. cit.

Pierson, P. 2004. *Politics in Time: History, Institutions, and Social Analysis.* Princeton, N.J.: Princeton University Press.

Plowden, W. 2003. "The Compact: Attempts to Regulate Relationships between Government and the Voluntary Sector in England." *Nonprofit and Voluntary Sector Quarterly* vol. 32(3): 415–32.

Putnam, R. 1993. *Making Democracy Work.* Princeton, N.J.: Princeton University Press.

———. 2000. *Bowling Alone: The Collapse and revival of American Community.* New York: Simon & Schuster.

Rhodes, R. A. W. 1996. "The New Governance: Governing without Government." *Political Studies* LIV: 652–67.

Ryan, W. P. 2001. "Nonprofit Capital: A Review of Problems and Strategies." New York: Rockefeller Foundation and Fannie Mae Foundation. Available at http://www.community-wealth.org/_pdfs/articles-publications/pris/paper-ryan.pdf.

Salamon, L. M. 2010. "Putting the Civil Society Sector on the Economic Map of the World." *Annals of Public and Cooperative Economics* vol. 81(2): 167–210.

Salamon, L. M., and H. K. Anheier. 1998. "Social Origins of Civil Society: Explaining the Nonprofit Sector Cross-Nationally." *Voluntas* vol. 9(3): 213–48.

Salamon, L. M., S. W. Sokolowski, and R. List. 2004. "Global Civil Society: An Overview," in L. M. Salamon, S. W. Sokolowski, and Associates. *Global Civil Society: Dimensions of the Nonprofit Sector.* West Hartford, Conn.: Kumarian Press.

Smith, S.R.. 2010. "Nonprofits and Public Administration: Reconciling Performance Management and Citizen Engagement." *American Review of Public Administration* vol. 40 (March): 129–15.

———. 2011. "Social Services" in L. M. Salamon (ed.) *The State of Nonprofit America.* 2nd ed. Washington, D.C.: Brookings Institute.

Smith, S. R., and M. Lipsky. 1993. *Nonprofits for Hire: The Welfare State in the Age of Contracting.* Cambridge, Mass.: Harvard University Press.

Smith, S. R., and J. Smyth. 2010. "The Governance of Contracting Relationships: 'Killing the Golden Goose' A Third sector Perspective," in S. P. Osborne (ed.) *The New Public Governance? Critical Perspectives and Future Directions.* London: Routledge.

Svedberg, L., and L. E. Olsson. 2010. "Voluntary Organizations and Welfare Provision in Sweden: Is There Such as Thing?" in A. Evers and A. Zimmer (eds.), op. cit.

Zimmer, A., and S. R. Smith. 2010. "At the Eve of Convergence: Social Services in the U.S. and Germany?" Report 42. Washington, D.C.: American Institute for Contemporary German Studies.

CHAPTER 4

DEVELOPMENT NGOs

ALAN FOWLER

SINCE the mid-1940s, nongovernmental development organizations (NGDOs) dedicated to promoting long-term economic, social, and political progress have proliferated across the world. Some, like Oxfam and World Vision, originated in Europe and North America to work across international borders, but have since spawned local entities with similar names and agendas. However, most NGDOs are located in developing countries. Over the last twenty years, their numbers, reach, and profile have expanded dramatically. Within the framework of international aid and development cooperation, a specific discourse has arisen around these organizations called "NGDO-ism," a discourse that gives rise to important questions about NGDOs, civil society, and social change (Hilhorst 2003).

This chapter traces the emergence of NGDOs from relative obscurity to a substantial presence in the international development community, a process that became more complex over time as NGDOs were conflated with a new discourse of civil society on the one hand and challenged by a human rights perspective on the other. Taking the long view, their history has been one of abrupt punctuations in an otherwise mutual, but nonetheless asymmetric, adaptation between government and NGDO practices and organizational behaviors, a process that has favored government and now threatens to dislodge NGDOs from their position in favor of support to new civic actors. Reflecting growing uncertainties about an emerging "world disorder," the chapter concludes by outlining some speculative future scenarios for NGDOs and their work.

1. NGDOs and Civil Society: Clearing the Analytic Ground

The formation of the United Nations (UN) in the aftermath of the Second World War provided both the label and a formal starting point for what today are known as NGOs. Alongside the General Assembly and Security Council, the new UN structure included a forum—the Economic and Social Council (ECOSOC)—dedicated to debate on economic and social issues. Long prior to this event, a number of transnational religious and "charitable" organizations had been working in such fields. To enable these and similar entities to be accredited as participant-observers of government debates at ECOSOC, forty-one were accorded consultative status as a nonstate institutional category of a nongovernmental organization (NGO) in 1947. This label has both remained and expanded into a complex, and often perplexing, global discourse far beyond its origins in the United Nations.

There are two critical points to bear in mind from this brief history. First, the formal label "NGO" was applied only to entities working internationally, which is no longer the case. Many organizations that are understood and legally defined as NGOs are domestic in their intentions and relationships. Second, whether gaining consultative status or not, NGOs were preoccupied with social and economic issues that, with the advent of foreign aid some fifteen years later, gained the additional attribute of being formally "developmental." These factors enabled a willy-nilly adoption by, or application of, the label "NGO" to entities that may or may not have any tangible affinity with the interventions, logic, or practices of foreign aid, a problem that has led to much analytic confusion that is discussed below.

Dissatisfaction with the catch-all nature of the negative descriptor "nongovernmental" abetted a terminological evolution including private voluntary organizations (PVOs) in the United States and voluntary development organizations (VDOs) in India; as well as nonprofit organizations (NPOs), third sector organizations (TSOs) and, more recently, civil society organizations (CSOs) worldwide. All these terms overlap with the attributes of NGOs as originally understood. This plethora of classifications is explored by Tvedt (1998:13–15) in terms of legal, financial/economic, functional, and structural-operational typologies. He argues for an agreed definition that can be relied on cross-nationally. However, there remains no universal definition, nor a robust or uncontested "positive" characterization of what NGOs or NGDOs are, what they do, and why they exist across the world.

Furthermore, a distinction is too seldom made between NGOs or, for that matter, NGDOs that serve third parties or external stakeholders (i.e., beneficiaries, target groups, and constituencies) and those that were established to serve their members, or to do both. By and large, however, NGDOs function as intermediaries between resource providers and those in populations whose ill-being justifies the organizations' existence (Carroll 1992; Fowler 1997, 26). Unless stated otherwise, this "positional" characterization in resource channels or chains from "developed" to "developing" countries—the North and the South—is used throughout the discussion that follows.

Also complicating matters is the thirty-year role of international aid in propagating NGDOs as a policy towards recipient countries. Regimes across the South have introduced legislation that often apply the label "nongovernmental" to all sorts of civic organizational forms and purposes in order to distinguish them from formal or informal enterprises and cooperatives.[1] Consequently, to a disproportionate degree, NGDO-ism prevails in official thinking, public and professional discourse, and practical imagery in terms of the interpretation of civic associations across the world. Legislative action has also stemmed from the infiltration into NGDO-ism of "pretenders" with self-seeking agendas or as ways for governments to attain "arms-length" control over civic actors. These motivations have given rise to a range of pejorative acronyms such as BRINGO (Brief Case NGO), MONGO (my own NGO), GONGO (government NGO), PONGO (Political NGO) and many more (Fowler 1977, 32).

Allied to these definitional problems are significant levels of uncertainty about the global numbers of NGDOs, especially given the problematic division between NGDOs and NGOs who are not involved in development. For example, of the estimated 277,000 "Hobbled NGOs" in Russia,[2] very few are NGDOs. Uganda alone boasted some 7,000 NGDOs in 2007 against 500 in 1992. Of India's estimated 1 to 2 million NGOs, very few are NGDOs registered to receive foreign aid, which is a legal requirement. Efforts at multi-country mapping of nonprofit and civil society organizations are only partial in their coverage and they are not consistent in their results, inviting caution about both classification and generalization in this arena (Salamon et al., 1999, 2004; Heinrich and Fioramonti 2007). There are also significant uncertainties about the amount of financial resources mobilized around NGDOs, since the multiplicity of channels involved, incentives to under- or over-report, and many other factors preclude the calculation of robust economic numbers. Estimates of NGDO funding or disbursement range from $15 to 25 billion annually (Fowler 1997, 133–136; 2000, 4), with an ever-increasing proportion from official aid allocations, accelerated by finance for post-conflict reconstruction. Moreover, there are signs of a skewed distribution of budgets and staffing. The six largest international NGDOs (INGDOs) alone are credited with an aggregate turnover in 2008 of $7 billion, while employing some 110,000 staff worldwide (Ronalds 2010). The Bangladesh Rural Advancement Committee (BRAC) had an annual budget in 2010 of $700 million and a staff complement of 130,000 people. Yet there are also many thousands of small and medium-sized organizations that are legally registered as NGDOs, some relying exclusively on volunteers. Nevertheless, taking these caveats into account, an estimate running into the hundreds of thousands of NGDOs operating globally would not seem unreasonable.

Against this cautionary backdrop, this chapter confines itself to a composite reading of the universe of NGDOs, understood in the following normative terms, which in practice may not all be found in every case: NGDOs (a) are separate in legitimacy and governance from governmental bodies; (b) acclaim and utilize the tenets of international aid as a substantive basis for their existence;[3] (c) gain direct or tax-based public support, in part because they are not established to generate wealth for their "owners"; (d) operate at any or all levels of socio-political organization from the individual, family, household, and local levels to transnational and global concerns, presence, and relationships; and (e) are not partisan in the politics of their endeavors. These attributes offer a lens through which the nature and evolution of NGDOs and NGDO-ism can be explored in the sections that follow, starting with their "articles of faith."

2. A False Promise of Alternatives?

The late 1970s can be regarded as the period when NGDOs started to lose the "security of obscurity" and enter the realm of recognition and embrace by the official aid system. Their entry was premised on the developmental value of being positively different to government and its community-oriented practices. The original notion of being "alternative" has been both a creed and a point of reference for defining and assessing NGDOs, though proving to be a mixed blessing that remains to this day (Bebbington, Hickey, and Mitlin 2008).

Throughout the 1970s, some International NGDOs (INGDOs) had been agitating to be seen and heard by the official aid system (Lissner 1977). Infused by campaigning for de-colonialization and agitating against military regimes, their arguments were twofold. First, the origins of INGDOs had informed a people-oriented approach to social change that had been honed over the years of pre- and post-independence engagement in developing countries. This experience offered valuable comparative advantages over government in micro, or community, development—articulated, for example, in Brown and Korten's (1989) seminal paper which spelled out for international bureaucrats what Tendler (1982) had described as NGDO "myths" or "articles of faith" (Tvedt 1998, 128). By this she meant self-referential premises of what NGDOs are and do which make them more effective in "soft" development initiatives that revolve around people, rather than "hard" technologies such as the creation of physical infrastructure. It is beyond the scope of this chapter to list and explore these myths in detail, other than to highlight the notions of people-centeredness, participation, and partnership as substantial sources of their comparative social value in development work. The critical point is that these myths and their later refinements provided a functional-technical metric against which NGDO performance was tracked and assessed throughout the 1970s and 1980s. This optic marginalized, but could not dispel, a more political interpretation of what alternative could mean, a perspective reinvigorated by global events that are discussed below.

Second, being and offering *alternatives* was not couched only in terms of operational functioning, but also in terms of bringing a different perspective and theory of change to the table that was premised on international solidarity. Articulated especially strongly in Latin America, this *anti-dependencia* view focused on how the liberal, capitalist economic system itself caused the underdevelopment it was purported to solve (Lehmann 1986). A radically different theory of the causes of, and remedies for, global poverty could and would inform NGDO strategy and practice, though their actual willingness and ability to pursue such an agenda has also been subject to dispute.

Arguments among NGDOs about what economics for development should look like emerged at a time of significant shifts in the domestic politics of donor countries, loosely termed the Reagan-Thatcher era of the 1980s. Through their dominance of multilateral institutions and bilateral agencies, the anti-"big government," pro-private sector policies of donor countries fed into changes in the foreign aid system. Consequently, recognition of nonstate development actors like NGDOs became an institutional imperative for foreign aid. For example, within its External Relations Department the World Bank established an NGDO office in 1982. The expansion of "private" aid supply channels matched an increase in demand driven by structural adjustment policies that were exacerbating poverty. As carriers of "alternatives," how did NGDOs respond to the move towards a pro-business ideological agenda?

The answer is that NGDOs resolved the moral issues stemming from their roots in "*caritas*," philanthropy, and voluntarism in favor of their own economic growth as a proxy for performance. Simply put, a *caritas* mentality means that a failure to raise as much money as possible is an affront to poor people and hence is unacceptable. Of course, negotiation on funding conditions is necessary, but in the last analysis, for most NGDOs most of the time, the "moral imperative" of growth wins out because it also makes "business sense." The prevalence of businessmen and women on the governing boards of large NGDOs is an ongoing reflection of this reasoning. It responds to an implicit assumption that NGDO staff are "amateurs" who require "guidance," in which professionalism is equated with adopting techniques from business management (Edwards and Fowler 2002). Moreover, as in other walks of organizational life, continuity and viability are normal expectations for staff and an enduring demand on leadership. The original NGDO mantra of "working oneself out of a job" as a measure of success was always a somewhat fictional aspiration.

A predisposition towards growth was abetted by the pro-NGDO policies of official aid and a rapid increase in resources, which fuelled a substantial increase in numbers, particularly in the South. The form and project-driven functioning of the organizations that were created corresponded to Northern role models, with varied degrees of affinity for local forms, norms, and practices. In some settings NGDOs appeared as suspicious foreign bodies. In others they were considered as variations on existing forms of organizing in which communities distributed resources for social ends. Of general significance, however, was the formation of an institutional type and scale that was not proportional to the local resource base. As a result, aid dependency was created, and remains a characteristic, of Southern NGDOs in a system of "partnerships" in which calls for their sustainability are not met with investments that would make this a reality. Further, the deep origins of Northern NGDOs in voluntarism seldom emerged in the less well-endowed circumstances of the South. Consequently, NGDO-ism evolved as a form of social entrepreneurship and employment-seeking, on occasion doing harm by undermining pre-existing coping mechanisms and institutions (Holmén 2010).

The donors' pro-NGDO policies of the 1980s also introduced an official cooptation of NGDO language, with interpretations of concepts such as "empowerment," "transformation," "participation," and "partnership" becoming increasingly state-centric. Some donors introduced internal reforms to make these rhetorical concepts more substantive in their own work. But, concomitantly, access to foreign aid became increasingly dictated by official perspectives and requirements which tended to standardize NGDO practices, thus eroding their potential comparative advantages and their vocabulary (Wallace et al. 1998). These coercive features of the aid chain have remained in play, reflecting the continued asymmetries of power between NGDOs and donors (Wallace et al. 2006). Finally, in addition to serving certain functional needs designed to improve development performance, on occasion NGDOs also provided donor countries with an informal presence in countries ruled by anti-Western regimes during the Cold War era. Consciously or not, NGDOs served the implicit geopolitical agenda of aid allocation to promote Western interests.

In retrospect, the 1980s were a "golden era" for NGDO expansion and accommodation within the official aid system, but one that had mixed long-term consequences. By and large, it can be argued that for both internal and external reasons, the formative period of NGDO-ism tilted NGDOs towards an apolitical economy of their own development. Contention around economic models and politics was not wholly jettisoned. Tacit acceptance of the donors' neoliberal economic solutions to poverty reduction was accompanied, for some NGDOs, by an agitatory, reformist, critical engagement towards the main players in the foreign aid system that gained traction at the beginning of the twenty-first century. By the end of the 1980s, NGDOs had come of age. They were now an acknowledged presence on the international development landscape, and some had global ambitions (Lindenberg and Bryant 2001). The notion of alternatives described above still held sway (Drabek 1987), but with relatively little by way of substantive evidence to test it or experience of government discomfort with their roles in the foreign aid system. This situation was to change markedly in the 1990s.

3. REVISIONISM AND RECONCEPTUALIZATION

The evolution of NGDOs over the past twenty years can be explained in terms of a continuation of earlier systemic processes, but within less benevolent environments that stem partly from critical evaluations of NGDO achievements and partly from disruptive "punctuations" in the global order. Previous trends and unexpected discontinuities have interacted in complex ways that are far from resolved, subjecting NGDO-ism to much uncertainty in the future. Four systemic trends have altered the generally positive NGDO trajectories of the 1970s and 1980s.

First, throughout the 1990s, studies and conferences on NGDO-ism and NGDO performance gave rise to increasing skepticism about their value-added and comparative advantages (Edwards and Hulme 1992, 1995; Sogge 1996; Smillie 1995; Hulme and Edwards 1997; Hossain and Myllylä 1998). Summative evaluations of NGDO performance at the end of the twentieth century could find no unequivocal support for the proposition that high expectations had been realized in practice (Fowler 2000a; Riddell 2007). The overall picture was one of occasional marked successes; some positive but scattered micro-level results; and generally very modest, uneven achievements. Little could be found in the way of systemic results in micro-development that was attributable to NGDOs as a distinct type of entity. In addition, the scale of their outreach to the poor was not particularly significant, and serious doubts had emerged about their ability to reach the very poor and the poorest.

Second, there was growing frustration within the NGDO community about the willingness and ability of Northern NGDOs to be authentic partners with their Southern counterparts by devolving, or at least sharing, power and decision making (Fowler 2000b). Compounding this trend was a strategic shift in many INGDOs to reposition themselves in relation to the decentralization of donor financing directly to the South. One result was to squeeze out local NGDOs from the foreign aid scene, which was already moving towards budget support to governments, tied to competitive bidding for donor-financed contracts. This led INGDOs to initiate processes to "localize" themselves on the one hand, while "federating" into more coherent transnational actors on the other. In sum, there was increasing evidence that Northern NGDOs were not living up to their own relational rhetoric (Edwards 2005). Instead they were seeking self-continuity by adjusting their geopolitical economy at the cost of solidarity as originally understood.

Third, and partly in response to Southern NGDO criticism, Northern NGDOs started to reduce their operationality and shift their focus towards national and international policy advocacy. The latter function has emerged with some success, as seen in the achievement of the anti-debt coalition, the International Coalition to Ban Land Mines (van Rooy 2004) and numerous national policy processes (Court 2006). This transnationalization of NGDO-ism gained momentum in global policy debates, increasingly framed in terms of a discourse around "global civil society" (Edwards and Gaventa 2001; Batliwala and Brown 2006). However, policy success invited greater government discomfort and a backlash against participation by entities that were seen as unaccountable, leading to a quest for stronger accountability in the late 1990s and early 2000s (Fox and Brown 1998). This remains a challenge for NGDOs, as evidenced, for example, in the adoption of codes of conduct to allow for self-, rather than state-, regulation.[4] The discomfort this created among Southern governments was a precursor to their behavior towards NGDOs in reaction to major disruptions in international relations as discussed below.

You need both!

Fourth, and potentially most far-reaching, the last twenty years of NGDO-ism have witnessed a confused displacement of identity and self-understanding which has many different origins. One was the emergence of a different "alternative" discourse on development premised on the logic of universal rights, rather than the logic of achieving a different economic model as it had been envisaged in the 1970s. The idea grew that inadequate NGDO performance during twenty years of satisfying basic needs could be redressed by concentrating on the causes of development problems, not their symptoms. Adopting power-related, rights-based approaches to development work was seen as the key to this reorientation. However, implementing this agenda remains a challenging, risk-strewn path. Notwithstanding high levels of commitment, marrying the logic of rights to the satisfaction of immediate needs has proved difficult to achieve in NGDO development practice (Elliott, 2008).

eg. HRW Freedom House

» it's not safe

Compounding these evolutionary pressures was a further change that stemmed from the abrupt, disruptive implosion of the Soviet Union. This event reinvigorated attention to civil society—a political category that, like rights, relies on citizenship as the defining relationship between a polity and a state. The triumphalist euphoria of Fukuyama's *The End of History* and the widespread adoption of civil society language opened new avenues for a more overt aid agenda around good governance and democratization (Clark 1991). Without much in the way of conceptual rigour, NGDOs and NGDO-ism were relocated by donors—and often repositioned themselves—in this new discourse, which called for different competencies in "building" civil society (VeneKlasen 1994). Paradoxically, one positive outcome of this unanticipated evolution was the stimulation of roles that NGDOs could play in the emerging ecologies of civil society as advisers, bridges, and nodes of networks, as well as intermediaries for resources that became available, particularly for democratic consolidation in post-Soviet countries (Pratt 2003).

Locating NGDOs in civil society meant that the parameters for judging their capacity and performance were shifted towards "small-p" politics. Consequently, throughout the 1990s, significant funds were allocated towards promoting and consolidating civil society, often with a naïve projectized approach that generated perverse effects (Ottaway and Carothers 2000). This approach permeated NGDO-ism still further. Liberal perspectives about civil society were propagated by Western governments, rather than by NGDOs articulating for themselves what it might mean to be part of civil society, however they understood that term. This lapse was characteristic of a generally self-disempowering reactive stance among NGDOs along the lines identified by Goldfarb (2006), in not being able to define and address new situations proactively, a form of behavior that abets their subordination to other civic actors that are driven "from below." Though too easily labeled as "social movements," these actors are often driven by a political entrepreneurship of the local that NGDOs are too often self-constrained to embark on, or are able to support, without distorting their purpose and identity.

A third major convulsion for NGDOs during the 2000s can be traced to the global "war on terror" that arose in response to the terrorist attacks on the United States on September 11, 2001. Important features of the NGDO operating environment changed almost overnight. One effect was the more active alignment by donors of development aid with diplomacy and defense: the three-dimensional triad of foreign relations (Beall et al. 2006). The reallocation of aid towards conflict areas such as Iraq and Afghanistan recalibrated where Northern NGDOs would focus their efforts and potential for financing in relief and reconstruction. However, there is increasing evidence that the allocational choices of Northern NGDOs already followed in the slipstream of their official funders, since their geographical distribution of aid correlates more highly with their governments than one would expect from a perspective of autonomy (e.g., Koch 2009). That NGDOs follow donor geo-priorities was not new; it simply became more obvious.

Reflecting the backlash of earlier years, the global war on terror has re-enabled governments everywhere to introduce legislation which curtails the space for civic agency. For NGDOs, this has proven to be a relational "stress test" (Fowler and Sen 2010), particularly with their counterparts in the Middle East. For example, Southern NGDOs work on the frontlines of anti-terror policies and domestic laws, and hence carry greater risks in embarking on rights-based approaches than their Northern partners. The South–North solidarity that had been built up over previous years faced serious challenges as Northern or International NGDOs complied with domestic rules and security-related tests of their overseas activities. Internal and external pressures on NGDOs to revert to the relative safety of increasing poor people's access to social services and material empowerment increased considerably, exemplified in the United Nations Millennium Development Goals. The demand for greater effectiveness in harmony with the policies of the official aid system under the Paris Agenda is another example of these pressures at work (Booth 2008). Thus, for NGDOs, the end of the first decade of the twenty-first century was characterized by shrinking room to maneuver and cooptation into the mainstream foreign aid system. How might these forces play out in the future?

4. NGDOs and the Certainty of Uncertainty

The end of the second millennium produced a plethora of predictions about NGDOs and NGDO-ism in the twenty-first century (Edwards and Sen 2000; Lewis and Wallace 2000; Fowler 2000c). Unforeseen disruptions in the past ten years, culminating in the near-collapse of the global financial system and the form of capitalism it supports, testify to the fallacy of prediction, scenario-building, and other forms of clairvoyance. Perhaps the only firm "futures" assertion is that the uncertainties associated with the interaction between technological advances, multicentric geopolitics, the volatile economics of globalization, and the impact of climate change, will continue to increase. A not unreasonable speculation, therefore, would be that states everywhere will become increasingly preoccupied with a basic raison d'etre of attaining and maintaining stability, domestically, and internationally. Overtly or otherwise, foreign aid will be framed and applied with this new reality in mind, and the allocation of official aid to different countries will reflect this political calculus.

Unlike civil society groups that are not dependent on foreign aid—which can disruptively agitate for change—NDGOs will find it difficult to embark on directions that differ from those which governments and official aid agencies expect, or will tolerate. Obviously, though, NGDOs could pursue "social justice" as a strategic contribution to a stabilizing imperative. Alternatives based around redistribution, inclusion, and civic action are all possible means to this end. Assuming the continuation of the "slipstream" character of much NGDO-ism, a point of reference for the future could also be the quality of the environments of the populations with whom they choose to work, loosely understood as the "stability" characteristics of nation-states that merit international aid. This measure can also accommodate recent scenarios that have informed a "new humanitarianism," which is certainly a strategic option for some NGDOs (Feinstein Centre 2010). This analysis posits conflict settings that call for a trifurcation of humanitarian action: one approach that requires total impartiality; another in which aid is an instrument deployed to affect conflict outcomes; and a third in which "failed states" lack robust or stable governance. The risks and implications of each are very different—for example, for NGDOs that interface with the military and security services.

In the case of development policy after the Millennium Development Goals, unless NGDOs quickly and seriously invest in their own transformation, their future scenarios will reflect expectations of what they do as harmonized complements to official foreign aid under different country conditions. Such organizational transformations are not considered very likely (Ronalds 2010), in part because they involve better ways of recognizing and equalizing power relations, both in development practice and in relationships within NGDO-ism itself (Groves and Hinton 2004). Transformation also requires a rethinking of growth as the metric which counts most of all. NGDOs that cannot take these steps, especially from the North, will be less well positioned to counter their continued incorporation into the official mainstream. Instead, they are likely to face increasing dependency on official aid priorities and stabilizing policies, and increasing pressure to satisfy the expectations they will bring. The general point is not to predict which scenario NGDOs will follow, but to suggest that international NGDOs may need to cope with macro-instability dynamics, while Southern NGDOs should be supported to deal with micro variations of instability within their countries.

A stability-driven picture of NGDO-ism in the years ahead will be subjected to many aid-related dynamics. Examples include the increasingly important behavior of mega-philanthropies, the role of diaspora transfers, and the rise of new bilateral donors such as China, India, and Brazil. Another dynamic already in play is the displacement of NGDOs by other civic actors and their agency, a trend that has nothing to do with foreign aid. These energies are often driven by citizens who engage in changing society as a political project, not as a technical exercise (Fowler and Biekart 2008). Perhaps, therefore, the future of NGDO-ism is really in the balance, not in the sense of their continued survival, but in the sense of their declining proportional relevance, resilience, fit, and embeddedness in civil society at large.

NOTES

1. See www.icnl.org and www.ijcsl.org.
2. See http://archives.chicagotribune.com/2008/may/07/news/chi-russia-civil_rodriguez mayo7.
3. This formulation includes "pretender" NGDOs as well as those who are antagonistic to the ways in which aid is both conceived and functions, and demanding its reform, replacement, or ending altogether. Foreign aid is still their point of reference.
4. See www.oneworldtrust.org/csoaccountability.

REFERENCES

Batliwala, S., and D. Brown (eds). 2006. *Transnational Civil Society: An Introduction.* West Hartford, Conn.: Kumarian Press.

Beall, J., T. Goodfellow, and J. Putzel. 2006. "Introductory Article: On The Discourse Of Terrorism, Security And Development." *Journal of International Development* vol. 18: 51–67.

Bebbington, A., S. Hickey, and D. Mitlin. (eds). 2008. *Can NGOs Make a Difference? The Challenge of Development Alternatives.* London: Zed Press.

Booth, D. 2008. "Aid effectiveness after Accra: How to reform the 'Paris Agenda.'" *Briefing Paper*, 39. London: Overseas Development Institute.

Brown, D., and D. Korten. 1989. "Voluntary Organizations: Guidelines for Donors." Working Paper, WPS 258. Washington, D.C.: The World Bank.

Carroll, T. 1992. *Intermediary NGOs: The Supporting Link in Grassroots Development.* West Hartford, Conn.: Kumarian Press.

Clark, J. 1991. *Democratizing Development: The Role of Voluntary Organizations.* London: Earthscan.

Court, J. 2006. *Policy Engagement for Poverty Reduction—How Civil Society Can be More Effective.* Briefing Paper, No. 3. London: Overseas Development Institute.

Drabek, A. (ed.), 1987. *Development Alternatives: The Challenge for NGOs, World Development*, vol. 15. Oxford: Pergamon Press.

Edwards, M. 2005. "Have NGOs Made a Difference? From Manchester to Birmingham with an Elephant in the Room." Working Paper Series 028. Manchester: Global Poverty Research Group.

Edwards, M., and A. Fowler. 2002. *The Earthscan Reader in NGO Management*, London: Earthscan.

Edwards, M., and J. Gaventa. 2001. *Global Citizen Action.* Boulder, Colo.: Lynne Reinner.

Edwards, M., and D. Hulme (eds.). 1992. *Making a Difference: NGOs and Development in a Changing World.* London: Earthscan.

—— (eds.). 1995. *Non-Governmental Organisations Performance and Accountability: Beyond the Magic Bullet.* London: Earthscan.

Edwards, M., and G. Sen. 2000. "NGOs, Social Change and the Transformation of Human Relationships: A Twenty-First Century Civic Agenda." *Third World Quarterly* vol. 21, no. 4: 605–16.

Elliott, J. 2008. "Development and Social Welfare/Human Rights", in Desai, V. and R. Potter, *The Companion to Development Studies*, Second Edition. London: Hodder Education.

Feinstein International Centre. 2010. *Humanitarian Horizons: A Practitioner's Guide to the Future.* Medford, Mass.: Tufts University Press.

Fowler, A. 1997. *Striking a Balance: A Guide to Enhancing the Effectiveness of Non-Governmental Organizations in International Development.* London: Earthscan.

—— 2000a. "NGOs, Civil Society and Social Development: Changing the Rules of the Game." *Geneva 2000 Occasional Paper*, No. 1. Geneva: United Nations Research Institute for Social Development.

——. (ed). 2000b. "Questioning Partnership: The Reality of Aid and NGO Relations." *IDS Bulletin*, vol. 31, no. 3. Brighton: Institute of Development Studies, University of Sussex.

——. (ed). 2000c. "NGO Futures: Beyond Aid", *Third World Quarterly Special Issue*, vol. 21, No. 4.

Fowler, A., and K. Biekart (eds.). 2008. *Civic Driven Change: Citizen's Imagination in Action.* The Hague: Institute of Social Studies.

Fowler, A., and K. Sen. 2010. "Embedding the War on Terror: State and Civil Society Relations." *Development and Change*, vol. 41, No. 1:1–47.

Fox, J., and L. D. Brown. 1998. *The Struggle for Accountability: The World Bank, NGOs and Grassroots Movements.* Cambridge, Mass.: MIT Press.

Goldfarb, J. 2006. *The Politics of Small Things: The Power of the Powerless in Dark Times.* Chicago: University of Chicago Press.

Groves, L., and R. Hinton (eds.). 2004. *Inclusive Aid: Changing Power Relationships in International Development.* London: Earthscan.

Heinrich, F., and L. Fioramonti (eds). 2007. *Global Survey of the State of Civil Society, vol. 11, Comparative Perspectives.* West Hartford, Conn.: Kumarian Press.

Hilhorst, D. 2003. *The Real World of NGOs: Discourses, Diversity and Development.* London: Zed Press.

Holmén, H. 2010. *Snakes in Paradise: NGOs and the Aid Industry in Africa.* West Hartford, Conn.: Kumarian Press.

Hossain, F., and S. Myllylä (eds.). 1998. *NGOs Under Challenge: Dynamics and Drawbacks in Development.* Helsinki: Department of International Development Cooperation, Ministry of Foreign Affairs.

Hulme, D., and M. Edwards (eds.). 1997. *NGOs, States and Donors: Too Close for Comfort?* London: Macmillan.

Koch, D-J. 2009. *Aid from International NGOs: Blind Spots on the Allocation Map.* London: Routledge.

Korten, D. 1990. *Getting to the 21st Century: Voluntary Action and the Global Agenda.* West Hartford, Conn.: Kumarian Press.

Lehmann, D., 1986. "Dependencia: An Ideological History." *Discussion Paper*, No. 219. Brighton: University of Sussex, Institute of Development Studies.

Lewis, D., and T. Wallace (eds.). 2000. *New Roles and Relevance: Development NGOs and the Challenge of Change*. West Hartford, Conn.: Kumarian Press.

Lindenberg, M., and C. Bryant. 2001. *Going Global: Transforming Relief and Development NGOs*. West Hartford, Conn.: Kumarian Press.

Lissner, J. 1977. *The Politics of Altruism: A Study of the Political Behaviour of Voluntary Agencies*. Geneva: Lutheran World Federation.

Ottaway, M., and T. Carothers (eds.). 2000. *Funding Virtue: Civil Society Aid and Democracy Promotion,* Washington, D.C.: Carnegie Endowment For International Peace.

Pratt, B. (ed.). 2003, *Changing Expectations? The Concept and Practice of Civil Society in International Development*. Oxford: International NGO Training and Research Centre.

Riddell, R. 2007. *Does Foreign Aid Really Work?* Oxford: Oxford University Press.

Ronalds, P. 2010. *The Change Imperative: Creating a Next Generation NGO*. West Hartford, Conn.: Kumarian Press.

Salamon, L., A. Sokolowski, and Associates. 2004. *Global Civil Society: Dimensions of the Nonprofit Sector, vol. 2*. West Hartford, Conn.: Kumarian Press.

Smillie, I. 1995, *The Alms Bazaar: Altruism Under Fire—Non-Profit Organizations and International Development*. London: IT Publications.

Sogge, D. (ed.). 1996. *Compassion and Calculation: The Business of Private Aid Agencies*. London: Pluto Press.

Tendler, J. 1982. "Turning Private Voluntary Organisations into Development Agencies: Questions for Evaluation." *Program Evaluation Discussion Series*, Paper No. 12. Washington, D.C.: United States Agency for International Development.

Tvedt, T. 1998. *Angels of Mercy or Development Diplomats? NGOs and Foreign Aid*. London: James Currey.

Van Rooy, A. 2004. *The Global Legitimacy Game: Civil Society, Globalization and Protest*. London: Palgrave.

VeneKlasen, L. 1994. "*Building Civil Society: The Role of Development NGOs.*" Concept Paper, No. 1. Washington, D.C.: InterAction.

Wallace, T., L. Bornstein, and J. Chapman. 2006. *The Aid Chain: Coercion and Commitment in Development NGOs*. Rugby, U.K.: Intermediate Technology Development Group.

Wallace, T., S. Crowther, and A. Shephard. 1998. *The Standardisation of Development: Influences on UK NGOs' Policies and Procedures*. Oxford: Worldview Press.

CHAPTER 5

....

GRASSROOTS ASSOCIATIONS

....

FRANCES KUNREUTHER

VOLUNTARY associations are often assumed to be synonymous with civil society and an engaged democratic citizenry. As the numbers and scope of voluntary associations have increased, civil society advocates have cited evidence that such associations advance the public good directly (by addressing issues such as poverty, inequality, and environmental degradation) and indirectly (by bringing people into democratic life individually and collectively). Associations provide spaces in which people can practice civic engagement and address problems that are unlikely to be resolved by government or the for-profit sector.

This chapter examines a subset of these associations that work primarily at the local level to promote strong grassroots participation in civil society. The chapter reviews the definition and scope of these associations and their relationships to other civil society groups, especially in the United States, and introduces another, overlooked, category of associations that are committed to the public good called "social change organizations" or SCOs. SCOs include grassroots associations and community organizing groups, and also other organizations that seek to change the underlying systems and structures of power in society. The chapter concludes with two examples that show how new alliances between these different types of grassroots association are emerging to link local work with larger efforts to build civic voice—a crucial task for the future.

1. THE THEORY OF GRASSROOTS ASSOCIATIONS

....

Grassroots associations are a subset of the associational universe and in many ways they capture the ideal of civil society. These are groups where people come together

Characteristics (

voluntarily to advance a concern or interest, solve a problem, take an action, or connect with each other based on something they share in common. Grassroots associations are characterized by more democratic and less hierarchical forms of governance and accountability, the predominance of volunteers as opposed to paid staff, and a local focus, factors which distinguish them from nonprofit, staff-driven organizations (Smith 2000). A grassroots association can be a self-help group such as a chapter of Alcoholics Anonymous (AA), an after-school program organized by parents, a storefront church, a neighborhood soup kitchen, a choral society, a block association, and many, many more, and because such groups are largely run by volunteers, their participants must accept or negotiate the terms on which the group organizes its purposes, activities, responsibilities, and outcomes. Key to these groups is the fact that those involved enter and leave voluntarily. Like others who promote their benefits, Smith asserts that most grassroots associations are light on ideology but strong in their commitment to teaching people the skills of democracy and participation.

The local, volunteer-driven character and small size of most grassroots associations often makes them hard to identify and quantify. In the United States, studies often rely on data collected by government agencies that require formally incorporated groups over a certain size to provide information about their finances and operations. This means that smaller groups are often overlooked, despite the fact that they number over 7.5 million in the United States alone (Smith 2000). However, it is precisely these characteristics—small in scale, voluntary, and local—that make grassroots associations so popular among advocates of civil society. By organizing around common interests, grassroots groups provide one way to address the isolation and sometimes overwhelming responsibilities that face individuals and families in the contemporary world. People come together to learn, act, share, discuss, and enjoy. Associations do not simply meet social needs, they also provide skills that help individuals to engage in the political and economic system, and build increased capacity at the local level for citizen interaction in democratic societies.

Grassroots associations are the often unrecognized places where a community's strengths can be identified and mobilized. Kretzmann and McKnight (1993) have pointed to the importance of acknowledging that all communities, even those that have serious social and economic deficits, are rich in associational life, a richness that helps to compensate for their lack of formal support systems and resources. The appeal of grassroots associations as the building blocks of civil society is that they offer venues in which people can convene across the lines of income, race, gender, geography, and other potential divides, in order to articulate and advance the interests they hold in common.

2. THE PRACTICE OF GRASSROOTS ASSOCIATIONS

These presumed advantages are often idealized, however. Although the number of grassroots associations has increased significantly on a macro level over the last few decades in the United States and elsewhere, economic inequality—an indicator of less rather than more democracy—has widened (Bartels 2008). Furthermore, if these associations are entry points for democratic practice and civic engagement, why have their numbers grown while the most direct expression of civic participation—voting—has declined? One reason is that, although at the micro level, the internal decision-making processes of grassroots groups may be less hierarchical and more democratic, these conditions support but do not guarantee participation in formal and informal politics.

Without paid, professional staff to make decisions and take action, the group must set their own direction, and decisions at volunteer-run organizations are less likely to be oriented towards the funding sources that are required to keep staff-driven organizations afloat. Grassroots associations *may* be places in which people can practice their civic involvement, but they are not *necessarily* spaces where deliberation and civic leadership are learned. A small local group with paid staff that is viewed by the community as a grassroots group may be democratically run, while a mostly volunteer-led affiliate of a larger federated group may be subject to decisions enforced by the national organization. One example is the Girl Scouts in the United States, where the national headquarters has been working to increase the group's overall effectiveness. The results may be mostly positive, but led to internal controversy when a decision to merge two affiliates was made over the objections of the local community (Boy and Girl Scouts 2008). Grassroots associations may be dominated by a volunteer founder or founding group that makes all major decisions, and volunteers in grassroots organizations may choose not to be engaged in decision-making processes at all. A person who joins a grassroots group as a friend to public parks may be perfectly content to pick up trash one day a month.

When one looks closely at the contributions of these groups, they do provide sites for citizens to express their interests, needs, and concerns, and at times they build the practices of civic engagement, but the link between grassroots associations and an engaged civil society is less clear. The right to association can benefit the common good, but is a chess club anything more than an association that is engaged in a private purpose? An association such as AA, which is frequently cited as an example of a group that is formal, voluntary, and grassroots, benefits society by helping individuals to stay alcohol-free, create networks of support, and become productive members of society, but does participation necessarily translate into involvement beyond the group itself? Does AA build civil society outside of its own private spaces? Does the organization work for the public good above and beyond the needs of its individual participants?

The debate over whether grassroots associations are expressions of civil society in these broader senses also depends on the relationships between civil society, the state, and the market. For example, the devolution of U.S. government functions over the past thirty years has resulted in nonprofits increasingly acting as private contractors to the state, taking on responsibilities that are required either by law or by social contract (Salamon 1995; Van Til 2000). In these circumstances, grassroots associations may differ from other nonprofits in their volunteer and locally driven orientation, but they also fill gaps left behind by a diminished public sector. In this context, do people in a community come together to establish more after-school activities because they are "civically engaged," or because cuts to public schools mean that government no longer accepts responsibility for running these much-needed programs, or because parent groups want to be more involved in government-sponsored activities in order to make them more accountable to their interests, or a mixture of all three?

In addition, the existence of grassroots associations adds value to a community, but that value is not equally distributed. Although associations cross all income boundaries, they may be more frequently used by—and be of greater benefit to—the wealthy, who already have more civic voice and power (Verba, Schlozman, and Brady 1995). For example, wealthy homeowners who form an association are more likely to influence laws, regulations, and policies than a tenants' association in a low-income community. A grassroots association in which local citizens come together to improve their schools, or clean up their neighborhoods, is easier to form and maintain in some communities than others, with income as a prime differentiating factor. This is not to say that low-income communities lack grassroots associations, but there are more factors that militate against their inception, ongoing existence, and impact. It is precisely because of continued inequalities of wealth and power and their disproportionate impact on civil society that a subset of grassroots associations called "community organizing groups" are important. They use the unequal distribution of influence and resources as their starting point for engaging with communities.

3. Community Organizing: Civil Society and Power

The visibility and popularity of community organizing groups increased in the United States when President Barack Obama identified himself as a former community organizer during his election campaign in 2008, but community organizing has a decades-long history and now a global presence. Community organizing groups have an explicit goal of addressing power and inequality by engaging people who have little influence as individuals, but who can gain voice and influence by working more closely together. Like other grassroots associations, community organizing groups are formal associations that stress democratic decision-making and the involvement of unpaid staff. Like social movements, most rely on mobilizing people to work collectively in order to accomplish their goals. Most organizing campaigns are not overtly ideological, but seek specific changes that focus on a public issue—from the need for a traffic light to protect children in the neighborhood, to closing liquor stores in order to reduce crime, to opening up schools to greater parent involvement and oversight.

Community organizing has a long history of mobilizing resources to fill unmet needs that range from building community capacity for self-help to solving community problems by shifting relationships of power. In its earlier manifestations, the field was primarily focused on local development, social planning or social action (Betten and Austin 1990). Today, community organizing is most frequently associated with the work of Saul Alinksy, who is known worldwide for the model he codified and promoted in the United States in the mid-twentieth century. Alinksy's background in the labor movement of the 1930s taught him how workers with little power used "controlled conflict" to gain basic rights and influence on issues such as wages, hours, and workplace conditions (Betten and Austin 1990). Applying these techniques to white working-class neighborhoods in Chicago, Alinksy focused on how the "have-nots" could gain power by working together. Change happens, he believed, through confrontation, using the strength of collective action to force concessions from politicians and other policy makers. Though Alinksy was a fan of de Tocqueville and acknowledged the importance of associations in making change, he also believed that "change comes from power and power comes from organization. In order to act, people must get together." (Alinsky 1969, 113). In Alinsky's model, organizers work through local associations such as churches, labor unions, book clubs, and others to build up their numbers. The Industrial Areas Foundation founded by Alinksy continues this tradition today through faith-based organizations in many parts of the United States (Warren 2001).

The landscape of community organizing has passed through a variety of modifications over the past fifty years. Many groups have adapted Alinsky's techniques, while keeping the emphasis on building power and changing power relations. For example, the United Farm Workers organized individuals (not organizations with constituencies) often through house meetings, and members were offered mutual benefits. The Association of Community Organizations for Reform Now (ACORN) evolved out of welfare rights organizing, focusing on reaching the very poor. Feminist critiques of Alinsky's emphasis on the public sphere recognized the need to organize in the private sphere in order to address issues such as domestic abuse. Others have promoted organizing in ways that take account communities of interest, especially race, where issues facing communities of color are highlighted and addressed. (Sen 2003; Jacoby-Brown 2006; Minieri and Gestos 2007).

These different approaches persist to this day. Smock (2004) identifies five prototypes: power, community-based, civic, women-centered, and transformative. The style of organizing promoted by Alinksy is the basis of the power model that emphasizes the need for confrontation. *Community-based* organizing, on the other hand, addresses the lack of infrastructure and capacity building in low-income communities and looks to solutions from the State. *Civic* organizing stresses the need for public order in order to stabilize and build safe communities, while *women-centered* groups organize in ways that challenge the divide between the public and private spheres in offering safe spaces and support. *Transformative* organizing focuses on how to rethink the ways in which public and private institutions operate in order to address the root causes of inequality. Smock's analysis separates groups according to the problems they are ultimately trying to solve. Groups that use power models see organizing as a tool of democratic pluralism, in which the goal is to enhance a community's ability to access more power and influence. Groups that stress transformative organizing are looking for changes that ultimately address the institutional injustices that are embedded in larger systems. More recent work by Su (2009) explores the differences that exist between groups, following Alinsky, that organize within systems in order to obtain a larger "piece of the pie," and those, following the popular education approach of Paulo Friere, that raise consciousness about the deeper problems of State and market institutions that must be addressed to change or enlarge the "pie" itself.

Social movement organizations also use community organizing strategies to create mass-based power for change (Ganz 2009), as in South Africa's anti-apartheid movement for example, where organizing took place not only within South Africa to mobilize support but also to inspire a worldwide divestment campaign which targeted governments and corporations. But not all community organizing groups are linked to movements. Most, like other grassroots associations, are confined to local communities, and even when they enjoy significant successes their results rarely add up to large scale, mass-based movement building across localities that creates significant social change.

Two basic tenets remain key to most community organizing practices today. The first is to identify common issues that affect a group of people and encourage them to address these issues *collectively*. The second is to move individuals and their private interests towards a common identity and a shared platform from which they can act together in this way (Chetkovich and Kunreuther 2006). Community organizing is therefore centrally concerned with preparing people to engage in the public sphere, especially those who are marginalized in the democratic process. In theory, organizing takes its cue for action from the individuals who are experiencing the problem, so that the issues are identified by the community and reflect their needs. In practice, some organizing efforts focus on a particular campaign that will benefit a community, and then members are enlisted to participate. Hence, community organizing can enhance or undermine equality, fairness, and sustainable development, because the organizing process can be used by any group of people to bring about the changes they desire. In the United States, for example, the recent Tea Party movement has used the Alinsky model to hold politicians accountable during town hall meetings held in their local communities, but in support of values and policies that Alinsky would never have endorsed (Stellar 2009). Hence, it is the combination of the *forms* of organizing with the *norms* of social change or social justice that is most important to long-term results.

4. Social Change Organizations: Creating the Good Society

If grassroots associations are too broad to be equated with a particular vision of the good society and community organizing is too narrow, a third group of social change organizations has arisen at the intersection of these two categories to offer a way to reconcile the dilemmas they evoke. Social change organizations (SCOs) are voluntary associations in local communities that address systemic issues in order to increase the power of marginalized groups, communities, or interests (Chetkovich and Kunreuther 2006). Over the past twenty years, the term social change organization has become commonplace among practitioners in the voluntary sector, but it is barely recognized in the academic literature on civil society, nonprofits or social movements. Community organizing groups are a subset of SCOs when they operate at a time or in a place where no mass-based social movements exist. Other social change organizations deliver services, engage in advocacy, and fight legal battles to solve problems caused by larger policies or systems. These are groups that are committed to a vision of the good society in which those with little influence because of their income, class, caste, immigrant status, race, gender, or sexual orientation are supported to build their voice and engage in a variety of ways to address imbalances of power.

Unlike grassroots associations, however, social change organizations may have a majority of paid staff, but they are also characterized by their commitment to involve their constituents in determining the direction of the organization and its work. This commitment extends to organizational leadership, which must manage both the operations of the group and the inclusion of the voices of staff members and constituents, even though internal governance structures range from traditional hierarchies to collective decision making. If civil society is a space for association and engagement in the public sphere oriented towards a vision of the good society that benefits all its citizens, then social change organizations are key (Chetkovich and Kunreuther 2006). They work in local communities to address critical issues such as environmental degradation, economic inequality, radical fundamentalism, identity-based discrimination, service needs, and the denial of basic human rights by states, though in practice their achievements indicate more success with engaging local constituents than in addressing the roots causes of problems. Like many grassroots associations, these organizations are entry points into the public sphere at a local level, and it is in the local arena that they are able to make a difference. However, the fact that many decisions are not made at a community level often thwarts social change organizations' efforts to build their vision of a good and just society.

Progress towards the good society is often seen in large-scale social movements, from the civil rights movement in the United States to the rise of Solidarity in Poland, which found support in civil society associations (Morris 1984; Walzer 1995). But in the absence of transformative movements, social change organizations can make systemic changes by joining forces in order to scale up their influence, working together across their local interests or acting as affiliates of a national organization. In the United States, the latter model has had more success than the former, but it has its own set of risks. National groups with local affiliates have a tendency to promote their own agendas and reinforce top-down control through their size and power (Piven and Cloward 1978), and it can be difficult avoid a command and control structure rather than building from the bottom up, from the local level to the national. In addition, the affiliates of national organizations may be torn between loyalty to national and local efforts. Even the process of creating local organizations may feel like an invasion of, rather than a support for, a community, especially if the group was not invited in by constituents. There can also be unseen vulnerabilities, as the case of ACORN in the United States demonstrates. Successful attacks on ACORN from conservatives in 2008 and 2009 not only jeopardized its mission (eventually leading to ACORN's disbandment), but also revealed a lack of internal transparency and accountability over finance and board governance that were in conflict with ACORN's public vision of social change (Cohen 2009).

Trying to scale up across different groups and localities through coalitions of membership organizations has, until recently, seemed unmanageable in the U.S. context, especially when they cross diverse issue areas, geographic boundaries, identity groups, goals, and constituencies. But now there are new formations that are attempting to do just this. Some are loose affiliations that raise funds together for a broad common agenda, and others are more structured. Among the former are the Pushback Network, "a national collaboration of indigenous, grassroots organizations and networks committed to building bottom-up, state-based alliances that change both the composition and levels of participation of the electorate."[1] The Pushback Network's members operate in eight states, and each has its own approach to winning power for social change. Sharing information and raising funds to support organizing and electoral work have been two important components of the network's success. Hence, organizing *above* the local level is a crucial ingredient of success.

5. Social Change Organizations in Action

a. The Right to the City

In 2007, a group of local community organizing groups formed the U.S.-based Right to the City (RTTC), a national alliance that "seeks to create regional and national impacts in the fields of housing, human rights, urban land, community development, civic engagement, criminal justice, environmental justice, and more."[2] With a core membership of thirty-seven "base-building" organizations in eight cities, RTTC is affiliated with the global Right to the City movement that grew out of the World Urban Forum in 2004. The agenda of Right to the City reflects its broad vision "that everyone, particularly the disenfranchised, not only has a right to the city, but as inhabitants, have a right to shape it, design it, and operationalize an urban human rights agenda."

Right to the City is a membership organization in which local organizing groups with similar analyses and goals find ways of working together to have a larger impact.

Jon Liss (2009), the director and one of the founding members of Tenants and Workers United, describes how the work of RTTC groups emerged in the void that was left behind by the decline of labor unions in the United States (organizations that historically tended to exclude people of color and women), the increase of immigrant workers in the labor force, and the breakup of the "new left." In the 1980s, new, power-based organizing groups emerged to challenge Alinksy's "color-blind" approach. They concentrated on transformational work with members as well as achieving concrete victories, but were unable to reach the scale required to give low-income communities, communities of color, and immigrant communities enough power to make significant systems change. Right to the City is an opportunity to address these shortcomings by building cohesion and sense of collective power, and developing a new generation of strategies around a shared ideology that offers member organizations a strong sense of belonging as well as concrete accomplishments on which to build their influence.

Liss is one of the members of the Right to the City working group on civic engagement, a strategy that promotes voter education, counts disenfranchised communities in the U.S. Census, and pursues other forms of action focused on energizing the public sphere. The working group members share information to strengthen civic engagement efforts in their own regions, and offer ideas to other RTTC groups across their different cities. For example, Tenants and Workers United has been organizing in Virginia for the past twenty years. Three years ago, Liss and his colleagues founded a sister organization called Virginia's New Majority to focus on voter engagement. New Majority was incorporated under a different tax status than Tenants and Workers; as a nonprofit, it is permitted by law to influence legislation and engage in some forms of political activity. Tenants and Workers United, like most organizations in the U.S. voluntary sector, is a charitable 501c3 organization that must remain nonpartisan.

More explicitly, Virginia's New Majority is a group that aims to "expand democracy in terms of who participates and maximize what democracy can look like…by building a new common sense or understanding about politics, policies, culture, and role of government…that moves hundreds of thousands of people" (Liss 2009, 1). Yet for Liss, civic engagement work is different than community organizing. While civic engagement has a broader reach, organizing still has a deeper impact on those involved. For example, Virginia's New Majority visited 300,000 homes in a two-year period, far exceeding the 10,000–15,000 homes reached by Tenants and Workers each year. But Tenants and Workers was able to recruit 600 to 1,200 volunteer activists with a deep commitment to organizing and service programs, while New Majority was only able to identify a few dozen new members. Trying carefully to balance scale, depth and commitment to deep change, Liss's work reflects some of the larger hopes and challenges of the Right to the City alliance and its members.

The members of Right to the City share a common theoretical framework based on French philosopher Henri Lefebvre's *Le droite à la ville* (for which the group is named). This shared analysis gives the group its cohesion, offering the potential to be more than a series of individual organizations that share information with each other. How and whether the members can really scale up their ideas and impact within and across communities is yet to be tested, but the Right to the City model is an important step forward for social change organizations, beyond allied relationships ("we like your work and you like ours") to the point at which strategic and ideological partners engage with each other in the public sphere in order to create the possibility of a good and just society.

b. Feminists Transformation Watch

While Right to the City aims is to strengthen local power as well as to work across geographic boundaries in the United States, the Feminist Transformation Watch (FTW) looks at how local grassroots efforts can be enhanced by working transnationally. Their methodology of building power in one locality by drawing on the resources and experiences of others is illustrated in the collaboration between Las Petateras, a Mesoamerican feminist group, and Just Associates, a U.S.-based intermediary that builds solidarity with women's groups in Mesoamerica, Southern Africa, and Indonesia, and which is dedicated to supporting the capacity of women to alter systems of power that perpetuate inequality and injustice. FTW is an innovative attempt to support women who are "questioning, confronting, and transforming power" to witness, document and bring attention to abuses of human rights, and to support women on the frontline in these situations (Arroyo et al. 2008, 2).

The FTW approach reflects an effort to "scale out" rather than scale up. It both supports and draws attention to the importance of women's ability to participate in the public sphere as visible actors, especially in countries where that ability is severely restricted by repression or cultural factors. The process begins when women in a given country issue a call for action that invites feminist media and international delegations to convene (virtually or in person) as witnesses to grassroots efforts to challenge existing power structures. Subsequent steps include the following:

- Designing and implementing a response to a particular situation affecting women, such as systematic state-endorsed or state-tolerated violence against women (for example in Ciudad Juarez and Oaxaca in Mexico).
- Calling on women and women's organizations from outside the country to serve as witnesses, amplify the issues, and generate more protection, especially in situations where protest is increasingly criminalized.
- Using the media, including radio and social networking, to reach out and involve larger audiences (for example, special broadcasts directly from sites of action where women call in from around the world and post statements of support online).
- Using statements provided by a group of women Nobel laureates who have been organized as strategic allies to spotlight or directly participate in FTW.

- Documenting lessons learned—both the impact of the action and the process of mobilization—in order to build the effectiveness of FTW and to continue to address the local issues at hand.

The idea for the Feminist Transformation Watch began in Mesoamerica where a multigenerational group of women from different countries and diverse backgrounds met at a workshop to talk about the need to weave their efforts together to create a stronger impact. Critical of the fragmentation and demobilization that stem from NGO politics and policy-driven forms of advocacy, they wanted to draw on the successes of earlier feminist movements that focused on grassroots activities to draw attention to injustices against women. Since 2006 there have been eight Feminist Transformation Watch activities in Nicaragua, Mexico, Guatemala, Costa Rica, Honduras, and the United States, ranging from fact-finding on violence against women in Guatemala to denouncing rights violations against pro-democracy activists after a state coup in Honduras. The results have heightened the FTW groups' understanding that there is a critical "erosion of already limited spaces of citizen participation" and a "dismantling of the social fabric and worldviews that sustain and nurture healthy and vibrant social and political relationships" (Arroyo et al. 2008, 19).

The FTW model is not so much about aggregating civic influence as about creating new ways of sharing power at and with the grassroots in order to highlight and address sites of injustice through information sharing, creative intervention, communications, and the collective strength that is achieved by weaving all of these elements together. Like Right to the City, Feminist Transformation Watch is a young civil society formation, yet it is already widely known and respected among Latin American social movements. The evidence of FTW's long-term impact is not yet clear, but a new level of engagement is already occurring. Those involved have been both excited by the possibilities and educated on the difficulties that small social change groups encounter when crossing national borders in their efforts to involve citizens in creating the good society.

6. Conclusion

Grassroots Associations are often equated with the ideals of civil society. They have become the entry points for nonstate and nonprofit activity outside of family life that provide much-needed opportunities for gaining civic skills and acting in the public sphere. Community organizing groups are a subset of these associations that focus on building the power and voice of disenfranchised communities, and social change organizations stand at the intersection of these two sets of groups, explicitly addressing the root causes of inequality but engaging in a wider range of strategies and forms of association which attempt to balance scale, depth, and commitment to deep-rooted social change.

All of these associations work primarily at the community level, and they have often been viewed as too localized to address larger, systemic barriers to the good society. But recent developments indicate that new approaches to working across organizational and geographic boundaries may be more successful in creating change on a larger scale and at a deeper level than before. These new formations are still nascent and their impact is unclear, but their attempts to address inequalities of power by increasing citizen voice are an indication that new routes to civil society through grassroots associations are constantly opening up, and must be nurtured.

NOTES

1. Pushback Network's official website is http://pushbacknetwork.org.
2. Right to the City's official website is http://righttothecity.org.

REFERENCES

Alinsky, S. 1969. *Rules for Radicals: A Pragmatic Primer for Realistic Radicals.* New York: Vintage Books.

Arroyo, R. et al. 2008. *Feminist Transformation Watch: Women Crossing the Line.* Washington, D.C.: Las Petrateras and Just Associates (JASS).

Bartels, L. M. 2008. *Unequal Democracy: The Political Economy of the New Gilded Age.* Princeton, N.J.: Princeton University Press.

Betten, N., and M. J. Austin. 1990. *The Roots of Community Organizing, 1917–1939.* Philadelphia: Temple University Press.

Boy and Girl Scouts. 2008. *The News,* Opinion, Advice Blog. Available at http://www .boyandgirlscouts.com/girl-scout-reorg/sheboygan-girl-scouts-fight-merger/ (accessed September 8, 2008).

Cohen, R. 2009. "An Independent Governance Assessment of ACORN: The Path To Meaningful Reform." *The Nonprofit Quarterly,* December 7, 2009. Available at http://www. nonprofitquarterly.org/index.php?option=com_content&view=article&id=1650:an-independent-governance-assessment-of-acorn-the-path-to-meaningful-reform&catid=149:rick-cohen&Itemid=117.

Chetkovich, C., and F. Kunreuther. 2006. *From the Ground Up: Grassroots Organizations Making Social Change.* Ithaca, N.Y.: Cornell University Press.

Ganz, M. 2009. *Why David Sometimes Wins: Leadership, Organization, and Strategy in the California Farm Worker Movement.* New York: Oxford University Press.

Jacoby Brown, M. 2006. *Building Powerful Community Organizations.* Arlington, Mass.: Long Haul Press.

Kretzmann, J. P., and J. L. McKnight. 1993. *Building Communities from the Inside Out: A Path Toward Finding and Mobilizing a Community's Assets.* Evanston, Ill.: Institute for Policy Research.

Liss, J. 2009. "Building New Majorities." *Engaging Power: How Community Organizing is Expanding Democratic Rights for New Urban Majority* 2: 1–5. Available at http://www .righttothecity.org/assets/files/EngagingPower_issue_2_web.pdf.

Minieri, J., and P. Gestos. 2007. *Tools for Radical Democracy.* San Francisco: Jossey-Bass.

Morris, A. D. 1984. *The Origins of the Civil Rights Movement: Black Communities Organizing for Change.* New York: The Free Press.

Piven, P. P., and R. Cloward. 1978. *Poor People's Movements: Why They Succeed, How They Fail.* London: Vintage/Anchor Books.

Salamon, L. 1995. *Partners in Public Service.* Baltimore: Johns Hopkins University Press.

Sen, R. 2003. *Stir It Up: Lessons in Community Organizing and Advocacy.* San Francisco: Jossey-Bass.

Smith, D. H. 2000. *Grassroots Associations.* Thousand Oaks, Calif.: Sage Publications.

Smock, K. 2004. *Democracy in Action: Community Organizing and Urban Change.* New York: Columbia University Press.

Stellar, C. 2009. "Pawlenty Comes from a Community that Alinsky Organized," *The Minnesota Independent*, September 21, 2009.

Su, C. 2009. *Streetwise for Book Smarts: Grassroots Organizing and Education Reform in the Bronx.* Ithaca, N.Y.: Cornell University Press.

Van Til, J. 2000. *Growing Civil Society: From Nonprofit Sector to Third Space.* Bloomington: Indiana University Press.

Verba, S., K. L. Schlozman, and H. Brady. 1995. *Voice and Equity: Civic Voluntarism in American Politics.* Cambridge, Mass.: Harvard University Press.

Walzer, M. 1995. "The Concept of Civil Society," in ed. Walzer, M. *Towards a Global Civil Society.* Providence, R.I.: Berghahn Books.

Warren, Mark R. 2001. *Dry Bones Rattling: Community Building to Revitalize American Democracy.* Princeton, N.J.: Princeton University Press.

CHAPTER 6

....

SOCIAL MOVEMENTS

....

DONATELLA DELLA PORTA
AND MARIO DIANI

ALTHOUGH empirically, collective actors defined as social movements on the one hand and as civil society on the other present several overlapping themes, in the social sciences these two fields of interest—both large and growing—have rarely interacted. In fact, while in political and media discourse particular organizations, individuals, and events are routinely described as stemming from one or the other, the social sciences have stressed different core conceptualizations for each of these two phenomena.

This chapter explores the interactions between the social science literatures in these two fields, and considers both differences and similarities in their conceptualization as well as in the actual evolution of the social actors that have been identified and recognized as social movements and as civil society. The chapter begins by discussing the analytical relationships between these two concepts, before moving on to illustrate some of the tensions that have emerged in their interrelationships and concluding by showing how these tensions have evolved over time and may be resolved in the future.

1. SOCIAL MOVEMENTS AND CIVIL SOCIETY: BASIC CONCEPTS

....

It is fair to say that analysts of social movements—or perhaps, more precisely, those associated with mainstream social movement analysis in North American (and American-influenced) social science—have paid little attention to the concept of civil society in their models (Snow, Soule, and Kriesi 2004). When they have done so, this has been in the context of other conceptual debates such as that inspired by "social capital," rather than in any explicit dialogue with social movement theory (Edwards, Foley, and Diani 2001). This does not mean that there are no logical areas of overlap. Depending on one's definitions, social movements may be seen as an integral component of civil society, and vice versa, associational life and participatory processes within civil society may be regarded as one instance of broader social movement dynamics. While there is no space here for a systematic discussion of these two concepts (Diani 1992; Kumar 1993; Edwards 2009), we can illustrate their relationships by looking at Diani's definition of social movements as informal networks created by a multiplicity of individuals, groups, and organizations, engaged in political or cultural conflicts on the basis of a shared collective identity (Diani 1992; della Porta and Diani 2006). Social movements are actually just one possible mode of coordination of collective action within civil society. Their peculiarity lies in the coupling of dense interorganizational networks and collective identities that transcend the boundaries of any specific organization and encompass much broader collectivities (Diani and Bison 2004). A good deal of collective action in civil society may also take the form of instrumental coalitions, in which collaboration neither relies on, nor generates larger identities. At other times, collective action is promoted by networks of like-minded people concerned with a specific issue or a broader cause (think, for example, of communities of practice or epistemic communities), rather than by organizations alone. Finally, collective action may take place within specific organizations without stimulating the growth of broader networks and identities.

Given this complexity of forms, and the fact that there is neither awareness nor consensus on the distinctiveness of the various types, it is no surprise that in practical terms researchers who claim to be primarily interested in social movements or in civil society end up with quite similar questions and empirical objects of analysis. For example, both lines of research share an interest in the mechanisms that facilitate or discourage citizens' involvement in collective action as individuals (Marwell and Oliver 1993; Wilson 2000; Diani and McAdam 2003). The two lines of inquiry also converge when movements are regarded primarily as sets of organizations with similar or at least compatible goals, rather than as networks of interdependent actors. If the focus is on voluntary organizations as organizations rather than on their networks, then the distinction between "social movement organizations" (the term favored by movement analysts), "voluntary associations," and "public interest groups" (the term favored by civil society analysts) loses some of its relevance. There is much common ground in considering how these organizational forms combine a quest for efficacy with a commitment to decentralized, participatory structures; how they coordinate resources; and other important issues (Kriesi 1996; Jordan and Maloney 1997; Anheier and Themudo 2002).

2. Conflictive and Consensual Collective Action

Having identified some areas of convergence, it is also important to recognize where these two fields of inquiry diverge. First, an emphasis on conflict is not as strong in

Conflict!

reference to civil society as it is to social movements. Social movement studies have since long stressed conflict as the key dynamic element of societies. The European tradition in social movement studies has looked at new social movements as potential carriers of a new central conflict in post-industrial societies, or at least of an emerging constellation of conflicts. In the North American tradition, the resource mobilization approach reacted to a then-dominant conception of conflicts as pathologies. However, from Michael Lipsky (1965) to Charles Tilly (1978), the first systematic works on social movements developed from traditions of research that stressed conflicts of power, both in society and in politics: "Social movement actors are engaged in political and/or cultural conflicts, meant to promote or oppose social change. By conflict we mean an oppositional relationship between actors who seek control of the same stake—be it political, economic, or cultural power – and in the process make negative claims on each other—i.e., demands which, if realized, would damage the interests of the other actors" (della Porta and Diani 2006, 21).

In contrast, analysts of civil society often focus on non- or less-contentious forms of collective action that give priority to largely consensual issues and agendas (Daly 2006; Edwards 2009): for example, campaigns promoting collective responses to pressing public issues that most people recognize as important (such as environmental degradation or the persistence of inequality between industrialized and developing countries). These campaigns are surely akin to coalitions if not to full-fledged social movements, since they involve multiple organizations and may also generate long-term solidarities. Yet conflict is not necessarily central to them, since civil society often acts in pursuit of goals defined broadly enough to make them acceptable—if not top-priority—to large sectors of public opinion. In an effort to bridge these two sectors of social life, social movement analysts have sometimes talked of "consensus movements" to identify instances of collective action in which conflict was either absent or peripheral (Lofland 1989).

Similar considerations apply to social movement practices, which are often defined as confrontational. Their tactics are disruptive in so far as, in order to capture the attention of the public and exercise pressure on power holders, they need to amplify their voice through a (more or less symbolic) challenge to law and order. Social movements are characterized by their adoption of unusual forms of political behavior. Many scholars pinpoint the fundamental distinction between movements and other political actors in the use by the former of *protest as* a form of exerting political pressure. Protest is defined as a nonconventional form of action that interrupts daily routines (Lipsky 1965).

Over the last few years, the analysis of social movements has been approached through the concept of contentious politics, defined as episodic, public, and collective interaction among claim makers and their targets (when at least one government is a claimant, an object of claims, or a party to the claim and the claims would, if realized, affect the interests of at least one of the claimants: McAdam, Tarrow, and Tilly 2001). By contrast, research on civil society has stressed civility, defined as respect for others, or tolerance, politeness, and the acceptance of strangers and their views (Keane 2003). In many reflections on contemporary societies, an autonomous civil society is referred to as being capable of addressing the tensions that arise between particularism and universalism, plurality and connectedness, diversity and solidarity. It is, in this sense, called to be "a solidarity sphere in which certain kind of universalizing community comes gradually to be defined and to some degree enforced" (Alexander 1998, 7). Linked to this understanding is a view of civil society as the texture of cooperative and associational ties that foster mutual trust and shared values, ultimately strengthening social cohesion (Putnam 1993). The implied link here between reducing conflict and increasing social cohesion has been criticized by those who argue that the articulation and explicit management of social conflict is essential for the survival of democracy (Mouffe 2005).

3. New Social Movements, Civil Society and the Autonomy of the Self

If the social science literature stresses different conceptual elements in the definition of social movements and civil society, empirical trends have increased their overlap. One such trend is the growing importance of the concept of *autonomy* in social movements, which has always been central to the definition of civil society. Dubbed as the "most favored export from sociological theory into politics" by Mitzal (2001) and "flattened out and emptied of content" by Chandhoke (2003), the concept of civil society has been used as a synonym for associational life and emancipation from authoritarian governments and corporate or commercial agendas. Inspired in particular by new social movements and the movement for democracy in Eastern Europe (Mitzal 2001), the revival of civil society in social theory in the 1990s coincided with the search for a space that was autonomous from both the state and the market.

Since the 1970s, some social movements that have developed have been labeled as "new," to stress their distance from the working-class and nationalist movements that had dominated industrial societies (Melucci 1996; Calhoun 1993). These included movements on environmental issues, women's and other human rights, gender and sexuality, peace and solidarity, as well as those advocating greater balance in North-South relations. While all of these movements were vocal in the public arena and provided political representation either to deprived social groups, unvested collective interests or both, they also contained strong elements that were explicitly nonpolitical.

More specifically, the new social movements focused their action on areas and issues that did not relate directly to the struggle for state power, but aimed instead at increasing the autonomy of individuals in relation to various political and institutional spheres. Some of these issues concerned the conditions under which knowledge is produced and used, both in its scientific and professional sense.

Environmental movements, for example, had a major interest in securing greater freedom for researchers operating in public institutions to explore important lines of research, such as alternative energy sources, that might not be relevant to established economic interests; or in granting researchers more freedom to speak out on issues of public concern, such as the risks associated with new technologies, regardless of the secrecy clauses that are often imposed by private companies that fund research on these topics. Likewise, women's movements developed a strong dialogue with certain sectors of the medical profession in areas like women's health, responsible maternity, and freedom of reproductive choice.

Common to these and to other new social movements, therefore, was a particular form of the struggle for autonomy that had been typical of civil society dynamics. In the examples cited above, autonomy was searched for in relation to technocratic apparatuses and corporate control over knowledge production. But the notion of autonomy was articulated in many other ways: by feminism, through its stress on the need to develop autonomy from male domination within the family, or from established institutions such as churches on moral and ethical matters; by environmentalism, through the promotion of sustainable forms of social organization, autonomous from the logic of private profit and from global economic interests; and by gay and lesbian movements, in terms of autonomy from heterosexual cultural models and stereotypes. From these different angles, it is clear that the idea of autonomy has become an important point of convergence between social movement and civil society theories and practices—for example, in the Habermasian version of movements as reactions to the attempted colonization of life-worlds by bureaucratic state and economic apparatuses, or in Melucci's (1996) view of movements attempting to redefine the relationships between individual and collective experiences through the elaboration of "challenging codes."

4. Social Movements, Civil Society and Social Conflict

Since the 1980s, many of the new social movements have taken considerable steps towards institutionalization and stronger ties to the political system. They have become richer in material resources, gained better access to decision makers, and become more and more focused on single issues. Indeed, an increasing focus on single issues came to be seen as characteristic of social movements, vis-à-vis political parties and labor unions (Kitschelt 2004). In parallel, recent literature on civil society has stressed the growing specialization of organizations on particular issues, often addressed within specific international regimes. A "global civil society" has emerged, consisting largely of organizations that are professionalized, institutionalized, and focused around specific causes (Kaldor 2003).

This image of post-materialistic and single-issue actors was shaken during the 1990s, and broke down after the year 2000. Since that year, reactions to what activists refer to as "hegemonic neoliberalism" have brought about a resurgence of interest in social issues, though blended with the concerns of the "new social movements." Does this signify a return to a class vision of society—the frame on which political sociology had been built in the past and whose recent waning has been considered as one of the causes of its decline (Savage 2001)? In the social movement field, these developments certainly indicate the limits of interpretations that stress the "institutionalization of class cleavages" or opposed postmaterialist to materialistic values. And in relation to civil society, they draw attention to attitudes among civic groups to the state and the market. However, the return of the social question cannot be read as a return to old-style class politics, for two main reasons. First, social concerns are linked with other issues, and second, the movements that are emerging tend to defend the autonomy of civil society, a position absent from traditional visions of class politics.

In recent times, various streams of social movements can be interpreted as a reaction to the retrenchment of the welfare state and to the increasing inequalities that this has promoted, revitalizing the social dimension of conflict—a "class cleavage" (Rokkan 1982)—that had appeared as pacified or tamed. If during the 1990s, the free market was considered as a solution to public deficits and unemployment, since the year 2000 the negative consequences of economic globalization have become more of a matter of public concern. In its different meanings and understandings, neoliberal economic globalization—or what Keane (2003) calls "turbo-capitalism"—is now perceived as the main target of both social movements and civil society actors. In Europe, the end of the "mid-century compromise" between capitalism and the welfare state (Crouch 2004) brought social rights to the center of these conflicts, albeit not without attention to new themes like environmental sustainability and gender that had emerged with the new social movements. These conflicts also stress that, as scholars of civil society had observed a long time ago, building a sphere of citizenship which is autonomous from the state and the economy does require inclusive citizens' rights.

5. Social Movements, Civil Society, and New Forms of Politics

By bringing social rights back into the debate, these conflicts also stress the role that politics has to play vis-à-vis the market. Politics has long been considered important for constituting the norms and institutions of civil society, and ensuring the conditions of equality and freedom in which civil society can prosper. If for Habermas the welfare state implies a risk that the life-world will be penetrated by the administrative state, it also represents a defense of the life-word against penetration by the capitalist economy. In similar vein, in 1992 Cohen and Arato had called for a reflexive continuation of welfare policies to counter both the risks of colonization by state power and the re-economization of society. Social movement studies, while emphasizing the differences between civil society and movement actors, have also considered the openness of institutions and the availability of alliances among institutional political actors as decisive for collective mobilization and its success.

In the past, old and new movements tended to align along existing political party lines or to form new ones. Since the 1980s, a de facto division of tasks between parties and movements has been noted, and often approved of. While social movements, civil society organizations, and NGOs retreated to or constituted the social sphere, political parties (especially on the Left) represented some of their claims in political institutions. At the same time, changes were underway in the repertoire of collective action. The social movement literature stressed a withdrawal of movements from protest. Movement organizations had become better structured at the national or even the transnational level, had acquired substantial material resources and a certain public recognition, had established paid staff thanks to mass membership drives, and had tended to replace protest by lobbying or other contentious actions. They had become interest groups, albeit of a public interest type; had entered the "third sector," acquiring professionalism and often administering public resources along the way; and/or had commercialized their activities by creating (sometimes successfully) new niches in the market. In parallel, the literature on civil society emphasized similar points by focusing on the richest and better-structured organizations, made more influential by their institutional contacts and legitimacy in the public eye. In this sense, global civil society could be said to have developed from the taming of social movements of the pre-1989 period as well as the decline of older civic associations such as labor unions and their transformation into NGOs (Kaldor 2003).

These emerging conflicts suggest that the professionalization of politics and citizens' withdrawal from participation in public life, are far from undisputed trends. Not only that: the grassroots conflicts of the late 1990s and the early 2000s seem to propose an alternative vision of politics itself. Although the interaction of institutional politics and politics from below—between *routine* and *contentious* politics—continues to be important, the image of a division of labor between political parties, especially on the Left, and movements is becoming more and more problematic, challenged by civil society actors that are elaborating a different vision of politics to underpin their changing roles. This is not "anti-politics," but "another politics." This new conception of politics is critical of the increasingly professionalized institutional processes that have developed in industrial societies. While stressing the need for political governance of the economy, these visions reflect an increasing tension between representative and participatory conceptions of politics. In the former, politics becomes an activity for professionals who take decisions that are legitimized by electoral investiture. In the latter, participatory processes and institutions are open to citizens, who regard themselves as the subjects and actors of politics itself.

This conception of "politics from below" does not imply withdrawal from relations with formal, institutional politics. Research confirms the openness of many social movement organizations to continued interaction with the institutions of multilevel governance. This attitude, which is at odds with interpretations of social movement organizations as focused solely on street protest or with civil society as antipolitical in nature, is clear in recent writing and research (della Porta 2009a and 2009b).

In summary, contemporary social movements and civil society activism indicate a return to politics in the street, but also stress an alternative conception of politics in response to the difficulties experienced by representative democracy such as the decline of political party loyalties, the retrenchment of the state, and the development of various forms of globalization. While the development of much prior reflection on civil society had taken state retrenchment for granted, more recent thinking reflects a growing demand to bring politics back into societies and into theorizing about them. Claims to autonomy from the state have not weakened, but a growing number of civil society organizations have accepted the increasingly political nature of their activities. At the same time, social movement studies need to address the challenges that have arisen to the conception of a division of labor between contentious and noncontentious politics, faced by the development of international governance institutions as well as the decline of national political parties.

In pursuing this line of inquiry, social movement analysts might well be inspired by the growing appreciation of the relevance of transnational processes that has spurred a growing debate on the emergence of global civil society (Anheier, Glasius, and Kaldor 2001; Kaldor 2003; Keane 2003). The role of protest organizations alongside other types of NGOs in global civil society has already attracted wide attention (Smith 2006; della Porta 2009a). The transnationalization of social movements has been strongly linked to their struggles to create new and different forms of the public sphere—spaces of autonomy from the mainstream corporate media (Hackett and Carroll 2006). This has taken multiple forms. Sometimes, the creation of new discursive spaces has relied on face-to-face interactions within specific sub-cultural communities and movements in specific locations, particularly in urban areas, and on the creation of local media. More frequently, however, it has been pursued through the use of the Internet and the emergence of new electronic media (Van de Donk, Loader, Nixon, and Rucht 2004). Well-known examples of these phenomena include the Association for Progressive Communication and the global justice network Indymedia. While many dispute the extent to which contacts created through electronic communication can replace real social ties and animate the mechanisms of trust and "civic-ness" associated with the classic public sphere, it is clear that such media will play a growing role in mobilization and campaigning.

6. CONCLUSION: CIVIL SOCIETY AS A PRODUCT OF PROTEST?

One element that is commonly stressed in both the social movement and civil society literatures is the relevance of a rich associational life for the development of strong movements and an autonomous civil society. Recent research points to the relevance of remobilizing previously existing networks (or movements), often with their roots in the global protest campaigns of the 1990s and the early 2000s (della Porta 2009a and 2009b). In this sense, the mobilizations of the 2000s are the outcome of a lengthy process of creating ties and intensifying solidarities between diverse strands of earlier progressive movements during transnational campaigns. From this point of view, contemporary social movements confirm the importance of the availability of resources for mobilization that social movement studies have stressed since the 1970s, and which reflections on civil society confirmed later on.

However, recent conflicts also point to the effects of protest itself on the creation of resources of trust and solidarity necessary for the creation of public spheres. In calling for social rights and the political responsibility to implement them, and in building concrete alternatives, social movement and civil society organizations not only deplete social capital but also produce it. While social movement studies have focused on protest as a dependent variable (looking at how it is supported by social capital), and the civil society literature has emphasized the role of nonpolitical and cooperative civil society groups, more recent conflicts point to the role of protest as an emergent event in producing civil society itself.

Research on networks in movement has long stressed that overlapping memberships facilitate the integration of different movement areas (Diani 1995; Carroll and Ratner 1996). Networking in-action increases the influence of each organization and individual. Coordination starts on the pragmatic grounds of facilitating mobilization, and then helps the development of inclusive norms. The logic of the network as an instrument for the coordination of activity facilitates the involvement of different political actors. The network is often kept together mainly through an emphasis on mobilization around concrete goals, but beyond this instrumental aim, protest campaigns are spaces for the development of mutual understanding (della Porta and Mosca 2007; della Porta 2008). The recognition of similarities across countries through action in transnational networks enables the construction of a transnational identity. In a scale-shift process (Tarrow 2005), activists begin to identify themselves as part of a European or even global subject. This reciprocal understanding is also considered by activists to be an antidote to single-issue claims: overlapping memberships and participation in organizational coalitions have been seen as preconditions for the spread of innovative ideas (as in the women's and peace movements: Meyer and Whittier 1994).

Participation in protest campaigns also develops reciprocal knowledge and, therefore, trust-in-action. From this point of view, activists interviewed in research on Social Forums in Italy stress the growing dialogue between leaders (or spokespersons) of different organizations as one clear effect of the reciprocal understanding developed during joint campaigns (della Porta and Mosca 2007). For rank and file members, these campaigns are perceived as enabling a mutual familiarity that favors the construction of shared objectives, as increased knowledge allows individuals to confront their prejudices.

These accounts of protest campaigns urge us to search for a balance between the venerable tradition in sociology that recognizes the fundamental role of conflict in creating solidarity, and concepts such as reciprocity, civility, and respect that have been pivotal in reflections on civil society. Far from making old sociological categories redundant, these challenges stimulate us to look at the emerging nature of social movements as actors capable of producing new resources-in-action.

From this perspective, a more intense dialogue between social movement and civil society scholars, as well as between social and political theorists and empirical analysts, might improve our understanding of major social transformations. As we have shown in this chapter, even though they developed apart from each other, social movement and civil society studies have addressed similar theoretical issues and covered similar empirical ground.

REFERENCES

Alexander, J. 1998. *Real Civil Society: Dilemma of Institutionalization*. London: Sage.

Anheier, H., M. Glasius, and M. Kaldor (eds). 2001. *Global Civil Society 2001*. Oxford: Oxford University Press.

Anheier, H., and N. Themudo. 2002. "Organizational Forms of Global Civil Society: Implications of Going Global," in M. Glasius, M. Kaldor, and H. Ahheier (eds.), *Global Civil Society 2002*. Oxford: Oxford University Press.

Calhoun, C. 1993. "'New Social Movements' of the Early 19th Century." *Social Science Journal* 17:385–427.

Chandhoke, N. 2003. *The Conceits of the Civil Society*. New Delhi: Oxford University Press.

Cohen, J., and A. Arato. 1992. *Civil Society and Political Theory*. Cambridge, Mass.: MIT Press.

Crouch, C. 2004. *Post Democracy*. London: Polity.

Daly, S. 2006. "For the Common Good? The Changing Role of Civil Society in the UK and Ireland." Dunfermline: Carnegie U.K. Trust.

della Porta, D. 2008. "Eventful Protest, Global Conflicts." *Dinstinktion* 17: 27–47.

———. (ed.). 2007. *The Global Justice Movement. Cross National and Transnational Perspective*. Boulder, Colo.: Paradigm.

———. (ed.). 2009a. *Democracy in Social Movements*. Basingstoke: Palgrave Macmillan.

———. (ed.). 2009b. *Another Europe*. London: Routledge.

della Porta, D., and M. Diani. 2006. *Social Movements*. Oxford: Blackwell.

della Porta, D., and L. Mosca. 2007. "*In movimento*: 'contamination' in action and the Italian Global Justice Movement." *Global Networks: A Journal of Transnational Affairs* 7(1): 1–28.

della Porta, D., M. Andretta, L. Mosca, and H. Reiter. 2006. *Globalization from Below*. Minneapolis: University of Minnesota Press.

Diani, M. 1992. "The Concept of Social Movement." *Sociological Review* 40:1–25.

———. 1995. *Green Networks. A Structural Analysis of the Italian Environmental Movement*. Edinburgh: Edinburgh University Press.

Diani, M., and I. Bison. 2004. "Organizations, Coalitions, and Movements." *Theory and Society* 33:281–309.

Diani, M., and D. McAdam (eds). 2003. *Social Movements and Networks*. Oxford: Oxford University Press.

Edwards, B., M. Foley, and M. Diani (eds). 2001. *Beyond Tocqueville: Social Capital, Civil Society, and Political Process in Comparative Perspective*. Hannover, N.H.: University Press of New England.

Edwards, M. 2009. *Civil Society*. 2nd ed.. Cambridge: Polity.

Hackett, R., and W. Carroll. 2006. *Remaking Media: The Struggle to Democratize Public Communication*. London: Routledge.

Jordan, G. and W. Maloney. 1997. *The Protest Business?* Manchester: Manchester University Press.

Kaldor, M. 2003. *Global Civil Society. An Answer to War*. Cambridge: Polity Press.

Keane, J. 2003. *Global Civil Society?* Cambridge: Cambridge University Press.

Kitschelt, H. 2004. *Landscape of Political Interest Intermediation: Social Movements, Interest Groups and Parties in the Early Twenty-First Century*, in P. Ibarra (ed.), *Social Movements and Democracy*. New York: Palgrave Macmillan.

Kriesi, H. 1996. "The Organizational Structure of New Social Movements in a Political Context," in D. McAdam, J. McCarthy, and M. N. Zald (eds.) *Comparative Perspective on Social Movements. Political Opportunities, Mobilizing Structures, and Cultural Framing*. Cambridge: Cambridge University Press.

Kumar, K. 1993. "Civil Society: An Inquiry into the Usefulness of an Historical Term." *The British Journal of Sociology*, vol. 44(3): 375–95.

Lipsky, M. 1965. *Protest and City Politics*. Chicago: Rand McNally.

Lofland, J. 1989. "Consensus Movements: City Twinnings and Derailed Dissent in the American Eighties." *Research in Social Movements, Conflict and Change* 11:163–89.

Marwell, G., and P. Oliver. 1993. *The Critical Mass in Collective Action. A Micro-Social Theory*. Cambridge: Cambridge University Press.

McAdam, D., S. Tarrow, and C. Tilly. 2001. *Dynamics of Contention*. Cambridge: Cambridge University Press.

Melucci, A. 1996. *Challenging Codes*. Cambridge: Cambridge University Press.

Meyer, D., and N. Whittier. 1994. "Social Movements Spillover." *Social Problems*, 41, 277–98.

Mitzal, B. 2001. "Civil Society: A Signifier of Plurality and Sense of Wholeness," in J. Blau (ed.), *The Blackwell Companion of Sociology*. Oxford: Blackwell.

Mouffe, C. 2005. *On the Political*. London: Routledge.

Oberschall, A. 1973. *Social Conflict and Social Movements*. Englewood Cliffs, N.J.: Prentice Hall.

Putnam, R. 1993. *Making Democracy Work*. Princeton, N.J.: Princeton University Press.

Rokkan, S. 1982. *Cittadini, Elezioni, Partiti*. Bologna: Il Mulino. [Original edition *Citizens, Elections, and Parties*. Oslo: Oslo University Press, 1970.]

Savage, R. 2001. *Political Sociology*, in J. Blau (ed.), *The Blackwell Companion of Sociology*. Oxford: Blackwell.

Snow, D., S. Soule, and H. Kriesi (eds). 2004. *The Blackwell Companion to Social Movements*. Oxford: Blackwell.

Tarrow, S. 1998. *Power in Movement*. Cambridge: Cambridge University Press.

——. 2005. *The New Transnational Activism*. Cambridge: Cambridge University Press.

Tilly, C. 1978. *From Mobilization to Revolution*. Reading, Mass.: Addison-Wesley.

Van de Donk, W., B. Loader, P. Nixon, and D. Rucht (eds). 2004. *CyberProtest*. London: Routledge.

Wilson, J. 2000. "Volunteering." *Annual Review of Sociology* 26:215–40.

CHAPTER 7

....

SOCIAL ENTERPRISE AND SOCIAL ENTREPRENEURS

....

ALEX NICHOLLS

SOCIAL entrepreneurship represents one of the most notable innovations in global civil society in recent times (Dees 1998). While many of the activities and approaches associated with this term are not in themselves new—for example, social enterprise's use of business models to generate income to support social programmes (Alter 2006)—the evolution of a discrete organizational field for such action does represent an important structural change in the institutions of social action (Dees 1994, 1996). Although the term "social entrepreneur" was first coined as long ago as the 1970s, it has only been in the past fifteen years or so that the term has started to gain traction within a range of interrelated discourses across civil society, government, and the private sector (Lounsbury and Strang 2009). Such discourses have been shaped and driven forward by a range of new field-building organizations. However, the institutionalization of social entrepreneurship as a new "conceptual apparatus" with which to make sense of innovation in civil society remains an ongoing, and sometimes controversial, project (Nicholls 2010a) not least because it is seen by some as signifying the marketization of collective action and of civil society activities previously based around participation, active citizenship, and political change. Indeed, social entrepreneurship has been conceived as a mechanism by which business (and the state) can co-opt and compromise the integrity and independence of civil society rather than reinvigorate and diversify its models of societal change. While such critiques represent a useful corrective to some of the hyperbole that is associated with social entrepreneurship, they also misinterpret the particular distinctiveness of this new field of action: namely, that it aims to generate outcomes that are superior to conventional models through innovation in, and disruption to, the status quo of public, private, and civil society approaches to the provision of social and environmental goods.

Social entrepreneurs represent a new generation of civil society actors who are driven to address the systemic problems facing the world today. Such individuals sometimes conform to the heroic norms and distinctive personality traits associated with conventional entrepreneurs such as risk-taking, creativity, an overly optimistic approach to analysis, and *bricolage*, but significantly, they are more likely to draw on the communitarian, democratic, and network-building traditions that have always underpinned civil society action (Nicholls 2006). Thus, social entrepreneurship is best understood in a linear—rather than disruptive—relationship with the historical norms of social and community action. For example, many social enterprises demonstrate a strong influence from the traditions of mutualism and cooperatives that go back to the nineteenth century. These traditions included space for distributed models of ownership, asset locks and dividend caps, democratic management structures, and organizational structures designed to reflect social mission rather than mimetic isomorphism (Michie and Llewelyn 2006). What is distinctive, therefore, about social entrepreneurship are not the institutional elements it embodies, but rather the patterns in which it assembles familiar material into new, sector-blurring, organizational logics and structures (Peredo and McLean 2006; Sud et al. 2009).

Actions of this kind are able to harness organizational hybridity to drive innovation and change that is focused on social and environmental outcomes, often by generating positive externalities and new market structures (Osberg and Martin 2007). For civil society, social entrepreneurship has come to represent a new stream of activity that aligns the objectives of achieving scale in systemic social change with the goal of empowering individuals as a "changemakers" (Drayton 2002). For government, particularly in the United Kingdom, the for-profit social enterprise model offers an attractive approach to marketizing social welfare programs without proposing a fully fledged privatization of the state (Social Enterprise Unit 2002; Cabinet Office 2007). For the private sector, social enterprise provides a model to access otherwise inaccessible market opportunities such as the poor at the Bottom of the Pyramid movement; state welfare budgets; and a growing body of "ethical" consumers (Nicholls and Opal 2005). Engagement with social entrepreneurship has also provided other commercial benefits, both as a means by which flagging Corporate Social Responsibility (CSR) strategies can be rejuvenated in the face of increasingly cynical consumers (Prahalad 2006), and as a new arena for investment that is typically uncorrelated with conventional capital markets (Nicholls 2010b).

1. The Institutional Drivers of Social Entrepreneurship

There have been a number of drivers behind the recent acceleration in the growth of social entrepreneurship. Most obviously, the demand for innovative social and environmental action has increased as global crises have proliferated and deepened in their impact (Bornstein 2004). Such crises include the effects of climate change and environmental degradation; new health pandemics; water and energy crises; growing migration; seemingly intractable issues of inequality and endemic poverty; the rise of terrorism and nuclear instability; and the "challenge of affluence" in many developed countries (Offer 2006). Beyond these urgent threats, a range of other influences can also be identified.

First, there are a number of important sociological factors. Technological innovations and the rise of improved global connectedness have played an important role in alerting potential social entrepreneurs to the need for action. Furthermore, technology has provided new pathways to empowerment for the individual as a social actor in the context of the development of a "pro-am" culture (Leadbeater 2008) and new social media. These innovations have altered the dynamics by which ideas are generated and disseminated, leading to societal shifts such as the rise of "new localism" and the splintering of much established political consensus (Murray et al 2010). The postglobal crisis landscape also offers a new context for individual social action as economic priorities are increasingly being judged by more sophisticated measures than financial criteria alone (Offer 2007).

Secondly, a range of political drivers can be identified, related to the redefinition of the role of the state that began with the rise of neo-conservative politics in the 1980s. The neoconservative ideological agenda gave preference to free-market deregulation and privatization, and sought to reduce and reform the state by cutting taxation and rolling back state provision of public goods (Grenier 2009). This ideological realignment encouraged a more managerialist focus on reforming the functioning of the state within the framework of the "new public management" and "reinventing government" (Osbourne and Gaebler 1992). Such a shift prioritized the promotion of more enterprising and entrepreneurial public-sector structures and behavior, and reached its logical conclusion with the introduction of internal "quasi-markets" within state welfare systems (LeGrand 2003). In parallel, a wider focus on enterprise and individualism across society in general lionized entrepreneurs as both economic heroes and strategic management "gurus" (Dart 2004). In the 1990s, as "third-way" (Giddens 1998) politics came to dominate in the United States and United Kingdom, market action and enterprise became further decoupled from business and allowed a new language of social provisioning to emerge that re-imagined public goods as best delivered by innovation outside—but contracted to—the state. As a consequence, by 2008, over half of all charitable income in the United Kingdom came from government contracts (NCVO 2009). These changes in the political landscape were evident across many countries and fundamentally altered the dynamics of the relationships between civil society, the private sector, and the state in the production and consumption of public goods. The consequence was simultaneously to generate both a range of market failures in the provision of welfare services and a variety of new opportunities for social innovation in addressing them.

Finally, the economics of civil society have changed significantly over recent years. As the number of civil society organizations has grown (Salamon et al 2003), the resources available from conventional funding sources such as philanthropic foundations came under increasing pressure, particularly during the economic recessions of 1990–91 and 2008–10. The result was that many civil society organizations had to become more entrepreneurial in terms of revenue generation, and increasingly looked to diversify their funding through profit-making opportunities and new partnerships with the state and the private sector (cf. Kanter 1999). The tightening of the market for conventional grant income caused civil society organizations to seek out independent revenue streams and to form social enterprises— the commercial model of social entrepreneurship. The development of viable profit streams also appeared to offer social enterprises the opportunity of greater independence from the influence of grant makers, the ability to innovate more quickly, and longer-term organizational sustainability. However, the real impacts (good and bad) of the social enterprise model on civil society are still are matter of debate, and they require further and much more rigorous research (Dart 2004).

2. Locating Social Entrepreneurship

Today, social entrepreneurship is a fluid and contested phenomenon. Indeed, in some senses, it is a field of action in search of an established institutional narrative (Nicholls 2010a). To a large extent, the diversity of discourses and logics that characterize social entrepreneurship reflect the internal logics and self-legitimating discourses of a broad range of influential, resource holding actors who are actively engaged in building the field, rather than any particular "reality" (Nicholls 2010a). Thus for government, social entrepreneurship is conceptualized as the solution to state failures in welfare provision (Leadbeater 1997). For civil society, it is conceived of as a space for new hybrid partnerships (Austin et al 2004), a model of political transformation and empowerment (Alvord et al 2004), or a driver of systemic social change (Nicholls 2006). Finally, for business, social entrepreneurship is cast as a new market opportunity (Karamchandani et al 2009) or a natural development from socially responsible investment (Freireich and Fulton 2009).

Despite evidence that social entrepreneurship is growing in influence as a field of action, significant questions remain concerning the definition of its limits and boundaries, particularly in terms of how broad or narrow its scope should be (Light 2008). Nevertheless, various attempts have been made to resolve some of the definitional questions concerning social entrepreneurship and there is now some broad agreement that a number of dominant characteristics are present in all such action (Dees 1998). Firstly, all social entrepreneurship shares a primary, strategic focus on social or environmental outcomes that will always override other managerial considerations such as profit maximization. Secondly, there is always evidence of innovation and novelty either in challenging normative conceptions of an issue, in the organizational models and processes that are developed, or in the products and services that are delivered (and sometimes in all three of these dimensions). Finally, there is always a strong emphasis on performance measurement and improved accountability, aligned with a relentless focus on improving the effectiveness of organizational impact and scale and the durability of outcomes. These three factors can be further refined under three headings: sociality, innovation, and market orientation (Nicholls and Cho 2006).

The "sociality," or social and environmental focus of social entrepreneurship, can be identified in three aspects of its operation: the macro-level institutional context in which it operates; the organizational micro-processes it employs; and the focus and nature of its impacts and outcomes. In terms of institutional contexts, social entrepreneurship is usually associated with six domains focused on the creation of public goods and positive externalities: welfare and health services (such as the Aravind eye hospitals in India);[1] education and training (such as the Committee to Democratize Information Technology or CDI in Brazil);[2] economic development (such as work integration social enterprises, or WISEs, in Europe);[3] disaster relief and international aid (such as Keystone's innovative "Farmer Voice" project);[4] social justice and political change (including race and gender empowerment, such as SEWA, the Self-Employed Women's Association in Pakistan);[5] and environmental planning and management (such as the Marine Stewardship Council).[6] With respect to organizational processes, social entrepreneurs have pioneered innovations that create new social value in terms of employment practices (by, for example, targeting excluded populations), supply chain management (such as Fair Trade),[7] energy usage and recycling (such as the "Green Thing"),[8] and financial structures (including Community Interest Companies, co-operatives, and "L3C" corporations). Finally, the outcomes of social entrepreneurship are defined by their social or environmental impact rather than their financial returns, with success or failure calibrated by outcomes rather than outputs within an explicitly values-driven framework of analysis (Young 2006).

Innovation, the second defining characteristic of social entrepreneurship, reflects many of the characteristics of similar processes that are found in commercial entrepreneurship. Drawing upon Schumpeter (1911; see also Swedberg 2009), innovation in entrepreneurship is defined by models that achieve macro-level "creative destruction" that change systems and realign markets around new economic equilibriums (Osberg and Martin 2007). Such innovation can range from incremental changes at the micro-level to disruptive interventions at the systems level.

Third, the market orientation of social entrepreneurship is most easily recognized in the profit-making business models of social enterprise that earn income by competing in conventional commercial markets (Alter 2006). However, this description only captures a minority of socially entrepreneurial activity across the globe.[9] For the noncommercial organizations in the field, a market orientation represents a broader set of issues that encompass a strong and relentless performance focus with enhanced accountability and an outward-looking strategic perspective. These aspects of organizational culture are reified in clear and effective impact metrics, robust systems to empower stakeholder voice, and a competitive attitude to performance improvement.

3. The Scope of Social Entrepreneurship

One of the challenges of mapping the field of social entrepreneurship is that only limited data are currently available to estimate its global size and structure. This is largely because unlike in the field of conventional not-for-profit organizations and charities, social entrepreneurship is not easily identifiable by a single legal form of incorporation or a distinct fiscal treatment in any country. Bespoke organizational forms do exist for social entrepreneurship, such as the Community Interest Company (CIC) form in the United Kingdom, Social Cooperatives (Types 1 and 2) in Italy, Social Solidarity Cooperatives in Portugal, and L3C organizations in the United States, but the field as a whole includes a wide variety of legal forms, from companies limited by guarantee, to Publicly Limited Companies (PLC), cooperatives and even unincorporated voluntary organizations, as well as hybrids that combine several of these forms (SEC 2005). For example, Hackney Community Transport (HCT) group in the United Kingdom includes five different legal forms across its subsidiaries.[10] As a result, data from national statistics are unhelpful as a source for delineating the field.

Nevertheless, other data sources that focus specifically on social entrepreneurship and social enterprise can be used to give a snapshot of the field in different contexts, notably in the United Kingdom where there has been a high level of institutional interest in, and support for, the field. The U.K. government took a lead in trying to quantify social entrepreneurship by commissioning a scoping survey of the national landscape of social enterprise in 2004–05. This survey calculated a total population of approximately 55,000 social enterprises (Cabinet Office 2007), and also concluded that these organizations constituted 5 percent of all businesses with employees, had a combined turnover of £27 billion, and contributed £8.4 billion to the economy each year. A subsequent survey for the U.K. government increased the estimate of the number of social enterprises to 62,000 across the country, calculating that small and medium-sized social enterprises contributed £24 billion GVA (Gross Value Added) to the economy across the period 2005 to 2007 (Williams and Cowling 2009; SEC 2009).

The Global Entrepreneurship Monitor (GEM) survey of worldwide entrepreneurial activity has included a survey of socially entrepreneurial activity in the United Kingdom since 2004. This research initially suggested that 6.6 percent of the total U.K. working population engaged directly with socially entrepreneurial activity (Harding and Cowling 2004; Harding 2004). However, for various methodological reasons, this estimate was later revised down to 3.2 percent, or roughly 1.2 million people, mostly in the form of new start-up organizations (Harding and Cowling 2006). The same figure grew to 3.3 percent in 2008 (Harding and Harding 2008). The GEM surveys also suggested that there was a clear bias towards women compared to men, and a strong ethnic minority bias, with Afro-Caribbean people being three times more likely to be social entrepreneurs than whites. The 2010 GEM survey took a worldwide perspective on social entrepreneurial activity for the first time (Bosma and Levie 2010). At a global level, the overall figures for direct engagement with social entrepreneurship are significantly lower, averaging between 1.6 percent and 1.9 percent depending on the region concerned and its level of economic development.

In 2010, Harding (2010) built on the GEM methodology to explore socially entrepreneurial behavior in mainstream businesses in the United Kingdom. Her work suggested a population of 232,000 "broad" social enterprises (defined as businesses that were designed to "make a difference" and that reinvested their surpluses according to their mission), and 109,371 "pure" social enterprises (defined as social enterprises that did not pay dividends, yet achieved sales revenues that exceeded 25 percent of their income). Harding suggested that the former contributed £97 billion and the latter £17.7 billion to the U.K. economy. Finally, Van Ryzin et al.(2009) expanded the GEM methodology to explore panel data from the United States and to establish key determinants of socially entrepreneurial behavior. However, they did not provide any statistically projectable data.

Information from the leading field-building actors in social entrepreneurship also provides relevant data. This evidence shows that more than £1 billion had been invested directly in over 8,000 socially entrepreneurial organizations globally. It is notable that of the total capital invested in social entrepreneurship, more than 68 percent came from the U.K. government. Some of the best-established examples of social entrepreneurship provide further data that demonstrate the scale of this field. For example, in terms of development and welfare, the Bangladesh Rural Advancement Committee (BRAC), founded in 1972, now runs more than 37,000 schools, provides microfinance products to over eight million poor people, engages 80,000 health volunteers, employs 120,000 workers, and serves over 100 million people (Dees 2010). In terms of social enterprise, the Fair Trade movement now generates more than £2 billion of sales from certified products worldwide and benefits more than seven million people across more than sixty countries (Nicholls 2010c). In terms of policy interventions, the U.K. government has invested more than £700 million directly into social enterprises (excluding contracts) since 2000, and other countries, such as the United States and Australia, are now following suit. Finally, evidence from organizations that support social entrepreneurship also suggests a vibrant and growing community: Ashoka's global Fellowship now numbers over 2000 members and, since 2001, UnLtd in the United Kingdom has supported more than 3,000 social entrepreneurs to initiate projects and take them to scale.

4. CONCLUSION

This chapter has suggested that social entrepreneurship represents a new, important, and growing subsector of civil society. It also proposes that this new field encompasses a variety of sector-blurring discourses that are being driven by significant institutional changes in modern societies. Research suggests that social entrepreneurship is something of an umbrella term for a wide variety of organizational forms and activities, but also that boundaries can be set for the field in terms of the presence of three qualifying factors at the organizational level: sociality, innovation, and market orientation.

However, despite evidence that social entrepreneurship is making an important difference globally (see for example, Ashoka 2010), there are also a number of critiques of the field that need to be taken into account (see also Grenier 2009). Firstly, research into social entrepreneurship remains in its infancy (Short et al. 2009). As such, robust data on the specific effectiveness of socially entrepreneurial outcomes and impacts remains underdeveloped, particularly in terms of deadweight calculations and counterfactual analysis. These gaps may give rise to a suspicion that social entrepreneurship is merely acting as an ill-proven proxy for improved outcome measurement in the social sector. Furthermore, in the absence of a convincing epistemological account of its distinctive value, the legitimacy of the field in a paradigmatic sense remains in some jeopardy (Kuhn 1962; Suchman 1995).

Secondly, the emphasis on the "hero" social entrepreneur appears to be as much a cultural product of those who propagate it as a reflection of the reality of the field (Lounsbury and Strang 2009; Nicholls 2010a). At least two other distinct categories of social entrepreneur can be discerned beyond the charismatic hero model that has received a disproportionate amount of foundation and media attention: "managerialist" social entrepreneurs, and "community-based" social entrepreneurs (Grenier 2009). The former category represents individuals who are skilled at managing hybrid organizations that deliver above-average levels of social-value creation (often balanced with financial-value creation), and who are often re-skilled voluntary sector managers. The latter category reimagines the individual within a community as a dynamic change agent, and stresses the importance of local structures—rather than top-down action—in bringing about meaningful and context-specific social change and social impact (Yujuico 2008). Moreover, it seems likely that networks and organizations that do not have charismatic leaders contribute far more to the landscape of social entrepreneurship than is suggested by the level of publicity they have received. The enduring impact and local significance of socially entrepreneurial cooperatives such as Mondragon in northern Spain is evidence of this observation.[11]

The institutional influence of certain field building actors in social entrepreneurship is also evident in some accounts of the field that are characterized by an overemphasis on the importance of business models, an overemphasis that appears to dismiss the logical proposition that business has as much to learn from civil society as civil society does from business (Edwards 2010). Moreover, such accounts of social entrepreneurship sideline the importance of political action in systems change, ignoring the historical evidence that shows that societal change is best achieved in tandem with social movements and by engaging with political structures (Davis et al 2005). Many social entrepreneurs across the world endorse this view, from Martin Burt of Fundación Paraguaya, for example,[12] to Harriet Lamb of the Fair Trade Foundation.[13] However, some commentators and field-building organizations—particularly those based in the United States—do not always agree that addressing politics at both the formal and informal levels is central to the long-term impact of social entrepreneurship (Osberg and Martin 2007).

Finally, there has yet to be any serious attention given to the "dark side" of social entrepreneurship—for example, in terms of the impacts of social enterprises that fail (Tracey and Jarvis 2006), and the potential that exists for crowding out existing civil society organizations and their support base. Furthermore, why should it automatically be assumed that social entrepreneurship always achieves positive outcomes? Under the tripartite definition suggested above, organizations as diverse as the Ku Klux Klan in the United States in the 1960s, the National Socialist Party in Germany in the 1930s, and the contemporary mega-churches in the United States could all be considered examples of social entrepreneurship, though the impact of all three would appear strongly negative to many. In this context, it should be noted that by no means all actors across civil society have embraced social entrepreneurship; indeed to many activists and voluntary-sector leaders, the field remains controversial and potentially threatening. This is, at least to some extent, because some of the logics of social entrepreneurship appear to challenge the established rationales for civil society (see Clotfelter 1992), particularly in terms of cross-sector hybrids such as social enterprise and "venture" philanthropy (Dart 2004; Edwards 2010).

For all these caveats, social entrepreneurship clearly brings an important new dimension to debates about civil society and its importance. In contrast to more established social organizations, the range of institutional discourses that are contained within social entrepreneurship give it a strategic advantage in terms of flexibility, adaptation, and speed of response to the complex market failures that characterize modern, global social and environmental issues. The field of social entrepreneurship is still developing, and its eventual scale, size, and impact are difficult to predict with precision. Nevertheless, it is already clear that the logics and models of social entrepreneurship have significantly recalibrated perceptions of the scope of civil society, its boundaries, and the potential impact it can achieve in the future.

NOTES

....

1. See www.aravind.org.
2. See www.cdi.org.br.
3. See Nyssens (2006).

4. See www.aline.org.uk/farmervoice.

5. See www.sewa.org.

6. See www.msc.org.

7. See www.fairtrade.net and www.wfto.com.

8. See www.dothegreenthing.com.

9. Almost all the social entrepreneurs supported by the Skoll Foundation, for example, are not-for-profits.

10. See www.hctgroup.org/index.php?sectionid=1.

11. See www.mondragon-corporation.com.

12. See www.fundacionparaguaya.org.py.

13. See www.fairtrade.org.uk.

REFERENCES

Alter, K. 2006. "Social Enterprise Models and Their Mission and Money Relationships," in Nicholls, A. (ed.), *Social Entrepreneurship: New Paradigms of Sustainable Social Change*. Oxford: Oxford University Press, pp. 209–32.

Alvord, S., L. Brown, and C. Letts. 2004. "Social Entrepreneurship and Societal Transformation: an Exploratory Study" *Journal of Applied Behavioral Science* 40(3): 260–83.

Ashoka. 2010. *Leading Social Entrepreneurs*. Arlington, Va.: Ashoka.

Austin, J., E. Reficco., G. Berger., R. Fischer., R. Gutierrez., M. Koljatic., G. Lozano., and E. Ogliastri (eds.). 2004. *Social Partnering in Latin America: Lessons Drawn from Collaborations of Businesses and Civil Society Organizations*. Cambridge, Mass.: Harvard University Press.

Bornstein, D. 2004. *How To Change The World: Social Entrepreneurs and the Power of New Ideas*. Oxford: Oxford University Press.

Bosma, N., and J. Levie. 2010. "A Global Comparison of Social Entrepreneurship." *Global Entrepreneurship Monitor 2009 Executive Report*. London, GERA, pp. 44–51.

Cabinet Office. 2007. *Social Enterprise Action Plan: Scaling New Heights*. London: Office of The Third Sector.

Clotfelter, C. (ed.) 1992. *Who Benefits From The Nonprofit Sector?*, Chicago: University of Chicago Press.

Dart, R. 2004. "The Legitimacy of Social Enterprise." *Nonprofit Management and Leadership*, vol. 14(4): 411–24.

Davis, G., D. McAdam., W. Scott., and M. Zald. 2005. *Social Movements and Organization Theory*. Cambridge: Cambridge University Press.

Dees, J. G. 1994. *Social Enterprise: Private Initiatives for Common Good*. Cambridge, Mass.: Harvard Business School Press.

———. 1996. *The Social Enterprise Spectrum: from Philanthropy to Commerce*. Cambridge, Mass.: Harvard Business School Press.

———. 1998. "The Meaning of Social Entrepreneurship." Available at http://faculty.fuqua .duke.edu/centers/case/files/dees-SE.pdf.

———. 2010. "Creating Large-Scale Change: Not 'Can' But 'How.'" McKinsey & Company: What Matters Report. Available at http://whatmatters.mckinseydigital.com/social_ entrepreneurs/creating-large-scale-change-not-can-but-how.

Drayton, W. 2002. "The Citizen Sector: Becoming as Entrepreneurial and Competitive as Business." *California Management Review*, vol. 44(3): 120–32.

Edwards, M. 2010. *Small Change: Why Business Won't Save the World*. San Francisco: Berrett-Koehler.

Emerson, J., and J. Spitzer. 2007. *From Fragmentation to Functionality: Critical Concepts and Writings on Social Capital Market Structure, Operation, and Innovation*. Skoll Centre for Social Entrepreneurship Working Paper. Available at www.sbs.ox.ac.uk/centres/skoll/research/Pages/socialfinance.aspx.

Freireich, J., and K. Fulton, K. 2009. *Investing For Social and Environmental Impact: A Design for Catalyzing an Emerging Industry*. New York: Monitor Group.

Giddens, A. 1998. *The Third Way*. Cambridge: Polity Press.

Grenier, P. 2009. "Social Entrepreneurship in the U.K.: From Rhetoric to Reality?," in R. Zeigler (ed.) *An Introduction to Social Entrepreneurship: Voices, Preconditions, Contexts*. Cheltenham: Edward Elgar.

Harding, R. 2004. "Social Enterprise: the New Economic Engine?" *Business Strategy Review*, vol. 15(4): 39–43.

———. 2010. *Hidden Social Enterprises*. London: Delta Economics and IFF Research.

Harding, R., and M. Cowling. 2004. *Social Entrepreneurship Monitor United Kingdom 2004*. London: Global Entrepreneurship Monitor and London Business School.

———. 2006. *Social Entrepreneurship Monitor: United Kingdom 2006*. London: Global Entrepreneurship Monitor and London Business School.

Harding, R., and D. Harding. 2008. *Social Entrepreneurship in the U.K.*. London: Delta Economics, Global Entrepreneurship Monitor, and Barclays.

Kanter, R. M. 1999. "From Spare Change to Real Change: The Social Sector as Beta Site for Business Innovation." *Harvard Business Review*, vol. 77(3): 122–32.

Karamchandani, A., M. Kubzansky., and P. Frandano. 2009. *Emerging Markets, Emerging Models*. New York: Monitor Group.

Kuhn, T. 1962. *The Structure of Scientific Revolutions*. Chicago: University of Chicago Press.

Leadbeater, C. 1997. *The Rise of the Social Entrepreneur*. London: Demos.

———. 2008. "We-Think." Available at http://www.charlesleadbeater.net/archive/we-think.aspx.

Le Grand, J. 2003. *Motivation, Agency, and Public Policy: of Knights and Knaves, Pawns and Queens*. Oxford: Oxford University Press.

Light, P. 2006. "Reshaping Social Entrepreneurship." *Stanford Social Innovation Review* Fall: 47–52.

———. 2008. *The Search For Social Entrepreneurship*. Washington, D.C.: The Brookings Institution.

Lounsbury, M., and D. Strang. 2009. "Social Entrepreneurship. Success Stories and Logic Construction," in D. Hammack and S. Heydemann (eds.) *Globalization, Philanthropy, and Civil Society*. Bloomington: Indiana University Press.

Michie, J., and T. Llewellyn. 2006. "Converting Failed Financial Institutions into Mutual Organisations." *Journal of Social Entrepreneurship* vol. 1(1): 146–70.

Murray, R., J. Caulier-Grice., and G. Mulgan. 2010. *The Open Book of Social Innovation*. London: NESTA and the Young Foundation.

National Council of Voluntary Organizations. 2009. *U.K. Voluntary Sector Almanac 2008*. London: National Council of Voluntary Organizations.

Nicholls, A. 2008. "Capturing the Performance of the Socially Entrepreneurial Organization (SEO): An Organizational Legitimacy Approach," in J. Robinson.,

J. Mair., and K. Hockerts (eds.) *International Perspectives on Social Entrepreneurship Research*. Basingstoke: Palgrave MacMillan.

———. 2009. "'We Do Good Things Don't We?': Blended Value Accounting In Social Entrepreneurship." *Accounting, Organizations and Society*, vol. 34(6–7): 755–69.

———. 2010a. "The Legitimacy of Social Entrepreneurship: Reflexive Isomorphism in a Pre-Paradigmatic Field." *Entrepreneurship Theory and Practice*, vol. 34(4) 611–33.

———. 2010b. "The Institutionalization of Social Investment: The Interplay of Investment Logics and Investor Rationalities." *Journal of Social Entrepreneurship*, vol. 1(1): 70–100.

———. 2010c. "Fair Trade: Towards an Economics of Virtue," *Journal of Business Ethics*. Available at http://www.springerlink.com/content/j15738378r7gtop3/abstract/ accessed January 14, 2011.

———. (ed.) 2006. *Social Entrepreneurship: New Models of Sustainable Social Change*. Oxford: Oxford University Press.

Nicholls, A., and A. Cho. 2006. "Social Entrepreneurship: The Structuration of a Field," in A. Nicholls (ed.) *Social Entrepreneurship: New Models of Sustainable Social Change*. Oxford: Oxford University Press.

Nicholls, A., and C. Opal. 2005. *Fair Trade: Market-Driven Ethical Consumption*. Thousand Oaks, Calif.: Sage.

Nicholls, A., and C. Pharoah. 2007. "The Landscape of Social Finance." Skoll Centre for Social Entrepreneurship Research Paper, Oxford University. Available at http://www .sbs.ox.ac.uk/skoll/research/Short+papers/Short+papers.htm.

Nyssens, M. 2006. *Social Enterprise Between Market, Public Policies and Civil Society*. London: Routledge.

Offer, A. 2006. *The Challenge of Affluence*. Oxford: Oxford University Press.

———. 2007. "A Vision of Prosperity." Sustainable Development Commission, London. Available at www.sd-commission.org.uk/publications.php?id=741.

Osberg, S., and R. Martin. 2007. "Social Entrepreneurship: The Case For Definition." *Stanford Social Innovation Review* (Spring): 28–39.

Osbourne, D., and T. Gaebler. 1992. *Reinventing Government*. Reading, Pa.: Addison-Wesley.

Peredo, A., and M. McLean. 2006. "Social Entrepreneurship: A Critical Review of the Concept." *Journal of World Business* vol. 41: 56–65.

Prahalad, C. K. 2006. *The Fortune at the Bottom of the Pyramid: Eradicating Poverty Through Profits*. Upper Saddle River, N.J.: Wharton Business School Press.

Salamon, L., H. Anheier., R. List., S. Toepler., and S. Sokolowski (eds.) 2003. *Global Civil Society: Dimensions of the Nonprofit Sector*. Baltimore: John Hopkins University Press.

Schumpeter, J. 1911. *Theorie der Wirtshaftlichen Entwicklung*. Leipzig: Duncker and Humblot.

Short, J., T. Moss., and G. Lumpkin. 2009. "Research in Social Entrepreneurship: Past Contributions and Future Opportunities." *Strategic Entrepreneurship Journal* vol. 3: 161–94.

Social Enterprise Coalition. 2005. *Keeping It Legal: a Guide to Legal Forms for Social Enterprises*. London: Social Enterprise Coalition.

———. 2009. *State of Social Enterprise Survey 2009*. London: Social Enterprise Coalition.

Social Enterprise Unit. 2002. *Social Enterprise: A Strategy for Success*. London: Department for Trade and Industry.

Suchman, M. 1995. "Managing Legitimacy: Strategic and Institutional Approaches." *Academy of Management Review* vol. 20: 517–610.

Sud, M., C. VanSandt, and A. Baugous. 2009. "Social Entrepreneurship: The Role of Institutions." *Journal of Business Ethics* vol. 85: 201–16.

Swedberg, R. 2009. "Schumpeter's Full Model of Entrepreneurship: Economic, Non-Economic and Social Entrepreneurship," in R. Zeigler (ed.) *An Introduction to Social Entrepreneurship: Voices, Preconditions, Contexts.* Cheltenham: Edward Elgar.

Tracey, P., and C. Jarvis. 2006. "An Enterprising Failure: Why a Promising Social Franchise Collapsed." *Stanford Social Innovation Review* (Spring): 66–70.

Van Ryzin, G., S. Grossman., L. DiPadova-Stocks., and E. Bergud. 2009. "Portrait of the Social Entrepreneur: Statistical Evidence from a U.S. Panel." *Voluntas* vol. 20: 129–40.

Williams, M. and M. Cowling. 2009. *Annual Small Business Survey 2007/08.* London: Department for Business Enterprise and Regulatory Reform.

Young, R. 2006. "For What It Is Worth: Social Value and The Future of Social Entrepreneurship," in A. Nicholls, A. (ed.). *Social Entrepreneurship: New Models of Sustainable Social Change.* Oxford: Oxford University Press.

Yujuico, E. 2008. "Connecting The Dots In Social Entrepreneurship Through The Capabilities Approach." *Socio-Economic Review* vol. 6: 493–513.

CHAPTER 8

GLOBAL CIVIL SOCIETY

LISA JORDAN

Most of the academic literature on global civil society maps its structural parameters or reviews its impact on specific social problems like poverty or environmental degradation (Florini 2000; Salamon 2004). By contrast, this chapter posits that global civil society should be understood as a force for democratic change, one which is implicitly making claims to global citizenship. Through protest and advocacy across national borders, activists in global civil society are assuming the rights and responsibilities of citizens, and while falling short of forcing the adoption of formal democratic structures, they and the networks, movements, and organizations in which they operate do promote transparency, accountability, and public participation in the evolving arrangements of global governance. In this sense, global civil society has promoted greater subsidiarity between local, national, regional, and global political arenas, thereby moving global governance one step closer to the governed. It has forced global institutions to recognize that technical deliberations and the standards they produce are forms of decision making with public responsibilities. And it has shown that, even in the absence of a global government, civil society can play a valuable role in democratizing the international regimes of the present and the future.

1. DOES GLOBAL CIVIL SOCIETY EXIST?

Over the past ten years, scholars have vigorously debated whether the fact that increasing numbers of people are associating with each other across national borders constitutes a "global civil society." It is certainly true that people are organizing to address issues that concern them in multiple political arenas—local, national, and international. But it is not clear that cross-border activism represents a genuine sense of global community, a global civic culture, or the emergence of global citizenship—as opposed to set of national interests that are increasingly active in the global arena. Skeptics argue that civil society can only exist in relation to a state; that new global social movements are predominantly nationally oriented; that those citizen formations that do exist between nation states are insufficiently "global" in their character and focus; and that global civil society is a Western construct (Tarrow 2005; Anheier 2003). Many intergovernmental organizations such as the Organization for Economic Cooperation and Development (OECD) and the International Monetary Fund (IMF) equate international nongovernmental organizations (INGO)s with global civil society, which further confuses the conceptual terrain.

Civil society has been defined in at least three ways: as the *forms* of associational life, such as NGOs, labor unions, social movements, and churches (Edwards 2009; Salamon 2004); as the *norms* of the good society, defined by values such as cooperation, nonviolence, and tolerance (Keane 2003); and as an *arena for public deliberation*, consisting of spaces that are relatively autonomous from both states and markets (Scholte 2000). These three definitions are also useful in considering the global arena.

Global civil society includes multiple forms of association such as international networks, social movements, and campaigns; international federations and confederations of churches, professional, and business associations; cross-border membership-based organizations of the poor; and nongovernmental organizations that are oriented towards the global arena. Unfortunately, there is no research that provides a reliable overview of the relative scale and density of these different forms of association (Anheier 2003, 2007). Only international NGOs have been studied in any depth (Union of International Associations 2010), and there is active debate within academia on whether other kinds of cross-border associations actually exist, especially global social movements (Tarrow 2005; Smith 2008). But it is known that over 60,000 NGOs and civic networks already operate on the international stage, 90 percent of which have been formed since 1970 (Edwards 2009, 23).

Normative definitions concentrate on the meaning of the "civil" as a positive moral force in international affairs, and as a mechanism through which new global norms are developed around universal human rights, international cooperation on global problems like climate change and poverty, and the peaceful resolution of national differences in the global arena. In this sense, global civil society is interpreted as a mechanism for the development of social compacts or contracts across national borders that solidify principled international action on common themes and priorities (Keane 2003; Kaldor 2003). Clearly, however, the forms of global civil society do not convey or carry a standard set of norms. As Bob (2005) and others have pointed out, global civil society is home to conservative and progressive interests, religious and secular groups, violent and nonviolent social action.

This is why a global public sphere or set of spheres is so important, providing the spaces in which different visions of globalization and conflicting global norms can be argued out, and—in the best manifestations of this process—moving towards an increasing cross-border consensus. Such spaces include open-access websites like Wikipedia and openDemocracy, new events and networks such as the World Economic Forum and the World Social Forum, global festivals organized by communities of practice to celebrate their identities and achievements such as the Fez Festival of Sacred Music, and international conferences which bring different interest groups together. Since the creation of the United Nations, civic associations have organized across national boundaries around issues of peace, social justice, and the environment. The World Federalist Movement,[1] for example, argued for a global government as early as 1937 to secure international peace, and began to emphasize building democracy on a global scale ten years later. Environmental organizations have organized globally to address the need for a common policy framework to preserve and protect natural resources since the early 1960s. And in the 1990s, the United Nations organized a series of global summits to address problems such as environmental degradation and discrimination, which acted as a catalyst for global civil society development (Pianta 2005).

Combining elements from each of these three definitions, Anheier (2007) concludes that global civil society is the sphere of ideas, values, institutions, organizations, networks, and individuals that are based upon civility; are located between the family, the state, and the market; and operate beyond the confines of national societies, polities, and economies. This definition is useful in defining the universe of actors that is concerned with affecting power and politics in the global political arena, but has a normative frame that limits its applicability. Nevertheless, while these norms may be contested, it is clear that global civil society is slowly emerging over time in all three of these guises, and will grow stronger as they continue to intertwine.

2. GLOBAL GOVERNANCE AND GLOBAL CIVIL SOCIETY

The arrangements of global governance are proliferating in a wide variety of issue areas and forums around the making and implementation of rules and the exercise of political power across national borders, though not necessarily by entities authorized by any general agreement to act (Keohane 2003). Global civil society is organizing to influence those who are exercising power in these ways, including INGOs like Oxfam and Greenpeace, global social movements like Via Campesina, and time-bound transnational actions such as the International Campaign to Ban Land Mines, the Global Campaign Against Poverty, and the Jubilee Debt Relief campaigns of the late 1990s, all of which had some impact on global public policy. Orchestrated, coordinated global protests and mass demonstrations have also been mounted around the war in Iraq—for example, to counter the official "coalition of the willing" in 2003. And identity-based solidarity groups are increasingly assuming citizenship rights at the global level, such as indigenous communities who succeeded in gaining recognition through the United Nations in 2008 after thirty years of trying, when the General Assembly passed the Declaration on Indigenous Peoples.

Most of these examples can be characterized as attempts to create new social contracts that reflect the realities of an increasingly interconnected world, in order to address the impact of globalization on social and economic conditions. Scholte (2011) calls these actions "enactments of citizenship, that is, they are practices through which people claim rights and fulfill responsibilities as members of a given polity." Global civil society activists recognize three realities that stem from Scholte's observation. First, that representative government at the national level is not a sufficiently effective arrangement to address domestic or cross-border social problems. Second, that representative governance does not naturally extend to the global arena. And third, that in order to resolve local problems, people sometimes have to organize globally. These realities speak to a new level of maturity in global civil society in formally positioning itself in relation to the institutions and processes of cross-border governance, which are fulfilling many of the functions that previously were undertaken at the national level. As this process evolves, members of global civil society are assuming the rights and responsibilities of citizenship. But when global civil society engages with intergovernmental institutions or organizations like the Bank for International Settlements, the Internet Corporation for Assigned Names and Numbers, or the Global Fund for Malaria, Tuberculosis, and HIV/AIDS, in what ways are they acting as "global citizens"?

First, their actions assume that intergovernmental organizations are governing bodies. This assumption *alone* has shifted the attitudes and practices of many global institutions. International trade experts, economists, and bankers do not perceive themselves as governing in the formal sense, yet when the institutions for which they work (such as the IMF and the WTO) build in mechanisms for public consultation, disclosure, and accountability, they inevitably assume some of the responsibilities of governance. Evidence of this shift is already visible in the mechanisms these institutions have established to communicate and respond to the public, for example, and in demands for whistleblower policies from staff associations in the United Nations and the Asian Development Bank (GAP 2005).[2] Naming global bodies as institutions of governance makes it more difficult for them to deny the power and impact they undoubtedly have. Exposing power relations within and between them has made it easier for civil society to claim citizenship rights, but it has also empowered governments to reflect on the growing role of intergovernmental organizations, discuss the consequences of ceding sovereignty to global entities, and argue for the right to maintain "policy space," which became a rallying cry among Southern governments in the Doha Round of WTO trade negotiations.

Secondly, it is increasingly recognized that global institutions bear an obligation to respond to those who are affected by their decisions. Almost all the intergovernmental organizations that have been targeted by civil society advocacy campaigns have subsequently instituted formal policies on transparency and public consultation. The exception is the Bank for International Settlements, which remains a veritable fortress of secrets. Consultation with affected communities is a commonly accepted practice in the Multilateral Development Banks and at the International Monetary Fund, the World Trade Organization, and the Internet Corporation for Assigned Names and Numbers (Clark Fox, and Treakle 2003). The call for greater consultation was the impetus behind the development of the Internet Governance Forum and of the creation of seats for civil society representatives on the Board of the Global Fund for Malaria, Tuberculosis, and HIV/AIDS. Even transnational corporations are developing mechanisms for community consultation. Ironically, the weakest efforts in this respect have come from INGOs, who are only beginning to review their consultation methods with the communities with whom they work (One World Trust 2007).

Third, in some instances, global activists have argued that international institutions must respond to them as taxpayers and constituents of shareholder governments, a tactic applied by Northern NGOs to the International Financial Institutions in particular. By challenging these institutions in this way, NGOs have successfully made the case for policy change.[3] Given that the citizens of middle income countries such as Brazil and China are in effect financing the operations of many global institutions through interest repayments on their loans, similar campaigns for tax-based accountability may arise in Southern countries in the future.

Fourth, global civil society activists insist that decisions should be taken in the public domain—that is, that they should be readily visible to all the relevant publics. This assumption has led to the emergence of transparency policies in most of the institutions where civil society has made this demand (The Bank for International settlements, again, is a noteworthy exception). Fifth, even if a group or community is not directly affected by the actions of an international institution, they may feel that they have the right to air their voices in the debate as informed members of the public who bring valuable experience and expertise to the table. Sixth, where governance arrangements are open to formal participation by multiple stakeholders, activists have demanded the right to a vote, not just a voice. The Global Fund for Malaria, Tuberculosis, and HIV/AIDS, for example, already includes civil society in its board. Clearly, standing for office in nondemocratic governance structures poses serious challenges of legitimacy, accountability, and representation for INGOs and global social movements (Peruzzoti 2006, Charnovitz 2006), but even though these questions have not yet been answered, the presence of civic activists in the governance arrangements of international bodies does deepen the debate around their evolving democratic nature.

All these "citizenship" claims are congruent with the rights and responsibilities of citizens in democratic societies at the national level. Even though no formal mechanisms of democratic practice exist beyond the nation-state (i.e., no representation, voting, or political parties), global civil society is increasingly arguing that it should be afforded democratic rights that are prefaced on the underlying principles of democratic practice, namely transparency in the process of exercising power; participation by affected peoples in the process of establishing policies; and downward accountability of the governors to the governed.

3. The Impact of Global Civil Society

[handwritten margin note: UN part of civil society?]

Thus far, the impact of global civil society on democracy in global governance has been limited. Citizens cannot vote for their representatives to the UN General Assembly or the Board of the IMF, or indeed to any other global body. The independent, cross-border judiciaries that have been formed in response to global civil society pressure, such as the International Court of Justice, do not act as a check or balance against the power of the UN or the WTO, and no international institution operates on formal mechanisms of representative democracy.

However, global civil society *has* been effective in promoting democratic principles and operating procedures in international organizations, especially in three areas: the accountability of governors to the governed; transparency in public policy deliberations and outcomes; and public participation in policy formation. This picture is complicated by the fact that each of these principles can be realized with negative impacts on democracy—as when accountability is only exercised upwards to a higher authority, for example (Scholte, 2011). Transparency, in and of itself, is a necessary but insufficient value for democratic practice (Fox and Brown 1998). Participation, if not undertaken with specific mechanisms to encourage the involvement of marginalized or minority populations, can reinforce hierarchy and patriarchy. Therefore, each principle has to be carefully qualified and specified in particular contexts in order to increase its democratic effects.

a. Transparency

Global civil society has pushed for transparency in the operating procedures of international institutions since the early 1980s in an effort to illuminate how power is exercised inside and between them (Fox and Brown 1998). Greater transparency has resulted in the reinforcement of democratic rights when, for example, freedom of information laws have been extended to transactions between international institutions and national governments. Such was the case in Mexico and Brazil when civil society groups worked simultaneously at the national and global levels to force the World Bank and the IMF to release documents pertaining to loans made in those countries.[4] Subsequently, members of parliament in Brazil and activists in Mexico were able to challenge the terms of loans from the World Bank and the IMF.

In 2007, disagreements over agriculture halted global trade negotiations at the World Trade Organization, and the Doha Development Round has yet to resume. Developing country governments refused to sign the WTO agreement because they had been educated by global civil society activists on the details of agricultural subsidies enjoyed by industrialized nations. These subsidies on cotton, sugar, peanuts, butter, and other dairy products were exactly what developing country governments thought were necessary for their own development, but they were blocked in the WTO negotiations by the United States and the European Union. Outrage over these double standards was widely credited for bringing the negotiations to a halt. By illuminating the links between national and global policies, the likelihood of greater public disclosure and transparency in future trade negotiations has been increased.

A third example of transparency lies in gradual reforms at the United Nations, where the selection and nomination processes for senior officials are shrouded in secrecy. Civic activists in the World Federalist Movement have been successful in convincing governments to be more transparent about potential nominees, in the wake of disappointing performances by many UN officials. These activists argued that officials with greater public backing would stand a better chance of taking on the power of the Security Council than those with no public legitimacy.[5] As a result, the UN is gradually opening up the process of nomination to public scrutiny.

b. Participation

The right of citizens to participate in governance lies at the heart of democracy, and action by global civil society has resulted in many marginalized communities being able to participate in global governance for the first time. For example, urban slum dwellers now participate in UN habitat meetings and on the governing council of the Cities Alliance, a World Bank-organized donor consortium. So-called safeguard policies at the Asian Development Bank are now written to protect those who are affected by projects from any unintended consequences. Most often, these are minority communities. At the UN, the inclusion of gender considerations in the Financing for Development negotiations was a huge victory, because the impact of development policies on women's lives is rarely taken into account. Similarly, the UN Peace Building Commission has formally extended invitations to local NGOs working in conflict zones to participate in consultations, and has established a working group to develop a formal mechanism for local NGO involvement in global plans to address future conflicts.

Most of the policies championed by global civil society allow for the general public or their elected representatives to participate, and are not specifically designed to empower marginalized communities, but these efforts can still be important. They include efforts to promote participation by parliamentarians, who constitute an important piece of a more democratic framework for governing the United Nations (Cardoso 2004).[6] Internet governance arrangements provide another target. In May of 2008, the U.S. National Institute for Science and Technology and a special deployment group of U.S. Homeland Security Department contractors proposed a new method of implementing a technical standard for authenticating and encrypting internet addresses. The proposal would have solidified U.S. authority over the internet by handing control of encryption keys to the Department of Homeland Security. Civil society activists who were monitoring internet governance realized the implications of this highly technical issue, alerted other governments to the implications (notably Canada, Germany, and Brazil), and proposed an alternative international repository which became the preferred solution (Internet Governance Project 2008).

c. Accountability

Accountability in the global political arena is complex. Essentially, the key questions are as follows: does action by global civil society bind the powers of an institution to the "rule of law"? Does it strengthen the responsibilities of the governors to the governed? Does it achieve redress when the rights of an individual or a community have been violated? Does it limit the abuse of political power? And are economic, social, cultural, and political rights recognized at the transnational level (Fox and Brown 1998)? In other words, the key questions are accountability to whom, and for what.

In global trade negotiations, for example, Our World is Not for Sale, a global social movement, pressed the Office of the U.S. Trade Representative (USTR) to accept that it was accountable to elected representatives operating at the local level within the United States, thus reinforcing principles of federalism and subsidiarity. The USTR had always taken for granted that it had the authority to negotiate on behalf of states within the United States, but it had never conferred with state representatives over the implications of trade negotiations in the global arena. The office even balked at conferring with the U.S. Congress, and for many years fast-track legislation suspended the power of Congress to contest specific trade provisions. In effect, USTR had no checks on its power and could negotiate whatever it felt to be in the U.S. national interest. Starting in early 2003, global activists began to educate state representatives such as attorneys general, governors, and state legislators on the specific provisions of the trade negotiations that were embedded in the WTO and bilateral trade agreements. The outcomes have been dramatic. Nineteen states have either opted out completely or given specific instructions to the USTR on how to represent their interests in international negotiations, forcing the USTR to reconsider, and in some cases renegotiate, many of its favored positions. After neutralizing Congress as a force for accountability, USTR is now forced to negotiate "down" the political system in order to secure the support of elected officials at the state level.

Accountability mechanisms at the United Nations are weak, but those that do exist have been developed in response to global civil society pressure. They include a whistleblower protection policy and the acknowledgment of Northern governments' legal responsibility to reach the Millennium Development Goals. Accountability outcomes in the international financial institutions have been a little more promising, reflecting many years of global civil society pressure to establish the impact of their activities on the poor, and push them to provide redress when institutional policies are violated. The bulk of these actions have been oriented towards creating mechanisms that offer compensation to communities that are impacted negatively by investments undertaken by these institutions (Clark, Fox, Treakle 2003). Broader victories include the removal of Paul Wolfowitz from his position as the president of the World Bank in 2007, an action that was ultimately successful as a result of rising internal and external pressure when violations of the Bank's own policies were made public.[7]

4. DEMOCRACY IN GLOBAL CIVIL SOCIETY

Global civil society has already begun to exercise a positive influence in democratizing global governance, but it would be even more effective if it could address two main problems that weaken its potential. The first problem concerns the elite nature of global civil society—meaning the lack of genuine grassroots participation in transnational networks, especially from the global South. This produces a limited pool of leaders, decreases accountability to mass-based constituencies, and encourages fragmentation along geographic or issue-based lines. Elitism makes it difficult for global civil society to defend itself against criticism from governments who question the legitimacy of groups who are active in the global arena. It also allows governments or intergovernmental bodies to create quasi-NGOs and then send them to international negotiations as civil society "representatives."

The second major problem is that global civil society networks rarely address their own internal power relations or reflect on the dilemmas of cross-border organizing and how best to address them. One cannot assume that global civil society is entirely democratic. The roles it has played are premised on well-developed privileges of citizenship as defined in a national political context, and while civil society has been adamant in extending the rights of citizenship into the global political arena, it has been less forthcoming in defining the responsibilities that go with them. Extending democratic principles into global governance requires that all of the actors in the global political arena acknowledge a balance between the rights and responsibilities of participation. This remains an enormous challenge (Jordan and Van Tuijl 2000). Power differentials arise through proximity to decision makers, the possession of superior forms of knowledge, unequal access to resources, varying levels of experience in organizing, and a host of other issues. Larger groups often have more power than smaller groups; and organizations from the global North have better access to powerful figures or information from official sources. But groups in the global South may have greater moral authority, access to specific details on the impacts of decisions, and sometimes better access to financial resources than their smaller counterparts from the global North.

Addressing these inequalities requires networks, coalitions, and individual civil society organizations to acknowledge and deal explicitly with the difficult issues of accountability, transparency, and representation within their own structures. Weak internal democracy can undermine the legitimacy of civil society organizations and global civil society as a whole, and entails precious resources being expended on the same issues over and over again. Battles over participation, for example, are refought in the context of every new institution or regime for global governance. Best practices are not carried over from one issue or segment of global civil society to another—for example, from human rights to the environment or trade. Civic associations following the World Summit on the Information Society and the Millennium Summit fought the same battle for the right to participate in total isolation from each other. Legal precedents are not recognized either by civil society or by intergovernmental organizations, in large part because there are very few groups that work across issues and constituencies. More concerted action in these areas is crucial.

5. CONCLUSION

Has the aggregate of global civil society influence reached a tipping point in reforming global governance? Clearly not, since that tipping point would only be reached when those charged with crafting new institutional arrangements understand themselves to be "governors" in the formal sense of that term, accept that they must make arrangements to consult and otherwise engage with the relevant publics, build in provisions for transparency from the outset, and create concrete accountability mechanisms. In some issue areas and intergovernmental organizations, some of these lessons have already been well-attended to. Trade negotiators, for example, are aware of their responsibilities, and both the UN and the international financial institutions have recognized that building their legitimacy with the public will help them in improving their performance and securing more resources.

These examples, and the accumulation of a rich body of research, indicate that global civil society is generally a positive force for democracy. Global civil society activists have achieved widespread public recognition for the notion that global governance is not just a technical matter for bureaucrats to resolve. By clarifying the nature of international institutions, civil society actors have created a sharper focus around demands for public accountability. And by challenging and clarifying the relationships between multiple governing authorities, global civil society has contributed to subsidiarity, the organizing principle that matters ought to be handled by the smallest, lowest or least centralized competent authority.[8] Participatory democracy at the global level both requires and can strengthen participatory democracy at the local and national levels. Perhaps the most telling example of this process at work has been the success of states within the United States in forcing the U.S. Trade Representative to renegotiate trade provisions within the WTO. When global governance arrangements run too far ahead of the populations they are supposed to serve, they can be reeled back through democratic means.

Civic engagement in global governance is increasingly supported by official bodies. The Group of Eight forum (G8), for example, spends millions of dollars on public consultations after having rejected this idea completely in its earlier years.[9] While civic associations are loath to lend legitimacy to the G8 itself, this is what consultation creates—a lesson that has not been lost when new regimes have been negotiated around climate change, communicable diseases, and the future of the Internet. In all three cases, global civil society has a seat at the negotiating table. Global civil society has also forced international institutions to develop accountability mechanisms that at least hint at the right of redress when basic human rights have been violated. Although these trends are fragile and limited in their effects, they represent potentially important breakthroughs that can be built on. The tipping point for democracy in global governance has not been reached, but everywhere that global civil society is engaged in claiming citizenship rights, it is likely that governance will become more democratic over time.

NOTES

1. See http://www.reformtheun.org.
2. See also www.ifitransparency.org.
3. See www.economicjustice.net.
4. See www.ifitransparency.org.
5. See www.reformtheun.org.
6. See also www.reformtheun.org.
7. See www.worldbankpresident.org.
8. In international affairs, subsidiarity is presently best known as a fundamental principle of European Union law. According to this principle, the EU may only act (i.e., make laws) where member states agree that action of individual countries is insufficient. The principle was established in the 1992 Treaty of Maastricht, and is contained within the proposed new treaty establishing a constitution for Europe. However, at the local level it was already a key element of the European Charter of Local Self-Government, an instrument of the Council of Europe promulgated in 1985 (see article 4, paragraph 3 of the Charter).
9. The Group of Eight consists of France, Germany, Italy, Japan, the United Kingdom, the United States, Canada, and Russia.

REFERENCES

Albrow, A., H. Anheier, M. Glasius, M. Price, and M. Kaldor (eds.) 2008. *Global Civil Society 2007/8*. Thousand Oaks, Calif.: Sage Publications.

Anheier, H. 2007. "Reflections on The Concept and Measurement of Global Civil Society." *Voluntas: International Journal of Voluntary and Nonprofit Organizations*; vol. 18(1): 1–15.

Anheier, H., M. Glasius, and M. Kaldor (eds.) 2003. *Global Civil Society 2003*. New York: Oxford University Press.

Bob, C. 2005. *The Marketing of Rebellion* New York: Cambridge University Press.

Cardoso, F. H. 2004. *We the Peoples: Civil Society, the United Nations and Global Governance*. Report of the Panel of Eminent Persons on United Nations–Civil Society Relations. Available at www.un-ngls.org.

Charnovitz, S. 2006. "Accountability of Non-Governmental Organizations in Global Governance," in L. Jordan and P. Van Tuijl (eds.) *NGO Accountability: Politics Principles and Innovations*. London: Earthscan.

Clark, D., J. Fox, and K. Treakle. 2003. *Demanding Accountability: Civil Society Claims and the World Bank Inspection Panel*. London: Rowman & Littlefield.

Council of Europe. 1985. European Charter of Local Self-Government, Article 4, Paragraph 3. Brussels: Council of Europe.

Edwards, M. 2009. *Civil Society*. 2nd ed. Cambridge: Polity Press.

Florini, A. 2000. *The Third Force: The Rise of Transnational Civil Society*. Washington, D.C.: Carnegie Endowment for International Peace.

Fox, J., and D. Brown. 1998. *The Struggle For Accountability: The World Bank, NGOs, And Grassroots Movements*. Cambridge, Mass.: MIT Press.

Government Accountability Project. 2005. "Whistleblower Promoted." Available at www.whistleblower.org. Washington, D.C.: Government Accountability Project.

Internet Governance Project. 2008. "Comments of the Internet Governance Project On Enhancing the Security and Stability of the Internet's Domain Name and Addressing System (Docket Number: 0810021307–81308–01)." Available at www.internetgovernance.org. Washington, D.C.: The National Telecommunications and Information Administration, U.S. Department of Commerce.

Jordan, L., and P. Van Tuijl. 2000. "Political Responsibility in Transnational NGO Advocacy." *World Development* vol. 28(12): 2051–65.

Kaldor, M. 2003. *Global Civil Society*. Cambridge: Polity Press.

Keane, J 2003. *Global Civil Society*. Cambridge: Cambridge University Press.

Keck, M., and K. Sikkink. 1998. *Activists Beyond Borders*. Ithaca, N.Y.: Cornell University Press.

Keohane, R. 2003. "Global Governance and Democratic Accountability," in D. Held and M. Koenig-Archibugi (eds.) *Taming Globalization: Frontiers of Governance*. Cambridge: Polity Press.

Khagram, S., J. Riker, and K. Sikkink (eds.) 2002. *Restructuring World Politics: Transnational Social Movements, Networks, and Norms*. Minnesota: University of Minnesota Press.

One World Trust. 2007. *Global Accountability Report*. London: One World Trust.

Patomaki, H., T. Teivainen, and M. Ronkko. 2002. "Global Democracy Initiatives: The Art of Possible." Working Paper 2. Helsinki: Network Institute for Global Democratization.

Peruzzoti, E. 2006. "Civil Society, Representation and Accountability: Restating Current Debates on the Representativeness and Accountability of Civic Associations," in L. Jordan and P. Van Tuijl (eds.) op. cit. 43–60.

Pianta, M. 2005. UN World Summits and Civil Society: The State of the Art. Paper no. 18. Geneva: United Nations Research Institute for Social Development.

Salamon, L., and S. Sokolowski. 2004. *Global Civil Society: Dimensions of the Nonprofit Sector*. West Hartford, Conn.: Kumarian Press.

Scholte, J. A. 2000. *Contesting Global Governance: Multilateral Economic Institutions and Global Social Movements*. Cambridge: Cambridge University Press.

——. 2004. "Democratizing the Global Economy: The Role of Civil Society." Center for the Study of Globalization and Regionalization, University of Warwick, Warwick, U.K.

———. (ed.) 2011. *Building Global Democracy? Civil Society and Accountable Global Governance*. Cambridge: Cambridge University Press.

Smith, J. 2008. *Social Movements for Global Democracy*. Baltimore: John Hopkins University Press.

Smith J., C. Chatfield, and R. Pagnucco (eds.) 1997. *Transnational Social Movements and Global Politics: Solidarity beyond the State*. Syracuse: Syracuse University Press.

Tarrow, S. 2005. *The New Transnational Activism*. New York: Cambridge University Press.

Union of International Associates. 2010. *Yearbook of International Organizations Guide to Global Civil Society Networks*. Germany: K.G. Saur Verlag.

PART III

GEOGRAPHICAL PERSPECTIVES

CHAPTER 9

....

CIVIL SOCIETY IN THE UNITED STATES

....

THEDA SKOCPOL

DEMOCRACY in the United States has long been admired by much of the world—and not just for its constitutional liberties and participatory elections. From early in the nation's history, Americans were preeminent organizers and joiners of voluntary associations that shape and supplement the activities of government (Schlesinger 1944). In the 1890s, Lord Bryce (1895, 278) observed that "associations are created, extended, and worked in the United States more…effectively than in any other country." Bryce echoed earlier observations by Alexis de Tocqueville ([1835–40] 1969), who visited the New World in the 1830s; and Bryce also foreshadowed the eventual findings of survey studies such as Almond and Verba's *The Civic Culture* (1963), which documented the unusual proclivity of Americans for participation in voluntary groups.

Although American voluntary groups have always been celebrated, their characteristics and political effects are not well understood. Understanding of U.S. civic history has been especially hazy—and as a result, scholars have been ill-equipped to grasp the momentous reorganization of U.S. associational life that took place in the late twentieth century. Between the late 1960s and the 1990s, Americans launched more nationally visible voluntary entities than ever before in the nation's history. They thus remained preeminent *civic organizers*. But late twentieth and early twenty-first century Americans simultaneously ceased to be such avid *joiners*—especially because they pulled back from organizing and participating in membership associations that built bridges across places and brought citizens together across lines of class and occupation.

To get a handle on civic reorganization in recent times, it helps to start with a snapshot of classic U.S. civic democracy, glimpsing the deep roots of the sorts of interest groups and voluntary organizations that held sway around 1950. In this chapter I highlight the major civic transformations that unfolded after 1960 and probe their impact on the broader workings of contemporary American democracy.

1. "Classic" American Civil Society

From the point of view of sheer numbers of groups, business associations predominated in the mid-twentieth-century United States. Groups representing businesses or business people constituted about half of all nationally visible associations in 1950 and more than 40 percent in 1960 (Fox 1952; Skocpol 2003, 146–47). Yet if we examine voluntary groups with large individual memberships, we see another side of mid-century civic life. Compared to citizens of Britain and Germany—the two other advanced industrial nations surveyed in Almond and Verba (1963)—mid-century Americans of both genders and all educational levels were more likely to join and hold office in voluntary associations. What is more, Americans were involved in distinctive types of groups. Americans, Britons, and Germans joined occupationally based associations at roughly equal levels (although the British were more often members of labor unions and did not join farm groups), and respondents of all three nationalities were comparably involved in social and charitable groups. But Americans were unusually likely to claim one or more memberships in church-related associations, civic political groups, and fraternal groups—and were also significantly involved in cooperative and military veterans' associations. The fraternal category especially stands out, in that Almond and Verba tallied it *only* for the U.S. case.

In short, as late as the early 1960s, Americans were avid participants in what I call *fellowship associations*—groups emphasizing and expressing solidarity among citizens, or among "brothers" or "sisters" who see themselves as joined together in shared moral undertakings. In 1955, more than two dozen very large membership federations enrolled between one and 12 percent of American adults apiece (Skocpol 2003, 130–31). Rooted in dense networks of state and local chapters that gave them a presence in communities across the nation, major fraternal groups, religious groups, civic associations, and veterans' associations predominated among very large membership associations (apart from the AFL-CIO). Beyond very large groups, smaller nationwide membership federations also flourished in the immediate post World War II era—including elite service groups such as Rotary and the Soroptimists; civic associations such as the League of Women Voters; and dozens of fellowship and cooperative federations with memberships restricted to African Americans or to particular ethnic groups.

Most of the business associations that were so numerous in the 1950s and early 1960s grew up over the course of the twentieth century; and the same was true of professional associations, which were also numerous by mid-century. But massive, popularly rooted fellowship federations had much deeper historical roots. They started to proliferate in the fledgling United States between the American Revolution and the Civil War, and then experienced explosive growth in the late nineteenth century, as civic organizers—some of whom had met during the Civil War struggles—fanned out across the United States, organizing state and local chapters in every nook and cranny of a growing nation. Millions of nineteenth-century Americans joined women's federations, fraternal and veterans' groups, and reform crusades. By the early twentieth century, the kinds of membership groups that had the most consistent presence, apart from churches, in towns and cities of all sizes were chapters of nation-spanning fellowship federations (Gamm and Putnam 1999, 526–27; Skocpol, Ganz, and Munson 2000, 535–36).

As the United States industrialized between the 1870s and the 1920s—an era during which business and professional groups and labor unions grew in this country as they did in other industrializing nations—fellowship federations remained a strong presence (though particular organizations came and went). In addition to the Civil War, World Wars I and II promoted the growth of fellowship federations, which worked closely with the federal government to mobilize Americans for wars (Skocpol et al. 2002). In an important sense, the United States continued preindustrial patterns of civic voluntarism through much of the industrial era, adding occupational and class-specific associations to its universe of associations while retaining older cross-class federations.

Fellowship associations usually claimed nonpartisanship, yet were often involved in public affairs. Half to two-thirds of the twenty largest membership associations of the 1950s were directly involved in legislative campaigns or public crusades of one sort or another (Skocpol 2003, 26–28). This is perhaps obvious for the AFL-CIO and the Farm Bureau Federation. But beyond these, the Parent-Teacher Association (PTA) and the General Federation of Women's Clubs were active in a variety of legislative campaigns having to do with educational and family issues, following long traditions in women's civic activism (Skocpol 1992). The Fraternal Order of Eagles championed Social Security and other federal social programs (Davis 1948). And the American Legion drafted and lobbied for the GI Bill of 1944 (Bennett 1996, Skocpol 1997).

2. CONTEMPORARY CIVIC REORGANIZATIONS

Three intertwined transformations fundamentally remade American civic life after the mid-1960s. In the first place, business groups gained in absolute numbers, but in the entire universe of groups, they lost ground compared to public interest groups—such as environmental associations, pro-choice and pro-life groups, human rights groups, family values groups, and good government groups. As the total number of national associations rose from about 6,000 in 1960 to about 23,000 in 1990, the share of business associations shrank from 42 percent to 17.5 percent, while groups focused on "social welfare" and "public affairs" burgeoned from 6 percent to 17 percent (Skocpol 2003, 146–47). The balance of organized voices in U.S. public affairs shifted markedly, as new public interest groups spoke for more causes and constituencies than ever before (Berry 1999, Hayes 1986).

Secondly, once-hefty blue-collar trade unions and fellowship federations went into sharp decline (Putnam 2000, 54). Mass memberships shrank, and networks of chapters grew sparse. Tellingly, however, elite professional societies experienced much less decline than popularly rooted membership organizations (see Skocpol 2004, 749–50).

Finally, voluntary groups founded in the 1970s and 1980s adopted new forms of organization. Some—such as public law groups, think tanks, foundations, and political action committees—are not membership groups at all. Many others are staff-centered associations that have few, if any, chapters, and recruit most supporters individually via the mail or media messages. With a few exceptions—such as the thirty-five-million-member American Association of Retired Persons (AARP)—most contemporary mailing-list groups have followings in the tens to hundreds of thousands, not millions (Smith 1992; Putnam 2000, 450).

Recently proliferating associations have other telling features. Even when they claim substantial numbers of adherents, they rarely have chapters, or they have very sparse networks of subnational affiliates (Berry 1977, 42; Putnam 2000, 51). In addition, many recently founded or expanding groups, such as environmental associations, have become more heavily invested in professional staffing (Baumgartner and Jones 1993, 187–89; Shaiko 1999, 12).

To the degree that there is any exception to the civic transformations I have just recounted, it is on the conservative side of U.S. civil society. Professionally managed advocacy groups have proliferated across the board, but present-day conservatives have done more than liberals to renew or reinvent massively large, popularly rooted federations. The National Right to Life Committee, the Christian Coalition, and the National Rifle Association are all extensive chapter-based membership federations that have flourished in recent times; and the Tea Party movement is a very recent addition to this panoply. Inspired by moral and ideological worldviews, conservative populist federations have recruited people across class lines through church networks or sports clubs, linking local units to one another and into the penumbra of the Republican Party (Guth et al. 1995; McCarthy 1987). The one unabashedly liberal membership federation to experience comparable massive growth in recent decades is the National Education Association, a teachers' union.

3. THE ROOTS OF CIVIC REORGANIZATION

Why did America's associational universe change so sharply in the late twentieth century? Some scholars argue that gradual changes in the choices made by masses of Americans are the principal reason for civic shifts (Putnam 2000). This is part of the explanation, but we must also focus on *a juncture of rapid civic reorganization* between the mid-1960s and the early 1990s—a juncture during which elite, well-educated Americans abandoned cross-class membership federations while launching professionally managed organizations. When a fundamental reorganization occurs as rapidly as it did in late twentieth-century America, a combination of causal forces—not just a single causal factor—is usually at work. In this case, a critical event, the Vietnam War, coincided with converging social, political, and technological trends to spur civic reorganization.

The Vietnam War broke the tradition of cross-class civic solidarity among men. Earlier wars across U.S. history encouraged men to band together in veterans and fraternal groups. But Vietnam was a losing war and especially unpopular with educated elites. In civic life, this war drove a wedge between social strata and generations. The human rights revolutions of the 1960s and 1970s were also pivotal, because they challenged the gender roles and racial divisions that had marked U.S. associational life in previous times (Skocpol 2003, 178–99). Young people and educated Americans became reluctant to join associations with histories of racial exclusion and separation of the genders. In the same era, given the entry of more and more women into the paid labor force and the proliferation of female-led families, women were no longer available as helpmates for men's groups, making it harder for those groups to flourish. Changes in work and family life also hurt groups that needed to coordinate people's availability for recurrent meetings, as most traditional male and female associations had needed to do.

Finally, as old-line membership federations declined, national government activism and new technologies spurred the formation of professionally managed advocacy groups and institutions. We often think of voluntary groups as making demands on government—yet it is also true that government institutions and policies influence group formation. From the late 1950s and the 1960s, the federal government intervened in many new realms of social and economic life—and thousands of new associations formed in response (Skocpol 2007). For example, new advocacy groups speaking for feminists and minorities proliferated, not before, but *after* the Civil Rights Act of 1964 and the establishment of federal agencies to enforce affirmative action regulations (Skocpol 2007, 47–49). As this happened in many policy areas, moreover, newly formed groups could maneuver more effectively if they hired professional staffers. Lawyers working for associations or public interest firms could bring cases before federal courts open to class action law suits. Expert staffers could manage relations with the national media, lobby proliferating numbers of Congressional aides, and contact expanding numbers of executive branch officials (Skocpol 2007, 51–52).

New technologies and resources allowed late-twentieth-century association-builders to operate from centralized offices in Washington, D.C. and New York City. Back in the nineteenth century, when Frances Willard worked to build a nationally influential federation, the Woman's Christian Temperance Union, she traveled all over the country recruiting organizers to found and sustain a nationwide network of local chapters. By contrast, when Marian Wright Edelman (1987) got the inspiration to found the Children's Defense Fund, she turned to private foundations for grants and then recruited an expert staff of researchers and lobbyists. And the founder of Common Cause, John Gardner, used a few large donations to set up a mailing-list operation (McFarland 1984, Rothenberg 1992).

4. THE IMPACT ON AMERICAN DEMOCRACY

Does civic reorganization matter for the health of American democracy? Democracy in the United States has been enlarged, say optimistic social analysts, by social movements and advocacy groups fighting for social rights and fresh understandings of the public interest (Berry 1999; Minkoff 1997; and Schudson 1998). Americans are reinventing community, too (Wuthnow 1994, 1998)—joining flexible small groups and engaging in ad hoc volunteering, while supporting expert advocates who speak for important values on the national stage. Many of these points are reasonable responses to pessimists who declare that contemporary civil society is falling apart. Yet those who look on the upside fail to notice that more voices are not the same thing as increased democratic capacity, and do not see that gains in racial and gender equality have been accompanied by declines in democratic participation and governance.

a. Dwindling Avenues for Participation

Scholars studying political participation have established that a combination of *resources, motivation,* and *mobilization* explains variations in who participates, how, and at what levels (Burns, Schlozman, and Verba 2001; Rosenstone and Hansen 1993; Verba, Schlozman, and Brady 1995). Individuals from privileged families have advantages of income and education, and also tend to be regularly contacted by civic organizers or election campaigners. What is more, people in managerial and professional careers are likely to gain skills at work that can be transferred to public activities. Nevertheless, such socioeconomic disparities can be partially counteracted if popularly rooted political parties, unions, churches, and associations mobilize and motivate average citizens and spread skills that facilitate participation.

Along with unions and farm groups, traditional U.S. fellowship federations were organizational mechanisms for widely distributing civic skills and motivation. Back in 1892, Walter B. Hill published a humorous piece in *The Century Magazine* purporting to explain to a foreign friend how the United States could be a country that encouraged every boy to aspire to be President and "every American girl to be the President's wife" when, in fact, there were not that many public offices to go around. The "great American safety valve," wrote Hill (1892, 384), is that "we are a nation of presidents" with an "an enormous supply of official positions" at the local, state, and national level in a "thousand and one societies."

Hill's (1892, 383) observations about "the significance of the non-political office-holding class in our country" identified a crucial aspect of traditional American civic life. Countless churches and voluntary groups of all sizes needed volunteer leaders. Indeed, the largest, nation-spanning voluntary federations could have as many as 15,000–17,000 local chapters, each of which needed twelve to eighteen officers and committee leaders each year. Considering just the twenty largest voluntary federations in 1955, I estimate that some 3 to 5 percent of the adult population was serving in such leadership roles. As they cycled millions of Americans through official responsibilities, classic voluntary federations taught people how to run meetings, handle moneys, keep records, and participate in group discussions. With fresh recruits to leadership ladders in each, so many officers and activists were required that there were plenty of opportunities for men and women from blue-collar and lower-level white collar occupations. Local activists, furthermore, regularly moved up to responsibilities at district, state, and national levels.

Unions, farmers' groups, and popularly rooted cross-class federations also conveyed politically relevant knowledge and motivation. The constitutions of voluntary federations taught people about parliamentary rules and legislative, judicial, and executive functions. Membership gave them experience with elections and other forms of representative governance, and drove home concrete lessons about the relationship between taxation through dues and the association's ability to deliver collective services. Whether or not they mobilized members for legislative campaigns, all traditional voluntary associations reinforced ideals of good citizenship. They stressed that members in good standing should understand and obey laws, volunteer for military service, engage in public discussions—and, above all, vote. Gerber and Green (2000) show that people are more likely to turn out to vote in response to face-to-face appeals, and America's traditional popular associations routinely provided such appeals.

Consider by contrast the workings of today's professionally run associations. To be sure, as the Children's Defense Fund exemplifies, certain kinds of advocacy groups can enlarge our democracy by speaking on behalf of vulnerable groups that could not otherwise gain voice. Nevertheless, in an associational universe dominated by business groups and professionally managed public interest groups, the mass participatory and educational functions of classic civic America are not reproduced. Because patron grants and computerized mass mailings generate money more readily than modest dues repeatedly collected from millions of members, and because paid experts are more highly valued than volunteer leaders, today's public interest groups have little incentive to engage in mass mobilization and no need to share control with state and local chapters.

In mailing-list organizations, most adherents are seen as consumers who send money to buy a certain brand of public interest representation. Repeat adherents, meanwhile, are viewed as potential big donors (Bosso 1995, 2002; Jordan and Mahoney 1997). Professional advocacy organizations have become more and more money-hungry operations, even as the United States has experienced growing inequalities in wealth and income (as documented in Danziger and Gottschalk 1995; and Mishel, Bernstein, and Boushey 2003). America today is full of civic organizations that look upwards in the class structure—holding constant rounds of fundraisers and always on the lookout for wealthy "angels."

Today's advocacy groups are also less likely than traditional fellowship federations to entice masses of Americans *indirectly* into politics. In the past, ordinary Americans joined voluntary membership federations not for political reasons, but also in search of sociability, recreation, cultural expression, and social assistance

(Skocpol 2003). Recruitment occurred through peer networks, and people usually had a mix of reasons for joining. Men and women could be drawn in, initially, for nonpolitical reasons, yet later end up learning about public issues or picking up skills or contacts that could be relevant to legislative campaigns or electoral politics or community projects. People could also be drawn in locally, yet end up participating in state-wide or national campaigns.

But today's public interest associations are much more specialized and explicitly devoted to particular causes—like saving the environment, or fighting for affirmative action, or opposing high taxes, or promoting "good government." People have to know what they think and have some interest in national politics and the particular issue *before* they send a check. And the same tends to be true of Internet-based movements, the latest twist in civic innovation. Such electronic movements can move quickly and connect citizens across many localities; but people often need to know they care, before they click on the site. Today's advocacy groups, in short, are not very likely to entice masses of Americans indirectly into democratic politics.

For the reasons just discussed, adherents of contemporary public interest associations are heavily skewed towards the highly educated upper-middle class (Skocpol 2007, 60–61). Of course, well-educated and economically privileged Americans have always been differentially likely to participate in voluntary associations. But there used to be many federations seeking huge numbers of members; and in a country with thin strata of higher-educated and wealthy people, mass associations could thrive only by reaching deeply into the population. Nowadays, we live in a country where the top quarter of the population holds college degrees, because higher education expanded enormously in the late twentieth century (Mare 1995, 163–68; National Center for Educational Statistics 2001, 17). In consequence, groups seeking mailing-list followings in the tens to the hundreds of thousands can focus recruitment on the higher-educated—aiming to attract the very Americans who are most likely to know in advance that they care about public issues. These are the people who appreciate the mass mailings that public interest groups send out. And because higher-educated Americans have experienced sharply rising incomes in recent decades, they are also the folks who can afford to pay for professionally managed advocacy efforts.

b. Upwards-Tilted Public Agendas and Policymaking

Apart from the participatory effects of recent civic transformations, what about their broader impact on agendas of public discussion and public policymaking? Evidence is spotty, but it points towards diminished democracy. Even for the middle class, professionally led associations with virtual constituencies may not deliver as much representational clout as we sometimes imagine. In a conceptually very interesting comparison of pro-life and pro-choice mobilizations in U.S. abortion controversies, McCarthy (1987) first measures public sentiments as reflected in national opinion surveys. At the time he wrote, such results showed that pro-choice sentiments were considerably stronger in the U.S. public, yet organized mobilization magnified the pro-life impact on public agendas and leg-islation far beyond what was achieved by the more popular pro-choice efforts. To see why, McCarthy argues, we must notice the gap between social movements that can build on already-existing social institutions and social networks—as the pro-life movement and other contemporary new right movements can—versus "thin infrastructure" movements run by "professional" social movement organizations that use direct-mail techniques. Although McCarthy does not deny that such thin infrastructure organizations can make some headway in translating widespread mass sentiment into publicity and legislative results, he sees them as far less effec-tive, relative to the proportion of citizens who may hold a given position, than movements that can build on already organized, network-rich institutions and associations.

More telling is the impact of recent civic reorganizations on America's capac-ity to use government for socioeconomically redistributive purposes. The decline of blue-collar trade unions is surely a case in point. Unions mobilize popular con-stituencies electorally as well as in workplaces to demand an active government role in social redistribution. A recent study investigating variations among nations and across the U.S. states argues that union decline helps to explain shrinking elec-torates. "Rates of unionization are important determinants of the size of the elec-torate...and, thus, the extent to which the full citizenry is engaged in collective decisions....Declines in labor organization....mean that the electorate will increas-ingly over-represent higher-status individuals," according to Radcliff and Davis (2000, 140). The result, presuming that elected officials are more responsive to those who vote than those who do not, will be public policies less consistent with the interests of the working class. Furthermore, Radcliff and Davis find that "given that unions also contribute to the maintenance of left party ideology, a declining labor movement implies that left parties may move toward the center. Shrinking union memberships...thus contribute to a further narrowing of the ideological space."

The dwindling of once-huge cross-class membership federations has also affected representation and public discussion. Ideologically, traditional voluntary federations downplayed partisan causes and trumpeted values of fellowship and community service, so their decline leaves the way clear for alternative modes of public discourse less likely to facilitate social inclusion or partisan compromises. Modern advocacy associations often use "human rights talk" and champion highly specialized identities, issues, and causes. Stressing differences among groups and the activation of strong sentiments shared by relatively homogeneous followings, advocacy group tactics may further artificial polarization and excessive fragmenta-tion in American public life (Fiorina 1999; McCarthy 1987; Skerry 1997). In Paget's (1990) eloquent phrasing, the proliferation of advocacy groups can add up to "many movements" but "no majority." Historically, popular and cross-class volun-tary membership federations championed inclusive public social provision—but contemporary advocacy groups plus business and professional associations are much less likely to do so.

Perhaps the most intriguing evidence on the distributive effects of recent civic changes appears in Berry's 1999 book, *The New Liberalism*. As his longitudinal research shows, professionally run public interest groups made quality of life causes such as environmentalism more visible and often prevailed in head-to-head legislative battles with business interests. But Berry also shows that, at least in the late twentieth century, public interest associations crowded out advocacy by unions and other groups speaking for the interests and values of blue-collar Americans; and liberal advocates rarely allied with traditional liberal groups on behalf of redistributive social programs. "Liberal citizen groups," Berry writes, "have concentrated on issues that appeal to their middle-class supporters. . . . as the new left grew and grew, the old left was . . . increasingly isolated" (1999, 55–7).

5. CONCLUSION

The upshot of recent, epochal changes in American civic democracy is paradoxical: Variety and voice have been enhanced in the new U.S. civic universe forged by the organizing upsurges of the 1960s to the 1990s. But the gains in voice and public leverage have mainly accrued to the top tiers of U.S. society, while Americans who are not wealthy or higher-educated now have fewer associations representing their values and interests and enjoy dwindling opportunities for active participation.

For all of their effectiveness in mobilizing citizens across class lines, traditional U.S. fellowship federations were usually racist and gender-exclusive, and they failed to pursue many causes that are vital for Americans today. Yet the recent proliferation of professionally managed civic organizations—from advocacy groups to nonprofit agencies to internet advocacy groups—creates a situation in which the most active Americans tend to be higher-educated and privileged people, Americans who know what to look for in the public realm, and who often do things *for* their fellow citizens rather than *with* them. On the liberal side of the partisan spectrum, especially, there are too few opportunities for large numbers of Americans to work together for broadly shared values and interests. This leaves U.S. public life impoverished, and suggests that those organizing to shape the political future must continue to look for innovative ways to recreate the best traditions of American civic life, while preserving and extending the gains of recent times.

For their own partisan purposes from the heyday of the Christian Coalition in the 1980s and 1990s to the outburst of the Tea Party movement from 2008, contemporary U.S. conservatives have created new combinations of centralized and local action. They have revived or newly built associational networks that link local energies with national lobbying, and that successfully engage a wide variety of Americans in civic and political action. Liberals have been slower to innovate in comparable ways, but there have been new efforts in the environmental and labor movements to combine national advocacy with community-building. What is more, from the 2004 through the 2008 electoral cycles, liberals did much innovative mobilization within the U.S. federal system, culminating in a remarkable engagement of young people and minorities in the 2008 presidential campaign of Democrat Barack Obama, whose organization creatively combined central discipline, the use of new information technologies, and local, face-to-face volunteerism.

But involvements and enthusiasms dwindled after Obama assumed the presidency and lobbyists in Washington, D.C. appeared to take charge once again. Electoral organizing alone is not enough to close civic engagement gaps in American civic and political life. Nor is any kind of politically partisan organizing likely to recreate the ongoing local and national ties that bound together so many millions of Americans of all walks of life from the early-nineteenth through the mid-twentieth century. Despite promising recent experiments, the future of democratic civic engagement in the United States is at best partly cloudy—and will remain so as long as inequalities of education and resources are so vast, and as long as there are so many incentives for elites to pull levers from above without inviting the sustained involvement of millions of fellow citizens.

REFERENCES

Almond, G.A., and S. Verba. 1963. *The Civic Culture: Political Attitudes and Democracy in Five Nations*. Princeton, N.J.: Princeton University Press.

Baumgartner, F. R., and B. D. Jones. 1993. *Agendas and Instability in American Politics*. Chicago: University of Chicago Press.

Bennett, M. J. 1996. *When Dreams Came True: The G.I. Bill and the Making of Modern America*. Washington, D.C.: Brassey's.

Berry, J. M. 1977. *Lobbying for the People: The Political Behavior of Public Interest Groups*. Princeton, N.J.: Princeton University Press.

———. 1999. *The New Liberalism and the Rising Power of Citizen Groups*. Washington, D.C.: Brookings Institution Press.

Bosso, C. J. 1995. "The Color of Money: Environmental Groups and the Pathologies of Fund Raising," in Allen J. Cigler and Burdett A. Loomis (eds.) *Interest Group Politics*. Washington, D.C.: CQ Press, 101–30.

———. 2002. "Rethinking the Concept of Membership in Mature Advocacy Organizations." Paper presented at the Annual Meeting of the Northeast Political Science Association, November 7–9, 2002, Providence, R.I.

Bryce, J. 1895. *The American Commonwealth*, 3rd ed, vol. 2. New York: Macmillan.

Burns, N., K. L. Schlozman, and S. Verba. 2001. *The Private Roots of Public Action: Gender, Equality, and Political Participation*. Cambridge, Mass.: Harvard University Press.

Charles, J. A. 1993. *Service Clubs in American Society: Rotary, Kiwanis, and Lions*. Urbana: University of Illinois Press.

Danziger, S., and P. Gottschalk. 1995. *America Unequal*. New York and Cambridge, Mass.: Russell Sage Foundation and Harvard University Press.

Davis, R. S. 1948. "Fifty Years of Service." *Eagle* 36(2): 7–9.

Edelman, M. W. 1987. *Families in Peril: An Agenda for Social Change.* Cambridge, Mass.: Harvard University Press.

Fiorina, M. P. 1999. "Extreme Voices: A Dark Side of Civic Engagement," in Theda Skocpol and Morris P. Fiorina (eds.) *Civic Engagement in American Democracy.* Washington, D.C.: Brookings Institution Press, and New York: Russell Sage Foundation, 395–425.

Fox, S. D. 1952. "Voluntary Associations and Social Structure." Unpublished Ph.D. dissertation, Department of Social Relations, Harvard University.

Gamm, G., and R. D. Putnam. 1999. "The Growth of Voluntary Associations in America, 1840–1940." *Journal of Interdisciplinary History* 29(4): 511–57.

Gerber, A. S., and D. P. Green. 2000. "The Effects of Canvassing, Telephone Calls, and Direct Mail on Voter Turnout: A Field Experiment." *American Political Science Review* 94(3): 653–63.

Guth, J. L., J. C. Green, L. A. Kellstedt, and C. E. Smidt. 1995. "Onward Christian Soldiers: Religious Activist Groups in American Politics," in A. J. Cigler and B. A. Loomis (eds.) *Interest Group Politics*, 4th ed. Washington, D.C.: CQ Press, 55–76.

Hausknecht, M. 1962. *The Joiners: A Sociological Description of Voluntary Association Membership in the United States.* New York: Bedminster Press.

Hayes, M. T. 1986. "The New Group Universe," in Allan J. Cigler and Burdett A. Loomis (eds.) *Interest Group Politics*. 2nd ed. Washington, D.C.: CQ Press, 133–45.

Hill, W. B. 1892. "The Great American Safety-Valve." *The Century Magazine* 44(3): 383–84.

Mahoney, J., G. Mahoney, and W. Mahoney. 1997. *The Protest Business? Mobilizing Campaign Groups.* Manchester: Manchester University Press.

Mare, R. D. 1995. "Changes in Educational Attainment and School Enrolment," in R. Farley (ed.) *State of the Union: America in the 1990s, Vol 1: Economic Trends.* New York: Russell Sage Foundaton.

McCarthy, J. D. 1987. "Pro-life and Pro-choice Mobilization: Infrastructure Deficits and New Technologies," in Mayer N. Zald and John D. McCarthy (eds.) *Social Movements in an Organizational Society.* New York: Oxford University Press, 49–66.

McFarland, A. S. 1984. *Common Cause: Lobbying in the Public Interest.* Chatham, N.J.: Chatham House Publishers.

Minkoff, D. C. 1997. "Producing Social Capital: National Social Movements and Civil Society." *American Behavioral Scientist* 40(5): 606–19.

Mishel, L., J. Bernstein, and H. Boushey. 2003. *The State of Working America 2002/2003.* Economic Policy Institute. Ithaca, N.Y.: Cornell University Press.

National Center for Educational Statistics. 2001. *Digest of Educational Statistics, 2000.* Washington, D.C.: U.S. Government Printing Office.

Paget, K. 1990. "Citizen Organizing: Many Movements, No Majority." *The American Prospect* no. 2 (Summer): 115–28.

Putnam, R. D. 2000. *Bowling Alone: The Collapse and Revival of American Community.* New York: Simon & Schuster, 2000.

Radcliff, B., and P. Davis. 2000. "Labor Organization and Electoral Participation in the Industrial Democracies." *American Journal of Political Science* 44(1): 132–41.

Rosenstone, S. J., and J. M. Hansen. 1993. *Mobilization, Participation, and Democracy in America.* New York: Macmillan.

Rothenberg, L. S. 1992. *Linking Citizens to Government: Interest Group Politics at Common Cause.* Cambridge: Cambridge University Press.

Schlesinger, A. M., Sr. 1944. "Biography of a Nation of Joiners." *American Historical Review* 50(1): 1–25.

Schudson, M. 1998. *The Good Citizen: A History of American Civic Life*. Cambridge, Mass.: Harvard University Press.

Shaiko, R. G. 1999. *Voices and Echoes for the Environment: Public Interest Representation in the 1990s and Beyond*. New York: Columbia University Press.

Skerry, P. 1997. "The Strange Politics of Affirmative Action." *The Wilson Quarterly* 21 (1) (Winter): 39–46.

Skocpol, T. 1992. *Protecting Soldiers and Mothers: The Political Origins of Social Policy in the United States*. Cambridge, Mass.: Harvard University Press.

——. 1997. "The G.I. Bill and U.S. Social Policy, Past and Future." *Social Philosophy & Policy* 14(2): 95–115.

——. 2003. *Diminished Democracy: From Membership to Management in American Civic Life*. Norman: University of Oklahoma Press.

——. 2004. "Civic Transformation and Inequality in the Contemporary United States," in Kathryn M. Neckerman (ed.) *Social Inequality*. New York: Russell Sage Foundation.

——. 2007. "Government Activism and the Reorganization of American Civic Society," in Paul Pierson and Theda Skocpol (eds.) *The Transformation of American Politics*. Princeton, N.J.: Princeton University Press.

Skocpol, T., M. Ganz, and Z. Munson. 2000. "A Nation of Organizers: the Institutional Origins of Civic Voluntarism in the United States." *American Political Science Review* 94(3): 527–46.

Skocpol, T., Z. Munson, A. Karch, and B. Camp. 2002. "Patriotic Partnerships: Why Great Wars Nourished American Civic Voluntarism," in Ira Katznelson and Martin Shefter (eds.) *Shaped by War and Trade: International Influences on American Political Development*. Princeton, N.J.: Princeton University Press.

Smith, D. H. 1992. "National Nonprofit, Voluntary Associations: Some Parameters." *Nonprofit and Voluntary Sector Quarterly* 21 (Spring): 81–94.

Tocqueville, A. de. [1835–40] 1969. *Democracy in America*, ed. J. P. Mayer and trans. George Lawrence. Garden City, N.Y.: Doubleday.

Verba, S., .K. L. Schlozman, and H. E. Brady. 1995. *Voice and Equality: Civic Voluntarism in American Politics*. Cambridge, Mass.: Harvard University Press.

Walker, J. L., Jr. 1991. *Mobilizing Interest Groups in America: Patrons, Professions, and Social Movements*. Ann Arbor: University of Michigan Press.

Wuthnow, R. 1994. *Sharing the Journey: Support Groups and America's New Quest for Community*. New York: The Free Press.

——. 1998. *Loose Connections: Joining Together in America's Fragmented Communities*. Cambridge, Mass.: Harvard University Press.

CHAPTER 10

··

CIVIL SOCIETY IN
LATIN AMERICA

··

EVELINA DAGNINO

EVERY notion of civil society implies some conception of how society should look
and how politics should operate. In this sense, different understandings of civil
society convey different political projects, and are always in dispute. This is especially true in Latin America, where intellectual and political debates are intimately
inter-twined. As in other parts of the world, the idea of civil society became prominent in the political vocabulary of the continent in the context of struggles around
democracy. From the mid 1970s onward, civil society came to be seen as the most
important source of resistance against oppressive States in countries under military
dictatorship such as Brazil, Argentina, Chile, and Uruguay; and under authoritarian
regimes such as those in Mexico, Peru, and Colombia. The re-establishment of formal democratic rule and the relative opening up of most political regimes in Latin
America did not remove the importance of civil society as some "transitologists"
had assumed (O'Donnell and Schmitter, 1986). On the contrary, it reinforced its
centrality in the building and deepening of democracy both theoretically and practically. Since 1990, the meanings of civil society have multiplied still further under
the divergent influences of neo-liberalism and the emergence of Left-leaning governments in some parts of the continent, the first trend consigning civil society to
the realm of "third-sector" service-provision and the second opening up new possibilities for participatory democracy.

Ideas about civil society in Latin America have to be understood within the
context of striking levels of inequality, and political societies that historically have
been unable or unwilling to address this problem; high levels of cultural heterogeneity, especially in countries with large indigenous populations; the predominance
of informal markets and endemic poverty; and a façade of liberal democracy that is

characterized by an enormous distance between political elites and institutions, and the great mass of Latin America's population. "Populist-developmentalist" arrangements of the kind that have been implemented in Argentina, Brazil and Mexico have tried to bridge this distance through the control and subordination of social organizations in order to guarantee political support and governability.

For some authors, these contextual characteristics mean that Western conceptualizations of civil society do not hold in Latin American societies (Zapata, 1999), but innovative, critical approaches have been developed across the continent in close collaboration with new experiences of civil society engagement such as participatory budgeting. As elsewhere in the world, the prominence of these ideas stems from the perception that civil society is a potent force in building an effective democracy, a perception that has not escaped some skepticism but remains alive across Latin America after more than thirty years. This chapter examines these various understandings of civil society and explores the factors underlying their diversity.

1. CIVIL SOCIETY: HOMOGENOUS OR DIVERSE?

Resistance against authoritarianism was able to achieve a relative unity across different social interests in many Latin American contexts, but it soon disappeared after the return to democratic rule, revealing the inherent nature of civil society as a field of different and conflicting views. However, these differences still tend to be ignored in political discourse, where civil society is often seen as a macro political subject, in some cases merely replacing older ideas about "the people." The widespread and persistent tendency to see civil society as the home of democratic virtues and the State as the "embodiment of evil" (Dagnino 2002), which had a clear sense under authoritarian rule, has been reinforced by the influence of leading theorists such as Habermas, Cohen, and Arato. Their tripartite models, in which civil society and the life-world are sharply distinguished from the market and the state, contributed to this sense of separation. Habermas's emphasis on communicative action as a privileged logic of civil society, and the risks of its colonization by both states and markets, helped to confer legitimacy on the demonization of the State.

The affirmation of civil society was also related to "a return to the values of an ethical life and social solidarity at a moment when the market becomes an irreversible element" (Pinheiro 1994, 7, 9). Leftist sectors, heavily affected by the failure of "real existing socialism," did not immediately react against this mythical view. Instead, they transferred their allegiance to social movements that emerged in the context of resisting authoritarianism, and which were considered, rather indiscriminately, as the new "heroes" of social transformation (Krischke and Scherer-Warren, 1987). The presumed connection between associational life and the "good society" is clear in this respect, and its premise is that the values of that society rest on the shoulders of ordinary people who organize and associate with each other to defend them. As a generalization about Latin America, or indeed any other place for that matter, this view is not defensible. Arato himself recognized that "the unity of civil society is obvious only from a normative perspective" (1992, 21).

The recognition of the heterogeneity of civil society is important not only in theoretical terms, as a field of conflict, but is also evident in empirical terms across the continent. From the paramilitary organizations of Colombia to market-oriented NGOs or entrepreneurial foundations in Brazil; corporatist trade-unions in Argentina to indigenous movements in Bolivia and Ecuador; and youth gangs such as the "maras" in Peru, associational life varies enormously. In Venezuela, for example, "civil society" has been appropriated by the middle class, and in President Hugo Chávez's discourse, the term has a pejorative meaning when used to refer to the privileged sectors of society. "For this reason, the poor have rarely identified with the term civil society, much less felt represented by the middle and upper classes." (García-Guadilla et al, 2004, 13). In Brazil after years of neo liberal rule, "civil society" has marginalized social movements and is increasingly restricted to denote the world of nongovernmental organizations (NGOs), itself an extremely heterogeneous field (Teixeira, 2003). This heterogeneity is exemplified in the role played by NGOs in Colombia, considered by President Uribe as serious adversaries, and in the insistence of ABONG, the Brazilian Association of NGOs, to resist the homogenizing denomination of "Third Sector" in order to affirm its own political identity.

Even when empirical research began to be undertaken on civil society in Latin America, it concentrated on assessing the size and levels of associational activity, assuming that a quantitative expansion meant favorable results for democracy (Avritzer, 2000; Scherer-Warren, Ilse et al., 1998; Santos 1993). Only recently has empirical research turned its focus to unveiling civil society's heterogeneity (Dagnino, 2002; Panfichi, 2002; Olvera, 2003; Gurza et al., 2005).

2. CIVIL SOCIETY AND THE STATE

Civil society and the state are always mutually constitutive. In fact, the kind of relationships that are established between them represent a crucial dimension in the building of democracy. In the 1980s and 1990s, most theoretical efforts to conceptualize civil society in Latin America were predicated on the need to affirm, not just its importance, but its very existence. In an academic and political landscape dominated by a "statist" conception of politics rooted in the developmentalist/populist tradition, the affirmation of "another space" of politics and of other actors who were entitled to participate in those spaces was a key concern, and an emphasis on separate spheres played a central role in that effort.

For similar reasons, Latin American social movements placed strong emphasis on their autonomy vis-à-vis the State and political parties, reacting against the control and subordination to which they had long-been submitted. This strategic emphasis has often been interpreted as a rejection or a "turning their back to the State" (Evers 1983). In fact, the State in Latin America has always been a mandatory interlocutor for social movements and other civil society organizations, even during the harsh times of authoritarianism.

Although they still predominate, the simplistic tone of these views has been increasingly contested in Latin America in both theory and in practice. The emergence of more complex approaches to civil society is in part a response to the concrete difficulties encountered in deepening democracy, which always implies an intricate interplay of forces and struggles across diverse actors and arenas. Simplistic views also created frustration, disappointment and disenchantment among civil society activists when the high expectations they had raised failed to be translated into reality (Olvera, 1999). Academics expressed the same reactions in an analytical wave that decreed the "death" or "crisis" of Latin American social movements.

At the theoretical level, alternative analyses of civil society took their inspiration from Gramsci and others in order to contest the false dichotomies of these dominant, homogenizing approaches. The Gramscian notion of civil society as a terrain of conflict and therefore, of politics, included an integral relationship with the State, without which the central notion of hegemony would make no sense. This framework has been used in several countries since the beginning of their anti-authoritarian struggles, where the role played by civil society in the destruction and recreation of hegemony was paramount to its embrace by the Left as an appropriate basis for the struggle for democracy. "Well familiar with 'frontal attack,' the Left had to learn how to conduct a 'war of position' and the multiplicity of trenches it implies" (Dagnino 1998, 41).

The notion of hegemony as a framework for analyzing civil society and its relationship to the state was reinforced by the gradual ascension to power in several countries of progressive and/or leftist forces that, in many cases, represented political projects formulated by or originating in civil society itself. The Workers' Party (PT) in Brazil is the most significant case. Emerging in 1980 from trade unionism, popular movements, progressive sectors of the Catholic Church, and a few intellectuals, the Workers' Party began its electoral trajectory in 1982 and gradually widened its access to government positions, from municipal administrations to state governments and finally, in 2002, to the presidency of the Republic. In other cases, such as the creation of the Partido Revolucionario Democratico (PRD) and the election of Mayor C. Cárdenas in Mexico City in 1997, and that of Alejandro Toledo in Peru in 2001, the articulation between politicians and civil society militants raised expectations and opened up more room for rethinking their relationship, in spite of subsequent, less positive developments. The movement of individuals in both directions intensified in many countries, with activists joining governments and politicians seeking civil society support. This pattern has been clear in the elections of presidents Tabaré Vasquez in Uruguay in 2004, Evo Morales in Bolivia in 2005, and Correa in Ecuador in 2006.

3. CIVIL SOCIETY AND PARTICIPATORY DEMOCRACY

The emphasis on the articulation of civil society and the state found expression in a whole variety of experiments around participatory democracy that developed throughout the continent from the 1990s onwards. The nucleus of these experiments was the need to deepen and radicalize democracy in response to the limits of liberal, representative models as a privileged form of state-society relations. Plagued by a resilient "crisis of representation" as a result of the exclusive and elitist nature of liberal regimes and their incapacity to tackle deep-seated inequalities across the continent, it was clear that representative democracy needed to be complemented by participatory and deliberative mechanisms that could increase participation in decision making (Santos and Avritzer 2002:75–76; Fals Borda 1996). When they translate to a central focus on equality, citizenship and rights become powerful components of democratization, activated through public spaces that enable greater participation in the formulation of public policies that are oriented towards this goal (Santos and Avritzer 2002; Murillo and Pizano 2003; Ziccardi 2004; Caceres 2004). These spaces are forums for deliberation and comanagement, implying more- or less-formal institutional designs and sets of rules, and directed towards producing decisions of a public nature. The state's presence in them distinguishes these experiments from Habermasian views of the public sphere. Civil society and public spaces are two distinct levels that correspond to the "socialization of politics" and the "socialization of power" (Coutinho 1980). Public spaces are spaces in which conflict is both legitimized and managed.

Brazil has been the pioneer in institutionalizing spaces like these within the frame of the 1988 Constitution, which provided for direct participation by civil society. Management Councils in several policy areas are mandatory at the municipal, state and federal levels, with equal representation from civil society and the state (Tatagiba 2002). The Participatory Budget process installed in Porto Alegre in 1989 under the Workers' Party Administration has been adopted in many cities in Latin America and increasingly in other parts of the world (Santos 1998; Avritzer 2002). The results of these experiments vary greatly, but, in some cases, they are proving to be reasonably effective in enabling government and civil society to take joint decisions, in spite of their limits and difficulties. It is not surprising that most of the initial theorizing on participation in Latin America has circulated around the Brazilian experience. The existence of the Workers' Party and of a dense and diversified civil society has allowed for significant reflective creativity through joint debates over an extended period of time that involve activists, party members, and academics. The same conclusion applies to the concept of citizenship, which has been significantly redefined by Brazilian theorists and activists since the mid-1970s, and which has also made important inroads in Colombia, Ecuador, Argentina, and

Uruguay. Even in Chile, where notions of citizenship were strongly influenced by the early rise of neoliberalism, a lively debate has ensued (De La Maza 2001).[1]

Advocates of participatory democracy envisage a role for civil society that rejects its traditional "self-limiting" character in order to engage with political activity and move beyond the strict separation from the state that characterizes the original approach of Jurgen Habermas (1986). These more radical visions define participation as shared decision making with the state, thus departing from the idea that civil society should refrain from political power and limit its actions to influencing those already in authority. Tarso Genro, once Mayor of Porto Alegre and subsequently Brazil's Federal Minister of Justice, has articulated the awkwardly named notion of "nonstate public spaces" to describe these experiments (Genro 1995). For Genro, these spaces—simultaneously materialized in and inspired by the experience of participatory budgets in Porto Alegre—enable civil society to penetrate the state in order to make it more responsive to the public interest, thus breaking the state's monopoly over decision making. This model obviously requires a willing disposition on the part of the state to share some of its power, and relies on a strongly organized civil society. Such conditions are comparatively rare in Latin America, which is why the Brazilian experience has proven difficult to replicate in other contexts. Furthermore, the autonomy of both partners in this relationship is crucial. Santos (1998, 491) sees citizens and community organizations, on one hand, and the municipal government, on the other, as converging "with mutual autonomy. Such convergence occurs by means of a political contract through which this mutual autonomy becomes mutually relative autonomy." Along the same lines, Oliveira (1993, 6) calls this process "convergent antagonism," emphasizing that such relationships are not a zero-sum game. In spite of their sometimes convoluted formulations, these ideas are important attempts to deal with the reality of state-society relations, a question that is often ignored even by analysts of participatory democracy.

The incorporation of participation by civil society in the constitutions of most Latin American countries is evidence that these concepts have been widely accepted, at least in theory. Between the early 1990s and the early 2000s, nineteen countries included some provision for citizen participation in their legal-institutional frameworks, seventeen approved mechanisms of direct political participation, and fourteen constitutions provide for public spaces with state and civil society representation (Hevia 2006).

Participatory experiences have proliferated across Latin America, marked by a great diversity in their forms, expressions, qualities, and results, and producing important demonstration effects through which one country learns from the experiences of others. This process has intensified with the growth of continental networking among social movements, NGOs, academics, and political parties. The most obvious example is the remarkable spread of participatory budgets, but others include the Mesas de Concertación in Peru (regional roundtables); the Auditorías Articuladas in Colombia (state-society partnerships in the oversight of public contracting, the execution of public works, and the accountability of state agencies); the

Conselhos Gestores de Políticas Públicas in Brazil; the Consejos Autogestivos in México (self-management councils in protected natural areas), and many others. These experiments show that alternative forms of "citizen politics" are possible, but they are limited in temporal and spatial terms, as well as in their cultural and political effects, especially when gauged against the expectations they have raised.

4. From Civil Society to Third Sector: The Impact of Neoliberalism

Neoliberal interpretations of civil society in Latin America stand in sharp contrast to participatory democracy. Although neoliberalism is associated with liberal, representative democracy, at its core is the notion that the state and its relationships to society have to adjust to the demands of a new moment in the development of global capitalism. This impulse defines the internal logic that structures the neoliberal project. It does not offer a diagnosis of society in which a concern for democracy is central. Instead, its goals are to adjust the economy by taking down barriers to international capital, removing any obstacles to the operation of "free" markets, and extending market principles as the basic organizing principle of social life. In this framework, states that are characterized by their large size, inefficiency, excessive bureaucracy, and/or corruption find new routes to more efficient forms of action and the optimal use of scarce resources (Franco 1999). In addition to the privatization of state enterprises, this process involves the transfer of the state's social responsibilities to individuals, civil society groups, and the private sector. Furthermore, the search for efficiency also works to legitimize the adoption of the market as the organizing principle of social, political. and cultural life, transforming governments into service providers and citizens into clients, users, and consumers.

How have these ideas translated into conceptions of civil society, participation, and citizenship in Latin America? From a neoliberal perspective, the role of civil society is twofold. On the one hand, it should supply the state and the market with information on social demands in order to increase efficiency. On the other, it should provide social organizations with the capacity to execute public policies that are oriented towards the satisfaction of these demands. Thus, civil society is conceived in a selective and exclusionary way, recognizing only those actors who are able to carry out these tasks. These ideas have been put into practice in powerful ways, reconfiguring civil society through the accelerated growth and expanded role of NGOs; the rise of the so-called third sector and of entrepreneurial foundations with a strong emphasis on redefining philanthropy in business terms; and the marginalization (or what some refer to as the criminalization) of social movements. The overall result has been a reductive identification of civil society with NGOs or the third sector. Latin American governments fear the politicization of their engagement with social movements and workers' organizations, and instead seek reliable partners who can effectively respond to their demands while minimizing conflict. This shaping capacity of state action is visible in what has been called the "NGOization" of social movements (Alvarez, 2009), not only in terms of their organizational structures and behavior but also in their political practices. Attracted by the opportunities offered by the state to engage in the execution of public policies, few social movements have been able to retain both their independence and their involvement in other kinds of political action. The Landless Movement in Brazil (MST) is one of the few that has.

Under neoliberalism, participation is defined instrumentally, in relation to the needs derived from the "structural adjustment" of the economy and the transfer of the state's social responsibilities to civil society and the private sector. For members of civil society such as NGOs, participation means taking on the efficient execution of social policies, even though the definition of those policies remains under exclusive state control. Participation is thus concentrated in the functions of management and policy implementation, not shared decision making (Teixeira 2003). The reform of the state that was implemented in Brazil in 1998 under the influence of Minister Bresser Pereira (who introduced the principles of the "new public management") is very clear in relation to the different roles of the "strategic nucleus of the state" and of social organizations. The former retains a clear monopoly over decision making (Bresser Pereira 1996).

All over the continent, the very idea of solidarity, whose long history is rooted in political and collective action, became the motto of neoliberal versions of participation. As part of a broader move to privatize and individualize responsibilities for social action, participation is relegated to the private terrain of morality where an emphasis on volunteer work and social responsibility (of both individuals and firms) becomes dominant. Along the same lines, the definition of the common or public good dispenses with the need for debate between conflicting views, replaced by "a set of private initiatives with a public sense" based on the moral thesis of "caring for the other" (Fernandes 1994, 127). The "public" character of the third sector and NGOs has been increasingly questioned on the grounds that they "lack the transparency and accountability in terms of finances, agenda, and governance necessary to effectively perform their crucial role in democratic civil society" (McGann and Johnstone 2006).

In this framework, associational life loses its public and political dimensions. In fact, third sector advocates and activists insist on emptying it of any conflictive or even political connotations (Franco 1999; Fernandes 1994). For these advocates, the replacement of civil society by the third sector would remove any sense of "systemic opposition to the state" (Fernandes 1994, 127). Thus, "the notion of civil society, and the critical field belonging to it, lose their meaning and only cooperation remains, under a new homogenizing guise. The main effect of this change has been the depoliticization of State-society relationships, with the question of conflict disappearing from the scene" (Dagnino, Olvera, and Panfichi 2006, 22).

Neoliberalism also redefines citizenship according to its own guiding principles, diluting exactly that which constitutes the core of this notion, which is the idea of universal rights. The way in which the meaning of citizenship is watered down can be seen in several dimensions of the neoliberal project. First, social rights, which were consolidated in some countries, in spite of the precarious nature of the Latin American welfare state, are now being eliminated, seen as an obstacle to the efficient operation of the market. Second, in the management of social policy, the conception of universal rights as an instrument for constructing equality is replaced by targeted efforts directed towards those sectors of society considered to be "at risk." Third, citizenship is pushed into the arena of the market and a seductive connection between the two is established. To become a citizen increasingly means to integrate into the market as consumer and producer. In a context where the state is progressively removed from its role as the guarantor of rights, the market is expected to step in to offer a surrogate space for citizenship. Fourth, when social policies are transferred to civil society organizations, philanthropy, and volunteer work, citizenship is both identified with and reduced to solidarity with the poor and needy. Those who are the targets of these policies are not seen as citizens with the "right to have rights" but as needy human beings who must be taken under the wing of private or public charities.

These ideas have been implemented by neoliberal governments throughout the continent with the heavy support of international agencies. After the pioneering Fondo de Solidaridad y Inversión Social (Solidarity and Social Investment Fund, or FOSIS) was created in 1990 in Chile—"especially tailored for NGO involvement" (Foweraker 2001, 18)—a number of similar agencies and programs materialized in the 1990s in Colombia, Peru, Bolivia, Venezuela, and elsewhere. In Brazil, during the eight years of the government of Fernando Henrique Cardoso, Comunidade Solidária, the agency in charge of social policies, became a powerful think tank, which was extremely effective in developing and disseminating this framework (Almeida 2009). These efforts have not been able to hinder the deepening of both poverty and inequality in most countries during the same period, but the number of NGOs multiplied geometrically, as did the growth of third sector employment (Salamon and Sokolowski 2004). The processes of decentralization that have taken place in most countries at different levels have contributed to this process through so-called partnerships between local governments and NGOs, but have also made possible a range of more participatory, democratic, and creative interactions between civil society and local governments.

5. CONCLUSION

These different conceptions of civil society coexist in a more or less tense relationship, according to different national contexts and historical processes. Other relevant dimensions that help us to understand this diversity have not been discussed here, including the weight and role of political parties (either as competitors or supporters of civil society's political actions), and the role of organized crime as providers of alternatives to civil society organizations among the popular sectors.

Recent political processes that have taken left-leaning forces into state power seem to indicate that the dominance of neoliberalism may be losing ground in the continent, although this does not necessarily represent a commitment to civil society or deliberative participation. In fact, in some of these cases such as Venezuela and even President Lula's Brazil, the presence of strong leaders committed to the popular sectors can, in fact, act as a deterrent to effective participation. In others like Bolivia, the strong and relatively autonomous organization of indigenous movements may serve as an antidote to this tendency.

In any case, the current condition of Latin America makes the centrality of the relationships between state and civil society even clearer. The extent to which civil society is seen as entitled to a share in decision making, and the extent to which conflict is seen as legitimate and public spaces are provided for its management, seem to be the crucial questions on which the future of civil society will hang across the continent.

NOTE

1. For a detailed account of the debate on citizenship in different Latin American countries see Dagnino (2005), as well as the special issue on this theme in Latin American Perspectives (2003).

REFERENCES

Almeida, C. 2009. "O princípio participativo fundado na solidariedade e a emergência de uma nova noção de responsabilidade pública." *Cadernos CIDADE*, 12(16):1–34.

Alvarez, S. 2009. "Beyond NGO-ization? Reflections from Latin America," *Development* 52(2): 175–184.

Arato, A. 1995. "Ascensão, declínio e reconstrução do conceito de sociedade civil: orientações para novas pesquisas." *Revista Brasileira de Ciências Sociais* 27: 18–27.

Avritzer, L. 2000. "Democratization and Changes in the Pattern of Association in Brazil." *Journal of Interamerican Studies and World Affairs* 42(3): 59–76.

———. 2002. *Democracy and the public space in Latin America*. Princeton, N.J.: Princeton University Press.

Bresser Pereira, L. C. 1996. "Da administração pública burocrática à gerencial." *Revista do Serviço Público* 47(1): 7–40.

Caceres, Eduardo. 2004. "La Participación Ciudadana desde un enfoque de Derechos." *Cuadernos Descentralistas*. 11. Lima: Propuesta Ciudadana.

Coutinho, C. N. 1980. *A democracia como valor universal e outros ensaios*. Rio de Janeiro: Salamandra.

Dagnino, E. 1998. "Culture, Citizenship and Democracy: Changing Discourses and Practices of the Latin American Left," in S. Alvarez, e. Dagnino, and A. Escobar (eds.) *Cultures of Politics/Politics of Cultures: Revisioning Latin American Social Movements*. Boulder, Colo.: Westview Press, 1998, pp. 33–63.

——. ——. 2005. "Meanings of Citizenship in Latin America." Institute of Development Studies Working Paper 258. Brighton: Institute of Development Studies.

——. 2002. (ed.) *Sociedade civil e espaços públicos no Brasil*. São Paulo: Paz e Terra.

Dagnino, E., A. Olvera, and A. Panfichi, 2006. "Introducción: Para otra lectura de la disputa por la construcción democrática en América Latina," in Dagnino, E., A. Olvera, and A. Panfichi (eds.) *La Disputa por la Construcción Democrática en América Latina*. Mexico City: Fondo de Cultura Económica.

——. 2008. "Civic Driven Change and Political Projects," in A. Fowler and K. Bierkhart (eds.) *Civic Driven Change. Citizen's Imagination in Action*. The Hague: Institute of Social Studies, 27–49.

De La Maza, G. 2001. "Espacios Locales y desarrollo de ciudadanía." In *Programa Ciudadania y Gestión Local*, Santiago: Fundación Nacional para la Superación de la Pobreza Universidad de Chile.

Evers, T. 1983. "De costas para o estado, longe do parlamento. Os movimentos alternativos na Alemanha." *Novos Estudos CEBRAP*, 2(1): 25–39.

Fals Borda, O. 1996. "Grietas de la democracia. La participación popular en Colombia." *Análisis Político* 28: 65–77.

Fernandes, R. C. 1994. *Privado, porém público: o terceiro setor na América Latina*. Rio de Janeiro: Editora Relume Dumará.

Foweraker, J. 2001. "Grassroots Movements, Political Activism and Social Development in Latin America. A Comparison of Chile and Brazil." *Civil Society and Social Movements Programme*, Paper Number 4. Geneva: United Nations Research Institute for Social Development.

Franco, A. 1999. "A Reforma do estado e o terceiro setor," in Bresser-Pereira, L.C., Wilheim, J. and L. Sola (eds.) *Sociedade e Estado em transformação*. São Paulo: Editora da UNESP.

García-Guadilla, M. P., A. Mallén, and M. Guillén. 2004. "The Multiples Faces Of Venezuelan Civil Society: Politization and Its Impact on Democratization." Paper delivered at the Congress of the Latin American Studies Association, Las Vegas, Nevada, October 7–9.

Genro, T. 1995. "Reforma do Estado e democratização do poder local," in Villas Boas, R. and V. S. Telles (eds.) *Poder local, participação popular e construção da cidadania. Revista do Fórum Nacional de Participação Popular* (1) 1.

Gurza Lavalle, A., P. Houtzager, and G. Castello, 2005. "In Whose Name?. Political representation and civil organization in Brazil." Brighton, UK:Institute of Development Studies: Working Papers 249.

Habermas, J. 1986. "The New Obscurity," in J. Habermas (ed.) *The New Conservatism*, Cambridge, Mass.: MIT Press.

Hevia, F. 2006. "Participación ciudadana institucionalizada: análisis de los marcos legales de la participación en América Latina", in E. Dagnino, A. Olvera and A. Panfichi, op. cit.

Krischke, P., and Scherer-Warren, I. (eds.) 1987. *Movimentos sociais: Uma revolução no cotidiano?* São Paulo: Brasiliense.

Latin American Perspectives. 2003. *Special Issue on Citizenship*. vol. 30(2).

McGann, J., and M. Johnstone. 2006. "The Power Shift and the NGO Credibility Crisis." *The International Journal for Non-Profit Law vol.* 8 (2): 65–77.

Murillo, G., and L. Pizano, 2003. "Deliberación y Construcción de Ciudadanía. Una apuesta a la progresión democrática a comienzos de nuevo milenio." Bogotá: Univ. de los Andes.

O'Donnell, G., and P. C. Schmitter (eds.) 1986. *Transitions from Authoritarian Rule: Tentative Conclusions about Uncertain Democracies*. Baltimore: Johns Hopkins University Press.

Oliveira, F. 1993. "Quanto melhor, melhor: o acordo das montadoras." *Novos Estudos Cebrap* 36: 3–7.

Olvera, A. J. 1996. (ed.) 1999. *La sociedad civil. De la teoría a la realidad*. Mexico City: El Colegio de Mexico.

———. (ed.) 2003. *Sociedad civil, gobernabilidad y democratización en América Latina: México*. Mexico City: Fondo de Cultura Económica.

Panfichi, A. (ed.) 2002. *Sociedad civil, gobernabilidad y democratización en América Latina: Andes y Cono Sur*. Mexico City: Fondo de Cultura Económica.

Salamon, L., and S. Sokolowski. 2004. *Global Civil Society: Dimensions of the Nonprofit Sector*, vol. 2. West Hartford, Conn. : Kumarian Press.

Santos, B. S. 1998. "Participatory Budgeting in Porto Alegre: Toward a Redistributive Democracy." *Politics & Society* 26(4): 461–510.

Santos, B. S., and L. Avritzer. 2002. "Para Ampliar o cânone democrático," in Santos, B. S. (ed.) *Democratizar a democracia. Os caminhos da democracia participativa*. Rio de Janeiro: Civilização Brasileira.

Santos, W. G. 1993. *Razões da Desordem*. Rio de Janeiro: Rocco.

Scherer-Warren, I. et al. 1998. *O Novo Associativismo Brasileiro*. Final report to the Ford Foundation, Rio de Janeiro office.

Tatagiba, L. 2002. "Os Conselhos Gestores e a democratização das Políticas Públicas no Brasil," in Dagnino, E. (ed.) *Sociedade civil e espaços públicos no Brasil*, São Paulo: Paz e Terra.

Teixeira, A. C. 2003. *Identidades em construção: Organizações não-governamentais no processo brasileiro de democratização*. São Paulo: Annablume.

Zapata, Francisco. 1999. "Presentación," in Olvera, A. J. (ed.) *La sociedad civil. De la teoría a la realidad*. Mexico City: El Colegio de Mexico.

Ziccardi, A., ed., 2004. *Participación ciudadana y políticas sociales en el ámbito local*. Mexico City: Universidad Autonoma de Mexico.

CHAPTER 11

....

CIVIL SOCIETY IN POST-COMMUNIST EUROPE

....

MARC MORJÉ HOWARD

Post-communist Europe presents a deep irony for scholars of civil society. On the one hand, the region is the source of the revitalization of the term "civil society" itself. Indeed, had it not been for Solidarnosc, the Polish opposition movement that mobilized ten million people, and the subsequent "people's revolutions" throughout Eastern Europe and some of the former Soviet Union, the term civil society would almost certainly not have become so widely used by academics or policy makers. On the other hand, post-communist Europe is an area of the democratic world where contemporary civil society is particularly weak. A closer look at the region shows that shortly after the "revolutionary" moment had passed, people left the streets and their civic organizations, leaving their societies largely passive and depoliticized.

Although historical precedents are important for understanding most social phenomena, they are vital for making sense of civil society in post-communist Europe. One simply cannot understand why so few post-communist citizens participate in the public sphere without grappling with the communist past and its combination with the post-communist present. This chapter takes a historical approach to civil society in the post-communist region, showing how the social legacies of communism have adapted and persisted, and how they may even have been reinforced by post-communist developments and experiences. It also addresses the growing differences across the region between countries that are democratic and those that are increasingly authoritarian, and also between countries that have now joined the European Union and those that remain firmly on the outside. The chapter then raises a broader set of questions about the applicability of the concept of civil society to nondemocratic countries and contexts. It makes the argument that communist and post-communist experiences with civil society show the need to distinguish between *types* of civil society—in particular "oppositional" and "democratic" forms—since otherwise it would make little sense for the strong civil society of the late communist era to have dissipated so quickly after the onset of democratization. Finally, the chapter concludes by assessing the implications of the weakness of post-communist civil society for democracy in the region. It argues that while the weakness of civil society certainly does not portend democracy's demise, it does suggest that post-communist democracy will remain unsettled and somewhat troubled in the foreseeable future.

1. Post-Communist Civil Society in Comparative Perspective

In order to be able to evaluate the strength and quality of civil society in any given region, it is helpful—if not crucial—to begin with a larger comparative perspective. In *The Weakness of Civil Society in Post-Communist Europe* (Howard 2003), I provide an empirical baseline that shows that post-communist citizens have extremely low levels of membership and participation in voluntary organizations. Moreover, when compared to other regions and regime types in the world, variations among post-communist countries are relatively small. Within post-communist Europe, the similarity in levels of organizational membership is especially striking in light of the wide political, economic, and cultural differences that exist between countries.

The drawback of a cross-national measure of civil society is that it focuses on a thin definition and conceptualization of the concept, namely organizational membership. While this approach can be complemented by case studies that go into greater depth, the broad approach nonetheless yields important comparative findings. For example, an analysis of the thirty-one democratic and democratizing countries included in the 1995–97 World Values Survey (WVS) shows that post-communist countries have significantly lower levels of membership and participation than older democracies and post-authoritarian countries, and that these levels actually declined from 1990–91 to 1995–97 (Howard 2003, 62–73). In fact, the WVS shows that citizens in post-communist countries belong to an average of 0.91 organizations per person, exactly half of the 1.82 organizational memberships per person in post-authoritarian countries, and much less than the 2.39 in older democracies (Howard 2003, 80). Moreover, organizational membership in post-communist Europe was lower than in post-authoritarian countries across eight of the nine types of organization that were included in the WVS (the exception being labor unions, which represent a special case in the communist and post-communist context).

Subsequent surveys and studies have not contradicted this basic pattern. An analysis of the next wave of the WVS, conducted in 1999–2003, confirms the same significant distinction between post-communist countries and other regions and prior regime types (Valkov 2009). Moreover, a more rigorous regression analysis that controls for other possible alternative variables—including economic, political-institutional, and "civilizational" factors, as well as several individual-level variables that are central to the literature on political participation and civil society—shows that a country's prior regime type (and in particular a prior communist experience) is the most significant and powerful variable for explaining organizational membership (Howard 2003, 81–90). These findings indicate the need for more in-depth consideration of the specific elements of that prior communist experience, in order to explain *why* post-communist countries have relatively low levels of organizational membership in comparison to older democracies and post-authoritarian countries. In short, in order to understand the common weakness of post-communist civil society, we need to take into consideration the common elements of the communist experience and its enduring legacy.

2. THE TRANSFORMATIVE IMPACT OF COMMUNIST INSTITUTIONS

Before turning to the contemporary period, it is critical to consider the transformative impact of the communist institutional system, which had a significant, decisive, and in many ways homogenizing effect on societies throughout the region. Prior to the establishment of the communist system—after World War I in Russia and in the early post-World War II period in Eastern Europe—the region consisted of a very diverse group of countries. In addition to having different religious faiths, having belonged to different historical empires, and having fought on different sides in both world wars, they had vastly different levels of industrialization and economic development, and different political traditions. By the 1950s, however, the communist leadership—enforced by the ruthless policies of "Moscow Center"—had succeeded in imposing and enforcing "replica regimes" that were characterized by the same institutional and ideological mechanisms throughout the Soviet bloc (Jowitt 1992). Although the communists certainly incorporated and reinforced pre-existing historical tendencies, over the next thirty years the "party of a new type" also succeeded in creating a "society of a new type."

Ken Jowitt, one of the most astute and original scholars in the field of comparative communism, has argued convincingly that the distinguishing feature of what he calls "Leninist" regimes was the concept of "charismatic impersonalism." In an essay written as far back as 1978 and reprinted in Jowitt (1992), he argued that just like the liberal societies of the West, communist societies were based on impersonal institutions and norms, but their central and defining feature was the existence of the Communist Party as the locus and core of all social organization, whose authority was transcendent, unquestioned, and charismatic. Although the extent of that authority did vary somewhat across the communist bloc, and it diminished slightly over the decades of communist rule, the institutional charisma of the Communist Party remained a defining feature that distinguished Soviet-type regimes from other forms of nondemocratic rule.

Valerie Bunce (1999, 21–25) also provides a very useful synthesis of the various elements of the communist experience, which she refers to as having been "homogenizing," by focusing on four central factors: 1) "the ideological mission of the ruling elite," 2) "the construction...of a conjoined economic and political monopoly that rested in the hands of the Communist Party," 3) "the fusion of not just the polity and the economy, but also the party and the state," and 4) "the extraordinary institutional penetration of the state." All four of these features existed in communist systems across the Soviet Union and Eastern Europe, with the partial exception of the more pluralist Yugoslavia and, to a lesser extent, Poland and Hungary. The fourth of Bunce's elements is the most important for understanding contemporary post-communist civil society, because it involves the party-state's attempt at complete penetration, surveillance, and control of all aspects of society. Unlike authoritarian regimes, which generally allow for the existence of independent social activities that are not directly threatening to the state (Linz and Stepan 1996), the party prevented "the existence of any associational life, political organizations, or social movements that existed separate from the party-state institutional web. As a consequence, mass publics were rendered dependent on the party-state for jobs, income, consumer goods, education, housing, health care, and social and geographic mobility" (Bunce 1999, 24).

Even further, the party actually attempted to supplant and supersede the very need for independent social activity by creating a dense institutional web of groups and organizations in which membership and participation were generally mandatory or coerced. Very few people could avoid this party-state control of the public sphere, since almost every child had to join the official youth organization, and almost every working adult belonged to the official trade union and to other mass organizations. Bunce (1999, 28) provides an evocative description of the "remarkably uniform set of experiences" of communist citizens: "Whether citizens engaged in political, economic, social, or cultural activities, they were controlled in what they could do by the party. Thus, the party did not just orchestrate elite recruitment, voting, attendance at rallies, and the content of the mass media. It also functioned in the economy as the only employer, the only defender of workers' rights (through party-controlled unions), the only setter of production norms, and the only allocator of vacation time (while being the only builder and maintainer of vacation retreats). At the same time, the party allocated all goods and set all prices. Finally, it was the party (sometimes through enterprises) that was the sole distributor of housing, education, health care, transportation, and opportunities for leisure-time activities."

In short, the Communist Party sought to monitor and control virtually every aspect of economic, political, and even social life, and this feature distinguished communism from other non-democratic authoritarian regimes. Another crucial element of the communist experience involves the peculiar social consequences of centralized economic planning. In an economic system with chronic shortages, only a few privileged people—usually elite members of the Communist Party who went shopping at special stores that had a full supply of western goods—could avoid the long lines, bland choices, and frequently missing necessities of daily life, from salt to toilet paper. The economic situation combined with Communist Party control of the public sphere in a mutually reinforcing relationship that constricted and sometimes reshaped the range of possibilities for thought and action. In other words, since the public sphere was so politicized, controlled, and monitored, and since valued goods and services were hard to acquire without connections or help, people developed common patterns of adaptive behavior.

The central characteristic of these social and behavioral patterns was the distinction between the public and private realms (Shlapentokh 1989; Kharkhordin 1999). As Jowitt (1992, 287) writes, restating his own argument from almost twenty years earlier, "the Leninist experience in Eastern Europe…reinforced the exclusive distinction and dichotomic antagonism between the official and private realms." Bunce (1999, 30) adds that "Homogenization also encouraged individuals within socialist systems to divide their personalities into a public and conformist self, on the one hand, and a private and more rebellious self on the other—what was referred to in the East German setting as a *Nischengesellschaft*, or niche society." With a public sphere that was entirely controlled by the Communist Party and its corollary organizational apparatus (including the secret police, trade unions, and many mass membership organizations), most communist citizens developed a cautious relationship to public and formal activities—recall Václav Havel's (1985, 27–29) famous example of the greengrocer who posts the slogan "Workers of the World, Unite!" in his shop in order to show that "I am obedient and therefore have the right to be left in peace."

Private relations, in contrast, became even more vibrant and meaningful, since people could only speak openly in front of others they knew and trusted, and also because connections took on an important role in the shortage economy, where people had to rely on their family, friends, and acquaintances in order to get things done, rather than going through official channels (Wedel 1986; Ledeneva 1998).

To summarize, the communist institutions that were established after 1917 in the Soviet Union and after World War II in Eastern Europe managed to reconfigure and homogenize an otherwise diverse set of peoples, even if not as originally intended. The result of the shortage economy and the Communist Party's ruthless control of the public sphere was that citizens throughout communist Europe developed adaptive mechanisms of behavior, centered on private networks, which augmented the sharp distinction between the public and private spheres.

3. The Social Legacy of Communism and Its Impact on Post-Communist Civil Society

One might have thought that the disappearance of the communist system and its mass organizations would lead to an outpouring of public participation in new organizations that were truly voluntary and autonomous. This is indeed what many analysts expected, especially following the remarkable spontaneous mobilizations that brought about communism's collapse between 1989 and 1991 (see, for example, Di Palma 1991 and Rau 1991). But, as it turns out, these new opportunities have *not* brought about an increase in participation.

The low levels of participation in civil society organizations in contemporary post-communist Europe can best be understood by taking into account the common elements of the communist experience, as well as the events since the collapse of that system. In particular, three important factors are common to the wide array of societies in post-communist Europe: 1) the legacy of mistrust of communist organizations; 2) the persistence of friendship networks; and 3) post-communist disappointment. Taken together, these three factors help to explain the lasting weakness of civil society in the region.

a. Mistrust of Organizations

As discussed above, one of the central features that distinguished communism from authoritarianism was the former's extensive repression of autonomous pluralism. Unlike authoritarian regimes, however, which tolerated nonstate activities so long as they did not threaten the state or the military, communist regimes not only attempted to eliminate any form of independent group activity but they also supplanted it with an intricately organized system of state-controlled organizations, in which participation was often mandatory. As a result, one of the most striking features of state-socialist societies was the clear distinction between formal institutions and informal behaviors that people made use of in their everyday lives. Every communist country was intricately organized with an array of formal organizations in almost the same institutional forms, including youth groups, the Communist Party, trade unions, cultural federations, peasant and worker groups, women's groups, and many others, as well as the less politicized (but still state-controlled) groups and organizations that ranged from sports clubs to book lover's clubs. Most people were members of multiple organizations, but membership itself was often mandatory, coerced, or used for instrumental purposes. In other words—to an increasing degree over the lifespan of communist regimes, as the party lost the legitimacy and popular enthusiasm that it had generated in its earlier stages—people often joined because they had to, because they were told that they could face negative consequences if they did not join, or because joining and participating improved their career chances. Only in the case of less politicized associations such as book clubs and sports clubs did people join for less coercive or instrumental reasons.

When they participated in quasi-mandatory organizations, most people did very little, aside from paying their small annual dues (which were usually deducted automatically from their salaries), attending a few compulsory meetings, and occasionally receiving some special benefits like vacation packages from the official trade union. Membership was mainly based on obligation, obedience, and external conformity, rather than on internal and voluntary initiatives. Due to this essentially negative experience with state-run organizations during the communist period, majorities of citizens throughout post-communist Europe continue to have a common sense of mistrust of organizations today.

As a direct legacy of the communist experience, most people in post-communist countries still therefore strongly mistrust and avoid any kind of formal organizations, even in newly free and democratic settings. Instead of drawing a clear distinction between the voluntary associations of today and the mass organizations of the communist past, most post-communist citizens view and evaluate organizations with a certain sense of continuity. The distinction they make is that previously they were essentially forced to join, while today they are free to choose *not* to join and *not* to participate.

b. The Persistence of Friendship Networks

The flip side of the public experience of communism—where membership in state-controlled organizations was more of a formality, born out of obligation and expediency rather than being deeply felt—was that relationships in the private sphere were extremely meaningful and genuine. Broadly speaking, there were two main reasons for this. First, because the formal and public sphere was highly politicized and also tightly controlled, people could only express themselves openly within close circles of trusted friends and family. Second, because of the shortage of available goods to buy, personal and social *connections* played an essential role in communist societies, whether used to obtain spare parts for fixing a car, or finding products that were rarely available in stores.

These two reasons also correspond to two different, although sometimes overlapping, *types* of private networks that existed in communist societies. The first encompassed how people socialized and with whom they spent their free time, and the second involved a more instrumental use of connections to acquire goods and services, and to get ahead in general (Ledeneva 1998). The first type of networks consisted primarily of a small number of close and trusted friends and family members, whereas the second included many distant acquaintances or people with whom one only interacted for the purpose of acquiring or receiving something in return. These two types of networks overlapped to the extent that close friends and family also helped each other instrumentally, but only rarely did instrumental acquaintances enter the small and trusted circle of close friends.

Today, long after the collapse of the system that had created and sustained this vibrant private sphere, networks of close friends and family remain extremely prominent and important throughout the post-communist region. These networks of instrumental connections, however, have changed to varying degrees across post-communist countries, since the market economy can eliminate the need to acquire goods and services through informal channels. Overall, however, unlike in many Western societies—where voluntary organizations have become a central part of social and political culture, and where people join organizations in order to meet new people and to expand their horizons through public activities—in post-communist societies, many people are still extremely invested in their own private circles. They simply feel no need, much less desire, to join and participate in organizations when they feel that, socially, they already have everything that they could need or want.

c. Post-Communist Disappointment

The third reason that helps to explain the particularly low levels of public participation in post-communist Europe is the widespread disappointment, and for some even disillusionment, with political and economic developments since the collapse of the state-socialist system. Although it is most pronounced among those people who were personally involved in the movements leading to the creation of a new institutional order, this third factor applies to the wider population as well. For most people throughout the former Soviet bloc, the years 1989–91 represent a unique, momentous, and fascinating time in their lives, when their world was changing rapidly and dramatically. Although they had many fears and uncertainties about where the changes would lead them, most people experienced at least a brief moment of genuine excitement, hope, and idealism during those times of rapid transformation. Moreover, they shared the belief that the end of Communist Party rule, the emergence of new democratic and market institutions, and at long last the freedom and right to speak freely, associate openly with others, and to travel beyond the "iron curtain," would change their lives for the better (Rose 1995).

In the years since those dramatic times, however, many post-communist citizens feel that they have been let down, perhaps even cheated, by the new system that quickly replaced the old one. Even though a vast majority in every post-communist country does not want to go back in time, the political and economic systems that have since taken root seem to have disappointed most people, who had hoped and believed that a new political and economic system would live up to their ideals. This sense of disappointment has only increased demobilization and withdrawal from public activities in the years since the collapse of communism.

Although this chapter has presented a rather homogeneous picture of post-communist civil society, there is also a great deal of—and perhaps growing—diversity within the region. Leaving aside the countries of Central Asia and the Caucasus, which do not fit into the geographic definition of post-communist Europe, there is a significant divide between countries that have been steadily democratizing since the demise of communism and those that have struggled with democracy (and in some cases have clearly become more authoritarian) over the past decade. This distinction was solidified and institutionalized in the enlargement process of the European Union (EU), which ten post-communist countries joined between 2004 and 2007. EU accession has not been a panacea for post-communist civil society. Nonetheless, there is clearly a greater need to distinguish between post-communist countries that have acceded and those that have not, even if the common social legacy of communism remains strong throughout the region.

4. CIVIL SOCIETY IN NONDEMOCRATIC CONTEXTS

An important question in the comparative study of civil society—one that is raised when considering the post-communist cases, both comparatively and historically —is whether civil society does (or can) exist in nondemocratic and/or nonwestern countries. There are a variety of possible answers to this question, spanning from a very narrow to a quite broad conceptualization of civil society. A narrow view posits that civil society derives from the particular theoretical tradition and practical historical experience of the West. According to this position, civil society refers specifically to the kinds of voluntary organizations that emerged from the American and West European models, and in some sense, civil society can only exist in societies that share this historical background. In other words, civil society is viewed as an inherently western concept that arose out of a distinct historical experience, giving it a decidedly ethnocentric bias.

In contrast, a broad view of civil society—of the type that is generally stressed by anthropologists—argues that its conceptualization and measurement should be expanded from its narrow focus on voluntary organizations in democracies, so that it can treat all forms of social organization and practices as different manifestations of the same general phenomenon. According to this perspective, each country has its own civil society, and any cross-national variation lies in the form that civil society takes, rather than in its level or strength.

A third approach occupies the middle ground between these two positions. According to this view, civil society is not a universal concept that exists everywhere, but it does take shape in many different guises. Therefore, the original definition and empirical manifestation of civil society should not be diluted and/or stretched in order to fit contexts that are vastly different, since this may result in the mischaracterization of some of the most interesting and unique forms of political and social action in many countries by forcing them into the "civil society" mold. At the same time, however, unlike in the first and narrow view, this approach does not restrict the applicable empirical terrain to countries that are culturally or historically "western." There is an actual substantive and practical basis for the study of civil society in nonwestern countries, even while still viewing it as a specifically western concept, since many of these societies have attempted over the past few decades to westernize and democratize. From this perspective, *regime type* is the crucial distinction, and what one might call "classical" civil society can only really exist within countries that have democratic institutions (regardless of their "western-ness"). This is not to say, however, that countries must be advanced liberal democracies in order for civil society to exist, but rather that they should meet the basic minimal criteria of procedural democracy. In other words, civil society is a legitimate, appropriate, and important object of exploration and analysis within countries that can be considered electoral democracies. But to extend the concept beyond those limits to various types of authoritarian regimes may risk lumping together too many different phenomena and forms of organization under one already beleaguered set of ideas.

This conclusion leads to an obvious rebuttal: what about Eastern Europe? Is it not true that civil society helped to lead to the collapse of communism? In some sense, the answer has to be "yes," especially since events in Eastern Europe (and Poland in particular) led to the rebirth and widespread popularization of the term "civil society" itself. But at the same time, the East European example shows precisely why it is so important to distinguish between civil society in democratic regimes and civil society in other types of nondemocratic regimes, for in just a few short years—as discussed above—the countries of post-communist Europe went from being the midwife of the term to having some of the least participatory civil societies in the world. In other words, the *oppositional* civil society of the late 1980s was clearly very different from the *democratic* civil society of today. This important distinction suggests that scholars should avoid the temptation of lumping different kinds of civil society together, and at the very least, that they should take care to develop subcategories such as these in order to capture the distinctive dynamics that occur in different types of countries.

This debate is by no means resolved. As the comparative study of civil society continues to grow and expand (see, for example, Heinrich and Fioramonti 2007), and as more scholars develop empirical indices to measure the strength of both civil society and democracy, the concept of civil society will continue to be applied to a wide array of countries and contexts—perhaps with mixed results for those concerned with systematic and meaningful comparisons.

5. Conclusion: Implications for Post-Communist Democracy

The consistently low levels of participation in civil society organizations that mark out large parts of post-communist Europe yield a host of different—and often emotionally charged—interpretations about the prospects for democracy in the region. On the one hand, the lack of engagement and participation by ordinary citizens can be viewed as indicative of the hollow, procedural, and formalistic character of post-communist democracy. Does democracy still mean "rule by the people" if "the people" choose not to participate in "ruling"? One could even argue that, with civic organizations lacking the active support of the population, such a hollow democracy will remain at risk of being toppled by hostile forces, whether based on nondemocratic historical traditions or on a new antidemocratic ideology.

On the other hand, a more optimistic interpretation would suggest that the absence of a vibrant civil society poses no obstacle to democracy and democratic stability. Indeed, political participation and trust in government are supposedly in decline throughout much of the world, as people withdraw from public activities in increasingly large numbers. Perhaps the post-communist present, having skipped or bypassed the "stage" of an active participatory democracy, actually resembles the democratic future of the rest of the world. Moreover, in terms of democratic stability, some argue that a strong and vibrant civil society can actually contribute to the breakdown of democracy (Berman 1997). If this is true, then democracy in post-communist Europe may actually be enhanced by the absence of citizen participation in voluntary organizations.

My own view of post-communist democracy differs from both these interpretations. Even if participation in voluntary organizations is declining in the older democracies, this does not mean that levels of organizational membership around the world are converging. More importantly, in terms of the breakdown or survival of democracy, I do not view post-communist democracy as doomed to collapse or failure, nor do I believe that the weakness of civil society is a good sign for the future of a healthy democracy. Instead, the weakness of civil society constitutes a distinctive element of post-communist democracy, a pattern that points to a qualitatively different relationship between citizens and the state, and one that may well persist throughout the region for at least several more decades.

REFERENCES

Berman, S. 1997. "Civil Society and the Collapse of the Weimar Republic." *World Politics* vol. 49: 401–29.

Bunce, V. 1999. *Subversive Institutions: The Design and the Destruction of Socialism and the State.* Cambridge: Cambridge University Press.

Di Palma, G. 1991. "Legitimation from the Top to Civil Society: Politico-Cultural Change in Eastern Europe." *World Politics* vol. 44/3: 49–80.

Havel, V. 1985. *The Power of the Powerless.* (ed. John Keane). Armonk, N.Y.: M.E. Sharpe.

Heinrich, V. Finn, and L. Fioramonti (eds). 2007. *CIVICUS Global Survey of the State of Civil Society.* 2 vols. West Hartford, Conn.: Kumarian Press.

Howard, M. M. 2003. *The Weakness of Civil Society in Post-Communist Europe.* New York: Cambridge University Press.

Jowitt, K. 1992. *New World Disorder: The Leninist Extinction*. Berkeley: University of California Press.

Kharkhordin, O. 1999. *The Collective and the Individual in Russia: A Study of Practices*. Berkeley: University of California Press.

Ledeneva, A. V. 1998. *Russia's Economy of Favours: Blat, Networking, and Informal Exchange*. Cambridge: Cambridge University Press.

Linz, J. J., and A. Stepan. 1996. *Problems of Democratic Transition and Consolidation: Southern Europe, South America, and Post-Communist Europe*. Baltimore: Johns Hopkins University Press.

Rau, Z. (ed). 1991. *The Reemergence of Civil Society in Eastern Europe and the Soviet Union*. Boulder: Westview Press.

Rose, R. 1995. "Freedom as a Fundamental Value." *International Social Science Journal* vol. 145: 454–71.

Shlapentokh, V. 1989. *Public and Private Life of the Soviet people: Changing Values in Post-Stalin Russia*. Oxford: Oxford University Press.

Valkov, N. 2009. "Membership in Voluntary Organizations and Democratic Performance: European Post-Communist Countries in Comparative Perspective." *Communist and Post-Communist Studies* vol. 42: 1–21.

Wedel, J. R. 1986. *The Private Poland*. New York: Facts on File.

CHAPTER 12

....

CIVIL SOCIETY IN THE MIDDLE EAST

....

EBERHARD KIENLE

IN the Middle East,[1] the fate of civil society has been closely tied to the political regimes in place and their transformation, or lack of it, over time, a fate crucially affected by the strong autocratic features that have characterized the exercise of state power in most of the region. The collapse of the anciens régimes in Tunisia and Egypt in early 2011, prompted by large-scale street protests initiated mainly by informally-organized young men and women, allowed people to associate without restrictions for the first time in decades. As a result, civil society organizations have grown in their visibility. However, other Arab regimes, and Iran, have so far managed to contain the effects of the "Arab spring" and remain largely authoritarian, in spite of regular but rigged elections and other forms of democratic "window dressing" (Schlumberger 2007; Azimi 2008). Turkey underwent progressive bouts of political change after World War II, and initiated a transition from authoritarian rule in the 1990s (Zürcher 2003). An independent state since 1948, Israel has been a democracy in the sense that its citizens are able to choose their rulers at regular intervals in free elections. Israel's Arab citizens are eligible and able to vote, though their liberties have been restricted in other domains. However, since the occupation of the West Bank, East Jerusalem, and Gaza in 1967, Israel has exercised de facto authority over a large Palestinian population that is excluded from the election of its Israeli rulers who moreover severely limit the jurisdiction of the Palestinian National Authority.

Coinciding with the end of the Cold War, the numerical growth of certain kinds of civil society organization (CSOs) in some authoritarian states of the Middle East seemed to reflect broader political changes that were captured by notions such as the "third wave" of democratization (Norton 1995/6; Huntington 1991). However, although ultimately related to transformations at a global scale, the "advent of civil society" in the Middle East was the direct result of government attempts to selectively redefine liberties in order to cushion external pressures for political liberalization and open up new funding opportunities that were technically reserved for nonstate actors. Under the political constraints prevailing in most Arab states and in Iran, the growth of CSOs since the 1980s has not significantly strengthened civil society as such, though conditions vary in line with the overall degree of political freedom that exists in each country. Even the more favorable situation in Turkey has not yet enabled civil society to assert itself as a major force. Only Israel, where strong CSOs predated the creation of the state, has continued to negotiate a range of accommodations with civil society similar to those found in North America and Europe. Roughly the same applies to the occupied Palestinian territories, where the Oslo accords of 1993 led to the broadly simultaneous growth of CSOs and political institutions. Attempts by Israel and its allies to contain and inflect statebuilding activities have strengthened civil society organizations in the territories even though military occupation has entailed a specific form of authoritarian rule.

Today the most hospitable grounds for CSOs are Israel, Turkey, Lebanon, the Palestinian Territories, Tunisia and Egypt. Morocco still compares favorably with Algeria, Jordan, and Syria; while in Iraq, CSOs are only just beginning to reemerge after decades of severe repression. In the Arab Peninsula, Kuwait is among the least restrictive countries and Saudi Arabia among the most. No CSOs are allowed to exist in Libya. Turkey counts several tens of thousands of CSOs, Egypt between 15,000 and 20,000, and Tunisia some 8,000, but such figures should not be confused with authentic measures of the strength or health of civil society.[2]

In most countries, CSOs continue to be heavily regimented and their independence is constrained by government interference. Overstepping the lines set by the state may result in the closure of CSOs, as happened in 2000 to the Ibn Khaldun Center in Cairo, for example. Most governments remain particularly hostile to organizations that promote human, civil, and political rights, while understanding the utility of those that promote human development activities in a period marked out by calls for the retreat of the state, and corresponding changes in international donor policies. Unsurprisingly, regional and national human development reports produced by the United Nations Development Program (UNDP) in cooperation with Arab governments mainly stress the development-related activities of CSOs. However, unlike their counterparts elsewhere, such CSOs have been unable to influence relations between state and society or among different social groups in any substantial way.[3]

Above and beyond the deleterious effects of authoritarianism, the weakness of civil society in most of the Middle East reflects the broad absence of the social and political transformations that were associated with the rise of capitalism and the industrial revolution as they unfolded in the global North from the eighteenth century onwards. Consonant with forms of social organization that are typical of peripheral capitalism, strong "imagined communities" based on family, religion, and other particularistic identities continue to govern the lives of individuals and to aggregate their interests. The societal divisions that ensue exacerbate the search for legitimacy, national identity, and independence from foreign domination by contested rulers and their attempts to dominate society by destroying all competing power centres.[4] In Israel the increasing importance of "imagined communities" other than the nation remains balanced by the living legacy of social transformations that historically affected Europeans, and therefore Jewish Europeans, whose modes of social organization strongly influenced Israeli civil society and the Israeli state.

These generally unfavorable conditions should not, however, obscure the many attempts by Middle Easterners to establish CSOs and similar organizations which date back to the nineteenth century or even earlier. Some of these attempts were highly successful, at least so long as generally difficult political conditions did not become entirely hostile. No less importantly, they served as precedents for later initiatives, thus establishing local traditions of collective action and voluntary association that predate the civil society enthusiasms of the late twentieth and early twenty-first centuries. Against numerous odds, individuals of all religious backgrounds have participated in these attempts, thus invalidating culturalist claims that civil society has no place in Islam (Gellner 1996; Lewis 1994).

1. The History of Civil Society in the Middle East

In many parts of the Middle East, CSOs and less formal voluntary associations began to be established well before the 1980s and 1990s. Some were based on religious forms of philanthropy and charitable giving such as the Islamic *waqf*, and others were secular in nature. Social networks and trade associations, for example, shaped urban life at least from the Middle Ages onwards (Raymond 1985; Massignon 1920). In the latter part of the nineteenth century, associations concerned with the equivalent of today's human development issues were created in the Ottoman Empire and Qajar Iran, alongside many other informal circles and networks. Inspired by Enlightenment ideas as well as their local critics these associations aimed at reforming religion, education, health services, gender attitudes, and society at large. Most operated within established religious boundaries, sometimes merely formalizing existing charitable initiatives by Muslims or representatives of other faiths. However, by the early years of the twentieth century, cross-religious and secular associations had developed in countries like Lebanon and Egypt. Most of the reforms they proposed were at least implicitly political since they questioned existing power relations, including arrangements through which Europeans dominated much of the Middle East. As such they were also promoted by secret societies and other nationalist groupings that emerged among the élites of the Ottoman Empire and at the eve of the 1906 constitutional revolution in Iran (Azimi 2008; Hourani 1983; Karam 2006; Ben Néfissa 1991).

In a number of Arab countries, membership-based professional syndicates were formed over the first half of the twentieth century, with the lawyers' syndicate (or bar association) in Egypt being registered as early as 1912. Established by law, they frequently managed to emancipate themselves from government tutelage, protect the interests of their members, and play an important role in regulating the activities of professions as diverse as engineers, physicians, accountants, and actors. Largely self-governing chambers of commerce and employers' associations catered to the needs of capital owners. Simultaneously, trade unions became active defenders of workers' rights. In Egypt, the Federation of Trade Unions was founded in 1921 and by the 1940s, some 170 unions were active in the country. In Syria the first trade union of sorts was set up by textile workers in 1925, to be followed by other more or less durable organizations in the 1930s and thereafter. In the 1950s the Union Marocaine du Travail (UMT) counted more than 570,000 members, thus constituting the largest of several tens of thousands of associations in the country at the time. The 1920s and 1930s also saw the formation of new organizations like the Muslim Brotherhood in Egypt (and beyond) and the (mainly Maronite Christian) Phalanges in Lebanon that catered to the social needs and demands of those lower-middle-class constituencies that defined themselves in religious terms. Seeking to establish political communities consonant with their social and religious values, these organizations frequently participated in power struggles and at times suffered from severe repression.

In the 1950s and 1960s, coups and revolutions in Egypt, Syria, Iraq, Yemen, Libya, and Algeria put an end to the colonial regimes, monarchies, and parliamentary republics that were dominated by foreigners, royal families, and other owners of land and capital. The so-called socialist regimes that replaced them dissolved existing CSOs or transformed them into corporatist tools to weaken potential opposition and control society. The consolidation of the Jordanian and Moroccan monarchies in the 1960s and 1970s had similar debilitating effects. Nevertheless, some constituencies managed to maintain a considerable degree of independence as illustrated by the Egyptian judges who in the late 1960s confronted President Nasser, or the Damascus Chamber of Commerce which helped the Syrian regime to overcome a major standoff with the Islamist opposition in the 1980s. Sufi orders also continued to exist and operate throughout this period. In some countries selective economic liberalization and political decompression from the 1970s onwards allowed various social forces to regroup and express themselves (Longuenesse 2007; Goldberg 1996; Beinin/Lockman 1988; Beinin 2010; Ashford 1961; Berger 1970; Blanchi 1989; Lawson 1982).

Following a different trajectory, Turkey eased restrictions on CSOs and trade unions after 1945, when political pluralism replaced single party rule. Trade unions and other CSOs were dissolved after the coup of 1980, but following years of repression, issue-based organizations came to the fore from the 1990s onwards (Zürcher 2003). In Iran, relatively formal ways to defend collective interests date back to the eve of the constitutional revolution. Printers established a union in 1906, and by 1944 the Central Council of United Trade Unions affiliated to the Communist Tudeh Party claimed as many as 400,000 members (Kazemi 1980). Increasing authoritarianism, in particular after the oil boom of 1973, entailed the growing domination of CSOs by the monarchy and then the Islamic Republic. Nonetheless, CSOs were active in the immediate aftermath of the 1979 revolution and regained some strength under Presidents Rafsanjani and Khatami who—following the Iran-Iraq war—sought a leaner state and the support of the middle classes (Azimi 2008).

Preceded by the voluntary organizations of the *Yishuv* set up by Jewish settlers under the Ottoman Empire and the British mandate, the state of Israel selectively incorporated some such organizations and established a division of labor with others. These arrangements included international NGOs such as the World Zionist Organization and the Jewish Agency for Israel that supported CSOs inside the country. Complex arrangements such as those established with the major trade union, the Histadrut, often blurred the boundaries between the state and civil society. Over time, the partial retreat of the state, funding from abroad, and differences over political choices (including the future of the Palestinian territories) strengthened CSOs in Israel. As in other countries, global developments increasingly favored issue-based approaches to social change (Horrowitz and Lissak 1978; Kimmerling 1989; Wolffsohn 1987).

The early emergence of CSOs in the Middle East does not signify the early emergence of a fully fledged civil society. In most places and periods, CSOs have had to cope with the various political restrictions referred to above, which have reduced their broader impact. They have also primarily furthered causes championed by numerical minorities such as the wealthy, the educated, organized labor, and activists. Challenging some definitions of civil society, a fair number have also played an active part in national and other political struggles, while others have represented the concerns of nonvoluntary "imagined communities" based on language or religion rather than citizenship. Hence, the organizational forms in which civil society manifests itself in most of the contemporary Middle East illustrate these continued weaknesses.

2. THE FORMS OF CIVIL SOCIETY IN THE MIDDLE EAST

History, politics, and the broader social context have come together to produce a range of civil society "ecosystems" in which different associational forms are layered one on top of the other. In their details these ecosystems vary across countries, but in nearly all cases they are fragile and incomplete. In most Arab countries and Iran, political restrictions limit larger, membership-based CSOs to professional syndicates, sports clubs, and development or community-based associations that seek to supplement inadequate government services. Except in Morocco, Lebanon, and Turkey, trade unions have been largely controlled by the state, but even in these countries some unions are close to the state or to political parties. There are no unions at all in Saudi Arabia. In Tunisia, unions partly escaped state control; in Egypt, fledgling, independent unions re-emerged in 2009. In both countries organized labor played a role in the 2010–11 "Arab Spring" protests.

In the Arab states and Iran, employers' organizations and chambers of commerce also frequently lack independence. Religious organizations with a political agenda such as the Muslim Brothers often have to operate in a semiclandestine manner, which reduces their active membership far below the numbers of sympathizers they have among the public. Membership in human rights and other advocacy organizations is also limited for political reasons. Exceptions are Turkey and now Tunisia and Egypt. Advocates of political reform sometimes prefer to register as companies to avoid restrictive legislation governing CSOs. Many CSOs consist of a relatively small number of committed activists who are morally supported by a board of public figures. Most activists hail from the educated and middle classes, or from specific social backgrounds such as organized labor. A more recent form of CSOs are the family-based philanthropic foundations that have become active in charitable work, health, and education in some countries, thus broadening the scope of activities carried out by the older *waqfs* or religious endowments (Peters and Deguilhem 2002; Ibrahim and Sherif 2008; Guazzone and Pioppi 2009; Norton 1995/6).[5]

The capacities of most CSOs in the Middle East are weak, although there are notable exceptions such as the Coptic Evangelical Organization for Social Services in Egypt and the Lebanese Union of the Physically Handicapped. Weak capacities reflect political restrictions on CSO development, but they also stem from patrimonial patterns of organizational governance. Though part and parcel of prevailing forms of social organization, these patterns are in turn reinforced by political repression, because CSO staff fear manipulation and subversion by regime supporters, and therefore avoid delegating responsibilities to others. In terms of their structure, organization, and governance, most CSOs are mere homonyms of their counterparts in the global North (Khallaf/Tür 2008).

In the broader sense, contemporary CSOs in the Middle East also include countless informal associations such as savings clubs that have been established in neighborhoods and workplaces. In the Arab Peninsula and Iran, people in search of status and influence often open their homes to *diwaniyyas* or *dowres* in which (mainly male) publics debate issues of common interest (Miller 1969; Tétreault 2000; Dazi-Héni 2005). Frequently, bonds based on family, religion, language, neighborhood, or professional identities are mobilized for collective action in line with interests and "opportunity structures" that range from lightly coordinated strategies of "quiet encroachment" to petitions, sit-ins, demonstrations, and strikes (Tarrow 1994).

The traditions of industrial action referred to above have often been interrupted by periods of political repression in which only small, clandestine groups of workers remained active. However, in some countries recent economic reforms have led to increasing unrest; in Egypt, for instance, some 1.5 million workers have gone out on strike since 2001 (Beinin 2010). Over the last decade or so, mobile phones, blogs, and electronic mail have further enabled people to act in concert, particularly under conditions of repression, and social media played an important part in the protests that culminated in the 2009 uprising in Iran and the "Arab spring" of 2010–11. Nonetheless, in the face of internet infiltration by the police, the efficacy of these technologies depended on elaborate modes of decentralized coordination by highly flexible, mostly young, protesters. Political repression continues to push many people to develop individual coping strategies rather than to coordinate activities collectively (Bayat 1997; Bennani-Chraïbi/Fillieule 2003; Zubaida 2008; Seib 2007).

Restrictions on political parties sometimes prompt opponents to act under the label of CSOs. In the 1980s and 1990s, the Muslim Brothers in Egypt, for example, sought to instrumentalize professional syndicates. Conversely, toothless opposition parties may be considered CSOs since they are effectively prevented from coming to power. Finally, authoritarian rulers, their friends, and family members have established a number of "royal" or "governmental NGOs" that benefit from official protection and attempt to crowd out other CSOs working in the same arenas (Kienle 2000; Schlumberger 2007; Hawthorne 2004). The defining impact that authoritarian rule and social fragmentation have had on the forms of civil society in the Middle East is highlighted by a comparison with the situation in Israel, where the polyarchic nature of the state and its social foundations has shaped CSOs in ways similar to those in the global North, despite the fact that the history of state-building, socialist, and cooperative traditions as embodied in the *kibbutzim* and *moshavim*, and external funding, continue to account for important specificities (Wolffsohn 1987; Laskier 2008).

3. THE NORMS OF CIVIL SOCIETY IN THE MIDDLE EAST

Subject to a history of authoritarian government and the continuation of so many political restrictions, civil society in the Middle East is often considered as a force that—almost by definition—opposes authoritarianism and works towards the liberal, democratic transformation of states and societies. However, the diversity of CSOs in terms of their forms, traditions, objectives, and positions with regard to ruling regimes and religion precludes any homogeneity in terms of the norms and values they publicly embrace.

In the Arab states, Turkey, and Iran, most CSOs that focus on human development continue to conceive of themselves as members of educated, modernizing elites that are fighting ignorance and backward traditions. More often than not their development strategies are built around the state and reveal a preference for top-down decision making. In the Arab states, moreover, they remain inspired by the largely egalitarian ethos of the socialist revolutions of the 1950s and 1960s. At the same time, these organizations grapple with the constraints imposed by international donors who increasingly advocate neoliberal values such as small government, market-based mechanisms of service delivery, and the privatization of risks and responsibilities. Foreign funding has become a key factor in determining CSO activities and the values that underpin them. CSOs in Iran cannot accept Western funding but are free to embrace globalized values such as those of economic liberalism, or at least those elements that the regime considers consistent with Islam.

Across the Middle East, private-sector sponsored research organizations such as the Egyptian Center for Economic Studies, and private-sector lobbies such as the Association of Turkish Industrialists and Businessmen, openly push for the neoliberal transformation of labor laws, welfare regimes, and education. Frequently these voices are close to authoritarian regimes which have increasingly allied themselves with business circles even when they defend egalitarian values rhetorically. On the other hand, organizations specializing in human rights and political reform tend to emphasize the values of political rather than economic liberalism. Alongside their traditional concerns for free speech, *habeas corpus* and political rights, they increasingly stress the importance of economic and social rights. Some CSOs such as Better Life in Egypt have also developed rights-based approaches to human development. However, mainstream conceptions of family values and gender roles are rarely challenged. While women's rights are gradually entering public debate, issues of sexuality (especially outside marriage) are advocated by very few CSOs, such as Helem in Lebanon.

Advocating for supposedly universal values and accepting foreign funds often go hand in hand with accusations of foreign interference, which result in part from recurrent attempts to de-legitimatize CSOs as "foreign stooges" by governments who themselves accept foreign funding. In addition, however, they also reflect deeply rooted concerns about "neoimperialist" designs of domination, including moral subversion. The generalized perception of asymmetrical relations with the global North has often led CSOs to stress national independence and anti-imperialism, sometimes to the point of defending authoritarian regimes. Simultaneously it has strengthened the identification with largely conservative cultural values considered as endogenous, in particular those associated with Islam and the Eastern churches. Numerous CSOs openly define themselves as Muslim or Christian, thus fuelling debates between advocates of religion-based and citizenship-based concepts of civil society.

However, the values that are actually practiced by CSOs converge to a far greater degree than those they publicly espouse. As modes of CSO governance remain largely personalized, paternalistic, and hierarchical, CSOs are frequently identified with their founders, who tend to stay in power over considerable lengths of time. Senior positions in CSOs are often used as sources of patronage and status, entailing symbolic and material rewards that outweigh incentives to promote social change. Therefore, broad-based participation, collective decision making, a search for consensus, the delegation of powers, and the division of labor are not common features of Middle Eastern CSOs, even though they are practiced by a number of organizations such as the Egyptian Initiative for Personal Rights. In Israel, CSOs are highly diverse in terms of the values they propagate, reflecting deep ideological divides between right and left, advocates of the religious and secular organization of the community, Jewish settlers in the Occupied Territories and the peace movement, and many others. Yet Israeli CSOs converge towards a comparatively more bureaucratic logic in their activities and internal procedures; reflecting societal transformations that in many ways have been similar to those in the global North.

Under pressure from major donors who are often ignorant of history and the complexities of social change, CSO governance worldwide, including in the Middle East, has become increasingly subjected to narrowly defined cost-benefit analysis and impact assessment techniques. Under the pretext of professionalizing CSO activities, this form of "results-based management" privileges simplistic, easily measurable, short-term objectives over broader, longer-term aims whose realization partly depends on uncontrollable actors and processes. The emphasis of these approaches on technical competence often limits broader civic engagement and creates new, unequal relationships between supposedly knowledgeable elites and the "ignorant masses."

In summary, gaps between the values that CSOs embrace and the values they actually practice, together with the sheer diversity of actors and the contexts in which they operate, translate into considerable normative pluralism. However, this pluralism remains heavily tainted by politically illiberal and socially conservative attitudes among CSOs that are close to the ruling regimes, defend "religious values," or simply seek to "develop" the poor and the underprivileged as passive recipients of charity or foreign aid.

4. MIDDLE EASTERN PUBLIC SPHERES

Across the Middle East, the ability of public spheres to mediate normative pluralism has been restricted by authoritarianism and by the broader historical processes that have reshaped societies and strengthened or weakened competing power centres (Göle 1996; Shami 2008). Some Arab countries had a relatively important public sphere in earlier periods of their existence. In Syria, Iraq, and Egypt, the increasing centralization of power after the revolutions of the 1950s and 1960s destroyed that sphere, as did the consolidation of monarchical rule in post-independence Morocco and Jordan. Only the plural politics of Lebanon enabled a public sphere to exist continuously after independence, even though it was affected by the various internal and other wars that the country experienced from the late 1950s onwards. In these earlier periods, public debate and deliberation were always enriched by CSOs and their more informal avatars, but they were ultimately dominated by privately owned media and political parties (Hourani 1983; Eickelman/Anderson 2003; Shami 2008).

In a number of countries such as Egypt and Morocco, the public sphere began to expand again in the late 1970s and the early 1980s, when governments selectively reformed the political system in order to perpetuate authoritarian rule under changing conditions. In other cases like Tunisia and Syria, similar controlled openings were soon closed again. In parts of the Arab Peninsula modest political adjustments in response to the challenges posed by the Iraqi occupation of Kuwait in 1990, the ensuing war, and later declines in oil and gas revenues allowed some expression of conflicting views, and in Iraq itself a new, putative public sphere came into being after the overthrow of Saddam Hussein in 2003. Especially in Tunisia and Egypt, the 'Arab spring' at least temporarily opened up the public sphere to an extent unseen in decades. The history of Iran and Turkey provides other telling examples of the degree to which public spheres depend on the centralization or decentralization of power. In Iran the 1979 revolution and the collapse of the monarchy temporarily opened up space for debate and deliberation, while in Turkey the 1980 military coup temporarily destroyed a public sphere that had been expanding for some years. As for Israel, the relative strength of the public sphere is an obvious corollary to a state that has been based on competing power centres from its inception, though external conflict and related factors have frequently contributed to narrowing the space for public debate, not unlike in the Arab states.

Advocacy and research organizations such as Partners in Development in Egypt, Muwatin in the Palestinian Territories, the Bouabid Foundation in Morocco, and Keshev in Israel have fostered contemporary debates about social, economic, and political choices. Among the earliest issue-based CSOs created by Arabs, human rights organizations broke the silence about state torture in the region and forced governments to openly confront human rights abuses. Unsurprisingly, however, sports and savings clubs, classical development organizations, and charities have had lesser effects on the public sphere. More recently, the target populations of attempts to build social justice—such as villagers deprived of drinking water, women refugees seeking professional qualifications, or factory workers on strike for decent pay—have entered the public sphere, largely on the back of successful attempts at collective action. Nevertheless, the public sphere remains largely populated and dominated by actors who are able to mobilize financial, intellectual, and social capital. In general, neither CSOs nor the masses enjoy such influence. In Egypt, for example, the majority of the poor who, depending on poverty lines and other criteria, account for anything between 40 percent and 80 percent of the population (Sabry 2009), largely remain on the margins of the public sphere as it is commonly defined. The most influential actors thus remain the increasingly lively print and audiovisual media as well as new websites and blogs run by commercial companies, public figures, or (would-be) politicians. One important exception is the expansion of the blogosphere and social media, where decentralized, multilateral conversations involving larger numbers of ordinary individuals have created the beginnings of an interactive public.

5. Conclusion

In most Arab states and Iran, authoritarian rule and strong non-voluntary forms of social organization continue to impose significant limits on independent associational life and the strength of public spheres. Though important in some respects, contemporary economic developments have rarely entailed the emergence of competing power centers or other societal transformations on the scale that helped independent organizations and public spaces to emerge elsewhere in the world. The privatization of public-sector companies, for example, has largely benefited entrepreneurs with close ties to ruling regimes. Thus far, the "facebook revolutions" of 2010–2011 have engendered counter powers of sorts only in Tunisia and Egypt. Though benefiting from existing civil society networks and capacities, they fed largely on virtual collective action that was mobilized independently of formal organizations. Able to mobilize intellectual, technological, organizational, and material resources, the protagonists of the "Arab Spring" also benefited from international support. By effectively challenging authoritarian rule these informal actors should strengthen the position of existing CSOs, and at the same time create new and more formal organizations.

While illustrating the limits of definitions that restrict civil society to formally-established CSOs, many of these actors also openly pursue political aims such as the departure of incumbent rulers and the exercise of influence over future appointments and policies. In countries where these efforts fail to replace authoritarian rulers, or at least force "historical compromises" onto them, political and civil liberties will continue to suffer from serious restrictions, and instead of shaping the state, civil society and the public sphere will continue to be shaped by it.

As far as Turkey is concerned, civil society is likely to grow further if the economic and political changes of the last decades maintain their momentum. Developments in Israel will continue to resemble those in the global North. A potential Palestinian state may face a relatively strong civil society that has been able to grow and consolidate itself thanks to the weakness of local political institutions. Provided that the gains of the "Arab Spring" are not rolled back by the restoration of authoritarian rule or captured by some of their own protagonists at the expense of others, the Middle East may henceforth provide more fertile ground for civil society to grow and develop in locally-grounded ways.

NOTES

1. By "Middle East" I refer to the Arab states, Iran, Turkey, Israel, and the Palestinian territories. Historically defined by political and strategic concerns, the region has little internal coherence in terms of political or social organization.

2. Extrapolations from UNDP (2002, 161)

3. See for instance Stiles (2002). The main exception is the Palestinian territories (cf Keating et al. 2005).

4. In the sense of the argument developed by Rueschemeyer et al. (1992); for the original concept of "imagined communities," see Anderson (1991).

5. For country surveys, summaries and comparisons see: Human Rights Watch (annual); Bertelsmann Foundation (ed., 2010 and www.bertelsmann-transformation-index.de); and the Arab Reform Initiative (ed.), 2010.

REFERENCES

Anderson, B. 1991. *Imagined Communities: Reflections on the Origins and Spread of Nationalism.* London: Verso.

Arab Reform Initiative. 2010. *The State of Reform in the Arab World 2009–10: The Arab Democracy Index.* Paris: Arab Reform Initiative.

Ashford, D. E. 1961. *Political Change in Morocco.* Princeton, N.J.: Princeton University Press.

Azimi, F. 2008. *The Quest for Democracy in Iran: A Century of Struggle against Authoritarian Rule.* Cambridge, Mass.: Harvard University Press.

Bayat, A. 1997. *Street Politics: Poor People's Movements in Iran.* New York: Columbia University Press.

Ben Nefissa, S. 1991. "L'Etat égyptien et le monde associatif à travers les textes juridiques." *Egypte/Monde arabe* no. 8: 107–34.

Beinin, J. (ed) 2010. *The Struggle for Labor Rights in Egypt.* Washington, D.C: The Solidarity Center.

Beinin, J., and Z. Lockman. 1988. *Workers on the Nile: Nationalism, Communism, Islam, and the Egyptian Working Class, 1882–1954.* London: I. B. Tauris.

Bennani-Chraïbi, M., and O. Fillieule. (eds.). 2003. *Résistances et protestations dans les sociétés musulmanes.* Paris: Presses de Sciences Po.

Berger, M. 1970. *Islam in Egypt Today: Social and Poitical Aspects of Popular Religion.* Cambridge: Cambridge University Press.

Bertelsmann Foundation. 2010. *Bertelsmann Transformation Index.* Gütersloh: Bertlelsmann Foundation.

Blanchi, R. 1989. *Unruly Corporatism: Associational Life in Twentieth Century Egypt.* Oxford: Oxford University Press.

Dazi-Héni, F. 2005. *Monarchies et sociétés d'Arabie: le temps des confrontations.* Paris: Presses de Sciences-Po.

Eickelman, D. F., and J. W. Anderson (eds.). 2003. *New Media in the Muslim World: The Emerging Public Sphere.* Bloomington: Indiana University Press.

Gellner, E. 1996. *Conditions of Liberty: Civil Society and its Rivals.* London: Penguin.

Göle, N. 1996. *The Forbidden Modern: Civilization and Veiling.* Ann Arbor: University of Michigan Press.

Goldberg, E. J. 1996. *The Social History of Labor in the Middle East.* Boulder, Colo.: Westview Press.

Guazzone, L., and D. Pioppi. 2009. *The Arab State and Neo-liberal Globalization: The Restructuring of State Power in the Middle East.* Reading: U.K.: Ithaca Press.

Hawthorne, A. 2004. "Middle Eastern Democracy: Is Civil Society the Answer?" *Carnegie Papers*, no. 44. Washington, D.C.: Carnegie Endowment for International Peace.

Horrowitz, D., and M. Lissak, M. 1978. *Origins of the Israeli Polity: Palestine under the Mandate.* Chicago: University of Chicago Press.

Hourani, A. 1983. *Arabic Thought in the Liberal Age, 1798–1939.* Cambridge: Cambridge University Press.

Human Rights Watch. 2009 and annual. *World Report.* New York: Human Rights Watch.

Huntington, S. P. 1991. *The Third Wave: Democratization in the Late Twentieth Century.* Norman: University of Oklahoma Press.

Ibrahim, B., and D. Sherif. (eds.) 2008. *From Charity to Social Change: Trends in Arab Philanthropy.* Cairo: The American University in Cairo Press.

Karam, K. 2006. *Le mouvement civil au Liban: mobilisations, protestations et revendications associatives dans l'après-guerre.* Paris: Karthala.

Kazemi, F. 1980. *Poverty and Revolution in Iran*. New York: New York University Press.

Keating, M., A. Le More, and R. Lowe (eds.) 2005. *Aid, Diplomacy and Facts on the Ground: The Case of Palestine*. London: Chatham House.

Khallaf, M., and Ö. Tür. 2008. "Civil Society in the Middle East and Mediterranean: An Exploration of Opportunities and Limitations," in: V. Finn Heinrich and L. Fioramonti (eds.) *CIVICUS Global Survey of the State of Civil Society* vol. 2: Comparative Perspectives. West Hartford, Conn.: Kumarian Press.

Kienle, E. 2000. A *Grand Delusion: Democracy and Economic Reform in Egypt*. London: I. B. Tauris.

Kimmerling, B. 1989. *The Israeli State and Society: Boundaries and Frontiers*. Albany: State University of New York Press.

Lawson, F. 1982. "Social Bases for the Hama Revolt." *Middle East Report* 12(9): 24–28.

Longuenesse, E. 2007. *Professions et sociétés au Proche-Orient: déclin des élites, crise des classes moyennes*. Rennes: Presses Universitaires de Rennes.

Laskier, M. M. 2008. "Les nouveaux mouvements sociaux," in A. Dieckhoff (ed.) *L'Etat d'Israël*. Paris: Fayard.

Lewis, B. 1994. *The Shaping of the Modern Middle East*. New York: Oxford University Press.

Massignon, L. 1920. "Les corps de métier et la cité musulmane." *Revue internationale de sociologie* vol. 28: 473–89.

Miller, W. G. 1969. "Political Organization in Iran: From *Dowreh* to Political Party." *Middle East Journal* vol. 23: 159–67.

Norton, A. R. (ed.) 1995/6. *Civil Society in the Middle East*. 2 vols. Leiden: Brill.

Peters, R., and R. Deguilhem. 2002. "Waqf," in H.A.R. Gibb and J.H. Kramers (eds.) *The Encyclopaedia of Islam*. (new ed.) vol. 11. Leiden: Brill.

Raymond, A. 1985. *Grandes villes arabes à l'époque ottomane*. Paris: Sindbad.

Rueschemeyer, D., J. D. Stephens, and E. Huber-Stephens. 1992. *Capitalist Development and Democracy*. Chicago: University of Chicago Press.

Sabry, S. 2009. "Poverty Lines in Greater Cairo: Understanding and Misrepresenting Poverty." Working Paper 21. London: International Institute for Environment and Development.

Schlumberger, O. (ed.) 2007. *Debating Arab Authoritarianism: Dynamics and Durability in Nondemocratic Regimes*. Stanford, Calif.: Stanford University Press.

Seib, P. (ed.) 2007. *New Media and the New Middle East*. New York: Palgrave Macmillan.

Shami, S. (ed.) 2008. *Publics, Politics and Participation: Locating the Public Sphere in the Middle East and North Africa*. New York: Social Science Research Council.

Stiles, K. W. 2002. *Civil Society by Design: Donors, NGOs and the Intermestic Development Circle in Bangladesh*. New York: Praeger.

Tarrow, S. 1994. *Power in Movement: Social Movements, Collective Action, and Politics*. Cambridge: Cambridge University Press.

Tétreault, M.A. 2000. *Stories of Democracy: Politics and Society in Contemporary Kuwait*. New York: Columbia University Press.

Wolffsohn, M. 1987. *Israel: Polity, Society and Economy, 1882–1986*. Atlantic Highlands: N.J.: Humanity Press International.

Zubaida, S. 2008. "Urban Social Movements," in P. Sluglett (ed.), *The Urban History of the Middle East, 1750–1950*. Syracuse: Syracuse University Press.

Zürcher, E. J. 2003. *Turkey: A Modern History*. London, I. B. Tauris.

CHAPTER 13

....

CIVIL SOCIETY IN CHINA

....

JUDE HOWELL

THIS chapter reviews the development of civil society in China since the start of economic reforms in the late 1970s, and analyzes the key constraints and opportunities shaping its past and future development. It argues that market reforms, subsequent socioeconomic changes, and technological and political factors have shaped the trajectory of civil society since 1978. Leadership concerns about political control and stability have been the overriding constraint on the full flourishing of civic organizing in China, leading to incremental cycles of expansion and contraction.

The term civil society is used here to describe the realm of independent citizen organizing around shared concerns and interests. It is thus distinct from the state and the market, though in practice the boundaries between these three domains are blurred and messy. This is particularly the case in China, where the state continues to wield considerable power and authority over society. Empirically, the realm of civil society encompasses a range of action and organising that varies in degrees of formality and legality. At one end of the spectrum it includes organizations that are closely related to the Communist Party such as the All-China Federation of Trades Unions (ACFTU) or government-sponsored nongovernmental organizations (NGOs); in the middle of the spectrum are more independent organizations with legal status such as professional associations or business associations; and further along the continuum lie more loosely organized, nonregistered networks, salons, and discussion groups. At the far end of this spectrum are illegal organizations, some of which would not enjoy legal status anywhere such as criminal gangs, trafficking networks, and drug cartels; and others which are prohibited for political reasons such as secessionist movements and religious sects that would be more likely to be tolerated in a liberal democratic polity.

The chapter begins by outlining the development of civil society in the post-Mao era. It then analyzes the social, economic, technological, and political factors that have shaped the contours of civil society. In particular it examines those variables that underpin the expansion of civil society spaces and those that have contributed to their contraction or stagnation. The chapter ends by considering the future prospects for civil society development in China.

1. THE DEVELOPMENT OF CIVIL SOCIETY IN CHINA AFTER 1978

In the three decades before the launch of market reforms in 1978, the state exerted tight control over the spaces for independent civic organizing. After Liberation in 1949 and years of civil war, the newly triumphant Chinese Communist Party (CCP) needed to consolidate its power, reconstruct the economy, and minimize both internal and external threats to its rule. The Cold War led not only to the economic blockade of China but also to its political isolation from the capitalist West, aggravated further by China's gradual break with the Soviet Union from the late 1950s onwards. The long enduring Cold War fostered increasing economic self-reliance along Maoist lines as well as the maintenance of tight societal controls through ideological and organizational means.

A key element of societal control was the establishment of intermediary organizations linking the party to society. These mass organizations served to transmit party policy downwards to key constituencies of society such as youth, workers, and women, and in turn reflect their views upwards to the party, thereby in theory realising the principles of democratic socialism. The largest such mass organizations were the All-China Federation of Women (ACWF), the ACFTU, and the Communist Youth League (CYL)[1]. These intermediary organizations formed an integral part of the Leninist style sociopolitical architecture of Maoist China, with their offices, staff, and activities being supported by the party-state. Apart from these key intermediary institutions, the work unit (*danwei*) and the rural commune were also key sites through which the party exerted control over society. As a result of the penetration of the state into the everyday life of Chinese society, there was little room for citizens to organize spontaneously or independently. Though occasional protests took place, such as the workers' protests in Shanghai in 1957 (Perry 1994), they were sharply put down, stymieing further collective action.

With the rise to power in 1978 of market-oriented reformers led by Deng Xiaoping, the economic and social infrastructure of Maoist China underwent fundamental transformation. The diversification of ownership systems, the relaxation of controls over rural-urban migration, the expansion of foreign trade, the introduction of foreign investment, and the dismantling of the rural commune system led to the pluralization of interests, and thereby increased social differentiation and stratification. Aware that the old systems for connecting with society—and in particular the mass organizations—were no longer adequate for reaching out to an increasingly complex society, from the late 1980s onwards the reformers began to encourage the development of new forms of association. These included, for example, trades associations, professional associations, learned societies, cultural and sports clubs, chambers of commerce, and business associations. A key protagonist of this opening up of space was the well-known economist Xue Muqiao. In an article written in 1988 he argued that as the state took on a more indirect role in economic management, so certain functions previously carried out by the state could be passed over to traders and business people. These economic associations could then "serve as a bridge between the state and enterprises."

From the mid-1980s onwards, new social organizations (*shehui zuzhi*) mushroomed across China. It was against this background that China-watchers introduced the concept of "civil society" into their analysis (White, Howell, and Shang 1996; Gold 1990; Gu 1993/4; He 1997; Huang 1993; Rowe 1993; Sullivan 1990). In doing so, many sought not just to use the term to describe a sociological phenomenon of increasing civic organization, but also to express a normative aspiration that such a development might herald the democratization of China. The embracing of this concept, moreover, reflected broader global trends whereby popular democratic movements in Eastern Europe, Latin America, and Africa had led to the overthrow of unpopular, authoritarian regimes. Indeed, East European scholars were the first to revitalize the idea of civil society to articulate their vision of a more democratic polity and society (Keane 1988).

The growth of social organizations reached a peak in the late 1980s, when the spread of China's democracy movement and the subsequent government clampdown in June 1989 brought their proliferation to a rapid halt. The party prohibited all organizations deemed a threat to its continued rule, such as the various autonomous students' unions and trades unions. The crackdown on protestors in Tiananmen Square on June 4 led Western observers to be far more cautious in declaring the emergence of a civil society in China and in predicting democratic regime change.

In October 1989, the party began to assert greater order over the sphere of social organizations by issuing new Management Regulations on the Registration of Social Organizations, replacing the 1950 regulations. These made the process of registration more complex and demanding, with prospective social organizations now required not only to register with the Ministry of Civil Affairs (MOCA) but also to identify a supervisory unit (*guakao danwei*) that would act as their sponsor and be responsible for supervising the activities of the appended social organization. The new regulations sought to establish a corporatist framework for governing social organizations, limiting, for example, the number of associations in any one domain to only one.[2] The issuing of the 1989 regulations clearly slowed the pace of growth of registered social organizations.

The tight grip of the party over society began to yield in the early 1990s as market reformers began to gain the upper hand over the more ideologically conservative elements of the party. Deng Xiao Ping's tour of Southern China in 1992 marked this subtle shift in power and heralded a further deepening of economic reform. It was within this context of political easing that the seeds of a new phase in the development of civil society were sown. Two outstanding features distinguished this new phase of development: first, the proliferation of associations addressing the needs and interests of social groups marginalized in the reform process; and second, the growth of new forms of association that skillfully bypassed the need to register as social organizations (Howell 2003). In the 1980s and early 1990s the majority of registered social organizations were found in the realms of academia, business, trades, culture, sports, arts, and professional interests. There were relatively few independent organizations that concerned themselves with issues of poverty, social disadvantage, or marginalization, or with public affairs. Pei's (1998) analysis of a sample of social organizations found that national-level charitable groups and foundations increased from two in 1978 to only sixteen in 1992, making up just two percent of all registered national social organizations. The paucity of charitable groups and foundations was due in part to the ongoing provision of basic social welfare through the urban state and collective sectors, albeit uneven in coverage. Though the production process had been opened up to private investment, both domestic and international, there was no for-profit or not-for-profit private sector in welfare provision.

From the early 1990s onwards, a new stratum of organizations emerged that sought to address the needs and interests of those who were vulnerable and marginalized in the reform processes. These associations took up issues such as HIV/AIDS, domestic violence, poverty, disability, migrant workers' rights, health and safety, and environment and industrial pollution. Since not all of these organizations are registered, establishing precise figures is not possible. Nevertheless, available evidence points to several hundreds by the end of the 1990s (China Development Brief 2001). Though this stratum of organizing has developed rapidly in the 1990s, their numbers remain limited, especially for groups such as sex workers or people living with HIV/AIDS, who face much social prejudice.

The second distinguishing feature of civil society from the mid-1990s onwards relates to the dynamic ingenuity of some Chinese citizens in bypassing the registration process. In November 1998 the party-state made further revisions to the regulations on social organization in an attempt to gain further control over the associational sphere. As a result the number of registered social organizations fell from 220,000 in 1998 to 136,841 in 2000, almost a third less than the 181,060 groups registered in 1993. Nevertheless this did not stop people from finding ways to organize around shared concerns. These included affiliating as second- or third-level bodies to a registered, established association, thereby obviating the need to register; forming networks that got around the regulatory restriction on forming branch organizations; organizing through projects sponsored often by foreign donors; meeting informally through salons, clubs, and loose networks; setting up research institutes and centers under the protective cover of universities; and registering as nonprofit companies with the Industrial and Commercial Bureau. In this way dynamic people maneuvered around the regulatory regime, recapturing associational space and pushing back the barriers that the party had tried to impose.

These two features of civil society in China have continued into the new millennium. At the same time, the party has introduced new laws to promote foundations and charities. It has also further parsed out registered organizations, dividing them into social organizations, foundations, and nonprofit enterprises, each with its own corresponding set of regulations. Apart from these registered entities the realm of nonregistered organizing has remained alive, provided it stays within the limits of acceptable activity as defined by the party. Nevertheless, there have been three key moments in the first decade of the new millennium that have prompted seemingly contradictory state responses of restriction and promotion.

The first of these relates to the more general global backlash against civil society that was becoming apparent at the turn of the millennium (Carothers 2006, Howell et al. 2007). A number of parallel trends were converging in the late 1990s to raise concerns about the probity, accountability, and legitimacy of nongovernmental organizations. These concerns gained increasing salience following the launch of President George W. Bush's "war on terror," which cast suspicion on charities as entities that were vulnerable to misuse by terrorist groups (Howell and Lind 2009). At the same time, President Vladimir Putin was also becoming increasingly concerned about the role of foreign-funded NGOs in national political processes. In particular he suggested that the Colour Revolutions that had occurred in the Ukraine, Georgia, and Kyrgyzstan were in part engineered by Western-sponsored democracy and rights groups. Putin's concerns caused alarm amongst China's political leaders, who from late spring 2005 quietly set about investigating international NGOs, foundations, and foreign-funded local nongovernmental groups. Part of this effort involved a review of NGOs that had registered under the Industrial and Commercial Bureau so as to avoid the more stringent requirements of the MOCA, and led to the closure of several NGOs deemed politically sensitive.

The second key moment was the boost given to volunteering and government perceptions of nongovernmental organizations in the aftermath of the earthquake in Sichuan province in 2008 (Teets 2009). This event brought into sharp relief the Janus-like response of the party to collective action in China: on the one hand, the party welcomed the contribution that volunteers and nongovernmental agencies could make in emergency relief situations, adopting as a result a more constructive approach towards such independent organizing. On the other hand, the party recoiled at spontaneous initiatives that criticized local government officials for corruption, which they saw as underpinning the poor quality of school construction. As a result, journalists, parents' groups, and dynamic, critical individuals encountered the heavy hand of the state in response to their calls for accountability and transparency, and their attempts to stimulate a public discussion about corruption.

The third key moment that shaped civil society's recent development were the Olympic Games, which were held in Beijing in 2008. Concerned about potential terrorist attacks and protests,[3] the party had already taken various measures in preparing for the Olympics to ensure the smooth running of the event. Internet cafes were closed down; websites blocked; human rights lawyers such as Teng Biao, who had defended AIDS activists and Falun Gong practitioners, were detained, and dissidents such as Hu Jia, a civic rights and AIDS campaigner, quickly removed from sight. The outbreak of demonstrations in Tibet in March 2008 led to a crackdown on protestors and monasteries in the province, enhanced surveillance of websites, and attacks in the media on the influence of external Tibetan campaigns. In addition, attempts to thwart the progress of the Olympic flame around the world so as to draw attention to issues such as Tibet, the Falun Gong (Ostergaard 2003) and secessionist struggles in Xinjiang province fuelled party leaders' concerns that external forces were seeking to interfere in China's affairs and destabilize the country.

The development of civil society over the last three decades has thus been characterized by cycles of contraction and expansion, with each cycle representing a gradual widening of associational space. Nevertheless the boundaries of what is possible continue to be contested and negotiated. Organizing around certain issues such as secession in Tibet or Xinjiang, legalization of the Falun Gong, democratic regime change, or independent trades unions remains out of bounds. In the next section I look at the combination of factors that have underpinned this incremental, cyclical pattern of civil society development.

2. Explaining Cycles of Contraction and Expansion

How can one account for this incremental, cyclical pattern of civil society development in China? Answering this question requires an understanding both of the economic, social, and political factors that have prompted citizen organizing and government tolerance, and of the forces that have constrained the expansion of civil society organizing. The first point to make is that market reformers recognized the need to open up intellectual spaces so that scientific and knowledge from the West could be used to accelerate economic growth. The reinvigoration of the China Association for Science and Technology and the growth of learned societies, professional associations, and academic associations reflect this drive to promote modernization and fundamental economic change.

Second, as the reforms deepened in the 1990s, the institutional architecture of social welfare was also gradually dismantled. In particular, the intensification of state enterprise reform from the mid-1990s onwards led to the streamlining and closure of state enterprises,[4] bringing in its wake the laying off of millions of workers (Lee 2007). The diversification of ownership systems along with state enterprise reform weakened the work unit (*danwei*) both as a site of political and ideological control over society and as a system for providing social welfare. Employees in state enterprises, particularly larger ones, had typically enjoyed guaranteed life employment, pensions, and access to schooling and health care, crèches, and kindergartens. With the introduction of the market and increasingly competitive pressures on the state sector, these systemic advantages have been gradually eroded. In response the party-state has gradually, albeit slowly, introduced new systems of social security, pensions, and social and medical insurance (Chan et al. 2008). However, migrant workers remain poorly covered by these schemes, while access to healthcare has become an increasingly divisive marker in society (Yao 2005).

The processes of state enterprise restructuring and social welfare reform have provided a context in which the CCP has recognized the need for a more diverse portfolio of service providers. Provincial governments across China have experimented with community-based social welfare provision and have welcomed the activities of newly established nongovernmental welfare groups, especially where these address sensitive issues such as HIV/AIDS that local governments find more difficult to deal with openly (Howell 2003). Furthermore, the service sector has also functioned as a way to absorb excess labor and workers laid off in the process of state enterprise reform. Awareness among party and government leaders of the potential contribution of nongovernmental organizations and voluntary activity to welfare issues was further heightened in the Sichuan earthquake of 2008. As volunteers from all over China raised money for earthquake victims and travelled to Sichuan to assist in relief operations, official appreciation and acceptance of the merits and utility of citizen action was strengthened. This not only reinvigorated discussions around creating a more enabling legal and regulatory framework for nongovernmental service-oriented organizations to operate, but also crystallized a picture of citizen action that was acceptable to the party—namely, a service-oriented, apolitical "harmonious" civil society.

The third factor favoring the expansion of nongovernmental initiatives was the need to address the increasingly diverse and differentiated interests that had emerged in China as a result of market reforms. With the weakening of the *danwei* system, the development of a private sector, and the deepening of state enterprise reforms, relying on the old mass organizations as the main intermediary channel between the party and society became increasingly inadequate. Though the mass organizations have adapted their structures, approach, and activities to relate to their increasingly complex and fluid constituencies more effectively, the need for new interests to find organizational expression was important for ensuring social stability and government control over society.

Technological change has also fuelled both the opening up of political space and the ferocity of state resistance. In 2009 there were over 384 million Internet users in China.[5] While the party has developed sophisticated means for blocking websites, blogs, and interactive media, such as the 2003 Golden Shield project, Chinese "netizens" have also become increasingly adept at circumventing and resisting these controls. For example, the well-known artist Ai Weiwei, who designed the beehive stadium for the 2008 Beijing Olympics, rallied Chinese netizens to stay offline on July 1, 2009 in response to the party's plans to introduce the new Green Dam Youth Escort censorship software into all new computers. Faced with widespread domestic criticism, the government backed down, declaring the uploading of the software as optional. Given the horizontal linkages that the Internet fosters both domestically and internationally, this will continue to be an important battleground shaping the limits of intellectual expression and mobilization in China.

Finally, China's engagement internationally has been a key spur to the development of civil society, as illustrated, for example, by the rapid growth of more independent women's organizations in the run-up to China's hosting of the Fourth World Conference for Women in 1995 (Howell 1997). Women across China began to set up salons, associations, and gender research groups, addressing the increasingly diverse interests and needs of women and promoting a gender analysis approach. The ACWF began to describe itself as an NGO and set about establishing new affiliated social organizations under its umbrella. External players have also contributed to greater political tolerance for citizen organizing. Relevant here is the growing layer of international development organizations that began to operate in China from the 1990s onwards, supporting and encouraging the growth of local nongovernmental groups to implement development projects aimed at poverty reduction.

While a combination of factors has hastened the emergence of certain kinds of civil society organizations in China, political and social factors have also constrained the development of civil society. Aware of the destabilizing effects of rapid economic reform and the growing socioeconomic and regional inequalities, party leaders have kept a wary eye on citizen organizing, particularly at the time of key political events such as the 17th Party Congress in October 2007 or the sixtieth anniversary of CCP rule in October 2009. The party has consistently opposed any form of citizen action around issues such as the separation of Tibet or Xinjiang from China; the Falun Gong; organizing independent trades unions; setting up alternative parties that challenge CCP rule; or initiatives calling for democracy. Moreover, the party's tolerance for criticism is still crucially low. Two recent incidents testify to this. First, citizens who protested the poor quality of construction that led to the collapse of schools in the Sichuan earthquake have been harassed by security agencies. Second, in the wake of the 2008 milk powder scandal, human rights lawyers and parents seeking compensation and disclosure of state involvement have similarly been harassed by the state. How much the party is prepared to tolerate has been subject to ongoing contestation within the party, among academics, and by civil society actors who test the boundaries in various ways. Maintaining social stability has been a key concern and legitimizing discourse for the party in both clamping down on civil society actors and in proceeding at a snail-like pace with improving the regulatory and legal regime.

The corporatist legal and regulatory framework has also had a constraining effect on the development of a legally based civil society. By 2009 the party had put in place a range of legal and policy measures to guide the registration and management of nongovernmental organizations. These included, for example, the 1998 Provisional Regulations for the Registration and Management of Popular Non-Enterprise Work-Units, the 1999 Law on Donations to Public Welfare Undertakings, the 2004 Regulations on the Management of Foundations and the 2008 Enterprise Income Tax Law, making it easier for companies to donate to charities. However, a planned charity law still remains in draft form. Similarly plans since 2004 to permit the legal registration of foreign social organizations have continued to drag on, not least because of underlying suspicion about the political intent of such organizations. While the development of such a framework testifies to the party's recognition of the relevance of these nongovernmental groups, the measures themselves still remain a barrier to their legalization and public recognition. Hence the tendency since the late 1990s has been for many groups to bypass these measures in innovative ways, and for local governments to cast a blind eye, aware that these groups are harmless and/or useful in addressing local needs and interests.

Another factor constraining the development of civil society has been party leaders' suspicion that external powers are trying to destabilize China. For example, during the July 2009 Xinjiang riots, the CCP accused Rebiya Kadeer, an exiled leader of the World Uighur Congress, of instigating the unrest. However China has also skillfully manipulated U.S. politics to counter secessionist tendencies in Xinjiang. After the U.S. government under President George W. Bush launched the so-called war on terror in 2001, China agreed to demonstrate its alliance with the United States in return for putting the East Turkestan Islamic Movement on the U.S. terrorist watch list. Chinese government suspicion of external influences also lay behind the investigation of international NGOs and foreign-funded Chinese NGOs in the mid-2000s.

A further constraint has been the lack of understanding among political leaders and the public about the role of nongovernmental agencies. The general public has remained suspicious about the purpose and intent of nongovernmental organizations seeking to harness their time or money, which has made fundraising difficult. A scandal surrounding the Project Hope campaign in the late 1990s did little to instill public confidence. In the run-up to the Fourth World Conference on Women the ACWF began to refer to itself as a nongovernmental agency, even though ACWF cadres at the time were not very clear about what a nongovernmental organization was, nor whether they were themselves governmental or nongovernmental, not least because many so-called nongovernmental organizations have often been supported by the state in terms of office space, equipment, and sometimes staff; some have been initiated by central and local governments; and some have very close connections with state officials at different levels (Chan 1993 Unger 2008,White, Howell and Shang 1996). Still, to suggest that civil society does not exist in China because of a lack of autonomy from the government fails to capture the dynamism and initiative that has come from independent actors driven to organize around a need, interest, or issue. Indeed, close cooperation with the state is a feature of many civil societies around the world, particularly in relation to governmental contracting out of service provision to the non-for-profit sector, the United Kingdom being a prime example.

Finally, foreign investors and companies interested in staking a share in China's domestic economy have also contributed to state controls over civil society, in part through their agreement to partake in censoring. For example, both Google and Yahoo signed agreements with the Chinese government to censor certain information on their sites in China in order to secure access to the Chinese Internet market. However, in early 2010 Google declared that it would no longer agree to censorship controls over the flow of information and websites. Though this move has garnered some domestic support, critics have condemned it as playing into the hands of the Chinese government by yielding space to alternative Chinese internet providers, who will willingly comply with government censorship demands.

3. Conclusion

The development of civil society in China has proceeded in an incremental, cyclical fashion, with periods of contraction followed by periods of expansion. Compared to the late 1970s when market reformers consolidated their power and embarked upon a fundamental program of economic reform, the spaces for independent organizing and the expression of ideas has widened considerably. Though the party maintains a tight hold over any organizing or expression of ideas that it deems threatening to social stability and the continuation of its rule, it is also increasingly receptive to the idea of a depoliticized, "third sector" of welfare-oriented social organizations, charities, and foundations. This incremental, cyclical pattern of development points to the ongoing contestation and negotiation of boundaries between state and civil society. In particular it highlights both the contradictory impulses of the party towards civil society organizing, and the growing resistance of civil society actors to restrictions on their freedoms of expression and association.

As China becomes more deeply integrated into the global economy and assertive in global institutions, it will also become increasingly subject to international scrutiny. Global economic, cultural, and social linkages as well as the Internet will make it harder for the party to control the supply of information, analysis, and opinion. Political leaders' concerns about social stability and potential threats to party rule will continue to drive a more restrictive approach to civil society organizing. At the same time, however, the need to address issues of social welfare and social inequality and to find new channels for the articulation of grievances calls for a more pragmatic and inclusive approach to governing society. Finding an effective way of addressing multiple, complex interests and channeling discontent will be crucial for the maintenance by the party of stability and its continued rule in China.

NOTES

1. On the ACFTU see Harper (1969) and Taylor et al. (2003) and on the ACWF see Davin (1976) and Howell (1996).

2. The classic work on corporatism is by Philippe Schmitter (1974). The concept has been applied to China by, for example, Chan (1993), Unger (1996, 2008), and White, Howell, and Shang (1996).

3. For a detailed survey of collective protests in China see Cheung et al. 2006.

4. Between 2001 and 2005 the number of state-owned enterprises had fallen by 48 percent (Du 2005).

5. See "China Internet Usage Stats and Population Report" in *Internet Usage and Population Stats*, www.internetworldstats.com (accessed on February 7, 2010).

6. On the increasing internationalization of China, see Zweig (2002).

REFERENCES

Carothers, T. 2006. "The Backlash Against Democracy Promotion." *Foreign Affairs* 85(2), March/April: 55–68.

Chan, A. 1993. "Revolution or Corporatism? Workers and Trade Unions in Post-Mao China." *Australian Journal of Chinese Affairs* 29 (January): 31–61.

China Development Brief. 2001. "250 Chinese NGOs: A Special Report from *China Brief*." Beijing: China Development Brief.

C. K. Chan, K. L. Ngok, and D. Phillips. 2008. *Social Policy in China: Development and Well-Being*. Bristol: The Policy Press.

Cheung, J. .H, H. Lai, and M. Xia, 2006, "Mounting Challenges to Governance in China: Surveying Collective Protestors, Religious Sects and Criminal Organizations." *The China Journal* 56 (July): 1–31.

Davin, D. 1976. *Women-Work: Women and the Party in Revolution China*. Oxford: Clarendon Press.

Gold, T. 1990. "The Resurgence of Civil Society in China." *Journal of Democracy* 1/1 (Winter): 18–31.

Gu, X. 1993/4. "A Civil Society and Public Sphere in Post-Mao China? An Overview of Western Publications." *China Information* 8/3 (Winter): 38–52.

Harper, P. 1969. "The Party and the Unions in Communist China." *The China Quarterly* 37: 84–119.

He, B. 1997. *The Democratic Implications of Civil Society in China*. London: Macmillan Press; New York: St. Martin's Press.

Howell, J. 1996. "The Struggle for Survival: Prospects for the Women's Federation in post-Mao China." *World Development* 24 (1): 129–43.

———. 1997. "Post-Beijing Reflections: Creating Ripples, but not Waves in China." *Women's Studies International Forum* 20(2): 235–52.

———. 2003. "New Directions in Civil Society: Organising around Marginalised Interests," in J. Howell (ed,), *Governance in China*. Lanham, Md.: Rowman and Littlefield.

Howell, J., A. Ishkanian, M. Glasius, H. Seckinelgin, and E. Obadare. 2007. "The Backlash Against Civil Society in the Wake of the Long War on Terror." *Development in Practice* 18 (1): 82–93.

Howell, J., and J. Lind. 2009. *Counter-terrorism, Aid and Civil Society: Before and After the War on Terror*. Basingstoke: Palgrave Macmillan.

Huang, P. (ed.). 1993. "Public Sphere/Civil Society in China: Paradigmatic Issues in China Studies, III." *Modern China* 19/2 (April), 183–98.

Keane, J. 1988. *Civil Society and the State*. London: Verso.

Lee, C. K. 2007. *Against the Law: Labour Protests in China's Rustbelt and Sunbelt*. Berkeley: University of California Press.

Ostergaard, C. S. 2003. "Governance and the Political Challenge of the Falun Gong," in J. Howell (ed.) *Governance in China*. Lanham Md.: Rowman and Littlefield.

Pei, M. 1998. "Chinese Civic Associations: An Empirical Analysis." *Modern China* 24(3): 285–318.

Perry, E. 1994. "Shanghai's Strike Wave of 1957." *The China Quarterly* 137: 1–27.

Rowe, W. T. 1993. "The Problem of 'Civil Society' in Late Imperial China." *Modern China* 19/2 (April): 139–57.

Schmitter, P. 1974. "Still the Century of Corporatism." *Review of Politics* 36/1 (January): 85–131.

Sullivan, L. 1990. "The Emergence of Civil Society in China, Spring 1989," in A. Saich (ed.) *The Chinese People's Movement: Perspectives on Spring 1989*. London: M. E. Sharpe, 126–44.

Taylor, B., C. Kai, and L. Qi. 2003. *Industrial Relations in China*. Cheltenham: Edward Elgar.

Teets, J. 2009. "Post-Earthquake Relief and Reconstruction Efforts: The Emergence of Civil Society in China." *The China Quarterly* 198: 330–47.

Unger, J. 1996. "Bridges in Private Business, the Chinese Government and the Rise of New Associations." *The China Quarterly* 147: 795–819.

———. (ed.) 2008. *Associations and the Chinese State: Contested Spaces*. Armonk, N. Y.: M. E. Sharpe.

White, G., J. Howell, and X. Y. Shang. 1996. *In Search of Civil Society: Market Reform and Social Change in Contemporary China*. Oxford: Clarendon Press.

Xue, M. 1988. "Establish and Develop Non-Governmental Self-Management Organizations in Various Trades." *Renmin Ribao (People's Daily)*, October 10.

Yao Shujie. 2005. *Economic Growth, Income Distribution and Poverty Reduction in Contemporary China*. London/New York: Routledge Curzon.

Zweig, D. 2002. *Internationalising China: Domestic Interests and Global Linkages*, Ithaca, N.Y.: Cornell University Press.

CHAPTER 14

....

CIVIL SOCIETY IN INDIA
....

NEERA CHANDHOKE

To suggest that concepts can neither be neutral nor transcultural, or that they bear
the imprint of the historical context in which they first emerged, is to reiterate the
obvious. Of more interest is the way the concept is reshaped in different social and
political settings. This chapter explores the specific features of civil society in India
and their implications for the concept of civil society in general.

1. THE DISCOVERY OF CIVIL SOCIETY
....

Much like Moliere's *Bourgeois Gentleman* Jourdain, who recognized with some surprise that he had been speaking prose all his life, scholars have documented, analyzed, and conceptualized associations, political movements, social engagements,
confrontations, and the politics of contestation and affirmation in India, without
realizing that they were theorizing a space that came to be known, particularly in
the 1980s, as civil society. The reasons why this concept was catapulted onto the
forefront of the political imagination are well known. First, civil society had waged
successful struggles against authoritarian state power in Central and Eastern Europe,
and elsewhere. Second, profound disenchantment with the developmental state, the
welfare state, and the socialist state motivated activists and scholars to look elsewhere for a resolution to their political predicaments, which they found in the associational life and social movements of civil society. Third, across the world the
English-speaking public was introduced to two significant works in the form of
Antonio Gramsci's *Selections from the Prison Notebooks* and Jürgen Habermas's *The
Structural Transformation of the Public Sphere* (translated into English in 1971 and
1989 respectively), both of which foregrounded the concept of civil society as the
public sphere. Finally, developments in the socialist world sharply illustrated the

problems that class projects and revolutionary transformations brought in their wake. The lesson was well learned. The future belonged to loose coalitions of issue- and identity-based movements, campaigns and civic associations, to projects that sought to monitor rather than take over the state, and to self-limiting political agendas. This realisation signified the arrival of civil society.

The concept of civil society does not only abstract from, describe, or conceptualize particular phenomena such as civic activism and collective action. It is normative insofar as it specifies that associational life in a metaphorical space between the household, the market, and the state is valuable for a number of reasons. For one, associational life neutralizes the individualism, atomism, and anomie that modernity brings in its wake. Social associations make possible multiple projects and thus engender solidarity. These projects range from developing popular consciousness about climate change to discussing and dissecting popular culture, to supporting needy children or organising neighborhood activities. Or they might simply aim to enhance sociability and dissipate alienation. Whatever the reason, associational life is seen as an intrinsic good.

Associational life is a good in another sense inasmuch as networks of associations facilitate collective action. And participation in collective action enables the realization of human agency insofar as citizens recognize and appreciate that they possess the right to take part in decision making, and the competence to do so. In other words, collective action brings to fruition the basic presumption of democracy: popular sovereignty. It follows that unless people are willing to come together across economic, social, and cultural divides, civil society cannot begin to engage with the state (Chandhoke 2009). Conversely, though associational life is of value in its own right it cannot be de-linked from the struggle for citizenship rights and state accountability (Gupta 1997).

Why is accountability important? One idea that lies at the heart of the civil society argument is that even democratic states are likely to be imperfect. Democracy is a project that has to be realized through collective action as well as sustained engagement with the state. Citizen activism, public vigilance, informed public opinion, a free media, and a multiplicity of social associations are necessary preconditions for this task. But precisely at this point of the argument a number of questions arise. Do all organizations in civil society bear the same sort of relationship with the state? Do they all follow the democratic script in terms of their constitution, decision making, perspectives, commitments, and the tasks they set for themselves? Are all organizations in civil society agents of democratization (Mahajan 1999, 1194)?

2. The Historical Trajectory of Civil Society in India

Civil society organizations in India cannot be seen as a distinct corollary of bourgeois society or what Hegel had termed *Burgerliche Gesellschaft*. These organizations were neither born out of experiences with an "autonomous" market, nor were they a product of a juridical order, of property relations, of individuation, and of the language of abstract rights. They emerged out of the twin processes of resistance to colonialism and the development of a self-reflective attitude to practices increasingly found unacceptable in the light of modern systems of education and liberal ideologies. From its very inception, civil society in India was a plural space, where at least seven categories of organizations and associations pursued different but not necessarily incompatible ends (Beher and Prakash 2004, 196–197; Jayal 2007, 144–145). First, in the nineteenth century social and religious reform movements such as the Brahmo Samaj and the Arya Samaj worked for women's education and widow remarriage; opposed the caste order, ritualism, and idolatry; and tried to rationalize and restructure a hierarchical and discriminatory Hinduism. Second, in the early decades of the twentieth century, Gandhian organizations engaged in what was euphemistically termed the "social uplift" of the doubly disadvantaged castes and the poor (e.g., the Harijan Sevak Sangh).

Third, a number of self-help organizations grew up around trade unions in industrialized cities such as Bombay and Ahmedabad, for example, Swadeshi Mitra Mandal and the Friends of Labourers Society. Fourth, movements against social oppression like the Self-Respect Movement in Tamil Nadu sought to overturn the hierarchical social order and establish the moral status of the so-called lower castes. Fifth, professional English-speaking Indians formed a number of associations to petition the colonial government to extend English education and employment opportunities to the educated middle classes (e.g., the Bombay Presidency Association). Sixth, the Congress party that led the freedom movement established a number of affiliated groups such as women and youth organizations. And finally, social and cultural organizations committed to the project of establishing a Hindu nation, such as the Hindu Mahasabha and the Rashtriya Swayam Sevak Sangh (RSS), formed the nucleus of what might be called uncivil organizations in Indian civil society.

After independence, as the leaders of the freedom struggle took over the reins of state power, organizations in civil society more or less retreated from engaging with the state. Since the political leadership was widely seen as legitimate, civil society organizations did not feel the need to politicize the population, make them conscious of their rights, or create a civic community in which the newly independent citizens of India could engage with each other and with the state. The situation was dramatically transformed barely two and a half decades after independence. The decline of the Congress party heralded the demise of representative and responsive politics. This naturally bred extreme discontent and anger. By the early 1970s the socialist leader J. P. Narayan succeeded in tapping into this simmering discontent by launching a major political movement against the authoritarianism of the central government headed by Prime Minister Indira Gandhi.

This movement provided one of the reasons for Indira Gandhi's decision to impose an internal emergency from June 1975 to January 1977. The emergency, which suspended normal democratic politics and in particular constitutional protections of civil liberties, was marked by high levels of repression. Paradoxically however, it also animated an entire range of social struggles *outside* the sphere of party politics. If there is one lesson to be learned from India and elsewhere, it is that authoritarian states trigger off the development and assertion of their own civil

societies. Arguably, civil society has won its most spectacular victories when confronted by dictatorships, for nothing arouses disaffection and political rage more
than the denial of civil and political rights. Not unexpectedly, civil society organizations in India took root to confront violations of democratic rights and to fill in the
developmental deficit of the state. Social activism at the grassroots prompted some
scholars to acclaim these new arenas of counteraction, countervailing tendencies
and countercultural movements as a "non-party political" alternative to the state
(Sheth 1983; Kothari 1988, 1989).

From the late 1970s, civil society mobilizations took place around the struggle
for caste and gender justice, the protection of civil liberties and the environment,
the struggle against large development projects that have displaced thousands of
tribal peoples and hill dwellers, and the rights to food, work, information, shelter,
primary education, and health (Shah 2004; Parajuli 2001; Katzenstein, Kothari, and
Mehta 2001). These movements have brought people together across social and class
divides and confronted state policies. By the year 2000, it was estimated that grassroots groups, social movements, nonparty political formations, and social action
groups numbered between 20,000 and 30,000 nationwide (Sheth 2004, 45).

In the 1990s, a striking shift from the vocabulary of social service and reform to
that of empowerment, rights, development, governance, and accountability heralded the advent of new forms of civil society organizing and activism. Political
democracy had been institutionalized throughout the country, yet large numbers of
people continued to exist on the margins of survival. Consequently, a large number
of civil society organizations became involved in development. Experiments in
alternative models of development had been initiated in the 1970s by educationists,
scientists, engineers, environmentalists, and social activists, including the Social
Work and Research Centre in Rajasthan and Kishore Bharti in Madhya Pradesh.
Increasingly, however, the field came to be dominated by professionalized nongovernmental organizations (NGOs), often sponsored and funded by donor agencies
in the West, and more than willing to partner with the state in the delivery of social
goods. This shift gained official recognition in the Seventh Five-Year plan (1985–
1990), with the government sanctioning considerable funds for service delivery. A
2004 study calculated that the total number of nonprofit organizations in India is
now more than 1.2 million and that 20 million people work for these organizations
either in a voluntary capacity or for a salary (PRIA 2003, 5,11).

3. The Professionalization
of Civil Society in India

In *Democracy in America,* De Tocqueville had suggested that "in democratic countries the science of association is the mother science, the progress of all others
depends on the progress of that one" (2000, 492). For highly individualistic modern

societies this observation was more than prescient. Social associations are of value because they make collective life possible, encourage citizens to participate in critical political and public discourse, and enable collective action to engage with the state. In the process, the basic presupposition of democracy—participation—is realized through citizen activism and various modes of civic engagement and protest.

Increasingly however, civil societies across the world have come to be dominated by highly professional NGOs, whose position in civil society has been questioned since they are neither social movements nor citizens' groups. The rise of NGOs has brought a qualitatively different way of doing things: campaigns rather than social movements, lobbying government officials rather than politicizing the population, working through networks rather than civic activism, and a high degree of reliance on the media and the judiciary rather than on direct action. This has been illustrated by four key campaigns in India that have focused on the rights to food, employment, information, and education. Their efforts have borne notable results in the form of specific policies and the grant of social rights, but these campaigns have been successful only when the Supreme Court has intervened (Chandhoke 2007). The problem is that whereas the court has adopted a proactive stance on social rights, it has dismissed the demands of movements that have demanded a more radical restructuring of power relations in the country. For example, in the 1980s the Narmada Bachao Andolan movement had highlighted the plight of thousands of people who had been displaced by the building of the Sardar Sarovar dam on the Narmada River in Western India. The movement had approached the Supreme Court and requested that work on the dam be stopped. However, in October 2000, the court, by a majority of one, permitted the raising of the height of the dam to 90 meters. The ruling not only resulted in the displacement of thousands more families, but amounted to a serious setback to critiques of large development projects as environmentally unsound and socially hazardous. This is not to suggest that judicial activism is unimportant, but too much reliance on judicial interventions can tame the agenda of civil society and force it to conform to what is politically permissible.

The Indian NGO sector is rarely in the business of acting, as one insider puts it, as "a catalyst for social, economic, and political changes favouring the poor, marginalized, and disadvantaged" (Beher and Prakash 2004, 199). It is difficult to expect the sector to mount a critique of the state when NGOs are heavily funded by it, and despite the tremendous contribution of the NGO sector to development, a concentration on specific issues leaves the big picture untouched—the huge inequalities in access to resources for example. Instead, NGOs aim to ensure that the state delivers what it has promised to deliver in the constitution, that policy is implemented effectively, that local authorities are made accountable, that government is transparent, that midday meals are provided to children in primary schools, that the poor get jobs for at least one hundred days a year, and that school enrolment increases. As a result, the quality of life for ordinary Indians may improve somewhat, but in the process participation and popular sovereignty might fall by the wayside.

These anxieties are not irresolvable, for no one group or set of strategies can tackle the sheer scale of problems that exist in India such as poverty, illiteracy, and health. The only alternative is to build networks between social movements, citizen groups, and professionalized NGOs and thereby pool their strategies and methods. This is politically sagacious for another reason. If social movements mobilize people and articulate their needs, the NGO sector can provide the expertise, publicity, and program strategies to meet them. Professional organizations might never engage in politicizing the population, but when they partner with social movements and other citizens' groups, they do come into contact with citizens, albeit indirectly.

In addition, in a globalized world it is no longer possible to insulate political struggles within a country from developments elsewhere. Globalization implies that people's lives are affected by decisions taken in the closed discussion rooms of the World Trade Organization and other distant institutions. Moreover, the intractable problems that confront humanity, like climate change, can only be negotiated through an amalgamation of ideas, energies, and resolutions. In recent years a space has been created for the emergence of global coalitions that speak for the poor and the oppressed across the world. What is important is that these coalitions have succeeded in putting issues on the domestic political agenda that have been neglected by national governments. For example, in the 1980s, global networks such as WIEGO (Women in Informal Employment Globalizing and Organizing) began to advocate for the right of unorganized workers to social protection. In India this sector constitutes almost 94 percent of the labor market. This strategy has been remarkably successful, for in December 2008 the government of India (which has sidestepped the problems that beset this section of the work force for so long) finally passed the Unorganised Sector Workers Social Security Bill. The bill provides social security and job protection to at least 375 million workers in the unorganized sector.

The experience of India's civil society has modified classical theories in at least three ways. First, if they wish their particular cause to achieve success, civil society organizations have to link up with like-minded groups across borders in loosely structured coalitions. Second, the professionalization of civil society organizations is likely to continue. Third, mobilization in civil society will most probably take the route of campaigns that aim to deepen democracy rather than to politicize constituencies or realize popular sovereignty through citizen engagement. Arguably these campaigns will achieve success only if the judiciary and the media are on their side. Deepening democracy might be achieved at the expense of realizing political rights, as well as representation and accountability. But perhaps this is the natural outcome of the professionalization of civil society, not only in India but elsewhere, as countertrends—such as workers' resistance—are no longer able to stand up for themselves.

4. INVOLUNTARY ORGANIZATIONS

The notion of social association presumes a high degree of voluntariness—that is, the ability of individuals to form, join, and exit associations out of their own free will. It is precisely here that one can locate the problem of civil society in countries like India, which are neither completely individuated nor wholly communitarian. Here people experience life as individuals in certain sorts of profession, relationships, vocations, and social commitments. But when they lay claim on the state for benefits such as affirmative action policies, people tend to act as members of a caste or religious group. That is, whereas membership in some associations is based on the principle of voluntary entry and exit, in other associations it is involuntary. The question then is whether involuntary groups are part of civil society or not?

Some scholars would say no. In order for an association to qualify as a civil society organization, its membership must be based on the principle of nondiscrimination, and all organizations must be open and secular. Therefore, the greatest threat to civil society comes from the intrusion of collective identities (Beteille 1999, 2589). I think two issues are at stake here. The first is that involuntary associations are necessarily exclusionary, and the second is that they are likely to put forth claims that are group specific. If, for example, group X demands affirmative action policies for its members alone, then not only are the many Y's excluded, but their demands can only be satisfied at the latter's expense. This breeds anxiety, because exclusions and partisan claims inhibit the capacity of civil society to launch collective action for the general good.

Susanne Rudolph (2000, 1767) points out that most associations are intentional, insofar as ascribed ethnic identities are the product of intention and cultural construction as much as birth. Therefore, these associations cannot be excluded from civil society. It is true that associational life is constitutive of these identities, but this does not cancel out the fact that both the membership and the agenda of these groups are restricted. The problem that such groups pose for the idea that civil society consists only of voluntary associations is, however, not intractable. Consider, for example, that in a plural society no one agenda can possibly be independent of all others. At some point associations of, say, the so-called lower castes will have to intersect with organizations of informal labor, simply because these two identities dovetail into one another. Women who work in the informal sector have to make common cause with women in other social locations, because they share certain problems in common, such as sexual harassment or domestic violence. And all these groups have to link up at some time with environmental groups because climate change affects everyone's lives. The forging of networks in civil society is of tremendous significance for strategic reasons, as well as for reasons of creating identities that overlap. But more importantly, in the process of creating networks and common agendas, partisan projects are modified and brought into line with other agendas that strive for democratization of the general social and economic order.

More important than the internal constitution of groups, therefore, is the process by which these groups and their platforms articulate with and modify each other in the spaces of civil society. From such intricate processes a critical public discourse is forged, and exclusive interests mediated. In other words, the processes by which civil society brings together different interest groups, and the manner in which groups are persuaded to collapse discrete individual interests into a critical public discourse, is as significant as the initial appearance of exclusive demands. This does not imply that organizations that represent discrete interests are compelled to water down their own demands when they enter into transactions with other civil society groups. Rather, it suggests that these demands acquire added political weight when other groups recognize that these are an indispensable component of democratic agendas (Oomen 2004, 128–143). The processes of "bridging" social capital are as politically significant as those of "bonding" social capital. If the former category facilitates the emergence of democratic coalitions, the latter lends political weight to the demand itself.

5. Uncivil Organizations

Despite the confidence that discrete individual agendas can and will be mediated by other platforms in plural civil societies, there is one set of organizations that defy this process. These are closed organizations that single-mindedly pursue a particular interest at the expense of others. Take the cadre-based organization of the religious right in India, the Rashtriya Swayam Sevak Sangh (RSS) or the National Self-Service Alliance. The professed objective of the RSS is not only the creation of a self-confident Hindu identity, but also the construction of a Hindu nation. As the RSS and other affiliates of the religious right have relentlessly pursued this objective since the early decades of the twentieth century, minorities have been put at risk.

The problem is that such organizations not only resist mediations of their own commitments, they also prevent the coming together of other associations. Taking his cue from Robert Putnam's thesis of social capital, Ashutosh Varshney (2002, 46–8) suggests that prior and sustained contact between members of different communities moderates tensions and preempts violence when such tensions arise due to exogenous shocks. Conversely, communal violence has occurred in precisely those cities in which these networks were either not present or had broken down. However, Varshney seems to underplay the contribution of the religious right to the breakdown of intercommunal relations, and to the build up of a climate of hatred, suspicion, and aggression. Research in one of the cities that has been marked by repeated communal riots, Ahmedabad, shows that the RSS and its affiliate organizations have since the 1960s systematically worked to instil in the majority community a profound hatred for the Muslim minority. This systemic mobilization shattered an already fragile associational life between communities. When in 2002 cadres of the Hindu right, backed by mobs, carried out a near-pogrom of the Muslim minority in the city, the civil society that was expected to keep watch on the excesses of power kept quiet (Oommen 2008, 74–75; Chandhoke 2009).

One cannot claim that the RSS is not a civil society association, because it represents itself as a cultural and a social service organization. It has established a network of educational institutions and social service organizations, and in moments of crisis such as natural disasters, RSS cadres are among the first volunteers to begin work in the affected area to rescue and rehabilitate those affected. For these reasons the organization has built up a high degree of trust among the population. From this and related examples, it is clear that civil society organizations need not be democratic nor subscribe to the same core values. Consequently, the only way in which uncivil organizations and their undemocratic agendas can be neutralized is through contestation in civil society itself. This means that democratic organizations in civil society have to be Janus-faced, with one face turned towards the state, and the other turned inwards. In the final instance, as Gramsci had theorized, civil society is a site of contestation.

6. The Relevance of Civil Society

Finally, is civil society relevant for countries like India that are marked by social exclusion, inequality, and poverty? In Europe, civil society emerged in tandem with the consolidation of bourgeois society. The unit of this society is the rights bearing individual who is protected by the rule of law. The problem is that in India, large numbers of citizens are relegated to the margins of society, and do not possess any kind of status. Nor are they protected by the law. Partha Chatterjee has therefore argued that in India civil society is restricted to a fairly small section of citizens, notably the middle classes who speak the language of rights (2001, 172). The poor, who negotiate the travails of everyday existence through the adoption of illegal means and clear violations of the law, occupy the space of political society instead. Though Chatterjee does not explicitly reject civil society, he sees it as irrelevant for a vast majority of Indians. And though he does not valorize political society, he seems to indicate that this space and its mediations are more authentic than those of civil society.

One can accept that the concept of civil society does not admit or sanction all sorts of practices, and that excluded practices need to be studied and conceptualized as well. But there are at least two difficulties that can be identified in Chatterjee's distinction between civil and political society. First, do practices in "political society," such as tapping water and electricity connections illegally, fall into the category of politics or proto-politics? As Hobsbawm puts it in his study of social banditry,

certain forms of politics are strictly speaking proto-politics—undetermined, conservative, and ambiguous (1959, 2). Proto-politics or semipolitics refer to those
practices that seek concessions for the individual or the group. But if the objective
of politics is to shape and reshape the political context in which we live, then we
need a politics that has a broader vision than merely negotiating the problems of
everyday life illegally. Such a politics demands that people be brought into a relationship with one another, that collective action be forged, that the universal be
mediated by the particular, and that citizens participate in the constitution of a
public and critical discourse. State concessions to proto-political activities neither
change formal institutions nor build solidarity. In fact, piecemeal practices might
even strengthen the power of the state. Though such forms of politics can exist in
modern civil societies as well, ultimately democratic agents have to take on the
responsibility of making the transition from short-term practices to long-term
engagement with real modes of power.

Secondly, the suggestion that subaltern groups are untouched by bourgeois ideology seems to overlook the fact that practices transcend the boundaries of discrete
spheres. In their struggles for land rights in squatter settlements, for example, the
poor can be motivated by bourgeois notions of entitlements and rights to property.
Furthermore, illegal transactions are not only a feature of noncivil society spaces,
since formal civil societies also engage in these transactions (Bardhan 2009; Coelho
and Venkat 2009). But more importantly, there is hardly any historical setting in
which a "pure" civil society has been lifted from a textbook and transplanted into
another specific context. The concept of civil society signifies a space and a set of
values, but this space and set of values are mediated and modified by historical contexts as the foregoing discussion has shown. In India's civil society, modern discourses
of rights coexist with practices that reinscribe collective identities, individual self-
consciousness is articulated with subordination to the dictates of the leader of the
caste or religious group, and legal practices intersect with other sorts of practices that
breach the law. In other words, the moment we think of civil society as a plural and
fragmented sphere, the distinction between political and civil society begins to blur.

7. CONCLUSION

This discussion of an actually existing civil society carries at least three implications
for the concept in general. First, since states are basically condensates of power, even
states that lay claims to democracy are likely to be imperfectly democratic.
 Democracy is a project that has to be realized through citizen activism in the space
of civil society. Second, civil society is plural in nature and in composition. Here one
finds chambers of commerce alongside workers' organizations, patriarchal groups
alongside groups that fight for women, caste and racist groups alongside democratic movements fighting for dignity. Civil society possesses no single essence, no

one set of practices that dovetail with each other. Third, one cannot assume that all organizations in civil society will always be democratic. Undemocratic organizations will, therefore, have to be engaged, countered, and even neutralized by groups committed to democracy. In the final instance civil society is a site of struggle between different sorts of groups and commitments (Chandhoke 2001). The example of civil society in India makes this crystal clear.

REFERENCES

Bardhan, P. 2009. "Notes on the Political Economy of India's Tortuous Transition." *Economic and Political Weekly* 5 (December): 31–6.

Beher, A., and A. Prakash. 2004. "India: Expanding and Contracting Democratic Space," in M. Alagappa (ed.) *Civil Society and Political Change in Asia: Expanding and Contracting Democratic Space*. Stanford, Calif.: Stanford University Press.

Beteille A. 1999. "Citizenship, State and Civil Society." *Economic and Political Weekly* September 4–10: 2588–91.

Chandhoke, N. 2001. "The 'Civil' and the 'Political' in Civil Society." *Democratization* vol. 8/2 (Summer): 1–24.

———. 2007. "Democracy and Well-Being in India," in Y. Bangura (ed.) *Democracy and Social Policy*. Basingstoke: Palgrave Macmillan.

———. 2009. "Civil Society in Conflict Cities." *Economic and Political Weekly* October 31: 99–108.

Chatterjee, P. 2001. "On Civil and Political Society in Post-Colonial Democracies," in S. Kaviraj and S. Khilnani (eds.) *Civil Society: History and Possibilities*. Cambridge: Cambridge University Press.

Coelho, K., and T. Venkat. 2009. "The Politics of Civil Society: Neighbourhood Associationism in Chennai." *Economic and Political Weekly*, June 27, 358–367.

De Tocqueville, A. 2000. *Democracy in America*. Transl. and ed. and H. Mansfield and D. Winthrop. Chicago: University of Chicago Press.

Gramsci, A. 1971. *Selections from the Prison Notebooks*. Transl. and ed. by Q. Hoare and G. Nowell. New York: International Publishers.

Gupta, D. 1997. "Civil Society in the Indian Context: Letting the State off the Hook." *Contemporary Sociology* vol. 26/3 (May): 305–07.

Habermas, J. 1989. *The Structural Transformation of the Public Sphere: An Inquiry into a Category of Bourgeois Society*. Transl. T. Burger. Cambridge, Mass.: MIT Press.

Hobsbawm, E. J. 1959. *Primitive Rebels*. Manchester: Manchester University Press.

Jayal, N. 2007. "The Role of Civil Society," in S. Ganguly, L. Diamond, and M. Plattner (eds.) *The State of India's Democracy*. Baltimore: John Hopkins University Press.

Katzenstein, M., S. Kothari, and U. Mehta. 2001. "Social Movement Politics in India: Institutions, Interests, and Identities," in A. Kohli (ed.) *The Success of India's Democracy*. Cambridge: Cambridge University Press.

Kothari, R. 1988. *State Against Democracy: In Search of Humane Governance*. Delhi: Ajanta Publications.

———. 1989. "The Non-Party Political Process." *Economic and Political Weekly*, February 4: 216–24.

Mahajan, G. 1999. "Civil Society and Its Avatars: What Happened to Freedom and Democracy?" *Economic and Political Weekly*, May 15: 1188–96.

Oommen, T. K. 2004. *Nation, Civil Society and Social Movements*. New Delhi: Sage.

———. 2008. *Reconciliation in Post-Godhra Gujarat*. New Delhi: Pearson Longman.

Parajuli, P. 2001. "Power and Knowledge in Development Discourse: New Social Movements and the State in India," in N. Jayal (ed.) *Democracy in India*. New Delhi and New York: Oxford University Press.

PRIA (Participatory Research in Asia). 2003. *Invisible yet Widespread: The Non-Profit Sector in India*. New Delhi: PRIA.

Rudolph, S. 2000. "Civil Society and the Realm of Freedom." *Economic and Political Weekly*, May 13: 1762–9.

Shah, G. 2004. *Social Movements in India: Review of Literature*. 2nd ed. New Delhi: Sage.

Sheth, D. L. 1983. "Grass-Roots Stirrings and the Future of Politics." *Alternatives,* vol 9(1): 1–24.

———. 2004. "Globalisation and New Politics of Micro-Movements." *Economic and Political Weekly*, January 1: 45–58.

Varshney, A. 2002. *Ethnic Conflict and Civic Life: Hindus and Muslims in India*. New Haven, Conn.: Yale University Press.

CHAPTER 15

CIVIL SOCIETY IN SUB-SAHARAN AFRICA

EBENEZER OBADARE

In recent times, scholarly enthusiasm about the idea of civil society appears to have waned somewhat, supplanted by something approximating a state of academic fatigue. Whereas in the early 1980s civil society enjoyed an intellectual renaissance that saw its widespread use by academics and activists alike, many scholars now openly express doubts about its usefulness as a concept, and some are already celebrating its demise (Shefner 2009; Wiarda 2003). In most of sub-Saharan Africa, old anxieties about the capacity of civil society to expound African socialities have also resurfaced. Should new life be breathed into this idea, and if so how? In reflecting on this question, this chapter provides a critical survey of the contemporary history of civil society in sub-Saharan Africa and concludes that, while the early promise of civil society may have been exaggerated there is equal danger in inflating current levels of disillusionment with a set of ideas that retain real analytic and practical utility.

1. Days of Enchantment

Civil society crept into academic discourse in sub-Saharan Africa in the early 1980s and was guaranteed a warm reception. The entire African continent was on the cusp of profound change. Three decades into the postcolonial era, political elites were having a turbulent time justifying their stay in power. The heady days of the immediate post-independence period seemed like another age, as countries faced up to prostrate economies, a listless youth demographic, and growing demands for political liberalization. This was the moment when civil society, fresh from its revolutionary feats in Eastern Europe, found its way into the vocabulary of opposition groups in Africa.

For those of a historical predilection, there was something familiar in all this. Specific moments in the evolution of the subcontinent have always produced or been animated by ideas. Accordingly, the state, the bourgeoisie, and voluntary associations have each, in their rise and fall, symbolized important milestones in the unending quest for the drivers of African development. Civil society seemed to be the latest incarnation of this chain of ideas, as well as its apotheosis. For members of the opposition, which in most parts of Africa meant anyone who, as Chabal (1991) might have argued "was not part of the state," civil society was an ideational godsend—a banner under which various groups, hitherto sundered by state manipulation, could rally. Civil society became not only a vehicle for ideological clarity and coherence, but also a space of sociability outside the reach of a traditionally overbearing state. From the expansive cloth of civil society, other forces fashioned designs to suit their own projects and objectives, deepening the frustration of purists who urged a more nuanced approach to its possibilities.

Two key points emerge from this analysis. The first is that the context in which these ideas were introduced into African academic and political discourse reinforced a tendency to understand civil society almost exclusively in relation to democratization and the state, though there is nothing culturally exceptional about this frame. As White (1994) has pointed out, civil society has always been an "analytical hat stand" on which different social forces have hung their agendas. And according to Paley, "Groups siphon vocabulary from internationally circulating discourses and enact distinctive meanings and practices" (2008, 7).

Second, a tendency for creative adaptation is part of the history of civil society thinking, since civil society has never enjoyed a single, uncontested meaning (Keane 1998). On the contrary, it has always been a "reactive idea" having "arisen and sometimes appealed quite widely in exceptional situations or moments of crisis, as a way of exorcising a certain type of threat" (Nairn 1997, 75). In the sub-Saharan Africa of the early and mid-1980s, that threat was a centralized state with overweening powers of coercion, and a determination to use them to force through an unpopular neoliberal economic agenda of "structural adjustment."

To the extent that it provided a battle cry against the state, civil society could be said to have met the needs of the moment, but this was not without its own problems as over time, the struggle against the state encouraged a tendency to define civil society in solely adversarial terms, thus stripping the idea of its all-important "historical density" (Honneth 1993, 19). By providing financial and material support to organizations and movements allied with this tendency, development agencies and international institutions played a crucial role in legitimizing a particular vision of civil society as a delegitimizing force, comprising a phalanx of largely urban-based associations.

2. A History of Tensions

To what enduring African problems should the language of civil society be addressed? Which particular sociocultural agents should be privileged in this conversation, and why? And where should civil society scholarship in Africa direct its gaze—to the past, where urgent work of cultural excavation is required, or to the present, where the task of economic and political reconstruction is no less important?

In raising these questions, my intent is to emphasize one perspective that is usually overlooked: that debates over the meaning and possibilities of civil society are more often than not a continuation of academic politics by other means. The intention here is not to demonize these politics, but to point to the existence of real epistemological differences among African/ist scholars which predate the arrival of the civil society debate. These differences have tended to reproduce and map onto the contours of preexisting rivalries. When, for example, Mahmood Mamdani questions "to what extent we can talk of the existence of civil society in contemporary African countries? What is the expression of its coming into being? And what is the significance of this process, particularly from the point of view of democratic struggle?" (1995, 604), it is clear that he is summating a genealogy of radical scholarship that tends to be on its guard against "a one-eyed vision of social and political processes" (1995, 3) in Africa, an attitude which evacuates ideas "of their moral contents" and "their substratum of implicating ethics" (Ekeh 1983, 17).

On one side of this debate are scholars who urge a critical distance from civil society because of the dangers they perceive in misapplying Western political constructs to African circumstances, especially when those constructs involve "such history-soaked concepts as civil society" (Ekeh 1992, 188). To varying degrees, this skepticism permeates the work of the Comaroffs (1999), Mamdani (1996), Mustapha (1998), Callaghy (1994), and Orvis (2001). In addition to its cultural and historical specificity, these scholars have genuine worries about the utility of civil society when confronted by sub-Saharan Africa's notoriously unstable social and political processes. In a memorable phrase, Callaghy equated the search for civil society in Africa with "the long Africanist flirtation with class analysis, [where] you often 'find' what you go looking for if you try hard enough. In the case of civil society, I would argue that there is even less reality out there than with 'classes'" (Callaghy 1994, 250).

For the skeptics, uneasiness with civil society's "ontological status" (Comaroff and Comaroff 1999) sets the tone for other grounds for caution. For example, African associational life is dominated by ascriptive (as opposed to voluntary) groups, and is thus perceived to be incongruous with the ideal of civil society in Western theory. For Ekeh (1992, 123) in particular, the problem lies not so much with ascriptive groupings in themselves, though it would help considerably if the individual had some leeway from the cultural obligations imposed by membership of associations they are born into. Rather, the real problem is that whereas "civil society requires that the worth of the unique individual be recognized beyond his or her ethnic group...the ideology of kinship imposes restrictions on the moral worth of individuals, with those from outside its domain being less morally valued than the kinsfolk....The universalism of civil society helps to offer common moral empathy, whereas kinship is restrictive in its meaning of freedom." If these problems are legitimate, and African associational life is indeed dominated by ascriptive groupings, does it not follow that civil society is "the prerogative of European-type industrialized societies?" (Jorgensen 1996, 40).

While not necessarily rejecting the assumption that ascriptive associations tend to impose cultural limits on individual agency, scholars on the other side of the civil society debate insist that that radical possibilities continue to exist within these associations. In addition, a variety of other institutions exist in Africa for protecting collective interests beyond ethnic and kinship associations (Bratton 1989, 411). The "habits of association," to borrow Alexis de Tocqueville's famous phrase, can be found in most societies, activated by the need "to organize to protect their families, develop their agriculture or crafts, form some health service or educational initiative, arrange for their burials and so on" (Jorgensen 1996, 40). Therefore, civil society is "indispensable to conceptualize politics in Africa" (Chabal 1991, 93). Indeed, for Harbeson (1994, 27), the language of civil society is best suited for this purpose because "civil society by definition roots political values in culturally specific value systems and is thus singularly valuable in overcoming and counteracting ethnocentrism."

Speaking of patrimonialism, Jean-Francois Medard (1996, 195) once observed that "the generality of the concept can be heuristically confronted to the singularity of historical situations." This seems to sum up the attitude of its supporters to the language of civil society in Africa, whereby a keen awareness of its limitations is balanced by an unquenchable faith in its adaptability to the singularity of historical situations. What, therefore, has civil society brought to the table in the contexts of sub-Saharan Africa, and how has its intervention shaped the changing balance of forces between state and society?

3. OPPOSITION, INFLUENCE, AND CHANGE

The 1980s were a critical period in the history of sub-Saharan Africa. Across the continent, the triumphalism that had greeted the transition from colonial overlordship to self-rule in the late 1950s and the 1960s had disappeared, to be replaced by a palpable disillusionment with postcolonial elites who, it was generally believed, had sacrificed the promise of the post-independence era on the altar of their own greed and incompetence. This sense of anomie was symbolized by the 1984–85 Ethiopia famine which resulted in the loss of thousands of lives, accompanied by the intervention of large numbers of Western NGOs and other development agencies.

Disappointment in Africa with the postcolonial elite was reinforced by the growth of a global ideology that focused on the perceived failings of the state as the supreme form of human solidarity. In the West there was considerable anxiety over what was widely seen as the welfare state's inexorable loss of influence and capacity, "too remote to manage the problems of daily life and too constrained to confront the global problems that affect us" (Guehenno 1995, 12–13). Some scholars (such as Bayart 2007) have disputed this assessment of the nation-state's performance, arguing that what many see as its failings are in fact proof of the state's tenacity and triumph, but the rise of anti-state ideology did create the discursive space required for the language of civil society to take hold. As John and Jean Comaroff put it, "at a time when distrust of sovereign authority across the political spectrum borders on paranoia, the Idea [of civil society] would have to be invented if it did not already exist. In Africa, Asia, Europe. Everywhere" (1999, 18).

In her analysis of civil society in Eastern Europe, Chandhoke (2001, 2) identifies three different "historical meanings" of these ideas: the wish "to limit formerly untrammeled power of the state by the institutionalization of political, but more importantly, civil rights and the rule of law;" "to carve out a domain that would function independently of state regulation;" and to assert "that the active engagement of ordinary men and women in groups, neighbourhoods, professional and social associations, and voluntary agencies, was a good thing in itself." All these meanings resonated powerfully in sub-Saharan Africa, where the maladroitness of the elite and the dysfunctionality of the state necessitated new patterns of social and political relations between governance and the governed.

While this resonance was dictated by obvious material circumstances, the idealization of civil society as the "good society" and as the prime vehicle for its accomplishment was championed by international financial institutions like the World Bank and the International Monetary Fund (IMF), often acting at the behest of Western countries, and supplemented by local NGOs (Edwards 2009). The role of NGOs in civil society in sub-Saharan Africa is already the subject of an extensive and often contentious literature which explains their role as institutions of "transnational governmentality" (Lewis 2002, 9).[1] In this role, NGOs often perform as analogues of similar institutions in Western countries, promoting a rhetoric that validates their existence and filling in for the state even as their expansion effectuates a diminution in the state's capacity to meet social needs. This is not always true. A tunnel-vision approach to the politics and practices of NGOs can occlude clear thinking about the social ecology in which they grow and flourish, the important role that NGOs have played in the delegitimizing of ossified political authorities, the bringing of African issues to wider international discourses, and their collaboration with aspects of political society that, in some notable cases, has led to the dislodgment of dictatorial regimes in Benin and Nigeria, to name but two examples. These experiences raise the crucial question: what possibilities do ideas about civil society in Africa create?

For Livesey (2009, 219), central to the recent popularity of civil society is its "capaciousness" and "capacity to comprise complexity and plurality." For Zakaria, part of the beauty of civil society lies in its ability to provide "the basis for a new liberal cosmopolitanism that guarantees the liberty of the individual against the populist temptations that are seen haunting all forms of democracy" (Zakaria 2003, cited in Livesey 2009, 5). And, most crucially, for the Eastern European resistance in the 1980s, the attraction of civil society resided in its perceived capacity to "tie together all the spheres of social action not belonging to state institutions, insofar as these spheres could serve as a basis for the construction of a democratic opposition. *In fact, it was precisely the vagueness of this concept which gave it a distinct strategical advantage*" (Honneth 1993, 19; emphasis added).

For the sub-Saharan African "resistance" which emerged in the early 1980s, civil society's utility in drawing up "a programme for radical democratization" (Honneth 1993, 19) was its most attractive feature. It was also expedient to belong to, or organize on the basis of, civil society, given that at this time there was no better guarantee of reliable access to foreign donors committed to "empowering" or "strengthening" civil society. These factors explain the frequency with which the language of civil society was employed in otherwise legitimate mobilizations across the continent by women's associations, labor movements, trade unions, student groups, civil liberties and human rights organizations, pro-democracy associations and citizen groups—in short, any group that opposed the status quo. To belong to civil society was to stake a certain claim to authenticity and morality, usually juxtaposed against the decadence of the state and its agents.

To the extent that these ideas about civil society as the "good" society succeeded, it was due in large part to the reluctance of its champions to admit to the essential moral and intellectual complexities involved. But as earlier in Eastern Europe, the romanticization of civil society by the African "resistance" and the widespread tendency to emphasize its presumed democratic properties were themselves a function of the demands of the historical moment. For many, it was civil society's utility, not its ambiguity, that really mattered.

4. THE DAWN OF REALISM

With initial exuberance on the wane, a greater sense of realism has emerged about what "actually existing civil societies" (Mamdani 1995) are capable of accomplishing in Africa. Three decades on, few expect civil society to be a magic wand for democratic stability or economic development in Africa, and in some quarters, civil society is blamed for the continent's failure to consummate the promise of the early post-independence period. What explains this sudden disillusionment? Why has civil society in Africa failed to live up to the grandiose claims of its pioneer proponents?

There is no shortage of answers to these questions. They range from a failure to appreciate the difficulties posed by civil society's roots in alien cultural soil (Guyer 1994), to the rush to equate a high-profile NGO sector with a resurgent civil society (Lewis 2004), to the willful inattentiveness of some to its moral ambiguity and the tensions and contradictions that are always present (Boussard 2002; Monga 1996), to an essentialism that invests civil society with democratic values when the evidence suggests that it has no determining properties at all, whether democratic or undemocratic (Bangura and Gibbon 1992, 21).

Other scholars have focused on the key assumptions that underpin state-civil society analyses in Africa, particularly those that define the political struggles of the post-independence era as between an inefficient, authoritarian, rent-seeking, coercive, neopatrimonial, and morally bankrupt state and a peaceful, transparent, democratic, and accountable civil society. Mustapha (1996) rejects this rigid bifurcation on the grounds that it reduces state processes to rent-seeking, thereby ignoring the role of the state "as the provider of services and facilities to underprivileged groups in society, within the context of the post-colonial nationalist project and the political coalitions built up around it" (1996, 226). Furthermore, he bemoans the refusal of civil society advocates to acknowledge that "power and exploitation is not limited to the state sector alone, for these are also to be found in the informal sector," and that "traditional values, purported to form the foundation of democratic associational life, are far from unambiguous" (1996, 227).

Perhaps the most damning indictment of civil society in Africa is that it has become an impediment to the emergence of a truly democratic political culture. Instead of providing viable alternatives, the organizational culture of civil society bears an uncanny resemblance to the verticality and personalism that characterize existing political culture at large. According to Boussard, "Besides being controlled by strong charismatic leaders, some civil society organisations have problems with lack of accountability, transparency, rotating leadership and representation" (2002, 163).

In sub-Saharan Africa, urban-based associations, and NGOs in particular, have become the *bête noire* of those who argue from this position. Their critique ranges from the reliance of most NGOs on foreign aid, which weakens their roots in domestic civil society constituencies and formations, to their alleged appropriation of the idea of civil society as a whole, thereby excluding rural and community-based associations which may have stronger and more organic linkages to the majority of the African population who live in villages and depend on the land for their subsistence. Suffice it to say that not all NGOs are alike in these respects, and their organizational cultures are certainly more diverse than the critics admit. But the criticism is valid and is itself a reflection of the long shadow that professionalized, urban-based NGOs have cast on the public sphere and the culture of social movements across sub-Saharan Africa, especially over the last twenty years. Indeed, some of the criticism seems unimpeachable. It is difficult to argue, for example, against Mamdani's contention that contemporary NGOs and civil society based movements

in sub-Saharan Africa are undermined by "their lack of a peasant base, and consequently their limited liberal agenda" (Mamdani 1993, 47); or that NGOs' reliance on
external funding has not influenced the issues and agendas that they have taken
up.

5. Conclusion: Beyond the Backlash

> In the developing countries that I know best, whether the issue is agrarian reform,
> community development, basic human needs, family planning, sustainable
> development, and now civil society, the same people always seem to form the
> local commissions and agencies that show the aid donors how and where to
> spend their monies. It is not merely love of public policy issues that motivates
> these persons; having been in quite a number of their homes, I can report that, as
> in political Washington, they have learned to "do well by doing good"; that is, by
> profiting personally and/or publicly by jumping quickly on the bandwagon of
> every new U.S. initiative that comes down the pike (Wiarda 2003, 144).

Wiarda's cynicism has also infected perceptions of civil society in sub-Saharan
Africa.[2] While in the early 1980s, civil society was hailed by some as the apotheosis
of the African quest for modernity, the mood in academic circles has become decidedly more somber. If the critics are to be believed, civil society has run its course,
and it is time that "the illusions of civil society" were jettisoned (Shefner 2009). For
Shefner, the concept of civil society has not merely run its course: "Civil society
analysis interferes with our understanding of what kinds of conflicts exist, who the
constituents of varied groups embroiled in conflicts are, and the differential results
of varied strategies and struggles" (Shefner 2009, 207). In short, civil society has
become a barrier to understanding the social and political realities and possibilities
of African development.

A number of responses need to be made to criticisms such as these. First, when
scholars criticize civil society, it is often difficult to establish whether the critique
applies to civil society as a concept or as a reality. Second, because African civil societies are shaped in many different ways and have specific strengths and weaknesses,
analytic generalization is always difficult. Third, when idealists emphasize the radical possibilities of civil society, problems arise not because of these ideas themselves
but because scholars fail to acknowledge "the dark side" of civil society and its
implications (Colas 1997, Obadare 2004). And fourth, radical and conservative critiques of civil society are necessarily dissonant, each informed by entirely different
expectations of what the concept means and the social and political projects that
civil society is supposed to sustain.

This fourth observation is arguably the most important. Most criticism of
civil society in sub-Saharan Africa has focused on the alleged weaknesses of

contemporary civil society associations, especially urban-based NGOs. Some of this criticism is justified, but it begs the question of whether such criticism itself rests on "a monistic view of the very area of life that is supposed to be the home of plurality" (Parekh 2004, 27). Put differently, the main problem with academic critiques of African civil societies is that they only make sense within a paradigm in which civil society is reduced to the realm of certain kinds of voluntary association.

By contrast, when civil society is viewed as an "ecosystem" which includes a wide variety of types of association, engagements in the public sphere, and relationships between civil and political action, it is clear that these ecologies have played an important role in the "third wave" of democratization in sub-Saharan Africa, even when certain types of association display behavior that is non-egalitarian and susceptible to "volatile individual impulses" (Edwards 2009; Parekh 2004, 29). Research has shown that "different degrees of direct and indirect compulsion are to be found within voluntary associations" and that many of their leaders "are themselves closely connected to the state, and many of the associations they lead exhibit different degrees of undemocratic practice" (Bangura and Gibbon 1992; Abrahamsen 1996; Mustapha 1998, 228). Hence, a healthy associational ecosystem does not automatically translate into a healthy civil society, but a focus on associations alone (even including ascriptive groups) imposes arbitrary limits on the plurality and spaciousness that the language of civil society encodes, and therefore on the utility of this concept in both theory and practice. The challenge before the next wave of civil society discourse in sub-Saharan Africa is to escape from the prison imposed by particular kinds of association in order to capture what Mbembe (2006) has described as "the power of the street" across the continent. This will involve an analysis of both old and new forms of politics in which participants draw on a range of cultural resources that do not necessarily lend themselves to the strictures of formal associations. Crucially, this will be in keeping with both the eclecticism that characterizes ideas about civil society and with subversive interpretations of these ideas which emphasize their capacity to inspire subaltern alternatives and actions (Obadare 2009; Chan 2002).

Thus, if civil society is to gain more analytic traction in sub-Saharan Africa, its discourse must be liberated from "orthodox confines" (Comaroff and Comaroff 1999, 33) in order to revalorize the questions that lie at the heart of radical scholarship about the African condition. How did Africa get into its current situation? What are the sociocultural determinants of the African crisis? How, if at all, can civil society illuminate an understanding of these questions, and how can it inspire new social movements and new forms of politics? Civil society cannot and should not be expected to eliminate the wide differences that exist between schools of thought and intellectual traditions. Instead, what it offers is a language that is rich enough to assist in the task of historical accounting, while at the same time being sufficiently flexible to accommodate the plethora of visions and approaches that scholars will continue to bring to their analyses of the African condition—past, present, and future.

NOTES

....

1. See Jorgensen 1996; Ndegwa 1996; Edwards and Fowler 2002; Kelsall and Igoe 2005; and Ndegwa 1996.

2. Chris Hann (2004) makes similar observations about what he refers to as the "mystery" of civil society in "post-socialist Eurasia," suggesting that it has no real existence in the absence of international aid funds and the "strategic managerialism" of its entrepreneurs.

REFERENCES

....

Abrahamsen, R. 1996. "Economic Liberalization, Civil Society and Democratization: A Critique of Some Common Assumptions in Contemporary Development Theory." in M. H. Hansen and A. E. Ruud (eds.) *Weak? Strong? Civil? Embedded? New Perspectives on State-Society Relations in the Non-Western World*. Oslo: Centre for Development and the Environment, University of Oslo, 15–25.

Bangura, Y. and P. Gibbon. 1992. "Adjustment, Authoritarianism and Democracy in Sub-Saharan Africa: An Introduction to Some Conceptual and Empirical Issues," in P. Gibbon et al. (eds.) *Authoritarianism, Democracy, and Adjustment: The Politics of Economic Reform in Africa*. Uppsala: Nordiska Afrikainstitutet.

Bayart, J. F. 2007. *Global Subjects: A Political Critique of Globalization*. Cambridge: Polity.

Boussard, C. 2002. "Civil Society and Democratization: Conceptual and Empirical Challenges," in O. Elgstrom and G. Hyden (eds.) *Development and Democracy: What Have We Learned and How?* London: Routledge.

Bratton, M. 1989. "Civil Society and Associational Life in Africa." *World Politics* 41(3): 407–30.

Callaghy, T. M. 1994. "Civil Society, Democracy, and Economic Change in Africa: A Dissenting Opinion about Resurgent Societies," in J. W. Harbeson et al. (eds.) *Civil Society and the State in Africa*. London: Lynne Rienner, 231–54.

Chabal, P. 1991. *Power in Africa: An Essay in Political Interpretation*. Basingstoke: Macmillan.

Chan, S. 2002. *Composing Africa: Civil Society and its Discontents*. Tampere, Finland: Tampere Peace Research Institute Occasional Paper 86.

Chandhoke, N. 2001. "The 'Civil' and the 'Political' in Civil Society." *Democratization*. 8(2): 1–24.

Colas, D. 1997. *Civil Society and Fanaticism: Conjoined Histories*. Transl. Amy Jacobs. Stanford, Calif.: Stanford University Press.

Comaroff, J. L., and Comaroff, J. (eds.) 1999. *Civil Society and the Political Imagination in Africa*. Chicago: University of Chicago Press.

Edwards, M. 2009. *Civil Society*, 2nd ed. Cambridge: Polity.

Edwards, M., and Fowler, A. (eds.) 2002. *The Earthscan Reader in NGO Management*. London: Earthscan.

Ekeh, P. P. 1983. *Colonialism and Social Structure*. Ibadan: Ibadan University Press.

———. 1992. "The Constitution of Civil Society in African History and Publics," in B. Caron et al. (eds.) *Democratic Transition in Africa*. Ibadan, Nigeria: Center for Research, Documentation and University Exchange.

Guehenno, J-M. 1995. *The End of the Nation-State.* Transl. Victoria Elliott. Minneapolis: University of Minnesota Press.

Guyer, J. I. 1994. "The Spatial Dimensions of Civil Society in Africa: An Anthropologist Looks at Nigeria," in J. Harbeson et al. (eds.) *Civil Society and the State in Africa.* London: Lynne Rienner, 215–29.

Hann, C. 2004. "In the Church of Civil Society," in M. Glasius et al. (eds.) *Exploring Civil Society: Political and Cultural Contexts.* London: Routledge, 44–50.

Honneth, A. 1993. "Conceptions of Civil Society." *Radical Philosophy* 64: 19–22.

Jorgensen, L. 1996. "What are NGOs doing in Civil Society?" in A. Clayton (ed.) *NGOs, Civil Society and the State: Building Democracy in Transitional Societies.* Oxford: International NGO Research and Training Center, 36–55.

Keane, J. 1998. *Civil Society: Old Images, New Visions.* Cambridge: Polity Press.

Kelsall, T., and Igoe, J. 2005. *Between a Rock and a Hard Place: African NGOs, Donors and the State.* Durham, N.C.: Carolina Academic Press.

Lewis, D. 2002. "Civil Society in Africa: Reflections on the Usefulness of a Concept." *Development and Change* 33(4): 569–86.

——. 2004. "On the Difficulty of Studying 'Civil Society': NGOs, State and democracy in Bangladesh." *Contributions to Indian Sociology* 38(3): 299–322.

Livesey, J. 2009. *Civil Society and Empire: Ireland and Scotland in the Eighteenth-Century Atlantic World.* New Haven, Conn.: Yale University Press.

Mamdani, M. 1993. "The Sun is not Always Dead at Midnight." *Monthly Review* 45(3): 27–48.

——. 1995. "A Critique of the State and Civil Society Paradigm in Africanist Studies," in M. Mamdani and E. Wamba-dia-Wamba (eds.) *African Studies in Social Movements and Democracy.* Dakar: Council for the Development of Social Science Research in Africa (CODESRIA), 602–16.

——. 1996. *Citizen and Subject: Contemporary Africa and the Legacy of Late Colonialism.* Princeton, N.J.: Princeton University Press.

Mbembe, A. 2006. "On Politics as a Form of Expenditure." in J. and J. L. Comaroff (eds.) *Law and Disorder in the Postcolony.* Chicago: University of Chicago Press, 299–335.

Medard, J.-F. 1996. "Patrimonialism, Neo-Patrimonialism and the Study of the African Post-Colonial State in sub-Saharan Africa," in H. Markussen (ed.) *Improved Natural Resource Management: The Role of Formal Organization and Informal Networks and Institutions.* Occasional paper No. 17, International Development Studies, Roskilde University, 193–206.

Monga, C. 1996. *The Anthropology of Anger: Civil Society and Democracy in Africa.* Boulder, Colo.: Lynne Rienner.

Mustapha, A. R. 1996. "Agriculture, Rural and Informal Sector Activities Under SAP," in A. Fadahunsi and T. Babawale (eds.) *Nigeria Beyond Structural Adjustment: Towards a Popular Democratic Development Alternative.* Lagos: Friedrich Ebert Foundation.

——. 1998. "When Will Independence End? Democratization and Civil Society in Rural Africa," in L. Rudebeck et al. (eds.) *Democratization in the Third World Concrete Cases in Comparative and Theoretical Perspective.* Basingstoke: Macmillan.

Nairn, T. 1997. *Faces of Nationalism: Janus Revisited.* London: Verso.

Ndegwa, S. 1996. *The Two Faces of Civil Society: NGOs and Politics in Africa.* West Hartford, Conn.: Kumarian Press.

Obadare, E. 2004. "In Search of a Public Sphere: The Fundamentalist Challenge to Civil Society in Nigeria." *Patterns of Prejudice* 38(2): 177–98.

——. 2009. "The Uses of Ridicule: Humour, Infrapolitics and Civil Society in Nigeria." *African Affairs* 108(431): 241–61.

Orvis, S. 2001. "Civil Society in Africa or African Civil Society?" *Journal of Asian and African Studies* 36(1): 17–38.

Paley, J. 2008. "Introduction," in J. Paley (ed.) *Democracy: Anthropological Approaches.* Santa Fe, N.M.: School for Advanced Research Press, 3–20.

Parekh, B. 2004. "Putting Civil Society in its Place," in M. Glasius et al. (eds.) *Exploring Civil Society: Political and Cultural Contexts.* London: Routledge, 15–25.

Shefner, J. 2009. *The Illusion of Civil Society.* University Park: Pennsylvania State University Press.

White, G. 1994. "Civil society, Democratisation and Development (I): Clearing the Analytical Ground." *Democratisation* 1(3): 378–89.

Wiarda, H. J. 2003. *Civil Society: The American Model and Third World Development.* Boulder, Colo.: Westview Press.

PART IV

THE NORMS OF CIVIL SOCIETY

CHAPTER 16

......

CIVIL SOCIETY AND SOCIAL CAPITAL

......

MICHAEL WOOLCOCK

OVER the last twenty-five years, the concepts of civil society and social capital have experienced a remarkable rise to prominence across many disciplines and sectors. Though they refer to broadly similar entities, it is generally agreed that civil society comprises those organizations that complement (and contextualize) states and markets, while at a lower unit of analysis social capital refers to the norms and networks that enable people to act collectively (Woolcock and Narayan 2000). Civil society may be the more encompassing concept and enjoy a longer intellectual history (Seligman 1992; Alexander 2006; Edwards 2009), but its operationalization in contemporary research and policy debates has often been made manifest through the concept of social capital.[1] The primary impact of both concepts, I argue, has come less through the novel empirical results they generate or their capacity to forge an inherently elusive scholarly or policy consensus on complex issues, than through their capacity to facilitate constructive dialogue on these issues between groups who would otherwise rarely (if ever) interact, and which necessarily require such dialogue in order to identify supportable ways forward.

This chapter is written in four parts. The first provides an overview of the concept of social capital, and the second provides a brief survey of the substantive issues to which it has drawn attention, especially as they pertain to the role of civil society organizations in facilitating collective action, economic development, and democratic governance. Part three considers some of the key implications of this research for policy and practice and part four concludes the discussion.

1. SOCIAL CAPITAL: AN OVERVIEW
OF ITS RISE AND RELEVANCE

In its most elementary form, the idea of social capital provides a name for an intuitive, transcultural recognition that we are inherently social beings, and that this has significant consequences for a host of other substantive issues we care about—variations on the maxim that "it's not what you know, it's who you know" are to be found in languages all over the world.[2] Social capital, defined as the norms and networks that enable people to act collectively, provides a common frame of reference for conducting conversations about these important issues across disciplinary, methodological, ideological, and cultural lines, conversations which are vital—indeed necessary to the resolution of many of the issues themselves—but which otherwise occur too rarely. Indeed, I argue that facilitating such conversations has been social capital's vital first-order contribution to scholarship and policy over the last twenty years. Pursuing these conversations in greater and contextually specific detail, however, requires recourse to terms and theories that are more precisely suited to the task.

Since the mid-1980s, both "social capital" and "civil society" have moved from the margins to the mainstream of social science terminology. From the publication of Coleman (1988) and then the famous work of Putnam (1993), social capital became, for better or worse, one of sociology's most high-profile "exports" (Portes 2000) to the realms of public policy and popular debates,[3] enjoying citation counts similar to other everyday terms such as "political parties" (see Woolcock 2010). In comparative terms, the use of social capital in academic discourse over the twenty year period from the mid-1980s to the mid-2000s increased by a factor of over one hundred, while the companion concept of "human capital" increased by roughly a factor of twenty, as did "civil society." Few terms other than "globalization" can make such claims.

Social capital has done much of its scholarly and policy work through its status as an "essentially contested concept" (Gallie 1956).[4] That is, its coherence and usefulness rests not on a clear consensus regarding its definition and measurement, but—like culture, power, and the rule of law—on its capacity to draw attention to salient features of the social and political world that are of significance in their own right and are valued for different aspects of everyday life (such as education, health, and crime prevention). The very fact that social capital has been used by everyone from Marxists to rational choice theorists to network scholars and structural functionalists means that a universally agreed-upon rendering cannot emerge. While vigorous debate is to be encouraged and expected, social capital is fated to be as controversial as the broader theoretical and epistemological debates in which it is inherently embedded.

Strictly speaking, one did not need the concept of social capital to have a conversation about the salience of social norms and networks prior to its rise in popularity, but to have such conversations in the public domain, and to have them across so many different sectors and countries, something is required that is more encompassing and tractable than these formal academic terms supply. For organizations like the World Bank, for example, which itself had only established a department for social development concerns in 1995, the timely emergence of social capital seemed to offer a convenient discursive bridge between economics (the dominant discipline at the bank) and the other social sciences (Bebbington et al. 2006). For its emerging portfolio of projects that stressed civic participation, harnessing and "building" social capital provided the necessary (if crude and imperfect) discursive justification that World Bank vice presidents and task managers needed to distinguish their proposals from those of more orthodox initiatives that focused on building "human capital" (schools and hospitals) and "physical capital" (road, bridges, and irrigation systems). Moreover, they rightly argued, even the efficacy of education and agriculture projects turns in no small measure on their engagement with the local social context. Community norms and civil society networks, for example, play a major role in shaping the extent to which farmers adopt technical innovations such as new fertilizers (Isham 2002). Independently of whether such projects worked or could be shown to be demonstrably better than their alternatives, they first had to be demarcated, justified, and promoted, and a constituency supporting them had to be mobilized. Using the language of social capital performed these tasks.

For some critics, however, any such efforts seemingly amounted to a sell-out, a naïve capitulation of social theory and social spaces to the ever-encroaching forces of economic logic, which in turn would only overwhelm and further marginalize anything that was distinctively "social" (Fine 2001, Somers 2008). But social theory is not so fragile, economic theory is not so robust, and some form of mutual exchange is needed for sensible resolutions to be crafted in all realms of life, especially those where the topics of debate are inherently contentious.[5] To be politically useful, concepts do not have to meet standards of academic purity. Rather, they need to generate productive debate within and across constituent groups, debates that should include highlighting the limits of those concepts. And while deploying different terminology is surely an insufficient lever of policy change, it is a necessary one (as every national election and marketing campaign attests), even as the use of particular concepts themselves must be adjusted with evolving circumstances and shifting audiences.

To this end, in the sections that follow I consider some of the key findings of social capital research and debate in the specific domains of collective action, economic development, and democratic governance, but laying greater stress on their outreach to other realms of the academy and to public debate rather than to their narrow technical merits. Understood in this way, social capital's positive impact largely takes the form of its status as a public discursive good, providing a common frame of reference around which a range of agreements and disagreements can be discerned and refined across disciplinary lines and professional boundaries, something that is especially important for civil society groups and the types of issues around which they mobilize. For many of the issues to which the language of social capital has been directed—such as social justice and equity, whose resolution largely requires political, not technical, answers—it was precisely these kinds of debates that were (and remain) necessary to craft legitimate, supportable resolutions.

2. Applications to Civil Society Research and Practice

A range of studies from across the sciences and social sciences have documented just how central are social relations for shaping, and in turn understanding, human behavior (see Woolcock and Radin 2008). As political theorists such as Aristotle, David Hume, and Alex de Tocqueville have long reminded us, however, and as Putnam (1993, 2000) made the centrepiece of his analysis, the nature and extent of participation in civic affairs matters not just for one's own individual and group well-being, but has larger social consequences. The manifestation of such consequences constitutes the epicenter of the social capital literature.

a. Collective Action

A central claim of Putnam's work (1993) was that social capital provided a mechanism for resolving otherwise pervasive collective action problems—namely, those situations where private individuals, rationally following what is best for them, leads to suboptimal public outcomes. The canonical case is the management of common pool resources (such as water and forests), wherein what is rational for the individual user (i.e., "appropriate as much as possible") has harmful aggregate consequences (such as depletion and inadequate maintenance). The most celebrated work on this topic is Ostrom's (1991), who at the time did not use the term social capital but later came to embrace it enthusiastically (Ostrom 2000). It is safe to say that Ostrom's work enjoyed much wider impact as a result, thereby embodying one of the central themes of this chapter: in and of itself, social capital was not really necessary to make a core claim about a pervasive empirical and policy problem, but casting such problems in social capital *terms* enabled them to be amenable to a vastly larger audience. Research on collective action problems with respect to the environment (Pretty and Ward 2001), community governance (Bowles and Gintis 2002), and climate change (Adger 2003) have all gainfully deployed the terminology of social capital to draw attention to important collective action problems.

b. Economic Development

Research on social capital (specifically) and civil society (more generally) has reinvigorated research on the social dimensions of economic development. At the micro level,[6] the work of economists such as Fafchamps (2006) and Barr (2003), among many others (see also Durlauf and Fafchamps 2005), is greatly refining our understanding of the ways in which different types of networks are used by the poor: immediate kinship systems are structured to minimize risk and retain identity, while a more spatially diverse set of ties are cultivated to enhance economic opportunities. Related work by political scientists such as Krishna (2002, 2006) has shown just how central are the interactions between networks and the prevailing local context in determining who moves out of (or remains mired in) poverty, and the mechanisms by which these different outcomes emerge. This is essentially a similar storyline to that formulated by sociologists of international migration such as Massey and Espinosa (1997). Again, a close reading of this type of scholarship shows a pragmatic, rather than ideological, commitment to social capital terminology: these scholars use the concept as and when necessary, depending on the audience. For the purposes of this chapter, it bears repeating that these types of studies from different disciplines encounter and constructively engage with one another because the language of social capital makes an opening conversation possible. Without it, they would likely operate in parallel universes.

c. Democracy and Governance

Perhaps the boldest claim of Putnam's book *Making Democracy Work* (1993) was that social capital—as measured by a dense, overlapping network of civil society organizations—not only facilitated collective action and economic development, but was ultimately the mechanism that connected the two together: aggregating collective action into broad-based prosperity turned on the construction and maintenance of effective local civic and political institutions that make democracy work.

Much of the subsequent work on this issue, following Fukuyama (1995), sought to make trust the centrepiece of the analysis. However, if one discerns in Putnam, not so much a clarion call to construct a clean empirical link that connects societal trust to effective government and the wealth of nations, but rather an invitation to revisit how the tone, level, and terms of everyday engagement in community affairs influence local politics, then there is considerable scope for advancement at the level of theory, evidence and policy. Yet again, one does not need the specific terminology of social capital to make such advances, and indeed for certain specialist audiences to do so could be a distraction. But the more diverse the audience and/or the less familiar any given audience might be with the finer points of social and political theory, then the stronger the case becomes for deploying a concept such as social capital which can bridge these divides.

Research in Indonesia on local government reforms is perhaps the best exemplar of this process at work, not least because the main project that was introduced to facilitate such reforms was explicitly designed on the basis of social capital theory (Guggenheim 2006). In the post-Suharto era, a succession of national governments pledged its full support for a major initiative to enhance the responsiveness and effectiveness of local government, especially with respect to its capacity to serve poor rural communities. The efficacy of this initiative has also been extensively examined, empirically and critically, by social scientists of all persuasions (Li 2007; Olken 2007; Rao 2008; Barron, Diprose, and Woolcock 2010). These studies make few grand claims about the capacity of such initiatives to single-handedly and uniformly reform local politics and reduce poverty, but it is important to note that social capital was here conceived as a mechanism by which civic participation—in this case, participation by otherwise marginalized groups in village-level decision-making bodies—could shape how decisions over the allocation of development funds were made and enforced. Specifically, it was hoped that by requiring funds to be allocated on the basis of the knowledge of everyday villagers (as opposed to external "experts"), and by requiring decision-making meetings to be (a) open to the public and journalists and (b) held only once proposals from at least two women's groups had been received, that the dynamics of decision making and enforcement would be different in kind from those that had prevailed during the autocratic Suharto era.[7]

3. Implications for Policy and Practice

The preceding discussion of social capital theory and research points to seven issues regarding the salience of civil society organizations. Some of the most salient examples are drawn from economic development, but they also apply more generally. First, civil society organizations help provide important insights for contributing to analyses of responses to poverty. In the face of pervasive risks and inadequate institutional mechanisms for addressing them, the poor have always drawn on their kinship systems, friends, and civic groups to help them survive and advance. Savings clubs, credit groups, and informal insurance systems, for example, even if imperfect, are actively created in many poor communities in very different countries. Chinese diaspora communities around the world are famous for this, actively helping recent immigrants to get their first foot on the economic ladder by supporting their entrepreneurial activities (Weidenbaum and Hughes 1996). A key question for public policy is whether and how external agents can work with and complement these informal ("organic") social mechanisms in poor communities to enhance their effectiveness in managing risk and vulnerability without undermining the other important social functions such groups perform for their members.

As neglected as the community-level focus may have been in the past, however, and as powerful as social ties can be in shaping survival and mobility strategies in poor communities, the evidence also shows how important it is to understand the nature and extent of social relations across formal and informal institutions, and especially across power differentials, such as those between police and citizens, teachers and students, doctors and patients, farmers and extension officers, lawyers and clients, and bankers and creditors—relationships that are central to the well-being of everyone, but especially to the poor. In this regard, organizations of the poor are critically important to enhancing their political strength in negotiations (or outright confrontations) with those who are more powerful (Gibson and Woolcock 2008).

Second, social capital theory and research evidence can be instructive in helping to improve the quality of service delivery. We are far beyond a consensus that funding should be provided to build schools and health clinics for all; we are still a long way, however, from realizing these commitments, with millions of children each day arriving at an empty school because their teacher has failed to show up for work (World Bank 2003). A key part of this failure of implementation is that the social relations binding teachers, parents and communities are inadequate, relations that are needed to underpin the accountability mechanisms that ensure that learning actually takes place. While there is considerable concern over the content of education (i.e., the curriculum), of more fundamental concern is that teaching and learning takes place in and through an ongoing social process, most particularly a face-to-face relationship between teacher and student that is sustained for six hours a day, two hundred days a year, for over a decade. Similar processes are needed to sustain medical, legal, and other social services (Pritchett and Woolcock 2004).

Third, a social capital perspective can be instrumental in helping to address a particularly difficult and complex set of development problems, namely those that require negotiated rather than technical solutions. While experts are necessary for addressing particular types of development problems (e.g., how to design roads that will function in high rainfall environments), there are many others—most especially those pertaining to political and legal reform—that are deeply context-specific and whose efficacy turns on the legitimacy that is afforded to them by virtue of the political contests through which they have emerged. A social capital perspective rightly places considerable emphasis on the vibrancy of the civic spaces that nurture and sustain such contests (Briggs 2008). As countries such as Indonesia, Vietnam, and China become more open societies, for example, the quality and accessibility of these civic spaces, and the degree of equity that characterizes the contests within them, will be central to identifying and implementing effective solutions to context-specific problems. In these realms, more experts, whether foreign or domestic, cannot arrive at *the* "right" answer (or even if they can, it is a qualitatively different answer if the same verdict is reached via a deliberative process).

Fourth, political movements towards greater openness and complexity in decision making will most likely entail increased demands for citizen participation. State-society relations will be a key arena in which change will occur as countries (especially those that are large and experiencing rapid growth, such as China and India) becomes more prosperous. Specifically, this will be an arena for reconceiving accountability mechanisms, from patronage arrangements that are almost exclusively upward to proto-democratic arrangements that are incrementally downward. Rising literacy, for example, will mean that citizens will be better positioned to more forcefully and accurately assert their demands and aspirations (by accessing the media and by harnessing data to support their arguments); their leaders in turn will face increasing pressures to be more responsive to them. The issuance of basic markers of identity and citizenship (such as birth, marriage, and death certificates) will also enhance these pressures (Szreter 2007). The social compact between citizens and politicians will therefore need to shift from one of intimidation, neglect or mistrust to more open collaboration.

Fifth, everything that is known from social and political theory suggests that organizational change, and especially rapid change, is associated with conflict (Bates 2000). This is already taking place across China (Muldavin 2006), and the pressures underpinning it are only likely to increase as a result of China's rapid growth. Importantly, these conflicts are a product of development *success*, not failure. Urbanization, migration, rising literacy, and changes in occupational categories, social status, and political influence are all factors that will alter the prevailing power structures, normative expectations, social identities, and systems of rules from the household level, to civil society, to the nation as a whole. The creation of new civic spaces for addressing these conflicts in a relatively peaceful manner, well before they become violent, will be crucial not only for sustaining growth, but nurturing a new and more dynamic social compact on which such continued growth will ultimately rest. In the decade following the East Asian financial crisis, Indonesia's triple transition—from autocracy to democracy, from corporatist to open economy, and from centralized to decentralized political administration—has been truly remarkable, not least because it has occurred with relatively minimal violent conflict, and it is at least plausible to argue that this is a result of development policies explicitly designed to work with and nurture Indonesia's civic organizations (Guggenheim 2006; Barron, Diprose, and Woolcock 2010).

Sixth, rising prosperity, mobility, and transportation and communication can only make countries more, not less, diverse in the coming decades. This is true for virtually all countries, but is especially significant for rapidly growing (and thus changing) countries such as India, Vietnam, and China. Not only will there be more diverse sources of identity (actually and potentially) from a strict demographic perspective (including occupation, language, and location) as populations expand and interact, but there will also be (a) greater awareness of it, (b) greater political salience attached to it, and (c) greater demands on individuals (and groups) to manage multiple forms and sources of identity at any given moment in time and over their lifetime. Moreover, social (and thus political) fault lines that are as yet unknown are likely to emerge in the future, especially as levels of inequality rise and economic (and political) opportunities, for some, expand.

Seventh, all these factors culminate in the need to reimagine and sustain a dynamic, genuinely inclusive sense of social cohesion (Easterly, Ritzen, and Woolcock 2006). Where and how the "us"-"them" divide is drawn is crucial in every society and constituent community; there cannot be a single invariant definition, but a flexible, legitimate, broadly shared and still coherent understanding is vital. This is especially important for the world's largest and fastest growing (hence potentially most rapidly changing) countries, and for those countries seeking to make a durable transition from autocratic to democratic governance. Nurturing the spaces, providing the resources, and enhancing the procedures for underpinning equitable contests between a country's different stakeholders is central to this challenge. These contests, by definition, cannot always be harmonious, but they can be waged in such a way that their outcomes are perceived as fair and legitimate.

4. Conclusion

For all the criticism that has surrounding it, social capital nonetheless remains unambiguously one of social science's most successful exports, and should be recognized as such. For this initial success to reach its full potential, however, the challenge remains to deploy a secondary set of tools and concepts that are better suited to enabling a more nuanced and sophisticated conversation on the wide range of specific issues that merit attention. There will always be a place for a term that can convey the essence of social science to larger audiences, but that term (whatever it is) should not be expected to carry a load it cannot bear. Social capital is destined to be as controversial as the broader theoretical, empirical, and epistemological debates in which it is necessarily embedded, and as such it will continue to occupy the beguiling status of a necessarily contested concept. It is to the substantive issues to which the social capital literature draws attention—and the accompanying debates that it has facilitated—to which we should be directing our energies in the years ahead, simultaneously encouraging broad participation using terms that are amenable (including social capital), *and* greater refinement in more specialized circles using the more precise terms, theories, tools, and evidence that serve that purpose.

Civil society organizations have been a key beneficiary of the emergence of social capital as the terminology of choice for facilitating dialogue and debate across diverse constituencies. Whether in public forums, corporate board rooms, the mass media, or the college classroom, social capital has enabled such organizations to be able to argue for and demonstrate the veracity of their concerns in ways that other terms have not. Even so, the core premise of this chapter still holds, namely that further advancements will require civil society organizations to deploy a dual discursive task: continuing to reach out to and engage an ever-widening spectrum of groups (a task for which the general social capital terminology is well suited), while simultaneously refining their theoretical moorings, evidence base and policy prescriptions—a task for which more specific concepts will be more useful.

NOTES

1. Social capital's intellectual history is explored in Portes (1998), Woolcock (1998), and Farr (2004); its development in applied research over the course of the twentieth century is explored in Woolcock and Narayan (2000).

2. Southern Africans, for example, refer to the delightful concept of *ubuntu*, which in its barest form translates as "I am because we are."

3. Tellingly, such claims were being made when social capital's citation count was five times lower than it is today.

4. See Collier, Hidalgo, and Maciuceanu (2006) for a broader discussion of such concepts.

5. Responses to the various criticisms that have been leveled at social capital are explored in Woolcock (2001).

6. Research at the "macro" level (using cross-national comparisons) was launched by Knack and Keefer (1997), but (as this section outlines) the micro-level work has been the most consequential in terms of its impact. See also the macro-sociological work inspired by Evans (1996).

7. Similar studies in this same category include the important work on participatory democracy (Fung and Wright 2003), decentralization (Heller, Harilal, and Chaudhuri 2007), local democracy (Baiocchi, Heller, and Silva 2008), accountability (Fox 2007) and empowerment (Alsop, Bertelsen, and Holland 2006).

REFERENCES

Adger, W. N. 2003. "Social Capital, Collective Action and Adaptation to Climate Change." *Economic Geography* 79(4): 387–404.

Alexander, J. 2006. *The Civil Sphere.* New York: Oxford University Press.

Alsop, R., M. Bertelsen, and J. Holland (eds.) 2006. *Empowerment in Practice: From Analysis to Implementation.* Washington, D.C.: The World Bank.

Barr, A. 2003. "Trust and Expected Trustworthiness: Experimental Evidence from Zimbabwean Villages." *Economic Journal* 113 (July): 614–30.

Barron, P., R. Diprose, and M. Woolcock. 2011. *Contesting Development: Participatory Projects and Local Conflict Dynamics in Indonesia.* New Haven, Conn.: Yale University Press.

Bates, R. 2000. *Violence and Prosperity: The Political Economy of Development.* New York: Norton.

Bebbington, A., S. Guggenheim, E. Olson, and M. Woolcock (eds.). 2006. *The Search for Empowerment: Social Capital as Idea and Practice at the World Bank.* West Hartford, Conn.: Kumarian Press.

Baiocchi, G., P. Heller, and M. K. Silva. 2008. "Making Space for Civil Society: Institutional Reform and Local Democracy in Brazil." *Social Forces* 86(3): 911–36.

Bowles, S., and H. Gintis. 2002. "Social Capital and Community Governance." *Economic Journal* 112 (November): 419–36.

Briggs, X. de S. 2008. *Democracy as Problem Solving: Civic Capacity in Communities across the Globe.* Cambridge, Mass.: MIT Press.

Coleman, J. 1988. "Social Capital in the Creation of Human Capital." *American Journal of Sociology* vol. 94: 95–120.

Collier, D., F. D. Hidalgo, and A. O. Maciuceanu. 2006. "Essentially Contested Concepts: Debates and Applications." *Journal of Political Ideologies* vol. 11(3): 211–46.

Durlauf, S., and M. Fafchamps. 2005. "Social Capital," in P. Aghion and S. Duraluf (eds.) *Handbook of Economic Growth* vol. 1, Amsterdam: Elsevier, 1639–700.

Easterly, W., J. Ritzen, and M. Woolcock. 2006. "Social Cohesion, Institutions, and Growth." *Economics & Politics* vol. 18(2): 103–20.

Edwards, M. 2009. *Civil Society.* 2nd ed. Cambridge: Polity Press.

Evans, P. 1996. "Government Action, Social Capital and Development: Reviewing the Evidence on Synergy." *World Development* vol. 24(6): 1119–32.

Fafchamps, M. 2006. "Development and Social Capital." *Journal of Development Studies* vol. 42(7): 1180–98.

Farr, J. 2004. "Social Capital: A Conceptual History." *Political Theory* vol. 32(1): 6–33.

Fine, B. 2001. *Social Capital versus Social Theory: Political Economy and Social Science at the Turn of the Millennium.* London: Routledge.

Fox, J. 2007. *Accountability Politics: Power and Voice in Rural Mexico.* New York: Oxford University Press.

Fukuyama, F. 1995. *Trust: The Social Virtues and the Creation of Prosperity.* New York: The Free Press.

Fung, A., and E. O. Wright. 2003. *Deepening Democracy: Institutional Innovations in Empowered Participatory Governance.* London: Verso.

Gallie, W. B. 1956. "Essentially Contested Concepts." *Proceedings of the Aristotelian Society* vol. 56: 167–98.

Gibson, C., and M. Woolcock. 2008. "Empowerment, Deliberative Development and Local Level Politics in Indonesia: Participatory Projects as a Source of Countervailing Power." *Studies in Comparative International Development* vol. 43(2): 151–80.

Guggenheim, S. E. 2006. "The Kecamatan Development Program, Indonesia," in A. Bebbington, M. Woolcock, S. Guggenheim, and E. Olson (eds.) op.cit.

Heller, P., K. N. Harilal, and S. Chaudhuri. 2007. "Building Local Democracy: Evaluating the Impact of Decentralization in Kerala, India." *World Development* vol. 35(4): 626–64.

Isham, J. 2002. "The Effect of Social Capital on Fertiliser Adoption: Evidence from Rural Tanzania." *Journal of African Economies* vol. 11(1): 39–60.

Knack, S., and P. Keefer. 1997. "Does Social Capital have an Economic Payoff? A Cross-Country Investigation." *Quarterly Journal of Economics* vol. 112(4): 1251–88.

Krishna, A. 2002. *Active Social Capital: Tracing the Roots of Development and Democracy.* New York: Columbia University Press.

——. 2006. "Pathways Out of and Into Poverty in 36 Villages of Andhra Pradesh, India." *World Development* vol. 34(2): 271–88.

Li, T. M. 2007. *The Will to Improve: Governmentality, Development, and the Practice of Politics.* Durham, N.C.: Duke University Press.

Massey, D., and K. Espinosa. 1997. "What's Driving Mexico-U.S. Migration? A Theoretical, Empirical, and Policy Analysis." *American Journal of Sociology* vol. 102(4): 939–99.

Muldavin, J. 2006. "In Rural China, a Time Bomb is Ticking." *International Herald Tribune*, January 1.

Olken, B. 2007. "Monitoring Corruption: Evidence from a Field Experiment in Indonesia." *Journal of Political Economy* vol. 115(2): 200–49.

Ostrom, E. 1991. *Managing the Commons: The Evolution of Institutions for Collective Action.* New York: Cambridge University Press.

——. 2000. "Social Capital: Fad or Fundamental Concept?" in P. Dasgupta and I. Serageldin (eds.) *Social Capital: A Multifaceted Perspective.* Washington, D.C.: The World Bank.

Pretty, J., and H. Ward. 2001. "Social Capital and the Environment." *World Development* vol. 29(2): 209–27.

Portes, A. 1998. "Social Capital: Its Origins and Applications in Contemporary Sociology."
      Annual Review of Sociology vol. 24: 1–24.
Portes, A. 2000. "The Two Meanings of Social Capital." *Sociological Forum* vol. 15(1): 1–12.
Pritchett, L., and M. Woolcock. 2004. "Solutions When the Solution is the Problem:
      Arraying the Disarray in Development." *World Development* vol. 32(2): 191–212.
Putnam, R. 1993. *Making Democracy Work: Civic Traditions in Modern Italy*. Princeton, N.J.:
      Princeton University Press.
——. 2000. *Bowling Alone: The Collapse and Revival of American Community*. New York:
      Simon & Schuster.
Rao, V. 2008. "Symbolic Public Goods and the Coordination of Public Action: A
      Comparison of Local Development in India and Indonesia," in P. Bardhan and I. Ray
      (eds.) *The Contested Commons: Conversations Between Economists and Anthropologists*.
      New York: Wiley-Blackwell, 168–86.
Seligman, A. 1992. *The Idea of Civil Society*. New York: The Free Press.
Somers, M. 2008. *Genealogies of Citizenship: Markets, Statelessness and the Right to Have
      Rights*. New York: Cambridge University Press.
Szreter, S. 2007. "The Right of Registration: Development, Identity Registration and Social
      Security—A Historical Perspective." *World Development* vol. 35(1): 67–86.
Weidenbaum, M., and S. Hughes. 1996. *The Bamboo Network: How Expatriate Chinese
      Entrepreneurs are Creating a New Economic Superpower in Asia*. New York: The Free
      Press.
Woolcock, M. 1998. "Social Capital and Economic Development: Toward a Theoretical
      Synthesis and Policy Framework." *Theory and Society* vol. 27(2): 158–208.
——. 2001. "The Place of Social Capital in Understanding Social and Economic
      Outcomes." *Canadian Journal of Policy Research* vol. 2(1): 11–17.
——. 2010. "The Rise and Routinization of Social Capital, 1988–2008." *Annual Review of
      Political Science* 13: 469–87.
Woolcock, M., and D. Narayan. 2000. "Social Capital: Implications for Development
      Theory, Research and Policy," *World Bank Research Observer* vol. 15(2): 225–49.
Woolcock, M., and E. Radin. 2008. "A Relational Approach to the Theory and Practices of
      Economic Development," in D. Castiglione, J. van Deth and G. Wolleb (eds.)
      Handbook of Social Capital. New York: Oxford University Press, 411–38.
World Bank. 2003. *World Development Report* 2004 *Making Services Work for Poor People*.
      New York: Oxford University Press.

CHAPTER 17

CIVIL AND UNCIVIL SOCIETY

CLIFFORD BOB

THE debate over civil society remains unsettled, with varying, often conflicting ideas about its definition, purposes, and effects. Lurking within this argument is another even more amorphous concept, "uncivil society." Proposed sometimes as a resonant and seemingly obvious contrast to the real object of interest, uncivil society has increasingly taken on a life of its own, particularly in the period after the terrorist attacks on New York and Washington, D.C. on September 11, 2001. This chapter argues that the concept of uncivil society should be strangled in the crib. In its various guises, it contributes to needless conceptual proliferation while adding little of analytic value. Worse, as typically used, uncivil society mixes a pretense at rigor with an overwhelming dose of obloquy. The term is used to place organizations, goals, or tactics beyond the political pale. Groups to the analyst's liking are starred as civil, while those she abhors are tarred as uncivil. Such labeling is both acceptable and expected as a rhetorical tack in the thick of ideological combat. But if scholars are serious about understanding rather than politicking, uncivil society should be unceremoniously dispatched. This is not to say that academics should abjure the quest for the good society or should remain neutral in the face of evil. But it is to say that these goals should be segregated from analysis—not least for the sake of achieving them—and that using uncivil society as a supposedly objective moniker fails this test.

Like civil society, its doppelganger is ill defined. Indeed, like it, uncivil society has acquired multiple, often muddled meanings darkly mirroring each of civil society's own. In the sections below, I survey and critique the meanings of uncivil society, some explicit, others implicit in the literature. These relate to the three primary, though overlapping, ways in which civil society is defined: as associational life, the good society. and the public sphere. Corresponding to each of these definitions, uncivil society is said to differ organizationally, normatively, and tactically from its twin.

1. Organizational Definitions
of Uncivil Society

In Tocquevillean terms, civil society is the realm of voluntary association among free individuals. Distinct from and by some accounts balancing the power of states and businesses, associational life is thought to be a crucial means of creating the trust and reciprocity on which both democratic and market interactions depend. In this view, a vibrant organizational life is thought to build strong and cohesive societies, particularly if it crosses primordial divisions such as ethnic and racial lines (Tocqueville 2004; Putnam 2001).

Following this logic, uncivil society would lack one or another of civil society's hallmarks. Most basically, it might refer to societies that lack significant numbers of voluntary associations. But the scholarly literature already includes more apt and specific terms. Without using the term uncivil society, Tocqueville (1998; 2004) contrasted early nineteenth-century America, with its numerous associations, to the atomism and conflict of pre-Revolutionary and, more pointedly, contemporaneous France. Others have analyzed "anomic" societies and "amoral familism" (Banfield 1967). Lacking in "civicness" due to an impoverished or predatory associational life, places like southern Italy suffer from backward economies and dysfunctional polities (Putnam 1994). Adding uncivil society to these existing terms is unnecessary.

More worryingly, because of the phrase's negative connotations, using uncivil society in this way could cast aspersions on functioning, even successful societies that have small voluntary sectors. The relationships between voluntarism, association, political democracy, economic development, and social welfare are poorly understood. The hypothesis that lively civil societies create the trust on which the latter are built might be turned on its head. It may be, for instance, that countries with strong welfare states do not develop large voluntary sectors, whereas in weak states or those with limited welfare policies such as the United States, they grow to fill the void. In the latter case, states may encourage community organizations—George H. W. Bush's vaunted "thousand points of light"—as a means of replacing state functions. It may also be that societies in which extended families remain vital develop weaker voluntary sectors than those in which family structures are disrupted, for instance by high levels of individual mobility. In any event, terming these societies uncivil would be unjustified.

Another alternative would be to label societies uncivil in which associational life exists but is coerced or controlled. But the term has seldom been applied in this way, and others are more apt. "Totalitarian" well describes those in which a state or ruling party obliterates autonomous social formations, commanding associational life from the top down, as in Nazi Germany or Maoist China. "Illiberal democracy" is now used to describe countries such as Russia that hold elections but limit other freedoms, including freedom of association. "Corporatist" has long been used to describe European states' formal recognition and strong support for privileged civil society interlocutors—and the states' reciprocal neglect or hostility to others. In

Japan, governmental policies have deliberately encouraged small local associations while inhibiting large, national, and political groups, creating a "dual civil society" (Pekkanen 2006). More generally, it is clear that state policies strongly shape civil societies.

In some societies, associational life is not managed by the state but nonetheless structures itself along racial, ethnic, or class lines. If associations reinforce rather than cut across these divides, an outcome that may occur naturally because of individual choices prompted by cultural norms, the results may be opposite to those expected by civil society enthusiasts. Trust may develop within associations, but simultaneously foster mistrust towards other groups (Tocqueville 1998, 161–62). Indeed the more organized one group becomes, the warier the other may be, potentially creating an ethnically based security dilemma and spiral of disorder. As Varshney (2002) shows in his study of India, communal organizations may embrittle societal bonds and facilitate communal violence, whereas cross-cutting associations may prevent it. But the long histories of stable consociational democracies such as the Netherlands, Switzerland, and to a lesser extent Belgium suggest that associational segregation may not cause or necessarily even contribute to conflict, and therefore should not be condemned as uncivil (Lijphart 1977). More broadly, it is not clear that the "violence" and "mischiefs of faction," a recurrent fear of liberal thinkers, need be solved only by enlarging the polity or encouraging cross-cutting associations (Madison 2003). Other forms of political engineering may work even as cultural differences and organizational insularity are preserved (Horowitz 2000). It may be, as Burke wrote, that "lov[ing] the little platoon we belong to in society, is the first principle (the germ as it were) of public affections...by which we proceed towards a love to our country, and to mankind" (2009, 47). In any event, labeling ethnic or class associations uncivil prejudges their effects.

Finally, uncivil might be applied to situations in which voluntary associations, whatever their ethnic or class composition, undercut rather than build trust. Societies marked by high levels of organized, apolitical criminality might come under this rubric. So might the global scene, which according to then-UN Secretary General Kofi Annan includes such uncivil society elements as "drug-traffickers, gun-runners, money-launderers, and exploiters of young people for prostitution" (1998). Calling such organizations uncivil is rather wan, however. More important, it is unnecessary when the sociological and criminological literatures already include a wealth of terms to describe such phenomena.

To take another approach, some fans of civil society draw sharp distinctions between the voluntary sector and both the political and economic spheres. In this view, even if civil society is said to undergird stable democracy and functioning markets, it stops where politics and markets begin. Some in this camp reserve the accolade civil society for the friendly societies and bowling leagues that only sporadically and narrowly (if at all) engage in conventional political activity (Putnam 2001). Others hold utopian visions for civil society, as a potent autonomous sector that might reshape the world for the better, on its own and against the pretenses of state power and corporate greed (Smith 2007; Kaldor 2003). But this rendering of civil society, whether national or global, is unrealistic because it provides no mechanism for resolving the conflicting impulses and interests that motivate a society's myriad associations. This is the function of political parties and ultimately the state. But suggesting that these entities are uncivil goes too far.

So does applying the term to companies. Some civil society devotees contrast the business world's competitive, profit-seeking activities with the harmony, sympathy, and cooperation supposedly prevailing in the voluntary sector. But this distinction is overdrawn. Most nonprofit organizations, a major part of the associational universe, inhabit their own Darwinian worlds, vying for members, funding, and recognition. Many are also highly professionalized bureaucratic institutions. Some have opened their own profit-making ventures as social entrepreneurs, even as many corporations take on new social responsibility principles. Many nonprofits rely on corporate, as well as philanthropic, largesse to operate. And many voluntary associations, like businesses, engage in political advocacy. This convergence of functions and approaches belies any sharp division of the nonprofit and for-profit worlds, making it untenable to suggest that the latter are somehow uncivil.

2. Normative Definitions of Uncivil Society

A second definition of civil society associates the term with the "good society," one marked out by norms of freedom, democracy, respect, tolerance, cooperation, and any number of other estimable values. At a minimum, civil society is said to model these virtues. More ambitiously, individuals and associations in civil society struggle to achieve them together. Maximally, civil society itself constitutes the good society. Any of these three formulations would suggest that uncivil society is problematic on normative grounds, because it fails to meet good society values or actively works to undermine them. Uncivil groups would be marked by internal hierarchies and lack of democracy; would fail to promote "progressive" ends; or would be exclusionary and belligerent.

But these normative definitions of uncivil society are also unsatisfactory. First, many of the most robust associations, nongovernmental organizations (NGOs,) and social movements in the world today and in the past do not embody the virtues of the good society. Often they are not governed democratically, even where they promote greater democracy, tolerance, or rights. For every Amnesty International and Sierra Club, which take a stab at member voting on selected policies and leaders, there are dozens of groups like Human Rights Watch and Greenpeace in which only "checkbook democracy" operates: members "vote" by contributing money to the NGO and voice disagreement chiefly by ceasing to do so. More generally, in the heat of political battle, civil society groups seldom welcome internal dissent, often leading them to splinter. Apolitical associations, even fraternal orders and mutual aid groups, suffer divisions for any number of personal, social, or financial reasons.

Importantly, this lack of collaborative spirit, democratic practice, or any of the other hallmarks of the good society has not stopped key civil society groups from achieving their goals. Indeed, some would argue that the most nimble and effective organizations are almost Leninist. Conversely, others would claim that real power emanates from the spontaneity of movements acting in the absence of formal organization and hierarchy, but such conditions often lack toleration and respect (Piven and Cloward 1978). The debate over the most effective way of achieving social change will not be resolved here, but calling groups uncivil based on their internal characteristics sweeps too much of associational life into the dustbin of incivility.

Rather than concerning themselves with such matters, analysts using public sociology, action anthropology, justice journalism, or other politically engaged methods often reserve the term civil society for groups seeking progressive ends domestically or fighting neoliberal goals internationally (Smith 2007). This categorization may be unintentional, simply a function of liberal predominance in the academy and a scholarly preference for studying groups with whom one sympathizes. Whatever the source of this bias, the literature implies, and sometimes states, that groups which oppose such goals should be labeled uncivil. But this view is based on two misconceptions: that civil society speaks or potentially can speak with one voice; and that this voice resounds in a left-leaning key.

Proponents of the first misconception seem to believe that civil society itself will aggregate the variety of interests and beliefs that comprise it. In this way, civil society may stand as a unified counterpoint to state or corporate interests. Along these lines at the global level, some see NGOs as the "conscience of the world" (Willetts 1996). Collectively, the World Social Forum is sometimes touted as a legitimate embodiment of all the world's peoples (Fisher and Ponniah 2003). In more utopian vein, international lawyers call for a global parliament of NGOs and social movements supplementing representation from states, even democratic ones (Falk and Strauss 2001).

In fact, however, civil society (whether domestic or global) is a turbulent sea of opinions and movements. Contending groups will of course clothe themselves in phrases like the "national interest," the "public good," the "global welfare," or the "future of humanity." But although abstract concepts like these are regularly deployed by right and left, their concrete meaning just as invariably ignites dispute. Only the democratic state has a viable if far from flawless mechanism for aggregating the diverse interests composing civil society, or at least coming to definitive policy decisions. Notably, however, such decisions are always temporary. Civil society's very diversity ensures that the losers—those for whom the new policy "solution" is in fact a problem—invariably reemerge to continue fighting. At the global level, the situation is more contingent still. The ad hoc agreements which pass for "global governance" are observed by states primarily when it is in their interest, and are continuously fought over by contending NGOs and social movements.

Talking about the "interests of civil society" is therefore inappropriate. This is true of social and political issues, from abortion to whaling. Much though some might want to believe otherwise, there are profound and often heartfelt, rather than merely tactical, disagreements within civil society. Rooted in contending values, worldviews, and emotions as well as material interests, professional identities, and scientific reputations, such disagreements are deep-seated (Sowell 2007). It is naïve to believe that, with a little more education or open-mindedness, the scales might drop from the eyes of the benighted (Mouffe 2005). More important, tarring as uncivil those who steadfastly oppose one's own pet aims is politically motivated and analytically unsound.

Nor does civil society have a unified view of its own scope or power relative to the state or market (beyond a likely baseline of agreement that civil society should at least exist). Interest groups and civic associations endlessly wrangle over this issue in policy battles. Meanwhile, intellectuals and politicians debate the question in more abstract terms. Even when it comes to matters as basic as the meaning of free association and expression, the concept of "civil society's interests" is problematic. Within many societies, there are sharp divergences. This is true not only in traditional or authoritarian societies, where cultures or states repress groups they consider dangerous, but also in modern, democratic countries. Consider Canada, where civil society organizations representing historically disadvantaged groups won hate speech cases in the country's Human Rights Commission in the 2000s. Quickly, however, the laws and their supporters came under fire, first from civil society challengers and later from court decisions. Who is uncivil in such contests?

Differences are even more jarring among states and within "global civil society"—witness the very different ways in which the United States and many European democracies define freedoms of association, speech, and religion. Groups banned as uncivil in the latter jurisdictions pass legally in the former. One minor but telling result has been sharp transatlantic disagreement over free expression among civil society proponents of a contemplated international charter of human rights and principles on the Internet. The broader point is that civil society itself has no interests precisely because its cacophonous components have so many different views. Thus, the term uncivil society is unhelpful not just when it comes to substantive issues but even regarding basic rules of association.

This misconception about the interests of civil society is often coupled with the notion that it is primarily composed of progressive groups. As already noted, a major reason for this belief is the comparative scholarly neglect of right-wing social movements. Using the term uncivil society to attack conservative groups only reinforces this neglect, fostering an unrealistic impression of civil society's composition. Civil society organizing is not exclusively or even primarily a progressive political project. European anti-immigrant and anti-Muslim groups are important contemporary examples. Indeed, it is probable that for every movement of the Left, there has been one on the Right. Consider the anti-suffrage and pro-slavery movements of the nineteenth century which, despite scholarly neglect, helped delay for decades the rights we now consider basic. The fact that these movements ultimately failed is no reason to ignore them. Their capacity to affect and hamper progressive movements must be considered as more than just the result of incivility. In any event, the progressive side is also strewn with movements that died, or more likely were killed by opposition.

Not to examine such groups leads to analytic one-sidedness. Overlooked is the chance to learn how sometimes highly successful social movements mobilized large populations, shaped political beliefs, and affected public policy. Scholars who ignore this universe miss a key source of empirical material. Theories about social mobilization, NGOs, and civil society should work regardless of ideology. They would be strengthened if they were built from and tested against movements espousing contrary, even "retrograde," ideologies. In any case, old ideological boundaries are breaking down or simply do not fit current realities. For example, Europe's anti-immigrant and anti-Muslim movements increasingly appear to be expanding from a right-wing fringe to encompass new and surprising constituencies such as homosexuals in Holland. In this, they resemble "sons of the soil" movements in India, Nigeria, Fiji, and many other countries, which challenge both foreign and domestic migrants and defy simple Left-Right distinctions. Again, dismissing these movements as uncivil may be valid in political debate but obscures key issues in scholarly endeavors.

But surely, those who promote intolerance, disrespect, hierarchy, authoritarianism, and conflict—who seek to destroy the good society—can legitimately be labeled uncivil? The problem is that all these concepts are hotly contested, just like their rosier opposite numbers. Calling their proponents uncivil impedes knowledge of civil society's ideological range. It also impairs comprehensive examination of civil society's dynamics, in particular contention between opposing camps. Such conflict is almost always part of activism, a point often missed in the myriad studies focusing on only a single (usually progressive) movement fighting a repressive state or an irresponsible corporation. Particularly in democracies and in the global arena, the battle for public opinion is crucial. Yet this cannot be studied effectively by focusing only on one side, rationalizing this because the other is supposedly uncivil. As a critical but largely unexamined matter, this conflict involves strategies aimed not only at convincing the public but also at undermining one's adversaries. Nor is this warfare conducted only or even primarily by politicians. Rather, on specific issues, it pits committed single-issue activists against one another (Bob, forthcoming). Finally, in some cases societal conflicts may only be solved by accommodations between groups supporting and opposing democratic ideals (Horowitz 1992). The U.S. Senate, with its vast disproportions in representation between America's most and least populous states, stands as a continuing monument to just such compromises (Dahl 2003).

If civil society writ large neither models nor seeks good society goals, and if therefore there is nothing substantive against which uncivil society can be counterposed, it is also the case that civil society does not itself constitute the good society. This view—civil society as a political endpoint (Hirst 1994, 19)—is associated with utopian visions of both left and right (although the right seldom uses the term good society to describe it). But the "withering away of the state," whether to be replaced by communal forms of socialism or "thousand points of light" conservatism, is not only unrealistic but also undesirable, given the unbridgeable divides that rend actually existing civil societies. For that reason, it is also untenable to brand societies in which this unwelcome vision has not materialized as uncivil.

3. TACTICAL DEFINITIONS OF UNCIVIL SOCIETY

A third view of civil society portrays it as the public sphere, the arena in which political ideas are raised, debated, and decided. In this view, contrasting with that of the neo-Tocquevillians, the essence of civil society is political. Private civic associations may foster norms of trust and reciprocity, but just as important are associations explicitly dedicated to achieving broader societal goals. Most public sphere theorists would also differ from the good society approach. Rather than denouncing as uncivil those who oppose a particular conception of the "good," public sphere theorists embrace plurality. The public sphere itself is the realm in which differences are resolved. This avoids relegating groups (usually conservative groups) to "uncivil" status on purely substantive grounds.

Yet public sphere theorists maintain at least an implicit conception of uncivil society based primarily on tactical factors and groups who reject the assumptions, processes, or outcomes of deliberative democracy. Consider the views of Jürgen Habermas (1991). His elaborate and impressive rendition of an ideal deliberative forum assumes at least basic agreement on certain foundational rules. These include equal consideration and hearing; fairness of the forum; and perhaps most importantly, acceptance of the substantive outcomes of such procedures.[1] These tenets may apply in forums such as courtrooms. They are less applicable to the free-wheeling and never-ending debates that characterize real political life. In these situations, much is up for grabs, including everything from the proper decision-making institution, to who may participate, to the validity of evidence. In addition, there is no guarantee that groups will accept decisions reached in the most rule-bound of institutions or by the most democratic of methods. Rather, many groups that are clearly part of the public sphere keep on fighting for their values indefinitely. On the right, consider anti-abortion activists in the United States who reject the Supreme Court's *Roe v. Wade* decision, or on the left, same-sex marriage advocates who repudiate popularly approved referendums defining marriage as between one man and one woman. Are they to be consigned to the uncivil realm?

Public sphere theorists would reject such a suggestion if based on substantive grounds, arguing, *contra* the good society view, that a Habermasian world leaves outcomes contingent on deliberative processes. From this same standpoint, however, those who reject the outcomes of deliberative processes might well be considered uncivil. But this way of defining uncivil society places too much weight on "civility" and leads to a *reductio ad absurdum*: Those who care most deeply about their values—the activists and advocates who keep on fighting for their goals no matter how deliberative the processes through which policy is made—are transformed into the uncivil.

This point becomes particularly clear when thinking of the most important political movements of the modern era. Much of civil society's power has come when such groups engage in "criminality for a cause," or civil disobedience, when they have refused to accept the outcome of deliberative processes deemed fair and adequate by their societies. Recent "people power" mobilizations from the Philippines anti-Marcos movement, to Mexico's 1994 Zapatista rebellion, to environmental protests in Europe, exemplify the use of force to challenge political regimes, social systems, and policy choices. One could argue that in these cases the laws that were broken were "wrong" because they were promulgated through objectively exclusionary and unfair processes or were transcended by some higher political purpose. Certainly, activists from India's nationalist movement to South Africa's anti-apartheid activists have justifiably made the former claim. Others such as the anti-nuclear and environmental movements have made the latter. But in both situations, governing institutions and the dominant civil society actors who bolster them have begged to differ. For scholars, however, accepting the authorities' charges about who is uncivil makes little sense. A better tack is to analyze equally both those who defend and those who defy deliberation in the public sphere.

What of groups that go beyond civil disobedience and people power to the strategic threat or the actual use of violence for political advantage? Surely, these at least should be defined as uncivil (Payne 2000). Again however, there are good reasons to avoid this label, at least for scholarly study. First, given the multitude of meanings associated with both civil and uncivil society, more specific terms are preferable. This is particularly the case because political violence takes vastly different forms and degrees, with targets ranging from public property to state officials to private citizens, each of which is better described narrowly rather than under the expansive and opaque umbrella of the uncivil. Second, many political associations and most social movements include a variety of tactics in their repertoire. Even those that self-consciously aim for nonviolence can seldom control all their adherents. This is particularly true of the largest and often most important movements. Their diverse and informal memberships make strategic control and tactical uniformity difficult. The responses of targeted authorities can also lead to spontaneous outbursts from movement constituents, even leaving aside the possibility of agent provocateurs. Given this diversity and ferment, uncivil society is too blunt a term to describe large-scale movements and associations.

Third, it is important for civil society scholars to acknowledge the possibility that violence may, for better or worse, be an effective means of reaching political goals, even estimable ones. This in no way suggests that it *should* be a preferred strategy but merely states a proposition that some civil society enthusiasts reject out of hand. Certainly, nonviolent activism has scored real political gains, as Europe's anticommunist movements, America's civil rights movement, and many other cases amply demonstrate (Sharp 2005).[2] But, all too obviously, violence by states and nonstate actors has also made history and continues to do so today. Certainly, it is legitimate for scholars to label groups that use certain tactics as violent or terrorist. Narrowly defined, such terms are analytically helpful even if political combatants also use them in far looser ways. The term uncivil, however, does not meet that test.

4. CONCLUSION

In recent years, uncivil society, civil society's dark twin, has increasingly appeared in scholarly and policy discussions. The temptations to use this term are great. Opposites often illuminate, and all that an analyst sees in civil society can seemingly be highlighted by contrasting it to the uncivil. Better yet, one can win points by doing so. Few admire incivility even if they deploy it in the heat of political infighting.

But using the term also exacts costs, particularly for scholars. A major reason is that civil society itself has multiple meanings. As a result, uncivil society's referent is never clear and unambiguous. More important, using the term can limit or foreclose much-needed analysis of powerful if sometimes repugnant organizations, goals, or tactics. A better strategy is to open analysis widely, to reject hazy terminology, and to avoid prejudicing scholarly debate with pejorative verbiage.

NOTES

1. Habermas holds that "state authority" is not part of the "political public sphere" but only its "executor," enacting laws rooted in democratic public opinion (1974, 49).

2. It is often forgotten, however, that important parts of the civil rights movement used deadly force in self-defense, as advocated by Robert Williams's 1962 book *Negroes with Guns*.

REFERENCES

Annan, K. 1998. "Secretary-General Describes Emerging Era in Global Affairs with Growing Role for Civil Society Alongside Established Institutions." Press release SG/SM/6638, July 14. New York: United Nations. Available at http://www.un.org/News/Press/docs/1998/19980714.sgsm6638.html.

Banfield, E. C. 1967. *The Moral Basis of a Backward Society*. New York: The Free Press.

Bob, C. Forthcoming. *Globalizing the Right-Wing: Conservative Activism and World Politics.* Cambridge: Cambridge University Press.

Burke, E. 2009. *Reflections on the Revolution in France.* Oxford: Oxford University Press.

Dahl, R. A. 2003. *How Democratic is the American Constitution?* 2nd ed. New Haven, Conn.: Yale University Press.

Falk, R., and A. Strauss. 2001. "Toward a Global Parliament." *Foreign Affairs,* 80(1), Jan./Feb, 212–20.

Fisher, W. F., and T. Ponniah, eds. 2003. *Another World is Possible: Popular Alternatives to Globalization at the World Social Forum.* London: Zed Books.

Habermas, J. 1974. "The Public Sphere: An Encyclopedia Article (1964)." Trans. S. Lennox and F. Lennox. *New German Critique* 3: 49–55.

——. 1991. *The Structural Transformation of the Public Sphere: An Inquiry into a Category of Bourgeois Society.* Trans. T. Burger. Cambridge, Mass.: MIT Press.

Hirst, P. Q. 1994. *Associative Democracy: New Forms of Economic and Social Governance.* Cambridge: Polity Press.

Horowitz, D. L. 1992. *A Democratic South Africa? Constitutional Engineering in a Divided Society.* Berkeley: University of California Press.

——. 2000. *Ethnic Groups in Conflict.* Berkeley: University of California Press.

Kaldor, M. 2003. *Global Civil Society: An Answer to War.* Cambridge: Polity Press.

Lijphart, A. 1977. *Democracy in Plural Societies: A Comparative Exploration.* New Haven, Conn.: Yale University Press.

Madison, J. 2003. "Federalist No. 10." *The Federalist Papers.* New York: Signet.

Mouffe, C. 2005. *On the Political.* New York: Routledge.

Payne, L. A. 2000. *Uncivil Movements: The Armed Right Wing and Democracy in Latin America.* Baltimore: Johns Hopkins University Press.

Pekkanen, R. 2006. *Japan's Dual Civil Society: Members Without Advocates.* Stanford, Calif.: Stanford University Press.

Piven, F. F., and R. Cloward. 1978. *Poor People's Movements: Why They Succeed, How They Fail.* New York: Vintage.

Putnam, R. D. 1994. *Making Democracy Work: Civic Traditions in Modern Italy.* Princeton, N.J.: Princeton University Press.

——. 2001. *Bowling Alone: The Collapse and Revival of American Community.* New York: Simon & Schuster.

Sharp, G. 2005. *Waging Nonviolent Struggle: 20th Century Practice And 21st Century Potential.* Manchester, N.H.: Extending Horizons Books.

Smith, J. 2007. *Social Movements for Global Democracy.* Baltimore: Johns Hopkins University Press.

Sowell, T. 2007. *A Conflict of Visions: Ideological Origins of Political Struggles,* rev. ed. New York: Basic Books.

Tocqueville, A. 1998 (1856). *The Old Regime and the Revolution,* vol. 1. Trans. A. S. Kahan. Chicago: University of Chicago Press.

——. 2004 (1835, 1840). *Democracy in America.* Trans. A. Goldhammer. New York: Library of America.

Varshney, A. 2002. *Ethnic Conflict and Civic Life: Hindus and Muslims in India.* New Haven, Conn.: Yale University Press.

Willetts, P. 1996. *The Conscience of the World: The Influence of Non-Governmental Organizations in the U.N. System.* Washington, D.C.: Brookings Institution Press.

Williams, R. F. [1962] 1998. *Negroes with Guns.* Detroit, Mich.: Wayne State University Press.

CHAPTER 18

CIVIL SOCIETY AND CIVILITY

NINA ELIASOPH

THEORISTS and policy makers hope that participation in "civic" associations naturally teaches people how to be "civil"—to be polite, respectful, tolerant, and decent to one another. They also hope that learning this face-to-face civility goes naturally with learning to act "civicly"—that is, to press for wider changes, including political policies, that will extend respect and decency throughout society. These three elements—civility, civicness, and the civic association—come from different strands of theorizing about civil society (Edwards 2009). They do not easily weave together, but any one strand separately is weak, so braiding them is an important though difficult task. How do civility and civicness materialize, together and separately, in everyday civic associations? How can people work together in a civil manner to change society? And what gets in the way of achieving this ideal synthesis in different types of civic association? These are crucial questions for the civil society debate.

Drawing on ethnographic studies from the United States and Europe, this chapter shows how these three elements of civic life are tangled up together and rearranged in everyday citizen action. The point here is not to prove theoretically that tensions between them are inevitable, but to see how they play out in practice and what might be done to lessen or resolve them. Only by allowing themselves to identify these tensions can people begin to tame them, so examining the realities of civility, civicness, and civic associations must be the first step in the argument—a careful inspection of people's everyday intuitions regarding different types of organizations, because people know that what is polite, decent, respectful, egalitarian, and easy to do in one situation would be difficult, and perhaps hopelessly out of place, elsewhere. What is polite in a civic association might not be polite in a family, a bank, or a school; and what is civil in one kind of civic association or culture may not be so in another.

When considering how any particular association shapes vague sentiments into collective action, the first question to ask is "What do the participants assume that they are doing together *here?*" Civic associations, however one defines this universe, are not all the same in this regard. Different implicit definitions of civility make it possible for participants to imagine different kinds of connections between good treatment of people face-to-face, and good treatment of distant strangers—between civility and civicness, politeness and politics. Therefore, the next stage in the argument is to explore some common obstacles in linking civility with civicness, particularly the roles played by inequality, diversity, conflict, and discomfort. Finally, the chapter examines how real civic associations manage to overcome these obstacles, making it possible for people to imagine their own everyday relationships in the light of a broader social context. They do so not by ignoring conflict, but by using it as a source of insight and a motor for social change. When civic associations bring civility (decent, face-to-face consideration of others) together with civicness (fighting for social and political change) they can find an important key to lasting transformation and the achievement of the good society (Edwards and Sen 2000).

1. Alexis de Tocqueville and Contemporary Civic Associations

Why would anyone imagine that civicness and civility would blend easily together in civic associations? Part of the answer to this question lies in the dominance of neo-Toquevillian perspectives in the contemporary civil society debate. Tocqueville makes the case for an explicit link when he describes the importance of local citizen's involvement in their communities: "To gain the affection and respect of your immediate neighbors, a long succession of little services rendered and of obscure good deeds, a constant habit of kindness and an established reputation for disinterestedness, are required" ([1840] 1969, 511).

Perhaps in communities of the sort that Tocqueville either saw or imagined in 1830s America, citizens knew each other, and were more or less equals. They could quickly see and feel the consequences of their interactions, and make judgments about how to be good citizens without needing much knowledge about distant places. If such communities existed, it would be easy to see how civicness and civility might merge imperceptibly in them through participation and interaction in informal associations.

This model is alluring, offering the vision of societies with no serious conflict, either visible or submerged; a world in which everyone could be equally qualified and no one needed any specialized knowledge; a society in which diverse individuals could easily find common ground and feel comfortable together; and a world in which civic participation felt civil and egalitarian. But the real world is not like this, being regularly fractured by behavior that is neither civil, nor egalitarian, nor comfortable. In a diverse, unequal and dizzily global society, in which people can inadvertently contribute to problems on the other side of the world or face problems that distant strangers help to cause, there are many reasons to think that civic associations might operate very differently to those described in Tocqueville's stories.

How does Tocqueville's vision play out in different contemporary types of civic association? Consider two distinct categories: one is the purely voluntary association—the contemporary embodiment of Tocqueville's ideal; the other is what I call the "empowerment project," a hybrid civic organization that blends elements from government, professional nonprofit, and volunteer identities and operates on multiple streams of revenue that impose different demands (Hall 1992). The universe of empowerment projects has expanded enormously over the last twenty-five years to include nongovernmental organizations (NGOs) of various kinds, advocacy groups, and nonprofits. Many of these organizations have a mission to "build community," increase participation, promote diversity, and strengthen civic engagement—to bring governance "closer to the people" and "the people closer to each other." When participants in empowerment projects try to connect civility and civicness, they face some of the same challenges that grassroots volunteers also face, and others that are quite different. While their bases of material support and the composition of their membership do tend to do differ, these organizations are not so starkly different in their everyday operations, and the differences within each category are just as wide. But although certain tensions are held in common, different organizations smooth them out in different—though probably not infinitely different—ways. Finding successful ways of doing this is key, because although the route to social transformation will probably never be perfectly smooth, it has to be smooth enough for people to be able to advocate dramatic change without having to resort to cruel incivility or violence.

2. Obstacles to Linking Civility with Civicness

In pure voluntary associations, there can be pressure to limit group discussion to problems that seem easy to solve: "How to transport cans of soda and keep them cold for the high school graduation?" or "How to roast twenty different kinds of hot dogs to sell at sports events to raise funds for the school?" rather than "How to protect ourselves from the radioactive emissions from the nearby military base?"—to take some examples from an ethnography of such groups I undertook in the town of Snowy Prairie in the American Midwest (Eliasoph 1998). Such groups are fragile; little holds them together but the continued optimism and good feelings of their members. Implicitly, members may assume that admitting to fear and acknowledging conflict could easily undermine this delicate, essential "can-do" feeling. Parents in a group that raised funds for the local high school, for example, knew about problems like radioactive emissions, race riots at the school, and government funding problems, which became hard to ignore when the school library roof caved in. They talked passionately about these problems when they were outside group meetings, but not when they were inside the meetings. Such potentially difficult and discouraging—and possibly conflicting expressions—were deemed out of place and uncivil.

Empowerment projects may share these reasons for avoiding major political issues that might evoke conflict or discouragement. They also may have financial reasons for doing so because of the reactions of their funders. For example in America's War on Poverty in the 1960s, government tried to defuse widespread inner city riots by inviting poor people to "participate" in tame, peaceful forums. But when poor people demanded money for schools, housing, or health care, the government canceled their invitation. Expensive or radical change was not the kind of participation that policy makers had hoped to find and fund (van Til and van Til 1970). If the War on Poverty is a valid example, then empowerment projects may have strong reasons to foster politeness minus politics. On the other hand, empowerment projects might have more tolerance for conflict and discouragement than purely voluntary associations, partly because paid employees cannot quit as easily as volunteers—their jobs, incomes, and reputations are at stake. So what is it that determines whether empowerment projects and voluntary associations press participants to connect their face-to-face civility with larger visions of social change?

The first issue concerns the role of equality and the distribution of expertise. In Tocqueville's model, local people's intimate familiarity with a place and with each other is crucial, on the assumption that they know their own lives best. But in the 1830s no one knew about global warming, for example, whereas contemporary citizens have to develop everyday habits that embody knowledge about the causes of, and solutions to, worldwide environmental problems (Luque 2005; Giddens 1991). Activists develop expertise in the course of many years of working on an issue, but egalitarian voluntary associations face a temptation to treat all newcomers as if they do not require specialized knowledge or training, in order to keep them in the group. In an ingenious interview study, Robert Wuthnow (1993) asked volunteers to retell the story of the good Samaritan, in which a passerby helps a man who lies bleeding by the side of the road. Neglecting any need for knowledge about how to help—how to move him safely, where to find safety, and how to find medical help—nearly all the interviewees focused only on the good Samaritan's good and simple heart.

To take an example from my own studies of Snowy Prairie (Eliasoph 2011), when a teen empowerment project resolved to feed the hungry, the head of the local food pantry and the adult organizers of the empowerment project talked past one another. The organizers said that the food bank head was missing the point, which was "all about participation and democracy," and improving the characters and lives of the volunteers. The food pantry head thought the point was food. The organizers told each other that the food pantry head was difficult to work with. To them, she seemed uncivil.

In empowerment projects, there is an additional temptation to ignore volunteers' possible need for specialized knowledge and experience because participation is assumed to help the volunteers themselves by improving their characters. This makes good sense, but it can become a problem when inexperienced volunteers resolve to help people who cannot wait for them to develop the required capacity and competence. These examples show that while treating people equally is a good long-term goal for civic organizations of different kinds, it is important to distinguish between the different kinds of equality that are required for different purposes. Time is also crucial: with a long time-horizon, people can treat each other as potential equals but do not have to be equals immediately on entering a relationship or group.

Secondly, purely voluntary associations tend to be socially homogeneous, so there is good reason to expect them to exhibit a comfortable, easy civility (Rotolo 2000). Even white racist "hate" groups in the United States hold picnics and gather clothing for needy families: members of the Ku Klux Klan or the White Aryan Nation say they feel like "family" or "Boy Scouts" in so doing (Blee 2003). Empowerment projects differ: they exist partly for the purpose of bringing diverse people together, and to build community, on the assumption that not enough of it is there already. Grassroots volunteers have, by definition, already gotten along civilly enough to band together. Empowerment projects, on the other hand, often have to build togetherness on purpose, to "rebuild social bonds" (Bacqué and Sintomer 2009) both to bring people out of their individual isolation and to overcome divisions between different groups.

Bonding with people whose backgrounds are very different from one's own is initially uncomfortable. In an organization whose members enter with diverse opinions and backgrounds, what feels comfortable to one participant in food, music, ideas, physical gestures, slang, and even vocabulary—may be annoying, puzzling, or disgusting to another. It takes a long time for such diverse people to make sense of one another, and even more for them to feel comfortable together. It probably only becomes a learning experience if participants open themselves up to a feeling of perplexity, and puzzle through this fruitful perplexity over a long stretch of time. The activist and philosopher Jane Addams, describing her work in a "settlement house" for early-twentieth-century immigrants to Chicago ([1901] 2001), went so far as to say that such openness to perplexity is a moral duty in a diverse society.

Personal bonding may seem like a perfect way of linking civility and civicness, if it is true that face-to-face contact makes people less likely to categorize others as evil. But when civic organizations try to speed up this process—as empowerment projects do, often under pressure to show some impact for the next round of funding applications—the effect can be inconsequential or even perverse. For example, to encourage young volunteers to "get out of their clumps," adult organizers in Snowy Prairie set up movie nights and dance nights, but young people from different walks of life stayed apart (Eliasoph 2011). Sometimes, familiarity breeds even more contempt than had existed previously: a quick foray into an impoverished school can reinforce stereotypes about poor people's apparent "bad habits." Nonprofit-organized discussion circles about race in the United States may teach black participants that whites are not as racist as they had thought; the whites are much *more* racist than the blacks had ever imagined (Walsh 2007). Holding community suppers, as suggested by the national Asset-Based Community Development Institute, provides another example.[1] Breaking bread together no doubt brings a certain companionship, but there are problems when the ideal of community building clashes with the reality of conditions on the ground. One is that people might do what some children did in one impoverished neighborhood in Snowy Prairie: bring large take-out containers to carry the "community dinner" home to their families. The dinners were supposed to promote civility, but material conditions made this hard. Instead of shrinking the distance between people at different ends of the social hierarchy, such dinners can easily make it grow, because poor people may appear uncivil in the eyes of their less disadvantaged counterparts.

Third, accountability requirements can affect the ways in which civility and civicness are linked together. Unlike the Klan or the Aryan Nation, empowerment projects are accountable to many kinds of stakeholders, including funders, and must prove that diverse groups participate in and appreciate their work. If the civility of the Klan or that of privileged property owners' associations that fight against low-income housing in their neighborhoods does not create civic equality with distant others, the impersonal bureaucratic rules of empowerment projects might actually help in this regard (Beem 1999; Cohen and Arato 1992). They do seem to help, but they also pose tensions for civicness itself. Documentation and transparency are important in empowerment projects, but this accounting is time-consuming and can be awkward. Many meetings in Snowy Prairie's empowerment projects are almost entirely devoted to finding means of documenting the numbers of volunteers, the numbers of hours they have served, the amount of food delivered to the needy, the number of hours spent reading to pre-school children, and numbers of pregnancies, drug abuse cases, and crimes averted in "at-risk" teen volunteers. To win the U.S. Presidential Hundred Hour Challenge Award for voluntarism, volunteers in these empowerment projects often spent more time discussing how to document their work than conducting the work itself, or reflecting on its successes and failures. Such long hours spent on accounting could make a civic imagination difficult to cultivate.

Because of the need to document their broad appeal and depth of local support, afterschool programs for disadvantaged youth have to welcome adult volunteers. These "plug-in volunteers" want a rewarding experience in a very short time, so they tend to ignore young people who are too hard to help. These volunteers want to forge an emotional bond quickly and easily—to become "like beloved aunties," in their words, over the course of an hour a week for six months or so (Eliasoph 2011). Paradoxically, this means that they often distract afterschool club participants away from their homework so they can have fun and bond, or have snowball fights in the middle of the road at twilight. Since it is important to prove quickly that the organization is "building community," welcoming these unhelpful volunteers is necessary, even though paid program organizers often suspect that those volunteers may be harmful to the project's long-term aims and objectives.

When, unlike in Tocqueville's day, and unlike in places in which people are more homogenous or genuinely share long-term bonds, civic organizations do not emerge from an already cohesive and active community, then connecting civicness and civility is hard, because activities that create civility also presuppose it. If the organization is working in an unequal, unjust society, and is trying to create a better one, then civility is a good long-term goal, but an organization will not be able to change society if members start with the assumption that agreeable, comfortable civility and good citizenship quickly and naturally emerge together from participation. Tensions between civicness and civility are not inevitable features of civic organizations, but they are real tendencies. Within these tendencies, purely voluntary associations and empowerment projects share a great deal, but they also differ in some systematic ways that make sense, given their different conditions of existence.

When we locate these points of tension with more precision, we see that blending civility and civicness may sometimes be easier in more composite, less purely voluntary associations. As Paul Dekker writes, "There may well be sound historical and political reasons for defining civil society as everything that is the opposite of an oppressive state, or as almost everything that falls outside a dominant market and opposes commercialization, but in highly differentiated Western societies the civil society sphere occupies a more complex in-between position" (2009, 226).

Dekker also suggests that we search not for a place—voluntary organizations defined as a place that is neither market, state, or family—but for a quality of interaction in "in-between" institutions such as consumer activism, corporate social responsibility, and public-private partnerships (Decker 2009, 234). These kinds of organizations blend more than one kind of moral metric, mixing market and state, charity and sociability so that participants are attached to each other in multiple ways, and not just through voluntary and personal bonds. Rather than assuming that we already know that there is only one place—the voluntary organizations—in which civicness and civility can blend together, we need finer concepts that allow us to observe the varied ways in which they are tangled up and rearranged differently in different settings.

3. MAKING CIVICNESS CIVIL

If conflict, inequality, and discomfort are inevitable in voluntary organizations, how do some groups manage to render them productive? In "mutual qualification" projects in France and the Netherlands, for example, which aim to improve infrastructure and civic participation in low-income neighborhoods, slum dwellers and public officials confront, rather than avoid, conflict (Carrell 2004). Project organizers recognize that neither side is qualified to come to judgment about priorities and solutions on its own. On the one hand, they assume that "experts in suits" rarely understand the lives of the poor they aim to help. On the other hand, they accept that there is no natural community already in place that is always adept at considering what will be good for all. The residents need to learn to be "qualified" too.

In a long, reflective and emotionally powerful process of mutual learning over the course of a dozen meetings and more, both sides express and analyze their own internal conflicts and the internal conflicts of their opponents, and begin to see how these can catalyze one another. Expressing anger in this context does not just mean allowing outbursts of random self-expression, but managing conflict. Managing conflict, in turn, does not mean making it disappear. Managing conflict means recognizing and making conflict useful. Teenage immigrant bus riders, for example, hear from bus drivers describing how they became angry after years of dealing with rude, fare-dodging passengers. The bus drivers, in turn, learn how the young bus riders became angry after being confronted by the surly bus drivers' decades-old anger. Purposely evoking conflict like this requires trained expertise, though even with expert facilitation these conversations do sometimes explode.

Similarly, participants in "public achievement," a project for young people in Minneapolis in the United States, are asked to make a commitment for a full school year to find and address a problem they want to fix in their community. But unlike in conventional empowerment projects, public achievement participants have to find a conflict in the issue they have chosen. If the problem is the quality of school lunches, for example, the question has to be "Who benefits from this situation?" Agribusiness, for example, might emerge as a culprit. As in mutual qualification projects, participants call this experience frustrating and difficult, but both examples transform conflict into an invigorating source of mutual understanding. This is risky, long-term, and can fail; the process both elicits and relies on step-by-step personal transformation all along the way (Edwards and Sen 2000). This is not the same as the "volunteering-as-therapy" described earlier, which uses volunteering instrumentally as a quick balm to smooth over very personal woes. Rather, this process enlists personal woes in the process of social transformation, each healing the other. It is this combination of personal change and collective action that leads to lasting results.

The problem of treating everyone as if they are already equals can also be surmounted. Making people into experts is not the same thing as excluding those without expertise. In Porto Alegre, Brazil, for example, impoverished citizens learn to make the city's annual budget together, but not simply by entering the process as if they were already equals in expertise. Rather, everyone has to build up, in steps, to a point of full participation. It takes months to learn how to be an effective, knowledgeable participant—to learn how to argue about the science and finance involved in paving the street with cement or asphalt, for example (Baiocchi 2002). Illiterate people might have more difficulty in reaching that point than others, so it is tempting for them to exit the conversation, but then no one would learn anything at all; or that no one should have to learn to master any skills in order to participate, in which case the tradeoff would be more equality against less effective problem-solving.

As in Porto Alegre and public achievement, the U.S. settlement house movement also had strict rules for learning how to become a volunteer (Hillman 1960). Settlement houses—like the one in Chicago that caused Jane Addams to make perplexity into a moral duty—spanned the nation, and surveys of them showed that volunteers were heavily screened: they had to make a heavy commitment, not just of feelings but of time; and they had to accept continuous guidance from expert social workers. Many dropped out before they had contact with the families they had hoped to serve, but at least this reduced the risk that they would promise solidarity and then vanish when their charges' problems seemed too hard to fix.

These examples share some common threads. First, they show that "the more fully public and democratic a conversation is, the more it calls for micro-management, rules, and procedures, to ensure that even inarticulate and shy people can feel safe in speaking up" (Schudson 1997, 301). No solution is entirely problem-free, which makes participation slower, less flexible, and less completely "grassroots." Second, these examples show that there is no substitute for time and commitment. Relationships unfold slowly. Comfort comes only over time. Embracing and working through disagreement is slow. There are no quick and speedy alternatives. This is especially difficult in empowerment projects that work on short-term grant money and constantly need to reconfigure their groups' membership and agenda to make them appealing to new funders each six or twelve months.

Building community by design is not as easy to solve. Often, when people do develop a sense of community, such feelings arise indirectly, rather than as a direct result of the organizations' aims and activities. For example, the famous Venezuelan music education program, "El Sistema," sounds very much like Snowy Prairie's empowerment projects when it describes itself as "the orchestra as instrument of community development".[2] But the similarity ends there: "The phenomenon of the Venezuelan orchestra is looked upon as a miracle. Nevertheless, the achievements are the result of constant effort and… [exemplify] what can be achieved through constant work and dedication." Community arrived indirectly, when people learned how to play their instruments well, over many repetitions. In contrast, Snowy Prairie residents were constantly told, directly, that volunteering builds community, and music programs got funding if they advertised loudly and publicly that they prevented drug abuse and pregnancy, with no mention of the quality of the music or diligence of the musicians. Their answer to the question posed at the beginning of this chapter—"What are we doing here together?"—was supposed to be "becoming friends, and thereby preventing drug abuse." The pressure was on, and it was direct: make friends now, and quickly, an observation that illustrates a conundrum facing many empowerment projects: often, if community, friendship, and social bonds arrive, they enter through the back door. Staring at them too intently makes them disappear.

Bridging diverse classes and cultures is also difficult. It would be tempting to say that problems of large-scale inequality simply cannot be solved in civic organizations but only at a higher level, through political policy making. But the examples cited above show that the conditions of different civic organizations, and social conditions more broadly, do not automatically encourage or prevent civility, or get in the way of making a connection between civility and civicness. Problems cannot be fixed unless someone fixes them, so we are thrown back to the question of how to make civic organizations work more effectively to put pressure on government and business to fix issues that can never be solved by civil society acting alone, especially in very inegalitarian societies.

4. CONCLUSION: UTILIZING ANGER AND DISCOMFORT

According to Schudson, "The fully public democratic conversation takes place...in situations that are bound to be uncomfortable. This is the kind of talk that people are particularly loathe to engage in...it invites conflict...people prefer sociable conversation to potentially explosive conversation" (1997, 306). Schudson is saying that discomfort might be the duty of citizens who want to act civicly, and even, on occasion, to be rude, so that "democracy may require withdrawal from civility itself" (1997, 308). As an American protest song puts it, "It isn't nice to drop the groceries. It isn't nice to go to jail. There are nicer ways to do it. But the nice ways always fail. It isn't nice...but if that's freedom's price, we don't mind.[3]" In the short run, some incivility may be a civic duty; and it may be important to separate politeness from politics in these cases. Assuming that all societies contain inequality and injustice, this problem—a clash between civicness and civility—will recur. But detaching civicness from civility will not suffice as a long-term vision for civil society. Sometimes, political conflict seems to be a simple win-lose situation, a competition between the rich and the poor, and in these cases the goal of incivility is to make it impossible for "business as usual" to continue. However, the people who might benefit from change are often those who most oppose it (Gaventa 1982), and no one ultimately benefits from problems like global warming, for example. Environmental problems continue partly because too many people are attached to routine ways of traveling and eating that feel too normal to disrupt without undermining their sense of reality. So in the longer term, conflict is rarely a simple win-lose competition: even the rich are not the ultimate beneficiaries if they have to cower behind locked metal grills in their houses, under police helicopters patrolling the night sky. Being a good citizen requires waking up and shaking up other citizens, and oneself as well, and hoping that the others will eventually shake themselves up too. This is not easy or comfortable, but treating any conflict as a cosmic split between pure good and evil will not transform anything.

Ignoring our differences and putting the past behind us may sound tempting. Volunteers in America, for example, often assume that looking forward, and working shoulder-to-shoulder, will solve problems more easily than looking backwards at the causes of a problem (Eliasoph 2011). Of course, citizens rarely benefit by being deliberately rude or disrespectful, but, as this chapter shows, repressed problems do not disappear. *Using*, and working *through* conflict and discomfort, is eventually necessary. When people are trying to change a divided, conflict-ridden society, civility arrives, in most cases, only as a hard-won achievement, and rarely as a starting point. Perhaps at some point civic relationships will overcome conflict and discomfort. In the meantime, the question should be if and how civic organizations can acknowledge real-life conditions and make conflict, discomfort and inequality *useable* in fashioning civil societies worthy of the name.

NOTES

1. See http://www.sesp.northwestern.edu/abcd/. See http://www.abcdinstitute.org/.
2. Fundación del Estado para el Sistema Nacional de las Orquestas Juveniles e Infantiles de Venezuela, 2008. *La orquesta cómo instrumento de desarrollo comunitario*, http://fesnojiv .gob.ve/es/historia/el-milagro-musical-venezolano.html
3. "It Isn't Nice," by Malvina Reynolds (original version 1964); additional lyrics by Betsy Rose (CODEPINK Songs, www.codepinkforpeace.org).

REFERENCES

Addams, J. [1901] 2002. *Democracy and Social Ethics*. Urbana: University of Illinois Press.
Baiocchi, G. 2002. *Militants and Citizens*. Stanford, Calif.: Stanford University Press.
Beem, C. 1999. *The Necessity of Politics: Reclaiming American Public Life*. Chicago: University of Chicago Press.
Blee, K. 2003. *Inside Organized Racism*. Berkeley: University of California Press.
Carrel, M. 2004. "Susciter un public local. Habitants et professionnels du transport en confrontation dans un quartier d'habitat social," in C. Barril, M. Carrel, J-C. Guerrero, and A. Marquez (eds.) *Le public en action: Usages et limites de la notion d'espace public en sciences sociales*. Paris: L'Harmattan: 219–40.
Cohen, J., and A. Arato. 1992. *Civil Society and Political Theory*. Cambridge, Mass.: MIT Press.
Dekker, P. 2009. "Civicness: From Civil Society to Civic Services?" *Voluntas*, vol. 20: 220–38.
Edwards, M. 2009. *Civil Society*. 2nd ed. Cambridge: Polity Press.
Edwards, M., and G. Sen. 2000. "NGOs, Social Change and the Transformation of Human Relationships: A 21st Century Civic Agenda." *Third World Quarterly* vol. 21(4): 605–16.
Eliasoph, N. 1998. *Avoiding Politics: How Americans Produce Apathy in Everyday Life*. Cambridge: Cambridge University Press.
———. 2011. *Making Volunteers: Civic Life After Welfare's End*. Princeton, N.J.: Princeton University Press.

Gaventa, J. 1982. *Power and Powerlessness: Quiescence and Rebellion in an Appalachian Valley*. Urbana: University of Illinois Press.

Giddens, A. 1991. *Modernity and Self-Identity*. Stanford, Calif.: Stanford University Press.

Hall, P. D. 1992. *Inventing the Nonprofit Sector*. Baltimore: Johns Hopkins University Press.

Hillman, A. 1960. *Neighborhood Centers Today: Action Programs for a Rapidly Changing World*. New York: National Federation of Settlements and Neighborhood Centers.

Luque, E. 2005. "Researching Environmental Citizenship and its Publics." *Environmental Politics* vol. 14 (2): 211–25.

Rotolo, T. 2000. "Town Heterogeneity, and Affiliation: A Multilevel Analysis of Voluntary Association Membership." *Sociological Perspectives* 43: 271–89.

Schudson, M. 1997. "Why Conversation is Not the Soul of Democracy." *Critical Studies in Mass Communication,* vol. 14: 297–309.

Tocqueville, A. de. [1835] 1969. *Democracy in America.* ed. J. P. Meyer, New York: Anchor Books.

Van Til, J., and S. Bould Van Til. 1970. "Citizen Participation in Social Policy: The End of the Cycle?" *Social Problems*, vol. 17 (Winter), 313–23.

Walsh, K. K. 2007. *Talking about Race: Community Dialogues and the Politics of Difference*. Chicago: University of Chicago Press.

Wuthnow, R. 1993. *Acts of Compassion*. Princeton, N.J.: Princeton University Press.

CHAPTER 19

CIVIL SOCIETY AND EQUALITY

SALLY KOHN

In the very first paragraph of his important treatise on American civil society, Alexis de Tocqueville wrote that "equality of condition is the fundamental fact from which all others seem to be derived" (1899, 3). It is no accident that one of the first texts that examines civil society opens with this refrain, for equality is an essential—if not *the* essential—undergirding premise of civil society in theory and in practice. High levels of inequality distort the ability of associational life and the public sphere to articulate a democratic path to the good society. Moreover, as a component part of any society that aspires to be fair and just, let alone that part of society that arguably is charged with promoting these goals, it is essential for civil society to both emulate and radiate equality. The relevant questions, then, are the extent to which equality actually exists in different civil societies, and whether those civil societies are committed to, and effective in, advancing equality more broadly. Is civil society equitable and, if so, does a more equitable civil society contribute to a more equitable world?

1. DEFINING EQUALITY

What is meant by equality? Tirades against equality as a destructive idea are plentiful,[1] but they are often built on an overly broad definition of the term, cast as a convenient straw person to attack more general notions of justice and fairness. For example, the early twentieth century social Darwinist William Graham Sumner wrote that "the assertion that all men are equal is perhaps the purest falsehood in dogma that was ever put into human language; five minutes' observation of facts will show that men are unequal through a very wide range of variation. Men are not simple units; they are very complex; there is no such thing as a unit man" (1913, 88). Such overly simplistic definitions of equality aim simply to fan the flames of opposition. To say that all people are equal is not to say they are identical. Egalitarians would just as quickly denounce this overly broad definition for its tendency to homogenize diverse societies under a dominant cultural and economic norm.

Centuries before Sumner, Aristotle outlined a much more complex and nuanced definition—that the idea of equality as a central pillar of a just society is to 'treat like cases as like' legally and politically. Building on this construct, Nancy Rosenblum has articulated a list of "key virtues for democracy" that include "treating people identically with easy spontaneity" (1998, 350). And, arguing from the inverse perspective of what needs to be avoided rather than developed, Charles Tilly states that democracy requires "insulating public politics from categorical inequality" (2007, 188). The Aristotelian definition of equality, inherited by liberal political thinkers like Rosenblum and Tilly, stresses that where *in certain key dimensions* two people are alike, then they should be treated equally under the law. The legitimate question, then, is what factors should count in determining likeness and how far we should cast our moral gaze in determining which groups fall within our sphere of concern. Is a same-gender couple equal to a heterosexual couple in terms of the quality and character of their relationship, and therefore to be treated equally under the law? Is a factory worker in China toiling away for fifteen hours a day entitled to the same compensation as British banking executive working these same hours? Definitions of equality are colored in morally complex shades of grey, not black and white. But the basic notion that people of equal condition should be treated equally can only be attacked by those who possess an explicit or concealed fondness for the spoils of inequality.

Nevertheless, even within the liberal political tradition there is disagreement as to whether inequality exists at a level that warrants particular and concerted attention. Among Neo-Tocquevillian civil society theorists, inequality is undoubtedly viewed as negative, but opinions vary as to whether it constitutes a significant problem in and for civil society to address. Liberal Egalitarians like Michael Walzer (1983) and William Galston (2000) go further in identifying inequality as a significant problem for the theory and practice of civil society, but deeper issues tend to be ignored. As Nancy Fraser argues, "liberal political theory assumes that it is possible to organize a democratic form of political life on the basis of socio-economic and socio-sexual structures that generate systemic inequalities" (1996, 79). Michael Tomasky, for example, has argued that the American Left was ruined by multicultural identity politics (1996). Reformers, adds David Brooks (2006), "have come to understand that they need to pay less attention to minorities and more to the white working class" if they want to succeed, and that economic inequality is a more pertinent cause than discrimination. Claims of racial, gender, and sexual discrimination are written off as "crying wolf," distracting from more important problems caused by economic structures that are seen as race- and gender-neutral. This overlooks the interlocking nature of racial discrimination, gender discrimination, and other forms of structural bias on the one hand, and economic inequality on the other. In a world where the darkest-skinned peoples are the poorest and where those with the lightest skin tend to fare best within industrialized and even most developing countries, it is naïve to try and disaggregate these factors. But more importantly, majoritarian theorists fail to recognize that the presumed dominance of their arguments may have something to do with the dominance of their own demographic groups in society at large. It is perplexing that supposed reformers can purport to attack inequality in society while denying its existence within their own ranks.

If one rejects fringe anti-egalitarians who attack equality and fairness by corrupting the definition of equality, and if one sees through the exclusionary arguments of others who in effect defend the status quo, it is clear that equality is an unarguable pillar of just societies and that furthering equality is essential to any effort at social improvement—civil society included. "The persistence of serious inequalities and insecurities endangers civil society as a democratic enterprise and places too much influence in the hands of elites," writes Edwards (2009, 111). Because inequality threatens civil society and democracy more broadly, the advancement of equality must be civil society's central agenda, operating both within itself and radiating out to society at large.

2. Radical Equality

The classic, liberal definition of equality in the operational sense belongs to Dworkin, who defines equality as an "envy free" distribution of resources which can include both political or participatory resources, economic or material goods, social capital, and even more abstract concepts like opportunity and aspiration (1981, 10). Envy, a morally grey emotion if ever there was one, signifies not simply that you want something but that you want something that you can't have but have reason to believe you deserve as much as the person who has it. Like the variegated and complex nature of inequality itself, Dworkin's definition is also fraught with complications. In the extreme, it might reward those with a grander sense of personal entitlement or simply fancier tastes, rather than the intended effect of providing equal resources for equal effort. Yet in a world in which some people can drive down the street freely while others are routinely stopped because of the color of their skin, where some live alone in mansions while others are crammed with their extended families into shacks, and where extremes of wealth and poverty persist, defining equality as the effort to combat *legitimate* envy seems reasonable and appropriate.

However, I want to introduce the term *radical* equality to push the definition even further. Classical liberalism, as noted above, tends to adopt a nice but somewhat innocuous concept of equality rooted mainly in political principles of opportunity and participation. Liberalism accepts a certain degree of inequality as unavoidable, and its primary response in this regard is to create structures such as public education and welfare which can supposedly offset such inequality.[2] Dworkin himself insists that "the liberal conception of equality is a principle of political organization that is required by justice, not a way of life for individuals" (1984).

Critiquing the limits of Dworkin's liberal framework, Stopler writes that "the equality espoused by modern liberalism is political equality owed to citizens by the government rather than private equality that reflects each person's individual conviction that all persons are equal, and therefore entitled to be treated equally in all spheres of life by every other person" (2005). In other words, liberalism is anything but inherently nor fully egalitarian. *Radical* equality—and radicalism in general—challenges inequality at its core. Radical equality aims to abolish oppression in all its institutional and interpersonal forms and replace them with values and structures that are premised on, and actively demonstrate, the fundamental equality of all people in the deepest sense. For example, articulating the premise behind critical legal studies, Matsuda (1987) argues such radicalism "is characterized by skepticism towards the liberal vision of the rule of law, by a focus on the role of legal ideas in capturing human consciousness, by agreement that fundamental change is required to attain a just society, and by a Utopian conception of a world more communal and less hierarchical than the one we know now." While the term "democracy" is arguably complex and easily co-opted (as Fraser, among others, suggest[3]), radical equality can lead to "democratic community"—"collective self-determination by means of open discussion among equals, in accordance with rules acceptable to all" (Anderson 1999, 313): a definition that links the debate over equality to the meaning and roles of civil society.

3. Radical Equality and the Aims of Civil Society

Conventional civil society theory often intimates that this sphere is substantively neutral—at worst, a passive, residual space in which forms of associational life not otherwise categorized can settle; and at best, a more active, discursive space in which the roles of government and the market are debated, but which harbors no consensus on the outcome. Yet in reality, both historically and structurally, markets and governments tend towards their own versions of radical inequality when left to their own devices. The market is based on dominant models of capitalism that breed economic and social inequality;[4] while the state is based on necessarily broad, essentialist operating assumptions that pretend natural or man-made inequality can be overlooked, therefore allowing inequality to continue.[5] Galston (1995, 521) has observed that "the standard liberal view (or hope) is that the autonomy of the market allows diversity to flourish while diversity promoted by government allows creative autonomy to be nourished." Yet not only does the market cut against diversity (for example, the trend towards monopoly if unchecked) but, Galston continues, "the decision to throw state power behind the promotion of individual autonomy can weaken or undermine individuals and groups that do not and cannot organize their affairs in accordance with that principle without undermining the deepest sources of their identity." Just as markets provide incentives to the sort of competition that takes advantage of and perpetuates inequality, state-based formations rely on a glue of shared identity whose manufacture may hide or trivialize important differences.

In the case of the private market, dominant models of capitalism rely on large inequalities between labor and the ownership of production, and those benefiting from these inequalities fight hard to preserve and perpetuate such imbalances. In the case of government, even for the most well-intentioned elected officials and bureaucrats, the need to maintain the image of "we, the people" conspires with the practical political risks associated with corrective measures to help particular, disenfranchised segments of the public. In addition, those who enjoy extraordinary benefits and privileges prefer to imagine their success as the just result of natural talent and hard work, rather than the unjust product of socially created inequalities. Pointing out the facts of such injustice is disruptive enough. Actually trying to root out inequality from institutions and interpersonal dynamics is even more so, because those at the top of the system may end up with significantly less—in material (though not moral) terms.

Moreover, government and the market are insufficient to balance out each other's dangers. Expanding democracy and participation, which appear to further equality, while masking deeper structures of hierarchy and unequal participation, not only legitimizes the democratic political enterprise as such but also perpetuates the social and political foundations on which inequitable capitalism thrives (Oxhorn 2003). Throughout modern history one can see how private enterprise can co-opt the state or vice versa and, ultimately, advance inequality. This is why civil society is so important, providing the only vehicle which can bring the "behemoth of the market" and the "leviathan of the state" into balance (Oommen 1996). Civil society exists to illuminate and critique inequality in government and the market and to affirmatively advance equality in all spheres. As Edwards puts it:

> The success of each of [the] three models of civil society is dependent on its
> interaction with the others. If these interactions are to operate effectively, there
> are certain things that have to be done almost regardless of the context, focused
> on the structural barriers that undermine the conditions in which such synergies
> can develop. Chief among those conditions are poverty and inequality, which
> remove the support systems people need to be active citizens and deprive them of
> the security required to reach out and make connections with others (2009, 110).

This more radical view is strongly rooted in civil society theory. Arendt (1998), for example, defined civil society (and specifically the public sphere), as the countervailing force against an unchecked government's inclination towards hyper-universality at the expense of individual liberty and expression, a process she labeled totalitarianism. Gramsci (1971) appropriated the term civil society to define a space of struggle against the inherent inequalities and injustices of capitalism and Eley (1991, 306) argues that civil society is "the structured setting where cultural and ideological contest or negotiation among a variety of publics takes place." In other words, civil society is the vital space in which minority interests establish the collective power and processes required to challenge majority operating principles and practices in society more broadly. Historically, this can be seen in examples that range from anti-apartheid activists in South Africa who mobilized in civil society and then formed a political party,[6] to labor unions in the Americas that operate from a base in civil society to check corporate interests.[7] If equality, or any approximation thereof, is to exist in the private market or in government, it must be generated from civil society pressure.

If the mandate of civil society is to advance radical equality, what does this mean in concrete terms? In particular, what does radical equality mean when applied to the three dominant formulations of civil society—associational life, the public sphere, and the good society itself?

4. RADICAL EQUALITY AND ASSOCIATIONAL LIFE

Because they exist within a larger society that is structured by racism, classism, and other forms of structural inequality, the forms of civil society cannot be magically immune from such injustice. Robert Putnam included equality in his definition of "civic community" and, in his studies of Italy, suggested that political and social equality strongly correlates with robust civic participation (1994, 88). Yet the reverse is also true—that inequality negatively affects civic participation (Verba et al. 1995). Rising inequality and increased concentration in the distribution of economic and political power has correlated with a decline in broad-based associational formations in the United States and elsewhere (Edwards 2009, 89). That so much is made of heightened and, implicitly, unexpected surges in participation—from the increase in voters of color in the 2008 United States presidential election to the participation of heretofore subjugated tribes in Iraq's imperfect 2010 elections—suggests that the exception proves the rule. Similarly, social movements from landless peasants in Brazil to slum dwellers in India to American feminists in the 1960s and 1970s have always created separate spaces for associational life in explicit acknowledgement of the closed and unequal nature of civil society more broadly.

As the sphere from which the agenda of equality is advanced, it is obviously vital that civil society must put "its own house in order" if it is to succeed in changing society more broadly. It is difficult to promote equality and participation in other institutions if one's own affairs are exclusionary. Large numbers of civil society associations have been formed with the explicit aim of advancing equality internally and transforming society as a whole. In the United States, for example, the civil rights movement was one of the first associational spaces in which blacks and whites socialized, learned and organized together—especially in the deeply segregated South, where associations like the Highlander Institute training center brought rare racial integration to divided communities and, from there, a divided land.

Yet throughout history, civil society has also been a breeding ground for increased inequality in some societies at certain times—for example, the white separatist movement in the United States, early Nazi formations in Germany, and the activist circles that schooled Pol Pot in Cambodia. Clearly, the commitment of different civil society groups to radical equality varies considerably, but even those associations with clear, activist agendas often perpetuate inequality within their structures and processes. Despite seismic demographic changes across the United States, in the nonprofit sector there, men are significantly overrepresented in leadership roles to the exclusion of women (Gibelman 2003). Similarly, one study of the nonprofit sector in California—the most racially and ethnically diverse state in the United States—found that at a time when people of color constituted 57 percent of the state population, they held a mere 25 percent of organizational executive directorships (De Vita et al. 2009). Kunreuther, Kim, and Rodriguez (2008) have documented how, even where there are people of color in leadership positions, they are overwhelmingly educated at elite, Ivy League universities. Similar observations about gender, race, and/or ethnic bias in nonprofit associations have been raised in South Africa (da Silva Wells 2004), India (Kirmani 2009), Latin America (Brysk 2000), and the Philippines (Clarke 1998). The outwardly focused rhetoric of equality espoused by civic associations makes them appropriate targets for criticism if their aims are limited to equality for members of their own excluded group. In this regard, the associational realm of civil society still has much to conquer.

5. RADICAL EQUALITY AND THE PUBLIC SPHERE

Jürgen Habermas (1989) first articulated the idea of the public sphere as a body of "private persons" assembled to discuss matters of "public concern" or "common interest," yet Habermas and other thinkers have since been criticized for assuming that differences between people are insignificant or otherwise avoidable in public discourse, an assumption that allows inequalities to persist. In fact inequality is the enemy of the public sphere and social equality is a necessary condition for political democracy. By prioritizing an aggressive agenda of equality, Fraser (1996) illuminates the embedded inequality in Habermas's analysis and, by extension, in civil society itself.

Habermas argues that a single, totalistic public sphere is preferable to multiple spheres or publics. If multiple public spheres exist, he contends, it can only be due to a failing of civil society to promote unity amid democracy. The parallels to Arendt's warnings about government totalitarianism are clear, and Fraser argues the exact opposite of Habermas—that the existence of multiple publics is actually a marker of a successful civil society and of democracy itself, and that people are expressing, not suppressing, their identities by finding their own voices amidst pluralism. Iris Marion Young places multiple publics not just in the context of seemingly independent identities but also in complex social relations and hierarchies. The public sphere can only be correctly understood "in relational conception," when such publics are constituted in relation to other groupings. As Young write, "class, gender, and race are some of the most far reaching and enduring structural relations of hierarchy and inequality in modern society" (1997, 389–90).

Herein lies another divide between classical liberalism and radical equality. As Galeotti (1993, 597) asks:

> What does the public recognition of collective identities imply in terms of public action and policies? The liberal purist might contend that the liberal democratic state has already answered this claim by means of the right to free association, granted and protected by the law. This right plus the principle of equal treatment under the law and some distributive mechanisms for balancing off the disadvantaged social positions is all the liberal democratic state can legitimately be asked to do in order to accord each member of the polity, whether belonging to majority or to minority groups, equal dignity and equal opportunity for his or her identity to flourish.

Galeotti counters that it is the job of society—the state and civil society—not just to create a space in which all identities can compete market-style, but to pursue parity between identity groups. "If social difference is denied public visibility and legitimacy in the polity, the group associated with it inevitably bear social stigma," he writes (Galeotti 1993, 597). If the public sphere can be imagined as a fluid space for back-and-forth discourse, such stigma inevitably "gums up" its workings.

Radical equality also challenges what we understand to be included in the public sphere, because historical assumptions about "the public" and "the common good" are often built on inequality. Fraser (1996, 86) gives a powerful example:

> Until quite recently, feminists were in the minority in thinking that domestic violence against women was a matter of common concern and thus a legitimate topic of public discourse. The great majority of people considered this issue to be a private matter between what was assumed to be a fairly small number of heterosexual couples (and perhaps the social and legal professionals who were supposed to deal with them). Then, feminists formed a subaltern counter-public from which we disseminated a view of domestic violence as a widespread systemic failure of male-dominated societies. Eventually, after sustained discursive contestation, we succeeded in making it a common concern.

In other words, both the process of public discourse and its outcomes must be dissected under the microscope of radical equality. It is not enough for marginalized communities to participate in so-called democratic discourse if the style of their participation is hindered and the outcomes favor existing patterns of domination. Presence is not the same as participation, just as the opportunity to compete is not the same as equality of outcomes. Without due attention to the corrosive effects of

unequal social and power structures in society, the public sphere will merely perpetuate such inequalities, rather than being a source of true, participatory, and
democratic debate that advances equality in society more broadly.

6. RADICAL EQUALITY AND THE GOOD SOCIETY

Few theorists would exclude equality from the "good society." Rather, the question
is how much equality and for whom, a question which points to the value of promoting equality in associational life and the public sphere so that the contours of
equality are very specifically discussed and debated, and the picture of the good
society comes into sharper focus. Polletta (2002) argues that rather than labeling
such practices as utopian (accompanied by condescension and a sense of impracti-
cality), equitable and democratic practices within civil society—especially the social
movement realm that Polletta studies—can be labeled as prefigurative, that is, illustrating the changes such movements seek to create.[8] Perhaps the best example of
this process is the global "social forum" phenomenon. First organized in Brazil in
2001, the World Social Forum and related regional and national social forums bring
together civil society actors and institutions, including large contingents from social
movements, in "a permanent world process seeking and building alternatives to
neo-liberal policies" (World Social Forum 2001). The tag line of the World Social
Forum further evidences this prefigurative agenda: "Another world is possible."

Historically, the United Democratic Front played a similar role in South African
politics, rehearsing collective participation and civic action for the nation's black
majority that would become the new norm after the fall of apartheid—imperfect in
practice, but still significant (Heller 2001). In a speech to the 2004 European Social
Forum, Wainwright laid out many other examples—from American feminist meetings that include child care provision to movements challenging corporate domination of food production by creating local, sustainable alternatives. As she noted, "we
need forms of political organization which can support and understand these practical alternatives and help bring about the wider political conditions in which these
alternatives can thrive" (Wainwright 2004).

The idea that the good society might be defined by radical equality begins to fill
the normative void at the heart of much current civil society thinking. According to
Cohen and Arato (1994, xi), "the demise of the most important radical-democratic
and socialist utopia of our time—Marxism—has already led thinkers to proclaim
the end of history." That a particular vision of equality failed in the form of the
Soviet state says little about the broader prospects for pursuing these objectives in
other contexts, but advocates of equality are often at such pains to distance themselves from Communism that they have distanced themselves from the idea of
equality altogether, especially radical equality. "Less inequality" is hardly a powerful
call to action or an inspiring vision of a better world, but the idea of radical equality

provides a bold and unifying vision for civil society, one that holds great potential to move all institutions in society towards greater equity and justice.

7. Conclusion

Towards the end of *Democracy in America,* de Tocqueville writes that "the tendency toward equality is general amongst mankind" (1899, 440). Perhaps he should have clarified that the tendency to *aspire to* equality is general amongst mankind, given that economic inequality has grown in nearly every society over the last twenty years while racism, sexism, and homophobia continue to persist. Given these realities, it would be naïve to suggest that egalitarianism is the default thrust of humanity. Rather, it can be said that people—certainly those in the liberal political tradition, but likely most people more broadly categorized—outwardly embrace the idea of equality even if they are inwardly skeptical or downright hostile about its full implications. These suspicions are only likely to multiply further under capitalism, which relies on greed and inequality to spur competition. If government risks swinging too far in the opposite direction, favoring cultural and political homogeneity as a corrective to the cutthroat nature of capitalist economics, some sphere of action must stand for the deeper ideal of radical equality, the idea that like shall be treated as like, envy free, despite the best or worst intentions of markets and the state. Both by necessity and design, civil society must fight the cause of radical equality. One cannot conceive of an associational space that is truly effective and democratic without embracing the principles of inclusion and fairness. Civil society as a discursive sphere is at best ornamental, and at worst a new space for marginalization, without aggressive efforts to ensure equality between the groups and individuals involved. And any prefigurative notion of the good society modeled in civic space that does not foreground the aim of equality arguably offers no alternative vision at all. But above all, if the agenda of civil society is to promote equality in society more broadly, it will have neither the expertise nor the credibility to pursue equality externally without doing so internally.

Equality is a very old idea, but it remains fiercely radical and subversive. The idea that the measure of society should not be judged by the average of its wealth or achievements—such that deprivation at the bottom is mathematically masked by blending it with outsized gains at the top—but by whether each person is given the opportunity and support throughout life to develop her or his own talents to the full and pursue their dreams, is a vision of radical equality that has the potential to transform the world. Civil society explicitly aims to change the world—to shape markets and government, and social, economic, and political norms more generally, through participation, public discourse, and revisioning the good society. The central requirement of an effective civil society in this sense must be equality within its ranks, or at least the active pursuit of equality in associational life and the public sphere. It is time for civil society theory to incorporate the central agenda of equality more explicitly by acknowledging the insights that critical theory has to offer, and by embracing the view that only by rigorously advancing equality will civil society play its full role in transforming the world for the better.

NOTES

1. See for example Ellis 1998; Rothbard 2000; and Reed 1995.
2. See for example Katznelson 1996, and Schwartzman 1999.
3. See also Oxhorn 2003.
4. See for example Marx 1993 (1889) and Moore, B. 1987.; Human Values; and Stevenson 1982.
5. See for example Arendt 1998 and Young 2000.
6. See for example Thorn 2009.
7. See for example Alvarez et al. 1998.
8. Polletta's main point is that deliberative democracy and other internal movement practices in the pursuit of equality are not *only* prefigurative but strategic and tactical as well, but her analysis with regard to the prefigurative aspects of social movement culture is most useful here.

REFERENCES

Alvarez, S. E, E. Dagnino, and A. Escobar (eds.). 1998. *Cultures of Politics, Politics of Cultures: Re-Visioning Latin American Social Movements*. New York: Worldview/ Perseus.

Anderson, E. 1999. "What Is the Point of Equality?" *Ethics* 109, 2: 287–337.

Arendt, H. 1998. *The Human Condition*. Chicago: University of Chicago Press.

Brooks, D. 2006. "The Death of Multiculturalism." *New York Times*, April 27, 2006.

Brysk, A. 2000. "Democratizing Civil Society in Latin America." *Journal of Democracy* vol. 11(3): 151–65.

Clarke, G. 1998. *The Politics of NGOs in South-East Asia: Participation and Protest in the Philippines*. London: Routlege.

Cohen, J. L., and A. Arato. 1994. *Civil Society and Political Theory*. Cambridge, Mass.: MIT Press.

da Silva Wells, C. 2004. "Changing the Way the Game is Played; Gender Equity in NGO Management," in M. Spierenburg and H. Wels (eds.) *Culture, Organization and Management in South Africa*. Hauppauge, N.Y.: Nova Science.

De Vita, C. J., and K. L. Roeger. 2009. *Diversity in California's Nonprofit Sector*. Washington, D.C.: The Urban Institute.

Dworkin, R. 1981. "What Is Equality? II. Equality of Resources." *Philosophy and Public Affairs* vol. 10(4): 283–345.

——. 1984. "Liberalism," In Sandel, M. (ed.) *Liberalism and its Critics*. New York: New York University Press.

Edwards, M. 2009. *Civil Society*. 2nd revised edition. Cambridge: Polity Press.

Eley, G. 1991. "Nations, Publics and Political Cultures: Placing Habermas in the Nineteenth Century," in C. Calhoun (ed.) *Habermas and the Public Sphere*. Cambridge, Mass.: MIT Press.

Ellis, R. J. 1998. *The Dark Side of the Left: Illberal Egalitarianism in America*. Lawrence: University Press of Kansas.

Fraser, N. 1996. *Justice Interruptus: Critical Reflections on the Post-Socialist Condition*. New York: Routledge.

Galeotti, A. E. 1993. "Citizenship and Equality: The Place for Toleration." *Political Theory* vol. 21 (4): 585–605.

Galston, W. 1995. "Two Concepts of Liberalism." *Ethnics* (105, 3).

——. 2000. "Civil Society and the 'Art of Association.'" *Journal of Democracy* vol 11(1): 64–70.

Gibelman, M. 2003. "The Nonprofit Sector and Gender Discrimination." *Nonprofit Management and Leadership* vol. 10(3): 251–69.

Gramsci, A. 1971. *Selections from the Prison Notebooks*. New York: Internal Publishers.

Habermas, J. 1989. *The Structural Transformation of the Public Sphere: An Inquiry into a Category of Bourgeois Society*. Trans. T. Burder and F. Lawrence. Cambridge, Mass.: MIT Press.

Heller, P. 2001. "Moving the State: The Politics of Democratic Decentralization in Kerala, South Africa, and Porto Alegre." *Politics & Society* vol. 29 (1): 131–63.

Katznelson, I. 1996. *Liberalism's Crooked Circle: Letters to Adam Michnik*. Princeton, N.J.: Princeton University Press.

Kirmani, N. 2009. "Claiming Their Space: Muslim Women-led Networks and the Women's Movement in India." *Journal of International Women's Studies* vol. 11(1): 72–85.

Kunreuther, F., H. Kim, and R. Rodriguez. 2008. *Working Across Generations; Defining the Future of Nonprofit Leadership*. New York: Jossey-Bass.

Marx, K. 1993 (1889). *Capital: A Critique of Political Economy*. 3 vols. Trans. D. Fernbach. London: Penguin Classics.

Matsuda, M. J. 1987. "Looking to the Bottom: Critical Legal Studies and Reparations." *Harvard Civil Rights – Civil Liberties Law Review* vol. 22: 323–400.

Moore, B. 1987. *Authority and Inequality Under Capitalism and Socialism: The Tanner Lectures on Human Values*. Oxford: Clarendon Press.

Oommen, T. K. 1996. "State, Civil Society, and Market in India: The Context of Mobilization." *Mobilization: An International Quarterly* vol. 1 (2): 191–202.

Oxhorn, P. 2003. "Social Inequality, Civil Society and the Limits of Citizenship in Latin America," in Eckstein, S., and T. Wickham-Crawley (eds.) *What Justice? Whose Justice? Fighting for Fairness in Latin America*. Berkeley: University of California Press, 35–63.

Polletta, F. 2002. *Freedom is an Endless Meeting: Democracy in American Social Movements*. Chicago: University of Chicago Press.

Putnam, R. 1994. *Making Democracy Work: Civic Traditions in Modern Italy*. Princeton, N.J.: Princeton University Press.

Reed, L. W. 1995. "The Quackery of Equality." *The Freeman* vol. 45 (12). Available at http://www.thefreemanonline.org/columns/the-quackery-of-equality/, accessed January 16, 2011.

Rosenblum, N. 1998. *Membership and Morals: The Personal Uses of Pluralism in America*. Princeton, N.J.: Princeton University Press.

Rothbard, M. N. 2000. *Egalitarianism as a Revolt Against Nature*. Auburn, Ala.: Ludwig Von Mises Institute.

Schwartzman, L. 1999. "Liberal Rights Theory and Social Inequality: A Feminist Critique." *Hypathia* vol. 14(2): 26–47.

Stevenson, P. 1982. "Capitalism and Inequality: The Negative Consequences for Humanity." *Crime, Law and Social Change* vol. 6(4): 333–72.

Stopler, G. 2005. "Gender Construction and the Limits of Liberal Equality." *Texas Journal of Woman and the Law* vol. 15: 43.

Sumner, W. G. 1913. *Earth-Hunger and Other Essays*. New Haven, Conn.: Yale University Press.

Thorn, H. 2009. *Anti-Apartheid and the Emergence of a Global Civil Society*. New York: Palgrave MacMillan.

Tilly, C. 2007. *Democracy*. Cambridge: Cambridge University Press.

Tocqueville, A. 1899 (1835, 1840). *Democracy in America*. Trans. H. Reeve. New York: D. Appleton and Co.

Tomasky, M. 1996. *Left For Dead: The Life, Death, and Possibly Resurrection of Progressive Politics in America*. New York: The Free Press.

Verba, S., K. L. Schlozman, and H. E. Brady. 1995. *Voice and Equality: Civic Voluntarism in American Politics*. Cambridge, Mass.: Harvard University Press.

Walzer, M. 1983. *Spheres of Justice. A Defence of Pluralism and Equality*. New York: Basic Books.

Wainwright, H. 2004. "Changing the World by Transforming Power—Including State Power!" Speech at European Social Forum. London, October 16.

World Social Forum. 2001. "Charter of Principles." Sao Paolo, Brazil. Available at http://www.forumsocialmundial.org.br/main.php?id_menu=4&cd_language=2.

Young, I. M. 1997. "Difference as a Resource for Democratic Communication," In J. Bohman and W. Rehg (eds.) *Deliberative Democracy: Essays on Reason and Politics*. Cambridge, Mass.: MIT Press.

——. 2000. *Inclusion and Democracy*. Oxford: Oxford University Press.

CHAPTER 20

CIVIL SOCIETY AND DIVERSITY

HILDE COFFÉ

AND

CATHERINE BOLZENDAHL

CENTRAL to the understanding of any democratic and well-functioning society is a focus on shared norms of civic responsibility and public participation in the polity and civic life. In democratic states such norms and patterns of participation explicitly or implicitly rely on concepts of citizenship. Put simply, the extent to which publics agree to, and act on, their roles as citizens determines the strength of democracy and the health of civil society. Yet this statement masks a variety of complicated questions: what constitutes a "good citizen" and which obligations should they fulfil? To what extent do different social groups have different ideas about "good citizenship"? Are some forms of participation privileged over others, and if so why and with what effects? Who is excluded from participating in public life, and are the causes and effects of exclusion similar for different social groups and different forms of participation?

These questions highlight the central role that is played by difference and diversity in determining the meaning of citizenship and the constitution of civil society. Traditionally, scholars have seen civil society as the "realm of particularity—the place where, whoever we are, we can find a home without asking for permission from above" (Edwards 2009, 54). All civil societies contain a wide variety of associations and agendas based on culture, religion, politics, ideology, and purpose, and the norms they represent and advance may diverge markedly, including their relative levels of tolerance concerning the views of others. This is why the public sphere is so important, in offering spaces in which these different normative and political agendas can be argued through to some sense of consensus. But the debate about civil society and diversity goes much further than a recognition that citizens and their associations express support for different social norms; it must also embrace the fact that there are varying normative understandings of citizenship and civil society themselves. As this chapter argues, the norms and practices of citizenship for diverse social groups may not revolve around simple questions of "more" or "less" participation, but around more complex questions that arise when some groups participate *differently* or have *different* norms about good citizenship. Both participation and citizenship embody a myriad of qualities, opening up the possibility that group membership may influence support for divergent norms and practices in many different ways. In order to investigate these questions, scholars must consider substantive variations in definitions of citizenship and measures of participation. By increasing our understanding of diversity in these arenas, we can position ourselves to appreciate what different groups can bring to the theory and practice of civil society, and what they can contribute to the vibrancy and vitality of the public sphere. Notably, such an expanded perspective may also serve to undermine persistent negative stereotypes about the *lack* of participation or commitment among nonmajority groups by showing that the fault may lie with overly narrow measures of participation and its meaning.

The remainder of this chapter is structured as follows. Section 1 provides an overview of the different meanings and practices of citizenship, highlighting how and why diverse social groups may have varying patterns of civic and political participation in both quantitative and qualitative terms. Section 2 illustrates the importance of this diversity across practices, meanings, and memberships through the lens of gender as the primary form of social difference in all societies. We show how a properly gendered analysis of civil society can reveal how and why women may be pressured to focus their participation on civil rather than political society, and around certain forms of associational life. These patterns may have important consequences for the ways in which political outcomes affect different social groups unequally. The chapter concludes with a summary of its arguments and findings, and an outline of some of the challenges that lie ahead for scholarship on this topic in the future.

1. THE MEANINGS AND PRACTICES
OF CITIZENSHIP

A participatory public is crucial for democratic responsiveness and is seen as an intrinsic democratic good (Verba 1996). Therefore, systematic and persistent patterns of unequal participation along existing lines of stratification, such as gender, class, race, and sexual orientation, are threats to both political equality and democratic performance (Sherrill 1996; Lijphart 1997; Burns, Schlozman, and Verba 2001). Most research highlights the ways in which white, male, heterosexual, and middle - and upper-class members of society tend to dominate civic and political participation. By being less involved in public life, nonwhites, women, and/or members of lower-class groups are thought to contribute less often to democratic processes, be less well represented among a variety of political offices, and benefit less from political policies and outcomes (Burns, Schlozman, and Verba 2001; Parry, Moyser, and Day 1992; Norris 2002; Inglehart and Norris 2003). For example, in the case of the United States, much research has pointed to lower levels of voter turnout among Latino citizens (Highton and Burris 2002; Uhlaner et al. 1989). In Europe and the U.S. higher levels of civic and political participation have been found among upper class individuals (Verba, Nie, and Kim 1978; Caínzos and Voces 2010), and in Belgium research has shown that women's levels of participation in formal civic and political associations are lower compared to those of men (Hooghe 2003).

Such findings highlight important inequalities in citizenship that remain to be addressed, but they suffer from two main limitations. First, most of this research has been focused on mainstream and/or institutional types of public participation, failing to recognize that groups may not only participate unequally, but may also participate *differently*. Second, such approaches fail to problematize differences in the ways citizenship is framed—that is, in what it means to be a "good" citizen and how citizens themselves describe their responsibilities to their communities, civil society, and the state. Just as citizens' behavior in public life can vary, so can their underlying understanding of citizenship, including concepts such as political participation, civic duty, social order, and social responsibilities. To the extent that beliefs about "good" citizenship are related to actual behavior, group differences in definitions may also explain variations in participation.

In fact, the evidence suggests that diversity in modes of participation may be more important to consider than ever before. Among industrialized nations there is evidence that people are changing the ways in which they participate, and that such changes vary according to group membership (Dalton 2008; Inglehart 1997). Older social cleavages may be shifting and/or taking on new meanings as citizens in industrialized democracies become more highly educated, technologically sophisticated, and policy- and issue-oriented. They are seeking out new ways of engaging with government, politics, and civil society that reflect such skills and goals (Dalton, Scarrow, and Cain 2003). To reflect these changes, research and theory must consider a wider range of forms of civic and political participation.

Group differences have the potential to both expand and limit a citizen's ability to, and interest in, engaging publicly (Dalton 2008; Norris and Curtis 2006; Pattie, Seyd, and Whiteley 2003). Specifically, American findings dispute the claim that younger citizens are disengaged by showing that, although traditional forms of political participation such as voting and party membership are more common among older age groups, participation in boycotts and attending demonstrations are more popular among younger age groups (Dalton 2008). Young people in Great Britain have also been found to be more likely to be part of informal networks compared to older age groups, but less likely to engage in formal associations, especially when compared to those in the middle age group (Pattie, Seyd, and Whiteley 2004).

Furthermore, cross-national European research shows that there are fewer class-based differences in participation in conventional, electoral politics than in protest-related politics (Caínzos and Voces 2010). Also in the United States, although Latinos have been found to be less likely to vote compared to white non-Latinos, their patterns of participation do not differ significantly in other forms of political participation including writing to elected officials, contributing money, and attending rallies (Hero and Campbell 1996). Finally, different social groups have been found to participate in different types of voluntary association. A straightforward example is the overrepresentation of more highly educated Americans in professional associations, as compared to labor unions to which people with less education are more likely to belong (Jacobs et al. 2005)

Research also suggests some important shifts and cleavages in understandings of citizenship itself. Theory has long considered citizenship as a multifaceted concept (Marshall 1950), and recently more limited empirical research also suggests that citizenship norms (particularly beliefs about "good" citizenship) are organized around three principal themes that are commonly reiterated in the literature (Bolzendahl and Coffé 2009; Lister 2003; Dalton 2008; Janoski 1998; Inglehart and Welzel 2005). First, citizens may consider *political activity* as the key denominator, such as a focus on participation in fair elections that select government officials, though nonelectoral forms of politics can also be included in this category. A second emphasis focuses on a commitment to *civic duty* and social order, highlighting the importance of abiding by the law, accepting state authority, and paying taxes. Finally, discourses surrounding the *social responsibilities* of citizenship such as maintaining a clean and safe environment, emphasizing tolerance, and accommodating the needs and interests of different groups, are increasingly influential.

Cross-national research demonstrates the importance of group stratification in influencing these divergent norms of citizenship. Among a large sample of Western democracies, Bolzendahl and Coffé (2009) found that respondents holding a university degree are more likely than those without such qualifications to focus on their political responsibilities (such as voting, participating in political organizations, and holding governments accountable for their actions), and their social responsibilities (such as shopping in a politically, ethically and/or environmentally responsible way, trying to understand people with opinions that differ from their own, and helping others inside and outside their society). Respondents without a university degree are more likely to prioritize civic duties as important aspects of being a good citizen. Similarly, in the United States, Dalton (2008) found that a focus on "duty-based" versus "engaged" meanings of citizenship varies according to group membership, highlighting the ways in which increased population diversity also shapes and expands diversity in citizenship norms. Younger generations are more likely to define "good" citizenship as being engaged in actions such as political consumerism, writing letters, signing petitions, and joining demonstrations, while older generations put more of a focus on duty-based aspects of citizenship such as voting and serving one's country. African Americans tend to place less importance than White Americans on duty-based norms, perhaps because—given a history of racist policies and direct government discrimination—African Americans have come to emphasize the types of empowerment that accompanied the civil rights movement and stimulated the rise of norms of engaged citizenship in the process (Dalton 2008).

Hence, diversity in civil society requires not only that we understand differences in participation among diverse social groups, but also that we reconsider and expand our approach to the meaning of citizenship and the definition of participation in and of themselves. In order to illustrate this point, we now turn to an analysis of civil society and citizenship through the lens of gender.

2. CIVIL SOCIETY, CITIZENSHIP, AND GENDER

Gender, while an important means of stratification in general, has also been found to be an important, specific marker in understanding unequal participation in public life. Obviously, gender cannot fully represent all the cleavages in citizenship that may be found in different societies, such as race and ethnicity, class, and sexual orientation. In some ways it provides a conservative test of the argument developed in this chapter, given that men and women are less segregated from each other in daily society, and less likely to face formal or informal discrimination in the public sphere, as compared to, for example, members of different ethnic groups, among whom variations in participation may be even greater. But because gender exists in every race, class, and sexual orientation it provides an important starting point for investigating other group differences, especially those that stand at the intersection of multiple status characteristics.

Citizenship has always been a gendered concept. Less than one hundred years ago most women did not have the right to vote in nations that were otherwise considered democratic, and even the granting of that right did not secure women's equal access to, or exercise of, social and political power—though,in the United States, at least, women played a crucial role in the development of many civil society organizations throughout the nineteenth and twentieth century (Skocpol 1992). Today, Western industrialized democracies have made great strides in promoting women and men's formal equality as citizens. Women's representation in parliaments has roughly doubled since 1970, and although early research suggested that women participated less in politics as a whole, more recent studies show similar—or even elevated—levels of female participation in terms of voting and other formal political activities (Paxton, Kunovich, and Hughes 2007; Burns 2007; Norris 2002; Parry, Moyser, and Day 1992).

However, gender differences continue to exist in other areas of participation in civic and political life. Among formal measures, Hooghe (2003) shows that Belgian women have fewer active memberships in formal associations than men, and that even those women who have an equal number of memberships devote less time to these associations than their male counterparts. In the United States, robust gender differences have also been found in political activities such as contacting public officials and discussing politics (Huckfeld and Prague 1995; Verba, Schlozman, and

Brady 1995; Verba, Burns, and Schlozman 1997), and studies across a range of countries indicate that, while gender gaps in some forms of participation are not large, they are certainly persistent (Burns 2007; Parry, Moyser, and Day 1992; Inglehart and Norris 2003). Research that attempts to explain these gaps highlights the fact that women are disadvantaged in the socio-economic resources that facilitate political activity. Namely, women and men have different demands on their time, both in terms of care work and employment. Women and men are also socialized to behave differently, and women still face a variety of forms of discrimination which may discourage or block their equal engagement as citizens (Burns 2007; Lister et al. 2007; Lovenduski 2005; Schlozman, Burns, and Verba 1994). For example, men are more likely to be employed full-time than women, and employment is positively related to political participation, information and efficacy among U.S. respondents (Schlozman, Burns, and Verba 1994; 1999). Thus, controlling for employment status may mediate a substantial portion of the gender gap in participation. Yet it has also been found that women's employment is not as strong a marker of different types of political participation as it is for men, a finding that has been related to cumulative, indirect disadvantages and a direct lack of leisure time that does not affect men's participation so strongly (Coffé and Bolzendahl 2010; Schlozman, Burns, and Verba 1999).

Research in the United States also suggests that women's lower levels of political information, interest, and efficacy are important explanations for gender gaps, independent of other characteristics (Verba, Burns, and Schlozman 1997). Women's lack of political resources may be rooted in social processes such as gender socialization (Burns 2007; Lovenduski 2005; Rapoport 1981; Verba, Burns, and Schlozman 1997). Women are socialized towards a gender role that is more passive, private, rule-abiding and compassionate, while men are encouraged towards public leadership roles, autonomy and self-reliance (Brownmiller 1984; Fox and Lawless 2004; West and Zimmerman 1987). This kind of socialization may contribute to women's lower levels of political engagement, with differences in political attitudes and participation beginning early in life and continuing over the life course (Atkeson and Rapoport 2003; Rapoport 1981; Fridkin and Kenney 2007; Hooghe and Stolle 2004; Alwin, Cohen, and Newcomb 1991).

One problem with these findings is the tendency to conceptualize civic and political engagement too narrowly. The possibility that the measurement of participation itself explains any gender gaps has been argued by scholars in the field of gender and politics who claim that research on political participation often focuses exclusively on formal organizations and voting (Goss 2003; Lister 2003; Orloff 1996). These scholars suggest that men and women have qualitatively different patterns of, and preferences for, participation (Bourque and Grossholtz 1998; Burns 2007; Sarvasy and Siim 1994; Young 2004). For example, women's lower average levels of socioeconomic resources may make it more difficult for them to engage in time-intensive, expensive, or highly skilled forms of activity such as campaigning for a candidate (Burns 2007; Lister 2003; Paxton, Kunovich, and Hughes 2007). They may find it easier to participate in ways that can be incorporated into daily life without putting more strain on already limited resources, such as participating in certain "private" forms of voluntary association or activity (Stolle, Hooghe, and Micheletti 2005).

The greater pressure on women to specialize in the private sphere of civil, as opposed to political, society, may contribute to gender differences in participation, with women participating less visibly and formally (Lister 2003; Lovenduski 1998; Risman 1998). Researchers have often demonstrated that women are more active than men in a number of nonpolitical voluntary organizations. Drawing on a Canadian survey, for example, Harell (2009) confirms that men are more likely to engage in political organizations, but women are more likely to be involved in social organizations with the exception of those focusing on sports and recreational activities. This pattern extends into volunteering, where men are more likely to coach or donate time spent on maintenance or repairs for voluntary organizations, and women are more likely to be involved in care work such as serving and delivering food. Similarly, Pattie, Seyd, and Whiteley (2004) show that British women are more likely to engage in personal support activities and less likely to belong to associations as compared to men. Norris and Inglehart (2005) find a global pattern in which men and women participate in different types of organizations, so that political parties, sports clubs, professional groups and labour unions are disproportionately male; and women are overrepresented in associations that work on education and the arts, religious and church organizations, the provision of social welfare services for the elderly or disabled, and women's groups. In some ways these different patterns may undermine women's contribution to, and impact on, formal political outcomes, but women's informal or nonpolitical activities may still have important political consequences (Burns 2007; Skocpol 1992; Koven and Michel 1993; Harrison and Munn 2007). For example, in explaining the unique trajectory of the U.S. welfare state, Skocpol (1992) found that women's groups exerted a powerful impact on policy choices despite their exclusion from politics, and in Sweden, Hobson and Lindholm (1997) have charted the dramatic role that women have had on national welfare policy.

Studying substantively disaggregated measures of political behavior, Coffé and Bolzendahl (2010) reveal that men and women do not differ in their electoral behavior across eighteen advanced Western democracies. However, once attitudinal characteristics are controlled for, women are more likely to vote than men. Thus, if women were to develop an interest in politics and feelings of political efficacy equal to that of men, women would vote *more* than men. Even though the gender gap often decreases significantly after controlling for attitudinal characteristics in this way, it appears that men are still more likely than women to join a political party, take part in a demonstration, attend political meetings, and engage in political contact making. Active engagement with a political party is not something most respondents report doing, but especially so among women. Such participation puts high demands on personal resources including time and money. In comparison to sending in a check, joining a demonstration or attending a political meeting takes time and planning, and women who are balancing greater family responsibilities along with work, friends, and nonpolitical engagement may be less inclined to take part in these more demanding forms of participation. By contrast, women, on average, are more likely to sign petitions, boycott or buy products for ethical or political reasons, and donate to, or raise money for, civic and political groups. This finding holds true even when socioeconomic and attitudinal differences are controlled for.

Tellingly, these private, individualistic actions are the least resource-dependent and the most easily incorporated into daily life.

Whereas gender gaps in civic and political participation have been studied extensively, much less empirical research has focused on gender differences in the conceptualization of citizenship itself. However, men and women across a number of Western democracies define "good" citizenship differently (Bolzendahl and Coffé 2009). In comparing support for a variety of beliefs about citizenship, women place more emphasis on social responsibilities than men. In other words, women are more likely than men to believe that good citizens should help others inside and outside their society, shop in a politically, ethically and/or environmentally responsible way, and strive to understand people whose opinions differ from their own. This gender gap holds regardless of socioeconomic and attitudinal characteristics. Moreover, women are more likely to focus on citizenship duties such as the importance of paying taxes and obeying the law. However, when it comes to defining a good political citizen, men and women do not differ. Women are just as likely as men to view politically oriented activities such as voting, being active in political associations, and keeping a watchful eye on the actions of government, as important aspects of good citizenship. Such findings suggest that, while women take a broader view of citizenship than men, these multiple emphases may make it more difficult for women to act on all the norms they subscribe to, thus forcing women to choose some areas in which to participate less frequently such as political party membership.

Given that men and women tend to define good citizenship in different ways, issues of gender-role socialization or specific life-course effects may provide one key to understanding the differences that exist between men's and women's support for civic rights and duties. Scholarship on childhood and adult socialization demonstrates that gender is ingrained early and often, and with this comes a set of overarching values and ideologies that may alter men and women's approach to civic and political issues (Martin 1998; West and Fenstermaker 1995). Thus, if women place more importance on social citizenship, this may be based on gender role expectations that women should be more submissive, private, rule-abiding, and compassionate, while men are oriented towards political citizenship since their gender role expectations emphasize public leadership roles, autonomy and self-reliance (Brownmiller 1984; Fox and Lawless 2004; West and Zimmerman 1987; Beutel and Marini 1995). Rather than adopting values of competition and aggression, women are pressured to develop an "ethic of caring," and this ethic predisposes women to think more in terms of the social whole and less in terms of individual gain than men (Cross and Madson 1997).

3. CONCLUSION

Citizenship is a very broad concept, but key aspects of citizenship include participation in civil and political society and the willingness to accept their associated obligations. These two related aspects of citizenship, involving beliefs about good citizenship on the one hand and actual behavior on the other hand, are necessary for a healthy civil society and political culture. The common thread that runs through this discussion is the need to consider a plurality of citizenship meanings and practices if we are to arrive at a fuller understanding of the significance of difference and inequality in civic and political life. Our main argument is that by looking beyond conventional beliefs and practices, we can see that some social groups not only participate more, or less, in civil society and politics, but that they also participate *differently*. Similarly, different social groups are not necessarily more, or less, concerned with their obligations as citizens, but rather have different ways of defining and realizing good citizenship in practice. In other words, rather than focusing only on differences in citizen participation between social groups, it is more useful to investigate the variety of gaps that exist across diverse modes of participation and ideas about citizenship themselves.

Focusing on gender differences, it is clear that women are significantly more likely to participate in private modes of participation, while men are more likely to participate in public modes. Women place more emphasis on social and civic responsibilities compared to men, even though both groups have similar views on the importance of their political responsibilities (Bolzendahl and Coffé 2009). These gender gaps may have important implications for political outcomes if policy responsiveness varies in response to different modes of participation. For example, politicians may pay more attention to the public actions in which men are more likely to engage, while ignoring or downgrading the interests and preferences of female voters. Such outcomes may be exacerbated by the tendency of men to be over-represented in political office, since research has shown that parliaments to which more women are elected tend to devote more resources to social policy (Bolzendahl and Brooks 2007; Bolzendahl 2010). Group differences also matter if they result in group-related social and political bonding. As Norris argues (2007, 729), "if horizontal segmentation into same sex-related bonding groups has positive functions for members," it may also generate negative externalities for society as a whole by reinforcing gender divisions. Similar arguments can be made for gaps across other social groups defined by race and ethnicity, class, and sexual orientation. This is obviously a matter of great importance for the functioning of democracy, the strength of civic life, and the health of society as a whole.

REFERENCES

Alwin, D. F., R. L. Cohen, and T. M. Newcomb. 1991. *Political Attitudes over the Life Span: The Bennington Women after 50 Years.* Madison: University of Wisconsin Press.

Atkeson, L. R., and R. B. Rapoport. 2003. "The More Things Change The More They Stay The Same: Examining Differences in Political Communication, 1952–2000." *Public Opinion Quarterly* 67(4): 495–521.

Beutel, A. M. and M. M. Marini. 1995. Gender and Values. *American Sociological Review* 60: 436–48.

Bolzendahl, C. 2010. "Directions of Decommodification: Gender and Generosity in 12 OECD Nations, 1980–2000." *European Sociological Review,* 26(2): 125–41.

Bolzendahl, C., and C. Brooks. 2007. "Women's Political Representation and Welfare State Spending in Twelve Capitalist Democracies." *Social Forces* 85:1509–34.

Bolzendahl, C., and Coffé, H. 2009. "Citizenship Beyond Politics: The Importance of Political, Civil and Social Rights and Responsibilities among Women and Men." *British Journal of Sociology* 60: 763–91.

Bourque, S., and J. Grossholtz. 1998. "Politics an Unnatural Practice: Political Science Looks at Female Participation," in A. Phillips (ed.) *Feminism and politics.* Oxford: Oxford University Press, 23–43.

Brownmiller, S. 1984. *Femininity.* New York: Simon & Schuster.

Burns, N. 2007. "Gender in the Aggregate, Gender in the Individual, Gender and Political Action." *Politics & Gender* 3(1): 104–24.

Burns, N., K. L. Schlozman, and S. Verba. 2001. *The Private Roots of Public Action: Gender, Equality, and Political Participation.* Cambridge, Mass.: Harvard University Press.

Caínzos, M., and C. Voces. 2010. "Class Inequalities in Political Participation and the 'Death of Class' Debate." *International Sociology,* 25(3): 383–418.

Coffé, H., and C. Bolzendahl. 2010. "Same Game, Different Rules? Gender Differences in Political Participation." *Sex Roles,* 62(5–6): 318–33.

Cross, S. E., and L. Madson. 1997. "Models of the Self: Self-Construals and Gender." *Psychological Bulletin,* 122(1): 5–37.

Dalton, R. J. 2008. *The Good Citizen. How a Younger Generation is Reshaping American Politics.* Washington, D.C.: CQ Press.

Dalton, R. J., S. E. Scarrow, and B. E. Cain. 2003. *Democracy Transformed?:Expanding Political Opportunities in Advanced Industrial Democracies.* Irvine, Calif.: Center for the Study of Democracy, University of California, Irvine.

Edwards, M. 2009. *Civil Society.* 2nd ed. Cambridge: Polity Press.

Fox, R. L., and J. L. Lawless. 2004. "Entering the Arena? Gender and the Decision to Run for Office." *American Journal of Political Science* 48(2): 264–80.

Fridkin, K., and P. Kenney. 2007. "Examining the Gender Gap in Children's Attitudes toward Politics." *Sex Roles* 56(3): 133–40.

Goss, K. 2003. "Rethinking the Political Participation Paradigm: The Case of Women and Gun Control." *Women and Politics* 25(4): 83–118.

Hagemann, K., S. Michel, and G. Budde. 2008. *Civil Society and Gender Justice.* London: Berghahn Books.

Harell, A. 2009. "Equal Participation but Separate paths?: Women's Social Capital and Turnout." *Journal of Women, Politics and Policy* 30: 1–22.

Harrison, L., and J. Munn. 2007. "Commentary—Gender, Citizenship and Participation: Opportunities and Obstacles in the Twenty-first Century Politics." *Parliamentary Affairs* 60(3): 424–25.

Hero, R., and A. Campbell. 1996. "Understanding Latino Political Participation: Exploring the Evidence from the Latino National Political Survey." *Hispanic Journal of Behavioral Sciences* 18(2): 129–41.

Highton, B., and A. L. Burris. 2002. "New Perspectives on Latino Voter Turnout in the United States." *American Politics Research* 30(3): 285–306.

Hobson, B., and M. Lindholm. 1997. "Collective Identities, Women's Power Resources, and the Making of Welfare States." *Theory and Society* 26:475–508.

Hooghe, M. 2003. "Why Should We Be Bowling Alone? Results From a Belgian Survey on Civic Participation." *Voluntas: International Journal of Voluntary and Nonprofit Organizations* 14(1): 41–59.

Hooghe, M., and D. Stolle 2004. "Good Girls Go to the Polling Booth, Bad Boys Go Everywhere: Gender Differences in Anticipated Political Participation among American Fourteen-Year-Olds." *Women & Politics* 26(3): 1–23.

Howell, J. 2006. *Gender and Civil Society*. London: Routledge.

Huckfeld, R., and J. Prague. 1995. *Citizens, Politics, and Social Communication.* New York: Cambridge University Press.

Inglehart, R. 1997. *Modernization and Postmodernization: Cultural, Economic, and Political Change in 43 Societies*. Princeton, N.J.: Princeton University Press.

Inglehart, R., and P. Norris. 2003. *Rising tide: Gender Equality and Culture Change Around the World.* Cambridge: Cambridge University Press.

Inglehart, R., and C. Welzel. 2005. *Modernization, Cultural Change and Democracy: The Human Development Sequence.* Cambridge: Cambridge University Press.

Jacobs, L. et al. 2005. "American Democracy and Inequality." *Dissent* 52(2): 80–84.

Janoski, T. 1998. *Citizenship and Civil Society: A Framework of Rights and Obligations in Liberal, Traditional, and Social Democratic Regimes.* Cambridge: Cambridge University Press.

Koven, S., and S. Michel. 1993. *Mothers of a New World: Maternalist Politics and the Origins of Welfare States.* New York: Routledge.

Lijphart, A. 1997. "Unequal Participation: Democracy's Unresolved Dilemma." *The American Political Science Review* 91: 1–14.

Lister, R. 2003. *Citizenship: Feminist Perspectives.* New York: Palgrave Macmillan.

Lister, R., F. Williams, A. Anttonen, J. Bussemaker, U. Gerhard, J. Heinen, and A. Gavanas. 2007. *Gendering Citizenship in Western Europe: New Challenges for Citizenship Research.* Bristol: Policy Press.

Lovenduski, J. 1998. "Gendering Research in Political Science." *Annual Review of Political Science* 1(1): 333–56.

———. 2005. *Feminizing Politics*. Cambridge: Polity Press.

Marshall, T. H. 1950. *Citizenship and Social Class,* Cambridge: Cambridge University Press.

Martin, K. A. 1998. "Becoming a Gendered Body: Practices of Preschools." *American Sociological Review* 63(4): 494–511.

Norris, P. 2002. *Democratic Phoenix: Reinventing Political Activism.* Cambridge: Cambridge University Press.

———. 2007. "New Feminist Challenges to the Study of Political Engagement," in R. J. Dalton and H-D. Klingemann (eds.) *The Oxford Handbook of Political Behavior.* Oxford: Oxford University Press, 724–43.

Norris, P., and J. Curtis. 2006. "If You Build a Political Web Site, Will They Come? The Internet and Political Activism in Britain." *International Journal of Electronic Government Reserach* 2(2), 1–21.

Norris, P., and R. Inglehart. 2005. "Gendering Social Capital: Bowling in Women's Leagues?" in B. O'Neill and E. Gidengil (eds.) *Unequal Returns: Gender, Social Capital and Political Engagement.* New York: Routledge, 73–98.

Orloff, A. S. 1996. "Gender in the Welfare State." *Annual Review of Sociology* 22: 51–78.

Parry, G., G. Moyser, and N. Day. 1992. *Political Participation and Democracy in Britain.* Cambridge: Cambridge University Press.

Pattie, C., P. Seyd, and P. Whiteley. 2003. "Citizenship and Civic Engagement: Attitudes and Behaviour in Britain." *Political Studies* 51: 443–68.

————. 2004. *Citizenship in Britain. Values, Participation and Democracy.* Cambridge: Cambridge University Press.

Paxton, P., S. Kunovich, and M. M. Hughes. 2007. "Gender in Politics." *Annual Review of Sociology* 33: 263–84.

Rapoport, R. B. 1981. "The Sex Gap in Political Persuading: Where the 'Structuring Principle' Works." *American Journal of Political Science* 25: 32–48.

Risman, B. 1998. *Gender Vertigo.* New Haven, Conn.: Yale University Press.

Sarvasy, W., and B. Siim. 1994. "Gender, Transitions to Democracy, and Citizenship." *Social Politics,* 1(3): 249–55.

Schlozman, K. L., N. Burns, and S. Verba. 1994. "Gender and the Pathways to Participation: The Role of Resources." *The Journal of Politics* 56(4): 963–90.

————. 1999. "'What Happened at Work Today?': A Multistage Model of Gender, Employment, and Political Participation." *The Journal of Politics,* 61(1): 29–53.

Sherrill, K. 1996. "The Political Power of Lesbians, Gays, and Bisexuals." *PS: Political Science and Politics,* 29: 469–73.

Skocpol, T. 1992. *Protecting Soldiers and Mothers: The Political Origins of Social Policy in the United States.* Cambridge, Mass.: Harvard University Press.

Stolle, D., M. Hooghe, and M. Micheletti. 2005. "Politics in the Supermarket: Political Consumerism as a Form of Political Participation." *International Political Science Review* 26(3): 245–69.

Uhlaner, C. J., B. E. Cain, and D. R. Kiewit. 1989. "Political Participation of Ethnic Minorities in the 1980s." *Political Behavior* 11: 195–231.

Verba, S. 1996. "The Citizen as Respondent: Sample Surveys and American Democracy Presidential Address, American Political Science Association, 1995." *The American Political Science Review* 90(1): 1–7.

Verba, S., N. Burns, and K. L. Schlozman. 1997. "Knowing and Caring about Politics: Gender and Political Engagement." *The Journal of Politics* 59(4): 1051–72.

Verba, S., N. Nie, and J.-O. Kim. 1978. *Participation and Political Equality: A Seven-Nation Comparison.* Cambridge: Cambridge University Press.

Verba, S., K. L. Schlozman, and H. E. Brady. 1995. *Voice and Equality: Civic Voluntarism in American Politics.* Cambridge, Mass.: Harvard University Press.

West, C., and S. Fenstermaker. 1995. "Doing Difference." *Gender & Society* 9(1): 8–37.

West, C., and D. H. Zimmerman. 1987. "Doing Gender" *Gender & Society* 1(2): 125–51.

Young, I. M. 2004. "Situated Knowledge and Democratic Discussions," in J. Anderson and B. Siim (eds.) *The Politics of Inclusion and Empowerment.* New York: Palgrave Macmillan, 19–35.

CHAPTER 21

....

CIVIL SOCIETY AND RELIGION

....

DONALD E. MILLER

RELIGION plays an important though complicated role in a healthy civil society eco-system, providing a location for moral debate and the articulation of competing social visions about what is good, right and compassionate (Edwards 2009; Casanova 1994; Neuhaus 1984; Dionne and Diiulio 2000; Bellah 1970, 168–192; Wuthnow 2004). Religious groups mobilize members to protest policies they consider unjust, draw-ing on the social capital of their members as well as their religious traditions for justification and ideological support (Smith 1996; Hondagneu-Sotelo 2007). Religious institutions also perform an important role in socializing children, pro-viding them with moral values as well as inspiring images of what it means to live a productive life (Fowler 1981). And religious organizations develop programs that serve people in need—especially people who lack healthcare, educational resources, and employment opportunities (Marsh 2005; Harper 1999; Elliott 2004). However, it is also true that religion has the potential to inflict great harm, especially if it becomes an instrument of the state or an uncritical advocate for sectarian or corpo-rate interests. For example, clergy have openly supported genocide and totalitarian leaders, and they have justified the privileges of the social elite, who sometimes are their patrons (Gourevitch 1999). In order for religion to contribute positively to civil society, its members must answer to a "higher power," appealing to values that serve all of humanity and not simply the self-interest of the few.

As a human invention, religion takes many forms depending on culture and historical circumstances (Berger 1967). Hence, given the diversity of religious expres-sion it is difficult to generalize about the relationship between religion and civil society. Nevertheless, there are distinct patterns that can be identified, some of which contribute to a vibrant civil society and others that are quite destructive.

Indeed, the history of sociological theory is replete with different normative evaluations of religion and its role in society. Karl Marx (Raines 2002) viewed religion as an opiate that dulls the pain of poverty and inequality and therefore is socially regressive because it inhibits revolutionary change. Emile Durkheim (1995) argued that religion potentially plays an integrative role in society, premised on the view that the objects of religious worship are the collective values of society. Max Weber (2002) had a much more complex view of religion, seeing its potential as a social change agent but also understanding its conservative and ideological role. Various permutations of these three perspectives continue to be relevant today in attempts to understand the complex interrelationship between civil society and religion.

1. DEFINITIONS OF RELIGION AND ITS SOCIAL ROLE

When religion is viewed as an element of civil society, the reference is typically to its institutional form, not to private experiences of prayer, meditation, and personal spirituality. Religion is often distinguished from spirituality in the following way: Religion is an institution that evolves over time and involves specific beliefs, rituals, and organizational forms, whereas spirituality refers to the ways in which individuals experience a transcendent dimension in their lives—what they refer to as God, a divine presence, or an alignment with a sacred path and way of life (Johnstone 1975; James 1961). In actual practice, religion and spirituality may interrelate, with institutional religion serving as the vehicle for mediating experiences of a transcendent or sacred dimension. On the other hand, there are increasing numbers of individuals in Western society who claim to be spiritual but not religious (Roof 1994; Flory and Miller 2008). For them, religion is a personal and private experience that does not require an institutional vessel. These individuals typically view institutional religion as a corrupt and hierarchical organizational form that impedes experiences of the sacred, reflecting practices and traditions that are irrelevant to contemporary society. In contrast, defenders of institutional religion often respond that privatized religion is narcissistic, contributing nothing to the common good. It is a palliative that serves the egoist need for individual meaning, but fails to address the larger causes of human suffering.

While there is some truth to both perspectives, the dichotomy between religion and spirituality is false, at least in healthy forms of institutional religion that contribute to civil society in creative ways (Stanczak 2006). Vibrant institutional religion engages "the spirit" at both the organizational and individual levels. The founders of the great religious traditions drew their inspiration from transcendent sources, or at least this is how the followers of these charismatic prophets experienced them. Likewise, when institutional religion becomes encrusted with layers of tradition and hierarchy, reformers often discard the organizational secretions that separate individuals from primal experiences of the sacred and attempt to return to the original vision (Hughes 1988; Miller 1997). And when one examines the lives of religiously motivated social transformers, as well as those individuals who live out their faith in incredibly hard circumstances—serving the homeless, people with AIDS, and those who are desperately poor—the thing that inevitably inspires them to act courageously or sustains them in the daily grind is a deep spirituality that connects them to something greater than themselves (Tutu 2004; King and Carson 1998; Ganz 2009).

When religion fulfils its social role in these senses, it intersects with civil society in five different ways. First, it provides a place where moral conversation is encouraged, where people can debate ideas and policies and hone their arguments about what is right and wrong. Second, vibrant religious institutions inspire their members to act out their convictions—through voting, public demonstrations, and other political acts that embody their moral values. Third, religious institutions have a long history of establishing schools, social service agencies, and responding to crisis situations related to natural disasters such as earthquakes, floods, and drought. Fourth, religious institutions provide opportunities for human community through music, the arts, and various means of caring for one another. And fifth, religious institutions have time-honored means of dealing with rites of passage: birth, puberty, marriage, childrearing, and death, the final passage.

What makes religion different from secular institutions that also play some of these roles is that religion claims a moral authority beyond the people who constitute its membership. Clubs, labor unions, and other civic organizations have rituals, creeds, and organizational structures. In this sense they resemble religious groups. But they seldom make claims about ultimate reality, and when they do they are accused of stepping into the realm of religion, whereas the task of religion, regardless of the particular tradition, is to make ultimate claims about truth, justice, and love. Nevertheless, religion is always a treasure in earthen vessels (Gustafson 2008). There are pedophile priests, clergy who are adulterers, and people who justify acts of bigotry and terrorism in the name of their religion. But hopefully these acts, these "bad apples" within the community, are distinguished from the ideals of the religion, thus enabling the conversation to continue about what constitutes the good society, the good person, or a world that is worth passing on to our children. When these conversations do not occur internally within religion, then one may rightly stand in judgment because at that point religion has engaged in an act of idolatry by substituting human self-interest for transcendent values.

2. Typologies of Religion and Civil Society Interaction

In his two-volume work on the history of Christianity, Ernst Troeltsch (1960) drew on Max Weber (1946) to distinguish sectarian expressions of religion from what he called "church" forms of Christianity. In addition, he identified mysticism as a third sociological form. Sectarian religion makes little contribution to civil society except as a "light on the hill" that exemplifies utopian manifestations of human community. In contrast, Troeltsch's church type represents a form of political realism that acknowledges human depravity and is premised on the idea that power is necessary to accomplish certain goals, while mysticism is an individualistic expression of religion that focuses on the divine-human encounter, including ecstatic states of consciousness.

Sectarian groups emphasis personal purity and therefore tend to withdraw from participating in political institutions they consider corrupt. Sectarians are typically pacifists, refusing to bear arms, although they sometimes serve as medics in the military. Sectarian groups are uncomfortable with hierarchical forms of authority, and emphasize the individual's relationship with God. In contrast, churchly expressions of religion understand the importance of compromise, the use of power to achieve worthy goals, and the value of hierarchical patterns of authority. Therefore, in contrast to the sectarian Anabaptist tradition which is pacifist, the Roman Catholic Church evolved theories that justified war under certain conditions and established distinctions between the duties of the priestly class and the laity (Bainton 1960). The mystic as an ideal type emerged within Roman Catholicism as a "safety value" for those who desired to live a more pure, uncompromised life. Mystics often separate themselves from society in monasteries and convents, seeking divine illumination in the act of giving up worldly possessions and living an unencumbered life. These three types—the sect, the church, and the mystic— operate synergistically within society. The sect holds up utopian visions of human possibility, the church engages with a sinful and corrupt world, and the mystic keeps alive in pure form the transcendent element that ultimately animates religion.

A variety of different typologies have been created in response to Troeltsch and Weber's church-sect distinction (Stark and Finke 2000, 259–276). For example, Brian Wilson (1982, 89–120) developed a number of sectarian subtypes, and H. Richard Niebuhr (1951) created a widely utilized typology in his book *Christ and Culture*, which was oriented around theological traditions within Christianity. In addition, Niebuhr (1929) recognized the development of the "denomination" as a sociological form that often evolves from sectarians who grow wealthy—in part because of their discipline and austere lifestyle—and decide that participating in the fruits of material culture is attractive. Today, denominations are the dominant sociological form among Protestants, and they no longer eschew participating in the institutions of society. In fact, evangelical denominations with sectarian roots began to form strong lobbying groups in the 1970s and 1980s—including the Christian Coalition, for example, in the United States—no longer ceding the public square to liberal advocates of the social gospel (Vaughan 2009).

In addition, sociological studies of congregational life have produced other useful typologies, such as the distinctions drawn by Roozen, McKinney, and Carroll (1984) after studying several hundred congregations in Hartford, Connecticut. They identified four orientations that cut across congregations from a variety of faith traditions and grouped their missions in public life in terms of activists, citizens, sanctuaries, and evangelists. The *activist* views the "here and now" as the main arena of God's redemptive work, and sees humankind as God's agent of social transformation. Clergy are expected to be public figures, mobilizing their congregations to political action even if this runs counter to prevailing power structures. In contrast, congregations that emphasize the *civic* role of their members tend to work within existing political and economic structures, educating their members about policy issues and stressing the right of individual members to engage and vote with their conscience. Congregations that operate as *sanctuaries* focus on the world still to come, with worship being a time to withdraw from the world as it is—not to engage in it. Members of *evangelistic* congregations believe that the path to individual and social transformation lies through personal salvation, and so they place a great deal of emphasis on sharing their belief system with those who are outside the fold.

While this typology is useful in identifying the various public roles of religion, one element is common to all religions: the communal. Congregations (especially large ones) offer divorce recovery meetings, programs for addiction counselling, seminars on how to cope with teenage children, retirement transition classes, musical productions, and religious education from the cradle to the grave (Thumma 2007). Individuals are attracted to these congregations, not primarily because of the political stance of the clergy or even the religious belief system of the tradition, but because they are vibrant communities where people can socialize and find support, including life partners. In urban mass society, human community is often a scarce commodity. Religious institutions therefore fill a vacuum in people's lives. Congregation members may be immigrants who left their extended family behind, or they may live in neighborhoods where people scarcely greet each other. Therefore, the neighborhood church, temple, mosque, or synagogue is a gathering place of human caring. And as a voluntary association, one can pick and choose among a variety of options. Gay or lesbian people can select a progressive Episcopal church rather than a conservative Southern Baptist congregation. African Americans can attend a black church, because this is one place where they can mix with people of their own race. Armenians, Vietnamese, or Filipinos can choose a congregation where they can sing and converse in the language of their home country as well as celebrate their homeland's customs and rituals (Kniss and Numrich 2007).

Many of these activities may appear to be therapeutic (Rieff 1966), but that does not make them narcissistic, especially if there is a strong element of communal support within the group. Congregations are places that the young, old, disabled, healthy, rich, and poor gather together, and in the liminal space of religious worship, all people are equal. It is this element of religion that many ardent atheists seem to miss in their critique of religion. They identify religion exclusively with a set of beliefs, many of which may seem outdated because they are anchored in tradition. They fail to see that religious institutions are gathering places where people can experience their common humanity, and be vulnerable about their fears, anxieties, defects, and strengths (Wuthnow 1996). Furthermore, the critics of religion also frequently fail to appreciate the need of people to create identities that are grounded in something deeper than their last consumer purchase. However, the worst shortcoming of religious naysayers is that they fail to account for the diversity of religion, including non-Western forms of spirituality. The goal of achieving an egoless state of being so that one can serve humanity more effectively is a much harder notion to critique than supernatural theories of divine intervention that inevitably raise thorny questions related to the perennial issue of theodicy.

3. CONSERVATIVES AND LIBERALS

While the typologies of social scientists are extremely useful, everyday distinctions between liberals and conservatives, progressives and orthodox, and modernists and fundamentalists also help to clarify the various ways in which religious groups relate to civil society (Hunter 1991). Liberals, progressives, and modernists tend to look to the future and acknowledge that religion needs to adapt to changes in culture and society. In contrast, conservatives, orthodox, and fundamentalists usually look back to a golden era when things were perceived to be better, less corrupt, and altogether purer embodiments of the religious ideals of the tradition. For conservatives, the goal is to return to this ideal state, rejecting many of the cultural elements that are associated with modernity. In contrast, progressives of different stripes do not identify their religion with any particular set of cultural trappings, but instead seek to create a society that both embodies the ideals and principles of the religion and takes account of new scientific information, new technologies, and changes in systems of governance. These two orientations result in quite different agendas in civil society. Conservatives typically focus on safeguarding institutions such as the family; they often reject intrusion by government into the socialization of children; and they are often nationalistic, perceiving threats to the homeland by foreign powers and/or immigrants. In contrast, progressives typically focus on poverty, injustice, and racism—seeing these as systemic problems that require government intervention.

While one might expect there to be substantial differences *between* various religious traditions, the differences *within* branches of a denomination or faith group are often even greater (Ammerman 1990). For example, progressive Muslims, Jews, Christians, and Buddhists may have much more in common with each other than they do with conservatives within their own denomination or faith group. Likewise, conservatives (whether Christian, Jewish, or Muslim) are typically "fundamentalists" when it comes to their sacred texts, believing that God inspires every word, while progressives from different religious traditions typically view their scriptures as reflecting cultural biases that are not identical with the central truths embodied in the stories and sayings of the prophet(s) of the tradition. For progressives, the challenge is to apply these principles to contemporary problems and issues.

Although opposing religious camps often demonize each other, in a vibrant civil society this contestation of viewpoints is valuable, providing locations where public policy can be debated and articulated with reference to clearly defined moral and theological positions. For this reason, religious freedom is an important element of civil society. To stifle religious pluralism is to diminish the opportunity for moral debate, which is the hallmark of democracy. Such debate ideally plays out in ways small and large—in committee meetings as well as in public forums. The obvious danger is that the contestation of religious and political views can become "uncivil," when violence in words or deeds is used to justify the ends of a religious ideal (Bellah and Greenspahn 1987). Killing doctors who perform abortions or innocent civilians in terrorist bombings are clearly outside the boundaries of any appropriate civic expression of religious-based commitments.

4. Contrasting Examples of Social Engagement

In the United States, there is a long tradition of community organizing that dates back to the beginning of the twentieth century, although it was ignited in the 1940s by Saul Alinsky (1989) who codified his philosophy and strategy of organizing in 1946 with the publication of *Reveille for Radicals*. Initially the prime audience for organizing were members of labor unions, but beginning in the 1970s and 1980s, as labor unions lost some of their power, many of the major organizing movements such as the Industrial Areas Foundation and People Improving Communities through Organizing (PICO) turned their attention to churches, where they could find large numbers of poor people as well as progressive people of faith who wanted to put their faith into action (Warren 2001; Wood 2002). In contrast to the "agency" model of social service, faith-based organizers followed Alinsky's "Iron Rule": "Never do for others what they can do for themselves" (Alinsky 1989). The goal of organizing, therefore, is to assist disenfranchised people to attain civic and political power by identifying the sources of pain in their lives and then capitalize on their anger by targeting specific policies or problems that require change.

These issues obviously differ from one community to another, but typical goals in faith-based organizing have often included securing a "living wage" from employers, advocating for higher quality schools in low-income neighborhoods, promoting the construction of affordable housing, and working to ensure safe neighborhoods. The key methods here are to engage people in one-on-one conversations, identify their most urgent needs, form a strong network of relationships at the neighborhood and congregational levels, target a winnable piece of legislation, and assemble large numbers of people at protests and rallies in order to demonstrate their collective civic and political power.

In broad-based community organizing, networks of religious groups from different faith traditions put aside their dogmas in order to focus on what is common to their traditions, most centrally a respect for people, regardless of their color, immigration status, or wealth. Professional organizers are trained and paid, and focus on developing leaders within the community who can carry out the fight for social justice. Concepts such as self-interest, conflict, and struggle are part of the vocabulary of successful community organizers who work with the faith community. They seek durable power and a place at the decision-making table, recognizing that power is not easily shared by corporate and political elites—it must be demanded.

Pentecostalism, on the other hand, represents a very different model of civic engagement. It is the fastest growing religious movement in the world, with approximately 500 million people identifying with a charismatic church or Pentecostal denomination (Cox 1995; Chestnut 2003). The "power" that Pentecostals embrace is the power of the Holy Spirit to transform individual lives, not political structures (Martin 2002). Drawing on the example of Jesus' disciples after his death and resurrection, Pentecostals believe in the gifts of the spirit: divine healing, prophecy, and speaking in tongues. Launched in 1906 in Los Angeles in an interracial church, Pentecostalism spread rapidly around the world, and in the 1960s and 1970s the charismatic renewal movement also transformed a number of mainline Protestant and Roman Catholic churches, inspiring contemporary forms of worship and an embrace of the presence of the Holy Spirit (Robeck 2006).

Based on five years of research among Pentecostal and charismatic congregations in twenty countries across Asia, Africa, Latin America, and the former Soviet Union, Miller and Yamamori (2007) show that, although many of these churches are sectarian in terms of their worldly engagement, there is also an emerging movement of socially engaged Pentecostal congregations, and the range of programs they operate is substantial, including: mercy ministries (providing food, clothing, shelter); emergency services (responding to floods, famine, earthquakes); education programs (providing day care, schools, tuition assistance); counseling services (helping with addiction, divorce, depression); medical assistance (establishing health clinics, dental clinics, psychological services); economic development projects (microloan programs, job training, affordable housing); programs in the arts (training in music, dance, drama); and policy change activities (opposing corruption, monitoring elections, and supporting human rights).

Among Pentecostals and charismatic Christians, there are also a number of "prosperity gospel" churches that emphasize health and wealth—often with a magical twist that is mixed with tithes and offerings to the church itself (Gifford 2004). These congregations fit Karl Marx's classification of religion as an "opiate" for the poor (Anderson 1979), although faith healing and ecstatic religious experience sometimes exist side by side with assistance programs for those in need (Miller and Yamamori 2007). In contrast to faith-based organizing or liberation theology (which sometimes go hand in hand), socially engaged Pentecostal and charismatic congregations are more likely to address people's needs one by one rather than confronting the systemic causes of poverty or human suffering. Hence, many socially engaged congregations run medical clinics, schools, feeding programs, and counseling services. However, only a few address political corruption in society or make demands for equitable social provision at the national level. Their strategy is to create an alternative social safety network rather than reform government policy. In this regard, Pentecostalism in the twenty-first century echoes its sectarian origins at the beginning of the twentieth century.

While critics from the Left may critique Pentecostalism for its individualistic approach to addressing social change, it is important to acknowledge the warm and caring relationships that exist within these congregations. Many of the fastest growing Pentecostal churches cope with their size by having cell groups that meet in member's homes, assuming responsibility for the care and nurture of their participants. Every congregation is filled with stories of conversion where husbands become less abusive and better fathers because they gave up drinking, gambling, and womanizing (Bomann 1999). In addition to informal means of caring for congregation members, many of these churches have compassion ministries that extend to the wider community. Central to the cell groups and combined gatherings is ecstatic worship, an experience that both comforts and inspires. Hence, it would be inappropriate to dismiss Pentecostal religion as irrelevant to civil society simply because it does not address social issues at a systemic level. For tens of millions of people, their church is their most important experience of community, and it is within the fold of religion that they raise their children, engage in volunteer work, and seek to make the world a better place.

Religion and civil society interact at the para-church, nongovernmental organization (NGO), and religious nonprofit levels as well as at the congregational level (Flanigan 2009). For example, many congregations develop separate nonprofit organizations in order to enable them to bridge beyond their own faith community as they develop social outreach programs. Likewise, there are dozens of large religious NGOs, such as World Vision, Catholic Relief Services, Lutheran Social Services, Adventist Relief and Development Agency, Food for the Hungry, and Compassion International that operate internationally (Lindenberg and Bryant 2001). Some of these organizations are extremely large and comprehensive, such as World Vision, which operates in a hundred different countries and has a budget exceeding $2 billion per annum. Other faith-based NGOs are small-scale operations that run after school programs, homeless shelters, and community development programs.

Several years ago I interviewed the leadership of most of the religious NGOs in the Republic of Armenia. Their programs resembled very closely the list described in the previous section on Pentecostalism, ranging from earthquake relief efforts to economic development, education, human rights advocacy, character development, and programs related to the arts. What surprised me was the range of religiosity in these "religious" NGOs. For example, there were NGOs that had a strong conversionist orientation with religion saturating all aspects of their work, and there were religious NGOs that bore the name of a denomination but otherwise were thoroughly secular. Some religious NGOs were highly ecumenical and others were focused exclusively on their own members. In addition, there was a substantial range of leadership styles; some depended almost exclusively on the charisma of the founder and others were bureaucratic, with senior personnel shifts barely causing a ripple in service delivery. While some of these NGOs were supported by the charitable contributions of their own constituencies, many of the groups were also partnering with external donor organizations such as the United States Agency for International Development (USAID), the Department for International Development (DFID) from the United Kingdom, and others, serving as vehicles for the delivery of millions of dollars of relief, development, and medical aid.

Religious NGOs play an important role in promoting different forms of social ties, though the balance between what Robert Putnam (2000) calls "bonding" and "bridging" social capital changes from one context to another, producing broader civic effects that are subject to conflicting interpretations (Flanigan 2009; Lichterman 2005). When religious NGOs make links outside their denominations and foster an open and self-critical culture, they can nurture bridging social capital that mitigates against intercommunal violence and strengthens cross-community engagement—by partnering, for example, on development projects at the village level with people who otherwise would not associate with one another, such as Catholics working with Protestants or Muslims working with Hindus (Varshney 2003). Key points of demarcation in these collaborations lie between projects that focus on relief versus those that emphasis development, and whether faith-based interventions create dependency or promote self-sufficiency. These distinctions are important in analyzing the relationship between religion and civil society in the following ways. If religious NGOs are building bonds of trust and cooperation between different religious and social groups, and if they are also contributing to self-sufficiency, then they serve an important social function. On the other hand, if they are creating long-term dependency and are perpetuating social inequities, then they may have a detrimental effect.

5. Conclusion

To summarize, religion is potentially part of a healthy associational ecosystem in societies where religious freedom is guaranteed and diverse religious views are allowed expression. In its healthy forms it stands against bigotry, intolerance, and the demonization of other groups and people. In its unhealthy forms, religion utilizes bonding social capital to create strong forms of internal community at the expense of pursuing the common good. At the root of all forms of healthy religion are love, compassion, and a concern for social justice (Edwards and Post 2008). On the other hand, when religion is a surrogate of the state or the market, it loses its ability to provide prophetic judgment, and some of religion's most unique qualities—such as mercy, forgiveness, and the promise of hope—are ignored. Therefore, healthy religion must always answer to a higher power if it is to perform its unique social role.

Religious institutions bring many assets to civil society. They have physical space, leadership, volunteers, and material resources, such as equipment and money. They are able to mobilize people around important social policy issues. They provide forums for debating as well as articulating the moral basis for civic responsibility. They also may attempt to fill a gap in the social safety net when government response is inadequate. And, on occasion, they create innovative programs that serve as models for social reform. This is the social dimension of religion. However, at the heart of all vibrant religion is worship. It is in periods of prayer, reflection, teaching, and preaching that people are internally renewed and sometimes inspired to undertake heroic acts of social transformation. When social engagement and worship lose their creative tension—failing to cross-fertilize each other—then religion becomes vapid and uninspiring.

REFERENCES

Alinsky, A. 1989. *Reveille for Radicals*. New York: Vintage Books.

Ammerman, N. T. 1990. *Baptist Battles*. New Brunswick, N.J.: Rutgers University Press.

Anderson, R. M. 1979. *Vision of the Disinherited*. New York: Oxford University Press.

Bainton, R. H. 1960. *Christian Attitudes Toward War and Peace*. New York: Abington Books.

Bellah, R. N. 1970. *Beyond Belief*. Berkeley: University of California Press.

Bellah, R. N., and Greenspahn, F. E. 1987. *Uncivil Religion*. New York: Crossroad Books.

Berger, P. 1967. *The Sacred Canopy*. Garden City, N.Y.: Anchor Books.

Bomann, R. P. 1999. *Faith in the Barrios*. Boulder, Colo.: Lynne Riennet.

Casanova, J. 1994. *Public Religion in the Modern World*. Chicago: University of Chicago Press.

Chestnut, A. 2003. *Competitive Spirits*. New York: Oxford University Press

Cox, H. 1995. *Fire from Heaven*. New York: Addison-Wesley.

Dionne, E. J., and Diiulio, J. J. 2000. *What's God Got to Do with the American Experiment?* Washington, D.C.: Brookings Institution.

Durkheim, E. 1995. *Elementary Forms of the Religious Life*. New York: The Free Press.

Edwards, M. 2009. *Civil Society*. 2nd ed. Cambridge: Polity Press.

Edwards, M., and S. Post (eds.). 2008. *The Love That Does Justice: Spiritual Activism in Dialogue with Social Science*. Cleveland, Ohio: Unlimited Love Press.

Elliott, B. J. 2004. *Street Saints*. Philadelphia: Templeton Foundation Press.

Flanigan, S. T. 2009. *For the Love of God: NGOs and Religious Identity in a Violent World*. West Hartford, Conn.: Kumarian Press.

Flory, R., and Miller, D. E. 2008. *Finding Faith*. New Brunswick, N.J.: Rutgers University Press.

Fowler, J. 1981. *Stages of Faith*. New York: Harper and Row.

Ganz, M. 2009. *Why David Sometimes Wins*. New York: Oxford University Press.

Gifford, P. 2004. *Ghana's New Christianity*. Bloomington: Indiana University Press.

Gourevitch, P. 1999. *We Wish To Inform You That Tomorrow We Will Be Killed With Our Families: Stories From Rwanda*. London: Picador.

Gustafson, J. 2008. *Treasure in Earthen Vessels*. New York: Library of Theological Ethics.

Harper, N. 1999. *Urban Churches, Vital Signs*. Grand Rapids, Mich.: William B. Eerdmans Publishing Company.

Hondagneu-Sotelo. 2007. *Religion and Social Justice for Immigrants*. New Brunswick, N.J.: Rutgers University Press.

Hughes, T. (ed.) 1988. *The American Quest for the Primitive Church*. Urbana: University of Illinois Press.

Hunter, J. 1991. *Culture Wars*. New York: Basic Books.

James, W. 1961. *Varieties of Religious Experience*. New York: Collier.

Johnstone, R. L. 1975. *Religion and Society in Interaction*. Englewood Cliffs, N.J.: Prentice Hall.

King, M. L., and Carson, C. 1998. *The Autobiography of Martin Luther King, Jr*. New York: Time Warner.

Kniss, F., and Numrich, P. D. 2007. *Sacred Assemblies and Civic Engagement*. New Brunswick, N.J.: Rutgers University Press.

Lichterman, P. 2005. *Elusive Togetherness: Church Groups Trying to Bridge America's Divisions*. Princeton, N.J.: Princeton University Press.

Lindenberg, M., and C. Bryant. 2001. *Going Global: Transforming Relief and Development NGOs*. West Hartford, Conn.: Kumarian Press.

Marsh, C. 2005. *The Beloved Community*. New York: Basic Books.

Martin, D. 2002. *Pentecostalism*. Oxford: Blackwell Publishing.

Miller, D. E. 1997. *Reinventing American Protestantism*. Berkeley: University of California Press.

Miller, D. E., and Yamamori, T. 2007. *Global Pentecostalism*. Berkeley: University of California Press.

Neuhaus, R. J. 1984. *The Naked Public Square*. Grand Rapids, Mich.: William B. Eerdmans Publishing Company.

Niebuhr, H. R. 1929. *The Social Sources of Denominationalism*. New York: Henry Holt.

———. 1951. *Christ and Culture*. New York: Harper and Row.

Putnam, R. D. 2000. *Bowling Alone: the Collapse and Revival of American Community*. New York: Simon & Schuster.

Raines, J. (ed.). 2002. *Marx on Religion*. Philadelphia: Temple University Press.

Rieff, P. 1966. *The Triumph of the Therapeutic*. Chicago: University of Chicago Press.

Robeck, C. M. 2006. *The Azusa Street Mission and Revival*. Nashville, Tenn.: Thomas Nelson Publishing.

Roof, W. C. 1994. *A Generation of Seekers*. New York: Harper Collins.

Roozen, D. A., McKinney, W., and Carroll, J. W. 1984. *Varieties of Religious Presence*. New York: Pilgrim Press, 1984.

Smith, C. 1996. *The Force of Faith in Social Movement Activism*. New York: Routledge.

Stanczak, G. C. 2006. *Engaged Spirituality*. New Brunswick, N.J.: Rutgers University Press.

Stark, R., and Finke, R. 2000. *Acts of Faith*. Berkeley: University of California Press.

Thumma, S. 2007. *Beyond Megachurch Myths*. San Francisco: Jossey-Bass.

Troeltsch, E. 1960. *The Social Teaching of the Christian Churches*. 2 vols. New York: Harper and Row.

Tutu, D. 2004. *God Has a Dream*. New York: Doubleday.

Varshney, A. 2003. *Ethnic Conflict and Civic Life: Hindus and Muslims in India.* New Haven, Conn.: Yale University Press.

Vaughan, J. 2009. *The Rise and Fall of the Christian Coalition.* Eugene, Ore.: Resource Publications.

Warren, M. 2001. *Dry Bones Rattling.* Princeton, N.J.: Princeton University Press.

Weber, M. 1946. *From Max Weber.* New York: Oxford University Press.

————. 2002. *The Protestant Ethic and Spirit of Capitalism.* New York: Penguin Books.

Wilson, B. 1982. *Religion in Sociological Perspective.* Oxford: Oxford University Press.

Wood, R. 2002. *Faith in Action.* Chicago: University of Chicago Press.

Wuthnow, R. 1996. *Sharing the Journey.* New York: The Free Press.

————. 2004. *Saving America?* Princeton, N.J.: Princeton University Press.

CHAPTER 22

....

CIVIL SOCIETY AND SPIRITUALITY

....

CLAUDIA HORWITZ

WHILE there are numerous impulses that inspire citizens to take collective action on the issues that concern them, spirituality may—paradoxically—be one of the most prevalent but least understood. A spiritually driven life may take formal shape through civic associations, but more often than not, it is expressed informally through a broad range of activities that take place in civil society and through civil society as the public sphere. The gifts of a spiritual path enable people to be more effective agents of change in countless ways, from improving the culture of civil society associations to transforming the nature of life in the public sphere. Spirituality lies at the core of what makes civil society possible. It strengthens the organizations that construct it, permeates the arenas that sustain it, and inspires the search for civil society itself. This chapter explores the neglected terrain of spirituality and civil society and argues that the spiritual character of much civil society action should be placed at the center of the analysis.

Because spirituality is understood, and misunderstood, in many different ways, the chapter opens by defining the terms of this debate and analyzing the linkages that connect spirituality to external or social action. Central to these linkages is a new relationship to collective suffering, a relationship that is explored in section 2. Section 3 considers the resources that spirituality provides to citizens and to activists so that they can be more effective in their civic activities in a whole variety of ways, both in associational life (section 4) and in their interactions in the public sphere (section 5). For example, spirituality helps citizens to confront their differences more successfully, and to build bridges across their identities. In these and other ways, spirituality helps citizens to create the good society together, which is the subject of the concluding section of the chapter. In essence, I maintain that the life of the spirit is a search *for* civil society, *by* civil society, and *through* civil society in ways that advance greater progress than would otherwise be likely.

1. What is Spirituality?

The word "spirituality" conjures up any number of definitions, images, and appraisals. In this chapter spirituality is understood as a doorway to the sacred, a response to internal suffering, and a quest for meaning that is accompanied by daily decisions to live in accordance with that search. Spirituality provides a lens through which people examine and navigate their most defining and complicated relationships: to each other, to themselves, and to the ineffable. In this sense, spirituality constitutes the more personal dimension of faith. For some, it is expressed through regular rituals that bring balance to a hectic lifestyle or healing from a crisis. For others, it is the alignment with particular teachings that cultivates the capacity for compassion or defines a path to wisdom.

In the way that it is understood in post-modern Western cultures, spirituality differs from religion in that it is less constrained, less beholden to a set of rules and traditions, and more closely aligned with the internal landscape of human experience. Religion gives rise to particular external expressions of text and theology, intrinsically located in communal realities. For centuries, religious institutions have anchored a sense of social mission for their followers, but over the last five decades rising skepticism about authority has led to a decline in trust in large institutions, be they from government, corporations, or organized religion. This, in turn, has created a strong momentum towards spiritual experimentation and self-determination. A number of significant impacts of this trend were reported by the Pew Forum on Religion and Public Life in 2008 (Pew Forum 2008), a survey of 35,000 adults in the United States which reported that religious affiliation is both very diverse and extremely fluid. More than 28 percent of adults have left their faith of origin, and the same proportion of young adults aged 18–29 years are unaffiliated with any particular religious path. More and more people are exploring alternative practices outside of the tradition in which they were raised, and often across different religious and spiritual traditions. Anecdotal evidence from the pages of any major newspaper fleshes out this story: Jews who are meditating, Christians who are practicing earth-based spirituality, Catholics who are leading the Sufi Dances of Universal Peace, and African-Americans who were raised in the black church and are now immersed in the Yoruba traditions of West Africa.

Frequently, spiritual experience is sought and embraced as a way of enlivening one's relationship to reality, and specifically of confronting the layers of separation—from one's ancestors, from the earth, and from our true human nature—that result from the conditioning imposed by entrenched patterns in families, societies, and cultures. Regular engagement in spiritual life holds the promise of wearing away the disconnection and suffering that results from separation of these kinds. Spirituality is often described as the experience of connectedness, a feeling of one- ness where the separation between human beings dissolves. Swami Kripalu, who inspired the Kripalu yoga tradition, described it as "a wave in love with the sea" (Mundhal 2008). Over time, new habits of understanding and contentment can take root, and the spontaneous and loving nature of the Self shines through. But funda- mentally, spirituality is also about freedom, the freedom to act in new ways once liberated from the constraints of inherited patterns of thought and action. It is this quality that makes spirituality such a compelling resource for the future of civil society.

2. A NEW RELATIONSHIP TO COLLECTIVE SUFFERING

In its current form, this search for meaning, fulfillment, and happiness is a relatively new phenomenon. As more people undertake their own conscious pursuit of tran- scendent wisdom, there is an implicit assumption that this wisdom, the search itself, or both together bring with them new levels of understanding and self-actualiza- tion. Postmodern culture is characterized by significantly heightened levels of alert and anxiety, caused by economic insecurity, ongoing threats of terrorism (real and perceived), environmental calamity, or simply the ever-quickening pace of life. In this context it is not surprising that many people have sought out practices that promise the potential of inner peace and an altogether calmer existence. When placed in the context of work for social change, this spiritual yearning takes on a new dimension and urgency. In their efforts to bring about social transformation, civil society activists, by definition, work in aggregate, and often experience intensi- fied levels of the anger, grief, and fear that are mirrored in wider society. The result- ing stresses and strains mean that leaders and their organizations do not always function with the level of excellence necessary to achieve a broader impact.

One potent remedy to this situation—the integration of spirituality and social activism—has blossomed over the past ten years. Civil society leaders and other practitioners are studying ancient wisdom, developing spiritual practices, and plac- ing these traditions in the context of their community and global responsibilities where they add value and strength to the work at hand. For these activists, spiritual- ity is both an individual and a collective enterprise, and it is inextricably linked to justice. In the face of hard realities, many are envisioning new forms of organization and organizing. As a result, they are creating new approaches to leadership and col- laboration that have the potential to strengthen social movements over time and increase their impact on society's most entrenched problems. An emphasis on inner work does not mean avoiding, denying or transcending external difficulties. Rather, the spiritual path serves as a way of turning towards society's most pressing challenges with a willingness to see, to feel, and ultimately to act from a place of wholeness. At its best, "spiritual activism" harnesses the passion that arises from witnessing the world's suffering, and redirects it in more effective ways.

The gradual transformation that is occurring in many voluntary associations is good news for civil society and the public sphere. This shift is heartening because engagement in civil society requires a capacity to turn towards suffering in the form of fear, sadness, and anger, over and over again. Without this capacity, the pull towards denial or demonization of the "other" usually proves to be too great. The United States sees occasional national expressions of grief (for example, after the terrorist attacks of September 11, 2001), outrage (such as disgust after Hurricane Katrina), and pity (including the response to the 2004 tsunami and more recent earthquakes in China and Haiti). But society as a whole is not very adept when it comes to embracing suffering and recognizing the impact of individual and collective decisions. As Parker Palmer notes, "Spirituality is not primarily about values and ethics, nor about exhortations to do right or live well. The spiritual traditions are primarily about *reality*. The spiritual traditions are an effort to penetrate the illusions of the external world and to name its underlying truth—what it is, how it emerges, and how we relate to it" (1999, 26).

Many ancient spiritual texts embody this wisdom. The yoga sutras collected by Patanjali in the first century B.C.E., for example, describe five roots of suffering: ignorance, ego, greed, aversion, and fear (Satchidananda 1990) It is easy to see how these states of mind obscure the capacity for clarity and discrimination and instead become a source of dissatisfaction. In the second sutra, Patanjali describes the benefits of the spiritual path as "stilling the fluctuations of the mind so that the Self can abide in its true nature." In other words, in their fullest expression, spiritual practices enable people to weaken the roots of suffering that take shape in the mind and to live in increasing states of freedom. Greater self-consciousness illuminates the five hindrances described by Patanjali so that they are visible, and in this way they become a messenger rather than an obstacle. With consistent effort, the practitioner develops the power of the witness, a presence that can see clearly without identifying with what is being seen. As the veil of illusion is pierced, the roots of suffering have less power to direct our actions. In this way, distress, crisis, fear, sadness, and grief can serve as an impetus to discover truth; and discomfort becomes a springboard to greater understanding.

In its fullest expression, spiritual practice sublimates the ego because it reveals the nature of impermanence and the inevitability of change. Over time, these practices strengthen one's capacity to be responsive rather than reactive and to rest in the unknown. It is clear that people want relief from their own suffering. Eastern traditions of meditation and yoga have been packaged in terms of "stress relief" and have become commonplace, not just in studios but in hospitals, prisons and workplaces. Chinese herbs can be purchased at the mall. Accessibility is good, but we privatize and commodify vulnerability and healing at our peril. If we hope for more than mere survival in close proximity to one another, then we need new, collective ways of turning towards suffering. This is not a comfortable task.

In the words of Sister Joan Chittister, the question is "how to make private spirituality the stuff of public leaven in a world fiercely private and dangerously public at the same time; how to end our public crucifixions while we say our private prayers. The fact is that simple spiritualities of creed and community and co-operation are obviously no longer enough. We need now, surely, a spirituality of contemplative co-creation." (2000) When confusion or pain are encountered, the tendency is to look for an escape route, a way to avoid feeling unhappiness, fear or anger. The other, more revolutionary choice is to experience whatever arises, *to simply be with what is.* This is a profound teaching: to surrender to the totality of the moment, whether it is grief over an act of senseless violence or anger with outdated public policies. Instead of meeting crisis with "fight or flight," we can find an intelligent and expansive response that points us towards collective liberation.

Individuals develop habits and patterns based on cultural legacies, family histories, and personal experience. When these habits are triggered by a negative event, an opportunity is presented to observe conditioned patterns like these; and over time, they can be weakened through greater exposure, awareness and compassion. Twenty-first century life is replete with conditioned patterns formed around oppression, violence and injustice. Spiritual wisdom teaches that it is possible to reveal these patterns in society—for example, in how wealth is distributed, how children are educated, and how resources are used and produced—in a way that allows for greater awareness and compassion. Instead of shame or guilt, suffering becomes a doorway to more effective understanding and action.

But how does this occur? In the work of Stone Circles, for example,[1] a civil society group based in North Carolina, individuals are invited to recall a recent incident of collective suffering, reconnect with the sensory details involved, and sculpt them into a snapshot of the event such as a confrontation between authority and a group of oppressed people, a meeting that disintegrates into chaos, or the collapse of a coalition. When asked to make one change that would have catalyzed a greater sense of freedom in the context of these experiences, the answers range from the subtle to the obvious—a finger pointed in someone's face that suddenly drops to the ground, hands clenched in a fist that gradually begin to open, or a figure that moves towards engagement with those on the other side of the fence. These shifts communicate clues about what it means to turn towards suffering in new ways, for example:

- Creating a bridge between two opposing entities
- Assuming a posture of neutrality to diffuse a charged situation
- Changing one's vantage point in order to see who else is suffering
- Eliciting an expression of pain that has been hidden
- Inviting others to join in collective action
- Risking engagement in a hostile climate
- And strengthening the bonds of mutual solidarity

People are more likely to choose these behaviors when they stand strong in their own power. When something difficult arises and causes suffering on the individual level, there is often a fear that it will last forever, even if intellectually this is clearly not the case, and the pull to denial or avoidance becomes too strong to resist. The same is true on the collective level. But instead of distracting oneself from the feelings or sensations that arise, there is always an option to stay present in the experience and to witness to the discomfort it creates. The experience is allowed to unfold, instead of always trying to control it. As a result, profound insights can be generated about the path to success.

3. Strengthening Associational Life

In some ways, it should come as no surprise that civil society activists are drawn to the benefits of spiritual practice. The pressure on workers on the front lines of the struggle for social justice is often very great. Many come to their work in response to the brokenness and suffering they have experienced or witnessed: the realities of economic injustice, racism and oppression, planetary degradation, and violence in any number of its forms. Close proximity to injustice provokes a reaction that can deepen their suffering in expressions of rage, grief, and frustration. People bind together based on shared commitment and shared anger; and for a while at least, occasional success and urgency are enough to sustain the work. But too many activists forsake personal well-being, and the culture of activism lends itself to addiction, illness, or exhaustion. Left unattended, these experiences can become a poison for body, mind, and soul, corrupting clarity, strategy, and tactics, and limiting the time that can be sustained in the field. Many civil society organizations struggle to survive, only to discover that their behavior is exacerbating the effects of burnout on their staff or members. The slow deterioration of physical, emotional, and mental health may go undetected for a time as practitioners inhabit a dangerous irony: complete dedication to external commitment, with virtually no awareness of how they are suffering themselves. Wake-up calls may come in any number of forms, from a crisis of physical health to the end of a significant relationship.

These personal trials arise in the context of complex and under-resourced work environments. Leaders of civil society institutions are vulnerable to a range of challenges: the tensions that arise between fulfilling their mission and securing the resources the organization needs to survive; balancing the needs of multiple constituencies and stakeholders; ensuring excellence in program delivery and evaluation; and navigating strategy and tactics in a rapidly changing world. A survey by CompassPoint of over 1,000 nonprofit leaders in the United States articulates the toll imposed by these challenges (Peters and Wolfred 2001, 3–4, 24):

- Fewer than half the executive directors in the sample plan to take on another position at the same level in the future; in most cases, executive directors stay an average of three to five years in their positions.

- "Finding meaning" and "contributing to others" were ranked highest in terms of the motivation for serving as leaders of nonprofit organizations.
- The most significant negative elements cited by respondents included high levels of stress and long hours, the anxiety caused by fiscal worries and fundraising, the challenges of managing staff, and high staff turnover, all of which create an atmosphere of scarcity.

In the same year, a study by the Center for Contemplative Mind in Society (Duerr 2002) surveyed seventy-nine leaders representing a broad cross-section of nonprofit and other civil society organizations and revealed a similar range of challenges: burnout, loss of perspective, lack of funding and appreciation, working from a place of self-righteousness and excessive anger, fears of replicating one system of injustice with another, and operating within larger cultural assumptions about busyness, materialism, product orientation, and individualism.

Nicole Lee of the Urban Peace Movement in Oakland, California once put it to me this way: "I've been doing community organizing for eleven years and there are lots of us in the movement who are not sure about our effectiveness. We're having epiphanies about where power really comes from and the relationship between other parts of our humanity and movement work. We're at different places with the conversation but there is a collective element. That's encouraging."[2]

In his essay on spiritual leadership, James Ritscher asserts that "only an organization that is well grounded in its spiritual nature has the will and the strength to survive" (2005, 69). Increasingly, younger civil society activists value the legacy of those from previous generations, but are reluctant to inherit the tradition of burnout that pervades the social movements they are beginning to lead. Many recognize the need to build stronger organizations from the inside out, because healthy and honest collectivities are the basis of everything civil society groups accomplish. In order to sustain social justice work and increase its effectiveness on the ground, the culture of organizations has to be transformed to reflect the values that activists are working to amplify in the wider world, including trust, compassion, equity, and love.

The Center for Contemplative Mind in Society's research also documented the impact of closer ties between inner awareness and work for social justice. Qualitative analysis identified several ways in which spiritual practices contribute to greater efficacy in social change, more sustainability for the long haul, the ability to process difficult emotions in constructive ways, and success in shifting entrenched power dynamics and power structures. The study was one of the first to reveal how activists are using spiritual practices to integrate personal with social transformation. As the connection between reflective individuals, healthy organizations and effective social movements has become clearer (though mirroring the lessons of an earlier generation of activism around civil and women's rights), new resources have been developed to meet their needs. Numerous organizations are resourcing civil society activists through education, training, retreats and materials. Leadership development programs provide intensive training that includes components on personal ecology and mastery, and what was largely a unrelated sprinkling of disparate efforts around the United States in the 1990s has become a more cohesive, connected network that is leveraging its power in a number of a large-scale collaborations.

More and more activists are experiencing firsthand the transformative power of combining the spiritual practices with the work they do in the world (Zimmerman et al. 2010). Imagine a community organizer participating in a training that values spiritual wisdom and incorporates the relevant practices. He arrives fresh from the most recent round of battles to protect undocumented farm workers. He is angry at the system, at the landowners, and even at some other immigrant rights leaders because they are prioritizing college access over farm worker health issues. During a guided meditation on the nature of leadership challenges, he sits with his anger and follows it to the root: a deep caring for his constituents. In a later session, he connects with two other organizers in a structured dialogue on strategy development. They discuss priorities, tradeoffs, and tough decisions. He is able to hold his current struggles in a larger and longer-term context, and gain insights into the choices other leaders in the movement are making. The evening closes with a session on mindfulness meditation. He experiences a deep level of compassion, first for the farm workers and their families, then for the people in his organization and other movement allies, and then, although perhaps fleetingly, for the landowners themselves. He returns to his work after the training with renewed energy and openness.

This is not to claim that spiritual practices automatically inspire holistic or inclusive thinking. If they did, the world would be different. If inner work is undertaken in isolation from the reflective mirror provided by real communities, the spiritual path merely bolsters individualism. The path becomes too self-referential, and the opportunity to contribute to the common good is lost. It is precisely the commitment to a world beyond oneself that saves spiritual practice from its potential narcissism. The web of interdependence necessitates great care and responsibility. As one moves into an awareness of interconnectedness, personal needs move out of the center of the universe. Over time, new structures, institutions, and organizations develop that reflect this shift. For activists, the fruits of a spiritual life inspire a desire to share their experience more widely; in the conviction that human beings come to realize their full potential in relationship with others. Indeed, all social movements have demonstrated the universal truth that individual freedom is not just dependent upon collective freedom, they are inextricably linked together.

4. NAVIGATING THE TENSIONS OF THE PUBLIC SPHERE

As society becomes more pluralistic, ignoring lines of difference is no longer a viable option. People must negotiate their differences in ways for which they have not adequately been prepared. The oft-learned tendency is to choose one side and demonize the other. Dynamic tensions arise which, when navigated poorly, diminish efforts at social change and fray the social fabric still further. When activists operate from fear, mistrust, anxiety, or anger, distinctions and tensions are magnified. When addressed skillfully, however, these tensions present an opportunity to look at duality in a different way. When activists operate from curiosity or compassion, these distinctions become the raw material that can assist in forging unlikely partnerships and a transcendent pluralistic narrative of human liberation through the life of the public sphere.

This shift entails a radical change in the dynamics between dominant and subordinate groups, or the mainstream and the margins. Jean Baker Miller (1991, 183) identifies the following five characteristics of a dominant group: they act destructively to subordinate groups; they restrict subordinate groups' range of action; they discourage the subordinate groups' full expression of their experiences; they characterize subordinates falsely; and they describe everything as the "way it should be." The psychologist and activist Arthur Mindell (1995) uses the terms "mainstream" and "margin" to describe a similar framework and this has been further expanded upon by Training for Change.[3] The mainstream exhibits the qualities, behaviors, and values that are more overtly recognized and supported, whether in an organization, a community, or society at large. The margin is made up of the qualities and behaviors that are pushed to the periphery and denied equal power. The mainstream uses its power to frame the discourse, set the tone and the terms of engagement, and define acceptable language, and these actions reinforce the power it already has.

The premise here is that mainstreams cannot grow or evolve without the wisdom that comes from the margin, and that mainstreams tend to be ignorant of their own behavior. This is clear when observing movements for social change, most of which emerge from the margin. And no matter how homogeneous or united an organization or community believes itself to be, a careful examination will show that some of its members or characteristics have been marginalized. A group that believes that it is mostly progressive politically has some members with more moderate or conservative views. An organization that uses email for internal communication has some staff members who like to talk things out face-to-face. Mainstream power is often hidden behind unexpressed assumptions about how everyone in a group should act, but mainstreams grow through becoming aware of, and then renegotiating, their relationships with the margins. Groups in which mainstreams refuse to do this eventually die. Groups and societies grow most robustly at their edges.

Spiritual practices reveal the possibility of a union of opposites—between movement and stillness, expansion and contraction, will and surrender, right and wrong. The intimate relationship that is inherent in every duality is revealed. In the presence of this intimacy, it becomes easier to deal with complexity, to hold two seemingly conflicting ideas in one's mind at the same time. Spiritual activism offers a middle way between "fight and flight"; the two responses that are instinctual, especially in times of challenge, crisis, or stress. Because of these advantages, spirituality can be of enormous assistance to the health and functioning of public spheres.

5. Conclusion: Spirituality and the Good Society

From ancient history through to the social movements of today, we find compelling examples of how spiritual conviction and consciousness can blossom into a compelling vision for the future of humankind. Spiritual wisdom sees beyond the mentality of "us versus them" to engage with the potential of commonality and radical equality. It has great potential to anchor visions of the good society in a commitment to concrete ethics and new forms of behavior, and to guide the actions of civil society groups as they labor to bring these visions to fruition.

To take but one example, "ahimsa," the Sanskrit word for nonviolence, defined a new approach to conflict and liberation from colonial rule in India. In *The Nonviolent Revolution*, Nathanial Altman (1988) describes it thus: "Instead of causing fear, the soldier of ahimsa seeks to instill confidence and trust. In place of antagonism, the spiritual warrior works to bring about communication and understanding. As opposed to the defensiveness and bullying of the traditional soldier, the soldier of ahimsa is protected by humility and vulnerability. In place of contempt for the 'enemy', the soldier of ahimsa offers goodwill and respect." In similar fashion, Martin Luther King, Jr. (1957) and other civil rights leaders placed love squarely at the center of nonviolent resistance, defining it as a refusal to hate and perhaps even more importantly, having "sense enough to cut off the chain of hate" completely. King's philosophy of the "love that does justice" is perhaps the best-elaborated framework of integrated social change of the kind that has been explored in this chapter. Built around a spirituality of cultivating unconditional or universal love for all human beings, King described his life mission as the translation of "love into justice structures," encompassing action at both the personal and the structural levels to create mutually reinforcing cycles of change that would spiral outwards to create what he called "the beloved community"—the ultimate synthesis of personal and social transformation (Edwards and Post 2009, 6). Jane Stembridge, one of the first white organizers to work with the Student Nonviolent Coordinating Committee expressed it like this: "Finally, it all boils down to human relationship...It is the question of whether I shall go on living in isolation or whether there shall be a we. The student movement is not a cause...it is a collision between this one person and that one person. It is 'I am going to sit beside you'...Love alone is radical" (Zinn 2002, 7).

Because unconditional love must consider the equal and general welfare of the whole, those who follow this path must also confront any factor that stands in the way of realizing the rights and dignity of every human being—whether rooted in personal prejudice and selfishness, or locked into the systems and structures of power that characterize all contemporary societies.

As Edwards and Post (2009, 7) put it: "Consider the volunteer working in New Orleans after Hurricane Katrina whose constant efforts, along with those of countless others, can achieve only a very partial alleviation of immense suffering. They inevitably begin to ask why it is that support and resources are not available from the corridors of power, and what forces are responsible for such neglect. This example shows how justice is *implicit* in love, and how justice-seeking is love's modulation or expression. 'Doing unto others' does require the irreplaceable face-to-face interpersonal works of love, but it also requires the courage to confront larger, systemic unfairness.... Love that does not 'descend' into the struggle for justice is incomplete, if not irrelevant." It is the same phenomenon that workers from the Student Non-Violent Co-ordinating Committee encountered in the Mississippi Delta four decades earlier, and that so moved Gandhi thirty years before.

A spiritually based activism makes all of this more than well-worn history or convincing theory. At its best, a dedication to the spiritual life ushers in a new sense of spaciousness that encourages people to take on more responsibility for their actions and begin to choose new responses to old and familiar questions. As these attributes continue to manifest in practice, activists find themselves grounded in an increased self-awareness, a place of readiness, and openness to change. They begin to know what is right in any given moment in time, and to trust that wisdom, whether it comes from within or from outside. Solutions can emerge at any time because the ground has been well prepared. The spiritual path to civil society does not generate ready-made answers to the deep-rooted and intractable problems of economic and social life, codified according to the conventional logics of Left or Right, or Jewish, Muslim, or Christian. Instead, it provides a different set of motivations from which alternatives can grow, eventually demonstrating how politics, economics, social relationships, and organizational effectiveness can be transformed through a radically different rationality. Marrying a rich inner life dedicated to the cultivation of loving kindness and compassion with the practice of new forms of politics, economics and public policy is the key to social transformation.

NOTES

1. See www.stonecircles.org.
2. Personal conversation with the author.
3. See www.trainingforchange.org.

REFERENCES

Altman, N. 1988. *The Nonviolent Revolution: A Comprehensive Guide to Ahimsa*. Brooklyn, N.Y.: Element Books.

Chittister O. S. B, J. 2000. "Spirituality and Contemporary Culture." Paper presented at the 2000 National Forum of The Center for Progressive Christianity, June 1–3, in Irvine, California.

Dass, R., and Bush, M. 1991. *Compassion in Action: Setting Out on the Path of Service.* New York: Random House.

Duerr, M. 2002. *Inviting the World to Tranform: Nourishing Social Justice Work with Contemplative Practice.* Northampton, Mass: The Center for Contemplative Mind in Society.

Edwards, M., and Post, S. 2009. *The Love that Does Justice: Spiritual Activism in Dialogue with Social Science.* Cleveland, Ohio: Unlimited Love Press.

Horwitz, C. 2002. *The Spiritual Activist: Practices to Transform Your Life, Your Work and Your World.* New York: Penguin Compass.

King, M. L. 1957. "Loving Your Enemies." Sermon presented at Dexter Avenue Baptist Church, November 17 in Montgomery, Alabama.

Miller, J. 1991. "The Construction of Anger in Men and Women," in Judith V. Jordan (ed.) *Women's Growth in Connection: Writings from the Stone Center.* New York: Guilford Press, 181–95.

Mindell, A. 1995. *Sitting in the Fire: Large Group Transformation Using Conflict and Diversity.* Portland, Ore.: Lao Tse Press.

Mundhal, J. (ed.) 2008. *From the Heart of the Lotus: The Teaching Stories of Swami Kripalu.* Rhinebeck, New York: Monkfish Publishing.

Palmer, P. 1999. *Let Your Life Speak: Listening for the Voice of Vocation.* San Francisco: Jossey-Bass.

Peters, J., and Wolfred, T. 2001. *Daring To Lead: Nonprofit Executive Directors and Their Work Experience.* San Francisco: CompassPoint.

Pew Forum on Religion and Public Life. 2008. *U.S. Religious Landscape Survey. Religious Affiliation: Diverse and Dynamic.* Philadelphia: Pew Research Center.

Powell, J.A. 2003. "Lessons from Suffering: How Social Justice Informs Spirituality." *University of St. Thomas Law Journal* vol. 1 (1):102–27.

Ritscher, J. A. 2005. "Spiritual Leadership," in John D. Adams (ed.) *Transforming Leadership.* New York: Cosimo.

Satchidananda, S. 1990. *The Yoga Sutras of Patanjali: Commentary on the Raja Yoga Sutras.* Buckingham, Va.: Integral Yoga Publications.

Segrest, M. 2002. *Born to Belonging: Writings on Spirit and Justice.* New Brunswick, N.J.: Rutgers University Press.

Shields, K. 1994. *In the Tiger's Mouth: An Empowerment Guide for Social Action.* : Gabriola Island, B.C.: New Society Publishers.

Straub, G. 2000. *The Rhythm of Compassion: Caring for Self, Connecting with Society.* Boston: Tuttle Publishing.

Zimmerman, K., et al. 2010. *Out of the Spiritual Closet: Organizers Transforming the Practice of Social Justice.* Oakland, Calif.: Movement Strategy Center.

Zinn, H. 2002. *SNCC: The New Abolitionists.* Cambridge, Mass.: South End Press.

PART V

THE SPACES OF CIVIL SOCIETY

CHAPTER 23

CIVIL SOCIETY
AND GOVERNMENT

NANCY L. ROSENBLUM
CHARLES H. T. LESCH

CIVIL society and government have their own conceptual and institutional histories, and each of these histories has a foot in both political theory and social and political developments. New institutions, shifting boundaries, and novel interpenetrations of civil society and government are a constant, but sometimes these changes amount to transformative moments. One such moment came when perceptions of civil society shifted from negative to universally positive, and civil society came to be identified as a separate sphere from the economy and from government, cast as the terrain of genuine moral and social life. As a result, civil society often escapes the critical analyses that have been leveled at government. Civil society, not the state, is the bastion of utopianism in political thought today. This chapter surveys the shifting boundaries of civil society-government relations and underscores the potentially transformative move towards partnerships that reach into areas that were previously marked out as separate terrains.

1. BOUNDARIES

Discussions of civil society and government pose difficult questions of boundary definition and boundary crossing. Assigning substantive purposes, designating the characteristics of their institutions, and identifying their shifting boundaries pose many analytic challenges. Moreover, locating the boundaries between civil society and government inevitably reflects moral norms and political ideology, and has implications for law and public policy. In addressing these questions, we adopt the spatial metaphors that have become indispensable to thinking on this subject.

Viewed from the perspective of government, the state is the encompassing sphere, the higher ground, and the controlling institution. Government is the inclusive, putative authorized voice of citizens, and bears principal responsibility for activities that serve common purposes. By means of law and public policy, government creates the institutional framework, the space in which the groups and associations of civil society take shape and carry out their activities. Government assigns the elements of civil society legal status, rights, and responsibilities; it outlaws certain groups and criminalizes certain activities. Public law sets the terms of cooperation and the permissible terms of conflict within and between these groups and associations. By means of coercion and incentives, government cultivates, constrains, regulates, directs, and supports the entire range of institutions and associations that comprise social life. From this perspective, government is "prior" to civil society, and the elements of civil society are "secondary" or "intermediate" associations. In one formulation, government represents "the social union of social unions" (Rawls 1993, 322). As such, government must insure that the partial social unions of civil society are congruent with, or not dangerously in opposition to, the requirements of stable democracy, and towards that end enforce equal protection of the law and due process over and sometimes against civil society groups. From this perspective, the obligations of citizenship outweigh the obligations of association membership, and one task of government is to cultivate public, democratic norms and a commitment to public purposes. At the same time, in recognition of the fact that individuals and groups find their meaning in associations, and on the understanding that for some people membership has priority over citizenship, government should also attempt to minimize conflicts between the obligations of citizenship and the demands of membership, in particular the demands of religious faith (Rosenblum 2000).

Viewed from the perspective of civil society, associational life encompasses activities and commitments as various as are human needs and imaginations, extending far beyond the business of government and citizenship: "our interests, convictions, cultural, religious and sexual identities, status, salvation, exhibitions of competence, exhilarating rivalries" are played out in these partial associations (Post and Rosenblum 2002, 15; 3). From the perspective of members, these groups bear a resemblance to government insofar as they are "jurisgenerative." Whether they are conceived as voluntary associations or as ascriptive religious, cultural, or ethnic groups, they impose laws and obligations, assign members rights and benefits, decide on collective purposes, and do so by instituting their own structures of authority and forms of internal governance. Unlike government, however, associations are plural, partial, and particularist, and participation in these groups and associations contrasts with singular democratic citizenship. They are partial in the sense that their membership is not inclusive, which is one reason why civil society is a terrain not only of myriad social differences but also of myriad inequalities. They are partial too in the sense that groups and associations do not occupy every moment or aspect of members' lives; men and women are also producers and consumers in the economy, family members, political actors, and citizens. Finally, associations are partial in that individuals typically belong to more than one group. They form multiple, diverse attachments over the course of a lifetime. Indeed, the possibility of "shifting involvements" and the "experience of pluralism" is a defining characteristic of life in civil society (Rosenblum 1998; Galston 2002).

This brief conceptual account brings us to the inescapable boundary question: what constraints should government impose on the formation, internal life, and activities of groups and associations, and what limits should it set to the authority that groups exercise over their own members and outsiders? In democratic theory there is general agreement that government cannot permit "greedy institutions" that take over every aspect of their members' lives or seriously inhibit their opportunity to exercise the rights and obligations of citizenship; the structure of exit must be deliberately constructed and enforced by law and made practicable by public provisions to meet the needs of those leaving closed communities (Warren 2009). Groups cannot, in classic Lockean terms, punish members (or outsiders) physically or by confiscating property. They cannot be permitted to act as private despotisms or to organize private armies. Less clear is the extent to which civil society is compatible with forms of pluralism that are closed and segmented such that society is composed of (often hostile) "pillars," or a collection of semisovereign ethnic, cultural, or religious communities, or some version of corporatism with fixed sectors.

In our view, some degree of fluidity, some mix of voluntary and ascriptive associations, must be present. "Escape from hereditary and ascriptive attachments (or their willing reaffirmation), the formation of new affiliations for every conceivable purpose, and shifting involvements among groups are essential aspects of liberty," Rosenblum writes (1998, 26). Exit from groups, if not costless, must be a real possibility. Where autonomy is accorded only to groups or subcommunities, and where government does not maintain personal legal rights and afford individual freedom of movement among partial associations, civil society as a conceptual entity hardly exists at all.

The boundary we have outlined, like every analytic approach to the subject, has normative and political implications. Government must be sufficiently strong and independent of civil society groups to maintain the conditions for pluralism and to insure that particularist and partial associations are not private despotisms. At the same time, civil society is inseparable from limited government and a degree of voluntarism and freedom of association. As members of groups and associations, men and women serve as countervailing forces against arbitrary or unlimited government intrusion on the internal lives, purposes, and organizational energy of groups; they must be on guard against even progressive, democratic colonization.

2. Civil Society and Government

The vision of civil society as an arena existing apart from, or antagonistic to, government propelled the concept's revival during the last years of the Cold War. In this capacity, theorists have frequently assigned to it two primary functions of particular importance to democratic viability. The first is as a sphere for popular resistance. The development of struggles against Soviet imperialism in Central and Eastern Europe led scholars and activists to develop its oppositional role as a "parallel polis" (Benda 1978), a site where some form of negative liberty might be distilled from an otherwise totalizing government hegemony. With open political opposition impossible, civil society came to be identified as an alternative source of struggle and solidarity. This image—the voice of an otherwise repressed mass bubbling up organically from below—became a feature of late-twentieth-century political theory, fueling efforts to make the concept portable to other parts of the world. In its role of empowering the powerless, civil society was also thought to perform a second, related function of organizing citizens for democratic participation. Political parties were only the most conspicuous vehicles for this task. Though a vast array of voluntary associations, groups might pool resources, fight for protection, and advance social policies. Particularly in the past, before they were given the vote, women and other marginalized social groups used associations to give themselves a voice that would not otherwise be possible through formal, political institutions (Kelley 2006). The voices of civil society spur popular discussion, turn the otherwise apathetic towards political participation, create democratic audiences, and demarcate deliberative spheres where policies, issues, and ideals may be affirmed or renegotiated.

As intermediaries between individuals and governments, voluntary associations may offer platforms for political participation, but this is not the limit of their function, nor need political advocacy, resistance, or agenda setting be their primary purpose. The ways in which group life intersects with political activity are neither clear nor predictable (Post and Rosenblum 2002, 18). Recent scholarship shows that in certain institutional, cultural, and historical contexts, civil society may have merely an auxiliary (Encarnación 2003) or even a negative (Berman 2003) role in democratization. Indeed in some circumstances, a once vibrant civil society may encourage an aversion to membership (Howard 2003, 124) or a "politics of anti-politics," with individuals living with their "backs toward the state" (Forment 2003, 438). That said, associations do provide a mechanism for political participation, raising crucial questions about the relationship between group membership and voice, the impact of unequal resources on political expression, and the multiple avenues by which organizations come to engage in political advocacy. Each of these areas reveals the complex and multivalent role that voluntary associations play; in finding their voice they simultaneously empower themselves politically and shape the identities of their members.

To begin, it should be plain that there is a direct relationship between associational membership and the voices that emerge from civil society. Thus, if association is compelled or otherwise involuntary, its voice may not represent all or even most of its members, and altered membership may change the message and the messenger dramatically. In this way, involuntary or coerced membership in an association may represent a kind of compelled expression. While such a proposition is anathema to classical liberals, it must also be reconciled with the needs of certain groups such as labor unions, whose effectiveness depends on presenting a united front (Rosenblum 1998, 215).

Associational voice may be strongly impacted by direct governmental efforts. These efforts may aim at limiting voices that are deemed too powerful—exercising undue electoral influence, for example. It is precisely this question of influence that is at issue in the relationship between expressive participation and large aggregations of money. The discussion is often framed in terms of the corrosive or distorting influence that corporations or large nonprofit groups endowed with substantial resources are thought to have on the integrity of the political process (*Austin v. Michigan Chamber of Commerce* 660, 668). Such concerns had led to the curtailment of certain kinds of speech, particularly around electoral campaigns. Alternatively, government policy may aim at enhancing the resources and opportunities for civil society voices that might not otherwise be heard, with a view to promoting more equal and universal participation or improving public debate (Gutmann and Thompson 2004).

A third point involves the connection between individual and group viewpoints. As deliberative theorists remind us, neither member nor group preferences are prefixed or pregiven. Associations cannot, in short, be reduced to an aggregation of atomized opinions. Group self-understanding is variable, and internal dynamics are often unplanned. Both constitutional law and political theory have, at times, made the mistake of essentializing political voices. Juridical rulings have given priority to freedom for avowedly political associations, but in many cases, groups form without the intent of engaging in political expression, and it is only later that associations enter the political arena, after fluctuations in membership, the influence of outside events, or a confluence of other factors. Women's groups are a prime example. Often formed initially for the purpose of providing fellowship or advancing charitable works, by the 1970s and early 1980s some of these groups had adopted an explicitly feminist and highly politicized message (Evans and Boyte 1992). For many associations, political expression may only be a small component of their larger purpose or mission. A decision to take a public stance on an issue is, with few exceptions, not delineated in a group's constitution or other guiding materials.

But associational speech *is* a function of its composition, and for this reason it is important to clarify further what is meant by "voice." When associations "speak," their ideas do not float freely within an ethereal public sphere (Habermas [1962] 1989). Rather, voices are necessarily linked to particular individuals or groups. As a consequence, voice plays a central role in determining not only what we say in the abstract, but also how we are perceived by others and how we perceive ourselves— that is, how we become who we are. Even if membership regulations do not affect the objective content of a message therefore, they will surely influence its impact.

This conclusion points to a final connection between voice and membership. Associations and the expression they produce do not enter the world stillborn. Together, they create *influence*, serving, with or without intention, to convince, persuade, and otherwise affect persons and policies both inside and outside of themselves (Dworkin 1987, 10). The unpredictability of political voice on the part of associations whose core activities are only tangentially related to politics or advocacy, the close connection between voice and membership, and the vulnerability of both to government regulation or compelled association, lead us to suggest that a wide degree of latitude be afforded to groups to control their membership and affairs.

3. Civil Society as a School of Citizenship

Seeing associations as a resource for political participation, advocacy, protest, and resistance does not adequately take into account the citizenship functions of civil society groups. Claims for the positive moral effects of associational life are familiar, and in recent decades attention has turned to the role of civil society in reproducing democratic citizens. The perceived decline of democratic participation, the rise of personal identities defined as consumers as a result of market forces and popular culture, and egoism and atomism, combine to cast civil society as a democratizing antidote. For critical theorists, associations comprise a comparatively egalitarian public space for deliberation that clarifies and legitimizes public values (Baynes 2002). Others emphasize that when the internal governance of groups is democratic, members develop organizational skills, habits of decision making, and a sense of political efficacy. Those who see civil society groups as so-called schools of citizenship focus on an array of democratic dispositions and practices, shaped directly through education or indirectly through some "intangible hand" (Brennan and Pettit 2004).

Critics have tempered these judgments. First, as an empirical matter they observe the prevalence of uncivil society that challenges an indiscriminate faith in the democratizing potential of associational life. They point to groups and associations that are dedicated to advocating and enacting discrimination and other anti-democratic values; or are organized hierarchically or by charismatic leaders, have internal structures that are rigidly authoritarian, or recruit and exploit anomic members from the disconnected margins of society (Chambers and Kopstein 2001; Berman 2003; Armony 2004). Second, some of the largest and most effective civic associations are national-level organizations, professionally led and managed; they do not cultivate membership and if they do have members they fail to provide them with opportunities for acquiring democratic commitments or skills (Skocpol 2003). Third, instead of creating public identities and platforms for democratic deliberation, civil society pluralism can produce a sense of "impotence in the face of impenetrable systemic complexity" (Habermas 1992, 453–6). Finally, school of citizenship arguments are vulnerable for often assuming—absent an articulated social dynamic and connecting structures—a "transmission belt" model that posits a spillover of democratic values, skills, and a sense of efficacy from associations into active participation in formal and informal democratic politics.

A principal caution against these accounts is that they often lead to a stringent "logic of congruence." The charge to reproduce citizens supports the idea that the internal lives and purposes of civil society groups should mirror the democratic values of equality and due process that (ideally) order public life. Advocates of a "seedbed of democracy" account of civil society propose that tutelary government should actively propagate and support groups that promote democratic practices and dispositions, and should outlaw or impose costs on those that advocate and enact ethnic, racial, or gender discrimination, deny members due process, or cultivate dispositions antagonistic to public values. The logic of congruence argues for "democracy all the way down," both as a matter of principle and as an empirical claim. In this view, congruence must be mandated by government, if not always coercively enforced. Principled justifications are given for such compelled association; for example, associations with social and networking objectives like the Boy Scouts should be required to admit gays as scout leaders. The caution here is plain: schools of citizenship thinking raises the prospect of government trespass across the boundary of civil society. In resolving tensions between citizenship and membership in favor of reproducing democratic citizens, the ecology of associational life may be interrupted (Rosenblum 1998). Adding to concern about the logic of congruence is the fact that it can be effected without direct public regulation and coercion, that is, by government acting as patron and enlisting civil society groups as partners, thus erasing the boundary of separate spheres.

4. Government as Patron

In accounts of civil society as the site of advocacy, participation, and resistance, and as the moralized terrain of voluntary cooperation and personal development, civil society is often represented as a spontaneous development that is independent of government (Post and Rosenblum 2002, 1). But government frequently provides more than just the infrastructure of public order and public services, the legal structure for forming organizations, and the parameters of civil and criminal law within which voluntary associations operate. Government is also a material patron, purchaser, funder, and partner in the presumptively beneficial activities of civil society groups.

Historians have documented the fact that governments have never been the sole provider of education and social needs, and that voluntary associations have not had the sole responsibility for caring for their members or communities (Novak

2009). In most societies, government recognition and direct and indirect support for associational activities is expanding, and the number of groups that benefit from public patronage continues to proliferate. Of course, the extent and methods of government support vary widely. In the United States, government provides financial support to civil society indirectly by awarding tax-exempt status and eligibility for tax-deductible charitable contributions to associations. Depending on the ideological baseline adopted, this is characterized as leaving civil society in its natural state, independent of government or as a public subsidy. In addition, government provides financial support for association activities directly through grants or vouchers that individuals can use for schooling and other services. Indeed, the most familiar area of government subsidy is education, where in the United States tax credits and vouchers underwrite school choice. Motivated by moral or religious duty and aimed at self-help for their communities, civic associations organize cultural events and create charities and mutual support networks to care for their own. Such groups have always been unequal in the resources their members can contribute and in their organizational capacity and leadership. Social and economic inequalities are replicated in civil society, and there is a class and race bias in associational life as well as in politics. Government subsidy and support for schools, mutual aid societies, and cultural institutions is potentially redistributive. It helps even poor groups provide services to their members, enabling "meat and potatoes multiculturalism" (Walzer 2004, 39). Apart from small, informal associations like private clubs, reading groups, or street corner churches, civil society groups increasingly depend on some form of public support, complementing and correcting both state and market failure in the provision of public goods and in the process encouraging volunteerism, collective responsibility, and cooperative provision. All the reasons for valuing pluralism and particularism generally operate to encourage a degree of government patronage, which benefits the self-chosen, self-directed purposes of associations.

Complicating this picture, however, are tensions between associational activities and public democratic norms of equality, inclusiveness, nondiscrimination, and due process. For strong advocates of the logic of congruence, it is the responsibility of government to democratize groups and liberalize their practices whether or not they receive public subsidy. Public funding lends added force to the argument: by subsidizing an association's nonprofit activity, government is seen as delivering the public message that it agrees with the association's broader purposes and practices. In this view, public support has symbolic and pedagogical as well as practical effects. Hence, public patronage of civil society raises the boundary question in acute form. Can religious groups subsidized by public funds be permitted to provide services only to coreligionists? Can they choose their constituency as they do their members? Do they violate laws prohibiting discrimination in hiring when they deny employment to workers of other faiths, or to gays because their doctrine declares homosexuality a violation of divine law? Similar questions arise for secular groups whose practices do not conform to norms of nondiscrimination or due process. Legislation in the United States requires government, and by extension public accommodations, to afford nondiscrimination protections to workers and due process to all recipients of services. As more and more associations receive government support, they are liable to fall under the public action umbrella. For those solicitous of the pluralism and independence of civil society, the concern is that groups and associations are liable to become artifacts of public policy.

5. From Patron to Partner

Recent developments in the United States and elsewhere pose a more radical challenge to the boundaries we have been tracing: "third party government" (Salamon 1995). The range of activities described as government-civil society partnerships is exhaustive, from drug rehabilitation centers and housing to social welfare. The scale and scope of direct grants and contracts is remarkable, made more so by the fact that these collaborations extend to the core activities of government. In addition to subsidizing the independent social and charitable activities of civil society groups, government increasingly contracts with these groups for everything from corrections, welfare provision, education, and job training to basic public services and inherently governmental functions such as emergency relief and military training and logistics (Minow 2009).

Policies about partnerships vary across countries, of course. Some countries have competitive bidding among nonprofit groups for block grants to deliver services (Goodin 2003, 43), while others have historically organized their welfare states around religious "pillars," so that segmented pluralism is built into the provision of important services. Some governments reserve more activities for the public sector, though there is a general trend towards functional privatization (Verkuil 2009, 330–31). In the United States, the menu of arrangements by which associations supplement or substitute for direct government services is fluid. Indeed, "partnerships" is an inadequate description of this terrain, since the mix includes voluntary associations, contracts with for-profit enterprises, and private foundations (Minow 2003, 8). An example of this fluid mix is "charitable choice," instituted by the 1996 Welfare Reform Act, by which federal dollars go to an array of groups including religious associations that mix services with worship.

Influential rationales for such partnerships do not always propose that there are specific advantages to social provision by civil society groups. Rather, conservative ideologies of small government, a general loss of trust in government, and the perennial challenges of social provisioning, combine to argue for more devolution. From this standpoint, the services provided by civil society groups are the equivalent of those provided by government, but with the added advantages of cost-cutting, less government, and the presumed efficiency of a competitive market in services. Other advocates of government-civil society partnerships claim that the provision of services by civil society groups is better and more humane, not just less costly or more efficient. For one thing, voluntary associations are seen as answers to political corruption. For another, these groups are said to be more creative, flexible, and responsive. Supporters have faith in the fine-grained knowledge and sensitivity that such groups exhibit when defining needs and serving their clients. Whereas recipients of public services are often demeaned and disrespected, voluntary associations are said to be more attentive to human dignity. Moreover, precisely because of their partial, particularist nature, pervasively religious groups and secular groups with strong moral or ideological commitments are said to do a better job at education or drug rehabilitation, for example, though the evidence for this proposition is contested (Glenn 2000; Wuthnow 2004).

Critics alert us to the potential moral and democratic tradeoffs of these developments. They raise questions from both directions: about the potentially deleterious consequences of partnerships for the values of pluralism and partial association on the one side, and for democratic responsibility on the other. The overarching concern is a lack of democratic deliberation about the appropriate division of labor between government and civil society. It is one thing for voluntary arrangements to supplement the public definition and provision of basic needs and services, and another for government to step back from these democratic responsibilities. Accountability is one concern, famously difficult to achieve even when activities are performed by public agencies, much less when they are the work of a wide array of dispersed associations. The reasons are plain. Legal assurances of public access to information do not always apply to private actors. Moreover, to the extent that government delegates public purposes to civil society groups, these activities may be buffered from due process and other constraints that govern direct state action (Metzger 2009, 292). In broad terms, the standard means of accountability do not apply to civil society groups. Associations are not subject to elections or the constraints of business enterprises, and are not responsible to voters or shareholders. Scholars have argued that civil society associations have developed their own, distinctive accountability regimes: they are constrained by their unique motivation and altruistic mission, and by reputational concerns. Nonprofit groups tend to develop networks with other associations that share their purposes and monitor their conduct (Goodin 2003). Government partnerships can weaken this accountability framework without effectively replacing it with another.

Oversight and accountability for outcomes is only one difficulty with partnerships from the standpoint of democracy. Diffusion frustrates deliberate democratic decision making when it comes to public provision, if only because innumerable subsidies, grants, and contracts obscure the character and dimensions of publicly mandated activities and services. Also from the government standpoint, there is concern that provision by particularist associations dilutes citizens' rights and benefits. Public funding of health care delivered through Catholic hospitals, for example, "affects the availability of reproductive services and assisted technology, abortion, counseling for persons who are HIV positive...and end-of-life choices" (Minow 2003, 13). Without alternative public providers or a plurality of civil society groups, individuals are necessarily directed to particular religious or secular institutions for services. Pluralism and voluntarism—the promises of civil society—do not hold when government contracts with particular groups to address social needs.

Finally, there is the question of diminished government capacity as public activities and the definition of public objectives are transferred to civil society and for-profit groups. Partnerships can drain public agencies of expertise, management skills, and the ability to provide regular oversight. They reduce government's ability to undertake energetic action, mobilize resources, and define and address collective problems. And partnerships may be hard to reclaim, leading one scholar to propose an "antidevolution principle" (Verkuil 2009, 316).

A different set of considerations arises from the perspective of civil society. The chief concern is whether public purposes are displacing the plural, self-directed purposes of associations as these groups initiate or alter their activities in order to receive government grants and contracts. Originally designed to underwrite the charitable activities of churches and other voluntary associations, government contracts now provide not only incentives for certain activities but impose requirements for management, record-keeping, audits, and transparency. Associations, at least in theory, are required to meet public measures of performance and outcomes. They are moved directly or indirectly to adopt professional norms and to replace the work of members and donors with professional staff. These developments pose many challenges to associations that value privacy, hold themselves to different measures of success, and seek to fulfill nonstandard needs. Forces push in the direction of convergence towards bureaucracy or towards modeling activities after businesses or establishing their own for-profit enterprises. The growing popularity of social entrepreneurship captures this trend. The overriding concern is that large swaths of civil society will be colonized by government.

6. CONCLUSION

Insofar as public values follow public dollars, the latitude to opt out of government support is vital to avoid compromising the independent life of associations (Minow 2003, 142). That explains why some religious leaders in the United States have refused to participate in government-civil society partnerships. Associations may lose the will and capacity to engage in activities and provide goods that neither markets nor government take on, or can even imagine. At stake is the self-direction that is characteristic of civil society: expressing and enacting plural visions of value, articulating their own missions, agitating for their independent ideas about public democratic purposes, and acting as vocal critics of government. If one of the imperatives of separating civil society and government is the preservation of countervailing authority and power, do partnerships weaken that capacity? If one reason for the mix of partnerships is to divide and distribute power, are these increasingly complex arrangements weakening this purpose? (Novak 2009, 33). Social scientists have the obligation to describe and explain, and political theorists to conceptualize and justify, the new contours of plural and partial civil society on the one hand and democratic capacity and control on the other. Is their increasing interpenetration irreversible, and if so why and with what effects? What boundaries remain, or should remain, and why? If we think that "the value of association is as encompassing as the value of liberty," we must continue to analyze, justify, and monitor the changing boundaries between civil society and government (Post and Rosenblum 2002, 3).

REFERENCES

Armony, A. C. 2004. *The Dubious Link: Civic Engagement and Democratization.* Stanford Calif.: Stanford University Press.

Austin v. Michigan Chamber of Commerce, 494 U.S. 675 (1990).

Baynes, K. 2002. "A Critical Theory Perspective on Civil Society and the State," in Robert C. Post and Nancy L. Rosenblum (eds.) *Civil Society and Government.* Princeton N.J.: Princeton University Press, 123–45.

Benda, V. 1978. "The 'Parallel' Polis," in Gordon Skilling and Paul Wison (eds.) *Civic Freedom in Central Europe: Voices from Czechoslovakia.* London: Macmillan, 35–41.

Berman, S. 2003. "Islamism, Revolution, and Civil Society." *Perspectives on Politics* 1(2): 257–72.

Brennan, G., and P. Pettit. 2004. *The Economy of Esteem: An Essay on Civil and Political Society.* New York: Oxford University Press.

Chambers, S., and J. Kopstein. 2001. "Bad Civil Society." *Political Theory* 29(6): 837–65.

Dworkin, R. 1987. "What is Equality? Part 4: Political Equality." *University of San Francisco Law Review* 1(22): 1–30.

Encarnación, O. G. 2003. *The Myth of Civil Society: Social Capital and Democratic Consolidation in Spain and Brazil.* New York: Palgrave Macmillan.

Evans, S. M., and H. C. Boyte. 1992. *Free Spaces.* New York: Harper & Row.

Forment, C. 2003. *Democracy in Latin America: Civic Selfhood and Public Life in Mexico and Peru, 1760–1900.* Chicago: University of Chicago Press.

Galston, W. A. 2002. "Liberal Egalitarianism: A Family of Theories, Not a Single View," in Robert C. Post and Nancy Rosenblum (eds.) *Civil Society and Government.* Princeton, N.J.: Princeton University Press, 111–22.

Glenn, C. L. 2000. *The Ambiguous Embrace: Government and Faith-Based Schools and Social Agencies.* Princeton, N.J.: Princeton University Press.

Goodin, R. E. 2003. "Democratic Accountability: The Third Sector and All." Working Paper No. 19. Hauser Center for Nonprofit Organizations, Harvard University.

Gutmann, A., and D. Thompson. 2004. *Why Deliberative Democracy?* Princeton, N.J.: Princeton University Press.

Habermas, J. [1962] 1989. *The Structural Transformation of the Public Sphere: An Inquiry into a Category of Bourgeois Society.* Trans. Thomas Burger. Cambridge, Mass.: MIT Press.

——. 1992. "Further Reflections on the Public Sphere," in C. Calhoun (ed.) *Habermas and the Public Sphere.* Cambridge, Mass.: MIT Press, 453–56.

Howard, M. M. 2003. *The Weakness of Civil Society in Post-Communist Europe*. New York: Cambridge University Press.

Kelley, M. 2006. *Learning to Stand and Speak: Women, Education, and Public Life in America's Republic*. Chapel Hill: University of North Carolina Press.

Metzger, G. E. 2009. "Private Delegations, Due Process, and the Duty to Supervise," in J. Freeman and M. Minor (eds.) *Governing By Contract: Outsourcing and American Democracy*. Cambridge, Mass.: Harvard University Press, 291–309.

Minow, M. 2003. *Partners, Not Rivals: Privatization and the Public Good*. Boston: Beacon Press.

——. 2009. "Outsourcing Power: Privatizing Military Efforts and the Risks to Accountability, Professionalism, and Democracy," in J. Freeman and M. Minow (eds.) op. cit., 110–27.

Novak, W. J. 2009. "Public-Private Governance: A Historical Introduction." In J. Freeman and M. Minow (eds.), op. cit., 23–40.

Post, R. C., and N. L. Rosenblum. 2002. "Introduction," in R. C. Post and N. K. Rosenblum (eds.) *Civil Society and Government*. Princeton, N.J.: Princeton University Press, 1–25.

Rawls, J. 1993. *Political Liberalism*. New York: Columbia University Press.

Rosenblum, N. L. 1998. *Membership and Morals: The Personal Uses of Pluralism in America*. Princeton, N.J.: Princeton University Press.

——. 2000. "Introduction," in N. Rosenblum (ed.) *Obligations of Citizenship and Demands of Faith*. Princeton, N.J.: Princeton University Press, 3–31.

Salamon, L. M. 1995. *Partners in Public Service: Government-Nonprofit Relations in the Modern Welfare State*. Baltimore: Johns Hopkins University Press.

Skocpol, T. 2003. *Diminished Democracy: From Membership to Management in American Civic Life*. Norman: University of Oklahoma Press.

Verkuil, P. R. 2009. "Outsourcing and the Duty to Govern," in J. Freeman and M. Minow (eds.) op. cit., 310–34.

Walzer, M. 2004. *Politics and Passion: Towards a More Egalitarian Liberalism*. New Haven, Conn.: Yale University Press.

Warren, M. E. 2009. "Exit-Based Empowerment in Democratic Theory." Paper presented at Political Ethics Working Group, American Political Science Association, September 3–6, 2009, in Toronto, Ontario, Canada.

Wuthnow, R. 2004. *Saving America? Faith Based Services and the Future of Civil Society*. Princeton, N.J.: Princeton University Press.

CHAPTER 24

CIVIL SOCIETY AND CIVIL LIBERTIES

MARK SIDEL

THE spaces of civil society provide the arenas in which "citizens engage with each other in the public sphere, argue and deliberate about the issues of the day, build consensus around the future direction of their societies, and participate in democracy, governance and dialogic politics" (Edwards 2009, 64). But the state governs those spaces, expanding and restricting them over time according to the interests, systems, parties, and individuals in power. In some countries, the mechanisms for such control rely solely on the raw exercise of state or party authority, but in most nations, the law is a key mechanism for regulating the spaces in which civil society functions. This chapter outlines some of the recent problems that civil societies have faced, both in dealing with their own liberties to operate and in representing and advocating for the broader liberties of citizens.

Democratic states, broadly defined, impose some constraints on the spaces, rights, and liberties of civil society and civil society organizations, but those constraints tend to be functional in nature. Democratic states may regulate widely on civil society, including such topics as the extent of advocacy activities by some kinds of civil society groups as a condition for providing them with tax incentives, or the extent to which organizations may engage in business activities without paying tax. Direct and highly controlling restraints on social and political advocacy by civil society organizations are less common in democratic states, and they tend to be couched in terms of restrictions applicable to individuals and groups throughout society rather than focused on a defined set of civil society, nonprofit, charitable or other groups. But there are times when the spaces, rights, and liberties of civil society groups are directly threatened in democratic societies, and such episodes can be serious. The destruction of nonprofit organizations in the United States and the silencing of nonviolent advocacy under McCarthyism during the 1950s was one such moment, a time of exceptional challenge both for the organizations that came under attack and because of the chilling effect it exercised on a wide range of nonprofit, charitable, academic, advocacy and other groups throughout American society (Cole 2003). Some developments in the United States and the United Kingdom since September 11, 2001 also raise these concerns, particularly the overbroad regulation of terrorist financing, overseas grant making, and statutes that criminalize providing some kinds of support to or on behalf of groups that a government has defined as a "terrorist" organization.

Constraints on the space for civil society in democratic states have followed a pattern of broad restrictions on a wide range of organizations and direct restrictions on a small number of groups, with widening ripples of chilling effects on a broader range of associations and their activities. But in democratic states, civil society can fight back through the legal and policy process. In undemocratic states, the situation can be far more serious, because such states can raise and lower restrictions on civil society at their discretion, carefully calibrating the space accorded to different types of organization, the work they do, and the needs of the state or ruling party. China and Vietnam illustrate this pattern of strong, direct, highly discretionary, and widely encompassing restrictions in undemocratic states on the space and freedom accorded to civil society groups.

1. The Dangers of Prosecution and Overregulation: Restricting Civil Society in the United States

These themes have emerged with particular force since the September 11, 2001 terrorist attacks on the United States. Direct restrictions have been placed on the rights and freedom of action available to a relatively small group of civil society organizations through a highly contested process that, in one important case, has reached the U.S. Supreme Court, focused on the question of how laws can criminalize the provision of certain forms of support such as humanitarian assistance, political advocacy, or distributing literature to or on behalf of groups that a government has defined as a "terrorist" organization.[1] These restrictions and other steps taken by the U.S. government have, at times, had a chilling effect on some activities carried out by the nonprofit sector (Sidel 2008, 2009a).

For the vast majority of American nonprofits and foundations, the primary impact of counterterrorism law and policy since September 11 has been the need for enhanced information gathering on partner organizations, including checks against government watch lists and the collection of "nonterror certifications"; and the shifting of risks for compliance downwards to the recipients of funds or to local affiliates of federated groups. For a minority of American organizations, however, counterterrorism law and policy has had an even greater effect. Some of the largest Muslim charities in the United States have been closed since 2001, their assets frozen, and in some cases the organizations and their leaders charged with material support for terrorism because of suspicion of their links with partner organizations in conflict areas overseas. The impact has also been felt directly by American public charities and foundations that work or make grants overseas, perhaps most acutely by organizations working in conflict areas where extremist groups and militant organizations operate. In a broad sense, the American nonprofit sector has sought to maintain its autonomy and vibrancy while agreeing and acceding to the government's interest in preventing nonprofit organizations from being conduits for terrorist finance or otherwise supporting terrorist organizations or their goals (Sidel 2009a; Guinane and Sazawal 2009).

The proscription and freezing of assets of several Muslim foundations on grounds of material support for terrorist organizations, and the attempt to promulgate new "voluntary" regulations governing the work of American organizations abroad, have been the most important regulatory actions in this area (Chesney 2005; Cole 2003; Crimm 2004). But the chilling effects of these measures went further than the letter of the law, as was their intent. These effects included the addition of unindicted "co-conspirator" organizations onto a government list that included many well-known and well-respected Muslim groups; civil actions against Muslim foundations; concerns in the American Muslim community about the impact of donating funds to organizations that might come under U.S. government scrutiny; and the impact of the Anti-Terrorist Financing Guidelines: Voluntary Best Practices for U.S.-based Charities that were issued by the U.S. Treasury in 2002.[2]

These guidelines provided a detailed range of new provisions for charitable and philanthropic organizations to use in their overseas giving that were intended to prevent the channeling or diversion of American funds to terrorist organizations or purposes. They included the collection of considerably more information about recipient organizations than is often available, the vetting of grantees, and the extensive review of their financial operations way beyond accepted voluntary sector norms. These guidelines were significant to the U.S. nonprofit sector because, although they were voluntary, nonprofit organizations faced considerable risks of being investigated and prosecuted for failing to carry out the required due diligence. In the words of Barnett Baron, Executive Vice President of the Asia Foundation, the 2002 treasury guidelines carried the danger of "setting potentially unachievable due diligence requirements for international grant-making, [and] subjecting international grant-makers to high but largely undefined levels of legal risk, [which] could have the effect of reducing the already low level of legitimate international grant making" (Baron 2004). Legitimate charities struggled to comply with the standards, while less professional or less well-intentioned groups could just ignore them.

However, measures with a narrow direct impact and a broad chilling effect can also spur opposition, and the guidelines did precisely that, provoking a widespread response by charities and foundations that were engaged in overseas giving who demanded their withdrawal or substantial improvement, while also proposing their own Principles of International Charity, a new self-regulatory approach to ensuring that charitable funds did not find their way to terrorists.[3] Partly in response to that opposition, the U.S. Treasury revised its guidelines in 2005 and 2006, but these changes did not satisfy the nonprofit sector. In 2007 the Treasury Department added a "risk matrix" for charitable institutions to use in connection with their overseas giving, also without consulting civil society groups themselves.[4] By 2009, civil society and the Treasury Department were at an impasse, with nonprofits refusing to recognize the legitimacy of the Anti-Terrorist Financing Guidelines, and the Treasury refusing to allow the Principles of International Charity to supplant them. In 2010, the new administration of President Barack Obama quietly opened discussions with representatives of the American nonprofit sector in an attempt to begin bridging some of these policy differences.

In practice, however, nonprofit fundraising and program activities had already begun to narrow, in part in response to concerns over U.S. government policies. Increasingly, overseas giving institutions were moving to a risk-shifting and risk analysis perspective in their activities, in line with the approach of the treasury's guidelines. The impact of government regulation was felt by prominent American foundations that were already concerned about potential investigations of their grant making by the U.S. government. For them, the stakes were high. Several of these organizations, most prominently the Ford and Rockefeller Foundations, responded by shifting responsibility to their grantees for terrorism-related risks through new language in their grant contracts. Ford introduced new language in 2003 that required grantees to promise not to "promote or engage in violence, terrorism, bigotry or the destruction of any State, nor ... make subgrants to any entity that engages in these activities." This new language prompted initial opposition from a group of elite universities and, for a time, from the American Civil Liberties Union who decided not to accept new funds from Ford (Sherman 2006; Sidel 2007). In 2007, a prominent Indian nongovernmental organization (NGO) also raised this issue with the Ford Foundation, requesting modification of the foundation's grant letter to restrict the very broad limitations to which it would have bound grantees.

In other cases, the American nonprofit sector has beaten back legal changes that would have restricted civil society advocacy and other activities. One example was an attempt in 2004 by the U.S. government agency that operates the Combined Federal Campaign (CFC), through which hundreds of thousands of federal employees donate to nonprofit organizations, requiring each nonprofit that receives CFC funds to investigate its own employees in order to certify that it "does not knowingly employ individuals or contribute funds to organizations found on the ... terrorist related lists promulgated by the U.S. Government, the United Nations, or the European Union' (Combined Federal Campaign 2003). This new requirement ignited a firestorm of opposition from the wide range of groups that received CFC funding. Eventually the American Civil Liberties Union and a number of other organizations filed suit against the federal government to overturn the new certification requirements (*New York Times* 2004; *Washington Post* 2004), and in November 2005 the federal government withdrew them (*New York Times* 2005).

The shifting of risk to recipient organizations goes even further than these examples suggest. In recent years, a number of local branches of the United Way in the United States have required that each nonprofit organization that receives funds—down to the smallest and most local charitable group—certifies that it complies with all anti-terrorist financing laws and regulations; that individuals or organizations that the organization works with are not on any government terrorism watch lists; and that no material support or resources are being provided to support or fund terrorism in any shape or form. In another example, it became clear in 2005 and 2006 that government surveillance of nonprofit organizations in the United States went far beyond the small number of Muslim charities and other groups that were suspected of direct terrorist ties. The American media revealed that the U.S. government had targeted a much broader swath of the nonprofit sector for observation. Hundreds of nonprofits have had their events monitored, their telephone calls logged, and their financial transactions examined by government agencies (*Washington Post* 2006).

In 2007, press reports indicated that the U.S. government was using software to search, track, and correlate donors to an undefined range of nonprofit organizations (*Los Angeles Times* 2007), and new reports emerged in 2007 and 2008 around government surveillance of nonprofits, particularly advocacy organizations, in several U.S. states. The *New York Times* and the New York Civil Liberties Union revealed in 2007 that the New York City Police Department had conducted surveillance on advocacy groups in at least thirteen states, as well as in Canada and Europe, before the 2004 Republican National Convention (*New York Times* 2007). In Maryland, the police and other security forces at the state and city level conducted surveillance on, and infiltrated, anti-war, anti-capital punishment and other nonprofit organizations in 2005 and 2006, with reports sent to "at least seven federal, state, and local law enforcement agencies" (ACLU of Maryland, 2008; Guinane and Sazawal 2009).

2. The Advantages of Quasi-Independent Regulation and Monitoring: Regulating Civil Society in the United Kingdom

British law also allows for the proscription of terrorist organizations and support for their meetings and other activities, bans fundraising and funding arrangements for "purposes of terrorism," and prohibits retention or control of "terrorist property," among other provisions (NCVO 2007). However, there are differences in the American and British approaches that offer useful lessons for the future in reducing the potential chilling effect of these restrictions on civil society. In particular,

Britain's approach to shutting off terrorist finance through charities relies in significant measure on charity regulators as "first responders," rather than simply shifting risks to recipients. The independent statutory regulator of charities in England and Wales is the Charity Commission, which has been at the forefront of charity-related terrorism financing investigations since before September 11, and which has played a key role in investigating, resolving, and where necessary collaborating in prosecuting ties between charities, terrorism and terrorist finance, while emphasizing the need for evidence and fairness in all such proceedings. The commission's central role was reaffirmed under the new Charities Act of 2006.

The Charity Commission's approach has been effective because of its wide investigatory and enforcement powers and its detailed understanding of developments in the U.K. charitable sector. In addition, the commission has had an array of means at its disposal to deal with failures to abide by the law, ranging from technical assistance and advice to, where needed, orders that can remove trustees, freeze funds, or close organizations, in partnership with security forces and prosecutors. Differences between the American and British approaches have emerged in several key cases. After the September 11 attacks, the U.S. government alleged that Interpal, a charity operating in both the United States and the United Kingdom, was supporting the political and/or violent activities of Hamas. After the U.S. government formally named Interpal as a "specially designated global terrorist" organization and proscribed its activities in the United States, the Charity Commission opened a formal inquiry and froze Interpal's accounts. The commission also requested "evidence to support the allegations made against Interpal" from the American government, but, according to a limited report from the commission, the U.S. government was "unable to provide evidence to support allegations made against Interpal within the agreed timescale." After the U.S. government failed to deliver the evidence, the commission decided that, "in the absence of any clear evidence showing Interpal had links to Hamas' political or violent militant activities," Interpal's accounts would be unfrozen and the commission's inquiry closed. Although the United States and the United Kingdom diverged publicly on Interpal, the inquiry also enabled the Charity Commission to reassert that it will "deal with any allegation of potential links between a charity and terrorist activity as an immediate priority...liais[ing] closely with relevant intelligence, security and law enforcement agencies to facilitate a thorough investigation." The Commission also re-emphasized that "as an independent statutory regulator the Commission will make its own decisions on the law and facts of the case" (Charity Commission 2003).

The July 2005 terrorist bombings in London and charges that other British-based charities were linked with terrorism brought renewed pressure to clamp down on terrorist networks and their financing. In February 2006, the then-chancellor of the exchequer, Gordon Brown, announced that the U.K. Government would review measures to combat the use of charities in terrorist finance and establish a new intelligence centre to investigate terrorist financing networks around the world and their impact on Great Britain (*The Guardian* 2006).

Increasingly, however, American officials and commentators were critical of the process-based British approach, calling the Charity Commission and other British institutions too lax (*New York Times* 2006). Sharper measures were announced in late 2006, when the British government said it would "use classified intelligence to freeze assets of those suspected of having links to terrorism," "allow law enforcement agencies to keep their sources of information secret after it is used to track down and freeze bank accounts," and seek pre-emptive authority to halt terrorist financing. These and other hardening moves came under criticism in a report from the National Council of Voluntary Organizations (NCVO) in early 2007 entitled Security and Civil Society (2007). The report called on the government to view charities as allies in the fight against terrorism rather than as adversaries and pointed out the fundamental sufficiency of the existing legal regime. It criticized the impact of some government actions in this arena on charitable activities in the United Kingdom and abroad, particularly with respect to Muslim organizations.

The Home Office and Treasury review of charities and terrorist finance was released in May 2007, and it called for tighter coordination between the Charity Commission and government agencies dealing with terrorism and terrorist finance, a move by the commission to undertake more prosecutions, increased funding for investigations rather than improved governance in the sector, and other measures.[5] The response from the NCVO on the potential impact of these measures on civil society was swift and critical: "By placing a veil of suspicion over all charities, the Government is in danger of damaging the trusted reputation of the voluntary sector and making people less likely to donate to good causes."[6] The Charity Commission's response, considered and drafted very carefully, described plans to accelerate its work on terrorist finance and to strengthen coordination with government agencies, but in ways that would avoid too deep a chilling effect on the sector: "The way we tackle the risk of terrorist abuse of charities falls squarely within our existing approach to regulation; we are uniquely placed to deal with abuse where it does occur, collaborate with other regulators and agencies and other parts of government and support trustees to protect their charities; when allegations of terrorist involvement or links with charities arise, we deal with them as a matter of priority. We will deal proactively, robustly, effectively and swiftly when we have evidence or serious suspicions of terrorist abuse involving charities; effective regulation involves putting a strong emphasis on giving support and guidance to charities to prevent problems and abuse occurring in the first place; we believe that the most effective way for the sector to minimize its exposure to the risk of terrorist abuse is through implementing strong governance arrangements, financial management and partner management" (Charity Commission 2008). The Charity Commission's firm actions against the misuse of charitable groups while maintaining its independence and advising the sector on effective measures to avoid involvement with terrorism and associated criminal penalties, have been a contrast to the harsher, broader, and arguably less effective policies of the United States.

3. THE IMPERATIVE TO CONTROL: RESTRICTING CIVIL SOCIETY IN CHINA AND VIETNAM

In democratic states, civil society can fight back. In undemocratic states, the situation is far more serious, because such states can raise and lower restrictions on civil society virtually at their discretion, carefully calibrating the space accorded different types of organization, the work that they do, and the needs of the state or ruling party. China and Vietnam illustrate this pattern of strong, direct, highly discretionary, and widely encompassing restrictions on the space and freedom accorded to civil society groups. The mechanisms used to impose such restrictions are clear, and they echo the use of measures already deployed in democratic and semidemocratic states.

These mechanisms include direct restrictions on registration and the status of civil society groups; broad and discretionary prohibitions on the purposes for which groups can be formed, often without grounds for appeal or any administrative or judicial process; broad government discretion to dissolve, terminate, or take over offending institutions and their assets, often without effective grounds for appeal or due process; limited tax incentives for civil society organizations and high levels of government discretion in implementing tax policy, including limitations on advocacy, representation, and other groups that the government disfavors; limitations on fundraising and foreign funding, particularly for advocacy, public interest, and other disfavored groups; high spending requirements and limitations on permitted investments; and discretionary requirements for organizational governance, including a plethora of required government approvals.

In China, civil society and its accompanying regulatory framework have become considerably more complex in recent years. The range of nonprofit, philanthropic, and other social organizations has expanded rapidly, as have their fields of activity. At the same time, the management of the emerging civil society sector by the Communist Party and state agencies remains exceptionally robust, highly discretionary and reactive, and extremely effective in controlling the organizations that the state seeks to control. Some social organizations are managed relatively lightly, including a significant number that provide social services or conduct other work that the state supports and that are not perceived as threats. But advocacy, religious, and policy-oriented groups are much more heavily managed and controlled by the authorities. In some cases, organizations have been closed and civil society activists have been detained, tried, and imprisoned for their activities.

The legal framework required to manage this highly differentiated process of state control has its origins in China's 1982 constitution and in an array of regulatory documents promulgated and enacted since the late 1980s. These documents regulate the full range of social organizations in China, including associations, often referred to as social organizations (*shehui tuanti*), foundations (*jijinhui*), civil non-enterprise institutions (*minban fei qiye danwei*), and quasi-governmental public institution (*shiye danwei*). Under the Chinese Constitution, particularly Article 35, freedom of association is guaranteed, at least in textual form. In practice, however, laws, regulations, and policies belie that broad constitutional freedom. The party retains strong authority and wide discretion to control the registration, activities, governance, fundraising, and voice of each kind of civil society group. In particular, the government erects strong, high, and discretionary barriers to entry based in policy, practice, and regulation. Registration procedures are complex and cumbersome, with extensive documentation and approval requirements. Many social organizations therefore operate without formal registration, making them even more vulnerable to state discretion and control.

Broad prohibition clauses bar the registration of groups that are perceived to oppose the state and/or the party, or challenge traditional customs. Barriers to operational activities are detailed and can be raised or lowered by the authorities at their discretion, depending in large part on which specific organizations are regarded as "oppositional" or "contributory." But even for registered organizations that have no significant issues with the state, registration, reporting and other requirements can be quite burdensome, particularly for small organizations. The regulatory framework allows for significant government intervention and interference and state security forces intensively monitor organizations of particular sensitivity to the party and the state. The enforcement of such rules can quickly halt the activities of disfavored groups, which are usually advocacy and public interest organizations, and send a clear, chilling message to other organizations that social services and related activities are the favored work that civil society groups should undertake (ICNL 2010).

One recent example is the case of the Open Constitution Initiative (*Gongmeng*), which provided public interest and civil rights advocacy support to a range of citizens and organizations in Beijing, including the investigation of major scandals such as the distribution of tainted milk in which dozens of children died. When the Chinese government decided to close the Open Constitution Initiative in 2009, it began by using nonprofit tax regulations and leveled a fine of 1.42 million Chinese yuan against the organization for tax evasion. Then the Initiative was raided by the civil authority responsible for nonprofit organizations, the Beijing Civil Affairs Bureau, which formally closed the office, while the organization's leaders were detained by security forces.[7] This tripartite use of civil affairs, security, and tax authorities in a coordinated set of actions killed off an important advocacy organization within days, while also sending a strong message to other advocacy, public interest, and representational groups around China to be cautious in their activities (Chinese Human Rights Defenders 2009). Other forms of civil society activity can be dealt with in even more summary fashion, including through the detention or trial of persons who sign petitions calling for more rapid political reform (such as Charter 08),[8] or those who criticized corruption in the building of schools in Sichuan province, a contributing factor in the deaths of many children after the 2008 Wenchuan earthquake.[9]

A similar range of methods is used in Vietnam, where efforts to enact a national law on associations foundered in 2005 and 2006, partly because of concerns from the party and the government that such a law could codify more expansive rights for civil society groups that might eventually come to threaten party control (Sidel 2009b). What remains in place is a strict 2003 decree on the organization, operation, and management of associations that severely limits the organization and activities of civil society groups and provides the government with wide discretion to challenge organizations, especially those undertaking advocacy and public interest representation. That decree provides for a long and complex process of organizational formation (thereby discouraging most organizations from forming); broad prohibition clauses barring a wide range of activities and maintaining exceptionally wide party and government discretion over associations; highly detailed organizational requirements and approvals for a wide range of organizational changes including board and staff; restrictions on branches and on bank accounts; retention of the traditional "dual master" or "dual management" system of associational governance by the state in which groups are controlled both by specialized line ministries as well as by a dedicated agency; and limits on advocacy in relation to the party and government policies that restrict "advice and criticism [to] matters within the association's scope of activities." In short, the 2003 Decree on Associations is a document to retain state control and send a strong message to civil society groups: that they should not challenge the party or the state.

Attempts to relax these restrictions have thus far failed, initially during an abortive attempt to adopt a broader law on associations in 2005 and 2006. Concerned with the potential impact of the law, the widespread debate that was occurring at the time on civil society regulation, and the role of NGOs in the "color revolutions" of eastern and central Europe, the law's progress towards passage was shut down by the party in 2006 (Sidel and Vasavakul 2006). The government continued to use older regulations both as a weapon and a message to the wider array of newly formed charitable and nonprofit groups in Vietnam. In particular, in 2009 the government closed a policy advocacy group, the Vietnam Institute of Development Studies (VIDS), which had angered some in the party and in government for its wide-ranging discussions of development alternatives and its commentaries on government policy (BBC 2009).

This closure was accomplished by an administrative regulation directed specifically against the institute, but with the clear implication that a line had been crossed for others. To reinforce the point, a list was included in the administrative regulation prohibiting policy and advocacy work in economic policy, public policy, political issues, and a range of other sensitive areas. According to the decision, "organizations "may only conduct activities within the areas under the List promulgated with this Decision. If they have views (*phan bien*) on the line, guidelines, or policies of the party or the state those views must be provided to party or state agencies with jurisdiction over such issues, and may not be released publicly."[10]

4. Conclusion

Every society provides some form of regulation, some restrictions or constraints, on the role of civil society and its organizations. The space provided by the state can differ dramatically from country to country, and is obviously more restricted in nondemocratic regimes, but it will not do to discuss the constraints on civil society in one-party states alone. Every government restricts civil society to one degree or another, and even in more democratic states there are times when those restrictions can have a significant impact. The decade following September 11, 2001 was one such time, especially in the United States and the United Kingdom, where enhanced government regulation has directly inhibited the activities and operations of a small number of organizations, and had a chilling effect on civil society as a whole in terms of the range of activities and innovations that organizations and foundations have been willing to fund or undertake. Elsewhere, states deploy severe restrictions on the space available to nonprofits not only in times of crisis but on an ongoing basis, seeking to mold a civil society that serves the state's needs for social service provision while discouraging—and at times even seeking to eradicate—advocacy, public interest lobbying, and other challenging activities. Both paradigms are at work across the world, and both serve to restrict the spaces of civil society which are essential to the prospects of democracy and social justice.

What should governments do to strengthen the role of civil society organizations under the law, while also maintaining a level of regulation appropriate to prevent the use of such groups for terrorist purposes (or as participants in terrorism); for fraud, or for other goals that states rightfully find unacceptable? Democratic states need to avoid overly broad and overly limiting rules that seek to restrict, channel, or excessively regulate some forms of conduct (such as overseas grants, or fundraising in Muslim communities), in the hope that actual criminal violations, which are much more rare, will be deterred by such restrictions. Nonprofits and civil society organizations are not the enemy of the state. In nondemocratic states, governments are clearly and intentionally focused on restricting the role of civil society groups through legal and political means. Where feasible, outside donors, foundations, governments, and NGOs should work with such states to help them recognize the benefits of civil society and the importance of guaranteeing nonprofit groups the freedoms that many of these states already enshrine in their laws and constitutions. But opening up to a broader role for civil society—particularly for advocacy, representative, and policy-focused groups—is a lengthy process that depends primarily on domestic developments. Helping such states with carefully drafted laws and policies that achieve a workable and gradually expanding balance between rights and responsibilities may bear fruit even in restrictive contexts.

NOTES

1. For more detailed information on this important case, *Holder v. Humanitarian Law Project*, see http://www.scotuswiki.com/index.php?title=Holder_v._Humanitarian_Law _Project.

2. For the revised version of the guidelines, see www.treas.gov/offices/enforcement/ keyissues/protecting/charities-intro.shtml.

3. See the Principles of International Charity at www.independentsector.org/ programs/gr/ CharityPrinciples.pdf.

4. For the treasury's risk matrix, see www.treas.gov/offices/enforcement/ofac/policy/ charity_risk_matrix.pdf.

5. The Home Office and Treasury Review is available at www.homeoffice.gov.uk/ documents/cons-2007-protectingcharities/Charities_consultation.pdf?view=Binary.

6. See NCVO, "Overstating the risk of terrorist abuse could damage trust in charities," available at http://politics.co.uk.

7. Among many newspaper and other reports on the Gongmeng closure, see Wong, 2009.

8. See, for example, articles in the *New York Times* on April 30 and December 24, 2009.

9. See *New York Times* 2010.

10. Decision 97 of the Prime Minister (97/2009/QĐ-TTg) Promulgating the List of Areas in which Individuals are Permitted to Form Science and Technology Organizations; Vietnamese text available at http://www.dost.hochiminhcity.gov.vn/web/data/ vanban/151/97-2009-QD-TTg.pdf(passage translated by Mark Sidel).

REFERENCES

Baron, B. 2004. "Deterring Donors: Anti-Terrorist Financing Rules and American Philanthropy." *International Journal of Not-for-Profit Law* 6(2): 1–32.

BBC. 2009. "New Law Closes Vietnam Think Tank." *BBC News*, September 15, 2009.

Charity Commission. 2003. *Inquiry Report: Palestinians Relief and Development Fund.* London: Charity Commission.

———. 2008. *Charity Commission Counter-Terrorism Strategy.* London: Charity Commission.

Chesney, R. 2005. "The Sleeper Scenario: Terrorism-Support Laws and the Demands of Prevention." *Harvard Journal on Legislation* 42(1): 1–89.

Chinese Human Rights Defenders. 2009. "Reining in Civil Society: The Chinese Government's Use of Laws and Regulations to Persecute Freedom of Association." Available at http://chrdnet.org/wp-content/uploads/2009/10/final.pdf, accessed January 16, 2011.

Cole, D. 2003. "The New McCarthyism: Repeating History in the War on Terrorism." *Harvard Civil Rights: Civil Liberties Law Review* 38(1): 17–30.

Combined Federal Campaign. 2003. "Combined Federal Campaign Memorandum 2003–10, New Certification for 2004 CFC Application." Available at http://www.opm

.gov/cfc/opmmemos/2003/2003-10.asp. Washington, D.C.: U.S. Office of Personnel Management.[11]

Crimm, N. 2004. "High Alert: The Government's War on the Financing of Terrorism and its Implications for Donors, Domestic Charitable Organizations, and Global Philanthropy." *William and Mary Law Review* 45(4): 1341–451.

Edwards, M. 2009. *Civil Society.* 2nd ed. Cambridge: Polity Press.

The Guardian. 2006. "Modern-Day Bletchley Park to Tackle Terror Finance Networks." February 11.

Guinane, K., and S. Sazawal. 2009. "Counter-terrorism Measures and the NGO Section in the USA: A Hostile Environment," in J. Howell and J. Lind (eds.) *Civil Society under Strain: Counter-terrorism Policy, Civil Society and Aid Post-9/11.* West Hartford, Conn.: Kumarian Press.

International Center for Not-for-Profit Law (ICNL) and World Movement for Democracy. 2008. *Defending Civil Society.* Washington, D.C.: International Center for Not-for-Profit Law and World Movement for Democracy.

International Center for Not-for-Profit Law (ICNL). 2010. "NGO Law Monitor – China Country Report." Available at http://www.icnl.org/knowledge/ngolawmonitor/.

Los Angeles Times. 2007. "Anti-Terrorism Program Mines IRS Records; Privacy Advocates are Concerned that Tax Data and Other Information May Be Used Improperly." January 15.

National Council of Voluntary Organizations. 2007. *Security and Civil Society.* London: National Council of Voluntary Organizations.

New York Times. 2009. "A Manifesto on Freedom Sets China's Persecution Machinery in Motion." April 30.

———. 2009. "Leading China Dissident Gets 11-Year Term for Subversion." December 24.

———. 2010. "Editor Reviewing China Quake Deaths is Sentenced." February 9.

Sherman, S. 2006. "Target Ford." *The Nation,* June 5.

Sidel, M. 2007. *More Secure, Less Free?: Antiterrorism Policy and Civil Liberties after September 11.* Ann Arbor: University of Michigan Press.

Sidel, M. 2008. "Counter-Terrorism and the Enabling Legal and Political Environment for Civil Society: A Comparative Analysis of 'War on Terror' States." *International Journal of Not-for-Profit Law* 10(3): 7–49.

———. 2009a. *Regulation of the Voluntary Sector: Freedom and Security in an Era of Uncertainty.* New York: Routledge.

———. 2009b. "Maintaining Control: Recent Developments in Nonprofit Law and Regulation in Vietnam." Report, December. Washington, D.C.: International Center for Not-for-Profit Law.

Sidel, M., and T. Vasavakul. 2006. "Report to the Vietnam Union of Science and Technology Associations (VUSTA) on the draft Law on Associations." Hanoi: Vietnam Union of Science and Technology Assocations.

Washington Post. 2006. "Surveillance Net Yields Few Suspects." February 5.

Wong, Edward. 2009. "China Shuts Down Office of Volunteer Lawyers." *New York Times,* July 17.

CHAPTER 25

CIVIL SOCIETY AND THE PUBLIC SPHERE

CRAIG CALHOUN

THE value of a public sphere rooted in civil society rests on three core claims: first, that there are matters of concern important to all citizens and to the organization of their lives together; second, that through dialogue, debate, and cultural creativity, citizens might identify good approaches to these matters of public concern; and third, that states and other powerful organizations might be organized to serve the collective interests of ordinary people—the public—rather than state power as such, purely traditional values, or the personal interests of rulers and elites. These claims have become central to modern thinking about democracy and about politics, culture, and society more generally.

Theories of the public sphere developed alongside both the modern state with its powerful administrative apparatus and the modern capitalist economy with its equally powerful capacity to expand wealth but also inequalities, tendencies to crisis, and intensified exploitation of nature and people. The public sphere represented the possibility of subjecting each of these new forces to greater collective choice and guidance. New media for communication have been important to this project, starting with print and literacy and extending through newspapers and broadcast media to the Internet and beyond.

This approach to public communication grew partly on the basis of active public debate in the realms of science (Ezrahi 1990), religion (Zaret 2000), and literature (Habermas 1962; Hohendahl 1982). Debates in these other spheres demonstrated that the public use of reason could be effective and schooled citizens in the practices of public communication. At the same time, this emerging notion of society treated the happiness and prosperity of ordinary people as a legitimate public concern—unlike Greek thought, in which such matters were treated as mere private necessity.

Classical republican thought was influential, with its emphases on the moral obligation of citizens to provide public leadership and service, and on the importance of
the public matters—*res publica*—that bound citizens to each other (Pocock 1975;
Weintraub and Kumar 1997).

Thinking about public life was also transformed by the rise of what by the eighteenth century was called civil society. This meant society distinct from the state,
organized ideally as a realm of liberty, with freedom of religion, association, business activity, conversation, and the press. The promise of civil society was that social
life could be self-organizing, even in complex, large-scale societies, and that it could
thereby be more free than if left to government officials or to technical experts. The
idea of the public sphere was crucial to hopes for democracy. It connected civil
society and the state through the principle that public understanding could inform
the design and administration of state institutions to serve the interests of all citizens. Obviously these ideals are imperfectly realized, and some of these imperfec-
tions reflect tensions built into the very starting points of civil society thinking. As
Hegel (1821) suggested, civil society reflects a struggle to reconcile individual self-
interest with the achievement of an ethical community. And while the ideal of the
public sphere holds that all participants speak as equals, the reality is that inequality
and domination constantly distort collective communication.

1. Five Visions of Civil Society

The first and most basic notion of civil society comes from urban sociability. People
interact, exchange goods or ideas, and form relationships, and especially in cities,
they are sociable with strangers. Social life is not restricted to family and kin, or to
neighbors, or to members of a single church. It reaches across the boundaries of different zones of private life to include those with whom there are no prior definitions
of mutuality or dependency. A cousin you have not met is still family, but the person
sitting next to you in the theater is very likely not. And during the early modern era
there were more and more such public spaces where people mixed with each other—
not just theaters but market places, coffee houses, streets, and squares. Urban life was
basic to the Renaissance, along with a renewed engagement with classical culture
which itself celebrated urban life: the Greek polis or Rome itself. But early modern
cities quickly surpassed their classical forebears in the extent to which they brought
strangers together. The London of Shakespeare and Elizabeth I was a vital node in
networks of culture, finance, and markets for goods and the movement of people.

Medieval cities had traditions of self-governance, notably through guilds of
craftsmen and merchants. They organized social life with some autonomy from the
feudal hierarchy. Likewise, though they were hierarchical and associated with the
church, medieval universities were generally urban sites of self-governance and
sociability among strangers as they attracted students and scholars from different

regions. Perhaps most importantly, the idea of self-government by communication among approximate equals, with respect for expertise not just inherited rank, was basic to the republican ideals of thinkers like Machiavelli (1513). John Locke (1690) extended this idea of society forged by lateral communication—initially mainly among elites—beyond its urban roots. But cities remained vital exemplars of the capacity for social self-organization. They drew ever-larger populations of strangers, people of diverse backgrounds and occupations, into interaction that required only a minimum of formal governance.

On a second account, the significance of markets shifted from physical spaces of direct interaction to larger-scale systems of exchange. This remained compatible, however, with the idea that freedom is maximized and the collective good achieved by relying as much as possible on individual choices, minimizing the role of government, of large-scale organizations, and of collective action. Adam Smith (1776) famously championed this view, though recent invocations of his name commonly offer caricatures of his theory. Markets, he held, made social self-organization possible not only by advancing exchange, reconciling supply and demand, and connecting those with different assets and needs, but also by leading individuals to serve the collective welfare—the wealth of nations—by producing to meet needs as efficiently as possible, and selling at prices set by the effort of each to buy cheap and sell dear. Markets thus produced a moral benefit by creating a collective good out of even self-interested individual action; in Bernard de Mandeville's (1714) phrase, markets made private vices into public virtues. For Smith, however, this only worked so long as all market actors were truly individuals, subject to the conditioning of market forces. Both joint-stock corporations and trade unions should be banned as constraints on trade that undermined the morality and psychological conditioning of markets. Absent such distortions, markets offered the public benefits of both wealth and the circulation of goods. Moreover, for Smith markets demonstrated that civil society could be self-organizing and operate by its own implicit laws rather than state governance or intervention (though Smith recognized that states were crucial for a variety of purposes where markets performed poorly). However, although markets translated private choices in potential public benefits, they did not in themselves provide the mechanism for self-conscious public choices.

On a third account, civil society is a matter of collective choice, but not government. The collective good is best achieved by the direct action of ordinary people organized in groups and associations (Edwards 2009). Civil society, in this view, is a matter of churches, charities, voluntary associations, and self-help movements. It is an arena in which people can do things for themselves and meet the needs of their fellow citizens. Here, freedom is not limited to individual choices in relation to markets, but also realized in collective, voluntary efforts. Neighbors may form an association to provide mutual security—a neighborhood watch—or to manage collective resources such as park or recreation facilities. Residents of a town or a country may collect funds and volunteer labor for purposes that are public insofar as they aim to advance a broader good than the sum of their selfish interests—for example, by providing food for the poor, running a recycling program, or supporting a public radio station. They may organize a social movement to try to persuade their fellow citizens that it would be in the public interest to take better care of the environment, or reduce poverty, or end a war. Of course, other citizens may believe the public interest lies in oil drilling not recycling, in the incentives that come with inequality, or in waging war. In this view, the essence of freedom lies in the right of people to form such self-organized efforts, with a presumption that where these are not in harmony with each other they will at least each be limited by respect for the others. What distinguishes civil society from the state in this view is pluralism and the absence of any master plan for progress.

A fourth view of civil society suggests that it is at best incomplete without a state to secure cohesion and provide a mechanism for concerted public action. While early theories of civil society generally emphasized its distinction from the state, most also saw the two as necessarily complementary and closely connected. The state gave society its form, even if civil society produced most of its internal web of relationships. The state offered laws that were enabling for civil society, providing a framework for the contracts central to market relationships and the judgments that balanced the agendas and interests of different actors in civil society—those who want more parks, for example, with those who want more housing or more job-creating industries. Some, notably Hegel, stressed the extent to which the state constituted society as an integrated whole, greater than the sum of its parts. This meant overcoming the "bifurcation" between family life, which he saw as guided by universal ethics but integrating only at the level of personal relations, and markets, which he recognized could be more general in their reach, but were based on particularistic self-interest. This distinction became basic to theories of social integration that contrasted the directly interpersonal relationships of family, community, and voluntary association to the impersonal and large-scale systems of market transactions. Without the state, on such a view, the market basis of civil society would always be disruptive to forms of social integration like the family, and would always be insulated from ethics by precisely the automatic, systemic character that Adam Smith celebrated as its invisible hand—good for generating wealth, but not social integration or justice.

The fifth view of civil society focuses on culture. A key eighteenth-century pioneer was Montesquieu (1748) who emphasized not just laws but the "spirit" that lay behind laws and mediated among the material conditions in different societies, the interests of individuals, and the institutions they formed. Montesquieu's specific ideas about how this mediation works are today followed less than his more general argument that laws and other conscious measures to organize social relations depend on the culture in which they are situated (Alexander 2006). At about the same time, David Hume (1739–40) developed an influential argument that keeping promises depends not just on good intentions—say at the moment a contract is signed—and cannot be explained simply by reference to nature (since human nature is all too compatible with evading obligations). Rather, promises and contracts are honored because failure to honor them is subject to widespread disapproval based not just on instrumental interests but on cultural traditions and norms. Moreover, the expectation of disapproval (or conversely respect as someone who honors his obligations) is not just a matter of conscious calculation but internalized into habit. To say "I promise" is thus a performative action that is only intelligible against a background of common culture that both recognizes what a promise means and provides for appropriate reinforcement—which in turn makes promise-keeping habitual most of the time and prudent when people think consciously about it. Culture is thus crucial to the capacity for agreements among individuals that is important to other conceptions of civil society. Culture also links the members of a society. This need not mean only a lowest common denominator of cultural uniformity; it may mean overlapping fields of cultural participation. Common religion may connect speakers of different languages (or vice versa). A shared business culture may connect people from different political cultures or with different musical tastes and so forth. Importantly, culture is not simply a matter of inheritance but of continued creativity, and processes of reproduction incorporate novelty, allow some practices to fade, and shift patterns of meaning—as languages add and lose words and adapt to new contexts.

Smith's account of the market was complemented, for Hume and for Edmund Burke, by the notion that there was another kind of invisible hand of historical trial and error that preserved useful customs and let others fade. More radical thinkers like Rousseau challenged this idea of cultural selection just as Marx would challenge Smith's account of markets. But each held that relations of power and property both kept practices in place that were not conducive to the public good, and drove cultural change in ways that served specific interests. Antonio Gramsci (1929–35) made the analysis of hegemonic culture basic to a theory of civil society. Society is held together not only by markets, formal agreements, and the power of the state but by common culture that underwrites consent. As Gramsci suggested, of course, hegemonic culture can also be contested. Thinking about nature as resources to be exploited may be dominant in a capitalist society but it is not impossible for Christians to contest this by expounding a view of nature as a gift of God demanding stewardship. The very organization of civil society is also shaped by culture. As Benedict Anderson (1983) has shown, we would be less likely to conceive of society as "nation" absent representations in novels, in museums, and on maps. Charles Taylor (2004) calls attention to modern social imaginaries like voting that depend on a cultural notion of what actions mean and what to expect of others, or the market as it is represented in the news and treated as a kind of collective reality. Similarly, the place and even reality of a business corporation depends on its cultural recognition, not just on laws or contracts.

2. THE IMPORTANCE OF THE PUBLIC SPHERE

Some eighteenth and nineteenth century writers argued that, contrary to Adam Smith and Edmund Burke, the visible hand of the state was better suited to providing public benefits than either the invisible hand of the market or cultural tradition that changed only incrementally, and mostly unconsciously. Jeremy Bentham (1789) founded utilitarianism on the notion that the greatest good of the greatest number depended on wise laws effectively administered. While some laws should provide for the vitality and liberty of civil society—for example by guaranteeing freedom of the press—others should put state administration to work in improving society. Bentham was a pioneer in both prison and educational reform. Over the ensuing centuries, states have been called on to build highways, run schools and health care systems, and generally advance the welfare of citizens. But there is recurrent public debate over what should be managed by states and what by markets or charities.

The public sphere is crucial to identifying the public good and to shaping both public and private strategies for pursuing it. This is not a matter of critical argumentation alone; it is also a matter of public culture that is shaped by creative and communicative processes as well as debate. Environmental discourse, for example, addresses the market choices of individuals, nongovernmental organizations developing alternative energy sources, and government agencies—and it addresses each with mixtures of rational-critical debate, attempts to change culture through art, and demonstrations of solidarity and commitment. To engage such questions, individuals refer not only to their private interests but also to ideas about the public good.

The scope given to the public sphere is smallest in the market-centered idea of civil society. Choices are made by individuals and connect to each other through markets, which have their own logics like supply and demand. But though these are in principle individual decisions, they are nonetheless influenced by public communication, such as advertising, and by the tastes and customs of specific communities and social groups. Such social influences on decisions can extend to ideas of the public good, like buying environment-friendly products or avoiding pollution. Markets themselves operate on the basis of public institutions and public knowledge—for example, publishing their financial results so that investors can make informed decisions. Of course, there are various ways in which the government may intervene to try to make markets perform for the public good: forming a central bank to insure financial stability, for example, or passing laws making bribery illegal.

The public sphere is also important where civil society is seen mainly in terms of the direct action of citizens—organized informally in communities or more formally in voluntary associations. Public communication shapes which civil society organizations are formed, from health clinics to Girl Scout troops, and what issues they address, from poverty to the environment. Not only do issues go in or out of fashion, the very forms and strategies of civil society organizations are matters of public knowledge, circulating in the media and first-hand reports, and offering a repertoire of models to each new organizing effort. Public discussion is also vital to evaluating the extent to which different civil society organizations or social movements do in fact serve the public good.

Urban sociability and public culture each evoke a public life that is not specifically political. Urban public spaces anchor face-to-face interaction, and promote serendipitous contact—and simple visibility—among people of diverse backgrounds.

Many of Europe's cities, especially older ones, were distinctive in their pedestrian character and their scale. Both suburbanization and larger-scale urban designs have changed the character of public interaction. Sennett (1977) argues that where eighteenth- and nineteenth-century urban life was vibrant and highly varied, twentieth-century development often reduced occasions for interaction across lines of difference. Citizens retreated into both privacy and the conformity of mass culture. This has negative implications for democracy. As Mumford (1938, 483) wrote, "One of the difficulties in the way of political association is that we have not provided it with the necessary physical organs of existence: we have failed to provide the necessary sites, the necessary buildings, the necessary halls, rooms, meeting places." As directly interpersonal relations organize proportionately less of public life, mediations of various kinds become increasingly important (Thompson 1995). The nineteenth and early twentieth centuries were the heyday of great urban newspapers; since then, media that transcend locality have become increasingly important. First radio and then television fundamentally altered the public sphere. They contributed to a shift in what was publicly visible as well as in how public discourse was organized (Meyrowitz 1985). New media shared both information and emotionally powerful images widely. Critics charged broadcast media with debasing reason by substituting powerful images for sustained analysis, appealing to a lowest common denominator in audiences, blurring the lines between entertainment and critical discourse, and centralizing control over messages in the hands of a few corporations. At the same time, however, formations of public culture expanded dramatically, stretching across the boundaries of nation-states. With films, music, and new media, public culture is increasingly global, though no version of it is universal. Much of it is centrally consumed as entertainment, but some also puts issues like human rights or humanitarian emergencies onto the public agenda.

The public sphere takes on its most specifically political import when civil society is seen as centrally related to the state. Whether the issue is waging war or financing health care or strengthening education, public discussion is the way in which ordinary citizens gain knowledge, form opinions, and express them— potentially influencing the state. Obviously some of these citizens have more knowledge than others; some have access to media platforms that give them greater influence. And some citizens grow quickly bored by political arguments and change their TV channel. Public discourse reflects the inequalities of civil society, but it also, at least potentially, compensates for them. Its very openness is an invitation to all citizens and a recognition that the opinions and emotions of citizens matter. As Hannah Arendt emphasized, politics includes not just petty struggles over power but public action that forms enduring institutions like the U.S. Constitution. Affirming the classical republican tradition, she suggested that it was a strange trend that treated civil society first and foremost as a realm of freedom *from* politics rather than freedom *in* politics, "to understand by political freedom not a political phenomenon, but on the contrary, the more or less free range of nonpolitical activities which a given body politic will permit and guarantee to those who constitute it" (1990, 30).

3. THE IDEAL OF PUBLICNESS

Without a vital public sphere, civil society is not inherently democratic. Certainly civil society organizations are not always constituted in democratic ways. They are usually more accountable to those who pay for them and work in them than to the general public. Nor do civil society organizations always pursue the public good, even by their own potentially competing definitions. While some are philanthropic in the sense that they exist to provide benefits to those who are neither members nor backers, others focus on serving specific interests—those of business groups, for example, or those of neighborhoods that use private security services to maintain their exclusivity. Many, like private clubs, simply serve their members. Only some civil society organizations exist mainly to serve public purposes. These include social movements that campaign on broad agendas like equal rights for women; service organizations that provide benefits for strangers like soup kitchens or homeless shelters; political parties, charitable foundations, and public information services. Only some work primarily in public ways, however, making their internal operations transparent and open, and inviting strangers to join. Many organizations in civil society take on what they regard as public purposes but remain "in-groups" of people knit together by personal relationships. Publics, by contrasts, are forged in sociability and communication among strangers (Warner 2001).

The public sphere is public first and foremost because it is open to all, not only in the sense that all can see and hear but also that all can participate and have a voice. In any modern large-scale society, this means that the public sphere is a matter of communications and other connections among strangers as well as among those networked by old school ties, church membership, or community. One may talk about politics or issues like climate change inside the family, but this becomes a public conversation only when it is open to, and informed by, others. This may happen in face-to-face meetings but also by reading newspapers or websites, by writing a blog or calling a talk radio show. A protest march is part of public communication—it is an effort to make a statement and show that many people are behind it. So is a petition. But publicness is not just a matter of large numbers. It is a matter of openness. Writing an article in a small journal still counts: it is available to strangers and through them may inform further conversations.

Although openness is basic to the ideology and theory of the public sphere, various forms of exclusion are basic to actually existing publics. Gender exclusion has been widespread, even in the ostensible golden age of the public sphere (Landes 1988; Ryan 1992). A state religion may exclude nonbelievers from public life, or a secular public sphere may limit the expression of religious views in public. Workers were largely excluded from the classical public sphere that Habermas analyzed (Calhoun 2010). Immigrants may be in a similar position today. Those who are excluded, or who disagree with the dominant organization of the public sphere, often build their own media and networks of communication and with them a counterpublic. Workers created a proletarian public sphere (Negt and Kluge 1972). The women's movement formed its own counterpublic and this enabled it to contest the terms of the hege-monic public sphere (Fraser 1992). Counterpublics challenge the apparent neutrality of more mainstream publics and reveal that hegemonic public culture reflects power relations, but as Warner (2001) suggests, claiming unfair treatment in the public sphere is a strategy, and one even powerful groups deploy.

Not all public communication is about weighty matters of politics or institu-tions. To the frustration of some, there may be more debate over the Academy Awards than over public policy. Such opinions may not matter much for the fate of democracy, but an open space in which to express and contest opinions does. Any effort to police the boundary between opinions that matter and those that don't potentially restricts the public sphere and political freedom. This is one reason why the United States and other constitutions protect free speech and freedom of expres-sion as such, and why limits on such freedoms—say, to restrict public obscenity—are serious and consequential matters. Some have argued, for example, that because family matters are essentially private, issues like spousal violence should not be on the public agenda. This view has changed for some publics but not all.

Not only must it always be possible for people to raise new issues or challenge dominant opinions, it must be possible for people to gain the information they need for informed discussion. This lies behind arguments for transparency in gov-ernment and business dealings, and also conflicts over censorship of the Internet, like that by the Chinese government. Chinese civil society is more and more active in response; and this brings greater public communication as well as state efforts to limit it (Yang 2009). Some matters of national security or trade secrets might legiti-mately by kept out of the public view, but for the public sphere to work effectively on behalf of democracy and citizens' rights to shape their own societies, it is impor-tant that information be accessible. A government that does not make it easy for citizens to get access to data it collects is trying to limit democracy by limiting pub-lic communication. Of course, the public sphere is limited not just by official secrets but also by lazy citizens. The ideal of publicness stresses active communication. In this sense it is at odds with reducing public opinion to the answers of separate indi-viduals to questions on opinion polls (Splichal 2000). Charles Horton Cooley (1909) argued that this debased the notion of public opinion, which ought to be conceived as "no mere aggregate of individual opinions, but a genuine social product, a result of communication and reciprocal influence."

The public sphere matters most for democracy to the extent that it is able to identify and constitute agreement about the public good and motivate people to seek it together. On Habermas's account, public opinion matters because it is achieved by reasoned, critical debate. But how to ensure that communication would be rational and critical is unclear. Hannah Arendt (1958) theorized "public" in terms of creative action, the making of a world shared among citizens, and saw the found-ing of the United States as a crucial example. Habermas idealized eighteenth-century English parliamentarianism, newspapers, and coffee house conversation. He pre-sented the public sphere as a realm of civil society in which private citizens could communicate openly about matters of public concern, transcending their particular statuses and addressing the state without becoming part of it. Such ide-alization commonly underwrites narratives of decline. In Habermas's classic *Structural Transformation of the Public Sphere*, for example, nineteenth- and twentieth-century public discourse is analyzed in terms of the loss of rational-critical capacity that followed the expansion of scale and the rise of public relations management that incorporated the public into the realm of administered society. Schudson (1998) has accordingly cautioned against such golden age concepts, argu-ing that the ideal of the good citizen as an active participant in the public sphere has long been contrasted with the failings of actual citizens.

Walter Lippman (1960) famously argued that most of the time citizens failed to educate themselves in public debate, and the effusions of opinion called forth in times of excitement were not to be trusted. John Dewey (1927) defended the capac-ity for reason in large-scale communication, arguing that participating in public argument was itself educative. As Iris Marion Young (2000) argued, the inclusion of diverse people in public discourse is not only an entitlement of membership in a democratic polity but also a tool for improving the quality of that discourse. Yet Young also calls attention to the extent to which reliance on sophisticated reasoning in public debates privileges the sophisticated. And democratic participation in the public sphere is not only a matter of rational-critical argumentation but of oppor-tunities to participate in shaping the formation of public culture.

Debates and institutions are public in their substance insofar as they extend beyond the simple sum of private interests to the fabric of shared concerns and interdependent processes that enable citizens to live together and pursue common projects. The topic can be banal. Traffic regulations, for example, affect each of us in our private efforts to get from home to work or to a stadium for a sports event. Where we drive our cars is primarily a matter of our private interests. But both the building of roads and the establishment of rules, including which side of the road to drive on, are matters of public interest. We cannot accomplish our private goals without public investments and public decisions; moreover, roads literally connect us to each other. In a democracy therefore, speed limits, fuel efficiency, and pollution controls are not merely technical decisions for transportation experts; they are matters of debate among citizens. The same goes for the infrastructure of communication in electronic media—or for that matter, whether to continue a war or create a national health care system.

In the nineteenth century, much political thought emphasized the fragility and limitations of the liberal democratic conception of the public. Tocqueville (1840, 1844), most famously, argued that the democratization of society tended to elimi-nate the *intermediary* public bodies that traditionally refined opinion and furnished individuals with a collective social identity outside the state. Engaged, politicized publics composed of distinct views and interests could be reshaped over time into mass publics—passive, conformist, and atomized before the state. Tocqueville's fear of the unmediated state would resonate with generations of critics of mass society. In a similar way, Arendt (1972, 232) suggested, also speaking of America, "since the country is too big for all of us to come together and determine our fate, we need a number of public spaces within it."

This issue comes even more clearly into the forefront as one considers civil society and the public sphere on a transnational scale. The globalization of civil society has created both connections among distant people and issues that cannot be resolved readily in national public spheres. Much of this is a matter of market structures that are seldom subjected to collective choice. Flows of goods, information, and people often linked global cities as much to each other as to their national hinterlands. More of public culture is transnational, and more voluntary organizations purse transnational agendas. Yet national states retain most of the capacity to act on public concerns, and they remain crucial arenas in which public discourse can influence public power.

4. CONCLUSION

A vibrant public sphere is the dimension of civil society most essential to democracy. It helps to constitute the *demos* itself—"the people"—as a collectivity able to guide its own future. The public sphere works by communication, combining cultural creativity, the selective appropriation of tradition, and reasoned debate to inform its members and potentially to influence states and other institutions. The public sphere is vibrant to the extent that engagement is lively, diverse, and innovative; its value is reduced when it is passive, or when it simply reacts to government actions or failures, or when mutually informing communication is sacrificed to the mere aggregation of private opinions.

Public communication does not simply flow in an undifferentiated fashion. Whether at a national or a transnational level, a public sphere is composed of multiple partially overlapping publics and counterpublics. These bring forward different conceptions of the public good and sometimes of the larger, inclusive public itself. They may be judged by their openness, creativity, or success in bringing reason to bear on public issues. The stakes lie in the double question of to what extent social life can be self-organizing, and to what extent social self-organization can be achieved by free human action. The public sphere is vital to that possible freedom, and to its exercise in pursuit of the public good.

REFERENCES

Alexander, J. C. 2006. *The Civic Sphere.* New York: Oxford University Press.
Anderson, B. 1983. *Imagined Communities.* (rev. ed. 2006). London: Verso.
Arendt, H. 1958. *The Human Condition.* Chicago: University of Chicago Press.
——. 1972. *Crises of the Republic.* New York: Harcourt Brace.
——. 1990. *On Revolution.* New York: Penguin.

Bentham, J. [1789] 1988. *An Introduction to the Principles of Morals and Legislation.* Amherst, N.Y.: Prometheus Books.

Calhoun, C. 2010. "The Public Sphere in the Field of Power." *Social Science History* 34(2): 301–35.

———., ed. 1992. *Habermas and the Public Sphere.* Cambridge, Mass.: MIT Press.

Cooley, C. H. 1909. *Social Organization: A Study of the Larger Mind.* New York: Scribner's.

Dewey, J. 1927. *The Public and its Problems.* Columbus: Ohio State University Press.

Edwards, M. 2009. *Civil Society.* 2nd ed.. Cambridge: Polity.

Ezrahi, Y. 1990. *The Descent of Icarus: Science and the Transformation of Contemporary Democracy.* Cambridge, Mass.: Harvard University Press.

Fraser, N. 1992. "Rethinking the Public Sphere: A Contribution to the Critique of Actually Existing Democracy," in Craig Calhoun (ed.) *Habermas and the Public Sphere.* Cambridge, Mass.: MIT Press, 109–42.

Gramsci, A. [1929–35] 1991–2007. *Prison Notebooks.* 3 vols. New York: Columbia University Press.

Habermas, J. [1962] 1991. *The Structural Transformation of the Bourgeois Public Sphere: An Inquiry into a Category of Bourgeois Society.* Trans. Thomas Burger. Cambridge, Mass.: MIT Press.

Hegel, G. W. F. 1821. *The Philosophy of Right.* Trans. T.M. Knox. Chicago: University of Chicago Press.

Hohendahl, P. U. 1982. *The Institution of Criticism.* Ithaca, N.Y.: Cornell University Press.

Hume, D. [1739/40] 1975. *A Treatise of Human Nature.* Oxford: Clarendon Press.

Landes, J. 1988. *Women and the Public Sphere in the Age of the French Revolution.* Ithaca, N.Y.: Cornell University Press.

Lippman, W. 1960. *Public Opinion.* New York: Macmillan.

Locke, J. [1690] 1980. *Second Discourse on Civil Government.* Indianapolis, Ind.: Hackett.

Machiavelli, N. [1513] 1975. *The Discourses.* London: Penguin.

Mandeville, B. de. [1714] 1997. *The Fable of the Bees: And Other Writings.* Ed. E. J. Hundert. Indianapolis: Hackett Publishing Company.

Meyrowitz, J. 1985. *No Sense of Place.* New York: Oxford.

Montesquieu, C. de. [1748] 1989. *The Spirit of the Laws.* Ed. A. M. Cohler, B. C. Miller, and H. S. Stone. Cambridge: Cambridge University Press.

Mumford, L. 1938. *The Culture of Cities.* London: Secker and Warburg.

Negt, O. and A. Kluge. [1972] 1993: *The Public Sphere and Experience.* Minneapolis: University of Minnesota Press.

Pocock, J. G. A. 1975. *The Machiavellian Moment.* Princeton, N.J.: Princeton University Press.

Ryan, M. 1992. "Women and Public Access," in C. Calhoun (ed.) op. cit. Cambridge, Mass.: MIT Press, 259–88.

Schudson, M. 1998. *The Good Citizen: A History of American Civic Life.* New York: The Free Press.

Sennett, R. 1977. *The Fall of Public Man.* New York: Knopf.

Smith, A. [1776] 1981. *On the Wealth of Nations.* Harmondsworth: Penguin.

Splichal, S. 2000. "Defining Public Opinion in History," in H. Hardt and S. Splichal (eds.) *Ferdinand Toennies on Public Opinion.* London: Rowman and Littlefield, 11–48.

Taylor, C. 2004. *Modern Social Imaginaries.* Durham, N.C.: Duke University Press.

Thompson, J. 1995. *Media and Modernity.* Stanford, Calif.: Stanford University Press.

Tocqueville, A. de. [1840, 1844] 1961. *Democracy in America.* New York: Scribners.

Warner, M. 2001. *Publics and Counterpublics.* Cambridge, Mass.: Zone Books.

Weintraub, J. and K. Kumar (eds.). 1997. *Public and Private in Thought and Practice.* Chicago: University of Chicago Press.

Yang, G. 2009. *The Power of the Internet in China.* New York: Columbia University Press.

Young, I. M. 2000. *Inclusion and Democracy.* Oxford: Oxford University Press.

Zaret, D. 2000. *Origins of Democratic Culture: Printing, Petitions, and the Public Sphere in Early Modern England.* Princeton, N.J.: Princeton University Press.

CHAPTER 26

....

CIVIL SOCIETY
AND PUBLIC WORK

....

HARRY C. BOYTE

WHEN civil society reappeared in democratic theory in the 1970s and 1980s, the concept of "space" was emblazoned on banners of sweeping social movements. Civil society formed a liberated zone from which to mount challenges to authoritarian governments—what Frances Hagopian called "the monster state"—in Eastern Europe, Latin America, Africa, Asia, and elsewhere. As Hagopian put it, "Horizontal solidarities in civil society challenged a corporatist state...in such a way that expanded the scope of freedom" (2006, 17). Today, civil society retains some of that aura of political freedom as a space for uncoerced civic agency in a world where manipulative techniques infiltrate every corner.

In continuing recognition of this history, theorists as diverse as Benjamin Barber and Jürgen Habermas see civil society as the citizen space. Barber, a powerful critic of "thin democracy" and an activist organizer of international connections among participatory democrats, created the definition of civic engagement that became dominant in the United States. Civil society, according to Barber (1995, 7), includes "those domains Americans occupy when they are engaged neither in government (voting, serving on juries, paying taxes) nor in commerce (working, producing, shopping, consuming)." His book *A Place for Us: How to Make Society Civil and Democracy Strong* (1998) developed this view, arguing that work is disappearing before the advance of technology and the market and proposing that the voluntary sector is the home for democracy. In this home, community service with civic reflection is the way to cultivate the identity of citizen as alternative to "producer" and "consumer." Barber also has strongly advocated for deliberative practices.

Habermas, a founding figure in deliberative democracy, has long sought to establish the theoretical grounds for a public sphere of communicative rationality rooted in civil society that separates deliberation from the entanglements of corporations and government bureaucracies (1998). In his view, civil society is "an open and inclusive network of overlapping, sub-cultural publics having fluid temporal, social and substantive boundaries." Though civil society is more vulnerable to inequalities than government, "it also is more open to new communicative insights" (1998, 307, 308).

In this chapter I argue that there are two very different ideas of civic agency embedded in the recent history of civil society, corresponding to different concepts of the citizen and civic education. They point towards very different approaches to change. The concept of civil society as a home for the deliberative citizen (and the related idea of volunteer service) has gained currency as an alternative to the rancor and fragmentation which are the stock-in-trade of public culture. In this usage, civil society is the place where people learn to be "civil," and in the process gain what is called "communicative power." As Fung and Wright (2001, 31) put it, "Through practice individuals might become better deliberators. By seeing that cooperation mediated through reasonable deliberation yields benefits not accessible through adversarial methods, participants might increase their disposition to be reasonable, and to transform narrowly self-interested preferences accordingly."

Deliberation is worthwhile, but the deliberative citizen is too narrow a conception of civic agency to make much change. Specifically, it cannot stem the metastasizing consumer culture which accompanies radical privatization. Deliberative theorists make the mistake of separating citizenship from work, or productive activity, paid or unpaid, that builds the common world as well as private goods. In so doing they remove from the civic animus its most important resource. In contrast, the concept of the citizen as a co-creator of democracy, understood as a way of life built through the public work of citizens, holds far more potential to challenge consumerism, to rebuild the commonwealth, and to develop robust civic identities. Public work, by which I mean sustained efforts by a mix of people who make the commons, or things of lasting civic value, puts the citizen at the center of public creation. As citizens create a commonwealth of public goods, they become a commonwealth of citizens. To take seriously developing the capacities of the citizen as co-creator requires theorizing the public dimensions of work, the capacities of civic agents to undertake it, and how and where they develop such capacities. Schools of civic agency understood as co-creative public work can be called "free spaces."

In this chapter, I outline the profound challenges that face democracy against the onslaught of a spreading consumer culture, detail the limits of civil society and the deliberative citizen, and argue that we need a different concept of civic agency and where it is developed.

1. DISMANTLING THE COMMONWEALTH

Commonwealth ideals once radiated across American politics and society (Boyte 1989), creating a vision of democracy as a way of life. In various formulations including the "cooperative commonwealth," the "maternal commonwealth," and the "commonwealth of freedom," the commonwealth was the idiom of choice for radicals and reformers, labor organizers, small farmers and business owners, suffragists and feminists, and those who struggled against racial bigotry and oppression. It challenged America in a prophetic voice to live up to its ideals.

An emphasis on the public dimensions of property drew from experiences of the "commons" such as grazing and pasture lands, streams, and forests for which whole communities had responsibilities, and in which they had rights of use. The commons also included public goods of general benefit built mainly through citizen labor, like schools, libraries, community centers, wells, roads, and bridges. For many immigrants, America represented a chance to recreate the commons that had been destroyed or privatized by elites in European societies (Bertoff 1982). Thus, Oscar and Mary Handlin used "commonwealth" to describe collaborative effort in Massachusetts: "For the farmers and seamen, for the fishermen, artisans and new merchants, commonwealth repeated the lessons they knew from the organization of churches and towns...the value of common action" (Handlin and Handlin 1969, 30). As the United States took shape after the American Revolution, the commonwealth approach continued in myriad forms of public work that was paid as well as unpaid.

Today, the attenuated qualities of the language of commonwealth make the term sound like a dusty museum piece. This declension highlights the erosions in civic life and in the civic identities of citizens. Consumer culture inculcates habits of what Barber calls "choice without consequence." As he put it, "Decades of privatization and marketization have obscured not only what it means to be a public...but also what it means to be free" (Barber 2006, 10). Studies document the damage wrought by the spread of the consumer culture into every corner of human experience. For instance, Susan Faludi describes the modern male condition in a consumer culture as like the "trapped housewife" of Betty Friedan (1963), experiencing an inchoate sense of lost identity and purpose hard even to name (1999). William Doherty details the spread of consumerism into marriages, transforming the concept of marriage as a life built over time in common, often through hardships and difficulties, into the idea of a search for consumer needs fulfillment (2001). Kerry Ann O'Meara (2007) has described the "striving culture" in higher education that turn students into customers and faculty into acquisitive awards-seekers. A recent World Bank study suggests that the utopian consumer images carried by the internet to rural youth in Thailand lure them away from supportive networks and communities into cities like Bangkok where they have few resources.[1] And as I have noted, "rural youth entering the cities with Playstation2 images of Laura Croft dancing in their heads may not be well equipped for the challenges that await them" (Boyte 2008, 212).

Habermas expresses concern about consumers' "privatistic retreat from the citizens' role" (1998, 78), but deliberative practices do little to halt the process. In fact, deliberation easily coexists with the consumer citizen, while separating those in government from their own citizenship. The problem is that civil society understood as the space of deliberative citizens severs the crucial connection between citizenship, and work.

2. THE DELIBERATIVE CITIZEN OF CIVIL SOCIETY

The western intellectual tradition of political theory conceives of public life as the democratization of aristocratic leisure, contrasting civic activity with work. As Barber (1998, 132) puts it, "To the Greeks, labor by itself defined only mere animal existence, while leisure was the condition for freedom, politics, and truly 'human' forms of being." Like the Greeks, Hannah Arendt (1958, 161–62) viewed work as part of the apolitical world. She saw "manual labor" as an undignified realm of necessity, "herd-like," while "work" was more creative and important, the activity of *homo faber*, or "man, the maker of things," the builder of the world. Yet Arendt still believed that work did not belong in the public arena of "deeds and action," and specifically of politics. She held that the worker's "public realm is the exchange market, where he can show the products of his hand and receive the esteem which is due him." Producers remained "private," or isolated: "*homo faber*, the builder of the world and the producer of things, can find his proper relationship to other people only by exchanging his products with theirs because these products themselves *are always produced in isolation*" (emphasis added). Arendt argues that the thought and manual art which produces craft—the creation of a "model" or idea in one's mind which one then reproduces through shaping materials of the world—necessarily requires isolation. Only apprentices and helpers are needed, she argued, in relations that are based on inequality.

Many civil society theorists follow Arendt in separating work from public life. Thus Cohen and Arato's *Civil Society and Political Theory* (1992, ix) took work off the map of civic engagement. Their book has democratic aspirations, but their idea of civil society, seeking to retain for the concept a critical edge, revised the classical notion of civil society as it descended from the Scottish Enlightenment and from Hegel, which *included* large institutions and commerce and *excluded* the family. Cohen and Arato argue for "a reconstruction [of the concept] involving a three-part model distinguishing civil society from both state and economy." They see this definition as the way to "underwrite the dramatic oppositional role of this concept under authoritarian regimes and to renew its critical potential under liberal democracies." Hence civil society becomes "a sphere of social interaction between economy and state, composed above all of the intimate sphere (especially the

family), the sphere of associations (especially voluntary associations), social movements, and forms of public communication."

Deliberative theorists draw on this map of civic space. Indeed, Habermas anticipated Cohen and Arato by decades in making a distinction between Greek democracy and contemporary circumstances in his classic work, *Transformation of the
Public Sphere* ([1962] 1989). For the Greeks, public judgment was conveyed by the
concept of *phronesis*, practical wisdom developed through public action around
common issues in the space of public life. For Habermas ([1962] 1989, 52), the public
sphere in the modern world is qualitatively different than that of the Greeks: "The
theme of the modern (in contrast to the ancient) public sphere shifted from the
properly political tasks of a citizenry acting in common (i.e., administration of law
as regards internal affairs and military survival as regards external affairs) to the
more properly civic tasks of a society engaged in critical public debate."

Habermas described a new deliberative role which emerged during the late
eighteenth and nineteenth centuries in a vibrant urban culture of debate and discussion, formed in a new spatial environment of lecture halls, museums, public
parks, theaters, meeting houses, opera houses, and cafes. In such social spaces, older
hierarchical principles of deference and ascribed social status gave way to public
principles of rational discourse. Emergent professional and business groups asserted
claims to a more general social and political leadership. In such spaces, patterns of
communication emerged that were characterized by norms of inclusivity, the give
and take of argument, and a relatively horizontal experience of interaction.
Arguments were judged by fit, by considerations of anticipated consequences, by
excellence of logic and so forth, not mainly by the social status of the speaker. By the
late eighteenth century or the beginning of the nineteenth (depending on the country), a public sphere grounded in civil society "was casting itself loose as a forum in
which the private people, come together to form a public, readied themselves to
compel public authority to legitimate itself before public opinion" (Habermas
[1962] 1989, 25–26).

In the late nineteenth century, Habermas argued, the public sphere atrophied as
the public began to break apart into myriad special interests. Technical and instrumental rationality replaced more interactive public dialogue. Technical rationality
depends upon a prior assumption of what the ends entail—how problems are
defined and what solutions are desirable—and concerns itself instead with the most
efficient means to reach them. After *Transformation of the Public Sphere*, Habermas
sought to sustain an enclave of "un-coercive interaction on the basis of communication free from domination" in theory and in practice (1971, 58). In this enclave he
hoped to "locate a gentle, but obstinate, a never silent although seldom redeemed
claim to reason, a claim that must be recognized de facto whenever and where ever
there is to be consensual action" (1979, 97). But his map separates citizens from the
work of actively building the commonwealth.

There is room for debate about the sharpness of distinctions between "communicative" and "practical" interests in Habermas's writings, but the general point
is clear. In *Between Facts and Norms,* he argued that the capacity of civil society "to

solve problems on its own is limited. The basic function of the public sphere is to move problems to the formal system" of politics and law-making. In the spaces of civil society, the goal should be "influence," not "power." Citizen efforts require translation into formal structures to amount to much: "Just like social power, political influence based on public opinion can be transformed into political power only through [formally authorized] institutionalized procedures." The power of citizens is sharply circumscribed, and Habermas asserts that "the public opinion that is worked up via democratic procedures into communicative power cannot 'rule' of itself but can only point the use of administration power in specific directions" (1998, 359, 362, 363, 300).

Civil society in such terms is the site for citizens who in their civic identities are separated from the work of those in government, the economy, or the professions. Like liberalism, Habermas said, "discourse theory...respects the boundaries between 'state' and 'society' but it distinguishes civil society." In particular, civil society in his view is the "social basis of the autonomous public sphere," distinct both from the economic system of markets and productive activity and from government. The strength of civil society is that it resists totalizing, technocratic impulses operative elsewhere. But its limits are also sharply drawn: "The success of deliberative politics depends not on a collectively acting citizenry but on the institutionalization of the corresponding procedures and conditions of communication, as well as the interplay of institutionalized deliberative processes with informally developed public opinions." For Habermas, there are clear "no trespass" signs; "democratic movements emerging from civil society must give up holistic aspirations to a self-organizing society... civil society can have at most an indirect effect on the self-transformation of the political system." He argues that "administrative power" is qualitatively and unalterably different than the space of civil society, and that "the administrative power deployed for purposes of social planning and supervision is not a suitable mechanism for fostering emancipated forms of life. These... cannot be *brought about* through [state] intervention [italics in original]" (1998, 299, 307, 308, 298, 372).

Dynamics which put citizens in the role of discussants *about* the common world, rather than active makers *of* it, correspond to formal distinctions in modern societies in which politics "belong" to the state system. In this theoretical frame, citizens have come to be consumers of the commonwealth, not its creators, even if the process raises some concerns. Thus the recent focus on "governance, not government" incorporates deliberative practices as a way to make government more responsive and interactive with citizens. This was a main theme in Fung and Wright's design principles drawn from case studies in what they called "empowered deliberative democracy," or EDD (2001). It is a major emphasis in approaches to governance promoted by the World Bank and other foreign aid groups around the world.

Deliberation by itself puts the citizen in the position of consumer. Government's role is to deliver services. Civil servants see themselves as outside the citizenry. This is a widely shared viewpoint far beyond the ranks of theorists. As Paul Light (quoted in Boyte and Kari 1996, 195) puts it, "Departments and agencies have plenty of advocates for doing things *for* citizens and *to* citizens, but there are almost no voices for seeing government workers as citizens themselves, working with other citizens." Politicians and government employees alike have psychologically removed themselves from being part of the citizenry. Yet deliberative and civil society theorists and others take conventional definitions of politics far too literally. Their arguments ignore the way "talk" is always connected to other processes of social reproduction. They slight the multiple ways in which constructions of the commonwealth can occur everywhere. Citizens need to be understood as at the center of the process if they are to care for a world created and shared in common. To offer an alternative to the deliberative citizen of civil society requires an alternative framework for thinking about civic spaces, the capacities and identities that are developed within them, and what it is that people do there.

3. WORKING THE WORLD IN PUBLIC WAYS

Cynthia Estlund (2000) has shown that work—understood as productive activity that makes things in the world—is a far more substantial way to bridge differences of "life worlds" than the search for truth and mutual understanding. She brings together a wealth of theoretical perspectives with a large body of social science research and examples from popular culture in order to remedy what she sees as the neglect of work and the workplace by communitarian and civil society theorists who focus on associational life.

Estlund makes a compelling case that, despite continuing patterns of hierarchy and discrimination, workplaces are still the only environments where most people are likely to have sustained encounters with people of differing racial, cultural, and ideological backgrounds. They also engage in such experiences with relative civility, and around practical, goal-directed tasks, making them relatively conducive to sustained experiences of collaboration. Her evidence shows that these features of work and workplaces enable people to develop enhanced respect for others, reduce their prejudices and stereotypes, build trust, develop civic skills, and create cross-group networks. Estlund observes that "it is not just the friendship potential of workplace relations that makes it a promising source of interracial contact." The work process itself "is generally cooperative and directed towards shared objectives; much of it is sustained, personal, informal, and one-to-one." Workplaces further democratic equality by "convening strangers from diverse backgrounds and inducing them to work together towards shared objectives under the aegis of the societally imposed equality principle" (2000, 25).

Estlund also shows how U.S. social movements such as union organizing efforts in the 1930s, the civil rights movement of the 1950s and 1960s, and the feminist movement of the 1970s and 1980s made the workplace more open and public. Thus, section seven of the Wagner Act, in part the product of New Deal reform and organizing, created "a kind of rudimentary system of civil liberties within the workplace" which in turn allowed further organization and action by workers. The equal protection of the law provision, enshrining in words "the notion that people should not be segregated or subordinated on the basis of their race or certain other immutable traits" was the result of civil rights efforts (Estlund, 85). Though the effort is not completed, it furthers democratic purposes.

Paying attention to work and the workplace raises questions of power, change, public creation, and social movements that are absent from conventional civil society theory. In particular emphasizing work in its public dimensions and possibilities has potential to reunite civic processes with civic consequences.

4. FREE SPACES AND CO-CREATION

Free spaces are the schools of democratic movements. The concept illuminates limits not only in deliberation but also in critical theory as conventionally developed. Modern critical theorists have posed the question of how can citizens, bemused by the socialization dynamics of modern capitalism, ever come to see themselves as other than free consumers, even though their apparent free choice itself functions to hide the oppressive relations of society? Karl Marx (1981–84) made the point about mystification—what he called false consciousness—in *The German Ideology*: "Thus, in imagination, individuals seem freer under the dominance of the bourgeoisie than before, because their conditions of life seem accidental: in reality, of course, they are less free, because they are more subject to the violence of things."

Prevailing intellectual fashions, updating such arguments in comparative and anticolonial terms and drawing on cultural theorists of power such as Frantz Fanon, Michel Foucault, and Claude Lévi-Strauss, focused on the ways in which cultural norms and practices operate in the spaces of everyday life to make oppressive assumptions seem normal and inevitable. Dominant cultural ideas, including those generated by the work of intellectuals themselves, shape, define, and circumscribe the life worlds and possibilities of ordinary people. For instance, the philosopher Rick Turner (Fluxman and Vale 2004) in South Africa observed how the apartheid system dramatized the "naturalization" of oppressive racial domination. Apartheid seemed self-evidently "the way things are" to whites and even to many blacks. Virtually every institution from family to church, from school to media, constantly reinforced white privilege and power.

Cultural theorists of power have brought important attention to previously invisible power dynamics. The problem is that when intellectuals develop a theory of what is to be done in response, they radically oversimplify the operations of cultural power. The result is a culturally estranged and alienated politics. Jean Paul Sartre's (Fluxman and Vale 2004) strategy of what he called "transcendence," or the act of standing outside prescribed roles and the commonplaces of culture with a sharply critical eye, can be taken as emblematic of the general stance of critical scholars. This stance is widely hostile towards rooted institutions such as religious congregations, ethnicity, family, and ties to place, as well as to the broader cultural traditions and symbols that constitute a sense of peoplehood. The view of liberated consciousness as a process of radical separation from roots and traditions was vividly summarized by Stanley Aronowitz in his essay titled, appropriately enough, "The Working Class: A Break with the Past" (1974, 312–13). According to Aronowitz, all particular identities of "race and nationality and sex and skill and industry" are obstacles to the development of genuinely oppositional, radical consciousness.

In contrast, a generation of social historians concerned with the actual development of popular movements—how it is that ordinary people, steeped in experiences of subordination, develop the courage and confidence to assert themselves and to become civic agents of their lives, not simply victims of larger social forces—has produced a rendering of the roots of democratic movements far more nuanced than the views of alienated intellectuals. Social history draws attention to the conflicted, contradictory quality of community settings and cultural traditions, full of oppositional currents, democratic elements, and insurgent themes as well as hierarchical and oppressive ones. Social historians richly describe the ways in which powerless groups draw inspiration from cultural elements that critical intellectuals write off as part of a monochromatically oppressive system.

Sara Evans and I, building on such history, have combined ideas of public space and freedom for democratic self-organization and co-creation in the concept of "free spaces" (1986, 1992). Free spaces, rooted in everyday life settings, are places in which powerless people have a measure of autonomy for self-organization and engagement with alternative ideas, and they are also places where people come to see themselves as makers of culture and producers of the world, not simply its consumers. Free spaces are places where people learn political and civic skills. They are also culture-creating spaces where people generate new ways of looking at the world. In free spaces, people simultaneously draw upon and rework symbols, ideas, themes, and values in their traditions and the culture to challenge conventional beliefs.

Thus, for instance, the historian E. P. Thompson in *The Making of the English Working Class* (1966) described places such as taverns and sectarian churches in which working people found space for intellectual life and democratic self organizations, separate from the gentry and the crown. Evans and I argued that free spaces also lay at the base of every broad democratic movement in American history, from the African American freedom struggle to the populist Farmers' Alliances of the 1880s, from labor struggles of the 1930s to feminist movements and modern community organizing. Such democratic movements show how complex are the power relationships of culture within and across societies.

Subterranean spaces for political agency and culture-making can be found even in settings that seem overwhelmingly oppressive. Thus, for instance, African American slaves in the American south found such spaces for self-definition and for insurgent cultural alternatives to conventional views of American democracy in the midst of extremely brutal circumstances. Christian religious services and practices were originally taught to slaves by slave owners in an effort to break their ties with their African roots and socialize them into passive, docile roles. Yet Christianity provided rich materials for strategies of everyday resistance (for instance, work songs and Gospel music) as well as far-ranging radical democratic visions of a transformed racial and political order. Martin Luther King and others built on this insurgent heritage to claim and transform definitions of American democracy, freedom, and citizenship.

Overlapping with civil society are qualities such as public space and freedom that are often found in voluntary and community settings. As the movements of the 1970s and 1980s illustrated, these can create seedbeds for democratic movements. In everyday community settings, people can find space for relatively uncoerced conversation, for self-organization, and for free intellectual life. Yet democratic movements arise to address patterns of power, not to find a home. Democratic movements subvert boundaries and cross categories. And they draw on the civic authority that comes from work.

5. DEMOCRATIC MOVEMENTS AND THE COMMONWEALTH

Free spaces often find hospitable ground in the life of communities and voluntary associations. But their qualities of freedom for self-organization, political education, and public co-creation are not the singular properties of community or voluntary groups. Nor is "volunteerism" or "deliberation" the best way to describe action within such spaces. Broad democratic movements incubate in diverse settings which people own, that have a measure of autonomy from dominant power, and that also have a public quality connecting people's efforts to the sense that they are helping to build a larger world. The concept of free spaces does not so much refute the idea of civil society as show its sharp limitations. Free spaces dramatize the necessity of bringing work into the equation. Throughout American history, democratic movements gained public power by drawing out the public dimensions of work. Such movements argued that the powerless, helping to "build the commonwealth," merit full recognition as citizens.

This claim was the central theme in the African American freedom movement. The civil rights movement built on the authority derived from making work visible and testifying to its strength and endurance. Cristina Beltrán has shown how the claim that "illegals" were "building America" was central to immigrant demonstrations in 2006 which called for reform in immigration laws (Beltrán 2009). Similarly, in women's history, women used claims based on their civic work (challenging the distinction between paid and unpaid) as the foundation for suffrage. Thus, Francis Willard, leader of the largest voluntary association of women in the nineteenth century, the Women's Christian Temperance Union, titled her book *The Work and Workers of the Women's Christian Temperance Union* (1972).

Free spaces reach beyond geographic communities through work and organizations associated with work. In the African American freedom struggle, for instance, groups like the Brotherhood of Sleeping Car Porters and community groups such as women's auxiliaries described in the study by Melinda Chateauwert, *Marching Together: Women of the Brotherhood of Sleeping Car Porters* (1997), sustained free spaces for political education and oppositional culture for generations. Free spaces are also foundations for the next wave of democracy-building.

6. Conclusion: The Democracy Movement of the Twenty-First Century

Commonwealth language has had particular power in the United States, where the concept of "commonwealth" has been widely used in democratic movements. But the commons, in fact, can be found in every society. Understanding of how common pool resources are sustained by citizen action and learning has advanced considerably through the theory-building of Elinor Ostrom and her colleagues at the Workshop in Political Theory and Policy Analysis, for which Ostrom shared the 2009 Nobel Prize in Economics (1990, 1999). Ostrom found that decentralized governance with high popular participation—what can be called productive activity that builds and takes care of the commonwealth—has key advantages in terms of efficiency, sustainability, and equity. These include the incorporation of local knowledge; greater involvement of those who are trustworthy and who respect principles of reciprocity; feedback on subtle changes in resources; better-adapted rules; lower enforcement costs; and redundancy, which decreases the likelihood of a system-wide failure. Ostrom argues persuasively for a mix of decentralized and general governance, what she calls "polycentric governance systems...where citizens are able to organize not just one but multiple governing authorities at different scales." Such mixed systems may be messy, but in studies of local economies, "messy polycentric systems significantly outperformed metropolitan areas served by a limited number of large-scale, unified governments" (Ostrom 1999, 37, 38, 40).

In shared governance a change in identifications and identities takes place. As people take care of the commons, they partly become the commonwealth they care for. There are multiple examples of growing attention to diverse forms of commons, from our common pool of knowledge to water resources, from public spaces to forests and fisheries.[2] The era of privatization requires a global movement to rebuild the commons, tied to skills, habits, and sensibilities of public work. Free spaces are the schools of such a movement. They are also the seedbeds of democratic hope.

NOTES

1. See http://www.digitaldivide.org/wp-content/uploads/2010/09/MBR2.0-broadband-Thailand-2015.pdf

2. The new commons movement is chronicled in websites such as On the Commons (www.onthecommons.org).

REFERENCES

Arendt, H. 1958. *The Human Condition.* Chicago: University of Chicago Press.

Aronowitz, S. 1974. "The Working Class: A Break with the Past," in C. Greer (ed.) *Divided Society: The Ethnic Experience in America.* New York: Basic Books.

Barber, B. R. 1995. "The Search for Civil Society." *The New Democrat* 7: 2–8.

——. 1998. *A Place for Us: How to Make Society Civil and Citizenship Strong.* New York: Hill and Wang.

——. 2006. "Civic Schizophrenia: The Free Consumer and the Free Citizen in a Free Market Society." *Kettering Review* 24: 10–21.

Beltran, C. 2009. "Going Public: Hannah Arendt, Immigrant Action, and the Space of Appearances." *Political Theory* 27: 596–622.

Bertoff, R. 1982. "Peasants and Artisans, Puritans and Republicans." *Journal of American History* 69: 579–98.

Boyte, H. C. 1989. *CommonWealth: A Return to Citizen Politics.* New York: The Free Press.

——. 2008. "Community Information Commons," in A. Fine, M. L. Sifry, A Rasiej, and J. Levy (eds.) *Rebooting America: Ideas for Redesigning American Democracy for the Internet Age.* New York: Personal Democracy Press.

Boyte, H. C., and N. Kari. 1996. *Building America: The Democratic Promise of Public Work.* Philadelphia: Temple University Press.

Chateauwert, M. 1997. *Marching Together: Women of the Brotherhood of Sleeping Car Porters.* Urbana: University of Illinois Press.

Cohen, J. L., and A. Arato. 1992. *Civil Society and Political Theory.* Cambridge, Mass: MIT Press.

Doherty, W. 2001. *Take Back Your Marriage: Sticking Together in a World that Pulls Us Apart.* New York: Guilford Books.

Estlund, C. 2000. "Working Together: The Workplace, Civil Society, and the Law." *Georgetown Law Journal* 89:1–96.

Evans, S. M., and H. C. Boyte. [1986] 1992. *Free Spaces: The Sources of Democratic Change in America.* Chicago: University of Chicago Press.

Faludi, S. 1999. *Stiffed: The Betrayal of the American Male.* New York: Harper Perennial.

Friedan, B. 1963. *The Feminine Mystique.* New York: W. W. Norton.

Fluxman, T., and P. Vale. "Re-reading Rick Turner in the New South Africa." *International Studies* 18:173–88.

Fung, A., and E. O. Wright. 2001. "Experiments in Empowered Deliberative Democracy." Available at www.ssc.wisc.edu/~wright/deliberative.html.

Habermas, J. [1962] 1989. *The Structural Transformation of the Public Sphere.* Cambridge, Mass.: MIT Press.

——. 1971. *Knowledge and Human Interests.* Boston: Beacon Press.

——. 1979. *Communication and the Evolution of Society.* Boston: Beacon Press.

——. 1998. *Between Facts and Norms: Contributions to a Discourse Theory of Law and Democracy.* Cambridge, Mass.: MIT Press.

Hagopian, F. 2006. "Latin American Citizenship and Democratic Theory," in J. S. Tulchin and M. Ruthenburg (eds.) *Citizenship in Latin America.* Boulder, Colo: Lynne Rienner, 11–58.

Handlin, O., and M. Handlin. 1969. *Commonwealth: A Study of the Role of Government in the American Economy, Massachusetts, 1774–1861.* Cambridge, Mass.: Harvard University Press.

Marx, K. [1846] 1981. *The German Ideology.* New York: International Publishers.

O'Meara, KA. 2007. "Striving for What? Exploring the Pursuit of Prestige," in J. C. Smart (ed.) *Higher Education: Handbook of Theory and Practice* 22, 121–79.

Ostrom, E. 1990. *Governing the Commons: The Evolution of Institutions for Collective Action.* Cambridge: Cambridge University Press.

——. 1999. "Polycentricity, Complexity, and the Commons." *A PEGS Journal: The Good Society* 9: 36–40.

Thompson, E. P. 1966. *The Making of the English Working Class.* New York: Vintage.

Willard, F. 1972. *Woman and Temperance: The Work and Workers of the Women's Christian Temperance Union.* New York: Arno Press.

CHAPTER 27

CIVIL SOCIETY IN THE DIGITAL AGE

ROBERTA G. LENTZ

A good deal of civil society action and deliberation, regardless of political persuasion, culture, or location, embodies what the celebrated theorist of everyday life Michel deCerteau once foretold: that "telecommunications practices have reorganized the speaking space." Though he was referring to the ordinary "oceans of communication" that surround us, deCertau noted how these oceanic waves and currents are amplified by electronic media such as telephones, radios, and televisions (1998, 252–53). Increasingly, we are witnessing how these speaking spaces now include electronic networks, both private and public, local, and translocal. The nodes, ties, and flows that characterize networks, both on- and offline (Barney 2004), augment and potentially redistribute communicative power. In their contemporary electronic online form, they enable millions of people worldwide to produce, distribute, exhibit, and exchange information, images, music, video, texts, talk, and data.

The many uses to which people and institutions now put these ever-expanding information, communication, and technology resources (ICTs) have led many digital enthusiasts to assume that increased access to new forms of communication provides a much-needed panacea for civic engagement and civil society empowerment in the twenty-first century: the "digital age" is upon us, and the so-called information society will inevitably reinvigorate democratic public spheres that can now be connected and animated electronically. Of course, such exaltations are not exactly new. Research and commentary about the role of ICTs in producing or reflecting social, cultural, economic, and political change has a very long history. Current configurations are only the most recent iteration of a series of moments that have celebrated new waves of technological innovation. At least since the 1950s with the advent of computing, scholarly, journalistic, business, and other forms of reportage have detailed the many ways in which technologies affect the workplace, personal interactions, and government processes. Each of these contributions pours more evidence into a steady flow of discourse about the so-called communication revolution or the network society. In terms of civil society and ICTs, the residue of these discursive flows takes two primary forms. The first is a utopian sensibility that argues that the evolution and intermingling of computers, information, knowledge, networks, and, more recently, a powerful array of mobile communication technologies, have changed just about everything for the better—so much so that civil society groups should wholeheartedly embrace these technological changes. The second is a more discerning vision that counters the enthusiasts by showing how societies have not changed in fundamental ways, but have merely evolved and adapted to successive waves of technological innovation. Power relations remain embedded in historically dominant patterns and institutions, and inequalities persist despite increased opportunities for access to new electronic consumer products and services (Bucy 2004). To skeptics, these rigidities prevent ICTs from having any truly transformative effects on civil society or indeed society at large.

This chapter argues for a balanced response to these viewpoints since the potential for civil society in the digital age situates the most interesting questions and possibilities between these two poles of thinking. For those immersed in either a celebratory or a skeptical orientation towards digital communications, it is often difficult to appreciate fully the other's point of view. In part this is due to the fact that both positions offer powerful evidence to counter their contrarians' positions. What seems "true" depends on the specific context in view, and particularly on the level of access to, material capacity to purchase, and skills at using, any type of electronic communications resource (Warschauer 2004). With this caveat in mind, the chapter briefly reviews both utopian and skeptical claims, while acknowledging the role that context and resources play in deciding how civil society actors approach the use and governance of electronic media resources. I argue that civil society and ICTs stand in reciprocal relationship to each other: politics and communication go hand in hand. This is why attention to the role that ICTs play in political communication anchors much of contemporary discourse about civil society and ICTs. However, it is shortsighted to focus only on how electronic media are used instrumentally for different civic and political purposes because such an orientation gives short shrift to those actors and institutions that—often silently and in the background—continue to build, own, control, regulate, and oversee the use of electronic media tools, architecture, and systems (Bollier 2003). Therefore, communications policy and the governance of ICTs are key *civil society* issues. In fact they are the issues that will ultimately determine whether ICTs offer any transformative potential for civil society in the future.

1. CAN NEW TECHNOLOGIES TRANSFORM CIVIL SOCIETY?

Advocates of a utopian sensibility claim that ICTs transform any number of things including notions of the self and human relationships; the design of corporate, government, and civil society institutions; the configuration of occupations and the workplace; the dynamics of political representation and civil society organizing; the way government functions, and even the structure of entire economies and societies. Such enthusiasts advance an emancipatory rhetoric that suggests that new technologies not only empower those who use them in unique ways, but that they also transform the very contexts in which people act and are empowered. These claims are fueled by a beguiling mythology that seems to resurrect itself at the beginning of each new wave of innovation; it woos many into thinking that *this* "next" will be different from the ones that preceded it. *This* one will change everything; and it will be decisive. To the optimists, the discourse around each wave of innovation—computing in the 1960s, the Internet in the 1990s, and more recently, the fascination with social media like Facebook, Twitter, and other electronic media tools—pulses with a fervor that makes it difficult to sound the alarm about previous waves of "the new" that have already come and gone with few signs of real or significant *social* transformation. So what is it that sustains the notion that technologies alone have the capacity to revolutionize society, politics, and markets? What tantalizes so many newcomers to embrace such an optimistic discourse?

One part of the answer lies in the allure of enticing concepts that tempt even the most critical imaginations. Key examples include the notion of the "cyborg" from feminist theorist Donna Haraway (1990), the concept of "cyberspace" as expressed by science fiction writer William Gibson (2004), and extensions of these concepts in myriad other renderings that include "cybersociety" and the "virtual public sphere," as well as the "network society," the "knowledge society," the "blogosphere," and "convergence culture." One of the most compelling of these images related to *political* communication is the notion of an electromagnetic cyberspace. Similar to the ways in which Jürgen Habermas's (1991) notion of a democratic public sphere has been mobilized into a new norm in the study of democratic and political communications, the idea of cyberspace also depicts a vast landscape of imagined potential for social transformation. To many, electronic spaces like the Internet are, in themselves, agents of change: such spaces offer up the potential to transcend the limitations of identity, space, time, and even the nation- state. The many declarations of an already converged communications environment predict tectonic shifts that are destined to release new waves in the electronic oceans of communication. As in a real tsunami, we are advised to get out of the way of these disruptions, to expect that our lives will be forever transformed, and to anticipate that everything must therefore be rebuilt as a consequence. Such assertions, however, pay little attention to how such convergences actually come into being in the first place. Many simply assume that they are irreversible, and must be dealt with.

The sheer size of the celebratory literature on this topic is daunting. Clay Shirky (2008) is only one of the most recent and highly celebrated "digerati" prophets of the optimistic view who focuses on the transformative power of the Internet. Shirky writes and lectures about how important things like open source software, web economics and social computing are transforming social relationships, and therefore the nature of institutions and society overall. His enthusiasm about social media and social networking tools such as blogs, corporate services like YouTube, and storage/replay technologies like podcasting, represents a contemporary version of the optimists' mythology (Li and Bernoff 2008). Clearly, social media do have civic and political effects, especially in reducing the transactions costs and increasing the speed and reach of information exchange—advantages that are extremely useful to civil society groups in their campaigns and fundraising. Social media make it convenient, for example, to contribute to nongovernmental organizations (NGOs) when responding to catastrophes like the 2010 Haitian earthquake, simply by texting a number that authorizes a withdrawal from a cell phone account (DeBrosse 2010). Technology certainly facilitated convenience voting during the 2008 United States Presidential elections for early and absentee voters (Leval and Marsico. 2008), and one-click access (which enables citizens to obtain information on public services and entitlements by calling a telephone number or visiting a website) are now features of many e-government portals in the United States, India, Brazil, and elsewhere (Peirce 2000).

Other examples of just-in-time electronic communications permeate practically every aspect of contemporary culture, at least in many higher-income societies: entertainment, healthcare, banking, education, transportation, and, as already noted, civil society activism. The recent film *Ten Tactics for Turning Information into Activism* tells the stories of twenty-five human rights advocates around the world who have successfully used information and digital technologies to create positive change.[1] The participatory potential of these technologies is celebrated through workshops, online seminars, symposia, and intensive courses for civil society groups where people can learn about new tools. For example, the New Organizing Institute (NOI) in the United States offers "webinars" focused on online organizing techniques. According to its website, the NOI is "the only progressive training program that integrates cutting-edge online organizing techniques, political technology, and field leadership. The Institute connects organizers to new organizing resources to enable them to support the progressive movement more effectively."[2] In addition, scholars, artists, educators, media makers, social movement organizers, journalists, and many others are gathering together to discuss the transformational potential of participatory forms of digital media production under the rubric of do-it-yourself, or DIY citizenship, and DIY media. Some of these new media practices are referred to as "tactical media," and their producers as "modders," "hacktivists," "prosumers," "remixers," and "user-generators."[3]

The discursive wave that was activated by the dot.com boom and wireless "adhocracies" in Helsinki and Tokyo during the 1990s (Rheingold 2003) also drew attention to dramatic personal stories that related how civil society activists were using ICTs to positive effect, to the drama and excitement, and often the conflict, that were involved in Belarusian "flash mobs," or rapid street-organizing in the color revolutions of eastern and central Europe, or Iranians using Twitter and text messaging to broadcast their opposition to rigged elections to an international audience in 2010. Adding to this enthusiasm were positive reviews about public journalism— the idea that ordinary citizens could help to reinvigorate the media by using interactive technologies to supply news just-in-time to large corporations from powerful new storytellers like grassroots and citizen journalists, or digital reporters. The ordinary people that deCerteau talked about were now allegedly empowered to "speak truth to power" by using their personal blogs, online chat groups, email, and other low-cost and user-friendly tools of publishing.

Another compelling contemporary example of these benefits comes from Benkler (2007), who offers persuasive evidence of the economic value to society of collaborative production of information and culture. Benkler analyzes networked systems of production like Wikipedia, the Creative Commons, and the blogosphere and asserts that collaborative, participatory communication in the form of these and other freely available or low- to no-cost tools provides larger-scale social and economic benefits than do closed systems of copyrights, patents, and other forms of intellectual property. The free and open-source software movement is another example of collaborative production and alternatives to restrictive licensing regimes, one that works from a specific political commitment to the development of commons-oriented tools and resources which, many would claim, are the essence of civil society (Coleman 2009).

Yet the key to sustaining the vibrancy of these ordinary "oceans of communication" is a clear-eyed understanding of how the political economy of electronic media and their governance affect civil society's communicative potential. A balanced view of ICTs in the service of civil society recognizes that discourses about the digital age are arguments that must be critically examined in terms of their effects on real policy change. Merely applauding the use of new media without also examining how they are produced and governed gives short shrift to the capacity of civil society actors to change the ways in which ICTs evolve as tools that can enhance popular participation in decisions that affect everyday life. Therefore, it is important to temper expectations about whatever the next "new" electronic media tools and spaces of the moment might achieve.

2. Tempering Enthusiasm about Civil Society in the Digital Age

An equally important but much less visible literature reviews and critiques the emancipatory discourse of the digital age. May (2002), Mattelart (2003), Barney (2004), Webster (2006), and Hindman (2008), for example, take a much more cautious stance, arguing that claims of the "new" divert attention from, and may even occlude, consideration of the structural conditions that reinforce long-standing patterns of inequality, domination and control. Such critics assert that the transformational view of ICTs errs in its underappreciation of history and its overreliance on traditional notions of modernity, progress, and the ability of technology to define and promote these things. In their view, critical perspectives on these issues provide a much more useful scaffolding on which to hang past, present, and future expectations about the promise of ICTs for civil society and civic and political engagement.

More than twenty years ago, Jennifer Slack questioned why another book on the information age was needed, adding in response that "the information age is a contested terrain: what it is—even *if* it is—how it is lived, how it is experienced, and how it is described differ remarkably...It is an ongoing articulation of political, economic, and ideological arrangements and relations.... descriptions of the information age are ideological, and ideology permeates what the information age is" (1987, 1–2). This conclusion is just as true today, and at least four major weaknesses of the enthusiasts' inclinations deserve particular attention. The first is technological determinism. Webster, for example, describes how proponents of digital-age discourse tend to focus on spectacular technological innovations and their transformative power as the "foundational elements of an information society." Those who proclaim that space and time have been completely transformed by symbolic interaction in cyberspace also advance, knowingly or unknowingly, this perspective, embodying a "genre of futurism.... full of dire wake up warnings, shallow analyses of the substantive realm, and the self-assurance that only the author has understood what most others have yet to comprehend" (2006, 7–8). Proponents of this discourse tend to overemphasize the changing value of information-related activities to economic productivity and social restructuring.

ICT enthusiasts tend to think that "the machines themselves, not the goals of progress, have come to play center stage.... Convenience, like progress, parades itself initially in fairly uncomplicated terms." Put simply, a better life means "having access to tools that help us save time, conquer space, [and] create comfort" (Slack and Wise 2005, 17, 28). Langdon Winner (1999, 43) defines this line of thinking as a belief that technology "is central to defining what culture is" and that technology itself drives cultural change. Winner also argues persuasively that artifacts actually embody politics rather than simply being instruments of them. He contends that "the things we call 'technologies' are ways of building order in our world," recalling Lewis Mumford's warning that both democratic and authoritarian tendencies are manufactured into the uses to which technologies are put by human beings: "What matters is not technology itself but the social or economic system in which it is embedded" (Winneer 1999, 32, 28), as is evident in contemporary examples of digital rights management (DRM), technologies that prevent the circumvention of locks on digital content distributed online.

The second weakness of uncritical techno-optimism is that it ignores the authoritarian tendencies and other problems that Mumford warned of, part of what Robins and Webster (2004, 65) call the "dark side of the information revolution." A key factor that gets lost in much of the hype about the digital age is the illusion that users control technology rather than being manipulated by it: being able to choose among a given plethora of electronic products and services that include cell phones, blogs, text messaging, pagers, personal data assistants, and high-technology phones says little about the real and lasting outcomes that these choices have on empowerment and social relations. Communication technologies facilitate and enhance the exchange of information and support online environments in which civic ties and political beliefs can be created, strengthened and potentially reshaped. Yet the nature and direction of these ties and beliefs, and whether ICTs weaken or reinforce the Balkanization of social life that is such a feature of civic engagement offline, are contested issues on which the evidence is ambiguous (Shah, Kwak, and Holbert 2001; Galston 2003). Nevertheless, these are important questions to be answered if communications technologies are to fulfill their potential in building alliances for change that are broad and deep enough to be effective and sustainable beyond episodic protest events or advocacy campaigns (Fine 2006; Leadbeater 2008; Harkin 2010). Equally important are the choices that are *not* being made available by technology developers, engineers, policy makers who approve patents, and many other kinds of decision makers. People must have the choice to opt in, not just to opt out of, already proscribed forms of digitally mediated forms of interaction or self-disclosure. By linking consumer activism with activism on digital rights, new choices can also be made more widely available.

Third, the literature that perceives technology "as imposing its character on the rest of society" (May 2002, 13) overestimates the power of ICTs to dislocate and democratize states and markets. May identifies four common claims that are especially problematic: that ICTs create a social revolution, give birth to a new economy, transform politics, and further the supposed decline of the nation state. He emphasizes how oftentimes online communities are purported to be "independent of geography," so that their presence changes the "character of democratic accountability and participation" (May 2002, 15). Although shifts are certainly occurring in the manner of political activity, critics like May are more sanguine about their political efficacy, partly because of the state's continued role in undermining privacy and imposing censorship online. Therefore, the arguments that are often made by ICT enthusiasts about the impotence of the state in the face of globalized information networks need to be tempered, even if new technologies, as they do, enable civil society to confront the state more effectively. The decline of the state rhetoric renders government as merely an untrustworthy and residual actor that is out of date and out of touch with technological developments. Yet it will be government intervention in many cases that will address concerns about the "digital divide" (Warschauer 2004). Those who would like to have access to digital forms of communication as well as the capacity to use these tools in ways that enhance their well-being rely on state intervention to support the necessary enabling regulatory conditions such as affordable prices, consumer protection laws, interoperability among networks, and nondiscriminatory services. Public interest policy advocates across the globe are working to develop these conditions, but they encounter many obstacles along the way including weak institutional capacity and a lack of resources to sustain their policy-advocacy efforts; constantly shifting policy-making forums in which to direct these activities; and an inability to communicate to non-experts what is at stake with regard to digital rights.

Finally, and following from this third point, all ICTs depend on communication infrastructure resources in order to function that are either owned by corporations or regulated in some way by governments. These resources include the radiofrequency spectrum for anything that travels over the airwaves, telecommunication networks for anything that requires a telephone connection, satellite dishes with up- and down-links for video content, cable connections for cable content, and software codes that control the switching involved in internetworking services like the Internet. All of these resources entail some form of government involvement, whether in the form of hard or soft law, light or heavy regulation. For this reason, ICT enthusiasts need to give equal attention to the intricate and reciprocal relationship that exists between those who design, finance, build, maintain, and govern electronic communication infrastructures and tools, and those who seek to use these resources for political, economic, social, or cultural ends. No technology is neutral and therefore no policy related to technological design or regulation comes without costs as well as benefits. The Internet is a case in point, designed as a decentralized, open architecture system that now facilitates a wide variety of speakers and speech forms that include pro-democracy supporters, media fan clubs, hobbyists, student groups, and scholarly networks—as well as pornographers, human traffickers, and weapons dealers. Whose and which rights should be protected when online are important questions for the new forms of governance that are emerging in the digital age. This is why civil society needs to pay attention to communication infrastructure policy *making* as much as to the various uses to which new digital tools and services are applied.

3. COMMUNICATION INFRASTRUCTURE POLICY IS A CIVIL SOCIETY ISSUE

Communication policy can be defined as "the principles and procedures of action that govern the uses of communication resources" (Rodriguez et al. 2009, 1), and encompassing "broadcasting, telephones, computers, and telecommunications, Internet, freedom of government information, privacy, and intellectual property" (Mueller, Page, and Kuerbis 2004, 169). Yet while these media and telecommunication systems clearly enable or disable the expression of other freedoms, rights, and capabilities, scholars who specialize in the study of social movements and human rights advocacy have largely ignored the role that communication media actually play in social, political, and economic struggles (Downing 2008). As Mueller, Page, and Kuerbis note, "recent literatures on global civil society and social movements contain numerous allusions to the importance of information technology (IT) in enabling activism, [yet] almost none of this literature looks at communication and information policy as the object of activism" (2004, 170).[4]

This blind spot becomes especially problematic when civil society's interests in communications policy are subordinated to the desires of industry and government. For example, the surveillance of civil society by corporations in collaboration with the state is increasing via data retention laws through which governments demand the collection of customer data by telecommunications companies, including internet service providers or ISPs (Costanza-Chock 2004). Corporate and government filtering of online content has also emerged as a new form of censorship (Diebert et al. 2008), using intellectual property law to restrict online behavior such as downloading restricted content, invoking libel laws to create a chilling effect on online critiques of corporate behavior, and interfering with network traffic speeds or blocking access to certain websites.[5] These interventions question the transformative civic and political power of ICTs: "instruments do not necessarily make for new politics" as Barney (2004, 130) puts it. Therefore, new and more democratic forms of ICT governance and control are essential if the potential for civil society engagement and participation are to be realized in the future.

At the same time, a specific group of civil society scholars and activists are increasingly active in challenging the control that intellectual property policies exert over online communications through digital rights management and other instruments (Jorgensen, 2006). For example, the Global Consumer Dialog on Access to Knowledge and Communication Issues, a project of Consumers International, the global network of some 220 consumer organizations worldwide, "seeks to harness the collective voice and effectiveness of consumer groups working around the world and across issue sectors, to guarantee that consumer interests are adequately represented in national and global debates around intellectual property and communications rights, and thereby to serve as a catalyst for policy change, by putting pressure on governments and international organizations to develop more balanced IP and communications regimes."[6] This project is one of many collaborative projects launched since the turn of the century in 2000 by civil society organizations around the world to ensure that digital rights are designed to benefit citizens and consumers, and not just corporations. These rights include such things as rights to privacy, freedom of expression, and access to electronically stored educational and government information. Effective advocacy in this area of public policy necessarily involves understanding the ways in which a variety of rights regimes intersect, and possibly collide or contradict one another, especially human rights and consumer rights.

Two successive United Nations Summits in 2003 and 2005 captured this dilemma under the rubric of the World Summit on the Information Society (WSIS) and resulted in the formation of the United Nations Internet Governance Forum (IGF). As Raboy (2004, 225) summarizes, civil society involvement in both the UN's WSIS and IGF meetings and processes has influenced civil society's expectations about new forms of governance. The WSIS highlighted a range of questions about issues and processes that characterize the governance of communications at the start of the twenty-first century. Without having resolved all these questions, which include issues of how to structure civil society participation, legitimacy, and accountability, WSIS and other similar processes illustrate an emerging paradigm for global governance generally, one in which information and communication issues are central and in which new actors, particularly global civil society, will have to be involved. Legal scholars such as Mueller (2002) and Zittrain (2008) have argued strongly for more, not less, attention to global governance issues, particularly those focused on the Internet.

4. CONCLUSION

In closing, this chapter has sought to emphasize the extent to which civil society deliberation and action in the twenty-first century both depend on, and are constrained by, electronic communication resources and their governance. The experiences of civil society actors in utilizing ICTs lie somewhere between the optimistic and skeptical perspectives. Associational life can obviously be enhanced by electronically networked communication; better communication and information transparency often make for richer democratic processes; and electronic public squares or spheres do provide spaces in which important civic and political work gets done. However, these spaces need to be recognized not just as something for civil society to use, but as something that civil society must work to preserve. This must include efforts to expand the adoption of open source software and its underlying philosophy, new frameworks for asserting civil society's rights in relation to electronic media, and policies that have the potential to sustain civil society media themselves as spaces and capacities that are relatively independent of governments and corporations—self-organized, community-based alternatives that are owned and managed by citizens, that are noncommercial and as open and participatory as possible (Hintz 2009).

Whether one thinks enthusiastically or skeptically about civil society in the digital age, or perhaps manages to balance elements of both perspectives, it is important to remember that "we are not the first generation to wonder at the rapid and extraordinary shifts...as a result of new forms of communication" (Marvin 1988, 1). Whatever advances technological innovations may provide, they never arrive without problems and inequalities that must be interrogated. In the inevitable delight that is certain to follow the arrival of the next new technology, it is important that civil society scholars and activists commit to a proper balance of expectations. The infrastructure policy of ICTs matters just as much as ICTs themselves in protecting and sustaining whatever is positive about electronic tools and spaces for civil society in any age.

NOTES

1. See http://thecoup.org/blog/10-tactics.
2. See http://www.neworganizing.com/about-us.
3. See http://diycitizenship.com.
4. A recent important exception is S. Milan (2009), "Stealing the Fire: A Study of Emancipatory Practices of Communication," available at http://www.eui.eu/Documents/

DepartmentsCentres/SPS/ResearchAndTeaching/ThesesDefended/THesesDefendedBio
Abs2009/MilanPhDThesisAbstractAndBio.pdf.

5. See, for example, http://opennet.net/blog/2010/02/pakistan-blocks-youtube-videos, http://www.spiegel.de/international/europe/0,1518,druck-678508,00.html, and http://opennet.net/blog/2008/10/oni-affiliate-reveals-chinese-surveillance-skype-messages.

6. See http://a2knetwork.org/.

REFERENCES

Barney, D. 2004. *The Network Society*. Malden, Mass.: Polity Press.

Benkler, Y. 2007. *The Wealth of Networks: How Social Production Transforms Markets and Freedom*. New Haven, Conn.: Yale University Press.

Bollier, D. 2003. *Silent Theft: The Private Plunder of Our Common Wealth*. New York: Routledge.

Bucy, E. P., ed. 2004. *Living in the Information Age: A New Media Reader*. 2nd ed. Belmont, Calif.: Wadsworth.

———. 2009. *Communication Power*. Oxford: Oxford University Press.

Costanza-Chock, S. 2004. "The Whole World Is Watching: Online Surveillance of Social Movement Organizations," in P. Thomas and Z. Nain (eds.) Who Owns the Media?: Global Trends and Local Resistances. London: Zed.

Coleman, G. 2009. "Code is Speech: Legal Tinkering, Expertise, and Protest Among Free and Open Source Software Developers." *Cultural Anthropology* 24(3):420–54.

DeBrosse, J. 2010. "Texting raises $24M for Haiti Earthquake Relief." *Dayton Daily News*, January 20.

deCerteau, M. 1998. *The Practice of Everyday Life, vol. 2: Living and Cooking*. Minneapolis: University of Minnesota Press.

Diebert, R., J. G. Palfrey, R. Rohozinski, and J. Zittrain. 2008. *Access Denied: The Practice and Policy of Global Internet Filtering*. Cambridge, Mass.: MIT Press.

Downing, J. D. H. 2008. "Social Movement Theories and Alternative Media: An Evaluation and Critique." *Communication, Culture and Critique* vol. 1(1): 40–50.

Fine, A. 2006. *Momentum: Igniting Social Change in the Connected Age*. San Francisco: Jossey-Bass.

Galston, W. 2003. "Does the Internet Strengthen Community?" *National Civic Review*, vol. 89(3): 193–202.

Gibson, W. 2004. *Neuromancer*. 2nd ed. New York: Ace Books.

Habermas, J. 1991. *The Structural Transformation of the Public Sphere: An Inquiry into a Category of Bourgeois Society*. Cambridge, Mass.: MIT Press.

Haraway, D. 1990. *Simians, Cyborgs and Women: The Reinvention of Nature*. New York: Routledge.

Harkin, J. 2010. *Lost in Cyburbia: How Life on the Net Has Created a Life of its Own*. New York: Knopf.

Hindman, M. 2008. *The Myth of Digital Democracy*. Princeton, N.J.: Princeton University Press.

Hintz, A. 2009. *Civil Society Media and Global Governance: Intervening into the World Summit on the Information Society*. Münster: LIT Verlag.

Leadbeater, C. 2008. *We-Think*. London: Profile.

Lentz, R. 2010. "Media Infrastructure Policy and Media Activism," in J. D. Downing (ed.) *Sage Encyclopedia of Social Movement Media*. Thousand Oaks, Calif.: Sage Publications.

———. 2002. *The Future of Ideas: The Fate of the Commons in a Connected World*. New York: Vintage Books.

Leval, J., and J. Marsico. 2008. "The Rise of 'Convenience Voting.'" *The American*, October 16.

Li, C., and J. Bernoff. 2008. *Groundswell: Winning in a World Transformed by Social Technologies*. Boston: Harvard Business Press.

Mansell, R., and M. Raboy (eds.) 2011. *The Handbook of Global Media and Communication Policy*. Oxford: Blackwell.

Marvin, C. 1988. *When Old Technologies Were New: Thinking About Electric Communication in the Late Nineteenth Century*. Oxford: Oxford University Press.

Mattelart, A. 2003. *The Information Society: An Introduction*. Thousand Oaks, Calif.: Sage Publications.

May, C. T. 2002. *The Information Society: A Skeptical View*. Boston: Polity Press.

———. 2003. *Key Thinkers for the Information Society*. London: Routledge.

Mueller, M. L. 2002. *Ruling the Root: Internet Governance and the Taming of Cyberspace* Cambridge, Mass.: MIT Press.

Peirce, Neal R. 2000. "E-Government More than Convenience." *Stateline.org*, August 14. Available at www.stateline.org/live/ViewPage.action?siteNodeId=136&languageId=1&contentId=14095 (accessed March 7, 2010).

Raboy, M. 2004. "The World Summit on the Information Society and its Legacy for Global Governance." *Gazette: The International Journal for Communication Studies* vol. 66(3–4): 225–32.

Rheingold, H. 2003. *Smart Mobs: The Next Social Revolution*. Jackson, Tenn.: Basic Books.

Robins, K., and F. Webster. 2004. "The Long History of the Information Revolution," in F. Webster (ed.) *The Information Society Reader*. New York: Routledge, 62–80.

Rodriguez, C., D. Kidd, and L. Stein. 2009. *Making Our Media: Global Initiatives for a Democratic Public Sphere: Creating New Communications Spaces*, vol. 1. Cresskill, N.J.: Hampton Press.

———. 2009. *Making Our Media: Global Initiatives for a Democratic Public Sphere: National and Global Movements for Democratic Communication*, vol. 2. Cresskill, N.J.: Hampton Press.

Shah, D., N. Kwak, and R. L. Holbert. 2001. "'Connecting' and 'Disconnecting' With Civic Life: Patterns of Internet Use and the Production of Social Capital." *Political Communication*, vol. 18: 141–62.

Shirky, C. 2008. *Here Comes Everybody: The Power of Organizing Without Organizations*. New York: Penguin.

Slack, J. D., and J. M. Wise. 2005. "Introduction" and "Section I: Culture and Technology: The Received View," in J. D. Slack and J. M. Wise (eds.) *Culture + technology: A primer*. New York: Peter Lang.

Warschauer, M. 2004. *Technology and Social Inclusion: Rethinking the Digital Divide*. Cambridge, Mass.: MIT Press.

Webster, Frank. 2006. *Theories of the Information Society*, 3rd ed. New York: Routledge.

Winner, L. 1999. "Do Artifacts Have Politics?" in D. MacKenzie and J. Wajcman (eds.) *The Social Shaping of Technology*. 2nd ed. Buckingham: Open University Press, 28–40.

Zittrain, J. 2008. *The Future of the Internet and How to Stop It*. New Haven, Conn.: Yale University Press.

Zuckerman, E. 2009. "Social Media In Iran: Lessons Learned." Available at http://www.boingboing.net/2009/06/21/social-media-in-iran.html

CHAPTER 28

CIVIL SOCIETY
AND PUBLIC JOURNALISM

CHARLES LEWIS

CENTURIES ago the great Italian astronomer Galileo Galilei wrote that "All truths are easy to understand once they are discovered; the point is to discover them." For people throughout the world, this has always been a formidable challenge, and it remains so today in the warp-speed, metamorphosing, multimedia Internet age of more than a hundred million websites, global search engines, instant messaging, and social networks. Facts are and must be the coin of the realm in a democracy, for government "of the people, by the people and for the people," to paraphrase Abraham Lincoln, requires and assumes an informed citizenry, at least to some extent. There can be no substitute for the truth about all the powers that be. On this point, Lincoln could not have been more emphatic: "I am a firm believer in the people. If given the truth, they can be depended upon to meet any national crisis. The great point is to bring them the real facts" (cited in Seldes 1985, 246).

And yet, regardless of the power of new media technologies, these "real facts" have proven to be ever more elusive to ascertain. In many nations including the world's oldest republic, there is a discernible pattern of laggard, inaccurate, and artificially sweetened information that distorts the political decision-making process, mutes popular dissent, and delays—sometimes fatally—the cold dawn of logic, reason, and reckoning that is so fundamental to an open democracy. The antidote to this problem is a vibrant and fearless civil society, including journalists and other watchdogs who provide citizens with correct, contemporaneous, and independent information about the decisions that affect their daily lives.

1. Defining Reality

Access to independent, accurate, and timely information by citizens is essential in order to hold any institution accountable. This is hardly a new notion—after all, freedoms of expression and information have long been recognized as universal human rights—but nonetheless it is often lost sight of. Throughout history, totalitarian regimes have restricted public access to information and further distorted popular perceptions of reality through disinformation. For example, in 146 B.C., on the northern coast of Africa, would the Carthaginians have agreed to relinquish their 200,000 individual weapons and 2,000 catapults to the Romans had they known that earlier the Roman Senate had secretly decided "to destroy Carthage for good" (Kiernan 2007)?

Secrecy, deception, and the abuse of power transcend time, geography, culture, language, and means of communication. The worst mass murderers in the twentieth century have had a common modus operandi, from Hitler's Third Reich to Josef Stalin's Soviet Union, and including Mao Tse Tung's Cultural Revolution (more accurately characterized as "China's Holocaust"), Pol Pot's Khmer Rouge "killing fields" in Cambodia, and "Hutu Power" in Rwanda. In this last case, the minority Tutsi population were demonized for weeks on the airwaves as *inyenzi* or "cockroaches" that needed to "disappear once and for all," and very soon thereafter, up to a million Tutsis were murdered within a few short months (Kiernan 2007, 536–8). Around the same time, in Bosnia, the Serbs described Islam as a "malignant disease" which would "infect" Europe, and their ethnic cleansing between 1991 and 1995 resulted in roughly 200,000 Muslim casualties (Kiernan 2007, 588–9). Most recently, in the first genocide of the twenty-first century in the Darfur region of Sudan, Arab Islamic Janjaweed militias, working in tandem with the Sudanese government, murdered hundreds of thousands of people and displaced millions more, with the brutality also spreading into Chad and the Central African Republic (Kiernan 2007, 594–6).

While the extent and predictability of human destruction certainly have varied, their enabling means have not. Those in power have always controlled the flow of information, corroding and corrupting its content using newspapers, radio, television, and other mass media to carefully consolidate their authority and cover their crimes in a thick veneer of fervent racialism or nationalism—and always with the specter of some kind of imminent public threat, what Hannah Arendt called "objective enemies" (Arendt 1951). Unfortunately, restricting and distorting information while also diverting the public's attention has not been the preserve of mass murderers and their regimes. Indeed, for those wielding power, whether in the private or the public sector, the increasingly sophisticated control of information is regarded as essential to achieving success, regardless of subject or policy or administration or country. Besides controlling the external message, strict discipline about internal information is also regarded as essential, severely limiting current and future access to potentially disadvantageous documents including calendars, memoranda, phone logs, and emails. In this 24/7, instantaneous, viral communications environment concerning the most controversial, politically inconvenient subjects, mere delay is the simplest, most efficacious public relations tactic available.

There are astonishing financial profits to be made in delaying and distorting the truth when investment banks misrepresent their financial conditions, or when companies knowingly manufacture harmful products, as the tobacco, asbestos, lead, and other industries have been found to have done many years later. There are immediate electoral rewards for delaying and distorting the political truth, as U.S. President Lyndon Johnson did in 1964, secretly girding for a major war in Vietnam while publicly promising not to send more soldiers off to war; and as President Richard Nixon did in 1972, secretly authorizing a political "dirty tricks" operation inside the White House, that, among many other things, effectively derailed the campaign of his most formidable Democratic foe, Senator Edmund Muskie. Both incumbent presidents breezed to their election victories in those years.

In the case of the Vietnam War in which hundreds of thousands of lives were lost between 1962 and 1975, the public learned over a period of years—with inculpatory revelations still seeping out four decades later—that the rationale for direct U.S. involvement was always a lie (Alterman 2004). Instead of the United States being attacked in a remote part of the world known as the Gulf of Tonkin by the North Vietnamese in 1964—as the President had announced to the world, precipitating congressional passage six days later of the Gulf of Tonkin resolution that authorized nearly all of the carnage that followed—the United States government had been engaged for months in top secret intelligence-gathering activities in flagrant violation of North Vietnam's sovereign land, air space, and territorial waters, including consciously planned, aggressive military provocations against that country. Remarkably, the American people then or since have never directly been told the truth by their government about what really happened in that remote part of the world, years before 24-hour cable news, cell phone cameras, video recorders, and the Internet.

Many of those lies and distortions were officially documented in the Department of Defense's secret, voluminous history of the Vietnam War known as the Pentagon Papers, which were leaked to reporters and courageously published by the *New York Times*, the *Washington Post*, and other newspapers in June, 1971. Publishing the Pentagon Papers and the media's coverage of the Nixon Watergate scandal still represent U.S. history's high-water mark in the longstanding struggle between raw political power and democratic values. But even with those emblematic moments of an independent, skeptical press in the American experience, important information about those in power took years to become known to the public. As the then-executive editor of the *Washington Post*, Benjamin C. Bradlee, mused two decades later, "What might have happened had the truth emerged in 1963 instead of 1971?" (Bradlee 1990).

With the advent of the atomic age after the Second World War and the demonstrated capacity for nuclear annihilation on an unprecedented human scale, the inclinations of those in possession of previously unimaginable power to operate in secrecy and deception were exacerbated. According to historian Garry Wills, the bomb "fostered an anxiety of continuing crisis, so that society was pervasively militarized. It redefined the government as a National Security State, with an apparatus of secrecy and executive control...The whole history of America since World War II caused an inertial rolling of power toward the executive branch...[and] the permanent emergency that has melded World War II with the Cold War and the Cold War with the war on terror" (Wills 2010, 237–8). Indeed, in a representative democracy such as the United States—in which by far the most extensive military operations, with no fewer than 761 bases around the world, are overseen by civilians led by the elected president who is also the commander-in-chief—national security and the political instinct to carefully calibrate and frame information to maximum public advantage are often melded together and eventually become indistinguishable (Hedges 2009, 144). As journalist Jacqueline Sharkey observed in her study of U.S. military restrictions on the news media over thirty years, from Vietnam to the military actions in Grenada, Panama, and the first Persian Gulf War in 1991, "Information-control policies designed to protect not military security but presidential approval ratings undermined...the right of the American people to receive unbiased, independent accounts of military conflicts, so they can pass judgment on the civilian and military leaders who took them to war" (Sharkey 1991, 40).

Each successive occupant of the White House has been more sophisticated and aggressive at controlling the message of his administration, technologically but also in terms of additional public relations money, personnel and outreach. For example, in its first term, the George W. Bush administration hired 376 additional public affairs officials to package information at an annual cost of $50 million (Brune 2005). Separately, $254 million was spent on "faux news" contracts, nearly double what the Clinton administration had spent during the preceding four years. Positive video news releases about administration policies were sent out to hundreds of commercial television stations and viewed by tens of millions of Americans, often with no on-air identification or disclosure (Barstow and Stein 2005). In March 2003, almost four decades after the Johnson administration had escalated the war in Vietnam under false pretenses, the Bush administration led the United States and several of its allies to war against Saddam Hussein's Iraq, also on the basis of erroneous information that it had methodically propagated. According to the Center for Public Integrity, in the two years following September 11, 2001, President George W. Bush and seven of his administration's top officials made at least 935 false statements about the national security threat posed by Iraq. The carefully orchestrated campaign about Iraq's supposed weapons of mass destruction effectively galvanized public opinion and, in the process, led the nation to war under decidedly false pretenses. The cumulative effect of these incorrect, bellicose statements—amplified by thousands of uncritical news stories and broadcasts—was immense. Much of the saturation media coverage provided additional, independent validation of the Bush administration's misstatements about Iraq (Lewis and Reading-smith 2008).

In addition, the New York Times discovered and reported years later that the Pentagon had quietly recruited seventy-five retired military officers to work as "independent," paid consultants and as radio and television analysts. They were secretly coached about how to make the public case for war in Iraq on the air, and many of them also had significant, undisclosed financial ties to defense companies that were benefiting from the policies they were supposedly analyzing (Barstow 2008). The broadcast media essentially ignored these revelations, neither reporting on their own dubious use of such compromised, closely tethered talking heads nor apologizing to the public for the gross misrepresentations they involved. Considering that most national reporters and their news organizations were figuratively embedded in official propaganda and misleading statements, what might have happened, to paraphrase Bradlee's question, if the public had discovered the truth about the actual extent of the national security threat posed by Iraq in late 2002 instead of some years later? Two distant quagmires, and twenty years of large-scale bloodshed in wars in Vietnam and Iraq, might have been avoided if the American people had been better informed with real-time truth about the specious official statements, faulty logic, and muscular manipulations of public opinion and governmental decision-making processes.

One of the most epiphanic public comments from the period of President George W. Bush's war on terror was made by an unidentified White House official, revealing how information is managed and how the news media and the public itself are regarded by those in power: "[You journalists live] in what we call the reality-based community. [But] that's not the way the world really works anymore. We're an empire now, and when we act, we create our own reality...we're history's actors...and you, all of you, will be left to just study what we do" (Suskind 2004). And yet, as aggressive as the Bush administration may have been in attempting to define reality, the subsequent administration of President Barack Obama may be even more so. With sixty-nine people managing the media and the message (compared to fifty-two under Bush and forty-seven under Clinton), the Obama White House press operation (which includes for the first time an Office of New Media) is the largest, most technologically advanced and most centralized in U.S. history. Meanwhile, because of the economic disruptions that are afflicting the commercial media companies, today there are *fewer* reporters covering the White House, and those who are there each day may be less relevant than their predecessors, partly because they now have less and less time to do any original reporting. As Peter Baker, the White House reporter for the *New York Times*, has complained, "We are hostages to the non-stop, never-ending, file-it-now, get-on-the-Web, get-on-the-radio, get-on-TV media environment." All of which leads to the widespread perception among journalists such as *Vanity Fair*'s Michael Wolff, "These people in this White House are in greater control of the media than any administration before them" (Auletta 2010; Wolff 2009).[1]

Setting the agenda and circumventing the news media has been the goal of every recent U.S. president's outreach strategy. Sidestepping full, televised news conferences with professional journalists and choosing more easily controlled venues instead—such as selected public questions on the video-sharing website YouTube without the risk of follow-up—epitomizes the difference between the aura of accessibility and actual accountability in the new media age (Kurtz 2010). Controlling the message and the news media has become easier with the increasing ability of the first Internet president and White House to get their carefully framed information out directly to the public via thousands of emails, blogs, and Tweets, not to mention using the electronic bully pulpit of numerous government, party and campaign websites; daily, televised White House press briefings; weekly radio addresses on YouTube; produced videos on Whitehouse.gov; official photos on the image and video-hosting website Flickr; and many more.

The realities of power in a 24/7 world are that now more than ever before, public perceptions and opinions are shaped in the first hours of any major event. Veteran journalist Hodding Carter, who served as assistant secretary of state for public affairs in the administration of Jimmy Carter, has observed that "if given three days without serious challenge, the government will have set the context for an event and can control public perception of that event" (Kovach and Rosenstiel 2007, 45). These new communications opportunities, set against the backdrop of economically emaciated media companies serving a thinner gruel of independently reported news (compared to the occasional "bisques" of yesteryear), illuminate just how difficult it is for ordinary citizens to get beyond talking points and their message, and to discover—indeed, decipher—important truths for themselves.

2. THE NEWS MEDIA CRISIS AND THE DECLINE OF THE PUBLIC SPHERE

The work of independent journalists is of course essential to any ostensibly free society, and yet their working conditions have never been typical compared to those of other professions. Besides the risk of being murdered with impunity, with most democratic governments doing very little if anything until after it occurs, journalists also face another real punishment for their truth-telling: being sued for libel and defamation by multinational corporations, organized crime, or wealthy individuals. Of course, journalists and their news organizations should be held civilly liable for their conduct on the same basis as everyone else in society, but as a practical matter, defending frivolous, financially threatening litigation can take years, be exorbitantly expensive, and end implausibly if the jurisdiction is inhospitable to the public scrutiny of those in power. Even worse, out of 168 countries recently surveyed, 158 have criminal defamation laws, which, according to Agnès Callamard, executive director of the human rights organization Article 19, "through enforced silence and imprisonment, stifle, censor and suppress freedom of expression., Defamation, both civil and criminal, is one of the greatest threats to freedom of expression in the world today. It is a global problem that requires global action" (Article 19 2007). The daily reality in much of the world is that journalism that speaks "truth to power" can result in financial ruin, imprisonment, or death for a reporter.

But by far the most significant threat to independent journalism is economic. In recent years in North America, Europe, and Japan, commercial, for-profit journalism has endured a difficult, historic transformation. Fundamentally, the relationship of classified and display advertising revenue to newspapers has been drastically disrupted by new online technologies and the simultaneous, declining interest of consumers in serious news. As a result, tens of thousands of journalists have been laid off in the United States, where the number of newspaper editorial staff fell by 33 percent between 1992 and 2009 (Downie Jr and Schudson 2009, 21–3). With the proliferation of online news sites and increasing broadband access, young adult citizens are increasingly getting their information digitally, via mobile phones and otherwise. The obvious result of this hollowing out process is that there are fewer people today to report, write, and edit original news stories about our infinitely more complex, dynamic world, and fewer journalists to hold those in power accountable. Put in perspective, at the same time as the historic shrinking of newspaper, radio, and television newsrooms across America over three decades from 1980, the number of public relations specialists and managers doubled from approximately 45,000 to 90,000 people. As Robert McChesney and John Nichols (2010, 49) have written, "Even as journalism shrinks, the 'news' will still exist. It will increasingly be provided by tens of thousands of well-paid and skilled PR specialists ready and determined to explain the world to the citizenry, in a manner that suits their corporate and government employers." The serious news and information void is also being filled increasingly by major nongovernment organizations (NGOs) specializing and implicitly or explicitly advocating in certain subject areas, such as the International Crisis Group, Global Integrity, Human Rights Watch, the Natural Resources Defense Council, and the Kaiser Health Foundation's Kaiser Health News. As the traditional, elite news organizations necessarily evolve from their condescending role as gatekeepers (deciding for the public what news is fit to print), the global nonjournalism, online marketplace of ideas, and information has exploded, though with widely varying quality and credibility of content.

Philip Meyer, professor emeritus at the University of North Carolina and author of two seminal books, *Precision Journalism* in 1973 and *The Vanishing Newspaper* in 2004, has written that "The hunter-gatherer model of journalism is no longer sufficient. Citizens can do their own hunting and gathering on the Internet. What they need is somebody to add value to that information by processing it—digesting it, organizing it, making it usable" (Meyer 2008). One of the most poignant and educative moments regarding the remarkable potential of citizen-journalists and hunter-gatherer collaboration occurred on July 7, 2005, when terrorist bombs exploded in the London subway. Within six hours, the British Broadcasting Corporation (BBC) had received more than 1,000 photographs, twenty video clips, 4,000 text messages, and 20,000 emails—all from citizens. For Richard Sambrook, the director of news there, it was a transformative illustration of the power and synergies of "crowdsourcing" when integrated with the editorial values and sensibilities of conventional journalism: "I believe that truth, accuracy, impartiality and diversity of opinion are strengthened by being open to a wider range of opinion and perspective, brought to us through the knowledge and understanding of our audience" (Sambrook 2005). Beyond the exigencies of breaking, daily news situations, the power and potential of citizen muckraking, with or without collaboration with professional journalists, remains relatively unrealized—but it will inevitably evolve over time as part of a new ecosystem for journalism (CPI 2000).

3. A New Journalism Ecosystem

What appears to be evolving across the world in the United States, Canada, and in parts of Europe, Africa, Latin America, and Asia in direct response to the commercial news media meltdown is the beginning of a new investigative journalism ecosystem, in which some of the most ambitious reporting projects will increasingly emanate from the public realm rather than from private, commercial outlets. From Britain to South Africa, the Philippines to Peru, Australia to the United States, philanthropically supported publishing centers are being founded and staffed by professional reporters and editors who have either lost their jobs or might do so soon, disconcerted veterans who are excited to be doing major important reporting projects once again.[2] It should be noted that nonprofit journalism itself is hardly a new phenomenon. For example, some of the most venerable media institutions in the United States have long operated this way, including the Associated Press, National Public Radio, and the Public Broadcasting System; well-known periodicals such as *National Geographic, Consumer Reports, Mother Jones, Foreign Affairs,* and *Harper's*; and the *Christian Science Monitor* and numerous other newspapers.

What is new is the recent proliferation of specialized, nonprofit, investigative, and public service journalism publishers online, who in many cases are working closely in partnership with existing "legacy" media institutions. The commercial, for-profit companies have smaller news-gathering capacities and less money, and are desperately seeking serious news content at little or no cost. The investigative nonprofit organizations have plenty of high quality content but are desperately seeking "eyeballs"—online visitors, page views, and traffic—to their online news sites. The two groups help and need each other in a marriage of convenience, with the public as the prime beneficiary.

The Associated Press, created back in 1846, announced in 2009 that for the first time, it will make investigative stories from four nonprofit national news organizations—the Center for Investigative Reporting, the Center for Public Integrity, the Investigative Reporting Workshop, and ProPublica—available to its newspaper clients. The two oldest investigative reporting nonprofits in the United States, the Center for Investigative Reporting in California and the Center for Public Integrity in Washington, D.C., were separately created by journalists in 1977 and 1989. ProPublica, based in New York, and the Investigative Reporting Workshop at American University in Washington, D.C., were separately founded in 2008. All four organizations share their content in partnership with major national news media outlets, from the *New York Times* and the *Washington Post* and many other newspapers to the television news programs such as *60 Minutes*, *Frontline*, and other major venues at CBS, NBC, ABC, CNN, and other broadcast and cable television outlets.

For example, the Center for Investigative Reporting, working with WNET and others, is reopening and investigating several cold cases from unsolved civil rights-era murders in the South, and separately has launched its California Watch project to investigate public issues in America's largest state, its stories being sold to more than three dozen news outlets. The Center for Public Integrity identified the top twenty-five subprime mortgage lenders in a "Who's Behind the Financial Meltdown?" series of stories in partnership with several major news organizations, and six months after the 2003 U.S. invasion of Iraq published *Windfalls of War*, an online posting of all war-related contracts in Iraq and Afghanistan and the political contributions of each contractor. Some of the best investigative reporting about federal stimulus spending amidst the recession of 2009 was carried out by ProPublica, and it has also partnered with the PBS program *Frontline* and the *New York Times* to investigate foreign bribery by the multinational company Siemens. The Investigative Reporting Workshop *BankTracker* project, in partnership with MSNBC.com, has been compiling and posting federal financial data and a troubled asset ratio analysis for every chartered bank in the United States; separately, the workshop is also coproducing television documentaries with *Frontline*, the first of which exposed unsafe working conditions inside regional airline carriers.[3] The AP announcement about collaborating with four nonprofit investigative centers came six months after the December 2008 statement by the Pulitzer Prize awards committee, declaring that the prestigious Pulitzer prizes, for the first time since their inception in 1917, could be awarded not just to newspapers, but other news organizations that publish only on the Internet, which are "primarily dedicated to original news reporting and coverage of ongoing stories," and that adhere to "the highest journalistic principles."[4] In 2010, ProPublica became the first of these investigative centers to win a Pulitzer prize, for a story published with the New York Times.

These historically significant developments are a direct response to the newspaper industry's financial crisis and the new nonprofit publishing environment. What does all this mean? It means that, in the foreseeable future, more and more investigative content from respected nonprofit news organizations will likely be included by the major media institutions in their news coverage offerings. Commercial and noncommercial news media organizations interested in investigative and other forms of public service journalism are increasingly collaborating and becoming intertwined with each other. A new way of doing in-depth journalism in the United States and elsewhere in the world is becoming increasingly common.

In recent years, as the quality and quantity of commercial news offerings have declined, local and national philanthropic foundations have recognized that a civic crisis of information exists. Between 2005 and mid-2009, at least 180 U.S. foundations spent nearly $128 million on news and information projects, half of that for investigative reporting by nonprofit centers. And these numbers do not include large-scale foundation and individual support given annually to public broadcasting (Schaffer 2009). What is most interesting is that before the fall of the Berlin Wall in

1989, there were only three nonprofit investigative reporting entities in the world; today there are literally dozens of them, and if professional membership and training organizations are included, the number is over forty (Kaplan 2007). In the United States, some nonprofit reporting centers are state-based, some are university-based, and some are both. In the latter case, college students collaborate with veteran journalists and the work is published in commercial or non-commercial outlets.

In 2009, twenty U.S. nonprofit news publishers came together for three days and issued the Pocantico Declaration, announcing that "We have hereby established, for the first time ever, an Investigative News Network."[5] Half of the groups represented had only begun since 2007. The new organization will likely grow to at least 50–100 nonprofit public service journalism organizations from around the world in the foreseeable future. It is unclear whether or not the network will evolve as one of the most important, online destinations for original, anthologized investigative reporting content, a mecca for editorial collaboration between news organizations across borders, or merely the first broad-based nonprofit news publishers association assisting organizations administratively and otherwise (Lewis 2009).

The global dimension and potential of this emerging ecosystem cannot be overstated. The Center for Public Integrity began the International Consortium of Investigative Journalism in 1997, containing 100 preeminent reporters from fifty countries on six continents who have produced cross-border content on everything from cigarette smuggling to the privatization of water, climate change lobbying around the world, and the proliferation of private military companies.(Lewis 2009) It was the first—and remains the only—working network of respected journalists who develop and publish international investigative stories about the most compelling public interest issues of the time. It will grow and, via the center's website, publish more frequently. Meanwhile, regional and subject-oriented reporting networks are also evolving in Latin America, the Middle East, Europe, and Africa. Another sign of the coalescing momentum for cross-border cooperation is the creation of the Global Investigative Journalism Network among different nonprofit investigative journalism organizations to support training and share information— but not to produce content—at international conferences. Six multi-day, multi-panel global conferences have been held in Copenhagen in 2001 and 2003, Amsterdam in 2005, Toronto in 2007, Lillehammer, Norway in 2008, and Geneva in 2010, cumulatively attended by more than 3,000 journalists from eighty-seven countries, with Kiev designated as the next conference site.[6]

4. Conclusion

Where all of this synergy and collaboration will lead, and whether new economic models can be created to help make this fragile ecosystem more financially sustainable, are unclear, but these developments are unprecedented and full of promise.

The American journalist A. J. Liebling once wrote that "freedom of the press is guaranteed only to those who own one."[7] For some of the boldest members of the current diaspora of immensely talented journalists with nowhere to work, starting a nonprofit, online news site is vastly more appealing than the bleaker specter of leaving the profession itself. The editorial freedom, excitement, and satisfaction of a journalist creating and running his or her own news organization are palpable—and the editorial, administrative, and financial management responsibilities are formidable. The ultimate winner, of course, is the public, supplied with independent, in-depth journalism that would not otherwise exist, in multimedia, infinitely more accessible forms.

As veteran journalists Bill Kovach and Tom Rosenstiel (2007, 255) observed, "Civilization has produced one idea more powerful than any other: the notion that people can govern themselves. And it has created a largely unarticulated theory of information to sustain that idea, called journalism. The two rise and fall together." Both ideas have evolved and been applied in various ways since the late eighteenth century throughout the world, and they will continue to be so. But neither can survive without the public's capacity to discover and understand the real-time truth about those who occupy positions of power. Civil societies must do everything they can to preserve and enlarge the public space for independent, investigative journalism in all of its evolving forms. For as Justice Hugo Black wrote in the historic Pentagon Papers Supreme Court decision, "Only a free and unrestrained press can effectively expose deception in government" (Kenworthy et al. 1971, 725).

NOTES

1. The White House staff numbers come from political scientist Martha Joynt Kumar, who has tracked presidents and the press for four decades. See http://marthakumar.com.

2. For a complete, updated, global list of nonprofit investigative news publishers, with vital organizational information and links, see "The New Journalism Ecosystem" at www .investigativereportingworkshop.org/ilab.

3. See www.cironline.org, www.publicintegrity.org, www.propublica.org, and www .investigativereportingworkshop.org.

4. See www.pulitzer.org/files/PressRelease2008PulitzerPrizes.pdf.

5. Available at http://cpublici.wordpress.com.

6. See www.globalinvestigativejournalism.org.

7. Liebling's well-known aphorism, among others, can be found at http://en.wikipedia .org/wiki/AJ_Liebling.

REFERENCES

Alterman, E. 2004. *When Presidents Lie: A History of Official Deception and its Consequences.* New York: Viking.

Arendt, H. 1951. *The Origins of Totalitarianism*. New York: Harcourt.

Article 19. December 11, 2007. "Defamation Mapping Tool Charts a Chilling Reality Spanning the Globe." Available at http://www.article19.org/pdfs/press/defamation-maps-pr.pdf.

Auletta, K. 2010. "Non-Stop News." *The New Yorker*, Januaqry 25: 38–47.

Barstow, D. 2008. "Message Machine: Behind TV Analysts, Pentagon's Hidden Hand." *New York Times*, April 20.

Barstow, D., and R. Stein. 2005. "Under Bush, a New Age of Prepackaged TV News." *New York Times*, March 13.

Bradlee, B. 1990. *Nieman Reports, Special Issue* (Winter). Harvard University: Nieman Foundation for Journalism. Available at http://nieman.harvard.edu/reports/issues.aspx.

Brune, T. 2005. "Cadre Grows to Rein in Message: Ranks of Federal Public Affairs Officials have Swelled under Bush to Help Tighten Control on Communities to Media, Access to Information." *Newsday*, February 24.

Center for Public Integrity. 2000. *Citizen Muckraking: How to Investigate and Right Wrongs in your Community*. Monroe, Maine: Common Courage Media.

Downie Jr., and L. M. Schudson. 2009. "The Reconstruction of American Journalism." *Columbia Journalism Review*, November/December, 48 (4): 28–51.

Hedges, C. 2009. *Empire of Illusion: The End of Literacy and the Triumph of Spectacle*. New York: Nation Books.

Kaplan, D. 2007. "Survey of Nonprofit Investigative Journalism Centers." Washington, D.C.: Center for International Media Assistance/National Endowment for Democracy. Available at http://www.ned.org/cima/CIMA-Investigative_Journalism_Report.pdf.

Kenworthy, E., F. Butterfield, H. Smith, and N. Sheeehan. 1971. *The Pentagon Papers: The Secret History of the Vietnam War*. New York: Quadrangle Books.

Kiernan, B. 2007. *Blood and Soil: A World History of Genocide and Extermination from Sparta to Darfur*. New Haven, Conn.: Yale University Press.

Kovach, B., and T. Rosensteil. 2007. *The Elements of Journalism*. New York: Three Rivers Press.

Kurtz, H. 2010. "Obama Embraces New Media, Which Piques the Old Guard." *The Washington Post*, February 8: C1, C3.

Lewis, C. 2007. "The Growing Importance of Nonprofit Journalism." Cambridge, Mass.: The Shorenstein Center on the Press, Politics and Public Policy, Harvard University. Available at http://www.hks.harvard.edu/presspol/publications/papers/working_papers/2007_03_lewis.pdf.

———. 2009. "Great Expectations: An Investigative News Network is Born. Now What?" *Columbia Journalism Review* 17–18 (September/October):25–28.

Lewis, C., and M. Reading-Smith. 2008. "False Pretenses," in *Iraq: The War Card*. Washington, D.C.: Center for Public Integrity. Available at http://projects.publicintegrity.org/WarCard.

McChesney, R., and J. Nichols. 2010. *The Death and Life of American Journalism*. New York: Nation Books.

Meyer, P. 2004. *The Vanishing Newspaper: Saving Journalism in the Information Age*, Columbia: University of Missouri Press.

———. 2008. "Phil Meyer, Raising the Ante Again." *Nieman Watchdog*, March 28. Available at http://www.niemanwatchdog.org/index.cfm?fuseaction=showcase.view&showcaseid=0076.

Sambrook, R. 2005. "Citizen Journalism and the BBC." *Nieman Reports*, Winter: 13–16. Available at www.nieman.harvard.edu/reports/05-4NRwinter/Sambrook.pdf.

Schaffer, J. 2009. "New Media Makers." Washington, D.C.: Institute for Interactive Journalism, American University School of Communication. Available at www.j-lab .org/new_media_makers.pdf.

Seldes, G. 1985. *The Great Thoughts*. New York: Ballantine.

Sharkey, J. 1991. *Under Fire: Military Restrictions on the Media from Grenada to the Persian Gulf*. Washington, D.C.: Center for Public Integrity.

Suskind, R. 2004. "Without a Doubt." *New York Times Magazine*, October 17.

Wills, G. 2010. *Bomb Power: The Modern Presidency and the National Security State*. New York: Penguin.

Wolff, M. 2009. "The Power and the Story." *Vanity Fair*, July: 48–51.

CHAPTER 29

CIVIC KNOWLEDGE

PETER LEVINE

CIVIL society and knowledge are connected in three major ways. First, in order for a civil society to function well, its citizens must know certain things.[1] They must have skills ("know-how") plus facts or concepts ("knowledge that"), plus knowledge that enables them to negotiate their views of right and wrong. Second, civil society *generates* knowledge, including certain kinds of knowledge that cannot be produced by other sectors or institutions. For example, science cannot produce knowledge of what is right or good in the way that citizens can when they are organized appropriately in civil society. The relationship between civil society and knowledge is reciprocal, with each contributing to the other. Third, civil society plays an essential role in preserving and nurturing the institutions that produce valuable knowledge. Knowledge is a public good, because excluding people from its benefits is difficult and expensive once it has been produced. Generating and protecting any public good raises special challenges that civil society is well equipped to address. In short, civil society both requires and produces knowledge, and protects and strengthens the conditions under which knowledge as a public good is produced.

1. CIVIC KNOWLEDGE AS KNOWLEDGE THAT ALL CITIZENS SHOULD HAVE

The knowledge that citizens need to participate in civil society depends on what we consider the role of civil society to be, which depends in turn on fundamental normative commitments. The libertarian Loren Lomasky presumes that one must be constrained by others' legitimate rights, but "how one comports oneself beyond that point is—if not exclusively, then predominantly—the agent's own business." In this view, civil society is the set of voluntary institutions and public forums in which people "advise, cajole, [and] remonstrate" with others to act well, given that they should be free to act as they wish (Lomasky 1999, 277–8).

In marked contrast, Henry Milner admires Nordic social democracies in which the state redistributes and regulates the economy to achieve equality of welfare. For Milner, civil society is the set of institutions that educate and moti-vate working-class people to press the state to redistribute welfare effectively and fairly. The state is the guarantor of justice, but an independent civil society is essential for holding the state accountable. In the Scandinavian model that he recommends, "an informed population supports policies that reinforce egalitar-ian outcomes" (Milner 2002, 10).

Once the normative purposes of civil society are settled, the levels and types of knowledge that citizens must possess for civil society to function become empirical questions. For example, Milner argues that citizens must have knowledge of politi-cal issues and processes. They must know where candidates or parties stand on issues and what tangible economic impact these positions will have. Such knowl-edge must be evenly distributed by social class, gender, race, and other demographic categories, or else participation will be unequal and democratic outcomes will be unjust. Civil society enters the picture mainly as the venue through which citizens gain political knowledge so that they can vote and otherwise influence public policy. For example, newspapers, labor unions, political parties, and social movements impart political information and ideas to their members.

Lomasky's account of civil society as a voluntary school of virtue suggests dif-ferent knowledge requirements, emphasizing personal "good behavior" and the ability to teach it to others. Similarly writes Richard Madsen, "In the Confucian vision...human flourishing can occur only if social relations have a proper moral basis. This means that people have to learn to discern what is the right way to behave, and that for the most part they voluntarily act accordingly." Neither pure self-interest nor pervasive state coercion is compatible with flourishing. Thus "the Confucian project requires moral cultivation at all levels of society. This cultivation is to develop the mind-and-heart, an inextricable combination of mental and emo-tional faculties." Although the extended family provides some of the necessary edu-cation, leadership also requires experience in community organizations such as temple groups, theater associations, and guilds. "To fulfill the purposes of self-cul-tivation, these institutions would have to be seen as educational, in the broadest sense of the word" (Madsen 2002, 196–7). Note Madsen's use of the words "discern," "learn," "mental and emotional faculties," and "education." Clearly, the Confucian model makes strong demands on citizens' knowledge, but in a way that emphasizes moral reasoning and character more than facts about the formal political system.

In Islamic societies, the body of trained religious scholars (the *ulama*), claims legitimate influence independent of the state precisely because of the knowledge it possesses. The *ulama* is one important antecedent of Islamic civil society, with knowledge an essential civic value. Secular intellectuals in Muslim societies have frequently contested the sole right of the *ulama* to influence public opinion. Today, as Masoud Kamali writes, "information technology is inclusive and increases the range of participants in discussions about Islamic values and practices and provides an opportunity to educate people who are not religious scholars to increasingly contribute to discussions" (Kamali 2001, 479). The vibrant blogosphere in countries like Egypt (where there were at least 1,400 blogs in 2007) reflects the growth of civil society (Radsch 2008), yet there is clear continuity with the classical Muslim idea that knowledgeable people should influence public opinion and the state.

In the United States, there is empirical evidence that certain values and skills are necessary, or at least helpful, to sustain a system that is moderately egalitarian, decentralized, and protective of minority rights. For example, Verba, Schlozman, and Brady (1995) argue that people need resources to participate in a political system that makes participation optional, and that these resources are unequally distributed, leading to inequitable outcomes. Among these resources are "civic skills," which include the ability to write a letter, attend a meeting and take part in its decisions, plan or chair a meeting, and give a presentation or speech. These skills can be understood as knowledge in the sense of "how-to," but they probably also depend on knowledge *of* specific topics. For example, one cannot write an effective political letter without understanding the political system and the issue that one wants to address.

Delli Carpini and Keeter (1996, 221, 224, 243, 253) find that knowledge of politics strongly predicts voter turnout, and knowledge of civil rights and political liberties correlates with tolerance. Thus, if a good civil society is one in which citizens tolerate one another and participate by voting, then knowledge of civil rights and politics are important preconditions. Nonpolitical civic participation, such as volunteering and belonging to associations, is not as clearly connected to knowledge, but research does show that residents who engage in their communities tend to seek information from high-quality news sources, such as daily newspapers. Obtaining information about current events probably provides relevant facts and motivations to participate in local volunteering efforts and associations; in turn, such participation encourages citizens to seek more information (Shah, McLeod, and Yoon 2001, 485).

Knowledge that is necessary for participation can be taught. For example, KidsVoting USA provides curricula, materials, and professional development for high school students and has been well evaluated. The program raises students' knowledge of politics (measured by current factual questions); reduces gaps in knowledge between the most and least knowledgeable students; and increases consistency between students' opinions on issues and their own voting behavior (Wackman and Meirick 2004; McDevitt and Kiousis 2004; McDevitt and Kiousis 2006). Perhaps the most intriguing result is that parents are more likely to discuss politics and current events if their children are enrolled in Kids Voting—a "trickle-up effect" (McDevitt, Kiousis, Wu, Losch, and Ripley 2003).

Kids Voting USA is a school curriculum, but institutions like newspapers and other news sources, labor unions, politically engaged religious congregations and social movements also have educative functions. The same can be said of formal political processes, such as elections and trials. John Stewart Mill argued that jury service, municipal elections, and "the conduct of industrial and philanthropic enterprises by voluntary associations" were valuable because they taught adults civic knowledge—"strengthening their active faculties, exercising their judgment, and giving them a familiar knowledge of the subjects with which they are thus left to deal" (Mill 1956, 133–4). A recent controlled study of jury service in the United States found that participants became more engaged in other aspects of civic life such as voting—unless the jury failed to reach a verdict (Gastil, Deess, and Weiser 2002). The authors' explanation involved "efficacy": by participating in a weighty and successful civic act such as a jury trial, people become more confident about their own civic potential. But Mill may also be correct that civic engagement deepens knowledge that assists with civic engagement, especially if one includes strengthened faculties and better judgment as forms of knowledge.

Studies that use actions (such as voting) as the dependent variables ignore an important normative question: when is engagement good? After all, Mussolini and his allies had civic skills, knew a great deal about Italian politics and society, and had substantial political impact. Their example is consistent with the studies cited above that show strong links between knowledge and participation, but it does not demonstrate that participation is desirable. One might therefore add that citizens should know right from wrong and justice from injustice (and act consistently with that knowledge).

2. CIVIC KNOWLEDGE AS KNOWLEDGE THAT SOME CITIZENS NEED

The argument thus far suggests that desirable forms of civic knowledge range from concrete civic skills (such as chairing a meeting), to a grasp of laws and rights, to awareness of current events, candidates, and ideologies, to moral knowledge or maturity that allows one to explore different interpretations of right and wrong. Historical, economic, scientific, and cultural knowledge are also valuable. For example, one cannot act effectively or responsibly on environmental issues without understanding biology, nor can one address racial tensions without knowing how they arose in history. These demands seem daunting, and surveys show that citizens in all the industrialized democracies are woefully ignorant of many important facts and concepts, but a division of labor can serve civil society, just as it serves a modern economy. Not everyone needs to know everything. In a pluralist society, individuals can specialize in particular issues—some working on environmental protection while others are concerned with spiritual matters or poverty. Moreover, civic associations have leaders as well as rank-and-file members, and the former need different knowledge to the latter.

Whereas the academic study of civic engagement investigates the knowledge that everyone needs, the field of leadership focuses on the more specialized skills and knowledge that individuals need when they assume leadership positions. Everyone should be able to vote, but only some people need to be able to negotiate with legislators. Everyone needs a general grasp of legal rights, but only some people need to know how to litigate. Everyone should be able to communicate effectively with strangers, but only some must be effective on national television. Furthermore, one's need for specialized factual knowledge rises as one becomes more influential within a movement. Members of environmental organizations need only a general commitment to policy, whereas leaders need to understand all the intricacies involved.

The leaders of successful social movements such as Mahatma Gandhi and Martin Luther King provide striking examples of skill and knowledge. The conventional view holds that the success of social movements depends on resources and conditions, not on the skills of those who lead them. But Peter Ackerman is one of several scholars who are revising that view, holding that strategic choices determine success and that leaders may either have or lack the skills to make good choices. Such skills are a form of knowledge (Ackerman 2007). Marshall Ganz holds that "mastery of specific skills—or how to strategize—is relevant, but so is access to local knowledge of the constituencies, opponents, and third parties with which one is interacting" (Ganz 2005, 220).

3. CIVIC KNOWLEDGE AS KNOWLEDGE THAT A CIVIL SOCIETY NEEDS

No individual can absorb all the information and knowledge that is accumulated in a traditional town archive, the clipping file of a conventional newspaper, or the vault of a local museum—let alone the vast expanses of the World Wide Web. Yet civil society is better off when such information is extensive, accessible, and secure. To hold a democratic state accountable and to accomplish voluntary collaborative projects, citizens need the opportunity to find data, knowledge, ideas, and interpretations on matters of shared concern: "*I* don't need to use such information if *someone* in my community can use it when it is needed."

Ostrom and Hess note that knowledge encompasses discrete artifacts (such as books, articles, maps, databases, and web pages), facilities (such as universities, schools, libraries, computers, and laboratories), and ideas (such as concepts, interpretations, hypotheses, and findings) (Ostrom and Hess 2007, 47). Thomas Jefferson already realized that ideas are pure public goods, for "he who receives an idea from me, receives instruction himself without lessening mine; as he who lites his taper at mine, receives light without darkening me" (quoted in Lessig 1999, 132). Knowledge artifacts and facilities are usually exclusive (my use of a computer terminal blocks yours), yet they can be shared—as Benjamin Franklin demonstrated when he founded the first public lending library.

The main challenges facing public goods are first, that individuals may not be motivated to produce things that benefit everyone (they can "free-ride" on others), and second, that individuals, firms, and governments may be tempted to privatize public goods for their own advantage. Today, many knowledge artifacts that once would have been exclusive can be digitized, posted online, and thereby turned into public goods. On the other hand, knowledge can be privatized and monetized, as when intellectual property is over-protected or when university-based research is influenced by corporate funding. It is also possible for knowledge to be underproduced, if there are insufficient incentives to develop and give it away. For example, too little research is conducted on diseases that affect the poorest people in the world.

Civic knowledge—knowledge of relevance to public or community issues—does not come into existence automatically, nor is it safe from antisocial behavior. The documents in a town archive, the reporting that fills a newspaper, and the artifacts in a local museum all take money and training to produce, catalog, and conserve. Once produced, these goods are fragile. They can literally decay, and they are subject to manipulation or inappropriate privatization. For example, access to state court decisions in the United States is provided exclusively by private firms, mainly the West Publishing Company and LEXIS/NEXIS. The public's interest in maintaining affordable and convenient access to public law would be undermined if these firms overcharged or provided poor quality information.

In 1998, with the Sonny Bono Copyright Term Extension Act, Congress extended most existing copyrights in the United States for 95 years. Congress thus granted monopoly ownership to works that had been created as long ago as 1903—requiring anyone who wanted to use these works to locate the copyright holder, seek permission, and pay whatever fee is demanded—and asserted a right to extend copyrights as frequently and for as long as it liked. In his dissenting opinion to the court decision that upheld this law, Supreme Court Justice Breyer wrote, "It threatens to interfere with efforts to preserve our Nation's historical and cultural heritage and efforts to use that heritage, say, to educate our Nation's children" (537 U.S. 26, 2003, 26). If Justice Breyer was correct, the Sonny Bono Act was an example of knowledge of civic value being turned from a public good into a private commodity by state power at the behest of private interests.

Given such threats, civil society can preserve and enhance civic knowledge by playing at least three roles. First, advocacy for policies that benefit the "knowledge commons" including the protection of free speech, appropriate copyright laws, public subsidies for libraries and archives, and public funds to digitize archives. Beneficial policies are public goods that often lose out to private interests that profit more tangibly from selfish policies. For example, everyone benefits from free access to historical texts, but a few companies profit much more substantially from their own copyrights. Independent, nonprofit associations can rectify this imbalance by recruiting voters, activists, and donors to promote the public interest in government. The American Library Association, for example, has been a strong advocate for knowledge as a public good.

Second, the provision of direct services by civil society groups. Many valuable archives and collections are funded and run by private, voluntary associations and their own donors and volunteers. Although the state has a role in producing and collecting knowledge, a state monopoly would be dangerous. And third, education, broadly defined. People do not automatically acquire an understanding and appreciation of valuable civic knowledge, nor the skills necessary to produce and conserve such knowledge. Each generation must transmit to the next the skills, motivations, and understanding necessary to preserve the knowledge commons. Again, government-run schools may have a role in this educational process, but they should not monopolize it. A more pluralistic and independent education system depends on nonprofit associations that recruit and train people to be community historians, archivists, naturalists, artists, or documentary filmmakers.

4. Civic Knowledge as Knowledge that Civil Society Generates

Most knowledge is created collaboratively. Scientists and other scholars collaborate on research projects and build on prior studies. Many scientists and scholars work for nonprofit institutions, such as universities and museums, and discuss and collaborate within voluntary professional associations. Because science and scholarship are collaborative, voluntary, and supported by nonprofit institutions, one might conclude that almost all knowledge is generated by civil society.

But that broad account would obscure important distinctions. Some knowledge is created by people who play specialized, professional roles. Scientists, for example, typically hold advanced degrees, receive salaries for working in scarce and competitive research or teaching positions, undergo various kinds of formal review (from tenure hearings to human subject review boards), and use funds from grants or contracts to collect and analyze data. Their training, funding, obligations, and guild-like organization separate them from civil society as a whole.

The more relevant question is what kinds of knowledge *citizens* can create collaboratively, if one defines citizens as all members of a civil society? Civic knowledge, in this sense, should be distinguished from knowledge that people create when they hold specialized professional roles. Civic knowledge should also be distinguished from knowledge that individuals create and use privately. Three forms of citizen-created knowledge seem especially important. First, empirical information and analysis can be collected or generated collaboratively by people who are not paid or credentialed as researchers. This was always possible: amateur botanists, genealogists, lexicographers, musicians, and many others contributed to the knowledge commons of the past. Yet the barriers to producing truly original and lasting work were high, and often amateurs invested substantial proportions of their time and energy to gain skills that made them comparable to paid professionals, and for that reason, they tended to be wealthy. Today's digital networks lower barriers to entry by making communication and publication extremely cheap, and by allowing large research projects to be broken into manageable parts.

Thus, for example, the *French Encyclopedia* of 1751–1772 was a major contribution to Enlightenment civil society. Not only did it contain knowledge as a public good, but it specifically expanded civil rights and liberties by promoting liberal positions contrary to absolute monarchism, the army, and the church. It had twenty-eight main authors, brilliant *philosophes* including Voltaire and Diderot, most of whom were amateurs in the sense that they were not paid to write—but they were a privileged and exceptional few. A new copy of the first edition cost about as much money as an unskilled laborer earned in sixteen months of work.[2] In contrast, Wikipedia, the online encyclopedia, has about 318 times more articles and roughly 85,000 active contributors, is completely free for anyone with Internet access, and expands freedom not because of a particular editorial commitment to liberal values, but because it is a massive, uncensored, public forum. Although it was set up for traditional encyclopedia articles, users now create live news pages as well. For example, the terrorist bombings in London in 2005 were tracked in real time on a Wikipedia page created within minutes of the first explosion (Shirky 2008, 116).

Wikipedia announces, "Visitors do not need specialized qualifications to contribute. Wikipedia's intent is to have articles that cover existing knowledge, not create new knowledge. This means that people of all ages and cultural and social backgrounds can write Wikipedia articles. Most of the articles can be edited by anyone with access to the Internet, simply by clicking the edit this page link. Anyone is welcome to add information, cross-references, or citations, as long as they do so within Wikipedia's editing policies and to an appropriate standard."[3]

Wikipedia is not evidently *better* than the *French Encyclopedia*: the former included many groundbreaking articles that changed disciplines and are still read today, whereas Wikipedia announces that its "intent [is not to] create new knowledge." But Wikipedia is a valuable resource that depends on citizen work. Like many other online tools and sites, it demonstrates that sheer numbers of people can generate useful knowledge that surpasses small numbers of experts. Another example would be search engines like Google that can identify material across an enormous range of topics, something that would be impossible for professional editors to achieve (Shirky 2008, 49).

A second form of knowledge that citizens can contribute is knowledge about their own needs, problems, goals, and interests. Democratic societies are supposed to pursue policies that people *want* (with appropriate regard for minorities as well as majorities). People know their own situations best; as John Dewey wrote, "The man who wears the shoe best knows where it pinches." In order to obtain just social outcomes, decision makers need to know what whole categories of people want and need. This is not easy. Elections convey relatively little information because voters must choose from finite lists of candidates, parties, or referenda. Surveys, focus groups, ethnographies, and "willingness to pay" experiments are among the techniques used to glean information about what people want, but all these methods are subject to inadvertent bias by researchers and deliberate manipulation by the institutions that commission them. The latter problem is most evident in authoritarian regimes, which systematically distort evidence about what people want. As Clay Shirky (2008, 163) notes, people not only need to know things; they must also know that everyone else knows these things, and that everyone knows what everyone else knows. For example, communist East Germany fell apart not when everyone knew that its system had failed, but when everyone could see that everyone else knew the same thing. Transparent public knowledge is a precondition for popular action, and is what authoritarian governments try to block by suppressing freedom of association and speech. The same danger is not absent in liberal societies.

Thus it is essential that many citizens should freely express their own values, goals, and concerns. People express what they want in many forms, including private conversations, consumer choices, protests, letters, songs, prayers, and gifts. They may even express their wants by *refusing* to act: silent noncompliance and foot-dragging are traditional modes of resistance by poor people around the world (Scott 1990, 198). Civil society plays an essential role in translating private goals and preferences into public opinion that can—in a democratic and liberal state—influence major institutions. In the terminology of Jürgen Habermas (1985, 113–197) the "lifeworld" consists of our ordinary, shared values and commitments, which develop in the course of daily life and face-to-face human interaction. The "system" means the formal processes by which governments, corporations, and other powerful actors allocate goods and rights. In a legitimate society, public debate and discussion *improve* the tacit norms of the lifeworld by addressing conflicts within the society and encouraging people to justify their beliefs to their peers. The results of this discussion become explicit as "public opinion" and influence the system. In practical terms, this process requires civic institutions, ranging from the coffee houses and newspapers of the Enlightenment to the activist groups and online social networks of today (Habermas 1991). Some institutions of civil society arise to make explicit, public claims on behalf of their own members. Interest groups and activist lobbies are examples. Some institutions attempt to create more or less neutral forums for discussion—for example, the opinion page of a traditional metropolitan daily newspaper or a civic lecture series. And some institutions simply make manifest the existence of social groups that have a claim to be recognized. For example, the mission statement of HispanicMoslems.com is "to show the diversity of the Muslim community by educating Muslims and non-Muslims about Hispanic and Latino Muslims."[4] Since Hispanics are often presumed to be Christian, and Muslims are often presumed to come from the Middle East, Hispanic Muslims need an association to obtain recognition, which is a precondition for being included in public dialog and influencing public opinion (Warren 2000, 132).

Habermas's theoretical perspective provides the basis for making normative judgments. Civil society is most helpful for generating knowledge about what people want and need when it is diverse, free, equitable, and anchored in the authentic values of the lifeworld. It is threatened when the system—dominated by money, wealth, and strategic communication—"colonizes" it. When the system dominates, public opinion is not true knowledge of what people want, but the spurious result of money and power.

Knowing what people want is insufficient for good decision making; for decisions also involve negotiations about what is right and just. At least since Socrates, theorists have searched for a technique that would determine what one should do, given an accurate description of the context plus valid rules of moral inference. Two modern secular techniques for this purpose are utilitarianism and Kantianism. Utilitarianism states that the right thing to do is that which would maximize the totality of human welfare. Although predicting the impact of any policy on objective net welfare is methodologically complex, utilitarians have developed methods for estimating welfare impacts, especially economic cost/benefit analysis. In contrast, Kantianism states that the right thing to do is that which is consistent with a general rule, binding on all. John Rawls (2005) applied Kant's position to politics by arguing that what is just is what one would decide under a "veil of ignorance" about his or her own social situation.

Although quite different in content, these techniques share the hope that people need not debate moral issues endlessly or face perennial conflicts of values and interests. Instead, these techniques promise a right answer that can be known by an individual armed with adequate information and the correct method. But that hope has been widely assailed. Utilitarianism is a minority viewpoint among philosophers, who have attacked it for, among other things, ignoring rights and presuming that one can compare welfare among individuals. Kantianism also has its critics, and even most of its proponents concede that it will not generate concrete decisions in many cases. Kant himself wrote that we need the "power of judgment sharpened by experience" to tell us how to apply moral laws to particular cases (Kant 1991, ix), and Rawls insisted that reasoning under the veil of ignorance could determine only very general rules such as those found in national constitutions. Ordinary decisions require public deliberation (Rawls 2005, 212–254).

If there is no technique for determining justice, then there is no escape from a permanent discussion among people who differ in their interests, values, and principles. But that discussion can be conducted in ways that are better or worse. Proponents of deliberative democracy advocate that moral discussions should be as equitable and free as possible. Participants should genuinely seek what is right, which involves listening to other perspectives and being open to change, rather than strategically seeking goals that they held before entering the discussion. Such conversations are most likely to occur within the institutions of civil society, rather than in markets, bureaucracies, or private homes. Indeed, some have *defined* civil society as the "private (nonstate) 'space' in which individuals without official status can communicate and attempt to persuade one another through argumentation and criticism about matters of general concern" (Cohen 1999, 55–85). In practice, public argumentation combines questions of abstract principle with expressions of personal and group identity and interest, because these matters cannot be sharply separated for human beings who are embodied creatures in specific cultural contexts.

Michael Sandel famously wrote that, "when politics goes well, we can know a good in common that we cannot know alone" (Sandel 1998, 183). Sandel argued that the characteristic knowledge that we must obtain together is moral knowledge, knowledge of the good. We need others to know it because moral judgments are heavily experiential, because any individual's perspective is biased and limited, and because there is no impartial algorithm or method that can identify the good for everyone involved.

5. Conclusion

Civic knowledge means the knowledge that people create, use, and preserve when they act as members of a civil society. A successful civil society requires a demanding range of these forms of knowledge, but fortunately, citizens can share the burdens that are involved in making and in using them. Because public issues and problems have moral dimensions, it is important for people to use knowledge deliberatively, in constructive and equitable discussions. The conditions that allow adequate levels of knowledge to be produced, shared, and applied do not arise automatically. The institutions and networks of civil society are also responsible for creating those conditions and protecting them against constant threats from both the market and the state.

NOTES

1. Here I define a "citizen" as a member of society, without assuming that they live in a nation-state or that citizenship is defined by legal rights.
2. The lowest subscription price was 546 francs (Watts 1958, 348). The market price of unskilled labor was 1.25 livres or francs per day (from the Global Price and Income History Group: http://www.iisg.nl/hpw/data.php#france).
3. See http://en.wikipedia.org/wiki/Wikipedia:About.
4. See http://hispanicmuslims.com/mission.html.

REFERENCES

Ackerman, P. 2007. "Skills or Conditions: What Key Factors Shape the Success or Failure of Civil Resistance?" Conference on Civil Resistance and Power Politics, St Antony's

College, University of Oxford, 15-18 March. Available at http://www.nonviolent-conflict.org/PDF/AckermanSkillsOrConditions.pdf.

Cohen, J. 1999. "American Civil Society Talk," in R. K. Fullinwider (ed.) *Civil Society, Democracy, and Civic Renewal.* Lanham, Md.: Rowman and Littlefield.

Delli Carpini, M., and S. Keeter. 1996. *What Americans Know about Politics and Why it Matters.* New Haven, Conn.: Yale University Press.

Ganz, M. 2005. "Why David Sometimes Wins: Strategic Capacity in Social Movements," in D. Messick. and R. Kramer (eds.) *The Psychology of Leadership: New Perspectives and Research.* Mahwah, N.J.: Lawrence Erlbaum.

Gastil, J., E. Deess, P. Deess, and P. Weiser. 2002. "Civic Awakening in the Jury Room: A Test of the Connection between Jury Deliberation and Political Participation." *The Journal of Politics* (64)2: 585–95.

Habermas, J. 1985. *The Theory of Communicative Action, vol. 2: Lifeword and System: A Critique of Functionalist Reason.* Trans. T. McCarthy. Boston: Beacon Press.

——. 1991. *The Structural Transformation of the Public Sphere: An Inquiry into a Category of Bourgeois Societ.* Trans. T. Berger with F. Lawrence. Cambridge, Mass.: MIT Press.

Kamali, M. 2001. "Civil Society and Islam: A Sociological Perspective, *European Journal of Sociology* 42: 457–82.

Kant, I. 1991. *Grundlegung zur Metaphysik der Sitten (Groundwork of the Metaphysics of Morals).* Ed. Wilhelm Weischedel. Suhrkamp: Frankfurt am Main:

Lessig, L. 1999. *Code and Other Laws of Cyberspace.* New York: Basic Books.

Lomasky, L. 1999. "Civil Enough: Toward a Liberal Theory of Vice (and Virtue)," in R. Fullinwider (ed.), op. cit.

Madsen, R. 2002. "Confucian Conceptions of Civil Society," in S. Chambers and W. Kymlicka (eds.) *Alternative Conceptions of Civil Society.* Princeton, N.J.: Princeton University Press.

McDevitt, M., and S. Kiousis. 2004. "Education for Deliberative Democracy: The Long-Term Influence of Kids Voting USA." Center for Information and Research on Civic Learning and Engagement (CIRCLE) Working Paper 22. University of Maryland.

——. 2006. "Experiments in Political Socialization: Kids Voting USA as a Model for Civic Education Reform." Center for Information and Research on Civic Learning and Engagement (CIRCLE) Working Paper 49. University of Maryland.

McDevitt, M., S. Kiousis, X. Wu, M. Losch, and T. Ripley. 2003. "The Civic Bonding of School and Family: How Kids Voting Students Enliven the Domestic Sphere." Center for Information and Research on Civic Learning and Engagement (CIRCLE) Working Paper 7. University of Maryland.

Mill, J. S. 1956. *On Liberty.* Ed. C. V. Shields. Indianapolis: Bobb-Merrill.

Milner, H. 2002. *Civic Literacy: How Informed Citizens Make Democracy Work.* Hanover, N.H.: Tufts University Press.

Radsch, C. 2008. "Core to Commonplace: The Evolution of Egypt's Blogosphere." Arab & Media and Society. Available at www.arabmediasociety.com.

Rawls, J. 2005. *Political Liberalism.* New York: Columbia University Press.

Ostrom, E., and C. Hess. 2007. "A Framework for Analyzing the Knowledge Commons," in C. Hess and E. Ostrom (eds.) *Understanding Knowledge as a Commons: From Theory to Practice.* Cambridge, Mass.: MIT Press.

Sandel, M. 1998. *Liberalism and the Limits of Justice.* 2nd ed. Cambridge: Cambridge University Press.

Scott, J. 1990. *Domination and the Arts of Resistance: Hidden Transcripts.* New Haven, Conn.: Yale University Press.

Shah, D., J. McLeod, and S-H. Yoon. 2001. "Communication, Context, and Community: An Exploration of Print, Broadcast, and Internet Influences." *Communication Research*, vol. 28, no 4: 464–506.

Shirky, C. 2008. *Here Comes Everybody: The Power of Organizing without Organizations.* New York: Penguin.

Verba, S., K. Schlozman, and H. Brady. 1995. *Voice and Equality: Civic Voluntarism in American Politics.* Cambridge, Mass.: Harvard University Press.

Wackman, D., and P. Meirick. 2004. "Kids Voting and Political Knowledge: Narrowing Gaps, Informing Voters." *Social Science Quarterly,* vol. 85, no. 5: 1161–77.

Warren, M. E. 2000. *Democracy and Association.* Princeton, N.J.: Princeton University Press.

Watts, G. 1958. "The Encyclopedie Methodique." *PMLA (Journal of the Modern Language Association of America)* vol. 73, no. 4: 348–66.

PART VI

THE ACHIEVEMENTS
OF CIVIL SOCIETY

CHAPTER 30

CIVIL SOCIETY
AND DEMOCRACY

MARK E. WARREN

THE two decades leading up to the end of the twentieth century saw a remarkable growth in the numbers of regimes that conduct politics through competitive elections. As of 2009, 116 countries counted as electoral democracies—slightly down from the high of 123 counted in 2006, but considerably more than the 69 registered two decades before (Freedom House 2010). But competitive electoral systems, though necessary for democracy, are not sufficient. Many new democracies—countries that have adopted the institution of competitive elections—fail to produce governments that are representative and responsive to those who fall within their jurisdictions. Many of the established democracies suffer from deficits of trust and citizen disaffection, leaving decisions to be made by elites under pressure from well-organized interests.

Can electoral democracies be deepened in such a way that they function to produce governments that are representative of, and responsive to, those within their jurisdictions? To ask this question is to ask about the ways in which people self-organize, such that they can form their interests and opinions, convey them to governments, hold governments accountable, and engage in collective actions oriented towards common goods. Elections are necessary enabling institutions. But robust civil societies provide the contexts within which elections function democratically (Dahl 2000). Indeed, the correlation between robust civil societies and functioning democracies has been so striking that we have come to understand them as reinforcing one another (Cohen and Arato 1992; Putnam 1993; Edwards 2009).

Civil society, as I shall use the term here, is the domain of society organized through associative media, in contrast to organization through legally empowered administration (the core of state power and organization), or market transactions mediated by money (the core of economic power and organization) (Warren 2001;

see also Cohen and Arato 1992; Habermas 1996, ch. 8; cf. Alexander 2006). Civil society is the domain of purpose-built, normatively justified associations. It is for this reason that civil society is as much a core feature of democracy as are competitive elections: it is through association that people organize their interests, values, and opinions and act upon them, some directly—as in religious and sporting associations—and some indirectly, as representations that organize public opinion, mobilize votes and other forms of pressure, and function to define "the people" whom a state can represent, and to whom the formal institutions of democracy can respond (Urbinati and Warren 2008). No civil society, no "people"—which is why the twenty-six or so countries that Freedom House (2010) lists as "electoral democracies" but not as "free" fail to function democratically. They lack the political protections for association, speech, and conscience that enable the modes of self-organization necessary for democratic institutions to function.

These democratic functions of civil society are contingent rather than necessary. Famously, civil society appeared to be robust in Weimar Germany before the rise of the Nazis (Berman 1997). And on the heels of enthusiasm for civil society in the 1990s, scholars pointed out that many kinds of civil society organization are bad for democracy since they can cultivate hatred, violence, and sectarianism (Chambers and Kopstein 2001). Some kinds of association underwrite networks that aid and abet political corruption, support clientelist political arrangements, and provide additional political advantage those who are already possess the advantages of income and education (Warren 2008).

From the standpoint of democratic theory, can we sharpen our focus? Can we distinguish the kinds, dimensions, and functions of civil society that are likely to deepen democracy from those that are not? We can, but to do so we must develop less abstract conceptions of both democracy and civil society, a task that is addressed in section 1 of this chapter. Section 2 analyzes the potential contributions of civil society to democracy, while section 3 distinguishes features of associations that are likely to determine their democratic contributions. Section 4 introduces ecological considerations by framing the question in terms of the optimal mix of kinds of association from the perspective of democracy.

1. DEMOCRACY AND THE "ALL-AFFECTED" PRINCIPLE

The potential roles of civil society in deepening democracy come into sharpest focus when institutional definitions of democracy—say, as constituted by competitive elections—are subordinated to a normative conception that focuses on what democracies should accomplish. Democratic theorists increasingly converge on the view that democracy requires that *all those potentially affected by collective decisions have opportunities to affect these decisions in ways proportional to the potential effects*

(Goodin 2007; Habermas 1994; Young 2000). The institutions, organizations, and practices that comprise democracy, then, would be those that enable those who are potentially affected by collective decisions to have opportunities to influence them.

Democratic theorists increasingly opt for this generic, normative conception of democracy for two reasons. First, institutional definitions of democracy conflate ideals of what democracy should achieve with institutional means for achieving them, thus making it impossible to judge particular arrangements to be more or less democratic. Distinguishing an ideal of democracy from its typical institutions—say, kinds of electoral democracy or deliberative forums—allows us to judge these institutions to be more or less democratic.

The second reason for preferring a normative conception of democracy is that the sites of collective decision making in today's societies are now so diverse that traditional sites of democracy—particularly elections based on territorial constituencies—are only one kind among many (Rehfeld 2005; Saward 2006). Not only are individuals affected by multiple levels of governments, but also by other kinds of collectivities, including corporations, religious organizations, schools, and other kinds of organizations. Moreover, because modern societies involve extensive divisions of labor and extensive interdependencies in areas such as security, environment, and migration, individuals are subject to what James Bohman (2007) has termed "chains of affectedness" that are global in scope and extensive in time and space.

For democracy to have meaning under these circumstances, it should refer to individuals' means and capacities to exert influence on these chains of affectedness, should they decide to do so. And for *influence* to have meaning under these conditions, we must also think about multiple possibilities beyond the democratic exercise of voting for governments—which, although it will always remain a foundational element of democracy, cannot encompass the many ways in which individuals are affected by collectivities. Thus, if we are to identify the democratic possibilities entailed by the contemporary conditions of politics, we must also consider potential avenues of influence more generically and abstractly.

As a general matter, individual influence can vary in two dimensions. In one dimension, influence can be *directive* or *protective*. Influence is *directive* when individuals exercise influence over collective decisions, as when they vote or participate in a decision-making venue. Influence is *protective* when individuals have the power to resist harms generated by other collectivities, as when they protest against collective decisions made elsewhere, or exercise veto powers, or organize to escape the potentially damaging consequences of a collective arrangement. That is, democracy does not necessarily mean that everyone is involved in making collective decisions—that is an impossible image of democracy under contemporary circumstances. Democracy can also mean that individuals have the powers to resist harms to self-determination, producing what contemporary republicans call "nondomination" (Pettit 1997; Bohman 2007).

Individual influence can also vary from *directly exercised* to *representative*. Individuals directly influence decisions when they vote in referendums, or participate in a neighborhood organization. They exercise influence through *representatives* when they vote for representatives, or join organizations that pressure, protest, sue, deliberate, or otherwise exercise influence on their behalf (Saward 2006). Because complex societies de-center sites of collective action, they open many new opportunities for direct democracy through civil society organizations (Warren 2002). At the same time, owing to the multiplication of influences in complex societies, most influences will be exercised through representatives—not simply elected representatives, but also interest and advocacy groups as well as other kinds of civil society actors.

In complex societies, then, *democracy* refers to the multiple means that individuals might use to affect collective decisions—not just voting, but also organization, advocacy, networking and deliberation, that may occur at multiple points in decision-making processes, from diffuse influences on public opinion to highly focused participatory inputs into specific decisions. And, indeed, in addition to the dramatic expansion of electoral democracy over the last three decades, we have also witnessed a rapid increase in social movements, interest groups, watchdog and oversight organizations, intensive media campaigns, network organizations, and new forms of direct action (Warren 2003; Rosanvallon 2008). Governments increasingly respond to these developments with the use of referendums, the devolution and de-concentration of decision making, new forms of network and collaborative governance, public deliberations and forms, stakeholder meetings, and other kinds of devices that often have little relationship to the institutions of electoral democracy (Warren 2009; Edwards 2009; Leighninger 2006).

Far from representing the failure of electoral institutions, the fact that much political work now takes place in other locations represents their success. Electoral institutions have had their most important impacts within constitutional regimes that protect and enable sites of collective organization, decision, and action within society. Over time, these kinds of arrangements disperse the powers and capacities for collective action, in this way transforming the very nature of governing from a sovereign centre. They reflect increasingly confident and capable citizenries, many with increasingly post-material sensibilities that include greater interests in self-government (Inglehart and Welzel 2005; Dalton 2007; Warren 2003). Some of the political responses to these trends, such as increasing reliance on processes of "governance"—partnerships between governments and civil society organizations—are incremental and experimental. Others are world-historical, such the European Union.

2. The Democratic Possibilities of Civil Society Associations

What all these developments have in common is that democracy has become ever more reliant on civil society for its realization. We can further specify these dependencies by classifying the potentially democratic effects of the associations in three broad classes, distinguished by level of analysis (Warren 2001; Edwards 2009). First, democracies depend on *individuals* with capacities for democratic citizenship. In a democracy, individuals should be able to understand and articulate their interests and values, have enough information and education to relate their interests and values to sites of collective decision and organization, have the political capacities to participate in collective decisions, and possess the civic dispositions that enable them to do so in ways consistent with democratic ways of making decisions: persuasion and voting. As Tocqueville famously noted, the associations of civil society should serve as "schools of democracy" (Tocqueville 1969 vol. 2, 517): they may provide individuals with information, educate them, develop their sense of political efficacy, cultivate their capacities for negotiation and deliberation, and instill civic virtues such as toleration, trust, respect for others, and sense of reciprocity.

Second, democracies are inherently *public:* rules, reasons, and decisions are knowable by those affected by them. Civil societies function as the social infrastructure, as it were, of the public spheres from which collective decisions ultimately derive their legitimacy. In a democracy, legitimacy stems from two sources. The first source is inclusion: the legitimacy of decisions rests on responsiveness to those affected—if not in substance, then because the views incorporated into decisions have been considered and deliberated. The associations of civil society provide the conduits of representation though advocacy and by framing the interests, values, and voices of those potentially affected, thus forming articulate constituencies (Young 2000, ch. 5). The second source of democratic legitimacy is public deliberation itself, through which representations are transformed into discourses which form public opinion, such that decisions have a locus of considered argument and agreement (Habermas 1996). The associations of civil society underwrite deliberation by organizing and communicating information to publics, provoking public deliberation, and monitoring public officials and institutions. Sometimes these functions are served by groups that specialize in public discourse, such as think tanks and media-oriented groups. Often, however, they are consequences of groups pursuing their agendas through public advocacy (Urbinati 2000). In short, civil societies can deepen democracy by underwriting the public spheres that guide and legitimatize collective decisions.

Third, civil society associations serve *institutional* functions that are necessary for a democracy to work. The advocacy organizations of civil society serve representative functions between elections, linking public officials with constituents, and often forming constituencies that are not formally represented by territorially based electoral institutions (Urbinati and Warren 2008). Multilateral and multistate institutions such as the United Nations and the European Union now include civil society organizations as part of their representative structures, in part to represent interests—such as basic human rights—that are not well represented through member-state channels. The development of governance structures also provides conduits of inclusion. Civil society is itself a key site of collective decision and organization: all countries now deliver services through partnerships, contracts, and other forms of devolved and de-centered forms of governance (Leighninger 2006).

And last but not least, civil society organizations provide sites of alternative voices and opposition when interests, values, or voices are not included (Young 2000).

3. Theorizing the Democratic Capabilities of Civil Society Associations

Listing the many possible political functions of civil society underscores the point that democracies today are complex ecologies which have come to depend upon the multiple contributions of civil society. This same list, however, makes the point that no single kind of association can perform all of these functions, and indeed some will not perform any of them, and may even be harmful to democracy (Berman 1997; Chambers and Kopstein 2001; Chambers and Kymlicka 2002). How should we develop our expectations? Following earlier work (Warren 2001), I suggest three kinds of theoretical distinctions which, when taken together, identify the features of civil society associations most likely to affect their democratic functions.

a. Voluntariness

It is common to refer to the associations that populate civil society as *voluntary* associations (e.g., Salamon 2003). The reason is normative rather than descriptive: as a pure ideal type, associations are constituted by individuals who share purposes, and who chose to associate to advance these purposes. There is also a normative relationship between the voluntariness of associations and democracy: social relations that are *chosen* rather than imposed will manifest rather than limit self-government. The legitimacy of collective choice follows from the voluntariness of the association—a normative relationship fundamental to liberal contract theory from Locke through Rawls.

As an analytic matter, however, no association is entirely voluntary or involuntary. Rather, there are degrees of voluntariness that will depend upon an association's control over the resources that people need or want, including identity resources such as religion, ethnicity, and culture. The degree of voluntariness has implications for democracy in three ways. The first relates to the association itself: a purely voluntary association has low normative requirements for democracy internal to the association just because members are free to exit. Freedom to exit— higher degrees of voluntarism—is likely to produce associations with more homogeneous purposes. And the more homogeneous its purpose, the more able the association will be to pursue goals that depend upon solidarity. Common purposes help to build what Putnam (2000, 336–49) calls "bonding" social capital, as opposed to the weaker "bridging" social capital that is created by internally diverse associations that cross ethnic, religious, racial, regional, and other divides. Members are better able to speak with one voice in the public sphere and represent positions or discourses within broad public conversations. Because voluntariness enhances solidarity, these associations are more likely to enable opposition to external sources of domination.

In contrast, associations with involuntary elements have potentials for exploitation and domination, as is evident in criminal and clientelist associations, and as is not uncommon in ethnic and religious associations too. Civil societies that are dense with these kinds of associations—as are many of the new electoral democracies—may function to reproduce social relations of power in ways that undermine the democratic effects of electoral institutions.

But involuntary associations can serve democracy in two other ways. First, from a normative perspective, the more involuntary an association is, the more democratic its internal decision making should be. Many common forms of association have involuntary elements, such as unions and workplaces, or residential communities and neighborhoods in which people have large sunk costs. Religious associations can be experienced as involuntary by those raised in the faith. These kinds of associations have the potential to serve a variety of democratic purposes, precisely because their involuntariness makes it difficult for them to externalize conflict. Members cannot "vote with their feet" (Hirschman 1970). For these reasons, involuntary associations must find ways of managing conflict. If they do so democratically, they can manage and protect against potential relations of domination, thus serving the goal of nondomination.

Second, to the extent that associations respond to their involuntary elements democratically with voice and votes, they are also likely to serve as schools of democracy, cultivating deliberative capacities, toleration, and political efficacy. In contrast, the more voluntary an association, the more likely it is to externalize conflict: members who are dissatisfied will often find exit to be easier than voice. Voluntary associations are subject to the dynamics of self-selection, which will create memberships that are more homogeneous in their purposes and social characteristics. They may be inclined to reinforce intolerance because they enable "enclave deliberation" in which members with similar opinions reinforce one another (Sunstein 2001).

b. Constitutive Media

The degree of voluntariness is only one of the features of civil society associations likely to determine their contributions to democracy. We can also distinguish associations along a second dimension—what I call their *constitutive media*. We need to know whether an association is primarily oriented towards (1) *social norms* such as shared identity or purpose, moral commitment, friendship, or other means of social solidarity; (2) *state power*, as are many kinds of advocacy and interest groups; or (3) *markets and money*, as are consumer cooperatives, social marketing associations, and labor unions. The medium towards which an association is primarily oriented—social norms, state power, or markets—determines much about the ways an association reproduces its identity and pursues its goals, which in turn affect its contributions to democracy.

An example will indicate why this set of distinctions is important. Consider the ways in which associations manage conflict, which in turn affects several potential democratic functions, including serving as "schools of democracy" and as sites of devolved or de-concentrated public purposes. All other things being equal, associations held together by social norms such as hobby groups or religious associations will have high degrees of solidarity, which will improve capacities for collective action. But these same characteristics will make it difficult for such associations to manage internal conflict, since conflict typically damages social solidarity—the constitutive medium of the association. From a democratic perspective, it might be good for members of an association to discuss and deliberate principled disagreements and delicate issues. But even civil argument tends to threaten social bonds, and will tend towards the equally antipolitical responses of exit (in the case of voluntary associations), or repression for the sake of civility (in less voluntary associations). More generally, associations based on social solidarity alone will tend to be robust in identity formation, and have high capacities for generating bonding social capital and the capacities for collective action that follow. But they will be fragile with respect to conflict resolution—and thus serve as poor schools of democracy with respect to deliberation, negotiation, and bargaining (Mutz 2006).

In contrast, associations that are oriented towards markets (such as labor unions) or political structures (such as community development associations or political interest groups), will depend more on *interests in strategic goals* than on social norms and identities. A community development association has interest-based inducements to set aside differences of race, ethnicity, and religious affiliation so that the organization can do its job. Indeed, like legislative bodies, such associations may develop norms of courtesy in order to prevent social cleavages from incapacitating deliberation and decision making (Warren 2006). All other things being equal, associations that are oriented towards interest-based goals will unburden social solidarity, which will in turn increase their capacities for political deliberation and problem solving. To the extent that interests cross-cut identity-based cleavages, these kinds of associations may foster the civic virtues of tolerance and reciprocity, while weakening representations of identity-based claims in public spheres.

It also makes a difference whether an association is vested or not vested in its constitutive medium: groups seeking to pressure market-based actors or political structures from without will have an easier time identifying a cause—and going public—than groups that have access to resources which they must manage, compromise, or distribute. When the German green movement, for example, was debating whether to become a political party in the 1970s, they recognized the tradeoffs involved. Transforming their organization into a party might give them a greater influence over policy decisions. But as insiders with influence, they would compromise their ability to criticize and oppose policies based on clear principles and purposes, which would in turn weaken their popular base in the green social movement.

c. Purposes

The final set of distinctions that make a difference to the democratic functions of associations has to do with their purposes. In complex societies the purposes of association are highly diverse—the Internal Revenue Service in the United States uses over 600 classifications of 501(c)(3) nonprofits alone. Fortunately, the features of purposes likely to make a difference to an association's democratic functions are much simpler, the most important of which have to do with whether an association seeks goods that are inherently public, identity-based, or status-based (Warren 2001, ch. 5). Associations devoted to *public goods* are especially important to deepening democracy. Public goods are nonexcludable goods subject to free-ridership—goods such as security, environmental integrity, and public health which must be provided to everyone if they are provided to anyone. These goods can only be gained through collective action, and so people must be persuaded to contribute. So associations devoted to public goods will tend to cultivate civic virtues, underwrite deliberation, represent common discourses and ideals, and increase common capacities for collective action.

In contrast, associations devoted to *identity goods* such as religion and ethnicity are more ambiguous in their effects: some—particularly minorities—may seek recognition and thus increase civic virtues such as toleration. Others—particularly majorities—often highlight in-group/out-group distinctions in order to produce internal cohesion, but at the cost of generating intolerance and exclusion. Such groups may contribute to public debate and group representation, but they are unlikely to enhance civic virtues or political skills of deliberation. Associations devoted to *status goods*—private clubs and connoisseur groups, for example—are unlikely to contribute to publicly represented dynamics of exclusion, but they will also tend towards exclusive status-based connections that contribute very little at all to democracy.

4. DEMOCRATIC ASSOCIATIONAL ECOLOGIES

A comprehensive research agenda on civil society's contributions to deepening democracy would map a region or country's associational landscape using these kinds of distinctions. We are far from having such maps (cf. Salamon 2003; Powell and Steinberg 2006; Hodgkinson and Weitzman 1996), but even if we did have them, our theoretical expectations would not yet be sufficiently developed to address the question of how civil societies might deepen democracy, especially across different contexts. The analysis above makes the point that no single kind of association can address the full range of functions civil society must fulfill, while also suggesting theoretical distinctions that should enable us to predict the contributions of distinct associational types (Warren 2001). The next task is to identify the mixes, balances, and distributions of associational types will serve to deepen democracy along the individual, public, and institutional trajectories suggested above. What would comprise a *democratic* _associational ecology_? To be sure, answering this question requires context-specific research into the mixes of associations that support or undermine democracy. But we can frame these research questions with several theoretical guidelines in mind.

a. Balance

A mix of associations that deepens democracy should be balanced: a political system needs the full range of potential contributions to function democratically. Imbalances may occur, for example, when civil society lacks interest-based associations to balance identity-based associations. Or, again, if a civil society is comprised primarily of associations that have vested interests in prevailing political or economic power structures—if most civil society associations are integrated into clientelist politics (as they are in many of the new electoral democracies), for example—civil society will tend to undermine democratic representation and public deliberation, and will certainly fail to provide citizens with means of oversight and accountability. Or, to take another possibility, if a civil society is comprised primarily of groups mobilized for opposition, the overall effect may be to create gridlock in government and undermine state capacities.

b. External and Internal and Checks on Associations

Certain kinds of civil society organizations are potential threats to democracy—particularly those which combine high capacities for collective action with narrowly focused interests or internally focused identities. Within authoritarian contexts, tribal or religious organizations may function as informal monitors and enforcers for governments. Associations populated by business people, for example, can serve to organize monopolies or oligopolies (as chambers of commerce have sometimes done in small U.S. towns), or as means for organizing the systematic corruption of a political system (as the Free Masons did in post-World War II Italy). Civil societies that deepen democracy will not lack such groups. But they are likely to have a mix of associations that check the potentials of such powerful groups to produce anti-democratic effects. A civil society with external checks on power will typically include, for example, citizens' watchdog groups, unions, associations of socially conscious investors, groups devoted to the provision of public goods, as well as a pluralism of identity-based groups. Of course, the mixes that provide such external checks typically depend on governments that protect pluralism, provide oversight of potential misuses of market power, and are relatively difficult for corrupting powers to penetrate—all reasons that democratic civil societies tend to be associated with the protections and supports of liberal-democratic regimes.

Other kinds of associations are subject to internal checks, so that even when they accumulate power they pose little risk to democracy. Internal checks are likely to be found within associations that combine lower exit with public purposes. Because associations with restricted exit will tend to internalize conflict, they will have inducements to manage conflict through processes that generate accountability (Hirschman 1970). These inducements are likely to be strongest within associations that seek public or common goods, since such goods can only be achieved, typically, with public justifications. Examples of these kinds of associations include groups devoted to civic, environmental, poverty, health, and other public goods-related causes, some kinds of political parties, public corporatist bodies, universities, much of the mass media, self-help and cooperative economic networks, and many other kinds of groups with these characteristics. Thus, we should expect civil societies with high densities of these kinds of associations to have relatively sturdy democratic associational ecologies.

c. Individual Attachments

We also need to think about associational mixes from the perspective of the individual attachments that form citizens' dispositions and capacities. Just as a civil society should have a mix of associations that cover the full range of democratic functions, individuals should have attachments that, in aggregate, provide a full range of developmental effects. Here again, there will be associational kinds that are more likely to provide developmental effects that enhance civic virtues and deliberative capacities: on average, these will include associations with somewhat restricted exit, have some responsibilities for resource distribution, and are oriented towards public or common goods. Examples include groups focused on education, health, and community development, and labor unions engaged in social issues.

In contrast, identity-based groups, exclusive social clubs, fundamentalist religious and ethnic groups, and business pressure groups, though perhaps important for the representative ecology of a democracy, also tend towards internal homogeneity of purpose, and so will lack one or more of the developmental experiences necessary for democratic citizenship. In associational ecologies in which individuals belong to these kinds of groups without complementary experiences, patterns of membership may produce rigid social cleavages which militate against political negotiation and deliberation. It is for this reason that activists seeking to move societies torn by ethnic or religious cleavages towards democracy will advocate forms of association focused on concrete projects such as community development: these kinds of associations cross-cut, and thus moderate, identity-based cleavages (Saunders 1999). Societies in which cleavages follow tribal, ethnic, or religious lines do not lack civil society associations, but they lack the kinds of associations that produce democratic citizens.

d. Distributions of Attachments

Finally, _who benefits from associational attachments_ also makes a difference: joiners will gain from advantages conveyed by social capital in ways that non-joiners will not. Thus, even if the mixes of associations in a society are balanced and checked in ways that favor democracy, it is still possible for patterns of associational attachments to mirror common resource advantages and disadvantages. In the United States, for example, many of the same factors that predict political participation—particularly education and income—also predict associational attachments, meaning that those who benefit from education and income also benefit from the distribution of social capital (Verba et. al. 1995; Pew Research Center 1997). A democracy should seek to cultivate association among the least advantaged, in part because association *in itself* is a precursor to democratic empowerment—moving a society closer to instantiating the all-affected principle (Warren MR 2001).

5. CONCLUSION

Democracy is a normatively ambitious goal: it requires that those affected by decisions have opportunities to influence them. Though ambitious, this democratic norm encompasses the increasingly common moral intuition that societies should maximize individual self-development and self-direction by altering power structures in favor of inclusion and voice. Yet under contemporary conditions of politics—scale, complexity, and pluralism—it is impossible to conceive of this ideal without the multitudinous sites of organization, experience, direction, and decision offered by civil society associations in the public sphere. Civil society is not only about *deepening* democracy: it is now impossible to *imagine* a democracy without the multiple effects of civil society on individual development, public deliberation and representation, and sites of organization and collective action. That said, none of these functions are necessary to civil society as such. Rather, they follow from democratic associational ecologies that are comprised of those kinds of associations whose characteristics incline them towards democratic effects.

REFERENCES

Alexander, J. 2006. *The Civil Sphere.* Oxford: Oxford University Press.

Berman, S. 1997. "Civil Society and the Collapse of the Weimar Republic." *World Politics* 49: 40–29.

Bohman, J. 2007. *Democracy Across Borders: From Demos to Demoi.* Cambridge, Mass.: MIT Press.

Chambers, S., and J. Kopstein. 2001. "Bad Civil Society." *Political Theory* 29: 837–65.

Chambers, S., and W. Kymlicka (eds). 2002. *Alternative Conceptions of Civil Society.* Princeton, N.J.: Princeton University Press.

Cohen, J., and A. Arato. 1992. *Civil Society and Political Theory.* Cambridge, Mass.: MIT Press.

Dahl, R. A. 2000. *On Democracy.* New Haven, Conn.: Yale University Press.

Dalton, R. J. 2007. *The Good Citizen: How a Younger Generation is Reshaping American Politics.* Washington, D.C.: CQ Press.

Edwards, M. 2009. *Civil Society*. 2nd ed. Cambridge: Polity Press.

Goodin, R. 2007. "Enfranchising All Affected Interests, and Its Alternatives." *Philosophy and Public Affairs* 35: 40–68.

Habermas, J. 1996. *Between Facts and Norms: Contributions to a Discourse Theory of Law and Democracy*. Translated W. Rehg. Cambridge, Mass.: MIT Press.

Hirschman, A. 1970. *Exit, Voice, and Loyalty*. Cambridge, Mass.: Harvard University Press.

Hodgkinson, V., and M. Weitzman (eds). 1996. *Nonprofit Almanac: Dimensions of the Independent Sector: 1996–1997*. San Francisco: Jossey-Bass.

Inglehart, R., and C. Welzel. 2005. *Modernization, Cultural Change, and Democracy: The Human Development Sequence*. Cambridge: Cambridge University Press.

Leighninger, M. 2006. *The Next Form of Democracy: How Expert Rule is Giving Way to Shared Governance*. Nashville, Tenn.: Vanderbilt University Press.

Mutz, D. C.. 2006. *Hearing the other side: Deliberative versus Participatory Democracy*. New York: Cambridge University Press.

Pettit, P. 1997. *Republicanism: A Theory of Freedom and Government*. Oxford: Oxford University Press.

Pew Research Center for the People and the Press. 1997. *Trust and Citizen Engagement in Metropolitan Philadelphia: a Case Study*, Washington, D.C.: The Pew Research Center.

Powell, W. W., and R. Steinberg. 2006. *The Nonprofit Sector: A Research Handbook*. 2nd ed. New Haven, Conn.: Yale University Press.

Putnam, R. 1993. *Making Democracy Work: Civic Traditions in Modern Italy*. Princeton, N.J.: Princeton University Press.

———. 2000. *Bowling Alone: The Collapse and Revival of American Community*. New York: Simon & Schuster.

Rehfeld, A. 2005. *The Concept of Constituency: Political Representation, Democratic Legitimacy, and Institutional Design*. Cambridge: Cambridge University Press.

Rosanvallon, P. 2008. *Counter-democracy: Politics in an Age of Distrust*. Cambridge: Cambridge University Press.

Salamon, L. 2003. *The Resilient Sector: The State of Nonprofit America*. Washington, D.C.: Brookings Institution Press.

Saward, M. 2006. "The Representative Claim." *Contemporary Political Theory* 5: 297–318.

Saunders, H. 1999. *A Public Peace Process: Sustained Dialogue to Transform Ethnic and Racial Conflicts*. New York: St. Martin's Press.

Sunstein, C. 2001. *Designing Democracy: What Constitutions Do*. Oxford: Oxford University Press.

Tocqueville, Alexis de. 1969. *Democracy in America*. 2 vols. Trans. G. Lawrence. Ed. J. P. Mayer. Garden City, N.J.: Doubleday.

Urbinati, N. 2000. "Representation as Advocacy: A Study of Democratic Deliberation." *Political Theory* 28: 758–86.

Urbinati, N., and Mark E. Warren. 2008. "The Concept of Representation in Contemporary Democratic Theory." *Annual Review of Political Science* 11: 387–412.

Verba, S., K. Schlozman, and H. Brady. 1995. *Voice and Equality: Civic Volunteerism in American Politics*, Cambridge, Mass.: Harvard University Press.

Warren, M. E. 2001. *Democracy and Association*. Princeton, N.J.: Princeton University Press.

———. 2002. "What Can Democratic Participation Mean Today?" *Political Theory* 30: 678–702.

———. 2003. "A Second Transformation of Democracy?" in B. Cain, R. Dalton, and S. Scarrow (eds.) *Democracy Transformed: Expanding Political Opportunities in Advanced Industrial Democracies*. Oxford: Oxford University Press, 223–49.

——. 2006. "What Should and Should Not Be Said: Deliberating Sensitive Issues." *Journal of Social Philosophy* 37: 165–83.

——. 2008. "The Nature and Logic of Bad Social Capital," in D. Castiglione and J. Van Deth (eds.) *The Oxford Handbook of Social Capital*. Oxford: Oxford University Press, 122–49.

——. 2009. "Governance-Driven Democratization." *Critical Policy Analysis* 3: 3–13.

Warren, M. R. 2001. *Dry Bones Rattling: Community Building to Revitalize American Democracy*. Princeton, N.J.: Princeton University Press.

Young, I. M. 2000. *Democracy and Inclusion*. Oxford: Oxford University Press.

CHAPTER 31

CIVIL SOCIETY
AND POVERTY

SOLAVA IBRAHIM
DAVID HULME

THE 1990s witnessed many changes as the Cold War ended and globalization deepened. Two of these changes are especially important for this chapter. First, the evolution of a global consensus that extreme poverty had to be tackled, and second, the belief that civil society should be a major player in this task by mobilizing communities, delivering services, and shaping policies. Yet the growing international interest in poverty reduction results mainly from the efforts of aid agencies rather than a self-sustaining social movement on poverty. The absence of committed leadership and the breadth and vagueness of the concept of poverty make it difficult to create the sharp messages that are required for large-scale social and political mobilization.

This chapter explores the achievements of civil society in the area of poverty reduction. Since both civil society and poverty are contested concepts, analyzing their relationship is difficult, but we argue that civil society organizations can promote poverty reduction by pushing for macro-level structural changes through advocacy, lobbying the government for policy change at the national level, and providing effective services directly to the poor at the grassroots. Success depends on the ways in which civil society groups integrate these three approaches together in different political contexts, since certain strategy mixes succeed in one context and fail in others. In Bangladesh, for example, the success of advocacy and policy change has been minimal due to the nature of that country's governance, while direct service provision has yielded significant results.

1. CIVIL SOCIETY AND POVERTY

Most of the literature on civil society and poverty reduction focuses on nongovernmental organizations (NGOs). Sometimes an NGO can act as an umbrella organization that works with pre-existing community groups, acting as a facilitator and providing technical support. Elsewhere, NGOs create community groups such as microfinance and women's groups to help the poor organize themselves and express their needs, though the sustainability of such imposed community groups is questionable. The very idea of poverty reduction seems to be associated with elite- and middle-class attempts to establish NGOs to help the poor, though faith-based organizations, religious communities, informal groups, cooperatives, recreational, and cultural organizations also play their roles. For example, mosque committees in Islamic cultures and temple and burial committees in Buddhism provide services and assistance to the poor. Unfortunately, these services are rarely documented except in a small number of ethnographic studies. Therefore, this chapter is focused on NGOs.

As for defining poverty, "there are heated debates about 'what' poverty is—a lack of income, a failure to meet basic needs, a set of multi-dimensional capability deprivations or an abrogation of human rights. These are not mere semantics as the way one envisions poverty has profound implications for the types of actions one believes are needed to eradicate or reduce it" (Hulme 2010, 37). Definitions of global poverty range from the narrow income concept of one U.S. dollar per day to the broader capability approach of enlarging people's freedoms and enhancing their human development. This chapter argues that in addition to using objective measures, subjective methods including the voices of the poor themselves should be used to evaluate the achievements of civil society in reducing global poverty on both its income and capability dimensions.

In terms of global trends, poverty in the developing world has declined as the number of people living on less than $1.25 a day in 2005 prices decreased from 1.9 billion (or 52 percent of total global population) in 1981 to 1.4 billion (or 25 percent) in 2005 (Chen and Ravallion 2009; Ravallion 2009). However, it is hard to tie the actions of NGOs to this decline because so many different national and subnational experiences underlie these figures. For example China, with a limited civil society, succeeded in reducing poverty effectively in the 2000s; while in Africa, a range of stronger NGO communities did not achieve much success, partly due to the difficult political contexts in which they operated. In contrast, NGOs in Bangladesh have played a major role in reducing poverty. The headcount poverty index in Bangladesh dropped from 52 percent in 1983–84 to 40 percent in 2000 (Hossain, Sen, and Rahman 2000). Some of this decline is clearly attributable to the efforts of the Bangladesh Rural Advancement Committee (BRAC), the Grameen Bank, and other NGOs. One might also argue that poverty reduction was a result of trade policy and growth in the private sector, but Sen and Hulme (2006) demonstrate that almost 25 to 30 million Bangladeshis have hardly benefited at all from the growth of the formal economy in Bangladesh—hence the importance of NGO efforts to reach the poorest. The impact of the 2008–09 financial crisis on the world's poor is still to be confirmed, though it is estimated that between 55 and 90 million more people live in extreme poverty as a result (United Nations 2009).

In assessing the role of NGOs in poverty reduction, one can examine four main dimensions: their structure, the space in which they operate, the values they advocate, and their impact on policymaking (Anheier 2004, 29–32). The focus of this chapter is on the values and impact of NGOs—that is, their ability to advocate for values that promote equity and their role in giving voice to the poor, in lobbying policymakers, and in expanding poverty-related service provision. This task is difficult because empirical studies yield ambiguous results. For example, NGOs often succeed in extending services to the poor and in improving their livelihoods; but the long-term social, economic, and political impacts of these projects are questionable. Nevertheless, it is possible to collate the available evidence along three approaches to poverty reduction by NGOs, namely: pushing for structural and social change via advocacy, lobbying the government for pro-poor reforms and changing government policy, and providing for basic needs via service delivery.

2. NGO ADVOCACY FOR GLOBAL POVERTY REDUCTION

In recent years the success of well-mobilized campaigns around debt cancellation, landmines, and fair trade has demonstrated the role that advocacy can play in promoting anti-poverty policies internationally. Coates and David (2002, 530) argue that "advocacy work has become the latest enthusiasm for most agencies involved in international aid and development." The use of advocacy work at all levels by NGOs is due to a number of factors. First, their understanding of poverty and deprivation has deepened as they have come to realize that despite decades of foreign aid, the deeper causes of poverty have yet to be tackled. Secondly, the context in which they operate has changed as a result of the growing size and capacity of NGOs in the South. As a result, "Southern NGOs and social movements have become more assertive in challenging power structures within their own countries and increasingly at the international level" through active advocacy campaigns (Coates and David 2002, 531). Thirdly, the role of Northern NGOs is shifting in the light of this development, making new and more effective advocacy campaigns possible in the form of coalitions of different organizations working across local, national, and international levels—Jubilee 2000, the global campaign for debt cancellation, is a good example (Edwards and Gaventa 2000).

However, have these campaigns had any impact on poverty reduction? Answering this question is difficult because the changes resulting from advocacy are nonlinear and long-term. Advocacy depends on cooperation, which is why its impact cannot be assessed by focusing on one organization alone, and attribution is almost impossible above the project level, especially because most of the forces acting on poverty are not controlled by NGOs or are susceptible to advocacy strategies. But there are certainly examples of NGOs that are using advocacy to change poverty policies and reshape patterns of aid and investment in a positive direction. Take, for example, the case of Shack Dwellers International or SDI.

SDI was established in 1996 as an international network of organizations from eleven countries representing more than one million of the urban poor, mostly women, to advocate for their rights and end coercive means of slum clearance. However, SDI does not occupy the leadership of the network; instead it plays a supportive role in monitoring public policy, mobilizing members, and creating new information resources through settlement surveys and the mapping of slums. SDI develops "leadership amongst the urban poor so that they themselves can lead the negotiations with the state and its agencies to extend and obtain entitlements" (Patel, Burra, and D'Cruz 2001, 47). Its main activities focus on building and strengthening community-based organizations of the urban poor and helping them to find and implement community-led solutions to housing and livelihood problems. The network uses saving-and-credit schemes to help members with housing loans, nurtures social capital, and supports them in their negotiations with local authorities and central governments, especially over security-of-tenure and the provision of adequate housing and infrastructure (Batliwala 2002, 403–404; Patel, Burra, and D'Cruz 2001, 47).

SDI's success has been well documented in the literature and is demonstrated in its growing size, its widespread impact on the lives of its members, and its ability to successfully advocate for change in housing and urban development policies at local, national, and international levels, including the investment policies of the World Bank (Patel, Bolnick, and Mitlin 2001; Mitlin and Satterthwaite 2004b, 288; Batliwala 2002, 407). Its success is due to at least four reasons. First, SDI enjoys high levels of legitimacy through representation because of its democratic nature, strong internal accountability systems and the constant reinvention of its relationships with grassroots actors (Edwards 2001, 148; Batliwala 2002, 406). Secondly, SDI has gained wide international recognition and has become a partner with the United Nations Centre for Human Settlements (Habitat) and the Global Campaign for Secure Tenure, but its main focus is on responding effectively to the specific needs of the urban poor in each locality (Patel Burra, and D'Cruz 2001, 52; Satterthwaite 2001, 135–138; Edwards 2001, 149). Thirdly, SDI's success is due to the use of knowledge and research to support its advocacy activities, knowledge that "is conceived as embedded in the lives and experiences of the poor themselves" (McFarlane 2006, 294). Fourth, SDI has created an empowering mindset among its members that encourages them to fight for their rights, making "community-based organizations the leading force in the struggle against poverty, with NGOs playing a supportive role, helping link people's organizations with mainstream governmental or private institutions, and acting as researchers and fundraisers" (Patel, Burra, and D'Cruz 2001, 48). The case of SDI thus demonstrates the importance of international partnerships, mutual learning, knowledge exchange, and community empowerment as strategies through which NGOs can promote poverty reduction through advocacy.

Advocacy movements bring the poor's struggles to public attention, spread the "politics of hope" and inspire the poor and disenfranchised by showing that change is possible. Rather than conventional approaches to advocacy in which NGOs generate campaigns on behalf of the poor, the success of SDI and others like it shows that effective advocacy rests on strengthening the bargaining power of the poor themselves to defend their rights and enhance their capacity for organization and collective action. As Mitlin and Satterthwaite (2004b, 282) explain, "poverty-reduction requires more than an official recognition of the poor's needs. It has to include strengthening an accountable people's movement that is able to renegotiate the relationship between the urban poor and the state (its political and bureaucratic apparatus at district, city and higher levels), and also between the urban poor and other stakeholders." One of the challenges that NGOs face is their reluctance to accept that groups of the poor often develop as alternatives to professionally driven solutions. It is therefore essential that when operating in the advocacy domain, NGOs view their role mainly as supporters and facilitators and do not "take on what individuals and community organizations can do on their own" (Mitlin and Satterthwaite 2004b, 283). NGO advocacy can best help the poor not by speaking on their behalf, but by helping them to express their voices, articulate their needs and defend their rights effectively.

3. CHANGING GOVERNMENT POLICY

NGOs can influence government to adopt pro-poor reforms through a number of strategies. First, by monitoring the allocation of government resources in favor of the poor—for example, by calling for participatory and gender-based budgeting. Second, by facilitating public debate around poverty-related problems so as to influence policy design, build new alliances, gain new supporters, and encourage policy-makers to establish programs that address these problems. For example, in Peru indigenous peoples have the right of prior consent before economic activities take place on their lands as a result of the efforts of indigenous peoples' movements and their NGO partners (Bebbington et al. 2009, 11). Many NGOs work with local governments to gain acceptability, and use a nonconfrontational approach to ensure that their suggestions are listened to (Mitlin and Satterthwaite 2004b, 286). Therefore, NGOs operating in this domain are also usually pragmatic and seek to cooperate with political parties who have a pro-poor agenda. Through partnerships with state agencies and by establishing a supportive institutional environment, NGOs can successfully scale up their initiatives to ensure their sustainability and reach.

The success of NGOs in affecting government policy depends on a number of factors, including the political context and the role of external actors in the formulation of poverty reduction strategies, and the policy capacities of NGOs themselves. The participation of NGOs in policy processes can become tokenistic because "although NGOs are working effectively to deliver services and care to poor and vulnerable groups...they lack the structures and mechanisms to work at the policy level" (Hughes and Atampugre 2005, 13). To improve their performance in the domain of policy change, it is therefore important to build NGO capacity to understand policy processes, access information more effectively, and improve their monitoring and evaluation skills. To effectively lobby government for policy reforms, it is also necessary that NGOs build partnerships and bridge the gaps that often exist between their staff, local communities, and policy-makers, and form stronger alliances with other organizations in civil society (Hughes and Atampugre 2005, 19).

As an example of these processes at work, take NGO participation in Poverty Reduction Strategy Papers (PRSPs). Endorsed in September 1999, PRSPs are "policy documents produced by borrower countries outlining the economic, social and structural programmes to reduce poverty, to be implemented over a three-year period" (Stewart and Wang 2003, 4). Although NGOs were mainly invited to participate in the PRSP process, they have tried to use these spaces to lobby for pro-poor reforms. In Bolivia, for example, the central government initiated a "national dialogue" and linked it to the PRSP process. As a result, nationwide consultations took place at the municipal, departmental, and national levels focusing on the provision of services to the poor in the first PRSP and on the importance of employment, productivity and commodity chains in the second (Molenaers and Renard 2002, 5–7; Curran 2005, 4–5).

Bolivian NGOs faced a number of challenges in using the PRSP process as an effective space to lobby for policy change due to the limited time frame of the process, the limited information available, the language in which the PRSPs were written, the lack of state commitment, the limited organizational capacities of NGOs, and their failure to form a unified front (Stewart and Wang 2003, 12–14; Surkin 2005). In many cases, NGOs were excluded from the design of frameworks and merely participated in "precooked" proposals for policy change (Stewart and Wang 2003, 15, Fraser 2005, 326; Curran 2005, 5; Eberlei 2007, 13). As a result, the consultation process raised expectations and led to frustration and social unrest when the state failed to meet them. NGOs expressed their frustration by sending a formal petition to the government expressing their disapproval of the PRSP document (Curran 2005, 4–9).

Nevertheless, there are two significant achievements of NGO participation in the PRSP process in Bolivia. The first is the establishment of a "social control mechanism" which allows NGOs to monitor the allocation and implementation of debt relief funds, and to follow up on the implementation and reformulation of the PRSP. The second is the Law of National Dialogue, which institutionalized NGO participation in policy formulation at the local level (Curran 2005, 8–9; Molenaers and Renard 2002, 8). NGO participation in these deliberative processes gradually "turned their attitude from 'Protesta' (protest) into 'Propuesta' (proposal)" (Molenaers and Renard 2002, 8). The PRSP process was therefore an entry point through which NGOs pushed the development process forward in a pro-poor direction.

4. SERVICE DELIVERY TO THE POOR

Rahman (2006) argues that "the NGO sector as a whole has shifted away from its initial focus on promoting political mobilization and accountable government, to the apolitical delivery of basic services" (Rahman 2006, 451). NGOs face problems because the services they provide are often unsustainable due to their dependence on external funding, the difficulties of going to scale, and their inability to recover costs through user charges. Evaluating the performance of sixteen NGO projects in the area of rural poverty reduction, Robinson (1992) concludes that "three-quarters of the projects were successful and had an impact in alleviating poverty" (Robinson 1992, 30), but NGOs faced a number of limitations on their service delivery projects including their inability to reach the poorest (Robinson 1992, 30–34). Effective service delivery requires an integrated approach whereby NGOs work with community groups to improve their conditions while nurturing their relationship with local government (Mitlin and Satterthwaite 2004a, 18). Otherwise NGO service provision may undermine government responsibility to provide adequate and efficient services to the poor (Collier 2000, 122), leading to a "franchise state" in which crucial public services are run by private programs (Rahman 2006, 455).

When these positive conditions are met, NGO service provision can be extremely effective in both the short and the longer terms. In their mapping of South African social movements, for example, Mitlin and Mogaladi (2009) point out that these movements were concerned with solving concrete problems related to poverty reduction, such as shelter, human rights, labor, gender, and the environment. To address these problems, they focused mainly on service delivery, especially the restoration of land to those who have been evicted (Mitlin and Mogaladi 2009, 21–22). NGOs contribute to urban poverty reduction by "often fulfilling the role that government agencies should provide—for instance, provision of water, waste removal, healthcare or the support of centres that assist particular groups (such as centres for street children)" (Mitlin and Satterthwaite 2004a, 18). In general terms then, the role of NGOs in service delivery should be complementary to the government and supportive to local communities. NGOs operating in this domain should emphasize the long-term effects of their projects by asking "how will this have to work in the future, after we leave?" (Collier 2000, 121). The answer to this question is crucial not only for the continuity of the services provided, but also for the sustainability of their poverty-reducing impacts on targeted communities. The case of the Bangladesh Rural Advancement Committee (BRAC) demonstrates how an NGO can successfully and sustainably provide a comprehensive package of services to the poor and even to the poorest.

Many NGOs help the poor directly through service provision, but BRAC occupies a particularly important position as "the developing world's largest NGO in terms of the scale and diversity of its intervention" (Chowdhury and Bhuiya 2004, 371). Founded as a charitable organization in 1972 to help in Bangladesh's reconstruction after the country's liberation war, its humanitarian efforts were later expanded to provide more permanent solutions to the problems of vulnerable groups (Lovell 1992, 23; Chowdhury Mahmoud, and Abed 1991, 4; Rahman 2006, 454). BRAC's development strategy stresses the importance of empowerment and conscientization, encourages participation and self-reliance, and adopts sustainable and people-centered approaches with a special emphasis on women and the poorest (Stiles 2002, 842; Lovell 1992, 24–33). This organization is worth careful examination because "it turns standard notions about development, business, poverty alleviation, and management on their head. And it confronts the idea that the drivers of development in poor countries must inevitably come from abroad" (Smilie 2009, 3).

Through its innovative services in education, health, agriculture, and income generation, BRAC has succeeded in bringing about lasting change in the lives of millions of poor people (Hulme and Moore 2010; Mustafa et al. 1996; Husain 1998). Four million children (70 percent of them girls) have graduated from its Non-Formal Primary Education program (NFPE) (Lovell 1992, 48–50), and "its extensive network of schools...provide[s] more non-formal education than the government" (Stiles 2002, 843). Millions benefit from BRAC's innovative community-based health care services and BRAC cooperates with the government to improve the national health system, with an emphasis on women's health and child survival programs (Lovell 1992, 58; Afsana and Rashid 2001, 79; Streefland and Chowdhury 1990, 263). BRAC also helps the poor through rigorous research that enhances the productivity of their enterprises, for example through new systems of chick rearing, poultry vaccination, and improved cattle breeding (Smilie 2009, 3). BRAC's poverty reduction program depends on creating an enabling environment for the poor by promoting gender equity and human rights; enhancing the poor's access to education, health care, housing, adequate technology, minimum income, and employment; and ensuring their entitlement to food and assets (Chowdhury and Bhuiya 2004, 373–376). Through the Rural Development Program, BRAC nurtures the entrepreneurial capabilities of the poor, while its Rural Credit Project serves the graduates of this program and helps them not simply by extending credit, but also by encouraging their collective activities (Chowdhury Mahmoud, and Abed 1991, 11). Its micro-credit schemes have made loans totaling more than $1 billion.

BRAC's most important contribution to poverty reduction is the Income Generation for Vulnerable Group Development Program, which aims at using "a combination of food aid, savings and training in activities with low capital requirements as a means of enabling the marginalized to climb the ladder out of ultra-poverty" (Halder and Mosely 2004, 387). The program has been very effective in reaching the ultra-poor and has successfully "deepened the outreach of its poverty-reduction activity and achieved impressive results" (Matin and Hulme 2003, 647). Although BRAC's main focus is on service delivery, it is "gradually moving beyond a 'supply side' approach, concentrating on the delivery of services or development projects, to a 'demand side' emphasis, helping communities articulate their preferences and concerns so as to become active participants in the development process" (Clark 1995, 593). The main reason for BRAC's unprecedented achievement in reducing poverty is the diversity and complementarity of its activities, which do not depend only on micro-credit, but use different paths to reduce poverty and vulnerability through income generation, asset building, and addressing immediate consumption needs (Matin, Hulme, and Rutherford 2002, 286–287). BRAC's comprehensive programs, innovative service delivery projects, empowerment strategies, people-centered approach, and focus on the poorest are the main reasons for its remarkable success in poverty reduction.

5. SYNERGIES AND LESSONS LEARNED

Each of the three strategies reviewed in brief above interacts with the others. For example, service delivery can create the necessary knowledge base for advocacy and policy change, since NGOs will be in a better position to collect the information required to advocate for pro-poor policies. However, when they operate in service delivery mode, NGOs also need to be careful not to adopt an exclusively needs-based approach that neglects the poor's human rights, and fails to challenge the structures and policies that brought about these deprivations in the first place. Given these mutually reinforcing linkages, an integrative and collaborative approach is the best way for NGOs to use the data and experience they gain through service provision to call for wider policy changes in favor of the poor and advocate for structural transformations that can help sustain these gains over time. NGOs can also focus on building the local organizational capacity of the poor, strengthening their ability "to work together, organize themselves, and mobilize resources to solve problems of common interest. Organized communities are more likely to have their voices heard and their demands met" (Narayan 2002, vii). But these strategy mixes are also dependent on the nature of the political environment in which NGOs operate, especially the effectiveness of the state.

The experiences reviewed in this chapter demonstrate that the success of NGOs in promoting poverty reduction is dependent on a number of factors. First, the quality of the relationships between NGOs and the poor is crucial: "the extent of success also depends upon the extent to which such organizations have resources or decision-making powers that can support urban poor groups, and on the space given by such organizations to urban poor groups in defining priorities and developing responses—or, more fundamentally...in actually conceptualizing participation" (Mitlin and Satterthwaite 2004b, 289).

Second, poverty is multidimensional, and therefore requires the adoption of a multifaceted strategy. For example, to address inadequate incomes, NGOs need to provide the poor with relevant training and the skills required to access better-paid jobs, widen their possibilities for self-production, extend the safety net through public works programs, and lobby for policy change in the provision of better and cheaper services. Inadequate and unstable assets can be addressed through emergency and asset building credit schemes, nurturing social capital for communal access to resources, and improving the poor's access to housing, health, and education. To overcome the problem of inadequate shelter, NGOs can help the poor to access new land and reduce building costs in addition to lobbying government to legalize informal settlements. Deteriorating infrastructure and social services can be addressed by increasing the capacity of local governments. The poor lack security, which is why NGOs need to lobby for the establishment of social safety nets, especially for the most vulnerable groups. Finally, through advocacy and policy reforms, NGOs can also protect the rights of the poor, enhance their bargaining power and help them overcome their lack of political voice.

Third, NGOs must personify the values they stand for. While calling for democracy, development, and social justice, NGOs need to demonstrate that their organizations adopt these values in their own activities and in their relationships with grassroots groups. Their role should be one of facilitating community-led solutions to ensure the sustainability of poverty reduction efforts. Fourth, the success of NGOs in tackling poverty depends on their adoption of an integrated approach that combines elements from all three strategies into a mutually supportive mix that is appropriate and effective in each context, combining practical and strategic actions by focusing on concrete, short-term solutions while also addressing the long-term dynamics that perpetuate poverty. Finally, knowledge and mutual learning are crucial for enhancing the effectiveness of NGO roles in poverty reduction. Knowledge helps NGOs not only to design more effective poverty reduction policies but also to enhance their bargaining power and credibility when calling for pro-poor reforms.

6. CONCLUSION

Although NGO achievements in the field of poverty reduction are not always easy to identify, it is clear that their efforts can help to disseminate a "politics of hope" and an empowering mindset that inspires the poor and helps them to voice their demands. NGOs should not lead this process, but they can act as facilitators in ways that leave enough space for the poor to articulate their own needs. If NGOs are to play a more effective role in poverty reduction, they need to overcome a number of limitations. First, they need to move away from a needs-based to an integrative approach that respects the rights of the poor and helps them to improve their living conditions in sustainable ways. Service delivery programs managed by NGOs should not replace government services, but rather complement and strengthen them—as is the case with BRAC.

Secondly, successful advocacy for the rights of poor people is based on adequate knowledge and deep understanding of their needs, context, and demands. Third, the impact of NGOs on policy change is limited so long as they maintain a competitive and mistrustful relationship with their governments. NGOs need not only to cooperate with government, but also to coordinate their own activities and thus create a unified front that can lobby for sustainable pro-poor national policies. To do so, they need to build their own capacities and improve the skills required to engage in policy dialogues, work with grassroots organizations, and develop and articulate credible alternative policy choices that can help to improve the lives of the poor.

REFERENCES

Afsana, K. and S. F. Rashid. 2001. "The Challenges of Meeting Rural Bangladeshi Women's Needs in Delivery Care." *Reproductive Health Matters* 9(18): 79–89.

Anheier, H. K. 2004. *Civil Society: Measurement, Evaluation and Policy*. London: Earthscan.

Batliwala, S. 2002. "Grassroots Movements as Transnational Actors: Implications for Global Civil Society." *Voluntas: International Journal of Voluntary and Nonprofit Organizations* 13(4): 393–409.

Bebbington, A., D. Mitlin, J. Mogaladi, M. Scurrah, and C. Bielich. 2009. "Decentring Poverty, Reworking Government: Movements and States in the Government of Poverty." Chronic Poverty Research Center Working Paper No. 149. Available at http:// www.chronicpoverty.org/uploads/publication_files/WP149%20Bebbington%20et-al .pdf (accessed December 3, 2009).

Chen, S. and M. Ravallion. 2009. "The Impact of the Global Financial Crisis on the World's Poorest." Centre for Economic Policy Research. Available at http://www.voxeu.org/ index.php?q=node/3520 (accessed April 10, 2010).

Chowdhury, A. M. R., and A. Bhuiya. 2004. "The Wider Impacts of BRAC Poverty Alleviation Programme in Bangladesh." *Journal of International Development* 16: 369–86.

Chowdhury, A. M. R., M. Mahmoud, and F. H. Abed. 1991. "Credit for the Rural Poor- The case of BRAC in Bangladesh." *Small Enterprise Development* 2(3): 4–13.

Clark, J. 1995. "The State, Popular Participation, and the Voluntary Sector." *World Development* 23(4): 593–601.

Coates, B., and R. David. 2002. "Learning for Change: The Art of Assessing the Impact of Advocacy Work." *Development in Practice* 12(3/4): 530–41.

Collier, C. 2000. "NGOs, the Poor and Local Government," in D. Eade (ed.) *Development, NGOs and Civil Society: Selected Essays from Development in Practice*. London: Oxfam GB: 115–23.

Curran, Z. 2005. "Civil Society Participation in the PRSP: The Role of Evidence and the Impact on Policy Choices." *PPA Synthesis Study*. London: Overseas Development Institute. Available at http://www.odi.org.uk/networks/cspp/activities/PPA0106/ ODI_PRSPsandCivilSociety.pdf.

Eberlei, W. 2007. "Accountability in Poverty Reduction Strategies: the Role of Empowerment and Participation," Social and Development Paper no. 104. Washington, D.C.: The World Bank.

Edwards, M. 2001. "Global Civil Society and Community Exchanges: A Different Form of Movement." *Environment and Urbanization* 13(2): 145–49.

Edwards, M., and J. Gaventa (eds.). 2000. *Global Citizen Action*. Boulder, Colo.: Lynne Rienner.

Fraser, A. 2005. "Poverty Reduction Strategy Papers: Now Who Calls the Shots?" *Review of African Political Economy* 32(104/105): 317–40.

Halder, S., and P. Mosely. 2004. "Working with the Ultra-Poor: Learning from BRAC Experiences." *Journal of International Development* 16: 387–406.

Hossain, M., B. Sen, and H. Z. Rahman. 2000. "Growth and Distribution of Rural Income in Bangladesh: Analysis Based on Panel Survey Data." *Economic and Political Weekly*, December 30, 4630–37.

Hughes, A., and N. Atampugre. 2005. "A Critical Look at Civil Societies' Poverty Reduction Monitoring and Evaluation Experiences." *Participatory Learning and Action 51: Civil Society and Poverty Reduction.* London: International Institute for Environment and Development: 10–20.

Hulme, D. 2010. *Global Poverty*. London: Routledge.

Hulme, D., and K. Moore. 2010. "Assisting the Poorest in Bangladesh: Learning from BRAC's 'Targeting the Ultra Poor' Programme," in D. Lawson, D. Hulme, I. Matin, and K. Moore (eds.) *What Works for the Poorest? Knowledge, Targeting, Policies and Practices.* Rugby: Practical Action Publishing: 149–87.

Husain, A. M. M. (ed.) 1998. *Poverty Alleviation and Empowerment: The Second Impact Assessment Study of BRAC's Rural Development Programs.* Dhaka: Bangladesh Rural Advancement Committee.

Lovell, C. H. 1992. *Breaking the Cycle of Poverty: the BRAC Strategy.* West Hartford, Conn.: Kumarian Press.

Matin, I., and D. Hulme. 2003. "Programs for the Poorest: Learning from the IGVGD Program in Bangladesh." *World Development* 31(3): 647–65.

Matin, I., D. Hulme, and S. Rutherford. 2002. "Finance for the Poor: From Microcredit to Microfinancal Services." *Journal of International Development* 14: 273–94.

McFarlane, C. 2006. "Knowledge, Learning and Development: a Post-Rationalist Approach." *Progress in Development Studies* 6(4): 287–305.

Mitlin, D., and J. Mogaladi. 2009. "Social Movements and Poverty Reduction in South Africa." School of Environment and Development, University of Manchester, research paper. Available at http://www.sed.manchester.ac.uk/research/socialmovements/publications/reports/Mitlin_Mogaladi_SouthAfricamappinganalysis.pdf.

Mitlin, D., and D. Satterthwaite. 2004a. "Introduction," in D. Mitlin and D. Satterthwaite (eds.) *Empowering Squatter Citizen: Local Government, Civil Society and Urban Poverty Reduction.* London: Earthscan: 3–21.

——. 2004b. "The Role of Local and Extra-Local Organizations," in D. Mitlin and D. Satterthwaite (eds.) op. cit., 278–305.

Molenaers, N., and R. Renard. 2002. "Strengthening Civil Society from the Outside? Donor-driven Consultation and Participation Processes in Poverty Reduction Strategies (PRSP): the Bolivian Case." Antwerp: Institute of Development Policy and Management, University of Antwerp.

Mustafa, S., I. Ara, D. Banu, A. Hossain, A. Kabir, M. Mohsin, A. Yusuf, and S. Jahan. 1996. *Beacon of Hope: An Impact Assessment Study of BRAC Rural Development Programme.* Dhaka: Bangladesh Rural Advancement Committee.

Narayan, D. (Ed.) 2002. *Empowerment and Poverty Reduction.* Washington, D.C.: The World Bank.

Patel, S., J. Bolnick, and D. Mitlin. 2001. "Squatting on the Global Highway," in M. Edwards and J. Gaventa (eds.) *Global Citizen Action.* London: Earthscan, 231–46.

Patel, S., S. Burra, and C. D'Cruz. 2001. "Slum/Shack Dwellers International (SDI)—Foundations to Treetops." *Environment and Urbanization* 13(2): 45–59.

Rahman, S. 2006. "Development, Democracy and the NGO Sector: Theory and Evidence from Bangladesh." *Journal of Developing Societies* 22(4): 451–73.

Ravallion, M. 2009. "The Crisis and the World's Poorest." *Development Outreach* 11(3): 16–18.

Robinson, M. 1992. "NGOs and Rural Poverty Reduction: Implications for Scaling-up," in M. Edwards and D. Hulme (eds.) *Making a Difference: NGOs and Development in a Changing World*. London: Earthscan, 28–39.

Satterthwaite, D. 2001. "From Professionally Driven to People-driven Poverty Reduction: Reflections on the role of Shack/Slum Dwellers International." *Environment and Urbanization* 13(2): 135–38.

Sen, B., and D. Hulme (eds.) 2006. "Chronic Poverty in Bangladesh: Tales of Ascent, Descent, Marginality and Persistence." Dhaka/Manchester: Bangladesh Institute of Development Studies/Chronic Poverty Research Centre. Available at http://www .chronicpoverty.org/uploads/publication_files/chronic_poverty_report_ bangladesh_200405.pdf.

Smilie, I. 2009. *Freedom from Want: The Remarkable Success Story of BRAC, the Global Grassroots Organization that's winning the fight against poverty*. Dhaka: The University Press Limited.

Stewart, F., and M. Wang. 2003. "Do PRSPs Empower Poor Countries and Disempower the World Bank, Or Is It the Other Way Round?" Working Paper No. 108. Oxford: Queen Elizabeth House.

Stiles, K. 2002. "International Support for NGOs in Bangladesh: Some Unintended Consequences." *World Development* 30(5): 835–46.

Streefland, P., and M. Chowdhury. 1990. "The Long-Term Role of National Non-government Development Organizations in Primary Health Care: Lessons from Bangladesh," *Health Policy and Planning* 5(3): 261–66.

Surkin, J. B. 2005. "Bottom-up Planning? Participatory Implementation, Monitoring and Evaluation of PRS processes in Bolivia." *Participatory Learning and Action 51: Civil Society and Poverty Reduction*. London: International Institute for Environment and Development, 53–58.

United Nations. 2009. *The Millennium Development Goals Report 2009*. New York: United Nations.

CHAPTER 32

CIVIL SOCIETY AND PEACE

JENNY PEARCE

CIVIL society has come to play a central role in the post-Cold War peace and peace-building agendas, mirroring its trajectory in the fields of development and democracy. As many have noted however, civil society is both a normative concept and one that can be empirically observed (Howell and Pearce 2001). The associational content of this concept can be valued but it can also be counted. Associations can become part of policy and practice, categorized, and funded. The problem arises when the normative and empirical aspects of civil society are elided in an effort to create a neutral tool for application across different contexts. In this process, civil society becomes used as a collective noun, aggregating multiple and diverse forms of associational life and assuming that what "it" *ought to* be is the same as what "it" *is*. In fact any claim to universality is difficult to sustain given the origins of this concept in the Western Enlightenment, and can easily become vacated of meaning, as Colas (1997, 39–40) has pointed out: "devoid of context, no longer linked to a particular period or a precise doctrine, gushing out of everyone's mouth at once, 'civil society' acceded at the end of the 1980s to a sort of empty universality. Now that it has become a label for all sorts of goods, and in certain cases even a mask for intellectual emptiness, 'civil society' allows people to speak without knowing what they are saying, which in turn helps them to avoid arguing with each other."

Despite these strictures, this chapter argues that the concept of civil society is significant for peace and peace-building, and that it is most useful when articulating the importance, and defending the possibility, of public disagreement and discussion when constructing shared ideas of the good society. Its normative power lies not in the specific values which different traditions attach to the concept, but in the general value of aspiring to such a society created through the contested values of what "good" actually means. Potentially, civil society has a deep affinity with "peace," another important idea that is often treated in uncontroversial terms as simply "the absence of war." If, on the other hand, peace is conceptualized as a highly complex idea that pertains to the human endeavor of building conditions in which societies can live without violence, it is evident that, like civil society, peace is a site of disagreement as well as the capacity to reach agreements themselves. Peace is "an activity of cultivating the process of agreeing" (Cox 1986, 12).

The first section of this chapter argues that civil society is conceptually relevant precisely because it concerns a plurality of visions that are articulated in a plurality of ways, all of which ultimately contribute to the peaceful interactions of human beings. However, this argument must not be confused with empirically observable patterns of associational life that do not necessarily point in this direction at all, in fact quite often the opposite. Distinctions between the "civil" and the "uncivil" therefore need to be explored and, it is argued, retained. The affinity of civil society with peace and peace-building becomes clear only if this distinction is clearly understood. A commitment to nonviolent forms of human interaction, for instance, must surely define a boundary for the idea of civil society if it is to be meaningful to understandings of human progress. Section 2 focuses on these key distinctions. Section 3 makes the case for maintaining an explicitly normative, but not hegemonic or homogenous understanding of civil society which aspires to distinguish itself from an uncivil "Other" by exploring the contribution of associations to peace-building in practice. Recognizing the legitimacy and significance of associational dynamics outside of the state has been of vital—though controversial—importance in efforts to build new norms for peace in the world, counter violent actors, and build peaceful outcomes after peace agreements. Civil society is therefore a vital conceptual source of agreement-building around such norms.

1. CIVIL SOCIETY AND PEACE: A NATURAL AFFINITY?

It is frequently argued that civil society and democracy reinforce each other. Is this also true of peace? What is it about the normative reading of civil society which makes this a pertinent question? A good starting point for this discussion is to clarify what "civil" might refer to. Dictionary definitions of "civil," from the Latin *civis* or "citizen," contain three main meanings: polite or courteous; concerned with the law in noncriminal cases; and ordinary, as in not military or religious. All three definitions point to the assumption that certain kinds of human relationships counter strife and bad behavior, and create a milieu of positive sociability that is independent of the forces of coercion and religious authority. There are also echoes of ancient Greek ideas about virtue here, and of the duties that good citizens share with one another. The Aristotelian version of these ideas added the participation of the citizen into the picture as "one who is entitled to share in deliberative or judicial office" (Aristotle, 1981, 87). The Greek *polis* was itself a response to war and the need for villages to come together for mutual protection and to overcome dissension between families or clans.

The first meaning of civil refers to polite or courteous behavior. During the Western Enlightenment, this idea became associated with an emergent ideal of "civility." At the time, however, this ideal developed in the context of an early-expansionist Europe and its efforts to distinguish itself from the "uncivilized Other" of the worlds it encountered. Adam Ferguson wrote that "the epithets of *civilized* or of polished properly refer to 'modern nations,' which differ from '*barbarous or rude*' nations principally because of their discretionary use of violence" (quoted in Keane 1996, 20). The emergent European civil society was counterposed in this way to the "barbarian" and the "savage" of the so-called new worlds. In the 1930s, Norberto Elias explored the civilizing process in Europe in terms of how Western societies, which in the early Middle Ages were ruled by numerous smaller and greater warriors, became the "internally more or less pacified but outwardly embattled societies that we call States" (Elias 2000, xii). He connected this process in Europe to both the formation of states and the diminishing of intra-elite violence. As the nobility lost their war functions, so economic and social interdependencies emerged and manners of social interaction were refined among elites. This culture filtered through to other social groups and, as the institutions which enforced the state's monopoly of power become more effective, greater levels of security in social life generated stronger social interdependencies. Martin Elsner (2001) has traced the decline in elite violence which ensued, and the rise of economic incentives to reduce violence and support an effective state monopoly over its use. A long-term decline in adult and male-on-male violence was accompanied by a "cultural model of the conduct of life, reinforced and reproduced through social institutions" (Elsner 2008, 301). While levels of homicide and interpersonal violence did decline in Europe, they did not disappear.

A parallel process witnessed the rise of organizations and movements against different forms of violence, from the abolition of slavery in the nineteenth century to organized campaigns against domestic violence and child abuse in the late twentieth century and beyond. Voluntary associations have played a very important role in de-sanctioning different forms of violence in these ways, and a strong case can be made that "empirical" civil society, and not just the state, has contributed greatly to the task of peace-building, understood as the process of building the conditions in which people can live without violence. Equally, the notion that the state unambiguously limits violence by persuading society of its right to monopolize its use has proven to be highly problematic. States themselves have been responsible for acts of extreme violence in their attempts to put down revolts, preserve elite rule or ethnic domination, and pacify populations.

A second meaning of civil lies in its association with the rule of law, and in particular with noncriminal disputes. At its origins, civil society referred to that form of association which upholds and promotes the regulatory mechanisms which enable citizenship to be a meaningful exercise, and which protect individuals from arbitrary acts of force. Eighteenth-century Europe was locked into a very limited understanding of citizenship and the law, which in practice were highly skewed towards the protection of property and wealthy white men. It was through the actions of new associations, forged first of all in the workplaces of the industrializing world, that emergent ideas of civil and political rights were democratized in a struggle which lasted into the twentieth century, and which continues in many parts of the world today. This initial struggle in Europe expanded from male workers in trade unions to associations which represented other sectors of society such as women, and black and ethnic minorities. However, it was not these mobilizations per se which articulated the idea of civil society. Rather, it was the way in which the interests of particular groups were defended, not *against* other groups, but in the name of deepening democracy and the rule of law for all. The democratizing and regulating character of empirical civil society has contributed to the diminishing of arbitrary state violence in Europe and elsewhere. Human and civil rights groups, and legal reform organizations, have made a huge contribution to the reduction of violence and to peaceful social interactions, as well as to democratization per se.

The third meaning of civil refers to the "ordinary" arena outside of the state, and originally constructed around autonomy from military and religious power. This came to be a very important dimension of the concept of civil society at its birth—as an arena which would tame absolutism and despotism—as well as its rebirth in the late twentieth century in the course of challenges to authoritarian, totalitarian, and militaristic states. Here, the normative concept of civil conjures up the participation of everyday citizens in seeking freedom from arbitrary authority and other forms of coercion, an idea echoed in the peace movements that have organized against militarization and the weapons of war, as well as against war itself, over at least the last one hundred years.

What does this discussion tell us about civil society? As a normative concept, civil society focuses attention on all the violence-reducing, civil, and civilizing components of human interaction. At the very least, it suggests a prima facie case for a connection with peace. However, its claim to some form of universality and relevance across cultures and societies is seriously undermined by its association with the particularities of the Enlightenment and the project of Western liberalism. Elias was not, in fact, suggesting that the Western trajectory was superior to others, or that it was complete, even though the discussion often seems to point to such claims. Ernest Gellner, for example, explicitly argued against the idea that ritual-based and communal groups belong in a conceptualization of civil society: "Whatever Civil Society turns out to be it is clearly something which is to be contrasted with both successful and unsuccessful *Ummas*, and also with ritual-pervaded cousinly republics, not to mention, of course, outright dictatorships or patrimonial societies" (Gellner 1994, 43). Instead Gellner turned to "modular man," who combines individualism and egalitarianism and is able to move into and out of his chosen social bonds without societal sanction, while still being able to construct effective social cohesion against the state.

Gellner's thinking is also relevant to the affinity between civil society and peace. When "modular man" is emancipated in the way Gellner suggests, the individual pursuit of self-interest, which was unleashed simultaneously with the rise of the market economy, generates new forms of competition and conflict in society as the moral bonds of communities of neighbors and kinship are loosened. Liberalism has not dealt very well with the conflict, antagonism, and radical disagreement that result (Mouffe 2005), in particular with group as opposed to individual claims to rights (Kymlicka 1995), but nor has it been very good in cultivating agreement, particularly moral agreement, as Alasdair MacIntyre (2007) has argued. In liberal thinking, civil society is seen as the way in which societies hold together in such contexts by reconciling the pursuit of individual self interest with the notion that society must be more than a set of individuals, but not, crucially, by building the common good.

It was not inevitable that liberal views of civil society would dominate. A parallel and very powerful idea of civil society emerged around cooperation and mutualism (Black 1984). While such ideas were eventually marginalized, they have been kept alive in various understandings of societal self-organization such as cooperatives, and in political ideas such as anarchism and some forms of socialism to this day. This suggests an alternative thread, even in the West, to the liberal concept of civil society—one which stresses a different set of values to individual freedom as negative freedom, of protection against the despotisms of either the state or the majority, and of values which promote the pursuit of the common good.

Although both understandings of civil society potentially contribute to the human project of civility, rule-bound governance and freedom from oppression—these providing a framework which enable people to live without violence—it is this other thread in civil society thinking which points to the components of the concept which aspire to promote the interests of all rather than those of the self-interested individual or advantaged groups of individuals, and thus construct the conditions for people to live without violence. The contesting values which flow through the civil society debate are precisely the reason why one version of this concept cannot be privileged over all the others. However, civil society does offer a means for addressing these competing values through the associational dynamics that operate independently from the state, the market, and the family, *so long as* they are embedded in the ultimate value of pursuing shared norms as a necessary goal. Peace is precisely such a goal—universal in its aspiration, but deeply contested in its content.

2. CIVIL SOCIETY AND VIOLENCE

The adjective "civil" can be attached to war or it can be attached to society, and the fact that many forms of associational life are rarely civil in the senses discussed above highlights the need to distinguish the normative aspects of civil society from empirical realities. Of course, the empirical must also be used to explore the normative potential of a concept. From his historical studies, Michael Mann has drawn the conclusion that "civil society may be evil":

In *civil society* theory, democracy, peace and tolerance are said to result when individuals are engaged in vibrant, dense social relations provided by voluntary institutions, which protect them from the manipulations of state elites (Putnam 1993, 2000). This is naïve. Radical ethno-nationalists often succeed precisely because their civil society networks are denser and more mobilizing than those of their more moderate rivals. This was true of the Nazis...and we see later that it was also true of Serb, Croat and Hutu nationalists. Civil Society may be evil" (Mann 2005, 21),

There is no doubt that people associate for multiple purposes including violence, and there is ample evidence that associations have been the means by which violent purposes and uncivil actions have been nurtured in pursuit of revolutionary, nationalist, and fascist goals. After 1925, the extreme Right in Germany permeated the associational culture of "bourgeois and workers," which had been predominantly liberal or socialist before 1914. In other words, "the Nazis conquered German civil society from within" (Ludwig Hoffman 2006, 83). Associational life has to be studied empirically to comprehend these processes. However, this vital empirical work should not be confused with the normative ideal which the concept of civil society has represented in its many metamorphoses in political sociology and philosophy. Therefore, we must unpack what it is that makes civil society "civil" as much as that which makes it "evil."

Social bonds exist in all societal contexts and are part of our humanity. In western liberal discourse, civil society contrasts the senses of belonging and identity that are fixed at birth with those of free association and the search for new identities in different associational modalities. In so doing, liberalism leads naturally to ideas about emancipated individualism and the capacity for independent and critical social action. At the same time, it seeks to distinguish itself from the bonds of solidarity and belonging which characterize societies which have not embraced the project of modernity, or which find themselves caught up in this project but at a disadvantage. The appeal of the liberal concept of civil society is that it emphasizes cross-cutting interests, so moving people closer to a less sectarian world view. The danger is that it dismisses all other bonds as unable to contribute to this process by their very nature, although they may in fact be a source of civility and peaceful interaction because they are based on alternative values to liberalism which may be more robust in promoting cooperation and solidarity.

Ethnic heterogeneity is correlated in statistical analyses with an increased possibility of civil war and violence (Hegre, Ellingsen, Gates, and Gleditsch 2001). However, particularistic solidarities are not inevitably a source of violence or solely a source of "cousinly ritual," as Gellner expressed it. They can provide precisely the kind of solidarities which protect people from adversity, as well as underpinning the cooperative values that are important to a more positive view of peace. Some particularistic groups may tend to look inward, precisely because the outside world is hostile in some way, or because they are protective of time-honored hierarchies. Others are hybrids, seeking to support their own group while engaging with the wider world. Overall, it may not be the mode of associational life that really matters (as Gellner implied) but the values which lie behind it.

During the 1990s and 2000s, it became commonplace for participants at civil society conferences to remind people that the bombers who blew up a federal building in Oklahoma City in 1995 were members of American bowling clubs, undermining the argument that only primordial ties generate violence as well as Putnam's emphasis on the positive social capital that bowling clubs supposedly generate (Putnam 2000). However, it should be pointed out that the Oklahoma bombers were not acting to defend their bowling club, and it was not the bowling club per se which generated the bombers. Timothy McVeigh, the driving force behind the bombing, was a disturbed ex-soldier. His mother had left his father at the age of ten; he was bullied as a child and fascinated by guns; and he was deeply affected by his experiences in the first Gulf war (BBC News 2001). McVeigh emerged out of the socializing process of a particular subculture in the United States, and today there are many forms of violence in the West that reflect an ongoing, unresolved tension between the way people fashion their individual life journeys and their interdependencies, which are replete with inequality, discrimination, and competition. High levels of violence are strongly correlated with high levels of inequality (Wilkinson and Pickett 2009). Individualistic forms of sociability can also generate conflict and violence.

From the forgoing, it is clear that civil society cannot be about every kind of social bonds or the trust that they generate, since trust can form among people who embark on acts of extreme violence. In fact all forms of sociability can generate the trust which Putnam and others have done so much to link with civil society. Therefore, trust can be used for adverse purposes too, as Putnam himself came to acknowledge: "Al Qaeda, for instance, is an excellent example of social capital, enabling its participants to accomplish goals they could not accomplish without that network" (2007, 138). So what is it about the nature of social bonds that strengthens the relationship of civil society to peace?

This question is often addressed in terms of the kinds of social capital that are generated through associational interactions. "Bonding" social capital is contrasted with "bridging" social capital, with the former bringing together people who are alike and the latter bringing together those who differ in some important way. Putnam (2007) suggests that these two forms of social capital are often erroneously counterposed to each other, as if high levels of bonding can never be compatible with high levels of bridging, but this depends on the values at stake. Civil society can diminish violence and build the kind of trust associated with peace only when it actively contributes to the conditions for nonviolence, encourages nonviolent forms of social interaction, and promotes processes for imagining and constructing the common good across social and other divides. This was the conclusion of Ahutosh Varshney's (2002) important study of ethnic conflict and civic life in northern India. Cross-communal civic life played a vital role in ensuring that triggers to conflict amongst Hindus and Muslims did not erupt into extreme violence in some cities in the region, but did erupt where similar civic interactions were absent. Such civic values do not necessarily translate into either bonding or bridging. Instead they are anchored in building certain kinds of human interactions and relationships. It is in this sense that Karstedt (2006, 58), in an essay on the relationship between democracy and violence, argues that it is universalistic bonds that matter when exploring this relationship—not an empty universality but one which explicitly promotes inclusionary and egalitarian values: "The associational bonds that develop within civil society provide mechanisms of outreach and generalized cooperation that can counterbalance individualistic practices…Trust relationships are produced through universal bonds and the inclusionary mechanisms of democracy, with democratic institutions as equally strong providers and enforcers of these bonds. These vital social bonds are endangered by processes like social inequality and ethnic and religious divisions that factionalize society."

Civil society as a normative concept is not "evil," since it contains the potential for building peaceful societies. However, empirical associations do not inevitably contribute to either peace or violence. It is only by building distinctions into the concept that we can enable civil society to be an impetus to peace-thinking and a stimulant to peace-building in practice. The concept must encourage us to imagine the possibility of peace as a common good, and a worthwhile goal. This runs the risk of constructing "uncivil" society as a dichotomous Other to its apparently benign "civil" sibling, and the real world is not usually so clear-cut. Nuance and complexity have to be invoked, and a lot of discussion and intellectual effort invested in deciding precisely what makes civil society civil in different contexts. However, by insisting on the distinction between civil and uncivil, attention is drawn to the danger of evacuating civil society of its content. Civil society must be invested of meaning, not emptied through particular experiences that masquerade as a universalizing discourse, or through a failure to give it a clear normative direction. The civil dimensions of the concept emerge clearly when examined in the light of their potential opposites. Therefore, civil society is worth retaining as a value-laden ideal, at least until something better replaces it. This is because it highlights the civil and nonviolent values that are essential to a project like peace-building. In this sense also, civil society provides a tool with intellectual and normative precision that can be used against states that oppress and repress civil society organisations in the name of their legitimate monopoly of violence. A normative conceptualization of civil society challenges such abuses morally and enables civil society organisations to offer justified resistance in the world as it is.

3. Civil Society and Peace-Building

Can civil society as a normative ideal illuminate the practice of peace-building? The complexity underlying the norm-building aspects of empirical civil society has already been acknowledged, but recognition of such complexity has rarely accompanied efforts to harness civil society for peace-building at the end of the twentieth and the beginning of the twenty-first centuries. Instead, peace-building became associated with what has been called the "liberal peace" (Paris1997; Richmond 2005), a partial vision based on neoliberal market values which many believe to have introduced new sources of division and competition into fragile societies recovering from prolonged war and violence. This has led many to abandon civil society as an ideal, precisely because it became associated with this vision. But rather than abandoning the concept completely, I argue that it should be retained and its normative content revitalized to embrace the contingent possibilities that empirical civil society participation in peace-building implies.

In 1992, in the wake of the end of the Cold War and in a moment of renewed optimism, the then-United Nations Secretary General, Boutros Boutros Ghali, outlined his "agenda for peace," in which post-conflict peace-building became a core element of international action. This new agenda coincided with the revival of civil society ideas in Eastern Europe and elsewhere. Peace thinkers such as John Paul Lederach (1997) were influential in drawing attention to the importance of civil society actors in ensuring that peace processes did not only involve armed parties at war. An unprecedented explosion of activity ensued among civil society organizations, many of which emerged with a dedicated portfolio of activities and interest in peace-building, encouraged by the international donor community.

As these activities began to be scrutinized and evaluated, however, they were often found to be wanting. As well as theoretical critiques of the entire enterprise, there were many specific criticisms of concrete practice in particular countries and contexts (Belloni 2001; Orjuela 2003; Pouligny 2005; Pearce 1999; Pearce 2005). Pouligny (2005, 499–500) sums up the arguments of these critiques as follows:

> Ultimately, most outsiders tend to reduce the main characteristics and richness of any civil society: its diversity. In our frequent quest for homogeneity, we tend to seek a "consensus" or a "common view"; however, this does not exist in any society, and certainly not in a post-war period. A so-called common belief is neither necessary nor even desirable for remedying the real problem: a long contradictory process of defining a new social contract. Historians and sociologists have shown us that such processes rarely unfold in sanctified harmony but are rather the outcome of successive negotiations or, indeed, of concrete struggles. Neither can they result from "dogmatic voluntarism" alone. Yet, most donors and agencies continue to believe in such a process, as shown by the creation and sponsoring of a countless number of consortiums and platforms—not to mention the multiplication of coordination meetings of all kinds that, amongst other consequences, justify the complaints of leaders of local organizations that they no longer have time to actually work!

Rather than facilitating activities in each context that supported civil society actors to open up new spaces, build relationships in and across society, and advocate to the state, these actors have been drawn into implementing particular models of peace by the availability and steering effects of funding. For example, a three-year study of civil society and peace-building by Paffenholz (2009, 2010) took a functional view of civil society's role in peace-building in order to put more empirical flesh on this critical debate. It identified seven such functions: protection, monitoring, advocacy, socialization, social cohesion, facilitation, and service delivery. It also used a wide definition of civil society which included traditional and clan groups as well as professional associations, clubs, and nongovernmental organizations (NGOs), but its understanding of peace-building was quite narrowly focused on the five to ten years after the end of large-scale organized violence. The study took a more measured view of the contributions of civil society organizations in such contexts than the overly optimistic claims of the donors, specifying the phases and moments in which civil society actors, as opposed to other actors, can play a positive role. It represents a new generation of efforts to understand the empirical potential of civil society organizations in particular contexts and moments of postwar recovery, and argues that they can indeed play a significant role alongside other actors. In this way, the study and others like it help to redeem the relationship between civil society and peace-building, demonstrating with precision the positive roles that some civil society organizations play while criticizing others which, for example, remain elite-based and distant from the main body of society, offering apolitical solutions to deeply political problems.

In Guatemala, for example, donor funding poured into the country in the wake of the Peace Accords of 1996, creating a well-funded sector of urban-based NGOs. Some of these NGOs became effective advocates for security sector reform and human rights protection, but with limited connections to the mostly indigenous and impoverished rural dwellers who had borne the brunt of army massacres during the country's protracted civil war (Howell and Pearce 2001). The state itself was increasingly undermined from within by criminal and parallel powers, and was unable to implement the reforms proposed by civil society organizations. Yet on the margins of donor funding circles, people did not stop organizing to protect their communities from mining companies, demand land reform, and promote the rights of indigenous women, for example. Some NGOs did manage to retain their roots in these struggles, enabling them to survive the subsequent decline in donor funding, albeit with difficulty.

The example of Guatemala highlights the need to distinguish between the roles of specific forms of organization at particular moments in time in enhancing the potential for fostering the conditions that encourage people to live without violence over the long term. Peace-building, at least in the sense discussed here, may be less about highly focused initiatives and more about contingent activities in the civil society arena which open up societies to competing ideas and values reflecting the complexity of the search for peace. They might involve challenges to the gender relationships and expectations of masculinity which perpetuate the male-on-male use of violence responsible for the vast majority of deaths and injuries in the world. They might question the assumption that violence in the private sphere is not a problem for the public policy arena. They might build space for new social actors or previously excluded and subordinated groups to feel part of the debate about the future of their society. They might question forms of wealth production, the distribution of resources, and the nature of security provision. They might, in other words, generate debate about the nature of the common good in any particular context. Enhancing our knowledge of civil society as a value-producing and value-contesting arena and how it transforms each society's understanding of the meaning of, and potential for, peace, could provide much sharper conceptual tools for recognizing when empirical civil society is truly able to move people in these directions. Such an unashamedly normative interpretation of civil society may challenge some of the liberal meanings attached to this concept, but it would also move us towards a shared ethical and moral interpretation of peace-building. Civil society, like peace, could once again become part of the political world, in which societies move towards nonviolent ways of addressing their differences and building the conditions required to live without violence.

4. Conclusion

This chapter has argued that conceptually, civil society has an affinity with the idea of peace, since both revolve around the process of constructing the common good. Peace must be understood positively as the process of building the conditions for human beings to live without violence, as well as negatively—as the absence of war, for example. In this process, empirical distinctions must be made between those forms of sociability that promote violence and those that build peace, contrasting civil to uncivil society. Civil society can then be defined in terms of the values which correlate positively with the goal-directed activities of peace-building. Such ideas are complex, and the values involved require ongoing public debate and disagreement. Universality must be constructed through a complex process of conflict and contestation in empirical civil societies. There will be no guaranteed outcomes, but striving for an outcome is a goal in and of itself. In this task, the normative content of civil society—the shared norms of the "good society"—are essential to the project of a common humanity. They must be defended if we are to preserve the space and independence that are necessary for associational life to play its full part in peace-building effectively.

REFERENCES

Aristotle. 1981. *The Politics*. Ed. T. J. Saunders and trans. T. A. Sinclair. Harmondsworth: Penguin Classics.

BBC News. 2001. "Profile of Timothy McVeigh." Available at http://news.bbc.co.uk/1/hi/world/americas/1321244.stm (accessed March 2, 2010).

Belloni, R. 2001. "Civil Society and Peacebuilding in Bosnia and Herzogovina." *Journal of Peace Research* 38:163–80.

Black, A. 1984. *Guilds and Civil Society in European Political Thought from the Twelfth Century to the Present*. London: Methuen.

Colas, D. 1997. *Civil Society and Fanaticism*. Stanford, Calif.: Stanford University Press.

Cox, G. 1986. *The Ways of Peace: A Philosophy of Peace as Action*. New York: Paulist Press.

Elias, N. 2000. *The Civilizing Process*. Oxford: Blackwell Publishing.

Elsner, M. 2001. "Modernization, Self Control and Lethal Violence: The Long-term Dynamics of European Homicide Rates in Theoretical Perspective." *British Journal of Criminology* 41: 618–38.

———. 2008. "Modernity Strikes Back? A Historical Perspective on the Latest Increase in Interpersonal Violence (1960–1990)." *Journal of Conflict and Violence* 2, no. 2: 288–316.

Gellner, E. 1994. *Conditions of Liberty: Civil Society and its Rivals.* London: Hamish Hamilton.

Hegre, H., T. Ellingsen., S. Gates, and N. P. Gleditsh. 2001. "Towards a Democratic Civil Peace? Democracy, Political Change, and Civil War, 1816–1992." *The American Political Science Review* vol. 95, no 1: 33–48.

Howell, J., and J. Pearce. 2001. *Civil Society and Development.* Boulder, Colo.: Lynne Rienner.

Karstedt, S. 2006. "Democracy, Values and Violence: Paradoxes, Tensions, and Comparative Advantages of Liberal Inclusion." *Annals of the American Academy of Political and Social Science* , vol. 605(May): 50–81.

Keane, J. 1996. *Reflections on Violence.* London:Verso.

Kymlicka, W. 1995. *Multicultural Citizenship: A Liberal Theory of Minority Rights.* Oxford: Oxford University Press

Lederach, J. P. 1997. *Building Peace: Sustainable Reconciliation in Divided Societies.* Washington, D.C.: United States Institute of Peace Press.

Ludwig, H. 2006. *Civil Society.* Basingstoke: Palgrave Macmillan.

MacIntyre, A. 2007. *After Virtue*, 3rd ed. London: Duckworth.

Mann, M. 2005. *The Dark Side of Democracy. Explaining Ethnic Cleansing.* Cambridge: Cambridge University Press.

Mouffe, C. 2005. *The Return of the Political.* London: Verso.

Orjuela, C. 2003. "Building Peace in Sri Lanka: A Role for Civil Society?" *Journal of Peace Research* 40:195–212.

Paffenholz, T. 2010. *Civil Society and Peace-Building: Summary of Results for a Comparative Research Project.* Geneva: The Centre on Conflict, Development and Peace-Building.

———. (ed.) 2009. *Civil Society and Peace-Building: A Critical Assessment* Boulder. Colo.: Lynne Rienner.

Paris, R. 1997. "Peace-building and the Limits of Liberal Internationalism." *International Security* 22(2): 54–89.

Pearce, J. 1999. "Peace-building on the Periphery: The Case of Central America." *Third World Quarterly* vol. 20, no. 1 (February): 51–68.

———. 2005. "The International Community and Peace-Building." *Development* August vol. 48, no. 1: 41–49.

Pouligny, B. 2005. "Civil Society and Post-Conflict Peace-Building: Ambiguities of International Programmes Aimed at Building 'New' Societies." *Security Dialogue* 36: 495–510.

Putnam, R. 2000. *Bowling Alone.* New York: Simon & Schuster.

———. 2007. "*E Pluribus Unum:* Diversity and Community in the Twenty-First Century." The 2006 Johan Skytte Prize Lecture. *Scandinavian Political Studies* vol. 30, no. 2: 137–74.

Richmond, O. 2005. *The Transformation of Peace.* Basingstoke: Palgrave Macmillan.

Varshney, A. 2002. *Ethnic Conflict and Civic Life.* New Haven, Conn.: Yale University Press.

Wilkinson, R., and K. Pickett. 2009. *The Spirit Level.* London: Allen Lane.

CHAPTER 33

CIVIL SOCIETY AND POWER

JOHN GAVENTA

CAN civil society transform power relations, and if so, how and under what conditions? These questions are not easily answered. Much depends on what one means by civil society and one's understanding of power, concepts on which there is little consensus. Even when agreement exists on the meanings of these concepts, further debates revolve around complex empirical issues: when is power transformed, and how do we know it when we see it? Generalizations around these questions are difficult and perhaps even dangerous, since civil society, power, and transformation are deeply embedded in specific social and political contexts, rooted in historical processes, and often dynamic and contested in theory and in practice.

Given these challenges, the goals of this chapter are limited. Section 1 briefly recounts the meanings of civil society and argues that each carries with it a parallel understanding of power and its components. Section 2 examines the changing forms and spaces of power, as well as the levels across which they occur, and explores some of their implications for civil society in practice. The third section of the chapter explores important, though inconclusive, empirical evidence of civil society's transformational role. Ultimately, the conclusion suggests, the issue must become more focused on questions of power for whom, civil society of what kinds, and which forms of transformation are desirable or desired.

1. CIVIL SOCIETY AND POWER

While there are multiple of definitions of civil society, three broad understandings stand out in the literature: civil society as a description of types of actors, as a public sphere or arena, and as a set of norms and values which promote a "good" or more "civil" society (Edwards 2009). Each approach also carries with it a different set of assumptions and—implicitly or explicitly—a parallel approach to the understanding of power.

In the first of these definitions, civil society is a seen as a set of nonstate, often nonmarket actors, most commonly including grassroots and professional associations, nongovernmental organizations (NGOs), labor unions, churches, and social movements. The assumption is often that such civil society organizations will serve as a counterforce to the unchecked power of state or market actors. Such organizations are seen as agents of empowerment through which citizens develop their capacities to become aware of their rights and agency, mobilize to act, and pursue democratizing or social justice aims. While there are many examples of such roles in practice, the literature is also filled with examples of the opposite behavior—pointing to the role that civil society organizations may play in legitimating, rather than challenging the status quo, as well as to huge variations of power within and between civil society actors themselves (Bebbington, Hickey, and Mitlin 2007; Shutt 2009).

Despite these variations, understanding civil society as a set of actors fits neatly with an actor-oriented approach to the understanding and analysis of power. In this view, perhaps most famously articulated by Steven Lukes in his seminal work *Power: A Radical View* (1974), power may be understood as the power of *A* (one actor or set of actors) over *B* (another actor or set of actors). "To put the matter sharply," Lukes writes, "*A* may exercise power over *B* by getting him to do what he does not want to do, but he may also exercise power over him by influencing, shaping or determining his very wants" (1974, 23). From this perspective, understanding civil society's transformational role would involve, therefore, examining when civil society organizations and actors are able to shape or alter the actions, agendas, or norms of other actors, such as states and markets. Such an approach can also be used to examine the nature of power between and across civil society organizations, such as in debates on whether larger international NGOs dominate or crowd out smaller community-based associations, or how decisions are shaped within coalitions and social movements. Note also that while Lukes's approach is very actor-focused, it also includes the power of actors to shape norms and values.

The second definition of civil society focuses on its role as an arena, space, or sphere in which public action occurs. This approach draws heavily from other theorists in the tradition of Habermas, who examines the nature of deliberation in the public sphere, and from Gramsci, who saw civil society as an arena standing in tension with "political society," and which could be a force for hegemony and counter-hegemony. To discuss civil society as an arena immediately raises questions about how power shapes the nature of deliberation inside it, as well as the boundaries which surround it. Hayward (1998, 2), for example, challenges the actor-focused approach and argues for "de-facing power" by reconceptualizing it as "a network of social boundaries that constrain and enable action for all actors." She argues that freedom is the capacity to "to participate effectively in shaping the boundaries that define for them the field of what is possible" (1998, 12), drawing heavily on Foucault's work that challenges the idea that "power is wielded by people or groups by way of 'episodic' or 'sovereign' acts of domination or coercion. Instead, Foucault sees power as dispersed and pervasive. 'Power is everywhere' and 'comes from everywhere,' so in this sense is neither an agency nor a structure" (Foucault 1998, 63, quoted by Pettit 2010). Rather, "it is a kind of 'metapower' or 'regime of truth' that pervades society, and which is in constant flux and negotiation." Power is also a form of ensuring conformity in society, as seen in Foucault's studies of prisons, schools, and mental hospitals where people learned to discipline themselves and behave according to established norms that are communicated through dominant forms of discourse. For Gramsci, civil society was an also arena where ideas and beliefs were shaped, especially through knowledge organizations such as the media, universities, and religious organizations, which in turn could both challenge dominant ideas in a counterhegemonic way and also "manufacture consent" and reproduce domination (Gramsci 1971).

In this approach, power is also linked to norms and values, but its key determinants are discourse, knowledge, and culture. Those who seek to understand civil society's role through this framework therefore focus on the nature of discourse and deliberation within and around the public sphere, as well as the nature of contestation inside it. For Chandhoke (2005, 3) for example, civil society, as distinct from society as a whole, "can be conceived as that part of society where people, as rights-bearing citizens, meet to discuss and enter into dialogue about the polity. It is in this sense that civil society is absolutely indispensable for democracy in its promise of an engaged citizenry." Chandhoke points out that the nature of deliberation within this arena may serve to re-enforce, as well as to challenge, established inequalities, a point developed by Cornwall and Coelho (2006), who interrogate in practice whether we can see participatory public spheres as "spaces of change." Others are even more skeptical about the possibility that civil society can transform power relations. Drawing on Foucault and others, for example, Lipschutz (2007, 225) argues that, far from being transformative of power, much of global civil society is "a central and vital element in an expanding global neo-liberal regime of governmentality. Global civil society is constituted out of social relations within that regime and…helps to legitimise, reproduce and sometimes transform *internally* that regime, its operation and its objectives."

The third definition of civil society as a set of values—including notions of solidarity and social capital, tolerance and respect for pluralism, courage and voluntarism—is heavily contested, with critics pointing to the "uncivil" aspects of some civil society associations, to growing intolerance, and to voluntarism and empowerment as neoliberal values which can serve to weaken state-based approaches to achieving the common good. This approach also carries with it a parallel understanding of power, understood in terms of the purposes for which it is used. One common understanding sees power as "oppressive" or as "power over" others. Others, however, see power as productive, as the power to bring about positive change, mutually constructed by multiple actors, and not a zero-sum game of winners and losers. This approach carries with it a focus on power *with* (similar to civil society concepts of building horizontal power through associations, networks, and coalitions), and power *within*, in which power refers to a recognition of one's internalized sense of agency and empowerment. In this sense, civil society's role in transforming power relations may be seen not only in how it confronts negative "power over," but also in how it co-constructs a new society with others (Eyben et al. 2006; Rowlands 1997).

However, for many theorists of power, the norms and culture of the "new" or "good" society are themselves intertwined with and part of power, not separate from it. In exploring the relation between culture and power, Bourdieu, for example, develops the concept of *habitus*, meaning "the way society becomes deposited in persons in the form of lasting dispositions, or trained capacities and structured propensities to think, feel and act in determinate ways" (Wacquant 2005, 316, cited in Navarro 2006, 16). Actors and their practices are both shaped by and help to shape these dispositions. As Haugaard (2002, 229) summarizes, "in this sense power is both interpersonal and systemic. Because individuals exercise it over each other, power is negative, but equally, since strategy entails *habitus*, order and culture, is simultaneously positively constructive."

Hence, for each approach to civil society—as an actor, arena, and set of values—there are parallel ways to understand and analyze power. Each approach finds within it examples of civil society both as transformative of power and also as shaped by and constitutive of it. While these broad schools of thought are useful, more specific tools are required to analyze the workings of power in any given context.

2. The Changing Nature of Power and the Challenges for Civil Society

Whatever conceptual approach is deployed, it is clear that the nature and manifestations of power are changing, with strong implications for civil society. The rise of concepts of co-governance, which link states and societies in new forums (Ackerman 2004), or of public-private partnerships, social enterprise, and "philanthrocapitalism" (Edwards 2010), mean that neat divisions between civil society, market, and state begin to give way, leading to a focus on "networked governance" or networks of power rather than on single actors alone (Hajer and Wagenaar 2003). With the rise of global governance and new sites of authority, the analysis of power must also address the multitiered and multilayered spheres that are emerging, and their interactions, rather than focus on any single public sphere (Bererenskoetter and Williams 2007). And with the growth of knowledge and expertise, social media, and the internet as tools of "soft power" for winning "hearts and minds" (Lukes 2007), more attention must be paid to how values and cultures of power and powerlessness are constructed and maintained, as well as resisted and challenged. As Beck (2005, 3–4) writes, "politics is no longer subject to the same boundaries as before, and is no longer tied solely to state actors and institutions, the result being that additional players, new roles, new resources, unfamiliar rules and new contradictions and conflicts appear on the scene. In the old game, each playing piece made one move only. This is no longer true of the new nameless game for power and domination."

In a long tradition of work on power and democracy, power is often understood in its visible forms, by focusing on who participates in, and benefits from, the shaping of decisions in public arenas. In an earlier work based on experience in an Appalachian valley where quiescence rather than voice seemed to be the response to high levels of inequality, I challenged that view, drawing upon Lukes's three "faces" or "dimensions" of power that sought to explain not only the visible, but also the hidden and invisible forms of power (Gaventa 1980). More recently, I have argued that these faces of power constitute but one continuum or dimension. When considered in relationship to civil society, power can also be understood in relation to the *spaces or arenas* of power from the claimed to the closed, as well as to the *levels* of power, from the local to the global. Linking these three dimensions of forms, levels, and spaces, one can construct a "power cube" in which power shapes and is shaped by each dimension, and in which power can simultaneously be used as a form of resistance as well as domination (Gaventa 2006).

This approach has already been used by civil society actors to analyze the possibilities and pathways for transforming power in their work (Participation, Power and Social Change Team 2010). While one can approach this task from any dimension of power, it is important to recognize that each dimension is only part of the picture, and is constantly interacting with the others. By understanding the interactive nature of power in this way, we can also begin to assess the transformative possibilities of civil society in challenging power, as well as how civil society itself is shaped by power relations of various kinds.

The first dimension of the power cube focuses on the forms of power, as they affect what voices and issues emerge and predominate in the public sphere. The first form (or what Lukes referred to as "face") of power refers to *visible* power and is closely linked to theories of how pluralist democracy is *supposed* to work. It may be seen, for example, through analyzing who wins and who loses in the public arena, such as town meetings, legislative councils, village councils, or other settings. Yet as power theorists confirm, power is rarely fully visible. Equally important are forms of *hidden* power which help to shape the public agenda, organizing some actors, issues, or values into the public arena and onto the agenda while discouraging or preventing the inclusion of others (Bachrach and Baratz 1962). As Schattschneider (1960, 105) put it: "whoever decides what the game is about decides who gets in the game." But even more insidious than the power to control the agenda through the suppression of voices and issues, argued Lukes (1974), is the power to keep issues from arising at all through the shaping of values and consensus, or the internalization of forms of powerlessness such that conflict does not arise in the first place— what we now know as *invisible* power (VeneKlassen and Miller 2002; Gaventa 2006).

These latter forms of power connect to Gramscian ideas of hegemony or to Foucault's understanding of how knowledge is used in disciplinary ways by shaping the boundaries and norms of public discourse.

For civil society actors and organizations that seek to promote transformation, each dimension of power has produced an array of political repertoires. Public arenas are full of interest groups, NGOs, professional associations, social movements, and others who use advocacy to debate, influence, and shape decisions on key public issues. Sometimes, such groups are critiqued for becoming more and more professionalized, encouraging a model of speaking *for* rather than *with* or *by* the people directly concerned. Other traditions have focused on mobilizing popular participation through people-based advocacy designed to challenge the hidden faces of power which keep certain voices or issues off the agenda (Clark et al. 2002). A third tradition has focused on challenging how power shapes ideas and socializes people to internalize a sense of powerlessness—as seen, for example, in the awareness-building and popular education work of Paulo Freire-inspired *conscientisation* programs or in feminist approaches that start at the personal level to build power "from within." Others have argued that only when all of these repertoires come together through advocacy, mobilization, and awareness-building does transformative change begin to occur.

While such approaches focus on the *forms* of power and how to challenge them, the second dimension of the cube looks at the *spaces* of power, at *where* as well as *how* power is made visible. As with the forms of power, one can think of a continuum of types of spaces. From the perspective of civil society actors, many decision-making spaces of the state and the market—and indeed of civil society actors themselves—remain highly closed, removed from public scrutiny and participation. At the other end of the spectrum are *claimed* or created spaces of engagement such as voluntary associations, social movements, and local debating or cultural groups, which ordinary people themselves create. Lying between these two positions are an increasing array of "invited," "cogovernance," or "hybrid" public spaces in which citizens engage states and markets through formal or informal consultative and decision-making mechanisms (Cornwall 2002).

Each of these types of spaces is filled with, and is reflective of, the power relations that surround them, and each is associated with distinct traditions of civil society action that try to challenge how power is manifested. Campaigns for greater transparency, freedom of information, and public accountability have tried to open up spaces that were previously closed, while other approaches have urged the responsible exercise of power within these campaigns themselves. At the other end of the spectrum a huge literature exists on the contribution of peoples' associations, social movements, and cultural groups to citizen empowerment, countering hegemonic ideas, and contesting power, as well as critiques of the forms of power and exclusion that develop within these spaces themselves. Increasingly, studies of hybrid public spaces are asking important questions about who participates and deliberates within them, what issues reach the agenda, and whether more participatory forms of governance which link civil society and the state in new ways lead to different and more democratic outcomes than more elitist approaches (Spink et al. 2009). Here too growing evidence exists that transformational change comes not through a single strategy or in a single space, but through alliances and mechanisms which link "champions" on the inside of closed spaces with pressures from outside, a conclusion which challenges the notion that civil society mobilization by itself is a sufficient condition for progressive change (Green 2008; Gaventa and McGee 2010).

These *spaces* of power—from closed to "claimed"—are cross-cut by the different levels of power and the dynamics that exist between them, constituting the third dimension of the power cube (Gaventa 2007). A growing literature on global governance warns of the dangers of focusing only on the "local," or the "national" in a globalizing world, requiring consideration of the role of global or transnational civil society in emerging political regimes (Edwards and Gaventa 2001; Batliwala and Brown 2006). To some extent the debate on the levels and sites of power is not new. For many years, those concerned with this subject have argued about where power is located. Feminist scholars have challenged the focus by political science on the search for power in the public sphere, arguing for the primacy of power relations at the intimate or household level. Some argue that participatory practice must begin locally, because it is in the arenas of everyday life that people are able to resist power and construct their own voice. Others argue for the importance of the nation state and its role in mediating power relations, suggesting that the possibilities of local spaces often depend on the extent to which power is legitimated and regulated nationally. But for many, the study of power can no longer be focused only on one particular level or place. As Held and McGrew (2003, 11) write, for example, "the exclusive link between territory and political power has been broken. The contemporary era has witnessed layers of governance spreading within and across boundaries."

For scholars and activists concerned with change, this reconfiguration of political power also has enormous consequences. On the one hand, the globalization of power has created a vast array of political opportunities beyond the national level in which civil society actors can engage, by demanding greater transparency and accountability, participating in policy formulation and monitoring, and pressing for formal mechanisms for redress (Scholte 2002). But not only do these shifts open up broader possibilities for action by relatively powerless groups at any one level, they also create new opportunities through the interaction of the different levels themselves. Those seeking to act on local or national injustices may choose to confront those perceived to be responsible by acting at other levels of power, in order to exercise their voice and express their demands. Keck and Sikkink (1998, 13), for example, demonstrate how advocacy networks may employ a "boomerang pattern," in which "state A blocks redress to organizations within it; they activate networks, whose members pressure their own state and (if relevant) a third-party organization, which in turn pressure state A."

However, just as new levels and spaces bring opportunities for civil society actors to engage with and confront power relations, so they also raise new challenges concerning civil society's own power and legitimacy. Increasingly in the civil society literature, questions are asked about representational issues such as "who speaks for whom" across boundaries, and about possible disconnections or tensions between civil society actors at the global, national, and local levels (Batliwala 2002; Van Rooy 2004). Demands for accountability among other state and nonstate actors have led to corresponding pressures for civil society organizations to strengthen their own accountability as well. Gaventa and Tandon (2010, 4) find that "for some citizens, there are new opportunities for participation in transnational processes of action, resulting in the emergence of a new sense of global citizenship and solidarity. Yet for many other ordinary citizens, changes in global authority may have the opposite effect, strengthening the layers and discourses of power that limit the possibilities for their local action, and constraining—or at least, not enabling—a sense of citizen agency." Much depends, they argue, on the forms of mobilization, the role of mediators, and the politics of knowledge that shape the possibilities and practices of citizenship in response to changes in the global landscape.

While looking at each dimension of power, it is equally important to understand the constant and dynamic interaction of these forms, spaces, and levels of power with each other. The spaces of power affect whose voice and knowledge are visible inside them, while mobilization across the levels of power can serve to strengthen certain voices in the public arena and create new forms of exclusion for others. To transform power fundamentally suggests that actors must be able to work across forms, spaces, and levels simultaneously ——a scope and range of action that few civil society organizations can accomplish alone. Ultimately, such an analysis suggests, a key challenge for civil society is how to develop more democratic and cross-cutting alliances which also address questions of representation and accountability. From this perspective, the power of civil society to foster change is deeply linked to how it engages with issues of its own power *within, with,* and *over* others.

3. The Transformative Potential of Civil Society

At least in the world of international development, there has been an implicit assumption over recent decades that greater participation by civil society actors will lead to outcomes that are positive. At the same time, the evidence surrounding this assumption, and the conditions under which it is correct, are mixed—with some arguing for the empirical virtues of civil society engagement and others stressing its risks and failures. In the larger literature on civil society and democracy one sees similar debates, with some pointing to the contributions of civil society to deepening democracy (e.g., Wainwright 2005), and others warning of the darker side of civic engagement. In attempting to shed light on these debates, Gaventa and Barrett

(2010) draw from one hundred case studies of citizen action across twenty countries to answer the following question: "What difference does citizen engagement make?" Using a meta-synthesis approach, they coded over 800 examples of citizen engagement in associations, social movements, and campaigns, or participatory forms of governance with the state, which produced both positive and negative outcomes. While the study does not focus on power per se, it provides a useful framework through which to explore how these forms of citizen action have contributed to broader processes of social and political change.

On the one hand, the study offers a fairly positive narrative. Of the 800 outcomes coded, 75 percent were considered "positive" in terms of their contribution to strengthening democracy and development. On the other hand, the study issues strong warnings about the risks of engagement; for every type of positive outcome, there are parallel or mirror images which can also be much more negative. The first important outcome of citizen engagement sounds almost tautological, but it confirms an argument long found in thinking on participation and democracy: citizen action serves to create "better citizens" (Pateman 1970). Engagement is itself a way of strengthening a sense of citizenship, and the knowledge and sense of awareness necessary to achieve and activate it. It can also strengthen the practices and efficacy of citizen participation through more effective action, the transfer of skills across issues and arenas, and the thickening of alliances and networks. These, the study argues, are not only "intermediate" outcomes, but they are also ends in and of themselves, and they help to measure the health of civil society and the dispositions and efficacy of the citizens who animate it. For example, Kabeer, Mahmud, and Castro (2010) explore the impact of membership in civil society organizations in Bangladesh and find clear evidence of how it helps to build awareness of rights and political capabilities among the citizenry—but also that it does not always do so. Much depends on the style of mobilization undertaken by the organizations themselves. Those that focused only on service delivery or the provision of micro credit, for example, were found to have little impact on political empowerment, whereas those that took a broader social mobilization approach were seen to bring about change in political and social as well as economic arenas.

In turn, greater awareness among citizens, coupled with stronger citizenship practices, can challenge the status quo more effectively, helping to contribute to the building of more responsive states which can deliver services, protect and extend human rights, and foster a culture of accountability. They can also contribute to a broader sense of inclusion among previously marginalized groups in society and—at least potentially—increase social cohesion across different communities. Strong examples may be seen, for example, in efforts by the Treatment Action Campaign in South Africa to challenge national policies as well as public norms on HIV/AIDS (Friedman 2010), and in the work of the freedom of information movement in India, which not only changed the law, but also helped to empower thousands of ordinary citizens to use the law for independent action (Baviskar 2010).

However, while providing compelling evidence of the positive outcomes of citizen engagement, the study also recognizes that such participation is not always used for positive purposes. It can lead to a sense of disempowerment and a reduced sense of agency, or to new knowledge dependencies, or to re-enforced exclusion due to new forms of awareness. Although engagement can contribute to strengthened practices of participation, at other times participation is perceived as meaningless, tokenistic, or manipulative. In other instances, it can contribute to new skills and alliances, but which are used for corrupt or other nonpositive ends, or are captured by elites, or raise new issues of accountability and representation. Participation can challenge state power but can also come up against bureaucratic "brick walls" and reprisals, including violence from state actors against those who challenge the status quo. And new spaces for civil society engagement can reinforce old hierarchies based on gender, caste, or ethnicity; and contribute to greater competition and conflict across groups who compete for recognition and resources in new ways.

4. CONCLUSION

As these findings make clear, civil society engagement is not in and of itself inherently transformative, though it has transformative potential. The studies from which they are taken go on to point to a number of factors that affect the degree to which this potential is realized. First, the nature and quality of mobilization and associational strategies matter greatly, not just the size or density of civil society organizations alone. Second, the ability to develop links and alliances with reformers inside the state and other institutions is critical, since civil society groups can rarely achieve major change alone. Third, changes in globalization, including the rise of new forms of communications and networking beyond borders, pose new opportunities for action, while also offering new barriers to inclusion. As section 2 concluded, the capacity to link action and activities across spaces, forms, and levels of power is necessary because transformation requires multidimensional and complex approaches to change, not a single magic bullet.

While these emerging lessons are important, more work is obviously needed. A key task for the future—for theorists and practitioners alike—is to move beyond simplistic debates about the "virtues" or "failures" of civil society. Through more rigorous empirical work, we need to develop higher-order and more nuanced theories of the ways in which states, markets, and civil societies interact in different regimes to explain differential outcomes. In turn, far more robust understandings are required of how concepts and practices of civil society intersect with theories and manifestations of power, and of how, and under what conditions, civil society actors, arenas, and values will transform, rather than reproduce, unjust and unequal power relations.

REFERENCES

Ackerman, J. 2004. "Co-governance for accountability: beyond 'exit' and 'voice.'" *World Development* vol. 32(3): 447–63.

Bachrach, P., and M. Baratz. 1962. "The Two Faces of Power." *American Political Science Review* vol. 56: 947–52.

Batliwala, S. 2002. "Grassroots Movements as Transnational Actors: Implications for Global Civil Society." *Voluntas* vol. 13(4): 393–409.

Batliwala, S., and D. L. Brown (eds.). 2006. *Transnational Civil Society.* West Hartford, Conn.: Kumarian Press.

Baviskar, A. 2010. "Winning the Right to Information in India: Is Knowledge Power?" in J. Gaventa and R. McGee (eds.) *Citizen Action and National Policy Reform.* London: Zed Books.

Bebbington, A., S. Hickey, and D. Mitlin (eds.). 2007. *Can NGOs Make a Difference? The challenge of development alternatives.* London: Zed Books.

Beck, U. 2005. *Power in a Global Age: A new global political economy.* Cambridge: Polity Press.

Bererenskoetter, F., and M. J. Williams. 2007. *Power in World Politics.* London: Routledge.

Chandhoke, N. 2005. "What the Hell is Civil Society." London: openDemocracy. Available at www.openDemocracy.net.

Clark, C., B. Harrison, V. Miller, J. Pettit, and L. VeneKlasen (eds.). 2002. "Advocacy and Citizen Participation." *Participatory Learning and Action* No. 43. London: International Institute of Environment and Development.

Cornwall, A. 2002. "Making Spaces, Changing Places: Situating Participation in Development." IDS Working Paper 170. Brighton: Institute of Development Studies.

Cornwall, A., and V. Coelho (eds.). 2006. *Spaces for Change? The Politics of Citizen Participation in New Democratic Arenas.* London: Zed Books.

Edwards, M. 2009. *Civil Society.* 2nd ed. Cambridge: Polity Press.

——. 2010. *Small Change: Why Business Won't Save the World.* San Francisco: Berrett-Koehler.

Edwards, M., and J. Gaventa (eds.). 2001. *Global Citizen Action.* Boulder, Colo: Lynne Rienner.

Eyben, R., C. Harris., and J. Pettit. 2006. "Exploring Power for Change." *IDS Bulletin,* vol. 37(6): 1–10.

Foucault, M. 1998. *The History of Sexuality: The Will to Knowledge.* London, Penguin.

Friedman, S. 2010. "Gaining Comprehensive AIDS Treatment in South Africa: The Extraordinary 'Ordinary,'" in J. Gaventa and R. McGee (eds.), op.cit. 44–46.

Gaventa, J. 1980. *Power and Powerlessness: Quiescence and Rebellion in an Appalachian Valley.* Urbana: University of Illinois Press.

——. 2006. "Finding the Spaces for Change: A Power Analysis," in R. Eyben, C. Harris, and J. Pettit (eds.) "Exploring Power for Change." *IDS Bulletin,* vol. 37(6): 11–21.

——. 2007. "Levels, Spaces and Forms of Power: Analysing Opportunities for Change," in F. Berenskoetter and M. J. Williams (eds.), op.cit., 204–24.

Gaventa, J., and G. Barrett. 2010. "So What Difference Does It Make? Mapping the Outcomes of Citizen Engagement." IDS Working Paper 347. Brighton: Institute of Development Studies.

Gaventa, J., and R. McGee. 2010. *Citizen Action and National Policy Reform.* London: Zed Books.

Gaventa, J., and R. Tandon. 2010. *Globalizing Citizens: New Dynamics of Inclusion and Exclusion.* London: Zed Books.

Gramsci, A., 1971. *Selections for the Prison Notebooks of Antonio Gramsci.* Ed. and trans. Q. Hoare and G. Newell Smith. London: Lawrence and Wishart.

Green, D. 2008. *From Poverty to Power: How Active Citizens and Effective States Can Change the World.* Oxford: Oxfam.

Hajer, M., and H. Wagenaar. 2003. *Deliberative Policy Analysis: Understanding Governance in the Network Society.* Cambridge: Cambridge University Press.

Haugaard, M. 2002. *Power: A Reader.* Manchester: Manchester University Press.

Hayward, C. R. 1998. *De-Facing Power.* Polity, vol. 31(1): 1–22.

Held, D., and A. McGrew (eds.). 2003. *The Global Transformations Reader: An Introduction to the Globalization Debate.* Cambridge: Polity Press.

Kabeer, N., S. Mahmud, and J. Castro. 2010. *NGO Strategies and the Challenge of Development and Democracy in Bangladesh.* IDS Working Paper 343. Brighton: Institute of Development Studies.

Keck, M. E., and K. Sikkink. 1998. *Activists Beyond Borders: Advocacy Networks in International Politics.* Ithaca: Cornell University Press.

Lipschutz, R. 2007. "On the Transformational Potential of Global Civil Society," in F. Berenskoetter and M.J. Williams (eds.), op.cit: 225–43.

Lukes, S. 1974. *Power: A Radical View.* London: Macmillan Basingstoke: Palgrave Macmillan.
———. 2007. "Power and the Battle for Hearts and Minds: On the Bluntness of Soft Power," in F. Bererenskoetter and M. J. Williams (eds.), op.cit: 83–97.

Navarro, Z. 2006. "In Search of Interpretation of Power: The Contribution of Pierre Bourdieu." IDS Bulletin vol. 37 (6): 11–22.

Participation, Power and Social Change Team. 2010. "The Power Cube." Brighton: Institute of Development Studies. Available at www.powercube.net.

Pateman, C. 1970 *Participation and Democratic Theory.* Cambridge: Cambridge University Press.

Pettit, J. 2010."Foucault: Power is Everywhere." Available at http://www.powercube.net/other-forms-of-power/foucault-power-is-everywhere/, accessed July 18, 2010.

Rowlands, J. 1997. *Questioning Empowerment: Working with Women in Honduras.* Oxford: Oxfam.

Schattschneider, E. 1960. *The Semi-Sovereign People: A Realist's View of Democracy in America.* New York: Holt, Rinehart, and Winston.

Scholte, J. A. 2002. "Civil Society and Democracy in Global Governance," in R. Wilkinson (ed.) *The Global Governance Reader.* London: Routledge.

Shutt, C. 2009. "Changing the World by Changing Ourselves: Reflections from a Bunch of Bingos." IDS Practice Paper 3. Brighton: Institute of Development Studies.

Spink, P. K., N. Hossain., and N. J. Best. 2009. "Hybrid Public Action." *IDS Bulletin* vol. 40 (6): 1–12.

Van Rooy, A. 2004, *The Global Legitimacy Game: Civil Society, Globalization and Protest.* Basingstoke: Palgrave Macmillan.

VeneKlasen, L., and Miller, V. 2002. *A New Weave of People, Power and Politics: the Action Guide for Advocacy and Citizen Participation.* Oklahoma City: World Neighbors.

Wacquant, L. 2005. "Habitus," in J. Becket and Z. Milan, *International Encyclopaedia of Economic Sociology.* London: Routledge, 315–19.

Wainwright, H. 2005. "Civil Society, Democracy and Power: Global Connections," in H. Anheir, M. Glasius, and M. Kaldor (eds.) *Global Civil Society 2004/2005.* London. Sage Publications.

CHAPTER 34

CIVIL SOCIETY
AND THE MARKET

SIMON ZADEK

ENCOUNTERS with business and the market have been woven throughout the history of civil society for at least three hundred years, but the pace and intensity of these encounters has increased dramatically since the fall of the Berlin Wall and the birth of corporate social responsibility in the late 1980s and early 1990s. Some see markets and civil society as natural allies, mutually dependent and working together to resolve social problems. Others see them as necessary antagonists, creating change out of conflict to avoid the co-optation that might strip them of their distinctive strengths and values. And a large and emerging middle ground finds inspiration in combining elements from both these views, celebrating the birth of new institutions that can no longer be categorized as belonging to one sector or the other. Can and does civil society transform markets, and if so how and to what long-term effect?

This chapter answers these questions by exploring three levels of effects of contemporary forms of civil society action on the behavior of market actors, and evaluating their social, environmental, and economic impacts. The *tactical* level of action concerns itself with the specific results of such efforts, such as a campaign against a corporation; the *strategic* level asks whether a more ambitious agenda and potential for change has been sacrificed in return for less substantive tactical successes; and the *systemic* level explores whether the underlying conditions for civil society action on market transformation are themselves shifting in the light of experience and broader global changes. If so, what are the implications of this shift? These three levels of action are woven through the analysis that follows, which begins by setting the debate in context and explaining the rise of "civil regulation," and then provides a brief summary of civil society's impact. Sections 3 and 4 explore new economic and geopolitical developments that complicate and enrich the encounter between civil society and the market, and section 5 concludes by re-evaluating the results of these encounters in the light of these new developments.

1. Civil Society and the Market

Civil society has always sought to influence markets and reshape their impact (Korten 1995). Contemporary experience should be appreciated in that context, but it must also be explored for its specific forms and outcomes (Zadek 2007). Since the late 1980s, the landscape of civil society engagement with business has been transformed, with many more, and more diverse, civil society actors, more extensive and intimate engagement between what historically were often oppositional forces, and more complex civil society strategies and tactics designed to affect the drivers of change, from traditional public pressure through to codesign with business, and even coinvestment and coproduction of innovative products and processes with potential for more benign societal impacts. Changing geopolitics are playing an increasingly important role, with the growing presence of civil society and business actors from the South mixed in with the voices of their governments and their underlying political cultures and institutional arrangements.

If ever a field of practice was in rapid flux, it is the relationship between civil society and markets. With this flux have come profound disagreements over strategic options and their consequences. The professionalization of large parts of civil society has brought with it not only pragmatic compromises necessary to satisfy their need for resources, but also new patterns of social identity among practitioners and in their politics, values and lifestyles (Chambers 1993; Said 1996). Multibillion-dollar programs to address health and education, for example, can only be accessed or mobilized if engagement with business is preferred to tackling the more profound challenges that concern ownership, governance, and the institutionalized objectives of profit. And even where deals are struck and new standards set, old battle lines are reopened when basic rights have to be renegotiated in the light of new cadres of businesses that emerge from political cultures unafraid to reshape priorities or even fundamental norms as enshrined in international conventions.

Whether or not to engage with business is no longer a useful question. Engagement covers a diverse range of options, and nonengagement is an increasingly implausible proposition given the interdependence of civil society actions with market-based technologies, communications pathways, and sources of expertise and resources (Elkington and Hartigan 2009). Autonomy must be an objective requirement of engagement, but it can no longer be synonymous with complete independence or other framing conceptions of purity of approach or community. The sheer range of these approaches belies comprehensive treatment in a chapter of this length. Therefore, the emerging—and contentious—roles of civil society as market actors themselves through procurement, ownership, and social enterprise, and their adoption of business-like institutional arrangements, processes, and cultures, are not considered here (Edwards 2010). My focus is on the successes and failures of civil society's attempts to shape markets through what has been called "civil regulation" (Zadek 2007).

2. The Successes and Failures of Civil Regulation

Civil regulation, the capacity of civil society to change market rules through direct pressure rather than the traditional route of lobbying for statutory changes, was born out of a particular moment in corporate development and broader political history (Vogel 2006). Neoliberal economic policies implemented during the 1980s undermined the social contract between business and Western societies, a fragmentation that was reinforced because the feared counterpoint of the Soviet Union could no longer be invoked (Gray 2000). At the same time, a rapid shift in the locus of economic value from production up the value chain towards the brand, marked out a period of remarkable success for Northern-based corporations across global markets, driven in particular by the ethos of privatization that opened markets up and at the same time further fractured the underlying social contract that was mediated by the state. Simultaneously, the rise of the Internet and the capacity of relatively resource-poor civil society organizations to mobilize media-friendly action was matched by the emergence of the first generation of multinational nongovernmental organizations (NGOs) such as Oxfam and the Worldwide Fund for Nature, which mirrored the rise of their corporate counterparts as had labor unions in the early development of industrial capitalism.

Civil regulation has largely relied on corporations' sense of brand vulnerability, which perhaps ironically increases in highly concentrated, oligopolistic markets.[1] In the second half of the 1990s, businesses increasingly yielded to civil society demands before stiffening their position because of concerns about brand damage and associated financial losses. Campaigning was founded on several iconic cases, including Shell's reversal of its decision to sink the Brent Spa Oil Platform in the North Sea in the face of a media-savvy Greenpeace campaign, and the anti-Nike sweatshop campaigns that, to some, demonstrated all that was wrong with globalization and capitalism in general (Zadek 2004). In some instances real damage was done by these actions, reinforcing the view for a time that campaigns of almost any form were a potentially lethal force. However, over the years this simplistic view has eroded with more experience of what does and does not count in practice, and as important, how best to inoculate the corporation against the force of civil society action. Nike still faces a steady stream of actions by anti-sweatshop campaigners, yet no longer reacts with the same fear that marked their earlier responses. Today, British Petroteum (BP), once a leading corporate advocate of sustainability, feels it can walk away from civil society-business coalitions such as the U.S. Climate Action Partnership despite this being a "significant blow for the campaign to bring in carbon dioxide emissions controls in the U.S.," with little fear of redress from civil society.[2]

Several changes underpin this shift in behavior. Through experience, businesses have learned to distinguish where real brand threats exist. Competitive pressures have intensified, making it harder for businesses to make changes that, even in the short term, disadvantage them in the marketplace. And new, less campaign-vulnerable business leaders are emerging in the South, a point I return to below. The most significant change, however, has been the development of closer relationships between business and civil society. Across many fields, their relationship has evolved from their traditional roles as "poachers and gamekeepers" to one of "uncomfortable bedfellows." The Worldwide Fund for Nature has led the way in creating global partnerships with individual corporations, including high-profile agreements with the Coca Cola Company and the French cement giant Lafarge.[3] Labor activists have joined with their erstwhile corporate targets in forming international, multicompany initiatives such as the Ethical Trading Initiative and the Fair Labour Association.[4] Human rights activists and anticorruption groups have joined forces with mining companies in the Extractive Industries Transparency Initiative and the Voluntary Principles on Security and Human Rights.[5] And health activists sit together with the world's largest pharmaceutical companies through the Global Alliance for Vaccines Initiative and other multi-billion-dollar partnerships designed to deliver health services to poor communities.[6]

Today, there are hundreds of initiatives that together have created a "soft governance web," spread across every market and issue from nanotechnology to fish.[7] These initiatives have sought to reshape markets by blending voluntary rules for business to follow, public and private finance, and the combined competencies of civil society, business, and government in delivering innovative designs and implementation practices. Some of these initiatives have achieved significant market penetration. The Marine Stewardship Council, for example, covers 10 percent of the global wild fish catch, and the Equator Principles cover more than 80 percent of cross-border project investments.[8] Such collaborative ventures have influenced the broader political narrative about public policy and international development. For example, President Lula of Brazil signaled a new contract with business as part of his election campaign's attempts to bridge the traditional gap between the Working Party's historical constituencies and business, especially financial capital (Zadek 2006a).

Civil society has and does transform how business is done, of that there is no doubt. Just as black South Africans boycotted white businesses during apartheid, so Chinese consumers vilified and abandoned French-owned shops, at least temporarily, when French President Sarkozy met with the Dalai Lama in December 2008.[9] Nestle, Nike, McDonalds, and Shell have joined a long list of global businesses that have visibly yielded to the perceived threat of damage to their cherished brand values created by targeted campaigns by community groups, environmental and human rights organizations, and labor unions. Such actions have clearly made a difference. Greater corporate transparency, new codes of conduct, a mainstream profession of social auditing that was considered exotic in the 1990s,[10] and collaboratively developed standards on everything from sustainable forestry to Internet privacy have shaped corporate practices and improved the lot of workers in global supply chains, communities located around mining operations, indigenous groups protecting their bio-homes, and endangered species from whales to tree frogs.[11] It is no longer possible to be a Western mainstream consumer brand and not commit to labor and environmental standards down one's global supply chain, just as it would be tough for any major Western financial institution funding major infrastructure projects not to sign up to the Equator Principles. In such senses, the basis on which business is done has been transformed, not merely the behavior of specific businesses that have been targeted by public campaigns. Progress has clearly been made through these new forms of collaborative governance (Slaughter 2005).

However, the disappointments have also been visible and troubling. An early casualty was the Global Alliance for Workers and Communities, which was closed down in 2004 after its main sponsors, the International Youth Foundation, Nike, Gap, and the World Bank, accepted that the initiative had failed to gain traction amongst the business, activist or development communities.[12] Far more disturbing was the effective collapse in 2006 of the much-vaunted Atlanta Agreement to secure child-free stitching of leather footballs in Sialkot, Pakistan. This turn of events was startling to many, if only because of the high-profile engagement of many international players in brokering and implementing the deal, notably the International Labor Organization (ILO), the Save the Children Fund, and the international labor movement. More generally, these new forms of collaborative governance, at least in their initial formulation, have succeeded in overcoming old impasses, but have only rarely generated the level of transformational change required to address the challenges at stake. Even those that addressed the roles of governments have had limited impact to date. This is obvious when it comes to corruption. Many anticorruption initiatives have emerged under pressure from civil society, governments, and sometimes business itself, including the Extractive Industry Transparency Initiative (EITI), the World Economic Forum-sponsored Partnership Against Corruption Initiative (PACI) and initiatives driven by single institutions such as Transparency International and the Soros-backed Revenue Watch Institute.[13] But corruption continues unabated. In Nigeria alone, an estimated $400 billion in oil revenues since the 1960s has been stolen by politicians and civil servants.[14]

Hence, one can also conclude that civil society has failed to transform the basis on which markets function, particularly the ways in which businesses profit from externalizing costs onto the shoulders of others. After two decades of global action on business accountability, the financial sector was still able to impose history's largest-ever exercise in taxation without representation during the crisis of 2009, destroying trillions of dollars of wealth in the process, accumulating trillions more in public debt, and putting tens of millions of people out of work. Despite the weight of public anger that resulted, the U.S. government failed to impose meaningful regulation on those who caused these problems, thus accelerating an underlying shift of power from the North Atlantic to Asia and the Pacific. Similarly, a global climate deal was not forged in Copenhagen in 2010, mostly as a result of the actions of several thousand corporate lobbyists in Washington, D.C. who successfully buried what might have been the last opportunity for concerted action on climate management, in exchange for a few additional percentage points in share values and short-term profits (Gore 2008). Corporate capture of the regulatory process, at least in the United States, is self-evident, rendering virtually irrelevant any theory that conceives of the state as an effective gamekeeper.

In each of these cases, civil society was actively engaged, but proved largely irrelevant in practice. It is true that organizations such as Ceres that represent many civil society organizations and progressive businesses in the United States have succeeded in persuading the Securities and Exchange Commission to mandate that companies report publicly on material climate risks.[15] But while this is a significant milestone in the evolution of corporate disclosure and the place of the environment in risk management, the evidence from earlier, comparable developments in U.K. company law is that such successes do not readily translate into substantive changes in performance. The global climate negotiations themselves were certainly amplified, but arguably weakened by, the incoherence of civil society either as a serious professional lobbying force or as a street-level platform for protest.

3. THE RISE OF NEW ACTORS

Realigning business responsibilities in society is never easy. Old ways are deeply embedded in the fabric of markets and the psychology of those who create and lead them. But such "old ways" are now themselves subject to a different challenge that threatens to overturn the terms of the debate about civil society and market transformation. That challenge is provided by a new cadre of emerging economic and political powerhouses, notably (and perhaps in order of importance) China, India, Brazil, Russia, and South Africa.

Existing global businesses complain that emerging economy businesses are competing unfairly by ignoring social and environmental standards. Emerging economy businesses and governments in turn accuse the international media of bias, and argue that sustainability standards institutionalize an uneven playing field in favor of European and North American firms. Since such standards emerge in most cases from the threat or actuality of destructive actions against business by civil society organizations, the perception in the South is that they are in effect policed by Northern NGOs on behalf of multinationals in the North. The good news is that responsible leadership is far from being the preserve of the Northern business community. The Brazilian body-care innovator, Natura, for example, the Indian conglomerate Tata, and South Africa's mining giant Anglo American are among a growing number of iconic emerging economy companies that match or exceed sustainability benchmarks set by the best practices of their Northern counterparts. The Global 100, a prestigious ranking of the world's one hundred most sustainable, publicly listed companies, includes twelve emerging economy companies in its list for 2010, up from zero in 2005.[16]

Leveraging such exemplary practices to the mainstream of the market requires generally accepted standards, the same challenge that drove campaigning NGOs to engage in the development of the first generation of sustainability standards in the 1990s. In this second round, the role of civil society in advancing such standards will be key, but this time faced by the growing importance of business communities in emerging economies. Civil society actors in Brazil and South Africa, for example, have extensive experience in sustainability standards. Post-apartheid South Africa has developed many voluntary social compacts between businesses, labor, civil society, and government, mainly focused on black empowerment, but also dealing with pervasive social and economic challenges such as HIV/AIDS. Similarly, Argentina and Brazil have advanced a raft of voluntary sustainability standards such as the Sustainable Soya Roundtable.[17]

Elsewhere the challenge for civil society is both greater and different. China, in particular, will be hugely influential for the next generation of business standards in international markets (Brautigam 2010). As one senior executive of a North American company based in Shanghai commented in 2010, "China is developing 10,000 new standards with every intention of placing them at the heart of tomorrow's global markets—the question is not whether these standards will be influential, but rather what will be in them."[18] Yet unlike in Brazil and South Africa, Chinese businesses and the Chinese government are both inexperienced in—and in the main resistant to—engaging with civil society actors in the development of such standards, let alone in their stewardship. There are exceptions: for example some Chinese companies have signed up to existing civil society-business partnership standards such as the Forest Stewardship Council and the Global Reporting Initiative, and China is an active participant in the development of the International Organization for Standardization (ISO)'s social responsibility standard (SR 26000). Yet as long as domestic experience of collaboration is weak, it is hard to imagine engagement with civil society becoming core to how China does business internationally.

Civil society's role in transforming markets is therefore further challenged by the growing economic power of the South. A new generation of global businesses may be less inclined to respond to civil regulation, especially if their domestic constituents (both governments and consumers) are less engaged or are actively disassociated with such issues. On the other hand, these profound geopolitical changes empower civil society to engage with a growing middle class in emerging economies in order to increase their interest and willingness to respond to the ethics of consumerism and employment choices. Recent public opinion polls of Chinese citizens indicate the rise there of the ethical consumer. Some 98 percent of respondents to one independent survey said they were likely to be more loyal and motivated as employees if the company demonstrated a strong commitment to social responsibility, and 81 percent said they felt their choices as consumers could affect company behavior.[19]

4. BEYOND THE BUSINESS CASE

The business case dimension of thinking has been the single most important driver behind mainstreaming the practice of corporate social responsibility, and lies at the heart of how civil society has sought to act directly in reshaping markets (Schmidheiny 1992). At its most straightforward, the business case describes a pragmatic need to convince corporations that it is in their narrow institutional interests to improve their social and environmental performance, even where relevant legislation is absent or unenforced. It is this approach that has allowed unlikely alliances to develop across a spectrum of players with diverse political views and interests, from the advocates of a free-market approach to those with a more radical change agenda (Klein 2002) However, much of the business case debate is misguided. The view that there is a stable relationship between, say, adhering to human rights and profitability is foolish. The much-vaunted positive impact of good corporate governance on business success is seriously overrated, or else poorly specified and understood (Zadek 2006b). There are many factors that mediate the relationships between context, drivers, enablers, and performance. Put simply, some businesses will work out how to make money from, say, improved environmental performance, while others will go bust in trying.

Civil society's business case approach has been predicated on the intensive accountability of most businesses, especially publicly listed companies, to shareholders with a predominantly financial interest. In its modern form this approach is associated with the failure of civil society in the 1970s and 1980s to successfully advocate for either renewed economic nationalization or a shift in international corporate governance towards more pluralistic accountability structures. In practice, there have been some gains in this latter respect, with extended trench warfare focused on definitions of materiality, public disclosure, and the rights of minority shareholders that has significantly increased accountability to nonfinancial shareholders in some countries, despite the resilience of the underlying Anglo Saxon model of fiduciary responsibility to financial capital.

However, this incremental, tactical approach to squeezing the last ounce of public good out of the Anglo Saxon model of corporate governance may come to be seen as a side-skirmish, or at least as an appetizer to more fundamental shifts that may accompany the growing importance of emerging economy businesses and governments. Core to this shift is the extensive role of the state in the ownership of economic assets in these countries. China's economy is dominated by state-owned enterprises, and the bulk of their international investments, notably in natural resources, are undertaken by publicly directed enterprises. Venezuela and other countries that pursue what might be called the "Chavez doctrine" are also focused heavily on state ownership, though here through renationalization framed by a vibrant political populism. Similarly, Russia has experienced a major backlash against poorly executed, post-Soviet privatization, with its political leaders driving a "grab-back" under dubious legal circumstances, linked to a subsequent opaqueness in the effective control of state assets.

The energy sector, more generally, is swinging heavily towards public ownership internationally, with the historically dominant North Atlantic global energy players rapidly dropping down the rankings by revenue and the all-important measure of exploitation rights. Sovereign wealth funds, especially those of China and the Middle East, are another major driver of the reemergence of state ownership of economic assets. And of course there is the small matter of the renationalization by Northern governments of failing financial institutions, notably in the United States and the United Kingdom. While positioned as temporary ownership and probably accurately described as such, there is no doubt that the ideology of private ownership for the public good has been severely damaged, opening the door to new civic and political discourses and actions about market transformation.

State ownership in these diverse forms might be good or bad news for social progress and sustainable development. In principle the state represents the public interest and can and should behave with this principle in mind. Negatively, state-capture by the business community, or cruder forms of political and bureaucratic rent-seeking using state-owned assets, might compromise or completely undermine the progressive role of the state as an economic actor. With both options in play, the ways in which civil society can transform markets will need to be reinvented or at least continuously evolved. Some forms of civil regulation might still be possible so long as state-owned companies are pushed to observe basic financial requirements. But state protection might dilute the impact of these strategies, as was observed, for example, in the Brazilian state-owned company Petrobras's refusal to respond to civil society demands for health-related improvements to their retail energy products.[20] Conversely, more classical forms of civic and political action might prove more productive in shifting the behavior of state-owned enterprises and the markets they dominate, most obviously when such behavior can be turned into a major political—and eventually electoral—issue.

what's that?

5. CONCLUSION

In its traditional form, civil regulation achieves incremental changes in business practices, but as it evolves in the changing context described above, it may be able to drive a wider redesign of economic institutions and how they are governed. Looked at through the first lens, civil regulation describes a way for business to achieve a comfortable accommodation to a negotiated set of norms. But through the second, more speculative, lens, one can see the possibility of a relatively unplanned and uncoordinated dismantling of distinct spheres of market and nonmarket action, and indeed of the distinction between the public and private spheres themselves.

In terms of the three levels of action described at the outset of this chapter, civil society has unquestionably had an impact at the *tactical* level on business behavior and thereby on people and the environment. Thousands of companies have developed or adopted collaboratively developed codes of conduct, and these codes have impacted millions of their suppliers and tens, if not hundreds, of millions of people working in global supply chains, along with their families and communities. Furthermore, some of these voluntary initiatives have been embraced in statutes covering corporate governance and reporting, stock exchange listing requirements, and public procurement conditions.[21] In the area of climate and carbon, such initiatives have engaged from the outset with multilateral negotiations, and in the case of business and human rights, the United Nations is seeking to establish an international framework that would (to date, uniquely), span international law, national regulation, collaboratively developed standards, and individual company behavior.[22]

Strategic impacts are more difficult to assess since they must compare actual practice to alternative scenarios that did not come to pass. Large-scale opposition to the fundamentals of free-market capitalism, perhaps signaled in venues such as the World Trade Organization meetings in Seattle in 1999, have not prospered, at least in Europe and North America. Smaller, radical skirmishes such as attempts to establish a pluralistic model of corporate accountability in a renewed company law in the United Kingdom have floundered, and the larger trend towards economic renationalization has been reversed, or at least slowed down in some countries, by the global recession of the late 2000s. In Brazil, for example, President Lula has protected private ownership and promoted almost every aspect of liberalized markets, and in so doing has weakened labor unions and other countervailing civil society groups. Brazil's home-grown, and now internationalized World Social Forum has sought to represent the real economic alternative to neoliberalism, but in practice it has largely shown itself, at least to date, as having a fragile intellectual, political, and economic grounding and potential.

Ironically, the *systemic* future of market transformation may be driven by forces largely antagonistic to civil society itself. Despite the Brazilian experience highlighted above, the new generation of political leaders that is emerging from the South has strong views about the limited role of civil society and the heightened role of the state in the context of markets designed to support national agendas and political interests. The Copenhagen climate talks probably marked the last time that such leaders allow themselves to be implicated in so unruly and unproductive an enterprise that sought to integrate civil society into an intergovernmental process. This experience will challenge the security of future open-source engagements by civil society in addressing major societal issues, at least in their current forms. If there is a serious systemic alternative to Anglo Saxon style economics, it is more likely to involve greater state control over, and engagement in, capital markets, and higher levels of state ownership and other less direct forms of control over economic assets.

Yet these directions, in some ways exactly what civil society has been calling for, are likely to come with a high price tag in terms of the erosion of human rights by more authoritarian states. They do not necessarily signify that markets will internalize social and environmental costs and benefits, and they are unlikely to empower civil society itself. Such a bittersweet scenario is not, of course, the only available future. Strategic gains could be forthcoming if the more engaged, collaborative pathways that have secured tactical successes could be eased into use in emerging nations, and these gains might eventually be converted into systemic change. After all, such approaches can be more effective modes of control than top-down models because of their flexibility, dynamism, and distributed responsibilities and investments, and this may make them attractive even to authoritarian and semiauthoritarian governments These features lie at the core of criticisms about their value as vehicles for radical change, and potentially constitute a source of strength in edging new political and economic elites to engage in the pursuit of improved livelihood strategies and the promotion of human rights. The dilemma of this pathway is most obvious for the human rights community, but can also be seen in other spheres (Sen 2000).

There are, then, a host of tactical, strategic, and systemic impacts and implications that emerge from the experience of civil society in seeking to shape business behavior and markets more broadly. Simply put, civil society engagement has delivered real and positive results, but it has not yet achieved the scale or depth of change required to lever a systemic impact, and even these potential systemic impacts may have effects that are unintended and possibly undesirable from a civil society point of view. Moreover, more of the same is unlikely to deliver better results, largely because conditions in the global economic context are changing so much. Therefore, civil society tactics and strategies must also evolve, rooted in a considered view of how civil society groups will function in a world with new and/or more extreme sustainability challenges, a clear need for business to be part of the solution and not merely not part of the problem, and a dramatic change in the cast of powerful political and economic interests that are seeking to shape tomorrow's agenda and how it might be advanced.

NOTES

1. "Ironic" in the sense that conventional economics holds that it is in these markets that the consumer surplus is most effectively captured by rent-seeking business, yet they have proved the most vulnerable to civil regulation, and have been the location of most modern innovations in the role of civil society in shaping changes in business behavior.

2. See the *Financial Times*, February 16, 2010. Available at http://blogs.ft.com/energy-source/2010/02/16/conocos-leave-from-uscap-underlines-congress-failure-to-act/.

3. See http://wwf.panda.org/what_we_do/how_we_work/businesses/corporate_support/business_partners.

4. See http://www.isealalliance.org/.

5. See http://www.voluntaryprinciples.org/.

6. See http://www.gavialliance.org/.

7. See www.iseal.org.

8. See Litovsky et al. (2008).

9. See http://www.dalailama.com/news/post/287-sarkozy-defies-china-with-dalai-lama-talks.

10. See the early path-breaking cases in Zadek et al. (1997).

11. See the reviews in Rochlin, Zadek, and Forstater (2008) and Zadek (2008).

12. See Radovich (2006).

13. See http://www.unglobalcompact.org/aboutthegc/thetenprinciples/anti-corruption.html.

14. See http://www.financialpost.com/news-sectors/energy/story.html?id=1856051.

15. See the Securities and Exchange Commission 17 CFR parts 211, 231, and 241 [Release Nos. 33-9106; 34-61469; FR-82] Commission Guidance Regarding Disclosure Related to Climate Change (www.sec.gov/rules/interp/2010/33-9106.pdf).

16. See http://www.global100.org/.

17. See http://www.responsiblesoy.org/.

18. From a personal discussion with the author.

19. See http://www.nationalgeographic.com/greendex/.

20. See http://www.ethos.org.br/DesktopDefault.aspx?TabID=3715&Lang=pt-BR&Alias=Ethos&itemEvenID=5069.

21. See http://www.isealalliance.org/.

22. See http://www.business-humanrights.org/SpecialRepPortal/Home.

REFERENCES

Barrientos, S., and S. Smith. 2006. *The ETI Code of Labour Practice: Do Workers Really Benefit?* Brighton: Institute of Development Studies.

Brautigam, D. 2010. *The Dragon's Gift: the Real Story of China in Africa.* Oxford: Oxford University Press.

Chambers, R. 1993. *Challenging the Professions.* London: Practical Action Publishers.

Edwards, M. 2010. *Small Change: Why Business Won't Save the World.* San Francisco: Berrett-Koehler.

Elkington, J., and P. Hartigan. 2009. *The Power of Unreasonable People: How Social Entrepreneurs Create Markets That Change the World.* Cambridge. Mass.: Harvard Business School Press.

Gore, A. 2008. *The Assault on Reason.* New York: Penguin.

Gray, J. 2000. *False Dawn: the Delusions of Global Capitalism.* London: The New Press.

Guoqiang, L., S. Zadek, and J. Wickerham. 2009. *Advancing Sustainable Competitiveness of China's Transnational Corporations.* Beijing: Development Research Centre of the State Council.

Klein, N. 2002. *No Logo: No Space, No Choice, No Jobs*. London: Picador.

Korten, D. 1995. *When Corporations Rule the World*. London: Earthscan.

Litovsky, A., S. Rochlin, S. Zadek, and B. Levy. 2008. *Investing in Standards for Sustainable Development*. Washington, D.C.: The World Bank.

Radovich, S. 2006. *The Global Alliance for Workers and Communities: Lessons Learnt From A Multi-Stakeholder Initiative*. London: AccountAbility.

Rochlin, S., S. Zadek, and M. Forstater. 2008. *Governing Collaboration: Making Partnership Accountable for Delivering Development*. London: AccountAbility.

Said, E. 1996. *Representations of the Intellectual*. London: Vintage.

Schmidheiny, S. 1992. *Changing Course: A Global Business Perspective on Development and the Environment*. Cambridge, Mass.: MIT Press.

Sen, A. 2000. *Development as Freedom*. London: Anchor.

Slaughter, A. M. 2005. *The New World Order*. Princeton, N.J.: Princeton University Press.

Vogel, D. 2006. *The Private Regulation of Global Corporate Conduct: Achievements and Limitations*. Thousand Oaks, Calif.: Sage Publications On-Line.

Zadek, S. 2004. "Paths to Corporate Responsibility." *Harvard Business Review* 82 (December): 125–32.

———. 2006a. *The Logic of Collaborative Governance: Corporate Responsibility, Accountability, and the Social Contract*. Working Paper 17. Corporate Social Responsibility Initiative, Kennedy School of Government, Harvard University.

———. 2006b. "Separating Smart from Great: Embedding Accountability into Business Practices Isn't Easy." *Fortune International* 30 (October): 74–77.

———. 2007. *The Civil Corporation*. 2nd ed. London: Earthscan.

———. 2008. "Collaborative Governance: the New Multilateralism for the 21st Century," in L. Brainard and D. Chollet (eds.) *Global Development 2.0*. Washington, D.C.: Brookings Institution.

Zadek, S., P. Pruzan, and R. Evans (eds.). 1997. *Building Corporate Accountability: Emerging Practices in Social and Ethical Accounting and Auditing*. London: Earthscan.

PART VII

SUPPORTING CIVIL SOCIETY

CHAPTER 35

CIVIL SOCIETY AND INSTITUTIONAL PHILANTHROPY

WILLIAM A. SCHAMBRA

KRISTA L. SHAFFER

INSTITUTIONAL philanthropy—by which we mean the universe of substantial, professionally staffed private foundations—is an outgrowth of civil society, yet it behaves as if it were somehow ashamed of its civil society origins. Indeed, if America's largest foundations were to have their way, they would dramatically alter the essential attributes of America's civic life. Given that American philanthropy is influential as a model in other countries too, these developments may also affect the health of civil society elsewhere. How did we arrive at this state of affairs and what can be done to change it? These are the questions we explore in this chapter.

1. ALEXIS DE TOCQUEVILLE, DECENTRALIZED ADMINISTRATION, AND LOCAL VOLUNTARY ASSOCIATIONS

Any discussion of American civil society must begin with Alexis de Tocqueville's *Democracy in America*, published in two volumes in 1835 and 1840. As many historians have noted, Tocqueville's description of the reality of American civic life at the beginning of the nineteenth century is not altogether historically accurate. To take Tocqueville seriously today, many scholars maintain, is a mistake—an exercise in nostalgia for a cozy, tightly knit community life that in fact only existed in Tocqueville's imagination, and that at any rate certainly does not exist today. But this is fundamentally to misunderstand the point of his account. It was never intended to be a Baedeker's guide to America, but rather a work of political philosophy. He meant to describe a radical and, to many, disturbing new political and social phenomenon, the spread of democracy around the world. America happened to be the nation where democracy had achieved its most advanced development. More to the point, and in spite of dire prognostications, America had managed to establish a temperate, self-controlled, orderly, liberal democracy. Tocqueville wished to distill from this experience the principles and practices that had brought out the best in democracy and suppressed the worst, so that other nations might similarly benefit. His account of American life, with what may seem to be its many omissions and exaggerations, is drawn with that pedagogical purpose in mind.

For Tocqueville, as for the American founding fathers, modern liberal democracy introduced the element of individualism into every aspect of national life. While this had produced a hitherto unimaginable degree of human freedom and prosperity, it also posed certain dangers. Individualism could turn humans into narrow-minded, petty, materialistic atoms of self-interest. It "disposed each citizen to isolate himself from the mass of his fellow." In individualistic democracies, "each man is thrown back on himself alone, and there is the danger that he may be shut up in the solitude of his own heart" ([1835] 2000, 482–4). If this was the prime danger posed by modern democracy, though, Americans had happily discovered a way to counteract it, according to Tocqueville. In this land, he found, individualism was moderated or attenuated by a series of devices, foremost among them administrative decentralization and voluntary association, that had in common a single principle: they compelled the individual to assume responsibility for a small portion of the public business—business that affects her immediate self-interest and is therefore important to her, but that nonetheless forces her to interact with others and thus gradually to see beyond her immediate self-interest to a larger common good.

Administrative decentralization is one of the most important tools for forging a responsible citizenry. Always a powerful tradition in America, local government had its roots in the New England town meeting. Even after the Union had been formed, though, Tocqueville notes, "the lawgivers of America did not suppose that a general representation of the whole nation would suffice" to ward off the dangerous tendencies of individualism; "they thought it also right to give each part of the land its own political life so that there would be an infinite number of occasions for the citizens to act together and so that every day they should feel that they depended on one another" ([1835] 2000, 486–7). Citizenly obligation can grow, however, only when it is immediately, tangibly clear to the individual that public matters affect his or her personal well-being: "It is difficult to force a man out of himself and get him to take an interest in the affairs of the whole state." In the regime of self-interest, public involvement and therefore social obligations are achieved only when the citizen experiences, in a concrete way, the connection between private interest and public affairs. Once the individual enters the public realm to deal with the question of the "road past his property," he is forced to act together with others, and "as soon as common affairs are treated in common, each man notices that he is not as independent of his fellows as he used to suppose and that to get their help he must often offer his aid to them" ([1835] 2000, 486). By dint of working for the good of his fellow citizens, he in the end acquires a habit and taste for serving them" ([1835] 2000, 488).

The voluntary associations of civil society operate in much the same way as administrative decentralization to produce a sense of citizenly obligation in the democratic individual. As the familiar Tocqueville quote puts it, "Americans of all ages, all stations of life, and all types of dispositions are forever forming associations" ([1835] 2000, 489). Typically, associations are formed to meet immediate, concrete problems that have a tangible bearing on individual self-interest: "If some obstacle blocks the public road halting the circulation of traffic, the neighbors at once form a deliberative body; this improvised assembly produces an executive authority which remedies the trouble" ([1835] 2000, 180–1). As citizens associate, "pursuing in common the objects of common desire," they have become accustomed to considering the interests of others, as well as their own self-interest; "feelings and ideas are renewed, the heart enlarged, and the understanding developed... by the reciprocal action of men upon one another" in associations ([1835] 2000, 491).

Decentralization and voluntary association characterized American political and social life for much of the first century of independence. The boundaries between public and private were by no means as clearly drawn as they were later, with much of the public's work—healing the sick, educating the young, caring for the poor—being done voluntarily or contractually by private groups. Because everyday political life was very much left to everyday citizens, the results were often inelegant, amateurish, duplicative, wasteful, and rooted in what may have seemed the incredibly diverse, peculiar, and irrational moral and spiritual beliefs of America's local communities. But this vast range of activity drew in and engaged productively and peacefully the full range of Americans—from the wealthy few, who formed philanthropies and private organizations to guard their interests once they had been excluded from public office by various populist movements, to women, poor farmers and laborers, despised religious sects, free blacks, and immigrants, who formed their own charities, burial societies, insurance companies, and cooperatives to look after their own interests (Hall 1982; Hall 1992, 140–206; McCarthy 2003).

2. THE RISE OF SCIENTIFIC PHILANTHROPY

While this immense outpouring of democratic energies in civil society would have been gratifying to Tocqueville, it was entirely inadequate to meet the needs of the nation as it approached the twentieth century, according to the American progressive movement. In its view, powerful new economic and technological developments—the development of factory production, mass markets, railroads, telegraph, and telephone—had shattered the old boundaries of what historian Robert Wiebe aptly called our "island communities," and rendered obsolete Tocqueville's decentralized, voluntary approach to public problems (1966, xiii, 4).

The everyday common sense of the citizen that had sufficed to understand public affairs on the local, community scale could not grasp the new technological interrelatedness that characterized public life. Citizens could only see the superficial, immediate manifestations of social problems—their symptoms—and could not understand their underlying root causes. That understanding depended on the new natural sciences that were revolutionizing medicine, public health, and agriculture, plus the new sciences of society that were explicitly based on their example. The professional social scientist—the economist, sociologist, psychologist, and political scientist—now had a critical role to play because, as Thomas Haskell points out, "it was largely through his explanatory prowess that men might learn to understand their complex situation, and largely through his predictive ability that men might cooperatively control society's future" (1977, 14). In Herbert Croly's formulation, "in the more complex, the more fluid, and the more highly energized, equipped, and differentiated society of today," the "cohesive element" would be "the completest social record," which could be only assembled by social science experts "using social knowledge in the interest of valid social purposes" (1915, 370).

Tocqueville's notion that *local*, voluntary action was essential to overcoming democratic individualism came to be seen as equally antiquated. Professionals believed that ordinary citizens were capable of only base self-interest, whereas those trained in the abstract, objective techniques of science, by virtue of their professional training and commitment to service, were alone able to transcend petty considerations and grasp the larger public interest, and lead the less enlightened closer to it. These new leaders would summon citizens out of the constraints of local communities and into a much grander and more compelling form of unity or oneness, now at the level of the nation as a whole. The great, national community would evoke a self-denying devotion to the "national idea" from the American people, a far-flung community of millions in which citizens nonetheless would be linked tightly by bonds of compassion, fellow-feeling, and neighborliness. In Croly's words, there would be a "subordination of the individual to the demand of a dominant and constructive national purpose." A citizen would begin to "think first of the State and next of himself," and "individuals of all kinds will find their most edifying individual opportunities in serving their country." Indeed, America would come to be bound together by a "religion of human brotherhood," which "can be realized only through the loving-kindness which individuals feel ... particularly toward their fellow-countrymen" (1909, 23, 406, 418, 453). As if taking aim squarely at Tocqueville's understanding of civil society, the sociologist Edward Alsworth Ross summed it up this way: America needed to transcend its fragmentation into "thousands of local groups sewed up in separatist dogmas and dead to most of the feelings which thrill the rest of society." This would be accomplished by the "widest possible diffusion of secular knowledge" among the many, which "narrows the power of the fanatic or the false prophet to gain a following." Meanwhile, university training for the elite would "[rear] up a type of leader who will draw men together with unifying thoughts, instead of dividing them, as does the sect-founder" (1921, 422).

The first large American foundations—Carnegie, Rockefeller, and Russell Sage—understood themselves to be instruments of this American progressive project. They were established, as had been the business corporations that produced their corpus, by "modern businessmen committed to notions of rationality, organization, and efficiency," who had become accustomed to subsuming smaller, less efficient units into nation-spanning enterprises with grand ambitions. So their new foundations were national in scope, established in perpetuity, and dedicated to the general welfare of mankind. The founders "were also imbued with the ethic of modern science." A "more scientific and businesslike approach" to problems, they believed, "was to attack the root causes of social dysfunction directly," which could be determined by "the scientific investigation of social and physical well-being" (Karl and Katz 1981, 236–270). Indeed, the essential self-understanding of the new foundations was that they would be, in John D. Rockefeller's description, "constantly in search for finalities—a search for cause, an attempt to cure the evils at their source" (Rockefeller 1913, 177). By contrast, Tocqueville's local communities could only understand and modestly ameliorate the symptoms of underlying problems.

The new foundations aimed their resources overwhelmingly at the generation and teaching of the new sciences of physical and social root causes, especially in modern research universities and institutes of public policy research. At the same time, they funded the rationalization, standardization, and modernization of the elite professions based on the new sciences, and the establishment of institutions that would insure their influence on public policy. Russell Sage, for example, was instrumental in converting social work from a local, community-based charitable activity into a genuine profession, reflecting foundation official Robert de Forest's conviction that, while social work must care for needy families, "the most effective work is to strike at those conditions which made these families needy, and so far as possible, to remove them" (Hammack and Wheeler 1994, 11). Mary Van Kleeck, director of the foundation's Department of Industrial Studies, believed that "the world *can* be controlled, if we release intellect" (Sealander 1997, 39).

Much of the Carnegie Corporation's work was similarly designed to establish uniform national standards in education, to insure that only the best were drawn into the new trans-local elites. Although the explicit function of the Carnegie Foundation for the Advancement of Teaching was to fund a pension fund for private college teachers, in fact, as first president Henry S. Pritchett noted, its scope "as a centralizing and standardizing influence in American education promises to outweigh in importance the primary purpose of the fund" (Lagemann 1983). Carnegie was behind the early efforts to standardize and rationalize the measurement of academic progress in high school, and to develop rigorous tests for admission to college and graduate school. Through a series of surveys of various professions, the most famous of which is the Flexner Report on medical education, the Carnegie

philanthropies sought to centralize and standardize the bodies of thought and practice essential to modern organization.

The Rockefeller Foundation committed itself not only to medical and public
health measures like the Rockefeller Institute for Medical Research and the
Rockefeller Sanitary Commission for the Eradication of Hookworm Disease (Ettling
1981), but also to a wide range of activities to develop and promote the social sciences in research universities and think tanks. Rockefeller's newly funded University
of Chicago boasted a strong emphasis on the social sciences, linked directly to practical application in public policy by a Rockefeller-funded building near the campus
that, at one time, housed twenty-two of the leading agencies of public policy and
public administration. Rockefeller was also the primary funder of the agencies that
would coordinate and centralize research in public policy like the Social Science
Research Council and the National Bureau of Economic Research. As a Rockefeller
mission statement put in the 1920s, its funding was designed to "increase the body
of knowledge which in the hands of competent social technicians may be expected
in time to result in substantial social control" (Fisher 1983, 208).

The work of the large foundations was designed not only to withdraw authority from citizens who had only imperfect and constrained understandings of social
causality and put it in the hands of experts who could penetrate to root causes in
their analysis. It was also designed to erect professional licensing and accreditation
barriers so that the new elites could be cleansed of any taint of the old irrational,
parochial views nourished within small, isolated communities. The reform of
medical education through the Flexner Report, for example, meant the closing of
scores of medical schools that, although deficient by scientific standards, drew the
poor and marginalized into medical practice. The number of medical schools serving African Americans, for instance, fell from eight to two after the report. But
Flexner "had little patience for the arguments of those who warned that closing
marginal schools would close medicine to poor boys and members of minorities,
and opposed offering fellowships on the basis of financial need" (Sealander 232).
Carnegie's work in professionalizing the legal profession was in part a response to
complaints like that voiced by Harlan Fiske Stone, dean of Columbia Law School,
that "the deterioration of the bar" has been a result of the "lowering of the average
by the influx to the bar of greater numbers of the unfit," especially the foreign born
(Lagemann 77).

Lagemann's comment about Carnegie's critics could apply to all the major
national foundations: "critics saw a peril" because they believed the foundations
were "supporting nationalism at the expense of localism ('provincialism'), universalism in standards at the expense of pluralism, expert participation in standard
making at the expense of lay participation, and private authority in policy making
at the expense of public authority" (1983, 180). The critics had a powerful argument.
In fact, the new foundations were dedicated to the proposition that significant
power should be wielded by professionally trained national elites rather than the
untrained, amateurish local communities so important to Tocqueville's account of
American democracy, or by those contaminated by their influences.

3. FOUNDATIONS AND GOVERNMENT: COLLABORATION AND OVERSIGHT

Throughout the twentieth century, the national elites who had been launched from the universities and think tanks funded by foundations increasingly wielded their power from the commanding heights of the federal government itself, as it expanded its reach over significant aspects of American life through Franklin Roosevelt's New Deal and Lyndon Johnson's Great Society. This meant that, by comparison, even the largest foundations played ever smaller roles in public policy, but since this trend towards centralized national administration had been propelled by its own expert professionals, philanthropy was content simply to seek a role for itself in the interstices of federal activity. It became the goal of the most sophisticated foundations to fund demonstration projects and trial interventions that, if proven successful, could then be passed on for "scaling up" through more substantial federal funding.

The most successful example of such demonstration and scaling up came with the Ford Foundation's Grey Areas project in the early 1960s, which became the basis of Johnson's community action notion in his War on Poverty. Interestingly, this was also the most significant instance of a major foundations flirting with the notion that citizens might be able to make a valuable contribution to solving public problems after all. Embedded in these approaches was the idea that the poor should have some say in the manner of delivery of services to their neighborhoods. But the orientation was still emphatically towards delivery of services by professionals, the coordination and effectiveness of which might be enhanced by community input. According to Francis Fox Piven, the aim was a "reorganization of services to procure rational, planned collaboration" (1967, 95). The far more radical notion that citizens in low-income areas might be consulted about what they considered problems, and that outside agencies should shape their assistance around solutions defined and organized by the community, was never considered. Writing about Philadelphia's experiment in community action drawn up by academics at Temple University, Charles Silberman pointed out that "the notion that citizens conceivably might want to speak for themselves obviously never occurred to the academicians, government officials, and 'civic leaders' who drew up the documents" (1964, 353).

Given that the Ford Foundation's venture into community action never departed very far from the model of professional service delivery, it is ironic that it managed to discredit the notion of active civic engagement in public policy for some time to come, only reaffirming the need for distance between the planning experts and planned-for citizens (Moynihan 1969). It also drew unwanted attention from Congress, which led to a tightening up of standards and procedures in philanthropy.[1] The result of both this flirtation with community empowerment and pressure from Congress was that foundations focused more and more on increasing the professionalism of their own internal management and grant-making processes, with less and less patience for the amateurish and slipshod projects brought to them by neighborhood nonprofits.[2]

4. The New Wave of Philanthropy and Its Impact

In spite of this history, wave upon wave of new philanthropists have arrived on the scene and, after cursory examination, announced, as if for the very first time, that philanthropy lacks rigor and expertise, and desperately needs a major infusion of rationalization, professionalization, and outcomes orientation (Edwards 2010). Many recent donors have entrepreneurial backgrounds in new technologies, and are confident that their business experience has given them peculiar and unprecedented insight about the need to solve problems, rather than simply treat their symptoms. They are either oblivious to, or unimpressed by, a full century of boastful discourse in philanthropy that surrounds its embrace of scientific solutions over the halting, disjointed, and superficial fumblings of charity.

In a typical pronouncement, Charles Bronfman and Jeffrey Solomon (2010, 23) write that until now, philanthropy was about "power, expectation, influence and yes, ego. It was rarely about impact." But now, apparently for the first time, "donors have sought to make a difference.... they are ready to make use of the sophisticated management instruments they have developed in their business life to achieve greater performance in this new, more challenging arena.... they give purposefully, think strategically, and rely on measurements and regular monitoring." Paul Brest, president of the Hewlett Foundation, and Hal Harvey similarly argue that rigorous thinking and strategizing is what has been missing from philanthropy. Their 2008 volume, *Money Well Spent*, argues that the central task of a truly strategic philanthropy is "designing and then implementing a plan commensurate with the resources committed to it." Then, in language that could have come straight out of a Rockefeller Foundation annual report in the 1920s, they add that "this, in turn, requires an empirical, evidence-based understanding of the external world in which the plan will operate." At the heart of effective philanthropy, they suggest, is constructing a "theory of change...an analysis of the causal chain that links your philanthropic interventions to the goals you want to achieve." Greater attention to scientific and logical rigor by foundation strategists will finally convert mere charity to truly effective philanthropy (2008, 7, 47–48).

As institutional philanthropy turns ever more to the need to shake up its own internal strategizing, planning, and measuring, the inevitable result is even further denigration of whatever thoughts and plans might occur to citizens who are organized in grassroots nonprofits. Indeed, many foundations proceed as if little or nothing of worth had been accomplished prior to the introduction of the newest techniques of planning and management. As David Hunter notes in *The End of Charity*, "there is virtually no credible evidence that most nonprofit organizations actually produce any social value." Furthermore, we "cannot rely on direct service nonprofits to fix themselves without a serious push." Only the nonprofit sector's funders can "take the lead in building a strong, effective and efficient nonprofit sector" (2009, 72). Many donors are clearly eager to become more directive about how nonprofits should behave. "Nonprofits should be run just a crisply as for-profits," insist Bronfman and Solomon. "Meetings should start on time and end on time too. They should not be social gatherings that drag on endlessly for no purpose. A nonprofit isn't a church either. It should not fall for a charismatic leader who gives the operation a charged-up, religious feeling—and loses sight of what it is actually created to do" (2010, 18).

Whether from philanthropy's initial enthrallment with social science or its more recent infatuation with business management, the long-term trend in the field has been to create ever more distance between the everyday citizen in his or her local nonprofit and the centralized, technocratic professional management of the modern foundation. Although organized within, and directing its funding towards, the institutions of civil society, philanthropy has become complicit in the disparagement of what Tocqueville regarded as civil society's primary task: the inculcation of democratic engagement in problem-solving and the development of community-mindedness. Nonprofits' meetings often are "social gatherings that drag on endlessly" (Bronfman and Solomon 2010, 18) for precisely that critical democratic purpose. As John McKnight notes about the larger problem of professionalization in modern society, "When the capacity to define the problem becomes a professional prerogative, citizens no longer exist. The prerogative removes the citizen as problem-definer, much less problem-solver. It translates political functions into technical and technological problems" (1995, 48).

5. Conclusion: What Should Foundations Do?

Were institutional philanthropy interested in a unique and immensely powerful role in American public life, it would stop denigrating civil society associations and attend to the alarming deficits in democratic engagement that it had a hand in producing (Gibson 2006). It would turn its attention to nourishing and supporting the Tocquevillian institutions of self-government. Building squarely on Tocqueville's insights, foundations might redirect funding to programs that originate with the views of citizens at the grassroots, with their understanding of the problems they face, and how they wish to go about addressing them.[3] Solutions tailored by citizens who actually live with problems are more likely to be effective for their own neighborhoods. Community ownership insures that these approaches will be supported and sustained over the long haul, rather than provoking the sort of resistance that often greets programs designed by remote experts and parachuted into neighborhoods, as had happened with the Great Society's community action program. Perhaps most important, the process of formulating and proposing solutions to their own problems cultivates in citizens the skills essential to democratic self-governance—the ability at first to endure, but finally perhaps to relish, the messy, gritty process of deliberating, arguing, and compromising demanded by American democracy's conviction that all citizens are to be treated with dignity and respect.

Tocquevillian or civic renewal philanthropy would reach out quietly but actively into the communities it wishes to assist, harvesting "street wisdom" about which groups genuinely capture a community's self-understanding of its problems (Somerville 2008). Such groups will more than likely have duct tape on their industrial carpeting and water stains on their ceilings. They will not be able to draft clever, eye-catching fundraising brochures or grant proposals. They will not have sophisticated accounting systems, or be able to lay out a schedule of measurable outcomes. They will not speak the language of the social sciences, but more often than not, the language of sin and spiritual redemption. They will not be staffed by well-paid credentialed experts, but rather by volunteers whose chief credential is that they themselves have managed to overcome the problem they are now helping others to confront. No matter what is stated in the group's formal charter, it will minister to whatever needs present themselves at the door, even if it means being accused of inefficiency or mission drift. In this spirit, each person is treated not as an inadequately self-aware bundle of pathologies, but rather as a unique individual, a citizen possessed of a soul demanding a respectful, humane response to the entire person.

This approach turns completely on its head the still-entrenched orthodoxy of institutional philanthropy. Indeed, it looks suspiciously like charity—the antiquated, discredited approach which nonetheless honored and ministered personally to the each individual. Charity does indeed deal with "mere symptoms" because they are what people themselves consider important, rather than with root causes visible only to experts who can "see through" the client. Because civic renewal philanthropy tackles social problems individual by individual, neighborhood by neighborhood, and because it relies on individuals and neighborhoods to define and solve their own problems, this approach calls for a degree of humility and surrender of control that will not appeal to professional experts.

Isn't this too humble a task for philanthropy? Isn't it an abject retreat from the promise of social science to get at the root causes of social problems once and for all? Do we have to revert to mere charity? Consider, though, that after almost a century of spending billions of dollars in root-cause philanthropy, it is difficult to name a single social problem whose roots philanthropy has reached. Meanwhile, everyday citizens have continued to form countless community associations to tackle their own problems in their own ways, usually in the form of neighbors caring for and nurturing each other directly and personally (McKnight 1995). One could look at this and see mere charity, or one could see vigorous civic engagement in self-governance. Tocqueville clearly saw the latter. On this modest, practical, local civic activity, he placed his highest hopes for the survival of the American experiment in democracy. Foundations supporting such activity need hardly be ashamed of helping to rebuild popular self-governance at the grassroots.

NOTES

1. The specific activities of the Ford Foundation that aroused Congressional ire are discussed briefly in Fleishman (2009, 325–26) and Reeves (1970, 20–22), and more thoroughly in Smith and Chiechi (1974, 43).

2. For more on the professionalization of foundations after the Tax Reform Act of 1969, see Frumkin (2006, 100–24), as well as the brief overviews in Hammack (2006, 80–82) and Abramson and McCarthy (2002, 343–44).

3. Examples of effective grassroots groups and the people who help fund them can be found in Woodson (1998) and Elliott (2004). For further, more policy-oriented background on supporting Tocquevillian institutions of self-government, as well as some examples, see Goldsmith (2002).

REFERENCES

Abramson, A., and R. McCarthy. 2002. "Infrastructure Organizations," in L. Salamon (ed.) *The State of Nonprofit America.* Washington, D.C.: Brookings Institution Press.

Brest, P., and H. Harvey. 2008. *Money Well Spent: A Strategic Plan for Smart Philanthropy.* New York: Bloomberg Press.

Bronfman, C., and J. Solomon. 2010. *The Art of Giving: Where the Soul Meets a Business Plan.* San Francisco: Jossey-Bass.

Croly, H. D. 1909. *The Promise of American Life.* New York: MacMillan.

———. 1915. *Progressive Democracy.* New York: MacMillan.

Edwards, M. 2010. *Small Change: Why Business Won't Save the World.* San Francisco: Berrett-Koehler.

Elliott, B. J. 2004. *Street Saints: Renewing America's Cities.* Philadelphia: Templeton Foundation Press.

Ettling, J. 1981. *The Germ of Laziness: Rockefeller Philanthropy and Public Health in the New South.* Cambridge, Mass.: Harvard University Press.

Fisher, D. 1983. "The Role of Philanthropic Foundations in the Reproduction and Production of Hegemony: Rockefeller Foundations and the Social Sciences." *Sociology* vol. 17 no. 2: 206–33.

Fleishman, J. L. 2009. *The Foundation: A Great American Secret: How Private Wealth is Changing the World.* New York: Public Affairs.

Frumkin, P. 2006. *Strategic Giving: The Art and Science of Philanthropy.* Chicago: University of Chicago Press.

Gibson, C. 2006. "Citizens at the Center: A New Approach to Civic Engagement." Washington, D.C.: The Case Foundation. Available at http://www.casefoundation.org/sites/default/files/citizens-at-the-center.pdf (accessed February 18, 2010).

Goldsmith, S. 2002. *Putting Faith in Neighborhoods: Making Cities Work through Grassroots Citizenship.* Washington, D.C.: Hudson Institute.

Hall, P. D. 1982. *The Organization of American Culture, 1700–1900: Private Institutions, Elites, and the Origins of American Nationality.* New York: New York University Press.

———. 1992. *Inventing the Nonprofit Sector and Other Essays on Philanthropy, Voluntarism, and Nonprofit Organizations.* Baltimore: Johns Hopkins University Press.

——. 2006. "American Debates on the Legitimacy of Foundations," in K. Prewitt, M. Dogan, S. Heydemann, and S. Toepler (eds.) *The Legitimacy of Philanthropic Foundations: United States and European Perspectives*. New York: Russell Sage Foundation.

Hammack, D. C., and S. Wheeler. 1994. *Social Science in the Making: Essays on the Russell Sage Foundation, 1907–1972*. New York: Russell Sage Foundation.

Haskell, T. L. 1977. *The Emergence of Professional Social Science: The American Society Science Association and the Nineteenth-Century Crisis of Authority*. Urbana: University of Illinois Press.

Hunter, D. 2009. "The End of Charity: How to Fix the Nonprofit Sector Through Effective Social Investing." *Philadelphia Social Innovations Journal* vol. 1(1): 72–77.

Karl, B. D., and S. N. Katz. 1981. "The American Private Philanthropic Foundation and the Public Sphere 1890–1930." *Minerva*, vol. 19(2): 236–70.

Lagemann, E. C. 1983. *Private Power for the Public Good: A History of the Carnegie Foundation for the Advancement of Teaching*. Middletown, Conn.: Wesleyan University Press.

McCarthy, K. D. 2003. *American Creed: Philanthropy and the Rise of Civil Society* 1700–1865. Chicago: University of Chicago Press.

McKnight, J. 1995. *Careless Society: Community and Its Counterfeits*. New York: Basic Books.

Moynihan, D. P. 1969. *Maximum Feasible Misunderstanding: Community Action in the War on Poverty*. New York: The Free Press.

Piven, F. F. 1967. "The Demonstration Project: A Federal Strategy for Local Change," in G. A. Brager and F. P. Purcell (eds.) *Communication Action Against Poverty: Readings from the Mobilization Experience*. New Haven, Conn.: College & University Press.

Reeves, T. C. 1970. "Introduction," in T. C. Reeves (ed.) *Foundations Under Fire*. Ithaca, N.Y.: Cornell University Press.

Rockefeller, J. D. 1913. *Random Reminiscences of Men and Events*. Garden City, N.Y.: Doubleday.

Ross, E. A. 1921. *The Principles of Sociology*. New York: The Century Co.

Sealander, J. 1997. *Private Wealth & Public Life: Foundation Philanthropy and the Reshaping of American Social Policy from the Progressive Era to the New Deal*. Baltimore: Johns Hopkins University Press.

Silberman, C. E. 1964. *Crisis in Black and White*. New York: Random House.

Smith, W. H., and C. P. Chiechi, 1974. *Private Foundations: Before and After the Tax Reform Act of 1969*. Washington, D.C.: American Enterprise Institute.

Somerville, B., with F. Setterberg. 2008. *Grassroots Philanthropy: Field Notes of a Maverick Grantmaker*. Berkeley: Heyday Books.

de Toqueville, A. [1835, 1840] 2000. *Democracy in America*. Trans. H. C. Mansfield and D. Winthrop. Chicago: University of Chicago Press.

Wiebe, R. H. 1966. *The Search for Order* 1877–1920. New York: Hill and Wang.

Woodson, R. L., Sr. 1998. *The Triumphs of Joseph: How Today's Community Healers are Reviving Our Streets and Neighborhoods*. New York: The Free Press.

CHAPTER 36

....

CIVIL SOCIETY
AND GRASSROOTS
PHILANTHROPY

....

G. ALBERT RUESGA

THE term "grassroots" is a powerful metaphor for many funders and activists in the field of philanthropy, and is often counterposed with ideas of top-down or elite-driven funding. The grassroots suggest the ground beneath our feet, something that is both anchored and anchoring. They are close to the earth, elemental, and connote a direct relationship with the sources of being and truth. They are rugged and hardy, and able over time to cover the wounds inflicted on the planet. The grassroots are also, ironically, something frequently trampled over and taken for granted, the universe of average or ordinary citizens and, in the parlance of philanthropy, members of "communities in need." As such, the grassroots have been both the subject and the object of a significant amount of individual and institutional giving to strengthen civil society in all of its guises.

Not surprisingly then, the term grassroots draws us immediately into a contested space, occupied by publics who have a vague but serviceable idea of what the term might mean and by individuals whose livelihoods depend on its precise interpretation, for funding streams may wend their way to those whose work embraces one definition of the term but not another. Some argue, for example, that a nongovernmental organization (NGO) ceases to be grassroots when it is no longer led by those directly affected by the problems the organization seeks to address. Others claim that when an association of ordinary citizens becomes formally chartered or incorporated, it leaves the realm of the grassroots and enters a world of professionalized activity that is inevitably more aligned with the purposes of society's elites.

While most people are not so demanding about the meaning of the term, a certain laxness about its use has led to an inflation of its meaning over time. As one commentator expressed it, "the rhetoric of resident engagement and community is now so banal as to render much of it meaningless" (Traynor 2002, 6). This has been the fate of many terms in currency in the world of philanthropy, including "social justice" and "social entrepreneur," not to mention the technical lexicon of formal evaluation methods and metrics that is much in vogue.[1] Therefore, some precision is important.

Many controversies surround the theory and practice of grassroots philanthropy. While some doubt that grassroots philanthropy can ever lead to significant social change, others argue that it is the only kind of philanthropy that ever has. Other debates relate to the engagement of ordinary citizens in efforts for social change. To what degree should these efforts be controlled by those who themselves are affected by problems rather than by trained professionals? Since poor people have direct knowledge of what it is like to live in poverty, can and should they be the prime movers in shaping programs that aim to change their condition? This chapter reviews these questions, suggests some ways to work through the thorny issues they raise, and advocates a critical stance on the assumptions that often surround the notion of grassroots giving.

1. WHAT IS GRASSROOTS PHILANTHROPY AND WHY IS IT IMPORTANT?

What makes a special kind of philanthropy necessary or desirable? The motivations for practicing grassroots philanthropy are many. Some see support for the grassroots as a good thing in and of itself. Helping to build a sense of community, enhancing a community's ability to address local concerns, and promoting a high level of civic engagement by ordinary people—these are all valuable, their proponents argue, whether or not they lead to specific outcomes such as higher birth weights or longer life expectancies. In most cases, however, funders see grassroots philanthropy as an essential, or at least an important, element of some broader theory of change—as a means to achieve specific social, economic, and political ends established, ultimately, by the donor.

If one thinks of philanthropy as the giving of time and money to activities of public benefit, three major strands of grassroots philanthropy can be identified. First, there is top-down support for activities that benefit the grassroots in some way. In this category of grassroots philanthropy, those directly affected by a problem are not involved in making funding decisions that are aimed at its resolution. A funder might, for example, make a well-intentioned effort to end homelessness without consulting the homeless in any way. This is philanthropy *to* the grassroots. A second approach includes support for activities that benefit the grassroots but also involve members of affected populations in grant-making decisions and/or the design, implementation, and evaluation of grant-making programs—at least to some degree. Some funders see meaningful citizen participation as the key to effective grant making, while others retain a greater measure of control, arguing that a division of labor between trained professionals and community residents yields better outcomes. This is philanthropy *with* the grassroots.

Third, grassroots philanthropy can mean the giving of time, money, and other forms of support *by* ordinary citizens to one another and to the collective activities of their own communities, defined either by geography, identity, or interest. The support of these givers is important to the health of many NGOs and other civil society groups and has played a critical role in many social change efforts. This is philanthropy *by* and *from* the grassroots. In many instances, funders are happy to provide support *to* the grassroots but not so eager to share control over decisions *with* affected communities or to cede ground to efforts supported by philanthropy *from* the grassroots. This ambivalence towards authentic citizen participation is characteristic of foundations and has many sources that are explored in brief below. It constitutes a central tension in debates about civil society and philanthropy.

Grassroots philanthropy is sometimes conflated with support for community-based organizations—a kind of NGO characterized by its rootedness in, and service to, a particular neighborhood or geographically defined community. While it is true that many community-based organizations are likely to have an accurate view of the concerns and aspirations of local residents, they are not necessarily resident-led or resident-staffed, and their goals and methods might put them at odds with the people they aim to serve. Grassroots Grantmakers, a U.S.-based association of funders, defines grassroots philanthropy as "a place-based grant-making approach that focuses on strengthening and connecting resident-led organizations and their leaders in urban neighborhoods and rural communities. Typically, it is aimed at strengthening the capacity of people who come together to improve their communities through projects and activities that they initiate and manage."[2] Grant makers who use this approach employ a number of methods to address local priorities, including small grants programs for organizations that might not otherwise qualify for funding, the sponsoring of community gatherings, the use of leadership programs to help develop and strengthen local leaders, and the provision of technical assistance and training to community-based groups.

It is worth noting that grassroots philanthropy has sometimes been characterized not by the nature of the recipients or the kind of work supported, but by the *style* of giving. Bill Somerville (2008, 25), for example, urges philanthropists to leave their offices so they can identify "outstanding people doing important work" more effectively. In this view, grassroots philanthropists should minimize bureaucracy and get out into the field in order to interact more freely with those who are making change happen on the ground. Of course these change makers might or might not be ordinary citizens or members of communities in need, and they might not be part of the grassroots defined in other ways. What is more important is that philanthropists of all shades move closer to the places where community needs meet institutional responses.

Given these diverse characterizations, it is easy to see why grassroots philanthropy is of interest to theorists and practitioners who care about the health and vigor of civil society. In its different manifestations, it appears to offer a promising route to supporting the engagement of citizens in voluntary action and public processes, thereby helping them to construct their visions of the good society (Edwards 2009). Grassroots philanthropy has proven to be a flexible tool in supporting the associational life of communities, helping funders to advance the common good, and shaping the content and character of the public sphere. However, given the substantial differences that exist between philanthropy *to*, *with*, and *from* the grassroots, one might expect these approaches to exhibit a range of strengths and weaknesses in relation to their ability to enhance civil society and civic engagement, with the authenticity of citizen control and direction (or at least their involvement and participation) as one key variable.

2. Philanthropy *to* the Grassroots

In philanthropy *to* the grassroots, ordinary citizens function primarily as beneficiaries. They are the objects of a donor's largesse, and often the clients served by funded activities. In this form of philanthropy, the role of impacted communities is to cooperate and, ideally, to be grateful. This holding of ordinary citizens at arm's length does not necessarily imply a lack of respect for the dignity or well-being of communities in need. For institutional funders who practice philanthropy to the grassroots, there may be any number of barriers to meaningful citizen participation, including limited staff resources and a lack of expertise in working with grassroots communities. In some cases a donor might enhance the grassroots character of his or her interventions by supporting only those groups and projects that are designed, managed, and evaluated by impacted communities.

There are some who opt to provide philanthropy to the grassroots simply because they wish to cut out the intermediaries that can skew relationships between donors and the objects of their generosity. Such funders prefer that their money goes directly to those affected by a problem rather than helping to pay the salaries of NGO staff members and other professionals. The Child Support Grants program of the Frank Buttle Trust in the United Kingdom, for example, accepts applications from social workers, health visitors, and others who work directly with low-income families. Grants awarded by the trust are used exclusively to provide necessities such as clothes, beds, bedding, and other essential household items.[3] Elsewhere, the choice to cut out the middle man may have less altruistic motivations. The November 13, 2009 issue of the *New York Times*, for example, reported that the United States was using small grants given directly to villagers in Afghanistan as part of a counterinsurgency strategy "aimed at drawing people away from the Taliban and building popular support for the Western-backed government by showing that it can make a difference in people's lives" (Tavernise 2009). In these situations there is no effort to deny the purely instrumental character of giving. While this is giving to the grassroots, it is clearly not *for* the grassroots but rather for the purpose of making a tactical or strategic gain in a broader geopolitical game.

It is important to note that philanthropy to the grassroots is championed by both conservative and liberal funders. In the U.S. context, for example, one of the goals of progressive philanthropists is to amplify the voices of those who are marginalized in society and empower citizens to become more engaged in the political processes that affect their lives, thus enabling them to address deeper issues of social and political injustice. These funders understand that in order to achieve significant social change, political action from above must meet agitation from below. This kind of "pincer" effect was much in evidence during the American civil rights struggles of the 1950s and 1960s, when sweeping legislative changes were insufficient and large numbers of ordinary people took to the streets to ensure that the new laws would be enforced (Levy 1998). It is clear, however, that a commitment to the goal of empowerment does not necessarily translate into the sharing of philanthropic decision-making. The Greater New Orleans Foundation's Community IMPACT Program,[4] for example, aims to help the poorest of the poor in the metropolitan New Orleans region by awarding grants to organizations that empower ordinary citizens. The program was designed in consultation with representatives from the region's NGOs, but it does not currently involve community residents in program leadership or grant decisions.

In a similar fashion, though arguing from a different ideological base, some so-called small government conservatives in the United States see grassroots philanthropy as a means of strengthening communities—both ordinary citizens *and* elites—against the intrusions of powerful, centralized governments intent on over-regulating markets, sanctioning allegedly immoral behavior, and illegitimately redistributing wealth through taxation. The Lynde and Harry Bradley Foundation, for example, supports projects that "seek to reinvigorate and re-empower the traditional, local institutions—families, schools, churches, and neighborhoods—that provide training in, and room for, the exercise of citizenship, pass on everyday morality to the next generation, and cultivate personal character."[5] The foundation also funds projects that "encourage decentralization of power and accountability away from centralized, bureaucratic, national institutions back to the states, localities, and revitalized mediating structures where citizenship is more fully realized." When set against a large and allegedly intrusive central government, just about any community of interest can claim the mantle of grassroots. This has been the case, for example, with the conservative Tea Party movement in the United States. Although championed by members of the political elite such as Sarah Palin and former congressman Tom Tancredo, the Tea Party movement characterizes itself as a "national collaborative grassroots effort" committed to exposing the "bankrupt liberal agenda" of President Barack Obama's administration and the Democratically controlled 111th Congress.[6]

How effective is philanthropy to the grassroots? While one can construct many plausible theories of change that lead from the funding of grassroots efforts to transformed societies, there is little documented evidence that philanthropy *to* the grassroots—at least as practiced by institutional funders—has ever played a determining role in securing deep-rooted social change. This may be due to a simple lack of evidence, given that the real efficacy of grassroots philanthropy of any kind has been so poorly researched, including its supposed impact on the strengthening of civil society. Most information is sketchy and/or anecdotal, and until recently there was no central repository even for program evaluations conducted and published by foundations in the United States.[7] But much depends on how one defines the goals of these kinds of intervention: while they may not have achieved large-scale gains in empowerment or poverty reduction, they have certainly brought concrete benefits to some communities and drawn others into the public policy process.

3. Philanthropy *with* the Grassroots

Partnerships with the grassroots, in which members of the community are involved in the decision-making structures of philanthropy, help funders to ensure that their efforts are rooted in the concerns of the people they wish to serve. By working with the grassroots they can avoid perpetrating yet another well-meaning but ultimately destructive intrusion into the lives of those who are most marginalized. Philanthropy with the grassroots can also bring significant benefits to funders themselves if the design and evaluation of programs are cogenerated and comanaged. According to the U.S. affinity group Grassroots Grantmakers, this approach can develop "new relationships and perspectives that inform other program areas, increased credibility as an entity that has deep knowledge and understanding about its community, and opportunities to create new partnerships with donors, local governments, and other philanthropies. Grassroots grant-making is a strategy that contributes to a funder's capacity to serve as a community leader, demonstrates its commitment to community accountability, and underscores the funding organization's unique position in its community."[8] One funder describes the building of relationships with neighborhood residents in these terms: "This is ground zero for kids and communities. It is where they are spending their time. Their relationships are here. The people who care for them are here" (Saasta and Senty 2009, 13). Thus, partnering with the grassroots can help funders to ensure that their actions are rooted in "the soil of people's hard necessities," to quote Senator Albert Jeremiah Beveridge, who is credited with coining the term grassroots (Safire 2008, 289). This, in turn, can lead to better and more sustained outcomes.

The Community Foundation for Northern Ireland, for example, has had significant experience developing participatory structures within its grant-making processes. As part of its work in the European Union Peace and Reconciliation

Program, it instituted seven committees to provide advice on grant decisions, one of which was made up of representatives of the victims of political violence in the province (Kilmurray 2009, 5). Kilmurray notes that these participatory structures have helped community-based activists to increase "their understanding of the quandaries of decision-making [about grants], an understanding that they, in turn, were able to relay to their local community and group constituencies. It has built the information and skills base of those involved, but most importantly of all in our divided society, it facilitated networking and the building of relationships" (Kilmurray 2009, 6). Or take the Fondo Centroamericano de Mujeres (FCAM) which has a program called Ola Joven (or "young wave") that focuses on groups led by young women aged sixteen to thirty. This program makes use of participatory evaluation and grant-making approaches. Funds are distributed through a process in which applicants are invited to vote on proposal summaries. In keeping with this spirit, grantees evaluate one another and themselves throughout the year using FCAM's evaluation tools.[9]

These success stories aside, a number of practitioners in the field of grassroots philanthropy have noted that efforts to strengthen civil society will be resident-led only up to the moment at which the funder decides that facilitators, trainers, and other professionals are required, at which point a grassroots project will begin to lose its bottom-up character. Along these same lines, when funders identify leadership in a neighborhood they will often look for people who can act as their proxies in carrying forward the funders' agendas—people who can be counted on, in other words, to share their values and behave accordingly. In these cases, grassroots philanthropy provides an illusion of democracy, but an unbridged gulf remains between the community and the funder. One might call this philanthropy in bad faith, when funders unconsciously use their partnerships with the grassroots as a fig leaf to cover their own intentions. In describing its Rebuilding Communities Initiative, for example, the U.S.-based Annie E. Casey Foundation laid out two apparently contradictory objectives (Traynor 2002). One of these was to "place residents at the center of the community-building effort," meaning that residents would be tasked with defining the change agenda. But at the same time, participating communities were required "to identify, reach out to, and involve traditionally disenfranchised constituents within their target areas," as well as "demonstrate that their…change agenda [addressed] systemic changes at the community level" (2002, 6). Participants were also asked to "[transform] the range of community-building activities in a given community into some form of collective agenda and action for change" (2002, 14).

In these cases, the culture of professionalized philanthropic activity clashes with the cultures of grassroots communities. One could, perhaps, make some headway in understanding the dynamics of these cultural clashes if the sociology and anthropology of philanthropy were better understood. Unfortunately, most of the information available about the cultures of individual and institutional givers comes from first-hand accounts by practitioners, occasionally published in articles and blogs but frequently communicated only in hallway conversations at conferences about philanthropy. As important, Kuhn's (1962) famous dictum reminds us that there are no theory-neutral observations in science. This principle applies *mutatis mutandis* to philanthropy: when funders make an effort to take their cues from the community, they will often be selective about who they listen to and, even after listening, what they decide to act on. In subtle and not so subtle ways, funders apply their own filters to what they hear. They look and listen for confirmation of their theories of social change but ignore information that might prompt too violent a reorganization of their world views. The listening tours that philanthropists like to conduct in the communities they support often conclude, after significant investments of time and money, that the poor are "just like us"—that they want a good education for their children, decent and affordable housing, quality health care, and meaningful, well-paying jobs. This much is uncontroversial, but problems arise when philanthropists begin to draw additional conclusions that are not rooted in the diverse, lived realities of communities.

In 1992, the Boston Foundation, for example, conducted a series of "community roundtables" under the aegis of its Persistent Poverty Project. It convened a forty-three-member Strategy Development Group representing a wide array of constituencies to study the problem of intergenerational poverty in Boston. According to Charlotte Kahn, the project director, "Through this process of 'deep listening' to the community and to one another, the Group concluded that we need a new broad-based approach to eradicating persistent poverty, one that turns conventional anti-poverty practice on its head. At its heart, this approach seeks to end poverty by building community. It calls for a fundamental shift from servicing low-income communities' deficits—treating the poor as 'clients'—to investing in their strengths as colleagues, neighbors, and citizens."[10] According to this paradigm, those who want to help the poor can do so most effectively by encouraging them to act on their own behalf. By investing in their strengths as colleagues, neighbors, and citizens, the poor would be empowered and encouraged to do such things as join their neighborhood councils, serve on commissions, and take more time to petition elected officials. Yet how many low-income citizens would forego a stronger social safety net for the vagaries of political activism? Would a larger or different sample of low-income people have led to the same conclusion? Many who work closely with poor communities in the U.S. context (or who have been poor themselves) have first-hand experience of mothers and fathers who are exhausted from working double shifts and dealing with the other daily challenges of living in poverty. Having already cooked an evening meal after a long day at work and given quality time to their children, how many people of limited means have sufficient energy to lead the charge at their town council meeting? As with the "noble savages" of eighteenth-century sentimentalism, the danger is that ordinary citizens become screens on which funders project idealized versions of themselves, backed up by closely held theories of social change in which the realities of the working poor are submerged.

One of the advantages of philanthropy *with* the grassroots is that the strengths and weaknesses of funders and communities can be harmonized in order to cogenerate a larger impact—an impact that is not limited by a wholesale reliance on the ideas and resources of either philanthropy or the grassroots itself. The poor, it might be argued, do not necessarily have any greater knowledge of how to change their underlying conditions than anyone else, while professionals from outside the community may have a clearer picture of how power and privilege are created, preserved, and brokered in particular sociopolitical contexts. Funders in Chicago, for example, expressed the issue in this way: "Sometimes a place-based strategy is not effective when broader forces are affecting an area...How do you understand that organizing is local but, if it's not connected to something larger, it can miss the mark? Small grants can isolate or work against larger systemic change if they simply stay small and don't link to the issues that drive what is happening in that community" (Saasta and Senty 2009, 36). Rather than err on the side of the philanthropist or rely overmuch on purely local knowledge, perhaps the best way forward is simply to acknowledge the tensions that exist and support a division of labor between funders and the community. People of good will who come together to effect social change will come from many walks of life and bring with them different skills and perspectives, all of them critical to social change efforts.

4. PHILANTHROPY *FROM* THE GRASSROOTS

Funding *by* and *from* the grassroots holds a special kind of promise. While the amounts contributed might be small when compared to some of the sums awarded by institutional funders, one can expect a high level of buy-in from members of a community who give of their own time and money to address issues that directly affect their lives. Examples from the United States include the individual contributions that made women's suffrage possible and the church collection plates that fueled the civil rights movement in the 1950s. In 2007, fully 74.8 percent of charitable contributions in the United States (a total of $229 billion) came from individuals, and only 17.7 percent came from foundations and corporations.[11] About a third of individual giving went to religious institutions, followed by education (14.1 percent), human services (9.7 percent), and health (7.6 percent). In 2007, some 61.3 million people volunteered in the United States, providing a total of 8.1 billion hours of service or 34.7 hours per resident.[12]

This outpouring of time, treasure, and talent by ordinary citizens is, of course, a global phenomenon, but its forms and motivations vary significantly from one context to another. In Mozambique, Namibia, South Africa, and Zimbabwe, for example, Susan Wilkinson-Maposa and her colleagues (2006) have demonstrated that giving among and between poor people is a much larger phenomenon than anticipated even though roughly 20 million people in southern Africa live below the poverty line of $1 a day, according to the United Nations Development Program's *Human Development Report*.[13] There are no natural cognates for the word "philanthropy" in the languages of these contexts, and even the concept of philanthropy itself fails to resonate given its monetary connotations and the fact that it typically implies that one person is the giver and another the recipient. Giving by the poor in these countries, the study found, is marked by a high degree of reciprocity. To get around these challenges, Wilkinson-Maposa and her colleagues used the term "help" instead of "philanthropy," and their findings call into question some of the assumptions often made about philanthropy by and from the grassroots. The poor, it turns out, are very active givers, but the archetype of the philanthropic act—a donor motivated by altruism and generosity to bestow his or her largesse on a grateful supplicant—is not instantiated in the Southern African contexts that were studied. According to these researchers, "help is not always, nor necessarily, a 'free' choice. Such behaviour can be driven by social duty as well as by a deep moral obligation emanating from a shared identity premised on a common humanity. My humanity is tainted if your humanity is not recognised and assisted when in need" (Wilkinson-Maposa 2006, xi).

In her book *Enrique's Journey*, journalist Sonia Nazario chronicles the odyssey of a young Honduran boy who faces unimaginable dangers to reconnect with his mother in the United States (Nazario 2006). Unable to feed her children, Enrique's mother had left Honduras eleven years earlier to find work in America. Enrique makes his way north, as many migrants do, by clinging to the tops and sides of freight trains. It's a dangerous journey. The trains travel through some of the poorest stretches of Mexico and Central America, and yet it is common for the people who live along the tracks to throw small bundles to the migrants as they pass by: "Families throw sweaters, tortillas, bread, and plastic bottles filled with lemonade. A baker, his hands coated with flour, throws his extra loaves. A seamstress throws bags filled with sandwiches...A stooped woman, María Luisa Mora Martín, more than a hundred years old, who was reduced to eating the bark of her plantain tree during the Mexican Revolution, forces her knotted hands to fill bags with tortillas, beans, and salsa so her daughter, Soledad Vásquez, seventy, can run down a rocky slope and heave them onto a train" (Nazario 2006, 105). These acts of kindness come at significant cost to the givers described in Nazario's book, and underscore the powerful motivations that often fuel giving by and from the grassroots.

It should be noted that grassroots giving is not always an individual affair. "Giving circles," for example, constitute a form of participatory philanthropy that has gained increasing visibility and support. In this form of giving, ordinary citizens typically pool their funds and meet with one another over a period of time to learn about issues and, ultimately, award grants collectively. A survey undertaken in 2006 identified 160 giving circles in the United States alone, involving 11,700 donors who raised more than $88 million for community needs (Bearman 2007). These largely self-organized groups support a wide array of causes and include a disproportionately higher number of women, younger people, and other "nontraditional" philanthropists. Giving circles provide an especially promising route to building and strengthening civil society. They bring citizens together to contribute to the common good, and they provide a structure through which people of modest means can participate in more formal giving.

5. Conclusion: Does Grassroots Philanthropy Really Make a Difference?

The paucity of research and data available leave many unanswered questions about grassroots philanthropy. Has it been, as some suspect, the key to fueling important social movements that have transformed societies? Or has it been a secondary influence, especially when its goals and methods have been dictated by society's elites? For those who aim to strengthen civil society, can infusions of money from outside a community really create lasting "ties that bind"? Or does a newly minted sense of social cohesion typically dissolve when the donors disappear? Certainly, local victories have been achieved with help from philanthropy here and there, but do these largely unconnected efforts add up to more than the sum of their parts? And what of those cases where grassroots philanthropy may have been counterproductive by weakening civil society and fueling intergroup divisions?

Part of the answer to these questions lies in the form and content of philanthropy to, with and by the grassroots. While poor people's giving to each other may in some contexts be a matter of sheer survival, a significant number of grassroots donors aim to generate social changes that—because they are defined and directed by the poor themselves—may have a broader and deeper impact than can be owned and sustained over time. In philanthropy to and with the grassroots, elite interpretations and institutional norms often clash with the cultures and priorities of ordinary citizens, but many of these donors act in good faith and have a genuine desire to reduce the dissonance between their work and the aspirations of the communities they aim to serve. Horror stories certainly exist,[14] but they do not invalidate the many acts of human goodness that have been attempted under the rubric of grassroots philanthropy. Going further, one can also look to these skirmishes as opportunities to model the kinds of relationships and interactions that are more likely to make philanthropy a handmaiden of broader social transformation. After all, a strong civil society is as much a container for healthy disagreement as a foundation for shared visions of the good.

Donors who aim to address the root causes of social problems through their giving will likely find grassroots philanthropy an indispensable tool. Clearly, there are conceptual difficulties in identifying anything like "a" root cause of poverty, beyond the condition of having few resources. The phenomenon of poverty is part of a dynamic system of many parts, all interacting with each other in complicated ways. This complex system has no discernible root that can be pulled out of the ground as one might do with the root of a noxious weed. Nevertheless solutions to poverty and discrimination will surely evade us until we learn to draw more consistently from the wisdom and activism that are rooted in ordinary peoples' lived experience of the problems that concern them. In that sense, philanthropy "with, by, and from" the grassroots is likely to be an important element of efforts to build the capacities and connections that are required to address social problems successfully in the future.

NOTES

1. On issues related to the definition of social justice, see Ruesga and Puntenney (2010), available at www.p-sj.org. The vagueness of the term "social entrepreneur" has been frequently commented upon.

2. Compare http://www.grassrootsgrantmakers.org/page11805.cfm.

3. The Child Support Grants program is described on the Frank Buttle Trust website at http://www.buttletrust.org/grant_aid/applying_for_a_child_support_grant/.

4. Compare the Greater New Orleans Foundation website at http://www.gnof.org/programs/community-impact/overview/.

5. From the Lynde and Harry Bradley Foundation website, at http://www.bradleyfdn.org/program_interests.asp.

6. Compare http://taxdayteaparty.com/about/.

7. The U.S.-based Foundation Center has attempted to address this gap in our knowledge by collecting and publishing the program evaluations commissioned by grant makers. These are currently available in the "PubHub" section of the organization's website at http://foundationcenter.org/.

8. From the Grassroots Grantmakers website, at http://www.grassrootsgrantmakers.org/page11805.cfm.

9. This profile is based on information supplied by FCAM staff in interviews conducted by William Niedzwiecki. These interviews were conducted to prepare case study materials for an international conference hosted by the Working Group on Philanthropy for Social Justice and Peace. More information about this group is available at www.p-sj.org.

10. In an article titled "Rebuilding Boston," available at http://bostonreview.net/BR19.3/kahn.html. Archives of Persistent Poverty Project publications and other materials are available at http://www.library.neu.edu/archives/collect/findaids/m127find.htm.

11. See *Giving USA 2008*.

12. From the Corporation for National and Community Service's Volunteering in America website, at http://www.volunteeringinamerica.gov/national.

13. See http://hdr.undp.org/en/reports/global/hdr2005/.

14. See, for example, Draper (2005).

REFERENCES

Bearman, J. 2007. *More Giving Together: The Growth and Impact of Giving Circles and Shared Giving*. Washington, D.C.: Forum of Regional Associations of Grantmakers.

Draper, L. 2005. "Funder's Little Shop of Horrors: Misguided Attempts at Nonprofit Capacity Building." *Foundation News and Commentary* vol. 46(5): 18–27.

Edwards, M. 2009. *Civil Society*. 2nd ed. Cambridge: Polity Press.

Kilmurray, A. 2009. *Grassroots Philanthropy: A Personal Perspective*. Belfast: Community Foundation for Northern Ireland.

Kuhn, T. 1962. *The Structure of Scientific Revolutions*. Chicago: University of Chicago Press.

Levy, P. 1998. *The Civil Rights Movement*. Westport, Conn.: Greenwood Press.

Nazario, S. 2006. *Enrique's Journey*. New York: Random House.

Ruesga, G., and Puntenney, D. 2010. *Social Justice Philanthropy: An Initial Framework for Positioning This Work.* New York: Working Group on Philanthropy for Social Justice and Peace.

Saasta, T., and Senty, K. 2009. "Building Resident Power and Capacity for Change." Available at http://www.diaristproject.org/files/Building_Resident_Power.pdf.

Safire, W. 2008. *Safire's Political Dictionary.* New York: Oxford University Press.

Somerville, B. 2008. *Grassroots Philanthropy: Field Notes of a Maverick Grantmaker.* Berkeley: Heyday Books.

Tavernise, S. 2009. "Afghan Enclave Seen as Model to Rebuild, and Rebuff Taliban." *The New York Times*, November 13.

The Center on Philanthropy at Indiana University. 2008. *Giving USA 2008.* Indianapolis, Ind.: Giving USA Foundation.

Traynor, B. 2002. *Reflections on Community Organizing and Resident Engagement.* Baltimore: The Annie E. Casey Foundation.

Wilkinson-Maposa, S., A. Fowler, C. Oliver-Evans, and C. Mulenga. 2006. *The Poor Philanthropist: How and Why the Poor Help Each Other.* Cape Town: University of Cape Town, Graduate School of Business.

CHAPTER 37

....

ASSISTING CIVIL SOCIETY AND PROMOTING DEMOCRACY

....

OMAR G. ENCARNACIÓN

In 2005, as part of its ambitious goal to transform Iraq into a "beacon of democracy" in the Middle East, the administration of George W. Bush sponsored the creation of a Ministry of Civil Society, a new addition to the architecture of the Iraqi state designed to complement other initiatives that included a new democratic constitution, liberalizing the economy, and granting some degree of home rule to minority communities. Although probably the only one of its kind in the world, the existence of an Iraqi ministry of civil society speaks volumes about the critical importance that U.S. officials have attached to civil society since the collapse of Communism in the early 1990s, a process which is credited with ushering in the view that civil society is the "oil" that greases the wheels of democracy (Bell 1989; Putnam 1993; Gellner 1994; Fukuyama 1995; Diamond 1999; Putnam 2001).

However, there are compelling reasons to believe that civil society could meet the same dispiriting fate that has been suffered by previous approaches to democracy promotion that were once heralded as a silver bullet (modernization theory comes rapidly to mind)—primarily because the embrace of this concept by the international development community, led by its largest and most influential member, the U.S. government, has been so uncritical and superficial. It is questionable whether a concept so closely identified with the West and its most transformative experiences—the Enlightenment, industrialization, and more generally, modernization—can be easily transported to the non-Western world. Civil society, at least in its liberal guise, appears to rest on social and economic transformations that cannot be created at will, however determined and well-financed the efforts may be.

A more serious problem is the impoverished view of civil society that animates democracy promotion, limited almost exclusively to nongovernmental organizations (NGOs) and especially to those that press for democratic freedoms. Although compelling, this view of civil society stands in striking contrast to the more expansive notions that inform academic discussions of the term, which emphasize a much broader universe of voluntary and nonpolitical organizations, social networks, and other forms of civic engagement. As presently conceived, civil society-based programs of democracy promotion may fall short of generating the pro-democratic virtues that scholars have attributed to a strong civil society, especially in nurturing the growth of a democratic public culture.

Finally, democracy promoters have erred in understanding the conditions under which civil society can be most effective in advancing democracy by neglecting the importance of the surrounding political environment. Broadly speaking, the international development community has banked on a strong civil society as a transformative political force capable of fixing the political system. But largely missing from this expectation is the possibility that under deteriorating political conditions, civil society can emerge as a foe rather than a friend of democracy, most likely by being hijacked by antidemocratic forces. In supporting civil society development at the expense of political institutionalization, democracy promotion may harm rather than advance the cause of democratization.

1. THE EMBRACE OF CIVIL SOCIETY

Two decades ago, the mention of civil society would have raised a quizzical eyebrow in discussions about democracy, but today the opposite is the case. This newfound affection for civil society was set in motion by the highly romanticized reading of the role of pro-democracy social movements in bringing about the demise of Communism. As noted by Carothers (2000, 19), "It was Czech, Hungarian, and Polish activists who wrapped themselves in the banner of civil society, endowing it with a heroic quality when the Berlin Wall fell." Notable among these activists were influential intellectuals such as Václav Havel in the former Czechoslovakia and Adam Michnik in Poland, whose writings depicted the collapse of Communism as a victory of civil society over a totalitarian state. From this era of post-Cold War exuberance emerged the view that civil society is "synonymous with empowered ordinary citizens and grassroots social movements working collectively from below toward forming a parallel democratic polis to that which represented the official Communist totalitarian system and party-state" (Encarnación 2002a, 117).

New academic theories of political development lent intellectual credibility to these ideas, and by the early 1990s, influential scholars such as Putnam (1993) were making the case for a strong civil society as the foundation for securing a viable and healthy democracy, an argument that borrowed generously from Alexis de

Tocqueville's views of voluntary associations as the bedrock of American democracy in the nineteenth century. In following this line of argument, Putnam placed civil society ahead of more conventional variables in determining the development of democracy, such as social and economic progress and political institutionalization. Using Putnam as a theoretical launching pad, other academics turned the concept of civil society into a magic cure for combating virtually all of society's ills, from corruption to poverty, and from ethnic conflict to mistrust in government (Fukuyama 1995; Gellner 1995; Diamond 1999).

No less impressive was the embrace of civil society by politicians from the left and the right, convinced that government alone could not solve all society's problems. Although the understanding of civil society among politicians has always been vague, the general discourse surrounding this concept has increasingly emphasized the core value of empowering the citizenry. For Hillary Rodham Clinton, grassroots movements and community leaders were the answer to the to failures of government in providing basic social functions such as education and child rearing, a point underscored in her bestselling book *It Takes a Village* (1996). For George W. Bush, private charities and religious organizations would improve the performance of government in the delivery of public services, a key assumption behind the agenda of "compassionate conservatism." Characterizations of civil society as the Zeitgeist of the post-Cold War era were not overstated (Carothers 2000).

2. Building the Infrastructure of Civil Society Assistance

The institutional infrastructure of U.S. civil society assistance that was prompted by this rising popularity was mostly developed under the presidency of William J. Clinton, who came into office in 1993, beginning a revival of democracy-promotion efforts as a central goal of U.S. foreign policy (Smith 1991).[1] Clinton successfully fought efforts by the U.S. Congress to shut down the National Endowment for Democracy (NED) that had been created by the Reagan administration in 1983 to fight the Soviet Union "in a war of ideas" (Carothers 1994, 123). For its critics, the NED was "a cold war relic that wastes taxpayers money on pork-barrel projects and political junkets abroad" (Carothers 1994, 125), but Clinton aimed to revive it and also created new government organizations to support his administration's emphasis on democracy promotion such as the Center for Democracy and Governance at the Agency for International Development (AID), and the State Department's Bureau for Democracy, Human Rights, and Labor. He also introduced a special assistant for democracy at the National Security Council.

In keeping with the fashions of the times, Clinton's post-Cold War democracy-promotion revival placed civil society development at the center of its mission. Throughout the 1990s, AID's civil society assistance budget skyrocketed from $56 million in 1991 to $231 million in 1999 (Carothers 1999, 50). This made spending on civil society AID's largest line item for democracy promotion between 1991 and 1999, exceeding the amount spent on the rule of law, governance, and elections and political processes. The post-communist world was the principal destination of this assistance, followed by Sub-Saharan Africa, Asia and the Middle East, and Latin America (Carothers 1999, 51). Private aid to civil society quickly followed suit, led by the Ford Foundation, the Rockefeller Brothers' Fund, and George Soros's Open Society Institute. Actual levels of private civil society funding are elusive, since although international philanthropies make transparency an intended goal of their civil society assistance, this is not a virtue they themselves regularly uphold (Quigley 1997).

Following in the footsteps of the United States, other leading Western democracies began to develop their own democracy-promotion institutions and programs, including Great Britain's Westminster Foundation for Democracy (WFD), which was created in 1992 to support the consolidation of democratic institutions and principles in developing countries, and the European Initiative for Democracy and Human Rights (EIDHR), launched by the European Union in 1994. Like their American counterparts, civil society assistance features prominently in these endeavors, representing something of a departure for European democracy aid which historically had focused on more overtly political operations such as strengthening parliamentary institutions, consolidating the rule of law, and electoral training. Multilateral lending agencies, whose concern for issues of governance has increased substantially in recent years, have also made civil society engagement and consultation a requirement throughout much of their operations. For example, World Bank-funded projects with a civil society component (mainly participation by NGOs) have risen steadily over the past two decades, increasing from 21 percent of total projects in 1990 to 72 percent in 2006 (World Bank 2010).

A more expansive approach to civil society developed under the presidency of George W. Bush, whose commitment to promoting democracy abroad among American presidents was exceeded perhaps only by that of Woodrow Wilson, the patron saint of American democracy promotion.[2] For President Bush, democracy promotion was deemed not just a good thing, but a very necessary one. In the wake of the terrorist attacks of September 11, 2001, the American government operated under the assumption that a lack of democracy in the Middle East posed a direct threat to the United States by turning the region into a center of radical anti-Americanism. This made democratizing the Muslim (and especially the Arab) world an imperative of American foreign policy, an approach epitomized by the invasion of Iraq in 2003. Announcing his view of democracy as the antidote to terrorism, President Bush (2003) noted that "the world has a clear interest in the spread of democratic values, because stable and free nations do not breed the ideologies of murder. They encourage the peaceful pursuit of a better life."

The Bush administration's flagship program of civil society assistance was the Middle East Partnership Initiative (MEPI), which according to the State Department was designed to "expand political participation, and strengthen civil society and the rule of law." Since its inception in 2002, MEPI has contributed over $530 million to more than 600 projects in seventeen countries, and has continued under the administration of Barack H. Obama, even though the rhetoric of democracy promotion has been dramatically toned down. As articulated by Secretary of State Hillary Clinton during her Senate confirmation hearings in 2009, the Obama administration seeks to emphasize defense, diplomacy, and development, not democracy. Not surprisingly, perhaps, Obama's high-profile Cairo speech of that same year, which was intended to reset America's relationship with the Arab world, was notable for its modest references to democracy promotion, but faith in civil society remains high in American foreign policy circles as Clinton herself noted in 2009: "Building civil society and providing tangible services to people help result in stronger nations that share the goals of security, prosperity, peace, and progress."

3. A QUESTIONABLE EXPORT

Perhaps the most immediate concern raised by the adoption of civil society as a focus in democracy-promotion programs is whether the concept can be effectively exported outside of the social and economic milieu that gave it birth. Civil society is one of oldest ideas in political theory, but its conceptual maturity arrived in the eighteenth century, when the term began to acquire its traditional connotation as the realm of associational life that is voluntary, self-supporting, and self-regulating, outside of the family, the market and the state (Seligman 1991; Hall 1995; Walzer 1998). This is hardly accidental given the economic and social developments that were transforming Western Europe at the time, especially the rise of capitalism that had been triggered by the commercialization of agriculture and the advent of industrialization, which developed hand in hand with the emergence of chambers of commerce and charities, learned societies, and later, the development of political parties, trade unions, and other working class and mutual-interest organizations (Bermeo and Nord 2000). This new sphere of private associations launched the idea that civil society was essential for securing and protecting liberty by creating a buffer zone between the state and the citizenry that kept in check the state's inherent authoritarian tendencies.

It is questionable whether this kind of organic development, where economic and social progress nurtured the rise of independent social organizations, is available in many parts of the world where Western donors are investing in democracy promotion, especially in the Middle East. Capitalism has made significant inroads in this region, but has not lead to the kind of social and economic development that boosts civil society by strengthening society vis-à-vis the state. The peculiarities of development in the Middle East, such as state-led industrialization fueled by oil revenues, have increased the state's capacity to control society through the expansion of the military and the bureaucracy (Owen 1992). For a whole host of reasons, including the failure of governments in the post-colonial era to efficiently manage the process of development, the bulk of the citizenry remains poor and uneducated, and the middle and working classes, where they exist, are relatively small and disorganized and hence severely limited in their capacity to affect politics. Labor unions, a primary component of civil society in the West, "remain either non-existent or are repressed by the state" (Abootalebi 1998, 47).

More recent developments, such as the advent of structural adjustment policies that were intended to liberalize the economy in the 1980s and 1990s, have weakened the state across the Middle East and have led to the rise of private associations of various purposes and sizes (Hawthorne 2005). In turn, these developments have given way to considerable hope for a breakthrough in civil society in the Middle East. But there are many reasons to be cautious about what this breakthrough might accomplish in terms of democratization. For one thing, "state financial and coercive power remains strong and far superior to the resources available to its social, economic and political opposition" (Abootalebi 1998, 46). Thus, it is not surprising that the challenge to the state posed by emerging civil society actors such as the Muslim Brotherhood in Egypt, Jordan, and Syria, has hardly been sufficient to push the state to change its domestic and foreign policies (Abootalebi 1998, 46).

More ominous is the fact that the fastest growing voluntary associations across the Middle East pose a real challenge to the rise of a liberal civil society. Arguably the brightest spot in the development of civil society in the Middle East in recent years is the so-called Islamic sector, the large network of "groups, associations, and movements whose common objective is upholding and propagating the faith of Islam" (Hawthorne 2005, 85). This outburst of associational activity is part of an Islamic resurgence in recent years, propelled in part by the desire to fill the void left behind by the failure of the state in areas such as healthcare, education, and housing, but the implications for democracy are hardly the ones that are usually associated with civil society. Some Islamic organizations are among the most vociferous denouncers of democracy as a corrupt liberal system, and they often use the services they provide to the public as a vehicle to spread antidemocratic views. As noted by Sheri Berman (2003), practical help is accompanied by a deeper message: "Islam is the way."

4. Contrasting Images of Civil Society

A second concern about democracy-promotion programs is whether they are targeting the most effective or potentially effective civil society organizations. When contemplating what matters most to democracy within the vast landscape of civil society associations, scholars and donor agencies see starkly different things. Although there is no consensus in the literature on civil society on what this term actually means, three definitions are generally emphasized: civil society as associational life, as a kind of society (marked out by certain social norms), and as a space for citizen action and engagement (the public square or sphere: Edwards 2009). Among these definitions, the first is the most popular, owing largely to the influence of Robert Putnam and other neo-Tocquevilleans who see civic, and essentially nonpolitical, associations at the heart of civil society. Recreational associations like choral societies, hiking and bird-watching clubs, literacy circles, hunters' associations, Lions Clubs, and others, are Putnam's most praised manifestations of a healthy civic life.

Aid agency officials engaged in democracy promotion, however, have shown very little interest in supporting the organizations championed by Putnam, even as they cite his writings to legitimize their advocacy for civil society assistance. As noted by Carothers (1999, 213), "although U.S. aid providers have nothing against choral societies, sports clubs and other forms of civil association that do not do much advocacy work, they are not inclined to devote aid funds to them in the belief that such groups are a less likely direct route to strengthening democracy than advocacy organizations." Instead, it is the NGO world that has captured the imagination of democracy promotion.

For many donors, civil society and NGOs are virtually synonymous. According to USAID officials, civil society refers to "non-state organizations that can or have the potential to champion democratic/governance efforts" (Hansen 1996, 3), and it is in the expansion of NGOs that American officials see the most tangible evidence of the effectiveness of their support for civil society development (USAID 1999). The roots of "NGO-ization" extend beyond the reputation of NGOs as groups that are indispensable for advancing transparency in government, respect for human rights, and the consolidation of the rule of law. NGOs are also seen as uniquely suited to receive and manage foreign aid. In the view of the U.S. government and many other international agencies, NGOs are lean in their organizational structure, nimble in their programmatic capacities, impervious to corruption and scandal, and accountable for their spending. As such, NGOs not only alleviate fears among international donors about the potential mismanagement of public funds, but they also allow donors to play an important role in the domestic affairs of foreign countries while avoiding the charge of "playing politics" (Ottaway and Carothers 2000, 12).

Unfortunately, much appears to have been sacrificed by reducing civil society almost exclusively to NGOs. Among the many things that made Putnam's work on civil society so provocative (if not outright controversial) was the argument that civil society's main contribution to a democratic public life was not its advocacy work on behalf of democracy but rather the production of social capital, or a culture of trust, reciprocity, and collaboration. Without a rich endowment of social capital, Putnam argued, democracy would find it difficult to survive and much less thrive. He focused on voluntary associations for one very specific reason: only this type of association can serve as a school for democracy by enhancing the democratic capacities and skills of the citizenry, bringing people together in "horizontal relations of reciprocity and cooperation" (Putnam 1993, 88).[3]

Little in the constitution of NGOs suggests that they possess any automatic capacity to advance the production of social capital. Although NGOs come in all shapes and sizes, few bring large numbers of citizens into close and sustained interaction with each other. In reality, the structure of most NGOs mirrors the kind of social organizations that Putnam regards an antithetical to the formation of social capital. These organizations include those that are highly bureaucratized and/or institutionalized, and those that generally involve the citizenry in their endeavors in "vertical relations of authority and dependency," such as trade unions and religious organizations (Putnam 1993, 88).

The democratizing capacity of advocacy NGOs is further diminished, paradoxically enough, by their connections to international donors. The Ford Foundation's attempts to build women's organizations in post-communist Russia, for example, illustrate how foreign donors' support for NGOs can actually undermine both civil society and democracy (Henderson 2003). Unintentionally, the Foundation's endeavors resulted in the creation of an oligarchy of powerful and well-funded groups that on the whole, has not been conducive to democratic development. Those groups lucky enough to be rewarded with funding have found themselves isolated from Russian society by the resentment they have generated among others that were denied foreign funding. This is thought to have exacerbated the lack of social trust that is already a serious concern in Russian society. To make matters worse, foreign assistance has made the groups that were funded more dependent on their donors rather than on their domestic constituencies, thereby weakening their roots in Russian society and their connections to other social forces.

5. Ambiguities and Paradoxes in Civil Society and Democracy

The most distressing thing about the embrace of civil society by democracy-promotion advocates, however, is that it has ignored the many ambiguities and paradoxes that make civil society both a friend and a foe of democracy. Whether civil society helps or hinders democracy appears to depend not so much on the constitution of its individual components but rather on the nature and characteristics of the surrounding political environment, a point stressed by many critics of the civil society revival (Berman 1998; Bermeo and Nord 2000; Encarnación 2006). When political institutions are effective in channeling citizens' demands and enjoy broad popular legitimacy, civil society can be counted on to buttress democracy. But in the context of a failing political system, civil society, especially if it is large and expanding, can serve to undermine democracy. By and large, democracy promoters have ignored the dependent nature of civil society's political impact, firmly believing that civil society is inherently democratic, and that its expansion is always an unmitigated blessing for democratic politics. Although appealing, this logic gets the sequence of political development backwards. Building a stable and legitimate political system that includes governments that are accountable, credible state agencies, and political parties firmly rooted in society, should always have priority over the development of civil society, whether this is understood as consisting of NGOs, voluntary associations, or social networks. Neither a well-functioning democracy nor a democratic associational landscape can be attained without a significant level of political institutionalization. Quite the contrary, as many societies have come to recognize, a civil society that thrives in the midst of failing political institutions can be a recipe for political disaster.

One of the clearest examples of this process at work is Weimar Germany. According to Berman (1997, 402), during the interwar era "Germans threw themselves into their clubs, voluntary associations and professional organizations out of frustration with the national government and political parties." But rather than serving to save the day for democracy, a stronger civil society became an essential element in democracy's breakdown by providing a ready-made base of support for Hitler's Nazi party in its conquest of German society. Ironically, democracy would have fared better under a less robust civil society. Berman (1997, 402) contends that had German civil society been weaker, "the Nazis would never had been able to capture so many citizens for their cause or eviscerate their opponents so swiftly."

A more recent drama about the perils posed by an invigorated civil society for democracy is playing itself out in Venezuela, where trade unions and business associations staged a civil society "coup" in 2002 that led to the temporary removal of Hugo Chávez from power, a democratically elected leader whose left-wing policies have upset the balance of power in Venezuelan politics dating back to the late 1950s. The U.S. government was quick to praise the actions of civil society groups in Venezuela as "a victory for democracy," before having to retract that statement with the following corrective: "defending democracy by undemocratic means destroys democracy" (Encarnación 2002b, 45). More embarrassing for U.S. officials were the persistent rumors that linked American civil society assistance to Venezuelan groups that were involved in the attempted coup. Just prior to the coup, the National Endowment for Democracy had stepped up its civil society assistance programs in Venezuela, quadrupling its budget to more than $877,000 (Marquis 2002).

6. Conclusion

Oddly enough, many of the criticisms highlighted in this chapter provide something of a roadmap for ensuring that the incorporation of civil society into democracy-promotion programs generates some positive results. The first lesson is not to neglect the prime importance of social and economic development in the promotion of democracy. If we have learned one thing about democratization over the last fifty years it is that there is no better guarantee than an educated and prosperous citizenry for the rise of a democratic public culture. Secondly, democracy promoters should think beyond NGOs when conceiving of civil society. Despite the lack of a scholarly consensus on what civil society stands for, there is widespread agreement that for civil society to realize its pro-democratic virtues, it must serve the functions of bringing citizens together and building bridges across different social groups. For all of their talent and their skill, NGOs are generally constrained in their capacity to unify society. Indeed, what makes them so effective as democratic watchdogs—especially their focus on specific concerns such as corruption and human rights—can often make them polarizing in the public sphere.

Finally, the expectation that nurturing the development of civil society in isolation from the messiness, corruption, and partisanship of politics will bring about a democratic transformation of the polity is far from realistic, and may in fact be counterproductive. At some level, civil and political society must meld together to form the "good society" that makes democracy both possible and enduring. How to bring about this union in radically different settings is one of the main challenges facing civil society assistance and democracy promotion in the many years ahead.

NOTES

1. Clinton's devotion to expanding the community of democracies flowed from his belief that democracy is the source of international order, a view rooted in the classic international relations argument that sees the spread of democracy as the key to peace owing to the rarity of wars between democratic states (Doyle 1993).

2. Wilson launched multiple military interventions in Mexico, the Caribbean, and Central America between 1911 and 1921 under the pretext of "making the world safe for democracy" (Smith 1991).

3. Putnam has been criticized for ignoring the fact that social capital is something of a double-edged sword. Social trust can further democratization or be employed for undemocratic purposes (Levi 1996). Other critics of Putnam such as Berman (1997) have argued that malevolent civil society associations often do a better job at promoting trust and solidarity than benevolent ones.

REFERENCES

Abootalebi, A. 1998. "Civil Society, Democracy, and the Middle East." *Middle East Review of International Affairs* 2(3): 46–59.

Bell, D. 1989. "American Exceptionalism Revisited: The Role of Civil Society." *The Public Interest* 9(5): 38–56.

Berman, S. 1997. "Civil Society and the Collapse of the Weimar Republic." *World Politics* 49(3): 401–29.

———. 1998. "Civil Society and Political Institutionalization." *American Behavioral Scientist* 40(5): 562–74.

———. 2003. "Islamism, Revolution, and Civil Society." *Perspectives on Politics* 1(2): 257–72.

Bermeo, N., and Philip Nord (eds.). 2000. *Civil Society before Democracy: Lessons from Nineteenth Century Europe*. Lanham, Md.: Rowman and Littlefield.

Bush, G. W. 2003. "Speech to the American Enterprise Institute." February 27. Available at http://www.guardian.co.uk/world/2003/feb/27/usa.iraq2 (accessed on June 9, 2009).

Diamond, L. 1999. *Developing Democracy: Toward Consolidation*. Baltimore: Johns Hopkins University Press.

Carothers, T. 1994. "The NED at 10." *Foreign Policy* 95: 123–38.

———. 1999. *Aiding Democracy Abroad: The Learning Curve*. Washington, D.C.: Carnegie Endowment for International Peace.

———. 2000. "Civil Society: Think Again." *Foreign Policy* (Winter 1999–2000): 18–29.

Clinton, H. R. 1996. *It Takes a Village and Other Lessons Children Teach Us*. New York: Simon & Schuster.

———. 2009. "The Role of Civil Society in Building a Stronger, More Peaceful World." Address to Indonesian Civil Society Dinner, February 18. Available at http://www.state.gov/secretary/rm/2009a/02/119425.htm (accessed October 16, 2009).

Doyle, M. 1983. "Kant, Liberal Legacies and Foreign Affairs." *Philosophy and Public Affairs* 12(3): 205: 235.

Edwards, M. 2009. *Civil Society*. 2nd ed. Cambridge: Polity Press.

Encarnación, O. 2002a. "On Bowling Leagues and NGOs: A Critique of Civil Society's Revival." *Studies in Comparative and International Development* 36(4): 116–31.

———. 2002b. "Venezuela's Civil Society Coup." *World Policy Journal* 19(2): 38–48.

———. 2006. "Civil Society Reconsidered." *Comparative Politics* 38(3): 357–75.

Fukuyama, F. 1995. *Trust: The Social Virtues and the Creation of Prosperity*. New York: The Free Press.

Gellner, E. 1994. *Conditions of Freedom: Civil Society and its Rivals*. London: Penguin.

Hall, J. 1995. *Civil Society: Theory, History, Comparison*. Cambridge: Polity.

Hansen, G. 1996. *Constituencies for Reform: Strategic Approaches for Donor-Supported Civic Advocacy programs*. Washington, D.C.: United States Agency for International Development.

Hawthorne, A. 2005. "Is Civil Society the Answer?," in T. Carothers and M. Ottaway (eds.) *Uncharted Journey: Promoting Democracy in the Middle East*. Washington, D.C.: Carnegie Endowment for International Peace.

Henderson, S. 2003. *Building Democracy in Contemporary Russia: Western Support for Grassroots Organizations*. Ithaca, N.Y.: Cornell University Press.

Ikenberry, J. 1999. "Why Export Democracy: The 'Hidden Grand' Strategy of American Foreign Policy." *The Wilson Quarterly* 23(2): 57–65.

Quigley, K. 1997. *For Democracy's Sake: Foundations and Democratic Assistance in Central Europe*. Baltimore: Johns Hopkins University Press.

Levi, M. 1996. "Social and Unsocial Capital: A Review Essay of Robert Putnam's *Making Democracy Work*." *Politics and Society* 24(1): 45–55.

Lipset, S. M. 1959. "Social Requisites of Democracy: Economic Development and Political Legitimacy." *American Political Science Review* 53: 69–105.

Marquis, C. 2002. "U.S. Bankrolling is Under Scrutiny for Ties to Chavez Ouster." *The New York Times*, April 15.

Ottaway, M., and T. Carothers. 2000. *Funding Virtue: Civil Society Aid and Democracy Promotion*. Washington, D.C.: Carnegie Endowment for International Peace.

Owen, R. 1992. *State, Power and Politics of the Modern Middle East*. New York: Routledge.

Putnam, R. 1993. *Making Democracy Work: Civic Traditions in Modern Italy*. Princeton, N.J.: Princeton University Press.

———. 2001. *Bowling Alone: The Collapse and Revival of American Community*. New York: Simon & Schuster.

Seligman, A. 1991. *The Idea of Civil Society*. Princeton, N.J.: Princeton University Press.

Smith, T. 1991. *America's Mission: The United States and the Global Struggle for Democracy in the Twentieth Century*. Princeton, N.J.: Princeton University Press.

U.S. Agency for International Development. 1999. *Lessons in Implementation: The NGO Story—Building Civil Society in Central and Eastern Europe and the New Independent States*. Washington, D.C.: United States Agency for International Development.

U.S. Department of State. 2002. "The Middle East Partnership Initiative." Available at http://mepi.state.gov/ (accessed February 2, 2010).

Walzer, M. 1998. "The Concept of Civil Society," in M. Walzer (ed.) *Toward a Global Civil Society*. Oxford: Berghahn Books.

World Bank. 2010. "The World Bank and Civil Society." Available at http://web.worldbank .org (accessed January 28, 2010).

CHAPTER 38

CONCLUSION: CIVIL SOCIETY AS A NECESSARY AND NECESSARILY CONTESTED IDEA

MICHAEL EDWARDS

As is obvious from the contributions to this handbook, civil society is not a concept that yields to easy consensus, conclusion, or generalization. Context is all, and ideology is closer to the surface of many analyses than their authors might admit, especially around contentious issues such as civil society's normative content and significance, and its relationships with government and the market. These are issues on which even the small numbers of contributors who are represented here sometimes disagree. But wholesale agreement is not essential to the utility of any set of ideas, whether in theory or in practice. As a "necessarily contested concept," to use Michael Woolcock's description in chapter 16, it is enough that civil society continues to prove itself to be a useful and motivational device in advancing our understanding of key social and political issues, and in channeling energy into action. And on this test it succeeds admirably. One would be hard-put to explain the course of politics, democracy, social relations, and societal change without some reference to the ways in which citizens organize themselves for normative purposes, articulate and argue about their ideas, and fashion some sense of vision and direction for the future of the communities to which they belong. Ideas about civil society do not resolve the tension between society and the market that has animated scholarship and debate for a century or more, for no such absolute resolution is possible. But without competing visions of the good society, public spheres in which they can be developed and solidified, and associations that create an infrastructure for collective action between the individual and the state, no democratic progress would be possible.

As the civil society literature is enriched by more non-Western and nonorthodox perspectives, the differences between schools of thought and their interpretations will grow, and many existing assumptions will be challenged much more deeply. This is surely a healthy development. It has always been somewhat ironic that ideas about collective action have been so influenced by thinkers in the United States—to many the home of individualism—and this tendency continues today with the rise of theories around social enterprise and "philanthrocapitalism" that treat civil society almost as a subset of the market. But as the U.S experience settles into a broader universe of knowledge shaped by ideas from China and the Arab world, Africa, and Latin America, this will change, and—though these societies may yet converge on a common pathway to the future—it is likely that much more attention will be paid to the distinctive characteristics they exhibit around issues of social identity, the role of the state, and other important matters. In addition, the ways in which different social groups understand and interpret these ideas should also find a more central position in the mainstream of civil society thinking, as Hilda Coffé and Catherine Bolzendahl enjoin us to do in their treatment of gender and citizenship in chapter 20. Many more layers of complexity and difference are waiting to be uncovered in the civil society debate.

Nevertheless, patterns do exist, some of which are anchored in common experiences of the challenges of capitalism and democracy and how civil society can help to meet them, and some of which are more superficial, perhaps even artificial, because they are generated by the fluctuating characteristics and preferences of donor support in places where civil society groups rely on outside assistance—for example, support to nongovernmental organizations (NGOs) that advocate for civil and political liberties, or to those that provide social and economic services to the poor, rather than to other expressions of associational life. These patterns indicate that there are forces acting both for and against indigenous articulations of civil society in both theory and in practice, and this is an important conclusion given that such articulations should have more chance of developing sustained and effective responses to the problems facing their communities. What is it, therefore, that underpins the achievements of civil society across so many different contexts, and what can be done to strengthen those achievements in the future?

1. THE CHANGING SHAPE
OF ASSOCIATIONAL LIFE

In every context, the structure of associational life is an important influence over outcomes, though clearly there is no automatic "transmission belt" that links the forms, norms, and achievements of civil society together. Yet despite wide differences in history and culture, regime types, funding arrangements, and other significant factors, the shape of associational life does seem to be changing in similar ways across the world, variously described as "professionalization," "NGO-ization," "hybridization," and the erosion of certain kinds of civic participation and engagement. The nonprofit sector has always an important component of associational life, but it seems to be increasingly dominant, especially in providing social services and advocating for change in public policy processes. By contrast, as Theda Skocpol shows for the United States in chapter 9, membership groups—and especially those that tie the interests of different communities together—have been declining for thirty years or more, and survey after survey shows a continuing fall in the proportion of respondents attending meetings, working on community projects, and reading newspapers from the early 1970s onwards.[1] In developing countries, NGOs already dominate the landscape of associational life (and are usually funded by foreign aid), even though most societies have their own rich traditions of organizing and debate, albeit in less formal ways. Using the analogy of civil society as an "ecosystem" introduced in chapter 1, it is clear that certain elements are being eroded and others strengthened, and that overall, greater homogeneity is being introduced into the forms of associational life. As in a real, biological ecosystem, this is bound to have significant effects over time.

Does this mean that civil society is in decline? In some ways and in some places, yes—though this decline may be offset, at least in part, by the rise of new forms of engagement, often based around social media and the Internet, and by new types of association such as social enterprise and social entrepreneurs, which Alex Nicholls sees as potentially revolutionary in chapter 7. As yet, it is unclear what the aggregate effects of these changes are going to be, but why are traditional forms of civic participation and activism under greater pressure? As Robert Putnam (2000) and others have tried to show for the United States, a myriad of factors are involved, ranging from structural changes in the economy and the workforce (which reduce the time available for voluntary activities), to rising factionalism in politics amid the "culture wars" of the last twenty years (which have destroyed bridges between different social groups), to the rise of more passive forms of media production and consumption, from television to Twitter. Widespread insecurity and inequality may be especially important, and are explored below. All these factors weaken large-scale, mass-based, bottom-up, cross-class, and multi-issue organizing and other forms of civic action.

But there are also more deliberate forces at work. Despite their stated support for democratization, donor agencies have consistently sought out and funded service delivery by NGOs, with some advocacy around the edges, ignoring or devaluing other roles and other expressions of associational life from burial societies to political-religious movements—despite the fact that such groups have stronger roots in their own constituencies and therefore more legitimacy and sticking power in terms of social action. The agenda of the "new public management" described by Steven Rathgeb Smith in chapter 3 has been a powerful force around the world in favoring more professional and/or bureaucratic civil society groups who can meet increased demands for reporting and accountability around public service and other contracts, a social and economic role that is welcomed by even authoritarian and semiauthoritarian regimes who are nervous about civil society's more political activities. At a more basic level, the struggle between "neo-liberal" and "participatory" models of civil society painted by Evelina Dagnino for Latin America in chapter 10 is playing out across a much wider range of contexts, often being decided in favor of the nonprofit sector in substitution for the state—so much so that civil society and the social economy of nonprofit service provision are often conflated. Such a dangerously reductive approach strips civil society of much of its meaning and potential, and this is why changes in the structure of associational life are so important, especially if they are engineered from the outside.

As Alan Fowler points out in chapter 4, development NGOs are much less likely to act as carriers of alternative ideas and energies if they captured by the foreign aid system and its priorities, managed through technocracy, and distanced from domestic social movements and other civic and political actors who have more purchase over the drivers of development. Spaces for "public work," as Harry Boyte describes them in chapter 26, have been systematically eroded in the United States by a rising predilection for service-providing nonprofits, and when the language and practices of contracting replace those of trust and solidarity, one would expect the normative effects of associational life to be somewhat different. These effects might be mitigated by combining different forms and roles together in creative ways, as in the "social change organizations" described by Frances Kunreuther in chapter 5, or when churches and other faith-based groups integrate service delivery with advocacy and community organizing, but these remain unorthodox approaches (Minkoff 2002). Elsewhere, the changing shape of associational life may indeed be damaging to the broader prospects of civil society, and to the "democratic associational ecologies" that Mark Warren highlights in chapter 30 as the key to civil society's long-term political impact. As a number of contributors put it for the Middle East, India, Sub-Saharan Africa, and elsewhere, "more NGOs" do not a civil society make. In that case, what does?

2. CIVIL AND UNCIVIL SOCIETY

A great deal of energy has been expended on defining "uncivil" society, perhaps because, once so defined, it might go away, or at least cease to complicate some models of civil society's normative content and significance. But as Clifford Bob points out in chapter 17, much, if not most of this effort is misguided. Persistent differences in norms and values are the reality of every human society, and inevitably they are expressed in, by, and through associations and the public sphere. Indeed, this is one of the prime purposes of public work and public deliberation—to provide spaces in which these differences can be aired and argued through to some sort of consensus. So rather than fretting in the abstract about which groups "qualify" for civil society membership, it is more productive to use conflict around different views as a pathway to the "good societies" that should emerge out of democratic negotiation. Writing about the Hindu nationalist Rashtriya Swayamsevak Sangh

(RSS) in India in chapter 14, which some would classify as a clearly "uncivil" movement, Neera Chandhoke concludes that "the only way in which such associations can be neutralized is through contestation in civil society itself."

As Donatella della Porta and Mario Diani point out in chapter 6, civil society theory and social movement theory have often been divided on the issue of conflicts over power and their value, and there is no doubt that this approach necessitates a celebration of diversity at a much deeper level, and a higher level of comfort with contestation, than have been present in much of the discussion to date—but it is the only way to advance civil society's *transformative* potential, since transformation implies the ability to break up and re-order power relations, norms, and values. As Jenny Pearce puts it in chapter 32, "the normative power of civil society lies not in the specific values which different traditions attach to the concept, but in the general value of aspiring to such a society, created through the contested values of what 'good' actually means." And even if these contestations take place in imperfect conditions of equality, nonviolence, and democracy in the deepest sense of that word, there is more of a chance that they will "bend towards justice" over the very long term, to paraphrase Martin Luther King's famous maxim, a point to which I turn next.

It is clear that successful, democratic negotiations of this kind require some boundaries—some norms and values of their own—since otherwise they would quickly break apart or be dominated by powerful interest groups, especially in settings where high levels of inequality and discrimination continue to exist. There are at least two ways of setting out these boundaries. The first is to insist on support for the "contested core conditions" of civil society that were described in chapter 1—those things without which no theory of civil society could function effectively in linking means and ends, even if some differences in interpretation continue to exist. Chief among these conditions are nonviolence and support for high levels of equality. A commitment to physical nonviolence ensures that no group can destroy absolutely the rights of others to participate, but it does not prevent the conflicts and contestations that are essential to a thriving civil society. "Peace is an activity of cultivating the process of agreeing," not simply the absence of war (Pearce, this volume), and to be effective and sustainable this "process of agreeing" must allow all voices to be heard. As Sally Kohn points out in chapter 19, and as many other contributors confirm, large-scale inequality impedes the functioning of civil society in all three of the definitions covered in this handbook—associational life, the good society, and the public sphere—and more particularly they also fracture the linkages that connect these three understandings together. Inequalities in associational life privilege civic and political participation by some groups over others, allowing them undue voice and influence in the public sphere and enabling them to skew collective visions of the good society towards their interests.

The second way of approaching the issue of civil society's normative boundaries is to focus on the connections that can be nurtured between the values of particular groups, and some larger set of norms that bind groups together in common cause, or at least in a common conversation about the shape of social progress. In times of war or national crisis this is obviously much easier, but the bonds of mutual sacrifice that are often forged during episodes like this rarely linger long—which is one reason why observers in the United States often lament the passing of high levels of civic engagement during and after World War II that underpinned the GI Bill of 1944 and other landmark social achievements (Skocpol, this volume). In chapter 18, Nina Eliasoph tackles this issue by exploring the relationships between "civility" (defined as interaction that is respectful, tolerant and decent) and "civic-ness" (defined as a commitment to press for wider changes that extend these values throughout society). By strengthening the ties between civility and civic-ness through associational life and public work, she argues, civil society takes on a more transformative persona. In this task, face-to-face interaction is essential, since—like rocks in a stream—the sharp edges of their differences can be softened over time as people knock against each other in the rough and tumble of civic life. Unfortunately for the "techno-optimists" that Roberta Lentz reviews in chapter 27, this is not a task that can be achieved in cyberspace or by using social media.

In many ways religion and spirituality are linked together in similar fashion. As the contributions from Donald Miller and Claudia Horwitz both make clear (chapters 21 and 22), only when religion is connected to, and anchored in, transcendent experience and universal human values does it become potentially transformative, building on, but not being imprisoned by, the particularities of each faith tradition, mosque or church. There are clear echoes throughout this conversation of "the love that does justice," Martin Luther King's philosophy that shows how personal and social transformation are intimately linked together (Edwards and Sen 2000; Edwards and Post 2008). Civil society can be, but is not necessarily transformative of power, as John Gaventa puts it in chapter 33. What seems to make the difference is the explicit articulation of these linkages and their use in guiding behavior at all times—among individuals, groups, and eventually whole institutions. When this happens, the means and ends of civil society are united, and a "strong civil society" can foster "societies that are strong and civil" (Edwards 2009). In other words, when certain conditions are present, the forms, norms, and spaces of civil society connect with each other in common purpose. But what if these conditions are not met? What if inequality and other barriers to participation are rooted in civil society itself? Can threats to the public sphere be dealt with simply through more debate and deliberation?

3. THREATS TO THE PUBLIC SPHERE

Placing one's faith in the theories of Jürgen Habermas has become a standard response in the civil society debate to questions of moral pluralism and consensus making, and there is no doubt that the debate has improved greatly as a result. Without a range of overlapping public spheres and the processes that take place inside them, even a rich fabric of voluntary associations could achieve little in the aggregate. However, as many contributors to this handbook point out, Habermas underestimates the forces that shape public spheres and interfere with their ability to generate democratic outcomes, and at a time of rising economic inequality across the world, increasing concentrations of corporate power, and continued political repression in many countries, these forces may be growing stronger. To imagine that one can strengthen civil society by eroding the things that people depend on to be active citizens makes little sense, yet inequalities and power relations of various kinds have often been ignored or devalued in discussions of civic life, perhaps because some have their origins in, or at least are mirrored by, voluntary associations themselves. This is why, contrary to much neo-Tocquevillean thinking, civil society cannot fix itself—and if it cannot fix itself then it is unlikely to be able to fix society as a whole. Confronting poverty, inequality, and discrimination requires action by states and markets too, but civil society cannot afford to be captured by these other institutions if it is to hold them accountable for their actions and fulfill its role as the carrier of different norms and values.

Inevitably then, civil society is forever positioned in a Janus-faced relationship with both government and business. On the one hand, equal protections must be anchored in the law and backed up by public policies and regulations, while the economy must be free to create jobs and expand the surpluses required for consumption and redistribution. This requires a stance of constructive engagement on the part of civic actors. On the other hand, without constant pressure and monitoring from civil society, neither governments nor businesses are likely to use their power in the public interest, and this necessitates a stance of critical distance, or at least independence. This is why some recent trends in civil society thinking and practice constitute both opportunities and threats, like the expansion of social enterprise and the rise of more overt forms of civil society organizing for political ends. The costs and benefits of these strategies must be carefully weighed to ensure that good intentions are not submerged by unintended consequences, and this requires a well-developed set of capacities that can help civic groups to come to informed decisions about strategy and tactics. In chapter 11, Marc Morjé Howard calls this a shift from "oppositional" to "democratic" civil society, and concludes that the weakness of associations and public engagement in post-Communist Europe can be attributed, at least in part, to a failure to make this transition.

Hence, the encounter between civil society and the market can foster both transformation and greater inequality, depending on the terms of this engagement, and on this question the contributors are divided. In chapters 7 and 34, Alex Nicholls and Simon Zadek argue strongly that closer relationships are positive, and indeed imperative, if civil society is to have more impact on poverty, injustice, and social needs. Sometimes these relationships will take the form of hybrid institutions, and at other times they will operate through what Zadek describes as "civil regulation"—or various forms of advocacy and co-governance that help to shape corporate activity. Taking a somewhat different view, John Ehrenberg concludes chapter 2 by stressing the paramount importance of economic democratization and democratic political action in addressing key structural problems in society. Civic traditions of voluntarism and localism are simply unable to cope with the rise of globalizing capitalism and the power of large, multinational corporations, and, as Lisa Jordan points out in chapter 8, global civil society has not yet reached the point at which it can act as an effective counterweight to global markets. In terms of the balance of power in most contemporary settings, markets outrank civil society at almost every level, and public spheres have been further eroded by the privatization and commercialization of the media, knowledge production, and large parts of education. The civic knowledge that Peter Levine describes in chapter 29 is in increasingly short supply. These trends make the protection and expansion of public spaces even more important, despite the difficulties involved, a point strongly made by Craig Calhoun and Charles Lewis in chapters 25 and 28. At all costs, such spaces must not be captured by business or other concentrated private interests, and clearly governments have a major role to play in ensuring that this does not happen.

Unfortunately, relations between civil society and government are not moving in this direction in many parts of the world. Authoritarian and semiauthoritarian regimes continue to constrain, and in some cases actively repress, civil society, at least in its political manifestations, though as Jude Howell shows for China in chapter 13, such strategies can be quite sophisticated in carefully calibrating different spaces for non-profit service provision and citizen advocacy at different times. Even in mature democracies, however, few governments are comfortable in actively promoting civil societies that are strong and independent enough to challenge their authority, especially after the events of September 11, 2001 and the ensuing war on terror which has exposed certain groups and activities to particular attention and interference. In chapters 23 and 24, Nancy Rosenblum, Charles Lesch, and Mark Sidel examine how to balance the rights and responsibilities of civil society in this context, highlighting the dangers of overregulation and advocating for approaches that are based on partnerships, mutual agreements, or "compacts" which protect zones of independent citizen action, even when large numbers of nonprofit groups are funded by government expenditure.

Whichever position one adopts, it is clear that the structure of the economy and the nature of the political regime are the most powerful factors in determining the shape and functioning of associations and the public sphere, including in settings where religion is sometimes assumed to be paramount—a point well-made by Eberhard Kienle in chapter 12 in relation to the supposed incompatibility between civil society and Islam. But if this is the case, where does this leave the growing industry of donor agencies, foundations and other institutions that aim to "build" or "strengthen" civil society by focusing on particular forms of association across radically different contexts?

4. CAN CIVIL SOCIETY BE NURTURED?

Omar Encarnación opens his account of donor assistance in chapter 37 with the story of Iraq's first Ministry of Civil Society, a peculiar priority in a country lacking basic security and services but not so strange given the influence of American democracy promoters after the deposition of Saddam Hussein's regime—who, not unnaturally, were no doubt enamored of Alexis de Tocqueville and his ideas. The point of this story goes beyond the obvious issues of sequencing and the dangers of inappropriate intervention, to pose more fundamental questions about the meaning of "civil society-building" at a much deeper level. If civil society means many different things and if these differences must be reconciled through dialogue and conflict over long periods of time, is there anything useful that can be done to accelerate the development of associations and public spaces in ways that are responsible, and to foster more interaction between them and with the state and the market in order to promote a more sustainable vision of the good society?

In many ways we know what *not* to do in answering this question, but we are much less clear about the alternatives. A forced march to civil society Western-style will do little to support the emergence of sustainable forms and norms in China, Africa, or the Middle East. An overemphasis on NGOs and service-delivery projects cannot change the civic and political cultures of India or Mississippi. And support for community media and public journalism won't, by itself, create a democratic public sphere. These are the priorities of most donor agencies and foundations, not because they are proven to be effective, but because they are easier to fund, report on, and manage. By contrast, the organic processes of civil society development are messy and unpredictable, and lie outside the control of the foreign aid system or philanthropy. As a result, even the more sophisticated efforts to nurture the ecosystems of associational life tend to short-circuit vital questions of culture, values, and politics, questions which do so much to determine the shape and functioning of civil society in all of its disguises. In his review of civil society in Sub-Saharan Africa in chapter 15, Ebenezer Obadare criticizes donor agencies for their tendency to substitute NGO capacity-building for the development of a "truly democratic political culture," echoing Encarnación's broader reservations about the sequencing of civil society assistance with political institutionalization. Leaving aside the question of whether these deeper and more overtly political tasks are amenable to outside assistance of any kind, these critics raise some very important points. Obviously context is important: as Solava Ibrahim and David Hulme emphasize in chapter 31, effective assistance to civil society poverty reduction efforts is not the same in India as it is in Bangladesh, where a much weaker state invites a larger role for NGOs in delivering basic social and economic services, ideally with some long-term impact on the claim-making capacities of citizens. But as a general conclusion, the priorities of civil society support have been inverted, with the least important factors receiving the most attention (like the number of NGOs), and the most important factors often being ignored—like indigenous expressions of associational life and their connections with political society, or at a more basic level, guarantees of human security.

In that case, what kinds of support would be more useful? In theoretical terms, though drawn from a wide range of empirical experiences explored in this handbook, the ideal would be a well articulated and inclusive ecosystem of locally supported voluntary associations, matched by a strong and democratically accountable state, with a multiplicity of public spheres that enable full and equal participation in setting the rules of every game. A society like this, in which different institutions consolidate their relationships with each other at a pace appropriate to the context around a gradually expanding economic base, would allow civil society to evolve organically and sort through the problems that are often associated with external assistance. Clearly, this type of society does not exist anywhere, particularly in low-income countries, but by working backwards from this ideal it is easier to identify what can usefully be done, and when.

First of all, there is a choice to do as a little as possible and simply let things take their course—to do no harm, so to speak, in the knowledge that any intervention runs the risk of producing consequences that are unforeseen. In a field as complicated and contingent as civil society, this is an attractive proposition, but it is unnecessarily restrictive because it ignores the fact that the preconditions for civil society—like security, equality, and the space to organize and express opinions— are all things that can be influenced without pushing associations in one direction or another. Support to these preconditions is one of the most useful things that donors can do, though clearly it does not produce the kind of short-term, quantifiable results that are so popular with a new generation of philanthropists and international bureaucrats. Once equipped with these basic elements of human flourishing, people can build whatever kind of civil society suits their interests and agendas. But what else can be done?

In chapters 35 and 36, the contributors offer different perspectives on this question from the viewpoint of philanthropy, which has always been an important support to associations and the infrastructure of the public sphere, at least in the United States. William Schambra and Krista Shaffer argue strongly for a minimalist approach in which philanthropic institutions support the self-organizing processes that mark out civil society, especially at the local level, and stay away from grand designs and the scientific analysis of "root causes." Albert Ruesga offers a modification of this approach, based on the recognition that local associations struggle to deal with problems of a broader, structural nature and have no monopoly over wisdom, so that philanthropy "with" and "from" the grassroots can play an important role in strengthening and connecting movements and networks that are still driven by authentically popular initiatives. By building the independent capacities of a broad base of citizens to engage with each other and take collective action, philanthropy can support civil society to shape itself with a little more help along the way—not in the short-term, highly targeted, pseudoscientific way that is favored by technocrats, but gradually, over time, and directed by people's own interpretations of root causes and the strategies that are required to address them. Support for social groups who are disadvantaged in some way is especially important, since this helps to level the playing field for associational life and public interaction. To take a non-Western example from Myanmar, local organizations, with support from outside the country, have adopted a range of lower-profile tactics after the suppression of street protests in 2009 which seek to take advantage of small-scale political openings and build some of the

preconditions for longer term civil and political engagement, including the introduction of new ideas and training in basic organizational skills. Over time, there
is some chance that these kinds of support will help to knit together a strong and
sustainable fabric of civic life and interaction.[2]

5. Conclusion

There are no final words on civil society, because civil society is constantly being
reinterpreted and recreated. This is particularly true at a time when emerging
superpowers like China, India, and Brazil are entering and beginning to reshape
global debates about politics and economics, often from the perspective of their
own knowledge base and traditions which, in civil society terms, may differ markedly from the trajectories of North America and Europe, from where most civil
society theory to date has emerged. In years to come, scholars and activists may be
learning about civil society from the experiences of Kerala, Bolivia, and South
Africa, and carrying these lessons back to California and London, as well as, one
hopes, the other way around. The civil society debate will certainly be all the richer
for it. Yet across very different contexts, as the contributions to this handbook
show, civil society is most valuable as a set of concepts and practices when it is
additional to, and not captured by, government and business—when it is seen and
supported as its own distinctive creation rather than as the consequence of state or
market failure.

As Ebenezer Obadare puts it in chapter 15, there has been much legitimate criticism of civil society ideas and assistance in Africa and elsewhere, but there is also a
need to move "beyond the backlash" in order to focus on developing a body of
scholarship that can yield more useful insights. This is only possible if the debate is
pluralized and opened up to new and different perspectives. To do otherwise—to
attempt to fix civil society in the context of one particular experience or
interpretation—would be against the spirit of civil society itself. It is that challenge—blending widespread differences into a "geometry of human relations," as
John Ehrenberg puts it in chapter 2—that will frame both the theory and practice
of civil society long into the future.

NOTES

1. Data from the General Social Survey and the DDB Needham Life Survey is available
at www.peterlevine.ws/mt/archives/2010/06/the-old-order-p.html, accessed August 22, 2010.
2. "Seeds of Hope in Burma," reprinted in the *Guardian Weekly* from the *Washington
Post*, November 9, 2009 (no author given).

REFERENCES

Edwards, M. 2009. *Civil Society*. 2nd ed. Cambridge: Polity Press.

Edwards, M., and G. Sen. 2000. "NGOs, Social Change and the Transformation of Human Relationships: a 21st Century Civic Agenda." *Third World Quarterly* vol. 21(4), 605–16.

Edwards, M., and S. Post (eds.). 2008. *The Love that Does Justice: Spiritual Activism in Dialogue with Social Science*. Cleveland: Unlimited Love Press.

Minkoff, D. 2002. "The Emergence of Hybrid Organizational Forms: Combining Identity-Based Service-Provision and Political Action." *Non-Profit and Voluntary Sector Quarterly* vol. 31(5), 377–401.

Putnam, R. 2000. *Bowling Alone: the Collapse and Revival of American Community*. New York: Simon & Schuster.

Index